Sixth Edition

MICROECONOMICS
PRIVATE MARKETS AND PUBLIC CHOICE

THE ADDISON-WESLEY SERIES IN ECONOMICS

Abel/Bernanke
Macroeconomics

Berndt
The Practice of Econometrics

Bierman/Fernandez
Game Theory with Economic Applications

Binger/Hoffman
Microeconomics with Calculus

Boyer
Principles of Transportation Economics

Branson
Macroeconomic Theory and Policy

Bruce
Public Finance and the American Economy

Burgess
The Economics of Regulation and Antitrust

Byrns/Stone
Economics

Carlton/Perloff
Modern Industrial Organization

Caves/Frankel/Jones
World Trade and Payments: An Introduction

Chapman
Environmental Economics: Theory, Application, and Policy

Cooter/Ulen
Law and Economics

Copeland
Exchange Rates and International Finance

Downs
An Economic Theory of Democracy

Eaton/Mishkin
Readings to accompany The Economics of Money, Banking, and Financial Markets

Ehrenberg/Smith
Modern Labor Economics

Ekelund/Tollison
Economics: Private Markets and Public Choice

Fusfeld
The Age of the Economist

Gerber
International Economics

Ghiara
Learning Economics: A Practical Workbook

Gibson
International Finance

Gordon
Macroeconomics

Gregory
Essentials of Economics

Gregory/Stuart
Russian and Soviet Economic Performance and Structure

Griffiths/Wall
Intermediate Microeconomics: Theory and Applications

Gros/Steinherr
Winds of Change: Economic Transition in Central and Eastern Europe

Hartwick/Olewiler
The Economics of Natural Resource Use

Hoy/Livernois/McKenna/ Rees/Stengos
Mathematics for Economics

Hubbard
Money, the Financial System, and the Economy

Hughes/Cain
American Economic History

Husted/Melvin
International Economics

Jehle/Reny
Advanced Microeconomic Theory

Klein
Mathematical Methods for Economics

Krugman/Obstfeld
International Economics: Theory and Policy

Laidler
The Demand for Money: Theories, Evidence, and Problems

Lesser/Dodds/Zerbe
Environmental Economics and Policy

Lipsey/Courant/Ragan
Economics

McCarty
Dollars and Sense: An Introduction to Economics

Melvin
International Money and Finance

Miller
Economics Today

Miller/Benjamin/North
The Economics of Public Issues

Miller/VanHoose
Essentials of Money, Banking, and Financial Markets

Mills/Hamilton
Urban Economics

Mishkin
The Economics of Money, Banking, and Financial Markets

Parkin
Economics

Parkin/Bade
Economics in Action Software

Perloff
Microeconomics

Phelps
Health Economics

Riddell/Shackelford/Stamos
Economics: A Tool for Critically Understanding Society

Ritter/Silber/Udell
Principles of Money, Banking, and Financial Markets

Rohlf
Introduction to Economic Reasoning

Ruffin/Gregory
Principles of Economics

Salvatore
Microeconomics

Sargent
Rational Expectations and Inflation

Scherer
Industry Structure, Strategy, and Public Policy

Schotter
Microeconomics

Sherman/Kolk
Business Cycles and Forecasting

Smith
Case Studies in Economic Development

Studenmund
Using Econometrics

Su
Economic Fluctuations and Forecasting

Thomas
Modern Econometrics

Tietenberg
Environmental and Natural Resource Economics

Tietenberg
Environmental Economics and Policy

Todaro
Economic Development

Waldman/Jensen
Industrial Organization: Theory and Practice

SIXTH EDITION

MICROECONOMICS

Private Markets and Public Choice

Robert B. Ekelund, Jr.
Auburn University

Robert D. Tollison
University of Mississippi

WITH INTERNET RESOURCES PROVIDED BY
Audrey B. Davidson
University of Louisville
AND
Barry Haworth
University of Louisville

 ADDISON-WESLEY

An imprint of Addison Wesley Longman, Inc.

Reading, Massachusetts • Menlo Park, California • New York • Harlow, England
Don Mills, Ontario • Sydney • Mexico City • Madrid • Amsterdam

Executive Editor: Denise J. Clinton
Senior Sponsoring Editor: Andrea Shaw
Senior Project Manager: Mary Clare McEwing
Supplements Editor: Deborah Kiernan
Senior Production Supervisor: Juliet Silveri
Cover Design: Regina Hagen
Marketing Manager: Amy Cronin
Composition, Illustration, and Packaging Services: Electronic Publishing Services Inc., NYC
Text Design: Electronic Publishing Services Inc., NYC, and Regina Hagen
Print Buyer: Tim McDonald
Printer: R.R. Donnelley & Sons Company

Text and photo credits appear on page 845, which constitutes a continuation of the copyright page.

Library of Congress Cataloging-in-Publication Data.

Ekelund, Robert B. (Robert Burton), 1940-
Microeconomics : private markets and public choice / Robert B. Ekelund, Jr., Robert D.
Tollison.--6th ed.
    p. cm. -- (The Addison-Wesley series in economics)
Includes bibliographical references and index.
ISBN- 0-201-68027-0
1. Microeconomics.   I. Tollison, Robert D.   II. Title. III. Series
HB172.E39 2000   99-049580
338.5—dc21   CIP

Printed in the United States of America.

2 3 4 5 6 7 8 9 10—DOW—03020100

In Memory of Tim Fowler,
Chuck Maurice,
and Margaret O'Donnell-Whitlock,
and for those who loved them
RBE

For Anna
RDT

CONTENTS

PREFACE   xxv

PART 1   THE POWER OF ECONOMIC THINKING   1

CHAPTER 1   ECONOMICS IN PERSPECTIVE   3

WHAT ECONOMICS IS   3

Economics: A Working Definition   4

The Economic Condition: Scarcity   4

Focus: Scarcity, Economizing, and the College Student's Time   5

Scarce Resources and Economic Problems   6

Other Factors Affecting Resources and Growth   7

KEY PRINCIPLES OF ECONOMIC THINKING   8

Resources and Activities Cost More than You Think   8

Economic Behavior Is Rational   9

Choices Are Made at the Margin   10

Prices Are Signals to Producers and Consumers   10

Public Choices Are Different from Private Choices   11

Economists Do Not Decide Who Gets What   11

Money Is Helpful, but Not Too Much   12

Voters Choose the Role of Government—The Economist Analyzes   12

THE ROLE OF THEORY IN ECONOMICS   13

THE ROLE OF ECONOMICS AND ECONOMISTS   13

Positive and Normative Economics   14

Microeconomics and Macroeconomics   14

Let's Get to Work   15

Application: How Economics Prepares You for Life and Work   15

SUMMARY   16

KEY TERMS   17

QUESTIONS FOR REVIEW AND DISCUSSION   17

WORKING WITH THE WEB   17

Appendix: Working With Graphs   19

The Purpose of Graphs   19

How to Draw a Graph   20

Slope of the Curve   22

Summary   24

Key Terms   24

Questions for Review and Discussion   25

CHAPTER 2

OPPORTUNITY COST, SPECIALIZATION, AND TRADE   27

SPECIALIZATION AND TRADE: A FEATURE OF ALL SOCIETIES   27

Focus: Economic Specialization in Everyday Life: Marriage and Roommate Selection   28

OPPORTUNITY COST AND PRODUCTION POSSIBILITIES: INDIVIDUALS AND SOCIETY MUST CHOOSE   29

The Law of Increasing Costs   30

WHY THE PRODUCTION POSSIBILITIES FRONTIER SHIFTS   31

The Shifting Frontier   31

Economic Growth: How Economies Progress   31

COMPARATIVE ADVANTAGE   33

Specialization   36

Trade: The Fruits of Specialization   37

Factors Explaining Comparative Advantage   38

Exchange Costs   39

Focus: Free Trade Associations, Past and Present   42

Application: AIDS and Reduced Production Possibilities in Africa   45

SUMMARY   48

KEY TERMS   48

QUESTIONS FOR REVIEW AND DISCUSSION   48

PROBLEMS   49

WORKING WITH THE WEB   50

CHAPTER 3

PRIVATE MARKETS AND PRICES: LAWS OF DEMAND AND SUPPLY   51

AN OVERVIEW OF THE PRICE SYSTEM   51

The Circular Flow of Products and Resources   52

Full Versus Money Prices   52

Focus: Full Price and a New Orleans Restaurant   54

THE LAW OF DEMAND   54

The Individual's Demand Schedule and Demand Curve   55

Factors Affecting the Individual's Demand Curve   56

Reviewing the Law of Demand   60

From Individual to Market Demand   60

THE LAW OF SUPPLY AND FIRM SUPPLY   61

Changes in Quantity Supplied and Shifts in the Supply Curve   63

Market Supply   65

MARKET EQUILIBRIUM PRICE AND OUTPUT   65

The Mechanics of Price Determination   66

Price Rationing   67

Effects on Price and Quantity of Shifts in Supply or Demand   68

SIMPLE SUPPLY AND DEMAND ANALYSIS: OTHER CONSIDERATIONS   72

Price Controls and Public Choice   72

Focus: Price Floors Cost You More than Peanuts   75

Application: Opportunity Cost, "Scalping," and Full Price: Waiting for Van Gogh   76

SUMMARY   78

KEY TERMS   79

QUESTIONS FOR REVIEW AND DISCUSSION   79

PROBLEMS   80

WORKING WITH THE WEB   81

CHAPTER 4   DEMAND AND SUPPLY: PROPERTY, MARKETS, AND PUBLIC CHOICE   83

INSTITUTIONS ARE "RULES OF THE GAME" THAT FACILITATE MARKETS   84

Property Rights and Contracts   84

Property Rights and Economic Incentives   85

Focus: Shipping Live Prisoners to Australia   86

Private Competitive Markets   87

WHY ARE PRIVATE COMPETITIVE MARKETS EFFICIENT?   88

Demanders Value Goods   88

Supply, Costs, and Value   90

Competitive Equilibrium and Economic Efficiency   92

THE ROLE OF GOVERNMENT   94

The Environment, Externalities, and Market Failure   94

Public Goods and Market Failure   96

Antitrust and Monopoly Regulation   97

PUBLIC CHOICE—THE RELATION BETWEEN POLITICS
AND ECONOMIC EFFICIENCY   98

Political Versus Economic Markets   98

Why Are Voters "Myopic"?   99

Focus: Politicians are Demanded and Supplied   99

Interest Groups Tend to Dominate   101

INTEREST GROUPS AND WEALTH TRANSFERS: THE CASE OF
BARBERS AND COSMETOLOGISTS   101

Application: Why Are There So Many Restaurants and Golf Courses in State
Capital Cities?   105

SUMMARY   106

KEY TERMS   107

QUESTIONS FOR REVIEW AND DISCUSSION   107

WORKING WITH THE WEB   108

Point/Counterpoint   109

PART 2   THE ARCHITECTURE OF PRIVATE MARKETS   113

CHAPTER 5   ELASTICITY   115

THE CONCEPT OF ELASTICITY   116

PRICE ELASTICITY OF DEMAND   116

Formulation of Price Elasticity of Demand   116

Elastic, Inelastic, and Unit Elastic Demand   117

Elasticity Along the Demand Curve   118

Relation of Demand Elasticity to Expenditures and Receipts   121

DETERMINANTS OF PRICE ELASTICITY OF DEMAND   124

Focus: How to Tell Who Your Friends Are   125

Number and Availability of Substitutes   126

The Importance of Being Unimportant   126

Time and Elasticity of Demand   126

OTHER APPLICATIONS OF ELASTICITY OF DEMAND   127

Income Elasticity of Demand   128

Focus: Elasticity and Your World   129

Cross Elasticity of Demand   129

ELASTICITY OF SUPPLY   130

Time and Elasticity of Supply: Maryland Crab Fishing   131

Application: Cigarettes, Elasticity, and Public Choice: The Effects of an Excise Tax   132

SUMMARY   134

KEY TERMS   134

QUESTIONS FOR REVIEW AND DISCUSSION   134

PROBLEMS   135

WORKING WITH THE WEB   136

CHAPTER 6

THE LOGIC OF CONSUMER CHOICE AND DEMAND   137

UTILITY AND MARGINAL UTILITY   137

CONSUMER EQUILIBRIUM: DIMINISHING MARGINAL UTILITY AT WORK   139

Basic Assumptions   140

Balancing Choices Among Goods   141

Focus: Menus and Marginal Utility: "Save Room for Dessert!"   142

The Budget Constraint and Consumer Equilibrium   143

Consumers Maximize Satisfaction Among Thousands of Goods   146

Consumer Rationality and a Famous Riddle: Marginal Utility and Smith's Diamond–Water Paradox   146

FROM DIMINISHING MARGINAL UTILITY TO THE LAW OF DEMAND   148

The Substitution Effect and Income Effect   148

Focus: "All You Can Eat" Pizza   149

Marginal Utility and the Law of Demand   150

SOME PITFALLS TO AVOID   151

Application: Is It Rational to Vote?   152

SUMMARY   153

KEY TERMS   154

QUESTIONS FOR REVIEW AND DISCUSSION   154

PROBLEMS   155

WORKING WITH THE WEB   155

Appendix: Indifference Curve Analysis   157

Indifference Curves   157

Characteristics of Indifference Curves   158

The Budget Constraint   160

Consumer Equilibrium with Indifference Curves   161

Indifference Curves and the Law of Demand   162

Substitution and Income Effects   163

Summary   165

Key Terms   165

Questions For Review And Discussion   165

Problem   166

CHAPTER 7   THE FIRM AND COSTS OF PRODUCTION   167

THE NATURE OF THE FIRM   167

HOW MARKETS AND FIRMS COORDINATE RESOURCES   168

COSTS IN A BUSINESS FIRM   169

Focus: Going into Business for Yourself   170

Explicit and Implicit Costs   170

The Nature of Economic Costs   171

Economic Profits Versus Accounting Profits   172

Private Costs and Social Costs   172

ECONOMIC TIME   173

SHORT-RUN COSTS: AN INTRODUCTION   173

Fixed Costs and Variable Costs   173

Diminishing Returns   176

Going into Business with Others—The Partnership   178

Diminishing Marginal Returns and Short-Run Costs   180

LONG-RUN COSTS   183

Adjusting Plant Size   183

Economies and Diseconomies of Scale   184

Focus: Big Business: The Corporation 185

    Other Shapes of the Long-Run Average Total Cost Curve 185

SHIFTS IN COST CURVES 186

COSTS AND SUPPLY DECISIONS 187

**Application: The Draft, Jury Duty, and Conscripted "Public Service":
    Opportunity Cost and You 187**

SUMMARY 189

KEY TERMS 189

QUESTIONS FOR REVIEW AND DISCUSSION 190

PROBLEMS 190

WORKING WITH THE WEB 191

CHAPTER 8   COMPETITIVE MARKETS   193

THE PROCESS OF COMPETITION 194

PURE COMPETITION 194

Focus: The Economics of Information: Searching for the Best Deal 194

THE PURELY COMPETITIVE FIRM AND INDUSTRY IN
    THE SHORT RUN 197

    The Purely Competitive Firm as a Price Taker 197

    The Demand Curve of the Competitive Firm 197

    Short-Run Profit Maximization by the Purely Competitive Firm 197

    A Numerical Illustration of Profit Maximization 200

    Economic Losses and Shutdowns 203

    Supply Curve of a Purely Competitive Firm 205

    From Firm to Industry Supply 206

THE PURELY COMPETITIVE FIRM AND INDUSTRY IN
    THE LONG RUN 207

    Equilibrium in the Long Run 207

    The Adjustment Process: Establishing Equilibrium 208

    The Long-Run Industry Supply Curve 210

PURE COMPETITION AND ECONOMIC EFFICIENCY 213

    The Competitive Market and Resource Allocation 213

Focus: Don't Buy a "Lemon": Information Problems and You 215

    Competition in the Real World 216

**Application: Do You Have a "Hunting License?": The Full Price of Parking
    on Campus 217**

SUMMARY   219

KEY TERMS   220

QUESTIONS FOR REVIEW AND DISCUSSION   220

PROBLEMS   220

WORKING WITH THE WEB   221

Appendix: The Economics of Agriculture in the United States: Toward a Market Approach   222

   Government Attempts to Solve Basic Agricultural Problems   222

   The Move to Markets in Agriculture   225

CHAPTER 9   MONOPOLY: THE FIRM AS INDUSTRY   229

WHAT IS A MONOPOLY?   230

Focus: Mercantilism and the Sale of Monopoly Rights   230

   Legal Barriers to Entry   231

   Economies of Scale and Natural Monopoly   232

MONOPOLY PRICE AND OUTPUT IN THE SHORT RUN   232

   The Monopolist's Demand Curve   232

   The Monopolist's Revenues   234

   Total Revenue, Marginal Revenue, and Elasticity of Demand   236

   Short-Run Price and Output of the Monopolist   237

   Monopoly Profits   238

   Comparing the Monopoly Firm and the Purely Competitive Firm   240

PURE MONOPOLY IN THE LONG RUN   240

   Entry and Exit   240

   Adjustments to Scale   240

PRICE DISCRIMINATION   240

   When Can Price Discrimination Exist?   241

   A Model of Price Discrimination   241

Focus: "Are You a Victim of Price Discrimination on Campus?"   243

THE CASE AGAINST MONOPOLY   244

   The Welfare Loss Resulting from Monopoly Power   244

   Production Costs of a Monopoly   246

   Monopoly and the Distribution of Income   246

THE CASE FOR MONOPOLY   246

Focus: Patents: The Inventor's Monopoly   248

Application: Technology, Economics, and the Postal Monopoly 249

SUMMARY 251

KEY WORDS 252

QUESTIONS FOR REVIEW AND DISCUSSION 252

PROBLEMS 253

WORKING WITH THE WEB 253

CHAPTER 10 — MONOPOLISTIC COMPETITION AND ADVERTISING 255

MONOPOLISTIC COMPETITION 256

    Characteristics of Monopolistic Competition 256

    Advertising and Monopolistic Competition 257

Focus: Let Your Fingers Do the Walking: Information in Markets 260

Focus: Advertising, Interest Groups, and the Price of Eyeglasses 261

    Short-Run and Long-Run Equilibrium Under Monopolistic Competition 262

    Does Monopolistic Competition Waste Resources? 263

    How Useful Is the Theory of Monopolistic Competition? 266

Application: What's in a Brand Name? The Consumer Chooses 266

SUMMARY 268

KEY TERMS 268

QUESTIONS FOR REVIEW AND DISCUSSION 268

WORKING WITH THE WEB 269

CHAPTER 11 — FEW COMPETITORS: GAME THEORY, OLIGOPOLY, AND CARTELS 271

GAME THEORY AND MUTUAL INTERDEPENDENCE 272

    Mutual Interdependence in the Economic World 272

    Game Theory: A Basis for Small-Numbers Behavior 272

OLIGOPOLY 276

    Barriers to Entry 276

    Models of Oligopoly Pricing 277

CARTEL MODELS 280

    Characteristics of Cartels 281

Focus: Bid Rigging: Cartels in Action   281

    Cartel Formation   282

    The Cartel in Action   282

    Cartel Enforcement   283

    Why Cartels May or May Not Succeed   285

FROM COMPETITION TO MONOPOLY: THE SPECTRUM REVISITED   285

Application: Diamonds, the De Beers Cartel, and the Russian Threat   287

SUMMARY   289

KEY TERMS   290

QUESTIONS FOR REVIEW AND DISCUSSION   290

PROBLEMS   291

WORKING WITH THE WEB   291

Point/Counterpoint   292

PART 3   INPUT MARKETS   295

CHAPTER 12   COMPETITIVE LABOR MARKETS   297

FACTOR MARKETS: AN OVERVIEW   298

    Derived Demand   298

    Firms as Resource Price Takers   298

MARGINAL PRODUCTIVITY THEORY   300

    The Profit-Maximizing Level of Employment   300

    Profit-Maximizing Rules for All Inputs   302

THE DEMAND FOR LABOR   303

    The Short-Run Market Demand for Labor   304

    The Firm's Long-Run Demand for Labor   305

    Changes in the Demand for Labor   305

    Monopoly and the Demand for Labor   307

Focus: The Marginal Revenue Product of Professional Baseball Players   309

THE SUPPLY OF LABOR   309

    Individual Labor Supply   309

    Human Capital   312

    Other Equalizing Differences in Wages   314

Focus: Politics and "Justice" in the Workplace: Comparable Worth   315

MARGINAL PRODUCTIVITY THEORY AND INCOME DISTRIBUTION   316

Application: Where Do You Live? Regional Wage Differences   316

SUMMARY   318

KEY TERMS   319

QUESTIONS FOR REVIEW AND DISCUSSION   319

PROBLEMS   320

WORKING WITH THE WEB   320

CHAPTER 13   LABOR UNIONS   321

TYPES OF LABOR UNIONS   322

Craft Unions   322

Industrial Unions   322

Focus: The American Medical Association as a Union   323

Public Employees' Unions   323

The Decline of Union Membership in the United States   324

UNION ACTIVITIES   325

Union Goals   325

Union Objectives and the Elasticity of Demand   327

Focus: "Services Pay" and the Restructuring of the American Economy   328

Increasing the Demand for Union Labor   328

MONOPSONY: A SINGLE EMPLOYER OF LABOR   330

Bilateral Monopoly and the Need for Bargaining   331

Collective Bargaining   332

Strikes   332

Public Choice and Union Bargaining   334

The Union as a Political Interest Group   335

THE IMPACT OF UNIONS ON LABOR'S SHARE OF TOTAL INCOME   336

CONCLUSION   338

Application: Should College Football Players Be Paid? The NCAA Monopsony   338

SUMMARY   340

KEY TERMS   340

QUESTIONS FOR REVIEW AND DISCUSSION   340

PROBLEMS   341

WORKING WITH THE WEB   341

CHAPTER 14   CAPITAL, LAND, AND ENTREPRENEURSHIP   343

THE ROLE OF CAPITAL   343

Roundabout Production and Capital Formation   344

The Rate of Interest   345

Demand and Supply of Loanable Funds   346

Focus: Should You Be Protected from High Interest Rates? Usury and Interest Groups   348

Interest as the Return to Capital   349

The Nature of Returns to Owners of Capital   350

The Present Value of Future Income   351

The Benefits of Capital Formation   352

THE CONCEPT OF ECONOMIC RENT   354

LAND RENTS   354

The Supply of Land to Alternative Uses   355

PROFITS AND THE ALLOCATION OF RESOURCES   356

Profit Data   356

Rate of Return on Capital   357

Accounting Versus Economic Profits   358

ENTREPRENEURSHIP   358

Entrepreneurs and Information: The Austrian View   359

Application: Trading Property Rights: Stocks and Bonds   360

SUMMARY   362

KEY TERMS   363

QUESTIONS FOR REVIEW AND DISCUSSION   363

PROBLEMS   364

WORKING WITH THE WEB   364

CHAPTER 15   INCOME DISTRIBUTION, POVERTY, AND HEALTH CARE   367

THE INDIVIDUAL AND INCOME DISTRIBUTION   368

Labor Income   368

Income from Savings and Other Assets   369

Taxes and Transfer Payments   369

HOW IS INCOME INEQUALITY MEASURED?   370

Interpretation of Money Distribution Data   370

The Lorenz Curve   371

INCOME DISTRIBUTION IN THE UNITED STATES   373

Adjustments to Money Income   374

Factors Affecting Income Distribution   377

Age Distribution and Income   377

Rags to Riches Mobility   377

Focus: Divorce, Single-Parent Families, and Income Distribution   378

CHARACTERISTICS OF INCOME DISTRIBUTION: POVERTY AND DISCRIMINATION   378

Poverty   379

Race and Sex Discrimination in Wages   380

Alleviating Poverty: The 1996 Revolution in Welfare   381

HEALTH CARE: AN ONGOING PROBLEM   383

The U.S. Health Care System   383

Focus: Should You Buy Health Insurance?   384

Health Care Reform: Some Models   385

Focus: Who Pays the Bill for Patients' Rights?   386

THE JUSTICE OF INCOME DISTRIBUTION   388

Application: Does Social Security Protect the Poor?   388

SUMMARY   391

KEY TERMS   391

QUESTIONS FOR REVIEW AND DISCUSSION   392

PROBLEM   392

WORKING WITH THE WEB   393

Point/Counterpoint   394

PART 4   APPLIED MICROECONOMICS AND PUBLIC CHOICE   397

CHAPTER 16   ANTITRUST, REGULATION, AND PUBLIC POLICY   399

MEASURING INDUSTRIAL CONCENTRATION   400
  Industry Concentration Ratios   400
PUBLIC POLICY: ANTITRUST   402
  Antitrust Law   402
  Antitrust Agencies   403
  Enforcement of Antitrust Policies   404
  Multinational Firms   407
  An Economic View of Antitrust Cases   408
PUBLIC POLICY: REGULATION   408
Focus: The Microsoft Case: Is It Monopoly, or Is It Envy?   409
  Regulatory Agencies   409
  The Purpose of Regulation   412
  Health and Safety Regulation   415
  Government Ownership   416
  Laissez-Faire   417
THE MOVEMENT TO DEREGULATION   417
Focus: Franchising Funerals in Nineteenth-Century London and Paris   418
Focus: Airline Deregulation: Success Story or Consumer Nightmare?   421
CONCLUSION   422
Application: The Telecommunications Act of 1996: Good Intentions Meet Market Realities   422
  Local Phone Service   422
  Payphones   423
  Credit Card Calls   423
  Cable Rates   423
  Radio and TV Markets   424
SUMMARY   425
KEY TERMS   426
QUESTIONS FOR REVIEW AND DISCUSSION   426

PROBLEMS   426

WORKING WITH THE WEB   427

CHAPTER 17   NATURAL RESOURCES, THE ENVIRONMENT, AND PUBLIC GOODS   429

NATURAL RESOURCES   430

The Market for Nonrenewable Resources   431

The Market for Renewable Resources   432

Focus: The Economics of Doomsday   433

THE ECONOMICS OF COMMON PROPERTY   434

Fishing in International Waters   434

Drilling for Oil   435

International Pollution Problems: Acid Rain and Global Warming   437

Focus: The Kyoto Treaty: Who Benefits from Global Warming?   438

EXTERNALITY THEORY   439

Negative and Positive Externalities   439

Determining the Need for Government Intervention   440

Correcting Relevant Externalities   441

PUBLIC GOODS THEORY   447

Public Provision of Public Goods   448

Free Riders   449

Pricing Public Goods   449

A ROLE FOR GOVERNMENT   452

Application: Can Economic Incentives Save the Elephant and Other Endangered Species?   452

SUMMARY   454

KEY TERMS   454

QUESTIONS FOR REVIEW AND DISCUSSION   455

PROBLEMS   455

WORKING WITH THE WEB   456

CHAPTER 18   PUBLIC CHOICE   457

SELF-INTEREST AND POLITICS   458

PUBLIC CHOICE ANALYSIS OF MAJORITY VOTING   459

PUBLIC CHOICE ANALYSIS OF POLITICS   461

Political Competition   461

Logrolling   462

Focus: Can You Buy an Election?   463

Voting   464

Interest Groups   466

Bureaucracy   468

Focus: Economics of the Birds and the Bees   469

CONSTITUTIONAL POLITICAL ECONOMY   470

Application: Registering Minority Votes   472

SUMMARY   474

KEY TERMS   475

QUESTIONS FOR REVIEW AND DISCUSSION   475

PROBLEM   475

WORKING WITH THE WEB   476

Point/Counterpoint   477

In this volume, Chapter 18 is followed by Chapter 30.

PART 8   INTERNATIONAL TRADE AND THE GLOBAL ECONOMY   769

CHAPTER 30   INTERNATIONAL TRADE   771

THE IMPORTANCE OF INTERNATIONAL TRADE   772

National Involvement in International Trade   773

Why Trade Is Important: Comparative Advantage   774

Tariffs and Quotas   780

THE EFFECTS OF ARTIFICIAL TRADE BARRIERS   780

Welfare Loss from Tariffs   781

Why Are Tariffs Imposed?   782

Nontariff Barriers to Trade   782

A Quota Is a Quota Is a Tariff   783

THE CASE FOR PROTECTION   785

National Interest Arguments for Protection   785

Focus: Autos, Peanuts, and Politics: How Quotas Affect You   785

Industry Arguments for Protection   787

Focus: "Fair Trade" and Protectionism: The Steel Industry   789

U.S. TARIFF POLICY   790

Early Tariff Policy   790

Modern Tariff Policy   790

Where Does the United States Stand in the Battle for Free Trade?   792

Focus: China and the World Trade Organization   793

Application: NAFTA: Free Trade or Free-for-All?   794

SUMMARY   795

KEY TERMS   796

QUESTIONS FOR REVIEW AND DISCUSSION   796

PROBLEMS   797

WORKING WITH THE WEB   797

CHAPTER 31   **INTERNATIONAL FINANCE   799**

THE FOREIGN EXCHANGE MARKET   800

Exchange Rates   800

Exchange Rate Systems   802

Focus: The Euro, Europe's New Money   803

FLEXIBLE EXCHANGE RATES   804

Exchange Rates Between Two Countries   804

Changes in Flexible Exchange Rates   806

FIXED EXCHANGE RATES   810

The Operation of a Fixed Exchange Rate System   810

Fixed Exchange Rates   812

MACROECONOMIC POLICY, EXCHANGE RATES, AND TRADE
BALANCE   814

Monetary Policy   814

Focus: Should We Return to a Gold Standard?   815

Fiscal Policy   815

THE BALANCE OF PAYMENTS   816

Exports and Imports: The Balance of Trade   817

Net Transfers Abroad   818

Current Account Balance   818

Net Capital Movements   818

Statistical Discrepancy   818

The Balance of Payments and the Value of the Dollar   819

THE EVOLUTION OF INTERNATIONAL MONETARY
INSTITUTIONS   819

The Decline of the Gold Standard   819

Bretton Woods and the Postwar System   819

The Current International Monetary System   821

Application: The Asian Economic Crisis   823

SUMMARY   825
KEY TERMS   826
QUESTIONS FOR REVIEW AND DISCUSSION   826
PROBLEM   827
WORKING WITH THE WEB   828
Point/Counterpoint   829

GLOSSARY   833

CREDITS   845

INDEX   847

PREFACE

Economic issues dominate the world we live in, affecting our perceptions about ourselves and our futures. Like it or not, we are faced with economic issues on television, in newspapers, in the voting booth, in career choice, and perhaps most significantly, in balancing our checkbooks every month! How do price controls affect consumers and producers? Will higher excise taxes deter teenagers from smoking? What does economics have to say about sound environmental policies? Is the government's case against Microsoft a good one? What is the role of labor unions in the economy? Is deregulation of markets a good thing? Do federally guaranteed entitlements—such as Medicare, Social Security, and welfare—have a future? Should government mandate a Patients' Bill of Rights for HMOs if it will contribute to higher premiums and less affordable insurance for more people?

A solid foundation in economics helps us answer such questions. In this sixth edition of our introduction to microeconomics, we again present economic ideas in a policy-real-world context that students—both those who continue the study of economics and those for whom this is the first and last class—can master and understand. Since our approach stresses the relationship between theory and policy, the technical presentations in this book are concise and straightforward. We rely heavily on examples to illustrate abstract theory, and describe graphs and graphical relationships in patient detail.

Our approach to economic study is "market oriented." It stresses that, in general, society's welfare is maximized when markets are used to allocate resources to their most desired private uses. Our approach goes further, however, to show (as early as the first chapter) how our public choices working through a political process can have a number of effects, not all of them desirable from the perspective of society. Democratic politics (as we make clear in Chapter 4) and interest groups may actually reduce society's welfare. In short, our approach to basic microeconomics is underscored by the integration of politics and markets and is illustrated by the complete title of our book—*Microeconomics: Private Markets and Public Choice.*

The sixth edition again covers microeconomics in clear and student-friendly prose with:

- Renewed emphasis on the use of markets to solve the basic economic problems created by scarcity;
- New and interesting examples of how economic and political markets interact and affect economic efficiency;
- Coverage of recent and continuing global events, including the Asian financial crisis and the advent of the euro as a common currency for Europe;
- Clear analysis of important domestic policies and proposals relating to such issues as health insurance, welfare reform, poverty, and deregulation; and
- Targeted, but streamlined discussions of theory and policy in a shorter presentation than that of the fifth edition (now 20 rather than 21 chapters).

CHANGES IN THE SIXTH EDITION

The overarching aims for the sixth edition have been to streamline the material for the typical principles course and to continue to enliven and enrich the material for students approaching economics for the first time. Among the main changes in the sixth edition are the following:

- *New material on the economics of information*, such as the problem of asymmetric information.
- *New, broadened discussion of environmental economics* and approaches to market failures such as pollution, overfishing, endangered species, and finite natural resources. The authors frame the discussion of renewable and nonrenewable resources in terms of the familiar concepts of supply and demand.
- *Tightening of the exposition of microeconomics,* including the subsuming of material on the firm into the chapter on competition.
- *A wealth of new applications.* About half of the Focus Boxes and lengthier end-of-chapter Applications are new to the sixth edition. These features spotlight the applicability of economic theory to real-world situations and scenarios. Among the many new topics and questions explored are whether Social Security protects the poor, how the Microsoft case can be viewed as monopoly or competitors' envy, what the repercussions of the Telecommunications Act of 1996 might be, how the "economics of Doomsday" has been part of environmental economics since the beginning of recorded history, and how the Asian financial crisis evolved.
- *The addition of Internet exercises to each chapter*. These exercises get students "working with the Web" in ways that help them see the relevance of the chapter material to all sorts of issues and situations—economic, political, and personal.

ENDURING THEMES

The public choice theme (present in all previous editions) continues in the sixth edition. In spite of the proposed public choice emphasis of other texts, we have found that the critical issue of how politics affects markets is not integrated into discussions of standard microeconomic issues. In our book we provide this coverage. In addition to carrying two full chapters dealing with public choice (Chapters 4 and 18), we provide in-text and "application-style" examples integrating public choice with discussion of basic economic issues. Thus, the student is introduced to such issues as how laws against scalping affect the revenue of public agencies (Chapter 3); the relationship between politics and excise taxes (Chapter 5); why voting is rational (Chapter 6); jury conscription (Chapter 7); campus parking politics (Chapter 8); the U.S. postal monopoly (Chapter 9); bid rigging (Chapter 11); the American Medical Association (Chapter 13); patients' rights (Chapter 15); and airline deregulation (Chapter 16).

There is an ongoing emphasis on the importance of all trade, including international trade. The principles of specialization, opportunity cost, and trade run throughout the book and are explicitly introduced to the student in Chapter 2, which explains the role of free trade associations such as NAFTA in producing greater economic welfare and integrates international trade and interest group considerations right from the beginning. The emphasis on the importance of international trade and markets is carried throughout the text. See, for example, discussions of tariffs and quotas in Chapter 30 and the discussion of international financial developments, such as the euro, in Chapter 31.

ORGANIZATION

The organization of *Microeconomics: Private Markets and Public Choice* is divided into four parts, consisting of 20 chapters:

Part One—The Power of Economic Thinking

Part Two—The Architecture of Private Markets

Part Three—Input Markets

Part Four—Applied Microeconomics and Public Choice

Part Eight—International Trade and the Global Economy

The object of our presentation of microeconomics is again to focus on an intuitive and carefully graded exposition of basic economic principles. The fundamental issues of supply and demand, elasticity, competitive and non-competitive markets, and input pricing are given this treatment right along with the topics that have become "standard" text material only recently (such as game theory in Chapter 11). In addition, we have attempted to include important and topical microeconomic issues, including free trade (Chapter 3), interest groups (Chapter 4), teen smoking (Chapter 5), agricultural policy and the Freedom to Farm Act (Chapter 8 Appendix), the U.S. postal monopoly (Chapter 9), advertising (Chapter 10), cartels (Chapter 11), regional wage differences (Chapter 12), labor unions (Chapter 13), entrepreneurship (Chapter 14), Social Security and health care reform (Chapter 15), antitrust policy (Chapter 16), deregulation (Chapter 16), environmental issues and finite resources (Chapter 17), expenditures and public goods (Chapter 17), and, of course, public choice (Chapter 18).

We have made two basic changes in the microeconomics presentation. Chapter 7 of this edition (on the firm and production costs) is now a combination of the previous Chapters 7 and 8, which treated these topics separately. The new Chapter 7 more effectively integrates the theory of the firm with the theory of costs. We have also expanded Chapter 17 into a full-scale presentation of environmental economics and issues in recognition of this increasingly important area.

Part Eight, International Trade and the Global Economy, includes Chapters 30 and 31, which are devoted to issues relating to international trade and finance, including recent major events such as the Asian financial crisis and the arrival of a common European currency, the euro. A number of instructors have told us that they prefer to teach these issues as a special unit or topic. These chapters have been streamlined and completely updated for that purpose. However, international trade issues and their relation to our economy and well-being are an integral part of our entire book. Our view is that these issues are not separate from trade issues in general. We therefore begin, in Chapter 2, with matters of specialization, comparative advantage, and trade from an international perspective. These ideas and applications are then carried throughout the book.

PEDAGOGICAL FEATURES

We have incorporated a number of learning tools for students to aid understanding and retention of material.

- Each chapter opens with an overview of the topics covered and a bulleted list of chapter objectives.
- Figures are drawn with consistent use of color, helping students understand key

concepts and the direction and magnitude of changes in economic behavior.

■ Key concepts and terms are boldfaced when first mentioned in the text, with definitions appearing in the margin.

■ Reader-friendly Focus boxes—at least one per chapter—provide interpretations and perspectives on critical or illustrative ideas or policies mentioned in the text. Many of the Focus features are new to the sixth edition. New examples include: "Price Floors Cost You More than Peanuts" (Chapter 3); "Shipping Live Prisoners to Australia" (Chapter 4); "Politicians Are Demanded and Supplied" (Chapter 4); "Elasticity and Your World" (Chapter 5); "All You Can Eat Pizza" (Chapter 6); "Going Into Business for Yourself" (Chapter 7); "Going Into Business With Others" (Chapter 7); "Big Business—The Corporation" (Chapter 7); "Let Your Fingers Do the Walking: Information in Markets" (Chapter 10); "The American Medical Association as a Union" (Chapter 13); "Services Pay and the Restructuring of the American Economy" (Chapter 13); "Who Pays the Bill for Patients' Rights?" (Chapter 15); "The Microsoft Case: Is It Monopoly or Is It Envy?" (Chapter 16); "The Economics of Doomsday" (Chapter 17); "The Kyoto Treaty: Who Benefits from Global Warming?" (Chapter 17); "Can You Buy an Election?" (Chapter 18); "Economics of the Birds and the Bees" (Chapter 18); and "The Euro: Europe's New Money" (Chapter 31).

■ Applications of key text material are again included in our presentation. These are in-depth discussions of issues or policies brought up in the text. New applications include: "How Economics Prepares You for Life and Work" (Chapter 1); "AIDS and Reduced Production Possibilities in Africa" (Chapter 2); "'Scalping' and Full Price: Waiting for Van Gogh" (Chapter 3); "The Draft, Jury Duty, and Conscripted 'Public Service': Opportunity Cost and You" (Chapter 7); "Do You Having a Hunting License?: The Full Price of Parking on Campus" (Chapter 8); "Does Social Security Protect the Poor?" (Chapter 15); and "The Asian Economic Crisis"(Chapter 31).

■ Every chapter contains a concluding summary of the major ideas and concepts of the chapter, a list of key terms, questions for review and discussion, and, where applicable, problems for the student to solve.

■ "Working with the Web" exercises, designed to give students research experience on the Internet, are new to this edition.

■ Point/Counterpoint features containing biographies of great economists, past and present, along with their contrasting ideas, conclude each book part.

■ A glossary of terms is provided at the back of the book, together with a useful and thorough index.

PRINT SUPPLEMENTS

The *Study Guide* by John Keith Watson of the University of Southwestern Louisiana is a comprehensive learning package containing chapter overviews; learning objectives; helpful hints; fill-in, true/false, multiple-choice, and short-answer questions; and "Something to Think About" segments.

The *Instructor's Resource Manual* by John Keith Watson of the University of Southwestern Louisiana is coordinated with the text and contains chapter overviews and outlines, learning objectives, answers to text questions, extra problems and essays with solutions, "One Step Further" segments, and suggestions for additional readings.

The *Test Bank* by John Thompson of Louisiana State University contains over 3,400 multiple-choice questions coded by level of difficulty. Ten percent of the questions are new to this edition and are identified with a marginal icon.

SOFTWARE SUPPLEMENTS

The *Instructor's Resource CD-ROM (Instructor's Resource Disk)* contains a Power-Point presentation, electronic Word files of the Instructor's Manual and Test Bank, and a Computerized Test Bank in TestGen-EQ 3.0.

The PowerPoint presentation contains all of the art from the book and is available in Macintosh and Windows formats. Those who have PowerPoint software can easily edit these slides to fit their individual teaching approaches. Those who do not have the software can still view the presentation through the PowerPoint Viewer provided on the disk.

TestGen-EQ 3.0, a computerized test generator that allows you to construct tests by choosing questions from the test bank, is available in Macintosh and Windows versions. If desired, test questions can be viewed on the screen, edited, saved, and printed. Instructors can also add or create their own questions.

ACKNOWLEDGMENTS

No book of this size and structure could be developed without the help of friends, colleagues, friendly critics, not-so-friendly critics, and editors. This book, both in its former editions and in the new sixth edition, is no exception. We gratefully acknowledge the following colleagues, friends, users, and students (past and present) whose generosity and advice fill these pages: John Allen, Gary Anderson, Leonardo Auernheimer, Andy Barnett, Raymond Battalio, Randy Beard, Richard Beil, Don Boudreaux, the late Katherine Boudreaux, Bill Biret, Butch Browning, Steve Caudill, Roy Cordato, Mark Crain, Elynor Davis, Charles DeLorme, David Gay, Kathie Gilbert, Cary Heath, Bob Hebert, Elmer Holt, Justin Issacs, John Jackson, Dave Kaserman, Roger Koppel, Dave Laband, Dwight Lee, Bobby McCormick, the late Charles Maurice, Francois Melese, the late Margaret O'Donnell, Karen Palasek, Chris Paul, Phil Porter, Ed Price, Morgan Reynolds, Richard Saba, Tom Saving, Bill Shughart, John Sophocles, Chris Thomas, Henry Thompson, Marc Ulrich, John Wells, and David Whitten. For special help and assistance on this edition we want to thank Roy Gilbert of Texas A&M University, Rand Ressler of the University of Southwestern Louisiana, and Bill Biret of Trinity University. John Thompson of Louisiana State University has offered valuable advice and provided an excellent and streamlined *Test Bank* for the sixth edition.

Several individuals deserve very special gratitude for helping us improve the quality and direction of *Economics* in both this edition and previous ones: Frank Adams, Troy State University; Richard Ault, Auburn University; Rob Blackstock, Auburn University; Audrey Davidson, University of Louisville; Paula Gant, Duke Energy; Rand Ressler, University of Southwestern Louisiana; David Saurman, San Jose State University; Keith Watson, University of Southwestern Louisiana; and Mark Thornton, Columbus State University.

Past and present graduate assistants—many of whom are now professors and productive contributors to economic research—were of help with all six editions of *Economics*: Manisha Perrera, Bharat Vijayan, Brian Goff, Ladd Jones, Cassandra Copeland, Dan Berry, George Ford, Elmer Holt, Yvan Kelly, Paul Gentle, Dwight Nystrom, Shawn Rittenour, Ken Somppi, John Thompson, Jim Tillery, Marc Ulrich, Deborah Walker, Doug Walker, and Biff Woodruff. Of special help in this sixth edition was Mark Thornton, Columbus State University.

We are grateful to Andrea Shaw and (in this and earlier editions) to Denise Clinton for unflagging support for our book. Most of all, however, we wish to sincerely thank Mary Clare McEwing, Senior Project Manager for the sixth edition, for her humor, intelligent criticism, good taste, and hard work in guiding our work. It could not have been done without her.

Official reviewers for this edition were Audrey Davidson, University of Louisville; Edward Flaherty, College of Charleston; Tom Means, San Jose State University; Ernest Morgan, College of The Albermarle; Mark Perry, University of Michigan; and Rand Ressler, University of Southwestern Louisiana.

Official reviewers and contributors for the earlier editions were Douglas K. Agbetsiafa, Indiana University; Ralph E. Ancil, Southwestern Missouri State University; Robert A. Baade, Lake Forest College; Dean Baim, Pepperdine University; Richard O. Beil, Jr., Auburn University; J. Lloyd Blackwell, IV, University of North Dakota; Robert Carbaugh, Central Washington University; Albert Celoza, Phoenix College; John Dennis Chasse, State University of New York-Brockport; George Shih-Fan Chu, University of Nevada at Reno; Paul A. Cleveland, University of Central Florida; Cheryl Cohen, Millikin University; Barbara Craig, Oberlin College; Robert D. Crofts, Salem State College; Steve Cunningham, University of Connecticut; William W. Davis, Western Kentucky University; David Denslow, University of Florida; Carl E. Enomoto, New Mexico State University; Donald H. Farness, Oregon State University; Arthur A. Fleisher III, Metropolitan State College of Denver; Andrew W. Foshee, McNeese State University; Robert Gillette, Texas A&M University; Richard F. Gleisner, St. Cloud State University; Jack Goddard, Northeastern State University; Anthony Greco, University of Southwestern Louisiana; Carole A. Green, University of South Florida; William B. Green, Sam Houston State University; Edward Greenberg, Washington University; Anthony O. Gyapong, Wayne State University; Jan M. Hansen, University of Wisconsin-Eau Claire; Cary Heath, University of Southwestern Louisiana; Steven C. Hine, State University of New York-Binghamton; George Hoffer, Virginia Commonwealth University; James H. Holcomb, Jr., University of Texas-El Paso; John B. Horowitz, Ball State University; Arthur Kartman, San Diego State University; Philip King, San Francisco State University; Gary F. Langer, Roosevelt University; Stephen E. Lile, Western Kentucky University; David MacPherson, Florida State University; Marvin S. Margolis, Millersville University; Lawrence W. Martin, Michigan State University; Warren Matthews, Texas A&M University; James N. McGowen, Jr., Belleview Area College; Mary Ann Meiners, Middle Tennessee State University; Charles C. Milliken, Siena Heights College; Khan Mohabbat, Northern Illinois University; Dan Myers, Western Kentucky University; Emmanuel Nnadozie, Northeast Missouri State University; Edd Noell, Westmont College; Terry Olsen; Don Owen, Ottawa University; Elliot Parker, University of Nevada at Reno; Ken Patterson, Oregon State University; Gerald Pelovsky, College of the Sequoias; Steven C. Pitts, Houston Community College; J. M. Pogodzinski, San Jose State University; Munir Quddus, University of Southern Indiana; Farhad Rassekh, University of Hartford; Rand Ressler, University of Southwestern Louisiana; Doralia Reynolds, Seward County Community College; Peter Rupert, West Virginia University; Carlos E. Santiago, State University of New York-Albany; Gerald W. Sazama, University of Connecticut; Phil Sorenson, Florida State University; Chaitram J. Talele, Columbia State Community College; Steven G. Thorpe, University of Colorado at Boulder; H. Bruce Throckmorton, Tennessee Technological University; Abraham Usumang, Bowling Green State University; James VanBeck, Blinn College-College Station Campus; John Wakemann-Linn, Williams College; Harold Warren, East Tennessee State University; Walter J. Wessells, North Carolina State University; Darrell Young, University of Texas-Austin; and Mahmood Yousefi, University of Northern Iowa.

Sixth Edition

MICROECONOMICS
PRIVATE MARKETS AND PUBLIC CHOICE

PART ONE

The Power of Economic Thinking

Economics
in Perspective

E conomics is the general study of human behavior in most, if not all, of its man-
ifestations. As such, it offers a way of thinking about how the world works
and a framework for making choices and decisions of all kinds. These choices
may be private choices about such issues as how much you should invest in
higher education, or they may be public choices about which candidate to vote for or
which public policy is most desirable. Close study of economics gives us a new perspective on a wide variety of human activities and institutions. When you finish Chapter 1 you should understand

- how individuals, societies, and nations solve the pervasive economic problem
  caused by scarce resources and unlimited wants.
- the functions of prices and how they act as signals to producers, consumers, and
  governments in any economy.
- how individuals actually make economic decisions.
- how economics gives insight into human behavior regarding the private and public
  choices that individuals make.

WHAT ECONOMICS IS

Economics is a social science—the oldest and best developed of the social sciences. As
such, it studies human behavior in relation to three basic questions about an economy:
What **goods** and **services** are produced? How are goods and services produced? For
whom are goods and services produced?

3

Goods
All tangible things that satisfy people's wants and desires.

Services
All forms of intangible but useful activities that are valued by people.

For at least 200 years, economists have tried to analyze how individuals and societies answer these questions. Communism, for example, appeared to be a viable answer to the questions *what, how,* and *for whom* in many countries throughout much of the twentieth century, but today it has largely been abandoned in favor of capitalism, free markets, and limited government.

Economics, particularly the study of markets, has much to say about the link between the amount of government economic control and personal freedom and democracy. The insistent questions—What? How? and For whom? —must be asked; for at least two centuries, economists have tried to analyze how individuals and societies answer them.

Economics: A Working Definition

A common thread runs through all definitions of economics. Each definition emphasizes the inescapable fact that **resources**—the wherewithal to produce goods and services—are not available in limitless quantities and that people and societies, with their unlimited desires for goods and services, must make some hard choices about what to do with the resources that are available. Our working definition of economics may be expressed as follows:

Resources
Those things used to produce goods and services. These include land, machines, energy, and human labor and ingenuity. Resources are also called factors of production.

> Economics is the study of how individuals, experiencing virtually limitless wants, choose to allocate scarce resources to best satisfy their wants.

Unlimited wants, scarcity, and the choices they force on us are thus the key elements in understanding economics.

The Economic Condition: Scarcity

Scarcity
The condition whereby the resources, goods, and services available to individuals and society are limited relative to the wants and desires for them.

What, exactly, is **scarcity**? More to the point, what are scarce resources? As individuals and as a society, we cannot get all of what we want because the amount of available resources is limited. The role of the economist and of economics in general is to explain how we can make the most of this problem of scarcity—how to get as much as we can of what we want.

The most important problem in economics is that while the wants of individuals and societies must be satisfied by limited resources, the wants themselves are not limited; they are endless. We are never satisfied with what we have. Individuals will forever be lured by more tempting foods, more cleverly engineered computers, more up-to-date fashions. We also desire safer highways, more national security, greater Social Security benefits, or more cancer research. Problems of scarcity and unlimited wants—economics itself—apply to all nations, regardless of political, social, and religious orientation. Moslems, Jews, and Christians all face the eternal problem of satisfying limitless wants with limited means. Methods of dealing with scarcity, of course, differ from society to society, depending on cultural differences and on particular endowments of resources within political boundaries, but the fundamental problem is the same everywhere and at all times.

Scarcity affects both private and public choices. We must choose virtually every day among items that we commonly purchase, such as food, transportation, and clothing, and we surely cannot have all of the things that we would like to have. How about a new Mercedes? And in our public choices as well, scarcity dictates that we must choose. Do we want to support candidates who want to spend more resources on public programs or less? How about increased space missions?

Economic goods and services
Goods and services that are scarce.

Costs
An implication of scarcity; the necessary sacrifices associated with making any choice.

All scarce goods—from television to chlorinated water—are called **economic goods**. Their scarcity leads to **costs**. While it is customary to associate cost with the money price of goods, economists define cost as the value of the good or activity given up in place of the good or activity actually chosen. Since all unlimited wants cannot be met with scarce resources, individuals have to make choices—between, for instance, more steaks and more computer games. Public choices have to be made between safer highways and more accurate missiles. Cost is, therefore, the direct result of the scarcity of resources. Scarcity of resources means that individuals, both in their public and private choices, must endure the costs of acquiring more of any good or service. That cost is the value of the good or activity given up in place of the good chosen.

Think for a moment about that scarce resource time. Being absolutely limited in supply for each of us, time—or rather, the use of time—bears a definite cost. No college student, certainly, has escaped being confronted with economic decisions arising from the need to allocate this costly resource. (See the Focus "Scarcity, Economizing, and the College Student's Time.")

Free goods and services
Things that are available in sufficient amounts and provide all that people want at zero cost.

You may feel that some things are not scarce and that some things—such as love, sunshine, and water—are free. In economic terms, **free goods and services** are goods that are available in sufficient amounts to satisfy all possible demands. But are many things truly free? Surface water is usually unfit for drinking except in areas far from human habitation. Water suitable for drinking must be raised to the

FOCUS

Scarcity, Economizing, and the College Student's Time

College students know the principle of scarcity all too well. Indeed, a successful student needs an ability to make sound and efficient economic decisions not only in the case of scarce monetary resources but in the allocation of scarce time resources as well. Time is a valuable resource to all human beings, but it exists in finite quantities of 24 hours a day, 168 hours a week, and (approximately) 720 hours a month.

Every student knows that he or she cannot have and do everything and that economic decisions, whether they are recognized as such or not, must be made every day. A student's time often must be allocated over a day or a week. A weekend trip to an out-of-town football game must be "paid for" not only in monetary terms but also in less time to work on the English paper due on Wednesday. The end of a term always necessitates economizing: Given the limited time available, should an additional two hours be directed to chemistry or art history? Actual choices will depend on perceived net gain or potential net gain from the array of alternatives.

College students are not alone, of course. For anyone, the choice may be between attending a rock concert or a Bach organ recital. We may have chosen a career in acting or dance instead of law or computer programming. A retiree may choose to return to the classroom rather than to spend time fishing or playing bridge. Economizing—maximizing the value of monetary or time resources under conditions of scarcity—forms the foundation of human behavior. Students, workers, politicians, philanthropists, business executives—all must make choices, and an analysis of these choices forms the basis of the social science of economics.

surface from deep wells or piped from reservoirs and treatment plants, operations involving resources that are scarce even when water itself is not. Scarcity of winter sun in the North leads many people to seek costly winter vacations in the snowbird states. And if you think love is free. . . .

Scarce Resources and Economic Problems

Human resources
All forms of labor and skill used to produce goods and services.

Nonhuman resources
All resources other than human resources, such as machines and land.

There are basically two categories of scarce resources: human resources and nonhuman resources. **Human resources** encompass all types of labor, including specialized forms of labor such as management or entrepreneurship. **Nonhuman resources** include land, natural resources such as minerals and water, and capital.

Examples of human resources abound. By definition, all human resources apply talent and energy to produce goods and services. The cook at the Chicken Shack, the hairstylist at the Mad Hacker, the chief executive of a computer firm, and the assembly-line worker at a General Motors plant all represent human resources. Obviously, labor includes a huge variety of skills, both general and precise. Knowledge, or know-how, is also part of human resources. Economists are interested not only in the scarcity of labor but in its quality. The quality of human resources can be enhanced through investments in education and training.

Economists view *entrepreneurship* as a special form of labor. An entrepreneur is a person who perceives profitable opportunities and who combines resources to produce goods or services. Entrepreneurs attempt to move resources from lower- to higher-valued uses in the economy and take the risk that they can make profits by doing so. Inventors, such as Thomas Edison, are good examples of entrepreneurs. *Management*, a second special form of labor, guides and oversees the process by which separate resources are turned into goods or services.

Human resources utilize nonhuman things such as land, minerals, and natural resources to produce goods and services. A commercial lot in Manhattan, a farm acre in Iowa, a coal deposit in Pennsylvania, a uranium mine in South Dakota, and a timber stand in Oregon are all scarce nonhuman resources. New deposits of minerals can be discovered, forests can be replanted, and agricultural land can be reclaimed from swamps. But at any one time, the available supply of nonhuman resources is limited.

Capital, another category of nonhuman resources, comprises all machines, implements, and buildings used to produce goods and services either directly or indirectly. A surgeon's scalpel, a factory, an electric generator, and an artist's brush are all used to produce goods and services and, thus, are considered to be capital goods.

Many different forms of capital may be needed to produce a single economic good. With a wheat harvesting machine, a South Dakota farmer can reap a huge crop. But the wheat must also be milled into flour and transported from South Dakota to bakeries in, say, California. Once the wheat has arrived, bakeries must utilize brick or convection ovens to produce bread. The harvesting and milling machines, the railroad, and the baker's ovens are all capital goods, created to increase the amount of final production.

Capital—and the resources used to produce it—is scarce. To create capital, we must sacrifice consumer goods and services because the production of capital takes time away from the production of goods that can be consumed in the present. Societies and individuals must therefore choose between immediate consumption and future consumption. That choice is crucial to economic growth and ultimate economic well-being.

Other Factors Affecting Resources and Growth

Quantities of human and nonhuman resources are only one prerequisite for economic growth and well-being in an economy. The institutional framework of an economy, such as the nature of its legal system and its form of government, is also critical for economic growth and development, as are factors such as technology and information. Consider, first, the nature of technology and information.

Technology and information assist resource utilization in a modern, functioning economy. **Technology,** in general, is composed of know-how, inventions, and innovations that help us get more from scarce resources. An improvement in technology implies that we can produce more from a given amount of resources. Existing technology is the outcome of many inventions, some of which were the invention of new resources—such as aluminum and hybrid plants. All inventions that increase the productivity of labor and capital can be considered improvements in technology. Innovation is the application of technology to the production of goods and services. Technology, then, helps make other resources less scarce.

Technology
Knowledge of production methods associated with producing a particular good.

Information is a scarce and costly ingredient in the economic process. The acquisition of information for economic decision making has never been free. In the nineteenth and early twentieth centuries, businesses hired armies of bookkeepers to provide sufficient information for managers to make decisions. The development of the digital computer in the mid-twentieth century made the storage and retrieval of information less costly. Technology has progressed so rapidly that the quantity of information that could be stored in a warehouse-sized computer in 1950 can now be placed on a chip the size of a fingernail. Information, then, helps us economize on the use of scarce resources.

Information
A costly but necessary input in the process of economic exchange and growth.

Resources, both human and nonhuman, never operate in a vacuum; they always exist in some real-world setting that includes government, a legal system, and a structure of property rights. **Property rights** are those rules that establish and govern the ownership and control of resources. Property rights are established by laws developed within a society's traditions and social relations. **Institutions** are the sum total of the traditions, mores, laws, and governmental structures of an economy. Institutions in the United States include the Constitution and the laws of the states. Some of these institutions restrict and define the rights to own and use resources. Others enhance the flow of resources among individuals and states. The U.S. Constitution, for example, guarantees the free movement of resources from state to state.

Property rights
Any legal and/or enforceable rights to the use of resources of any kind.

Institutions
The sum total of the traditions, mores, laws, and governmental structures of an economy.

These institutions represent a type of capital that is the result of public choices that citizens and leaders in a society make. We live in a world filled with many governments representing many different institutional structures. Some countries are blessed with huge quantities of land and natural resources but still do not manage to achieve economic growth and development beyond the barest minimum. Prior to the 1980s, China's communist government directed almost all human and non-human resources from the highest levels of bureaucracy. Despite China's huge resource base, these institutions reduced the country's ability to achieve economic development. More recently, and in spite of periodic political repression, the Chinese government has tentatively embraced some elements of a Western-style free market system, in which some areas of the economy, such as agriculture, are given over to self-interested production, distribution, and exchange. However slowly, Western institutions and technology are being adopted in China because they have encouraged a more efficient use of human and nonhuman resources in producing goods and services.

When property rights are not assigned to scarce resources, the resources tend to be wasted. The old adage "What is owned by all, is cared for by none" means the failure to legally assign property rights to specific resources will ensure that the resources will not be utilized in the most efficient fashion. Most Western economists believe that private rights over property—combined with free and unregulated private markets for human and nonhuman resources—are essential to economic growth in any nation. The success stories of relatively free and unrestricted economies such as Hong Kong, Taiwan, and Singapore—each endowed with very modest quantities of resources—are often presented as evidence that noninterventionist institutions contribute greatly to economic development. The lesson to be learned from these cases is that institutions—especially the form of government and the nature of controls over resources and resource utilization—are keys to productivity and economic growth in any society.

When it comes to material goods, most people throughout history have believed that more is better than less. Accordingly, economic growth has been defined as *more* housing, *more* food, *more* health care, *more* leisure, *more* of everything. Growth, however, may be defined to include the attainment of less tangible environmental goals as well as an increase in the output of physical goods and services. Today, some people prefer the kinds of "goods" associated with a simpler, safer, and cleaner life for society. The acquisition of these goods also requires public decisions and public choices about the expenditure of scarce resources.

Scarcity of resources and scarcity of imagination in designing institutions to facilitate resource use are at the heart of all economic problems. Resources can be augmented over time; indeed, we are much better off materially than our grandparents, and our grandparents were better off than their grandparents. At any one time, however, individuals and societies cannot get all of what they want. Given scarcity, individuals and societies must make choices, and a primary role of economists is to analyze scarcity and the process of choosing.

KEY PRINCIPLES OF ECONOMIC THINKING

All economists share certain ways of thinking. These perspectives, which form the core of the science of economics, appear many times throughout this book. A look at these economic perspectives in simple, commonsense language should convince you that economics and economic reasoning are closely related to the private and public decisions you make every day.

Accounting costs
Actual money expenditures associated with any activity; out-of-pocket costs.

Explicit costs
Accounting costs.

Implicit costs
Nonpecuniary costs associated with the consumption of a good or service.

Resources and Activities Cost More than You Think

What does it cost you to take a skiing weekend in the mountains or to make a trip to the beach during spring break? Your reply might include the costs of gasoline, auto depreciation, airfare, lift tickets, food, drink, entertainment, and a motel room. These money expenditures are called **accounting costs,** or explicit money costs.

Economists define *costs* more broadly than accountants do. In addition to the **explicit** (money) **costs** considered by accountants, economists consider additional **implicit costs** associated with an action. In the case of a ski trip, an economist would recognize that an additional implicit cost of a ski weekend is the forgone opportunity of using the time in its next most valuable use when all viable alternatives are considered. For example, if the student who goes skiing would otherwise have spent the weekend working at a part-time job, an implicit cost of skiing is the income that would otherwise have been earned, if working is the highest-valued alternative. Therefore, the full economic cost of the ski weekend—the **opportunity cost**—equals the explicit money costs (that money does have an alternative use) plus the implicit costs of forgone income.

Opportunity cost

The highest-valued alternative forgone in making any choice.

Such opportunity costs also exist for public choices. Use of government lands in Wyoming and Montana as national forests entails a cost. Through lease or purchase, these lands could be used as a source of oil, minerals, and timber. Such use would contribute to society's well-being, but park land serves the recreational needs of society as well. Whatever public choices we make for the use of land will imply a cost in economic terms. An opportunity must be forgone when the land is used in either manner.

A favorite saying of economists is "There is no such thing as a free lunch." The first fundamental principle of economics is that most things in life come at the opportunity cost of something forgone. They are never free. In economics, opportunity cost is the true measure of the costs of anything.

Economic Behavior Is Rational

A second fundamental principle of economics is that people behave according to **rational self-interest.** Economists focus on a particular view of human behavior— that of *homo economicus* (economic man or woman). Economists argue that human behavior is predictably based on a person's weighing the costs and benefits of decisions. Simply stated, individuals pursue their goals, whether public or private in nature, in a purposeful fashion. A student will choose to eat lunch at the local health-food restaurant rather than the fast-food cafeteria on campus if the perceived personal benefits of doing so—eating nutritious food in a pleasant atmosphere, say—outweigh the perceived costs, such as longer lines and a greater distance to be walked.

Rational self-interest

The view of human behavior espoused by economists. Given circumstances and preferences, people weigh the costs and benefits of choices in order to do the best they can for themselves.

The view of the individual espoused by economists has always been subject to misinterpretation. When economists say that humans are self-interested, they do not mean that other aspects of human behavior and motivation are unimportant or irrelevant. Altruistic or charitable behavior, for example, is perfectly compatible with *homo economicus*. If a person values altruism, then an act that benefits others will carry personal benefits and will therefore be in that person's self-interest. Economists simply maintain that people consider the costs and benefits of their decisions and act in their own self-interest.

No economist would deny that love, charity, and justice are important aspects of human behavior. Economists have merely advanced the simple but powerful proposition that, given personal tastes, values, and social philosophy, rational self-interest is a better guide to predicting behavior than any other assumption about why people act as they do.

The economist's view of the rational self-interested individual applies not only to economic behavior, but also to other realms of behavior. Economics as a social science includes observations of what people, motivated by self-interest, actually do. Politicians maximize their self-interest by wooing voters to elect and reelect them. Even activities such as dating, marriage, and divorce have been analyzed using the self-interest assumption! After more than 200 years of economic theorizing, self-interest remains a most powerful predictor of human behavior.

Choices Are Made at the Margin

Margin
The difference between costs or benefits in an existing situation and after a proposed change.

Economists are typically concerned with decisions made at the **margin**—the additional costs or benefits of a specific change in the current situation. An individual consumer, for example, does not spend his or her entire budget solely on food, cassette tapes, or weekends at the beach. Consumers purchase hundreds of goods and services. Their choice to purchase or not purchase additional units of any one good is based on the additional (or marginal) satisfaction that that single unit would bring to them.

Marginal analysis
Looking at changes in the costs and benefits of a change from the status quo to a proposed new situation. These marginal changes in the costs and benefits are the basis for rational economic choice.

Marginal analysis is a method of finding the optimal, or most desirable, level of any activity—how much coffee to drink, how much bread to produce, and so on. In an economic sense, every activity we undertake involves both benefits and costs, so an optimal level of an activity is the point at which the activity's total benefits outweigh its costs by the greatest amount.

Students make marginal decisions all the time, whether studying for exams, purchasing a new sweater, or voting. Clearly, additional study for a mathematics examination will improve the grade you receive. But doing your best will not mean devoting all available time to the project. The total gain in terms of grade achieved will rise, but the total costs due to the opportunity cost of time will rise also. Additional hours spent studying math may require forgone activities such as work, sleep, studying history, or even recreation. The rational student will stop studying for an examination when the marginal benefits from another hour of study equal the marginal costs of study. Beyond this point, additional study hours would likely raise the exam grade by a few more points, but the additional study would not be worth the additional cost in terms of other activities given up. The net benefits of studying math (net benefits = total benefits − total costs) are always maximized where the marginal benefits equal the marginal costs. It is the same for all choices that individuals make, even highly complex ones such as voting, buying a house, and so on.

Prices Are Signals to Producers and Consumers

Market
A collection of buyers and sellers exchanging resources, goods, or services.

Prices
The market-established opportunity costs of goods and services obtained through exchange.

Consumers decide what is to be produced—TVs, automobiles, public parks —with the scarce resources in our society. Economists say that consumers transmit their desires through **markets,** which are simply arrangements where buyers and sellers exchange goods or services for money. In a market economy **prices** are the essential signals that tell producers and resource suppliers what and how much to produce. Take, for example, a fairly new product, the compact disc (CD) player.

What happened when consumers suddenly wanted more CD players than cassette decks or turntables in their homes and automobiles? Consumers expressed this desire by buying many more CD players and leaving cassette decks and turntables to gather dust on store shelves. Meanwhile, the relative unavailability of CD players caused their price to rise, because, temporarily, there were insufficient resources and production to meet the new demand. Manufacturers observed the increased sales and rising prices and realized that producing more CD players would be profitable. They reacted by producing more players, which meant ordering more electronics and circuitry and plastics, and hiring more labor and machinery. Higher prices for integrated circuits, fabricated metals, and wiring gave producers in Silicon Valley and other resource suppliers a signal to supply more of their inputs and services. Why did they do it? Because higher prices mean greater profitability to resource suppliers as well. Resources were diverted to CD players as both demand for and production of cassette decks and turntables declined.

Consumers also view prices as signals that help them decide what, and how much, to buy. Prices are both a mechanism that signals the degree of scarcity of goods and services to consumers and an allocator of the available quantities of goods and services among consumers.

Prices serve two basic functions in an economy. They serve to determine how much and what goods and services are produced by producers. They also serve to allocate available commodities among different consumers and competing end uses.

Public Choices Are Different from Private Choices

Private choice
Any choice made through private markets.

Public choice
The economic analysis of political decision making, politics, and the democratic process.

Individuals make private and public choices. Their **private choices** are made through markets, and involve the supply and demand of cars, housing, and other private goods. **Public choices** are also made by that individual with respect to the things that he or she wants government to do. How much should we spend on national defense versus national parks, for example?

The individuals who make public choices are the *same* individuals who make private choices. We thus make the same assumption about their behavior—that is, they act in their self-interest, broadly defined as before, when they make public choices.

What is different about public choices is that the setting or constraints that affect public choices are different from those that affect private choices. Public decisions in democracies are made by voting, and voting does not work in the same way as markets. To understand how voting and the market differ is to study public choice. This is the study of the behavior of self-interested political actors—voters, politicians, bureaucrats, regulators, judges—as they go about their "ordinary" business of governing. Economics is concerned with both private and public choices and how they are made, and with the consequences of allocating resources through markets and voting.

Economists Do Not Decide Who Gets What

Economists study poverty and wealth, but as economists they have no unique knowledge to make judgment about how rich people should be or how much poverty (if any) is tolerable. Economists basically explain that the economic value of all individuals—expressed as their income—is determined by the relative desires for their services and by the relative scarcity of their talents and abilities.

Most products and services—such as food and vacations—are allocated to those with the greatest desire and ability to pay for them. Our ability to pay is determined by the economic value of our own particular services or resources in the marketplace. This value depends on our education, on-the-job training, health, luck, inheritance, and a host of other factors.

The distribution of publicly provided goods and services—such as highways and bridges and space weapons—is conducted by governments through the filter of politics and voting. Ultimately, therefore, decisions on how public resources are to be distributed are made by voter choices. In government, as in the workings of the market, the chief role of economists is not to say who should get what, but to describe and analyze the process—the costs, benefits, and incentives—through which the distribution of all products and services takes place.

Money Is Helpful, but Not Too Much

Barter
Direct exchange of one good
or service for another without
the use of money.

Economists also place a special significance on the role of money in our lives. The trade of goods for goods, called **barter,** will not work in any economy that completes billions of transactions every day. Barter may have been sufficient in primitive societies where few things were produced and traded, but as the number of commodities grew, the cost of transacting by barter grew enormously. Low-cost trade demanded a double coincidence of wants—you had to demand the corn I produced at the same time and place that I demanded the baskets you produced. A common denominator, acceptable to all, developed within economic societies to reduce the costs and inconveniences of barter. That common denominator is **money,** which serves as a medium of exchange.

Money
A generally accepted medium
of exchange.

Money is not limited to coins and paper dollars. Throughout history many things—shells, feathers, paper, gold, and cattle, for instance—have served as money. The important point to economists is that money, whatever it is, reduces the costs associated with barter and increases specialization and trade. At the same time, economists are concerned that money should not be available in such quantities as to become unacceptable and valueless to people who produce, buy, and sell. For society, at least, huge increases in the money supply may be too much of a good thing.

Inflation
A sustained increase in the
general level of prices;
inflation reduces the
purchasing power of money.

When the quantity of money increases beyond its use as a means of making transactions, confidence in the medium of exchange and its value (in terms of the quantity of goods and services a unit of it can purchase) deteriorates. Economists call this phenomenon **inflation.** Inflation was a fact of American life during the 1970s, and it is a persistent element in nations around the world, as in the republics of the former Soviet Union. Inflation, if left untamed, can result in the collapse of entire economies, with reversion to primitive barter conditions. Economists therefore are very concerned with the relation between the production and trade of goods and the quantity of money available to facilitate these crucial activities.

Voters Choose the Role of Government— The Economist Analyzes

In a functioning democratic system, society chooses an economic role for government by electing politicians. In general, that role has included such activities as taxation for and provision of collective goods such as national defense, highways, and education; the regulation of monopoly; pollution control; control of the money supply; and alleviation of poverty through welfare programs. In its economic role of taxing and spending, government can affect economic factors such as inflation, the degree of unemployment, economic growth, and international trade.

Economists have always been concerned with the effects of government activity in these areas. In the United States, economists are in the thick of government policy-making. Since 1946 an official Council of Economic Advisers has been appointed by the president to aid in the formulation and implementation of economic policy. Almost every agency of government employs economists to provide analysis in their areas of expertise.

In their role as advisers, economists primarily evaluate, from the perspective of economic theory or analysis, the effects of proposals or, more correctly, of changes in economic policies. Economists are not confined to giving advice on specific issues such as the Social Security program or the effects of advertising regulation by the Federal Trade Commission. Larger issues are within economists' purview as well. Predicting the effects of government taxing and spending policies on employment, interest rates, and inflation is a very large part of economists' role. As such, economists are concerned with economic stabilization.

Despite economists' influence, however, the economic role of government is ultimately decided by voters in periodic elections. Economists evaluate the implications of government's economic policies. They do not make ultimate decisions about what the government should do.

THE ROLE OF THEORY IN ECONOMICS

Economists organize their thoughts about human behavior and its results through models. Economists, like all scientists, construct models to isolate specific phenomena for study. Constructing a **model** requires assumptions and abstractions from the real world.

Model

A simplified abstraction of the real world that approximates reality and makes problems easier to analyze; also called a theory.

Economists must *abstract* from extraneous factors to isolate and understand some other factor because, as one economist has put it, people's minds are limited and nature's riddles are complex. Economists must assume that the extraneous factors are constant—that "other things are equal"[1]—or that, if altered, they would have a predictable effect on the relations or model under consideration. Humanity has never progressed very far in understanding anything—be it chemistry, astronomy, or economics—without abstracting from many factors that are not central to a given problem. *Thus, all economic models are of necessity abstractions. Good models, those that perform and predict well, use relevant factors; poor models do not.*

An economic model (or, essentially the same thing, a theory) can be expressed in verbal, graphical, or mathematical form. Sometimes verbal explanation is sufficient, but graphs or algebra often serve as convenient shorthand means of expressing models. Economics is like other sciences in this regard. A complicated chemical or physical process can be described in words, but it is more convenient to use mathematics. All methods of expressing models will be used in this book, but we rely primarily on words and graphs. The appendix to this chapter explains how to read and interpret graphs.

Since a complex world is the economist's workshop, economic theory cannot always be tested in the way chemical or physical theories can. The accuracy of economics is like that of meteorology. Total accuracy is not within the meteorologist's abilities.

In economics, the problem of imperfect conditions for testing is a limitation to theory, but theory is essential nonetheless. Nothing can substitute for the usefulness of theory in organizing our thoughts about the real world and in describing the regularities of economic behavior.

THE ROLE OF ECONOMICS AND ECONOMISTS

Economics—and its practice by economists—permeates society. University-trained economists wear many hats and perform diverse roles within the profession. Most economists specialize in some area of particular concern. Some economists work as researchers in think tanks, such as the Hoover Institution at Stanford University or the Brookings Institution in Washington, D.C. Others serve as corporate

---

[1]The Latin phrase *ceteris paribus*, meaning "other things being equal," is common economic shorthand for this assumption about human behavior.

forecasters for private businesses. Every conceivable area of the economy—health, energy, agriculture, research on the role of particular technologies—is part of the research program of these economists. Many economists don policy hats and advise federal, state, and local governments on a huge variety of matters—including budgets, taxes, government spending, and policies toward business. Last, but not least, economists teach economics. In virtually every college and university in America, economists perpetuate their field by teaching undergraduate and graduate courses and conducting research. Since 1969, a Nobel Prize has been awarded in economics, underlining the special prestige of the discipline as a social science. The Nobel Prize has been awarded to an impressive number of economists at American universities (How and in what manner economics may be of value to you is explored in the Application at the end of this chapter, "How Economics Prepares You for Life and Work").

Positive and Normative Economics

Positive economics

Observations, explanations, or predictions about economic life; scientific economics.

Normative economics

Value judgments based on moral principles or preferences about how economic life should be.

Economics is primarily a positive rather than a normative science. **Positive economics** describes what is or predicts what will be under certain circumstances, whereas **normative economics** entails value judgments about what should be. For the most part, economists confine themselves to positive statements. This does not mean that economists as individuals act always as pure scientists. They most certainly do arrive at normative positions based on their own personal values in addition to their positive analyses.

Consider U.S. welfare programs. To say that additional tax dollars should be spent on welfare would involve a normative (or value) judgment on the part of economists. Once society has decided to spend more on welfare, however, economists can make positive statements about the effects of such spending. Or economists may observe the welfare system and analyze how the system could work more efficiently in achieving its goals. In other words, economic analysis can show, once society has decided on a welfare system and on some dollar amount to be devoted to welfare, how alternative systems of welfare distribution would alter the effectiveness of the program.

Microeconomics and Macroeconomics

Microeconomics

Analysis of the behavior of individual decision-making units, including individuals, households, and business firms.

The first half of this book concerns what economists call microeconomics, while the second half deals with macroeconomics. **Microeconomics,** like microbiology, concerns the components of a system. Just as a frog is made up of individual cells of various kinds, individual sales and purchases of commodities from potatoes to health care are the stuff of which the whole economy is composed. Microeconomists are thus concerned with individual markets and with the determination of relative prices within those markets. Supply and demand for individual goods, services, and factors of production are the subject matter of microeconomics. Microeconomists address questions such as the following: Will the use of larger quantities of solar energy reduce the total energy bill of Americans? Will an increased tax on cigarettes increase or decrease federal revenues from the tax? Will the quality and quantity of nursing services in the state of Wyoming be changed by the licensing of nursing in that state?

Macroeconomics

Analysis of the behavior of an economy as a whole.

Macroeconomics is the study of the economy as a whole. The overall price level, inflation rate, international exchange rates, unemployment rate, economic growth rate, and interest rate are issues of concern to macroeconomists. Macro-

Gross domestic product (GDP)
A measure of the final goods and services produced by a country with resources located within that country.

Gross national product (GNP)
The value, measured at market prices, of all final goods and services produced in an economy in one year.

economists analyze how these crucial quantities are determined and how and why they change. The most common measures of macroeconomic well-being are **gross domestic product (GDP)** and **gross national product (GNP).**

Some issues contain elements of both microeconomics and macroeconomics—for instance, a proposed U.S. tariff on Japanese auto imports. Microeconomists would be interested in the effects of the tariff on auto prices, on the American auto industry, and on the quantity of cars bought by U.S. consumers. Macroeconomists would be primarily interested in the effects of the tariff on economic growth, employment, international trade, the balance of payments, and total spending.

Let's Get to Work

Economics, like meteorology, is an inexact science, and it is likely to remain so. But economic theory and prediction provide extremely important insights into numerous issues that touch our lives. And the science of choice and scarcity is constantly being improved from both theoretical and empirical perspectives. The well-established power of economic thinking is the result of 200 years of such continuing improvements. Sound understanding of the principles of economic thinking will improve your understanding of the world.

APPLICATION

How Economics Prepares You for Life and Work

Economics is a way of thinking about all kinds of events. More precisely, economics prepares you to think about all behavior—particularly about how consumers' and producers' behavior is influenced by certain events (changes in prices, changes in interest rates, new government regulations, marriage rules, and so on). Even more particularly, it is a method for organizing your thoughts based on a long-tested theory about human behavior—self-interest.

The principle that individuals act rationally and in their own self-interest has far-reaching implications. After some necessary technical training regarding the working out of this principle, you will learn the how and why of many things: why the value of some goods and services rise and fall—why, for example, Picassos, gym memberships, tech stocks, and avocados vary in price over time. You will, with some creativity and basic economic tools, be able to pinpoint areas where new products and market innovations may be expected, such as fast foods, talking books, pool cleaning equipment, and audio-visual communications facilities and equipment. You will come to understand why information and time are considered valuable commodities. Economics even extends into sociological areas—helping you to understand law, marriage, divorce, and child bearing and rearing. (Indeed, economics is one of the most popular preparations for the study of law.)

Your education in economics (especially as a college major) thus prepares you for employment in a wide variety of jobs, from policy-oriented work with foundations and trade associations to technically oriented work with public utility commissions and private firms. Virtually every large corporation in America, as well as numerous medium-sized firms, employs economists to help make appropriate pricing decisions for their products, to evaluate the impact of government regulations, and to forecast future demand and supply conditions and product innovations within their industry. Trade organizations, representing small firms, also make much use of economists.

Public sector agencies at the federal, state, and local levels hire economists to monitor performance of the economy, to assess the desirability and impact of regulations, and to contribute to ongoing discussions of policy formation. Nonprofit groups such as hospitals, community foundations, charitable organizations, and schools employ economists as well.

After all is said and done, economics is important because it provides an essential means of thinking about the world and your place in it. Economics is not like accounting or physics in that it does not provide specific work skills. But unlike management or marketing, there *is* a widely accepted body of knowledge attached to economics. Further, and perhaps most importantly, you will be entirely flexible in the workplace armed with a good understanding of economics. The days of having only one or two jobs throughout a lifetime are gone forever. Learning to construct and manipulate a web page or a spreadsheet is a specific (and important) skill. Learning to adapt to a changing business or personal environment—*what*, in effect, to put on a spreadsheet or the computer and how to analyze it—is even more important. The flexibility that economic understanding provides will help you make wise business and personal choices for a lifetime.

QUESTION

Can you name any trade or occupation over the next fifty years that will escape the necessity of learning economics, as defined in this chapter?

SUMMARY

1. Economics is basically concerned with three questions: What goods and services are produced? How are goods and services produced? For whom are goods and services produced?

2. Economics is the study of how individuals make private and public choices to allocate scarce resources given unlimited wants.

3. Scarce resources include human and nonhuman resources as well as time, institutions, and technology. Human resources consist of labor, including entrepreneurship and management. Nonhuman resources include land and all natural resources, technology, information, and capital.

4. All scarce resources bear an opportunity cost. This means that individuals forgo other opportunities whenever scarce resources are used to produce specific goods and services.

5. Economic behavior is rational. Human beings are assumed to behave predictably by weighing the costs and benefits of their decisions and their potential actions.

6. Economic choices are made at the margin—that is, they take into account the additional costs or benefits of a change in the current situation. Prices are the signal that indicates individual choices for goods and services as well as the relative scarcity of the resources necessary to produce the goods and services.

7. Private and public choices are made by the same persons, but public choices are made by voting while private choices are made in markets.

8. The study of prices of individual products and inputs is called *microeconomics*, and the study of inflation, unemployment, economic growth, and related problems is called *macroeconomics*.

9. Economics is a science. It predicts much economic behavior and provides insight into a large number of important problems.

KEY TERMS

goods
services
resources
scarcity
economic goods and services
costs
free goods and services
human resources
nonhuman resources
technology
information
property rights

institutions
accounting costs
explicit costs
implicit costs
opportunity cost
rational self-interest
margin
marginal analysis
market
prices
private choice
public choice

barter
money
inflation
model
positive economics
normative economics
microeconomics
macroeconomics
gross domestic product (GDP)
gross national product (GNP)

QUESTIONS FOR REVIEW AND DISCUSSION

1. What problem creates the foundation of economic analysis? Is this problem restricted to the poor?

2. Can wants be satisfied with existing resources?

3. What are resources? How is the resource capital different from the resources land and labor?

4. What is the difference between behaving in one's self-interest and behaving selfishly?

5. What functions do prices have in the economy?

6. You have already paid your tuition. What does it cost you, at the margin, to attend your afternoon economics class on Friday? On Tuesday? (Remember: The margin refers to the additional cost of attending one additional class.)

7. Is air a free good? Is clean air a free good? Is cleaner air a free good?

8. Why do economists abstract from reality when formulating theories? Does this imply that their theories have no relevance in the real world?

9. "The distribution of income in the United States is not fair." What type of statement is this? Can "fair" be used to describe something without being normative?

10. To what extent can we say that economics is an accurate science?

11. John gives an annual contribution of $500 to his church. By doing so, he is acting in his own self-interest. Explain.

12. Would you expect a discussion of the Great Depression of the 1930s to be covered in a macroeconomics class or a microeconomics class?

WORKING WITH THE WEB

1. The impact of economics throughout history has been significant. While you have not yet been introduced to many of the famous economists throughout history, you will be learning about them throughout the course. To get a quick introduction to the scope of economic thought and its contributors, go to http://www.frbsf.org/econedu/curriculum/great/frames.html. Once there, take a tour of this site by clicking on the links on the right-hand side of the page (Contents). After reading the material, you are ready for the Treasure Hunt. Click on the link "play the treasure

hunt" and answer the questions here to test your understanding of the scope of economics. You can either submit your answers or simply choose "Complete" to finish the game.

2. The Application in Chapter 1, "How Economics Prepares You for Life and Work," discusses the role of economics in everyday life. It discusses how economics can help you understand not only business–related issues, but also sociological issues such as marriage and divorce! In 1992, the Nobel Prize in economics was awarded to Gary Becker, an economist at the University of Chicago. Go to http://nobelprizes.com/nobel/economics/1992a.html and click on the link "Chicago's Becker Wins Nobel Prize." Briefly explain how Becker's ideas correspond with sociological issues.

Working With Graphs

APPENDIX

Economists frequently use graphs to demonstrate economic theories or models. This appendix explains how graphs are constructed and how they can illustrate economic relations in simplified form. By understanding the mechanics and usefulness of graphs, you will find it much easier to grasp the economic concepts presented in this book.

THE PURPOSE OF GRAPHS

Most graphs in this book are simply pictures showing the relation between economic variables, such as the price of a good and the quantity of the good that people are willing to purchase. There are many such pairs of variables in economics: the costs of production and the level of output, the rate of inflation and the level of unemployment, the interest rate and the supply of capital goods, for example. Graphs are the most concise means of expressing the variety of relations that exist between such variables.

Many of the graphs in this book use the Cartesian coordinate system, which consists of points plotted on a grid formed by the intersection of two perpendicular lines. See Figure 1.1. The horizontal line is the **x-axis,** and the vertical line is the **y-axis.** The intersection of the two lines is the point 0, called the *origin.* Above the origin on the vertical axis, all values are positive. Below the origin on the vertical axis, all values are negative. Values to the right of the origin are positive on the horizontal axis; values to the left are negative. The economic variables we use in this book are usually positive; that is, to plot economic relations we will usually use the upper-right portion, or quadrant, of a graph such as the one in Figure 1.2.

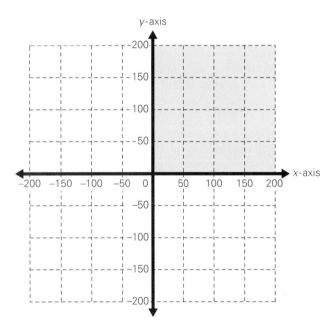

FIGURE 1.1

A Grid for Plotting Graphs

Any pair of numerical values can be plotted on this grid. The upper-right quadrant, shaded here, is the portion of the graph most often used in economics.

19

FIGURE 1.2

A Simple Line (or Linear) Graph

Curve *AE* shows the essential relation between two sets of variables: the number of words memorized and the number of minutes spent memorizing. The relation is positive; as the variable on the *x*-axis increases or decreases, the variable on the *y*-axis increases or decreases, respectively. A positive relation is shown by an upward-sloping line tracing the intersection of each pair of variables.

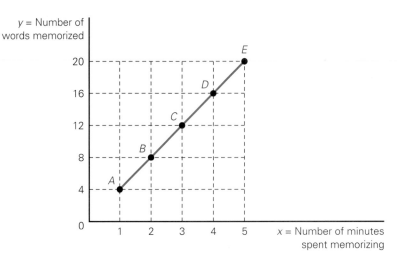

HOW TO DRAW A GRAPH

Suppose you wish to graph the relation between two variables. Variable *y* is the number of words memorized, and variable *x* is the number of minutes spent memorizing words. Table 1.1 presents a set, or schedule, of hypothetical data for these two variables.

We can plot the data from Table 1.1 on a graph using points in the upper-right quadrant formed by the *x*-axis and the *y*-axis. See Figure 1.2. The variable, number of words memorized, is measured along the *y*-axis and is considered the *y* value. The variable, number of minutes spent memorizing, is measured along the *x*-axis and is the *x* value. From the data in Table 1.1 we see that each increase of 1 minute of memorizing resulted in 4 more memorized words. The graph in Figure 1.2 illustrates this relation.

The points marked as large dots in Figure 1.2 represent pairs of variables. Point *A* represents the pair on the first line of Table 1.1: 4 words and 1 minute.

TABLE 1.1

Schedule of Hypothetical Data

Number of Words Memorized (*y*)	Number of Minutes Spent Memorizing (*x*)
4	1
8	2
12	3
16	4
20	5

Point *B* represents 8 words and 2 minutes, and so on. When we connect the points, we have a straight line running upward and to the right of the origin. Lines showing the intersection of *x* and *y* values on a graph are referred to as **curves** in this book, whether they are straight or curved lines.

Curves show two types of relations between variables: positive and negative. The relation between the *x* and *y* values in Figure 1.2 is positive: As the *x* value increases, so does the *y* value. (Or, as the x value decreases, the y value decreases as well. Either way, the relation is positive.) On a graph, a **positive,** or **direct, relation** is shown by a curve that slopes upward and to the right of the origin. In a **negative,** or **inverse, relation,** the two variables change in opposite directions. An increase in *y* is paired with a decrease in *x*. Or a decrease in *x* is paired with an increase in *y*. Figure 1.3 shows a negative, or inverse, relation on a graph. The curve for a negative relation slopes downward from left to right—the opposite of a positive relation.

General Relations

Throughout this book, some graphs display general relations rather than specific relations. A general relation does not depend on particular numerical values of variables, as was the case in Figure 1.2. For example, the relation between the number of calories a person consumes per week and that person's weight (other things being equal) is positive. This suggests an upward-sloping line, as shown in Figure 1.4a, with calories on the *x*-axis and weight on the *y*-axis. Figure 1.4a represents a general relation, so it does not need numerical values on either axis. It does not specify the

FIGURE 1.3

A Negative Relation Between Two Variables

As the price of a cup of coffee increases, the number of cups drunk each day decreases. When variables move in opposite directions, their relation is negative, or inverse. Negative relations are shown by a curve that slopes downward and to the right of the origin.

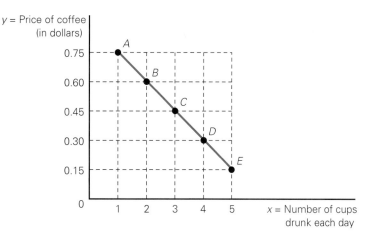

particular number of calories required to maintain a particular body weight; it simply shows that an increase in the number of calories consumed increases body weight. Figure 1.4b shows an inverse relation between body weight and the amount of exercise per week, again a general relation. Sometimes two variables are not related. Figure 1.4c shows that a person's weight is independent of a neighbor's caloric intake. Thankfully, no matter how much your neighbor eats, it has no effect on your weight.

At this point you should be able to construct a graph showing simple relations. For example, graph the relation between the weight of a car and the miles per gal-

lon it achieves or between the length of the line at the school cafeteria and the time of day. If the relationship between any two variables you select is represented by a straight line, it is said to be a **linear relation.** A linear relationship means that for every unit change (increase or decrease) in one of the variables (the weight of a car), the other variable (miles per gallon of gasoline) changes (increases or decreases) by some fixed amount.

Nonlinear Relations

Often, relations between two variables are not the simple linear relationships depicted in Figures 1.2, 1.3,

(a)

(b)

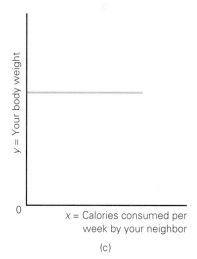

(c)

FIGURE 1.4

General Graphical Relations

General relations are (a) positive, (b) inverse, or (c) independent. General relations are not measured numerically on the y- or x-axis.

and 1.4. For example, unlike in Figure 1.2, where each additional minute spent studying enables one to memorize 4 additional words, it may be that the number of additional words memorized changes as the number of minutes changes. Such a **nonlinear relation** is depicted in Figure 1.5. There, 1 minute of studying enables a student to memorize 6 words, but 2 minutes of studying enables a student to memorize only 11 words—the second minute adds only 5 additional words to the total. Additional minutes of studying beyond 2 lead to even smaller increases in the total number of words memorized. Therefore, there is a positive relationship between the two variables, but the relationship is *nonlinear*.

Occasionally, nonlinear relations are more complex than the one depicted in Figure 1.5 and do not fall into the simple categories of positive or negative. A U-shaped curve, as graphed in Figure 1.6, shows that the x value is at first inversely related to the y value and then positively related. After some critical value, x^*, the y value begins to rise as the x value increases. The y-axis in this example might represent the probability of having an accident on an interstate highway, and the x-axis might show the miles per hour at which a car travels. To avoid accidents, x^* is the optimal, or "best" speed. Driving at speeds lower than x^* increases the probability of an accident, but rates faster than x^* mph also increase the chances of an accident.

SLOPE OF THE CURVE

In graphical analysis, the amount by which the y value increases or decreases as the result of an increase or decrease in the x value is the *slope* of the curve. The slope of the curve is an important concept in economics. Much economic analysis studies the margin of

FIGURE 1.5

A Nonlinear Graph

Curve *AE* shows the nonlinear relation between the number of minutes spent studying and the number of words memorized.

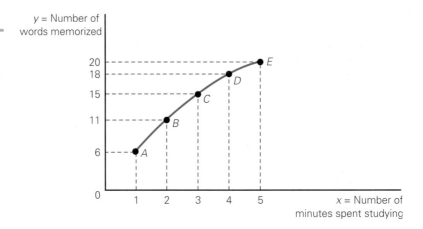

FIGURE 1.6

A U-shaped Curve

Some relations yield a U shape. Variables along the *x*- and *y*-axes are inversely related at first, but after some critical value, here shown as *x**, they become positively related. Naturally curves may also be bow-shaped with relations reversed.

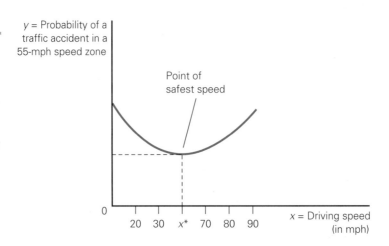

change in a variable or in a relation between variables, and the slope of a curve measures the marginal rate of change. In Figure 1.2, for example, every change in the x value—every increase of 1 minute—is associated with an increase of 4 words memorized. The slope of the curve in Figure 1.2 is the rate of change. Economists express the concept "change in" with the symbol Δ. So in Figure 1.2 the slope of the line AE is $\Delta y/\Delta x = 4/1 = 4$.

For the straight-line curves in Figures 1.2 and 1.3 the slope is constant. Along most curves, however, the slope is not constant. In Figure 1.6, an increase in driving speed from 55 to 60 mph will increase the probability of an accident only slightly, but an increase from 60 to 65 mph would increase the probability by a greater amount. Not only does the probability increase for each mile-per-hour increase in driving speed, but it increases by a progressively greater amount. This indicates that the slope not only is positive but also is increasing.

The slope of a curved line is different at every point along the line. To find the slope of a curved line at a particular point, draw a straight line tangent to the curve. (A tangent touches the curve at one point without crossing the curve.) Consider point A in Figure 1.7. The slope at

A on the curved line is equal to the slope of the straight line tangent to the curved line. Dividing the change in the y variable (Δy) by the change in the x variable (Δx) yields the slope at A. In Figure 1.7, every change in x from 0 to 1, 1 to 2, and so on, results in a change in y along the curve. At point A, $\Delta y = 4$ on the tangent line. So $\Delta y/\Delta x = -4/1 = -4$. At lower points along the curve, such as B, the curve is flatter—that is, less steep. The line tangent at B has a slope of -1. As we move from point A to point B, equal increases in x result in smaller and smaller decreases in y. In other words, the *rate* at which y falls decreases as x increases along this particular curve.

Other relations lead to different slopes and different changes in the slope along the curve. Along the curve in Figure 1.8, not only does the y value increase as the x value increases, but the slope increases as the x value increases. For equal increases in the x value, the incremental changes in the y value become larger.

Interpreting the essential concepts illustrated in graphs is a necessary part of learning economic principles. Should you encounter difficulty in interpreting any of the graphs in later chapters, a brief review of this appendix will prove helpful.

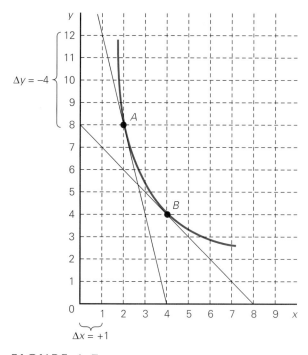

FIGURE 1.7

Slope Along a Curve

The slope of a curve at a particular point is the slope of a straight line tangent to the curve at that point.

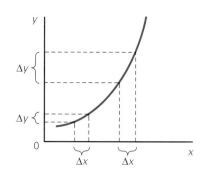

FIGURE 1.8

A Curve with an Increasing Slope

As the x variable increases, the change in the y variable increases.

SUMMARY

1. Graphs are a concise expression of economic models, or theories. Graphs usually show the relation between two variables, such as price and quantity.

2. Linear graphs are drawn with two perpendicular lines, called axes. The *x*-axis is a horizontal line. Variables measured along the *x*-axis are called *x* values. The *y*-axis is a vertical line. Variables along it are called y values.

3. Lines showing the correlation between *x* and *y* values are called curves. An upward-sloping curve indicates a positive, or direct, relation between variables: As the *x* value increases or decreases, the *y* value increases or decreases. A downward-sloping curve indicates a negative, or inverse, relation between variables: As the *x* value increases, the *y* value decreases, and vice versa.

4. Relations between variables may be specific or general. Specific relations are based on numerical quantities measured on either the *x*- or *y*-axis or both. General relations are not based on specific numerical quantities.

5. Relations between two variables can be either linear (straight lines) or nonlinear (curved lines).

6. Variables can be both positively and negatively related over certain ranges. In such complex relations, a curve is either bow-shaped or U-shaped.

7. The slope of a curve measures the ratio of change in the *y* value to change in the *x* value, expressed as $\Delta y/\Delta x$. Along a straight-line curve, the slope is constant. Along a curved line, the slope is different at every point.

KEY TERMS

x-axis, *y*-axis
curve
positive (direct) relation

negative (inverse) relation
linear relation
nonlinear relation

slope

QUESTIONS FOR REVIEW AND DISCUSSION

1. Explain how the slope of a line tells you whether the relation between the two variables illustrated is direct or inverse. If you drew a line illustrating your score on a history test as you study more hours, what would its slope be?

2. Plot the following points on a graph with X on the horizontal axis and Y on the vertical axis. Connect the dots to show the relation between X and Y.

	X	Y
A	0	2
B	2	4
C	4	8
D	6	14
E	8	22

What is the slope of the line between points A and B? What is the slope between C and D? Is this a straight line?

3. Curves can be represented in algebraic form by an equation. For example, the points along a certain line can be demonstrated by the equation

$$Y = 10 - 2X.$$

The value of Y can be found by inserting different values of X and solving the equation for Y.

Some of the values of Y for different values of X are shown in the following table. Fill in the blanks by solving the equation for the value of Y for each value of X given.

X	Y
0	10
2	6
4	—
6	—
8	—
10	—
12	—

Draw this set of points on a graph. Does this show a direct or inverse relation between X and Y? What is the slope of this line between the first and second points? Between the second and third? Is this a straight line?

4. If you measured body weight on the horizontal axis and the probability of dying of heart disease on the vertical axis, what would be the slope of a curve that showed the relation between these two variables?

Opportunity Cost, Specialization, and Trade

The essence of the economic problem is how to get as much value as we can from limited and costly resources. To do so, we constantly make choices. Economists emphasize that decisions to use scarce resources bear an **opportunity cost**. The opportunity cost of a decision is the next most preferred or next-best alternative to a good or activity that one must forgo in order to obtain some other good. Economists have developed tools for expressing that choice and opportunity costs are central to all decisions. After reading Chapter 2 you should understand

- the role of specialization and trade for individuals and societies.
- how individuals actually make decisions given that they are always costly.
- how specialization and trade increase quantities of output for parties who exchange goods and services.
- how exchange, transaction costs, and certain public choices to erect barriers to trade reduce the benefits from specialization and trade.

SPECIALIZATION AND TRADE: A FEATURE OF ALL SOCIETIES

Specialization refers to a situation in which the tasks associated with the production of a product or service are divided—and sometimes subdivided—and performed by many different individuals to increase the total production of the good or service. Virtually all known peoples have engaged in specialization and trade, and theories and principles related to specialization and trade have been part of economists' tool kits for more than 200 years. Adam Smith (1723–1790), the Scottish philosopher and recognized founder

Opportunity cost
The highest-valued alternative forgone in making any choice.

Specialization
An economic entity producing only one good or service, or the performance of a single task in a production process by an individual.

Division of labor
Individual specialization in separate tasks involved with a production process; the result of specialization.

of economics, published his great work *An Inquiry into the Nature and Causes of the Wealth of Nations* in 1776 (a year of declarations). It formally established the science of what we now call economics. (For more information about Adam Smith, see Point/Counterpoint, pp. 109–111.)

At the very core of economics, according to Smith, is the ability of individuals and societies to deal with the facts of scarcity through specialization and trade. When tasks are divided, permitting each individual to concentrate on a single element in the production of a good, output increases over what it would be if each individual produced the entire good. Specialization and the **division of labor** lead to increased output. As a result, people became more dependent on one another for all goods. We may work in an automobile plant, for example, but we still want eggs for breakfast. Think of any organization and try to list the number of distinct divisions of labor in it. Think of a larger factory, a steel mill, a football team, a fraternity, a church. Specialization exists in almost everything we do. (See the Focus "Economic Specialization in Everyday Life: Marriage and Roommate Selection" for illustrations.)

FOCUS

Economic Specialization in Everyday Life: Marriage and Roommate Selection

Specialization and trade have increased economic welfare and human progress from the very beginning of time. These gains have depended on the diverse talents of individuals as well as the different resources of great nations. Consider two examples that do not often come to mind when considering the economic principles of specialization: the selection of a marriage partner and selection of a roommate.

Although relationships like marriage have many bases—love, security, and so on—one of them is surely economic. The greatest gains from trade occur when individuals (or countries) with widely differing skills or resources trade. In a society in which males and females acquire widely different skills, the incentive to marry is quite strong. If, as in primitive society, women do not know how to hunt or fish and men cannot prepare food or make clothing, the gains to both partners in a marriage relationship are immense. In fact, survival outside of a marriage-type relationship may be impossible. In such societies, nearly everyone would marry, and individuals would abandon a marriage relationship only to enter another one. In societies where men and women acquire similar skills, the gains from exchange between marriage partners are much smaller. Individuals, therefore, have a weaker incentive to marry or to remain married. The slowing marriage rate and the growing divorce rate in Western societies in recent decades may partly be attributed to greater occupational equality. As the incomes of women rise (and the opportunity cost of child rearing), a lower birth rate may be expected. Specialization may even be reversed, with men taking more active roles in raising children. "Mr. Mom" may become more common due to economic specialization and trade.

Roommate selection, an activity perhaps closer to your experience, also takes place, in part, on the basis of economic specialization and trade. Students room together to save money, but they also do so, in part, because of the gains from specialization and trade. Communal arrangements ranging from fraternities and sororities to clubs and study groups work best when the participants have tradable skills. Ideally, then, one roommate would be an excellent cook, say, while another roommate would be an expert carpenter, and yet another would be adept at yard work. Even if individuals' skill levels are pretty much the same, trade is still profitable when roommates' tastes and preferences for specific jobs differ and trade is possible. Problems and disputes arise most often between roommates when trade agreements or "contracts" are not enforceable. You may do the cooking, but can you "force" your roommate to clean up the kitchen—assuming you both agreed she would?

The benefits of specialization and trade are not just of academic interest, nor do they pertain only to trade in goods and services between nations such as Japan and the United States. As workers, club members, marriage partners, roommates, or friends, these principles affect us every day.

All modern nations, states, firms, and individuals specialize in the production of economic goods and services, in varying degrees. The individual, the most basic economic entity, specializes to the greatest extent. Your teacher for this course specializes in economic research and teaching. Other people specialize in mechanical engineering services or in breeding thoroughbred racehorses. Some businesses produce only one product, whereas others offer a multitude. One very critical point must be made about all specialization and trade—it is as significant as having more and better resources or improved production techniques. Specialization and division of labor lead to increased output without any additional resources. The gains from specializing in and exchanging goods and services are, in effect, equivalent to acquiring or developing additional natural resources or capital.

OPPORTUNITY COST AND PRODUCTION POSSIBILITIES: INDIVIDUALS AND SOCIETY MUST CHOOSE

Imagine a society in which the following things are true:

1. Only two goods are produced;
2. Supplies of resources are fixed; and
3. Technology is held constant, and no economic growth occurs.

Our hypothetical (theoretical) society can produce cheeseburgers and/or automobiles. Note that it is an example of an economic model where signifying assumptions are used to abstract from nonessential aspects of the problem.

Given the state of technology and assuming that the society uses all its resources, the society could produce either 100 million cheeseburgers or 16 million automobiles (see Table 2.1). Or the society may choose to devote some of its resources to producing cheeseburgers and some to producing automobiles. These choices, called society's *production possibilities*, are listed *A–E* in Table 2.1. From this information a production possibilities curve can be constructed (see Figure 2.1). A production possibilities curve depicts the alternatives open to society for the production of two goods, given full utilization of all existing resources, human and nonhuman, and an existing state of technology at some point in time. When resources are fully employed, moreover, society is said to be producing on its **production possibilities frontier**.

At choice *A* in Figure 2.1, society produces 100 million cheeseburgers and no automobiles, whereas at choice *E* society uses all its resources in automobile

Production possibilities frontier

The curve that graphs all the possible combinations of two goods that an economy can produce given the available technology, the amount of productive resources available, and the full utilization of these resources.

TABLE 2.1

Society Decides: Cheeseburgers or Automobiles
Society must choose among many alternative combinations of goods to produce. The cost of one good is the lost production of other goods.

Choice	Cheeseburgers (millions)	Automobiles (millions)
A	100	0
B	90	4
C	75	8
D	50	12
E	0	16

FIGURE 2.1

Production Possibilities Curve

As more and more automobiles are produced, the opportunity cost per automobile increases. The opportunity cost of producing the first 4 million automobiles is 10 million cheeseburgers. The opportunity cost of producing the next 4 million automobiles is an additional 15 million cheeseburgers, and so on.

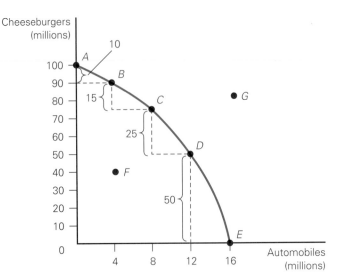

production. Choices in between, with some of both commodities produced, are shown at points *B*, *C*, and *D*. Continuous choices of all other possible combinations are shown along the curve; resources are assumed to be fully employed at all points on the curve. The curve therefore shows all of the possibilities for the production of automobiles and cheeseburgers, assuming resources are fully employed at present or at some given point in time. Points such as *G* lie beyond the production possibilities frontier. The country's resources and technology do not permit it to produce at points, such as *G*, that lie outside the frontier.

The Law of Increasing Costs

There is an opportunity cost for society in any choice between producing cheeseburgers and automobiles.

Consider a society that produces nothing but cheeseburgers, choice *A* in Figure 2.1. The opportunity cost of that choice is that no automobiles can be produced. A move to choice B, representing a movement of some resources from cheeseburger production to automobile production, means a sacrifice of 10 million cheeseburgers, but society gains 4 million automobiles. Thus the opportunity cost of producing the first 4 million automobiles is 10 million cheeseburgers. To get the second 4 million automobiles, however, a larger quantity of cheeseburgers must be given up—15 million. Thus as society becomes more specialized in production of either automobiles or cheeseburgers, the opportunity cost per unit of the good rises. This effect is called the **law of increasing costs**.

Law of increasing costs

As more scarce resources are used to produce additional units of one good, production of another good falls by larger and larger amounts.

Why does the law of increasing costs hold? Resources, training, and talents are not all alike and are not perfectly adaptable to alternative uses. Capital suited to cattle raising or dairy farming is not equally suited to steel making or automobile manufacturing, and vice versa. Cowboys and farmers are not equally adept at the manufacture of seat covers for automobiles or metal fabricating without additional training. The most-suited human and nonhuman resources are moved into production first, but as production of a good increases and becomes more specialized, less-adaptable resources must be used to produce it. The costs of producing additional units of the good rise because larger amounts of these increasingly less-adaptable resources are required to produce each successive unit. This means that greater quantities of another good do not get produced and must therefore be sacrificed in the process.

Unemployment of resources
A situation in which some human and/or nonhuman resources that can be used in production are not utilized.

The law of increasing costs always applies when resources are fully employed. When there is a degree of **unemployment of resources,** however—such as a certain amount of land lying idle—society finds itself producing at a point within the production possibilities curve. Point F in Figure 2.2 represents such a situation. From point F to the curve, additional cheeseburgers or automobiles can be produced without any increase in opportunity costs until resources become fully employed. The production possibilities curve is thus referred to as a *frontier* because it represents full employment of resources. Full employment means that society is realizing its maximum output potential.

Choices at the margin
Decisions based on the additional benefits and costs of small changes in a particular activity.

This society (or the individuals in it) must choose the level of cheeseburger and automobile production that it prefers. Such a choice involves trade-offs among the alternative possibility. To have more cheeseburgers means having fewer automobiles. Choices are made at the margin and balanced accordingly. If individuals want to increase automobiles from 8 to 12 million in Figure 2.1, the opportunity cost is 25 million cheeseburgers. The final outcome will depend on how individuals weigh the costs and benefits of these **choices at the margin**. Remember: When we say "society," we mean the individuals who make up that society. Societies do not make decisions, individuals make decisions.

WHY THE PRODUCTION POSSIBILITIES FRONTIER SHIFTS

If we keep in mind the meaning and assumptions of the production possibilities frontier, we will also understand that an increase or decrease in society's human or nonhuman resources can shift society's output potential. An understanding of such changes is central to an understanding of economic growth—or the lack of it.

The Shifting Frontier

The production possibilities frontier can shift leftward or rightward in response to any change in the quantity of human resources, any change in the quantity of nonhuman resources, or any change in technology. Changes in these factors, which we previously assumed to be constant, shift the production possibilities frontier.

In Figure 2.2, a general change in productivity, technology, or resource supply is assumed. An increase in the quantity of labor (through a simple growth in population), for example, shifts the entire production possibilities frontier rightward from PP_1 to PP_2. Suppose society now chooses the cheeseburger/automobile combination A_1. More of both goods are produced and consumed as a result of the technological improvement. But society faces new trade-offs once it is producing on its new frontier. Opportunity costs arise again in resource utilization, just as they did at combination A on production possibility curve PP_1. Society cannot escape scarcity, yet it can improve its production possibilities through growth in technology, quantity of human or nonhuman resources, or resource productivity.

Economic Growth: How Economies Progress

We can understand the nature of economic growth with the aid of the production possibilities curve model. The key to economic growth in society is related to the growth or change in capital stock and other crucial resources.

FIGURE 2.2

Shifting the Production Possibilities Frontier

A general increase in technology or resource supply shifts the entire production possibilities curve outward.

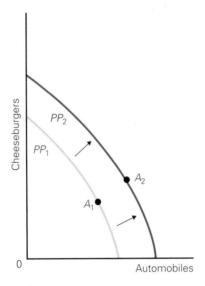

Capital stock

The amount of nonhuman resources available in the economy. These include tools, land, machinery, equipment, and so on.

The creation of **capital stock** (a supply of items used to produce other items) takes time and bears an opportunity cost in present consumption. The benefits of creating capital, however, are in increased amounts of future consumption. In other words, forming new capital stock requires that people save—that is, abstain from consuming in the present. When investment in capital stocks results from this saving, capital formation and growth occur. The formation of capital goods—tools, tractors, computers and so on—requires a redirection of resources from consumption of goods to production of capital goods. The opportunity cost of acquiring capital is thus consumption goods forgone, but the reward for society is an increase in future productive capacity in consumption goods, capital goods, or both.

We can illustrate this phenomenon with the production possibilities curve. Figure 2.3 shows two production possibilities frontiers that contrast capital goods production (the vertical axis) with consumption goods production (the horizontal axis) for two hypothetical societies with initially similar production possibilities curves. Consider society A's choice of consumption and capital goods in 2000, represented by point E_A in Figure 2.3a. Clearly, society A devotes a larger proportion of its resources to capital goods production than to consumption goods production. Saving (abstaining from current consumption), investing, and capital formation are all high in that society. The payoff for society A will come later, say in 2010, with vastly enlarged productive capacity, designated by the shift of the production possibilities curve to PP_{2010} in Figure 2.3a.

Society B chooses to use almost all of its resources in 2000 for consumption goods, with only a small quantity of resources devoted to capital goods, a combination represented by point E_B in Figure 2.3b. The consequence of this choice is low economic growth over the following decade. By 2010, the production possibilities of that society have grown by only a small amount, as curve PP_{2010} in Figure 2.3b indicates. Thus **economic growth** in the future is largely determined by current decisions about production. Technological changes are important factors in the progress of society, but to take advantage of technology, society must sacrifice some present consumption. With reductions in human or nonhuman resources, societies can actually regress. After World War II, for example, the production possibilities of Germany

Economic growth

A permanent increase in the productive capacity of the economy.

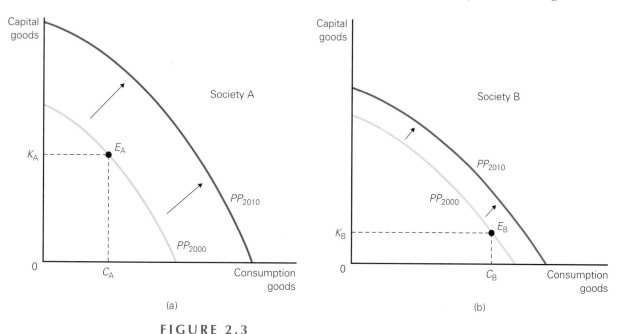

FIGURE 2.3

Growth Choices on the Production Possibilities Curve

(a) By producing more capital goods, K_A in 2000, society A can produce more consumption goods in the future than (b) society B, which produces only K_B capital goods in 2000.

and Japan were virtually smashed, leading to a massive shift to the left of their relevant production possibilities curves. Production possibilities may be reduced by other kinds of disastrous events as well. See the Application at the end of this chapter, "AIDS and Reduced Production Possibilities in Africa," for example.

And keep in mind something we have not addressed so far. We have discussed trade-offs and opportunity costs, but we have not told you how individuals make private choices or public choices about these tradeoffs. In short, where on the production possibilities curve does one end up or choose to be? Individuals make these choices in both private and public settings, and we will explore how they do this throughout the rest of the book.

In addition to making choices between consumption now and later, both individuals and societies can increase their output by specializing in and trading, or exchanging, goods and services. The manner in which both individuals and societies specialize is related to an important principle—the law of comparative advantage.

COMPARATIVE ADVANTAGE

While Adam Smith developed the fundamentals underlying specialization and trade, it was left to his English followers, David Ricardo (1772–1823) and Robert Torrens (1780–1864), to develop the critically important principle of specialization—the theory of comparative advantage. Comparative advantage (and its relation to specialization and trade) is best understood with a simple, hypothetical example. Table 2.2 describes three combinations of silver and lumber production for two different countries, Canada and Mexico. The production possibilities information in Table 2.2 is represented graphically in Figure 2.4. The production possibilities curves of Figure 2.4 do not look exactly like the production possibilities curves we have discussed so far. For simplicity, we have temporarily assumed that the law of increasing costs does not hold in the two countries—at least not where lumber and silver production are concerned. Instead, we assume that in each country both silver and lumber production are subject to constant opportunity costs of production. This means that the production possibilities curves are straight lines instead of curves.

Table 2.2 indicates that production of the first 30,000 ounces of silver in Canada means 300,000 board-feet of lumber do not get produced. Moving from point *A* to point *B* on Canada's production possibilities curve reduces the production of lumber from 1 million to 700,000 board-feet. In such a move, each additional ounce of silver produced has an opportunity cost of 10 board-feet of lumber. If Canada is producing 30,000 ounces of silver and shifts productive resources from the lumber industry to produce 70,000 more ounces of silver (for a total of 100,000 ounces), lumber production drops by 700,000 board-feet. Each additional ounce of silver produced has a constant opportunity cost of 10 board-feet of unproduced lumber, regardless of how many ounces of silver are already being produced.

The same information may be expressed in a different manner. In Canada, the additional cost, or **marginal opportunity production cost,** of 1 board-foot of lumber is constant and equal to 1/10 of an ounce of silver. Silver and lumber production in Mexico are also subject to constant (marginal opportunity) production costs. For each additional ounce of silver produced, only 1 board-foot of lumber goes unproduced. The marginal opportunity cost of producing 1 ounce of silver in Mexico, 1 board-foot of lumber, is less than it is in Canada, where it is equal to 10 board-feet of lumber. Mexico is said to possess a comparative advantage over Canada in producing silver. A comparative advantage exists because the marginal opportunity cost of producing an ounce of silver in Mexico (1 board-foot of lumber) is less than it is in Canada (10 board-feet). So, any locale with a lower marginal opportunity cost of producing a good possesses a comparative advantage over some other locale in producing that good.

Marginal opportunity production cost

The number of units of one good that do not get produced when one additional unit of another good is produced.

TABLE 2.2

Production Possibilities in Canada and Mexico

Canada has a comparative advantage in lumber. If Canada were to move to producing combination *A* instead of *B*, 300,000 board-feet of lumber could be had at an opportunity cost of 30,000 ounces of silver. Each board-foot of lumber has a marginal opportunity cost $\frac{1}{10}$ of an ounce of silver going unproduced. If Mexico were to move from *B* to *A*, 40,000 more ounces of silver could be had at an opportunity cost of 40,000 board-feet of lumber. Each ounce of silver costs Mexico 1 board-foot of lumber. Conversely, Mexico has a comparative advantage in producing silver. In Canada an extra ounce of silver costs 10 board-feet of lumber.

	CANADA'S PRODUCTION POSSIBILITIES			MEXICO'S PRODUCTION POSSIBILITIES		
	A	*B*	*C*	*A*	*B*	*C*
Silver (ounces)	0	30,000	100,000	0	40,000	80,000
Lumber (board-feet)	1,000,000	700,000	0	80,000	40,000	0

FIGURE 2.4

Canada's and Mexico's Production Possibilities Curves

Both countries agree that each 1000 ounces of silver trades for 5000 board-feet of lumber, or a board-foot of lumber for 1/5 of an ounce of silver. Each agrees to trade on these terms because obtaining a good through trade is less costly than obtaining the good by producing it at home. After specialization and trade, each country will consume combination *D,* a combination that lies beyond each country's production possibilities curve.

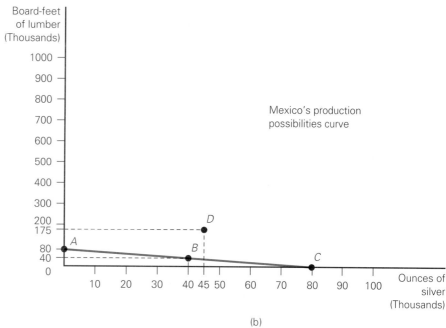

Canada has a comparative advantage over Mexico in lumber production, as indicated in Table 2.2. Canada can produce lumber at a lower marginal opportunity cost (1/10 of an ounce of silver) than can Mexico (1 ounce of silver). If Canada has a comparative advantage in lumber production, this necessarily means that Mexico has a **comparative advantage** in silver production. One ounce of silver costs Mexico only 1 board-foot of lumber, whereas in Canada the cost is 10 board-feet. Each country has a comparative production advantage over the other, but in a different good.

Comparative advantage

An economic entity's ability to produce a good at a lower marginal opportunity production cost than some other entity.

Suppose that both Mexico and Canada are initially self-sufficient in silver and lumber. That is, each country produces and consumes some of both goods and does not trade with the other nation. Specifically, suppose that both countries produce and consume the combination of silver and lumber labeled *B* in Table 2.2 and Figure 2.4. We assume that combination *B* represents the most desirable consumption combination for both Canada and Mexico that is attainable from self-production.

How might Mexicans and Canadians be made better off economically? Excluding economic growth, residents of each country could improve their economic situation through specialization and trade. Each could specialize in producing the good for which that locale has a comparative advantage and then trade some of its output for the other good. The residents could consume more of both goods or more of one good and the same quantity of the other good.

Specialization

Suppose that Mexico and Canada happen to hire the same economic consultant to help them improve their respective economic fortunes. After a study of each economy, the consultant brings representatives of both countries together and suggests a plan that will leave each better off economically: Specialize according to comparative advantage and trade with each other.

The benefits of specialization and trade are shown in Tables 2.3 and 2.4, and Figure 2.5. Table 2.3a shows the situation in each country before specialization and trade occur. Specifically, it reproduces combination *B* from each locale's production possibilities curves shown in Figures 2.4a and 2.4b. Combination *B*, recall, is assumed to be the most desirable consumption combination for each country. Also shown in Table 2.3a is the sum total of both countries' production and consumption of each good. It is assumed that Canada and Mexico constitute the "world."

TABLE 2.3A

Canada and Mexico Before Specialization and Trade

The amounts actually produced and thus consumed in Canada and Mexico are the combinations labeled *B* in Table 2.2. Amounts of each good for the "world" are the sums of the two countries' production.

	Canada Produces and Consumes	+	Mexico Produces and Consumes	=	World Produces and Consumes
Silver (ounces)	30,000		40,000		70,000
Lumber (board-feet)	700,000		40,000		740,000

TABLE 2.3B

Canada and Mexico After Specialization, but Before Trade

Specialization in production according to comparative advantage yields a world gain in the output of both goods.

	Canada Produces	+	Mexico Produces	=	World Produces	World Gains
Silver (ounces)	0		80,000		80,000	+10,000
Lumber (board-feet)	1,000,000		0		1,000,000	+260,000

FIGURE 2.5

The Trade Between Canada and Mexico

Canada and Mexico agree that each ounce of silver trades for 5 board-feet of lumber, or a board-foot of lumber trades for 1/5 of an ounce of silver. Each agrees to trade on these terms because obtaining a good through trade is less costly than obtaining it by producing it at home.

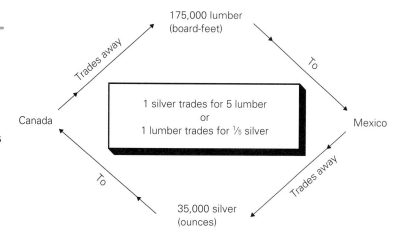

Table 2.3b depicts the production situation in each country, and, therefore, the world, after Canada and Mexico have specialized in production according to comparative advantage. After specialization, total world output of silver is 10,000 ounces greater than it was at combination B on the production possibilities curve in Figure 2.4. World production of lumber has also increased. It is 260,000 board-feet more than before specialization. The world is better off economically (more of both goods), but we have yet to show that each individual country is made better off as a result of specialization according to comparative advantage. There is one more step to the process, that of trade.

Trade: The Fruits of Specialization

Our consultant realizes that neither Canada nor Mexico would voluntarily agree to an exchange that would leave them worse off (than before trade). For voluntary exchange to take place, each nation must end up better off economically. With this in mind, the consultant proposes that Canada trade 175,000 board-feet of lumber to Mexico in exchange for 35,000 ounces of silver, or 5 board-feet of lumber for each ounce of silver. The Canadians would agree to this trade since domestic production of the 35,000 ounces of silver would cost them 10 board-feet of lumber each, for a total of 350,000 board-feet. This exchange allows the Canadians to obtain silver from the Mexicans more cheaply than it costs to produce it themselves.

The Mexicans would also agree to the proposed trade. Each board-foot of lumber costs them 1 ounce of silver to produce, but the proposed trade allows them to obtain each board-foot for 1/5 of an ounce of silver. The trade with Canada enables Mexico to obtain 175,000 board-feet of lumber for 35,000 ounces of silver. The opportunity cost to Mexico of producing 175,000 board-feet of lumber would be 175,000 ounces of silver. It is less costly for Mexico to obtain lumber through trade than through self-production. This trade is depicted in Figure 2.5.

The number of board-feet of lumber that trade for an ounce of silver is called the **terms of trade.** The terms of trade is really a price that is not measured in terms of either country's money. In this example, Canada pays Mexico 5 board-feet of lumber for each ounce of silver. Mexico pays 1/5 ounce of silver for each board-foot of lumber. The terms of trade is a price that defines the number of units of one good that exchange for one unit of some other good. The terms of trade will always fall somewhere between the marginal opportunity production costs of a given good in each of the two countries. In this case, an ounce of silver has an opportunity cost

Terms of trade

The number of units of one good that exchange in the market for one unit of some other good. Although not expressed in terms of money, it is a price nonetheless.

of 10 board-feet of lumber in Canada and 1 board-foot of lumber in Mexico, so the terms of trade will be at least 1 board-foot of lumber for 1 ounce of silver and at most 10 board-feet of lumber for 1 ounce of silver. Terms of trade outside these limits would cause trade to be counter to the interests of citizens in one of the countries—for instance, Canadians would be better off producing their own silver than paying more than 10 board-feet per ounce for Mexican silver.

Table 2.4 summarizes the economic positions of Canada and Mexico after specializing in production and trading. Most important, both countries end up with more of both goods to consume than before trade. Canada consumes 125,000 more board-feet of lumber than it did initially; Mexico, an additional 135,000 board-feet. Both enjoy 5000 more ounces of silver than in the period before specialization and trade. In Figures 2.3a and 2.3b, both countries are consuming combination *D*—combinations of goods that lie beyond the respective production possibilities curves. Without specialization and trade, these combinations could only be attained through economic growth. It is as if additional resource quantities of silver and lumber were actually created through specialized production and division of labor. Residents in each country are better off economically. Specialization according to comparative advantage and trade has led to increased living standards in both parts of the world.

Factors Explaining Comparative Advantage

There are basically two reasons that a locale would have a comparative advantage over some other locale in producing any given good relative to other goods—differences in technology or differences in the quantities of productive inputs in the two locales. Relative differences in production technologies of the goods in the two locales can lead to a comparative advantage for each locale. Certain institutional factors can also affect both the level of technology utilized and costs. One country may impose minimum wage laws on employers. Another may contain effective environmental laws that create different costs to producers.

Alternatively, if production technologies are identical in both locales, an abundance of the productive resources used in producing lumber in Canada compared

TABLE 2.4

Canada and Mexico After Specialization and Trade
Specialization in production according to comparative advantage and trading yields a world gain and a gain for each country.

		CANADA			
	Produces	**Trades For (+) Away (−)**	**Consumes After Trade**	**Produced and Consumed Before Trade**	**Gains from Trade**
Silver (ounces)	0	+35,000	35,000	30,000	+5,000
Lumber (board-feet)	1,000,000	−175,000	825,000	700,000	+125,000
		MEXICO			
	Produces	**Trades For (+) Away (−)**	**Consumes After Trade**	**Produced and Consumed Before Trade**	**Gains from Trade**
Silver (ounces)	80,000	−35,000	45,000	40,000	+5,000
Lumber (board-feet)	0	+175,000	175,000	40,000	+135,000

with Mexico's amounts of these resources could exist. This would give Canada a comparative advantage in lumber. Patterns of comparative advantage may, of course, shift over time with either natural or artificially induced changes in resource prices and supplies or with changes in technology.

Consider another aspect of the situation in Mexico and Canada. Table 2.2 indicates that Canada has the ability to produce more lumber in absolute terms than Mexico if each country produces only lumber (1 million board-feet versus 80,000 board-feet). Canada also has the capacity to produce absolutely more silver (100,000 ounces versus 80,000 ounces) than Mexico. Canada has what economists call an absolute advantage in production of both goods. That is, Canada can specialize in silver production and simply produce more silver than Mexico. The same holds for lumber production. Any time a country can specialize in producing a good and produce absolutely more of it than some other country, the first country has an absolute advantage over the second. An absolute advantage can arise because of technological factors or because one country possesses a larger quantity of productive resources. Although Canada has an absolute advantage in producing both goods, it has a comparative advantage only in lumber. Mexico has an absolute disadvantage in both goods, but it still can produce silver at a lower marginal opportunity cost than Canada. Both countries still benefit from specialization and trade according to comparative advantage.

It is important to understand the simplification attached to the preceding discussion of comparative advantage. Differences in marginal opportunity costs explain comparative advantages, but the economic system does not actually require an "economic consultant" to tell countries (or businesses or individuals) about the potential gains from specialization and trade. Relative scarcities based on differences in marginal opportunity costs are transmitted to producers and consumers through the price system. Prices "inform" producers and consumers about what, how much, and when to supply and consume millions of goods and services. The details of how prices are formed through the interaction of supply and demand are reserved for Chapter 3. Nonetheless, it is useful to remember that prices, not hypothetical economic consultants, "discover," signal, and reflect the comparative advantages that exist between nations, businesses, and individuals.

Exchange Costs

The model of comparative advantage and trade—along with all other economic models—is a simplification of reality. A number of important assumptions hide behind our simple discussions. But there are also costs to the process of exchange that must be accounted for when calculating the benefits of specialization and trade. We classify these **exchange costs** as transaction costs, transportation costs, and artificial barriers to trade.

Exchange costs
The opportunity costs of the resources used in making trades; includes transaction costs, transportation costs, and artificial barriers to trade.

Transaction costs
The opportunity costs of the resources directly associated with trade; includes time costs, brokers' fees, and so on.

Transaction Costs   Transaction costs are all the resource costs (including time-associated costs) incurred because of exchange. Transaction costs occur every time goods and services are traded, whether exchanges are simple (purchase of a pack of gum) or complex (a long-term negotiated contract with many contingencies). Here's a simple example: Gwen goes to the supermarket to purchase a pound of coffee. What are the costs of the transaction? Gasoline and auto depreciation must be considered as resource costs, of course, but the principal cost is the opportunity cost of Gwen's time. Gwen might have spent this time working or playing tennis instead of grocery shopping. Gwen's wage rate might then serve as her opportunity cost. If the shopping trip takes 30 minutes and if Gwen's wage rate is $15 an hour, the time part of her transaction costs is $7.50.

In this simple case the contracting and negotiating are instantaneous—Gwen simply gives the money to the checkout person, takes her coffee, and the transaction is complete. In other, more complex exchanges—such as the purchase of a house, a car, or a major appliance or the negotiation of a long-term labor contract—contracting and negotiating costs can be substantial. Think of the time and other resource costs associated with long-term supply contracts such as U.S. arms deals with allies or negotiations for ammonia plants in China. Every detail must be studied, formulated, and then spelled out.

The important point is that transaction costs include resources used by each party to the exchange. The higher the resource costs, the lower the benefit that comes from specialization and trade. Institutions—new legal arrangements, new marketing techniques, new methods of selling—have emerged, and are continually emerging, to reduce all forms of transaction costs. Gwen could have purchased coffee at a convenience store nearer to her house. The price of the coffee might have been somewhat higher, but Gwen's time costs, and therefore her total transaction costs, would have been lower. In a broader sense, laws about contracts, and law itself, are means by which transaction costs are reduced. The invention of money and the development of various forms of money and financial instruments are responses to transaction costs associated with barter and more primitive means of exchange.

In addition to money, intermediaries such as wholesalers and advertisers developed over the ages to facilitate exchange. The creative marketing of goods and services from bazaars to discount stores to media advertising has increased consumer information and thus reduced the costs of making transactions. Intermediaries have lowered transaction costs by decreasing the risk of exchange. The production of some goods entails some risk and uncertainty on the part of buyers and sellers. Planting wheat in the spring for sale in the fall obviously entails some uncertainty about what prices will be at harvest. Intermediaries-speculators who deal in futures provide sellers and buyers assurance of prices in the future. This type of intermediaries makes profits on the miscalculations of buyers and sellers but reduces uncertainty and thereby increases trade and specialization.

Transportation costs

The value of resources used in the transportation of goods that finalize any trade.

Transportation Costs   Transportation costs, resource costs associated with the physical transport of products from place to place, are also an impediment to trade. The higher these resource costs are, the lower the benefits from specialization and trade.

We did not include transportation costs in our initial examples of comparative advantage with Canada and Mexico. Let's do so now. Suppose that transportation costs associated with the trade amounted to 10,000 board-feet of lumber to each country. Even after paying these transportation costs, Canada and Mexico still enjoy more lumber than they did before specializing and trading (see Table 2.4). However, if transportation costs were high enough, possible advantages to specialization and trade could be wiped out completely. Cheaper transportation costs permit more trade and open up opportunities for new forms of and increases in specialization. The invention of the railroad in the nineteenth century, the spread of the automobile and the truck, and the dawning of air freight transport in the twentieth century were all boons to specialization and increased output.

Artificial barriers to trade

Restrictions created by the government that inhibit or prevent trade; includes import quotas and tariffs.

Artificial Barriers to Trade   The final impediments to specialization and trade are government-imposed restrictions such as tariffs, quotas, and outright prohibi-

Tariff
A tax or levy on imported goods.

Quota
A restriction or limit on the quantity of an imported good.

tions on the import or export of goods. **Tariffs** are taxes or levies on imported goods. **Quotas** are quantity limitations on imports of products purchased from abroad. Such impositions, known as artificial barriers, either reduce or eliminate the benefits of specialization and trade.

Governments always have reasons for these restrictions, but the reasons must be closely scrutinized because the benefits from international and domestic specialization and trade are potentially huge for all consumers. Artificial barriers have the power to reduce economic welfare by reducing or eliminating the benefits of specialization according to the law of comparative advantage.

The possible effects of restrictions on trade can be seen in the growing volume of trade between Japan and the United States in commodities such as TVs, automobiles, stereo equipment, and musical instruments. Special-interest groups—such as American autoworkers and manufacturers—have lobbied for import tariffs and other trade restrictions to protect their own interests, which include increased demand for American-made products and therefore increased domestic production. Government-enforced tariffs make Japanese goods more expensive, however, causing a reduction in the general well-being of Americans. Artificial restrictions on trade, whatever their purpose, reduce the advantages of specialization and trade. As a matter of economic principle, therefore, most economists generally advocate free trade over any type of trade restriction. Further, any institution or mechanism that reduces the costs of exchange usually gets the support of economists because greater specialization permits better utilization of scarce resources. Specialization, in other words, helps us get more of what we want, given a limited amount of resources.

Tariffs, Trade, and Trade Zones   In both the modern and ancient worlds, trade and specialization take place when countries agree to special trade arrangements. Fine details of free trade zones differ, but the basic idea is that certain nations agree to have free trade with each other while continuing to have trade barriers—tariffs or quotas, for example, against other countries. Currently the best known, but by no means the only, free trade association affecting the United States is the North American Free Trade Association, or NAFTA. It is composed of the countries of Mexico, Canada, and the United States. NAFTA went into

Mexican workers assembling shoes at a plant in Guadalajara, Mexico.

effect on January 1, 1994, creating the largest free trade association in the world and affecting more than 360 million consumers. (See Focus: "Free Trade Associations, Past and Present" for details about these important international trade organizations.) We will have more to say about such associations in this book, but a simple example will help you understand how tariffs and trade agreements affect the quantity and directions of trade. Consider a simple example of computer trade between three countries, the United States, Mexico, and Taiwan.

Table 2.5 illustrates several points concerning real-world patterns of trade. It shows the potential effects of a free trade zone on Mexican consumers. Assume that Mexico, the United States, and Taiwan are all able to produce computers, and that computers are subject to a Mexican tariff rate of 40 percent. The Mexican pro-

FOCUS

Free Trade Associations, Past and Present

Economic unions, taking advantage of the principles of specialization and trade, have been common since ancient Greek and Roman times and even before. As such, the North American Free Trade Agreement is only one of the latest in a long list of arrangements for economic gain. All unions—for economic betterment and growth, for defense, or for any political purpose—presuppose that mutual gain can be had by enacting policies that are beneficial to all parties. However, the extent of the union may vary from full political and economic unification, where separate countries may in fact become one, to far less extensive agreements on tariffs and other trade restrictions.

The prototype for a popular form of modern union was the Zollverein or customs union of the last century. The name was given by the Prussians to a union established in 1833 to set uniform tariffs among separate German states (initially comprising Hesse Cassel, Hesse Darmstadt, Bavaria, and Wurtemberg) and the rest of the world. The agreement specified no tariffs or trade restrictions among these states. The Zollverein was the nineteenth-century model for many other unions.

These nineteenth-century agreements provided models for contemporary trade blocs in North America and Western Europe. The most famous economic union in the post–World War II period was the European Economic Community or Common Market, which formed the basis for the European Union (EU) of today. The EU is the most important present-day regional trading bloc, and there are fifteen member countries (Belgium, France, Luxembourg, Germany, Italy, the Netherlands, Denmark, Ireland, the United Kingdom, Greece, Spain, Portugal, Austria, Finland, and Sweden.) In 1999 the euro became the common currency of eleven European countries, with an initial value set at 1 euro = \$1.16. It is used for all official and interbank transactions plus securities quotations and transactions. National currencies still exist for *private* transactions. On January 1, 2002, euro coins and bank notes will be introduced to replace all national coins and notes. The union will make trade within Europe as regulation-free among the countries of Europe as it is between the states of Massachusetts and New Hampshire. Eventually, all tariff and nontariff barriers will fall to zero and the EC will, after the NAFTA countries, become the largest and most populous trading area of the world.

Many unanswered questions accompany this new-world scenario of "competing Zollvereins." Not to be minimized is the potential for dissolution of any trade bloc from internal disagreements and dissension. For example, the debate over the net benefits of NAFTA within the United States did not end with its passage in January 1994. Financial problems in Mexico, U.S. loans to bolster Mexico's currency, and the (inevitable) adjustments in domestic employment in some fields have led to much dissension in the political arena.

TABLE 2.5

Example of Potential Effects of a Free Trade Zone on Mexican Computer Consumers

Producer of Computers	Domestic Price of Computers		
	MEXICO'S TARIFF RATES ON COMPUTERS		
	0%	20%	40%
Mexico	$2000	$2000	$2000
U.S. before NAFTA	$1800	$2160	$2520
U.S. after NAFTA	$1800	$1800	$1800
Taiwan	$1600	$1920	$2240

ducers can make a computer for $2000 and do not pay a tariff. U.S. producers can make a computer for $1800. With a 40 percent tariff, their price is $2520 in the Mexican market. Taiwanese producers can make a computer for $1600 and, under the same tariff rate, their price is $2240 in the Mexican market. Mexican firms emerge, as a result of the 40 percent tariff, as the low-cost producers in their domestic market and supply the entire market demand; thus, there is no international trade.

Now consider the trade-creating effects of the North American Free Trade Agreement (NAFTA). The fundamental premise behind NAFTA is the creation of a free trade zone (no tariffs) between Mexico, the U.S. and Canada only. In other words, the agreement establishes a system of preferential treatment for particular trading partners. If Mexican tariff rates on imported computers are 20 percent, the United States will emerge as the low-cost producers ($1800) following the implementation of the Agreement. This result emerges from tariff-free trade between the United States and Mexico while trade in computers between Mexico and Taiwan would still be subject to a 20 percent tariff and, thus, a higher price ($1920). In this example, NAFTA's creation of a free trade zone diverts trade from the low-cost producer, Taiwan, to a relatively higher-cost producer, the United States.

Notice that only when tariff rates are 0 percent between all three countries will an efficient pattern of production and trade result with the low-cost producer, Taiwan, supplying the Mexican (and the American) market. Trade diversion is not a problem for the member nations, but from a global perspective trade diversion results in inefficient production, because the more efficient producer loses sales to a less efficient producer. Thus a key feature in the debate over free trade zones is the debate over whether the free trade zone results more in trade creation or more in trade diversion. But economists are almost uniform in their support of free trade and would almost unanimously support a worldwide reduction in tariff and nontariff barriers to trade. For the United States, there are many benefits from the creation of free trade zones such as NAFTA. One is the reduction in the prices of imports to U.S. consumers because of reduced tariffs. Another benefit is the increased efficiency of production and the increased competition that comes from a larger market. Some estimate that after the ten- or fifteen-year phase-in period, NAFTA could yield additional trade of $1 to $2 trillion. But there will be winners and losers as free trade becomes a reality between the United States, Mexico, and Canada. Over the fifteen or so years of adjustments, in 2010, some U.S. business owners and employees of those businesses that cannot compete with Mexican and Canadian producers will lose. Some business owners will lose their investments, and some workers will lose their jobs. Some textile firms, for example, will lose their production facilities to Mexico since labor is cheaper there.

Economists argue that the *net effects* of tariff reduction through free trade associations and other means is positive. But even if economists condemn tariffs and quotas, they also recognize how individuals in their public choices may be able to convince government to pass a tariff. Think of it. The benefits of the tariff to a domestic industry may be highly concentrated on the workers and owners in the industry. New trade agreements that lower tariffs and quotas ordinarily create jobs and destroy other jobs. The costs of the tariff in terms of higher prices and costs are spread across the general public so that they may not even notice the effects. Government decision makers respond to this concentrated benefit–diffused cost condition by "supplying" a tariff to the industry. We will have a great deal more to say about this process later in this book. The point is that government can and often does override comparative advantage in order to respond to political pressures for protection.

Real-World Patterns of Trade The previous sections suggest that trade occurs between two countries when the countries have differences in opportunity costs of producing various goods (i.e., when comparative advantages exist), when transaction costs and transportation costs are small, and when the countries promote free trade. Real-world evidence reported in Table 2.6 and Figure 2.6 supports these arguments. For example, Canada is the leading trade partner of the United States. Transportation costs between the two countries are very low, and the two countries have one of the freest trade relationships in the world. In contrast, the United States trades substantially less with the United Kingdom and other European

TABLE 2.6

Leading Trading Partners of the United States
In terms of exports, Canada is the biggest customer of the United States. In terms of imports, Canada is also the biggest supplier of the United States.

Country	Value of U.S. Imports (billions)	Value of U.S. Exports (billions)
All countries, total	$870.6	$689.2
Canada	168.2	151.8
Japan	121.7	65.6
Germany	39.0	24.5
United Kingdom	32.7	36.4
Mexico	86.0	71.4
France	20.6	16.0
South Korea	23.2	25.1
Hong Kong	10.3	15.1
Singapore	20.1	17.7

Source: U.S. Bureau of the Census, *Statistical Abstract of the United States,* 1998 (Washington, D.C.: U.S. Government Printing Office), pp. 801–804.

FIGURE 2.6

Leading Trading Partners of the United States

In terms of both import and export values, the greatest amount of trade takes place between Canada, Mexico, and Japan. These high values are best explained by comparative advantage.

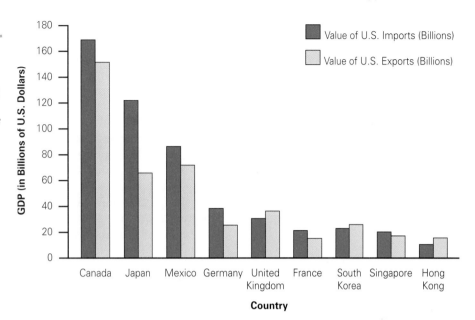

nations because their trade policies are more restrictive and transportation costs are much greater than those for trade with Canada.

Other factors explain the relative importance of foreign trade in the economies of different nations. Foreign trade is relatively more important to the Hong Kong and Singapore economies than to the German or Canadian economies, although it is quantitatively less important in trade with the United States. Geography and transport costs are part of the explanation, but the resource endowments (or lack thereof) is another principal explanation for larger volumes of trade. Further, nations pursuing less restrictive trade policies may, other things being equal, be expected to engage in more foreign trade.

The tremendous volume of trade between the United States and other nations is best explained by strong comparative advantages. Because the types of productive resources found in the countries differ greatly, certain goods that have high opportunity costs elsewhere have low costs in the United States, and vice versa. A huge trade volume, therefore, exists between nations of the world despite transportation costs and the fact that many nations pursue policies to restrict trade. The gains to specialization and trade are enormous, no less between nations as between individuals and all other trading units.

APPLICATION

AIDS and Reduced Production Possibilities in Africa

Almost everyone is familiar with the devastating toll the AIDS (autoimmune deficiency syndrome) epidemic has taken on individuals, families, and communities. In light of the huge number of personal tragedies resulting from the disease, it is unsurprising that the societal impact of AIDS has received relatively little attention. However, it is important not to overlook the extent to which the AIDS crisis could wreak havoc with the economies of certain developing nations, particularly those in sub-Saharan Africa.

More than a decade ago (in 1987) the World Health Organization estimated that about two and a half million adults in Africa were infected with human immunodeficiency virus (HIV), the pathogen that causes AIDS. By 1990 that figure had tripled for many countries. Now, as the millennium is crossed, the infection rate in most central African nations exceeds 10 percent, and several have rates well above 15 percent. (By contrast, less than 1 percent of American adults are thought to be infected.) Unlike many other diseases, which primarily affect the very young or the old, AIDS has its greatest impact on people between the ages of twenty and forty. In economies dominated by agriculture and light industry, these are the most economically productive years of a person's life. Another characteristic of AIDS in African nations is that incidence rates are approximately the same for men and women. As a result, many children are losing both parents to AIDS at a very early age and there is a high incidence of mother-to-child (intrauterine) transmissions. Further, although many new drugs (protease inhibitors) have had significant effects in slowing or, in some cases, preventing the development of the virus in developed countries, such medicines are costly and less available in developing countries. The result is that because AIDS affects all socioeconomic groups, the ranks of the political and entrepreneurial leaders of many African nations are being thinned.

In the late 1980s, experts believed that AIDS would reduce population growth rates throughout Africa by as much as 3.5 percent per year. They further predicted that certain African nations could find particular populations devastated. These dire and economically significant predictions have been borne out. The 1998 Revision of the World Population Estimates and Projects of the United Nations reveal a devastating mortality toll. One in four adults are infected with HIV in Botswana. Life expectancy at birth in Botswana is anticipated to fall from 61 years in 1990–1995 to 41 years by 2000–2005. Based on these projections, Botswana's population may be 23 percent smaller in 2025 than it would have been without the AIDS epidemic. The pre-AIDS life expectancy in Zimbabwe of 65 years sank to

The human tragedies of the AIDS virus in Africa are accompanied by a reduction in production possibilities.

FIGURE 2.7

Production Possibilities and AIDS in Africa

A loss in labor resources caused by AIDS shifts the production possibilities curve toward the origin. A higher percentage of resources must be devoted to consumption goods after the crisis.

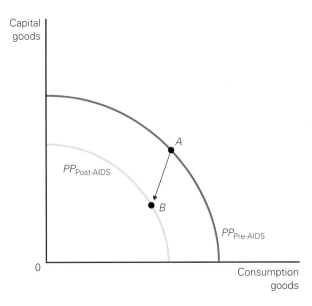

39 in the post-AIDS period. Such reductions are similar in countries such as Malawi, Kenya, Uganda and the Ivory Coast.

Figure 2.7 shows what happens to a nation's production possibilities curve when a large percentage of the nation's working population is decimated. Note that these plunging life expectancies do not eliminate the trade-off between consumption goods and capital goods. Because labor has been cheap and plentiful relative to other resources in central African nations, agricultural methods have been oriented to the large, untrained labor supply. A scarcity of labor caused by the AIDS epidemic in a particular country would mean that that country would have to devote a larger proportion of its resources to consumption goods in order to survive (point *B* in Figure 2.7). In other words, labor-saving technology would be employed to economize on scarce labor inputs.

The development of an AIDS vaccine, the deployment of life-extending drugs, or the implementation of more effective AIDS education would prevent a reduction in the output potential of the developing countries of central Africa. Still, the AIDS crisis provides convincing evidence that disease can create reduced production possibilities even in modern societies.

QUESTION

How do you think the following catastrophic events would affect the production possibilities curve? A hurricane that kills hundreds of thousands in a small developing country? A war that devastates both population and machinery and buildings? A drug that eradicates all infectious diseases?

Sources: Information for this discussion was drawn from Ken Sidey, "AIDS Reshapes African's Future," *Christianity Today* 34 (October 22, 1990), p. 47; Gary W. Shannon, Gerald F. Pyle, and Rashid L. Bashshur, *The Geography of AIDS: Origins and Course of the Epidemic* (New York: The Guilford Press, 1991); and the United Nations, *Revisions of the World Population Estimates and Projections*, Department of Economic and Social Affairs, Population Division, 1998.

SUMMARY

1. Economic choices, both for the individual and for society, always involve an opportunity cost.

2. Opportunity cost is the highest-valued alternative forgone in the decision to engage in a particular activity.

3. The law of increasing costs means that as more of one good is produced by a society, the opportunity costs of obtaining additional units of that commodity rise. The increase in cost is the result of resources becoming less adaptable as production becomes more specialized.

4. Specialization—the division of tasks to produce goods and services—takes place in all known societies. The principles of specialization are thus related to the decisions all societies and economic organizations face in trying to overcome the basic problem of scarcity.

5. The production possibilities curve shows the possible quantities of two goods that could be pro-

duced given the state of technology and society's scarce resources.

6. Changes in technology or increases (or decreases) in the amount of resources cause rightward (or leftward) movements in the production possibilities frontier.

7. Greater quantities of output can be obtained with society's scarce resources when people specialize and trade. Trade takes place according to the principle of comparative advantage.

8. Trade can take place between two individuals or economic entities even if one of the entities is more efficient at producing all goods. All that is required is that each entity be relatively more efficient than the other in some production.

9. Transaction costs, transportation costs, and artificial trade barriers such as tariffs and quotas reduce the benefits obtainable from specialization and trade.

KEY TERMS

opportunity cost
specialization
division of labor
production possibilities frontier
law of increasing costs
unemployment of resources
choices at the margin

capital stock
economic growth
marginal opportunity production
   cost
comparative advantage
terms of trade
exchange costs

transaction costs
transportation costs
artificial barriers to trade
tariff
quota

QUESTIONS FOR REVIEW AND DISCUSSION

1. What did reading this chapter cost you? Did you include the price of the book? What will reading the next chapter cost? Does that include the price of the book?

2. Do government-sponsored financial aid programs for college students influence the amount of education produced? Do these programs shift the production possibilities curve?

3. What does a movement along the production possibilities frontier suggest? What does a point inside the curve suggest?

4. A subsidy to farmers who purchase combines and tractors increases the production of this farm machinery. Does this cause an increase in the production possibilities curve or just a movement along the curve? Can subsidies cause economic growth?

5. Why would a country with an absolute advantage in the production of all goods be willing to trade with other countries?

6. Alpha can produce 60 bottles of wine or 40 pounds of cheese. Beta can produce 90 bottles of wine or 30 pounds of cheese. Both have constant

costs of production. Draw their production possibilities curves. What is Alpha's cost of 1 bottle of wine? What is Beta's cost of 1 pound of cheese? If they trade, who should specialize in cheese?

7. What are the costs of going to college? Does the marginal benefit outweigh the marginal cost?

8. Is the lost present consumption associated with the production of capital goods worth the benefit of the new capital?

9. Does Japan have an absolute advantage over the United States in the production of televisions and stereo equipment, or is it just a comparative advantage?

10. Who is hurt by and who benefits from an import quota on foreign beef?

11. How does the cost of purchasing a loaf of bread at a supermarket compare with the cost of purchasing a loaf of bread at a convenience store?

12. What is the law of increasing costs, and why does it hold?

13. When the gains from specialization and trade are assessed, exchange costs must be considered. What are these costs?

14. If the United States opened its border with Mexico and lowered all tariffs and quotas, what would happen to the production possibilities frontier of the United States?

PROBLEMS

1. Countries A and B both produce golf balls and golf clubs. The table shows what each country can produce at full employment.

A		B	
Golf Balls	Golf Clubs	Golf Balls	Golf Clubs
1200	0	900	0
1000	50	750	25
800	100	600	50
600	150	450	75
400	200	300	100
200	250	150	125
0	300	0	150

a. Graph the production possibilities curve of each country.
b. Do both production functions exhibit constant costs?
c. Who has the absolute advantage in both golf ball and golf club production?
d. Who has the comparative advantage in the production of golf balls?
e. Who has the comparative advantage in the production of golf clubs?

2. Consider the following data concerning the production possibilities of the countries Alpha and Beta.

ALPHA		BETA	
x	y	x	y
0	20	0	60
20	15	10	45
40	10	20	30
60	5	30	15
80	0	40	0

a. Which commodity, X or Y, does Alpha have a comparative advantage in producing?
b. Where does Beta's comparative advantage lie?
c. Show the results in a graph.

3. Consider the following production possibilities for the United States and France for two commodities, steel and concrete:

	United States	France
Steel	100 tons	25 tons
Concrete	200 tons	100 tons

a. Which country has the comparative advantage in the production of concrete? Carefully explain why you believe your answer to be correct.
b. What would be the "loss" if both countries became self-sufficient and did not exchange?

WORKING WITH THE WEB

1. The theories of specialization and division of labor are at work in many careers. Go to the web site http://sports.yahoo.com/mlb/players/ and scroll through the players whose last name begins with A–D. How do the concepts of specialization and division of labor apply to the lives of these major league baseball players?

2. Consider trade that exists between the United States and Canada as well as the United States and China, where both Canada and China produce and export household furniture (wood and upholstered) as well as cutlery to the United States.

   First, go to http://www.ita.doc.gov/ocg/imp2511.htm and look at the statistics for both countries (Canada and China) in 1998 regarding the level of household furniture imported by the United States (measured in dollars). Next, go to http://www.ita.doc.gov/ocg/imp3421.htm and do the same comparison for each country in 1998 for U.S. imports of cutlery. If Canada and China were to decide to only manufacture one of these two types of products (and assuming each faces similar marginal opportunity production costs), which country has a comparative advantage in the production of household furniture and which country should produce cutlery? Why?

Private Markets and Prices: Laws of Demand and Supply

S imple specialization began to take place in primitive cultures as individuals recognized unique abilities in themselves and in others. As we have seen, increasing
specialization led to organized markets where people bought and sold goods, to
the use of money, and to increasingly large groups of buyers and sellers. Economists define these organized markets—such as bazaars, the stock exchange, or Saks Fifth
Avenue—as places or circumstances that bring together demanders (buyers) and suppliers (sellers) of any goods or services. After reading Chapter 3 you should understand

- the motivations of demanders and suppliers in the exchange of goods and services
  in markets.
- how and why some goods and services get produced and sold at certain prices
  while other items are not produced or sold at all.
- what happens to demand and supply when governments or other agencies institute
  price or rent controls.
- that the full price we pay for goods and services includes the money price and such
  things as time and the other costs involved in a transaction.

AN OVERVIEW OF THE PRICE SYSTEM

In the familiar economic transactions of everyday life, we enter markets where buyers and
sellers congregate to buy and sell a great variety of products and services. The typical American supermarket sells thousands of products, and as we wander through the store we can
view a price system in action. In the produce section, for instance, quantities and prices of

fruits and vegetables depend on the quantities consumers want and on the season. Early crops usually bring in the highest prices. Watermelon may sell for more than $2 per pound in March but only $0.15 per pound by the Fourth of July.

What determines who will get the early melons or how they will be rationed among those who want them? Why are prices and quantities constantly rising and falling for millions of goods and services in our economy? How do new products find their way to places where buyers and sellers congregate? The answers are simple. In a market society, the self-interest of consumers and producers, of households and businesses, determines who gets what and how much. To paraphrase Adam Smith, it is not to the benevolence of the butcher and the baker that we owe our dinner but to their self-interest. The primary way that consumers and producers express their self-interest is through the economic laws of supply and demand. Sticking a price tag on a product does not imply price-setting power, as anyone who has run a garage sale knows. In a market system, demand and supply determine prices, and prices are the essential pieces of information on which consumers, households, businesses, and resource suppliers make decisions. High melon prices in March will encourage suppliers and discourage demanders, whereas low prices in July will encourage demanders and discourage suppliers. Before investigating the mechanics of these laws of supply and demand, we consider a simple overview of the price system.

As market participants, households and businesses play dual roles. Businesses supply final output of products and services—rock concerts, bananas, hair stylings—but also must hire or demand resources to produce the outputs. Households demand rock concerts, bananas, and hair stylings for final consumption. But they also supply labor and entrepreneurial ability, as well as quantities of land and capital to earn income for the purchase of products and services.

The Circular Flow of Products and Resources

Products market
The forces created by buyers and sellers that establish the prices and quantities exchanged of goods and services.

As Figure 3.1 shows, businesses and households are interconnected by the **products** (outputs) **market** and by the **resources** (inputs) **market**. Each market depends on the other; they are linked by the prices of outputs and inputs. The particular mix of goods and services exchanged in the products market depends on consumer demands in that market plus the cost and availability of necessary resources. Similarly, the particular mix of resources available at any one time or through time is determined by what households are demanding—subject also to the availability of the resources. If land suitable for banana growing is available, it is most likely to be sold for banana plantations if households are demanding a lot of bananas, thereby making it possible for banana growers to pay landowners for their land.

Resources market
The forces created by buyers and sellers that establish the prices and quantities exchanged of resources such as land, labor services, and capital.

Prices are the impulses of information that make the entire system of input and output markets operate. The prices formed in both product and resource markets reflect the relative desires of consumer-demanders for particular goods and services as well as the relative scarcity of the resources required to produce them. The very fact that a product or service bears a price means that scarcity exists. Supply and demand in all markets is at the core of scarcity and, therefore, of economics.

Full Versus Money Prices

Money price
The dollar price that sellers receive from buyers; a price expressed in terms of money, not in terms of an amount of another good.

A distinction must be made about prices resulting from the forces of supply and demand: There is a difference between the **money price** of a product or service

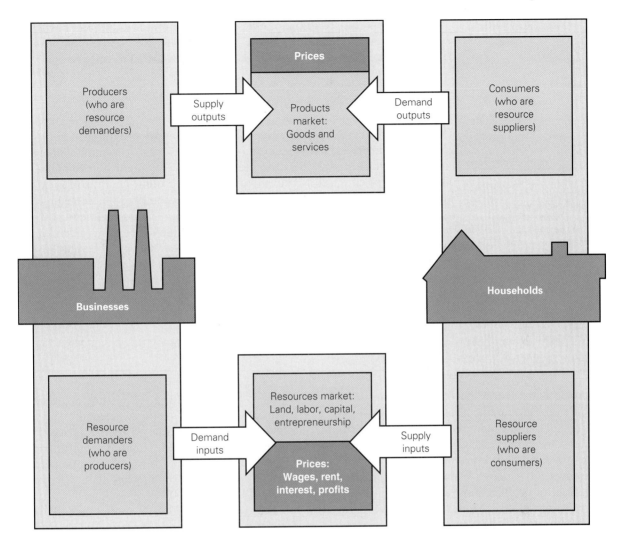

FIGURE 3.1

The Product and Resource Markets: A Circular Flow

Businesses play a dual role in the market economy: They are the suppliers of goods and services as well as the demanders of resources. Households also have a dual role. They are both demanders of goods and services and suppliers of resources.

Full price

The total opportunity cost to an individual of obtaining a good; includes money price and all other costs, such as transportation costs or waiting costs.

and the **full price**. Consider the money price of a haircut for which the customer pays $12.50 in cash. Is this the full price of a haircut?

Money price is often not the only cost to consumers. In the case of a haircut, we must account for the time spent traveling to and from the salon, the time spent waiting, and the time spent with the hairdresser. Time is a scarce resource, and it bears an opportunity cost. Time costs are often estimated in terms of the wage rate forgone, the leisure time forgone, or, generally, as the opportunity cost of the consumer's next-best alternative. Thus the full price of a haircut or any other good or service includes the price in money terms plus any other resource costs required in the purchase of the commodity. (See the Focus "Full Price and a New Orleans Restaurant.") Prices as interpreted in the simple model of demand and supply of this chapter are to be regarded as full prices.

THE LAW OF DEMAND

Relative price

The price ratio or "trade-off" in consumption between one product (or service) and another product (or service) or between one good and other goods taken as a whole.

The concept of demand is intuitive. The notion that the amount of goods sold depends on the prices charged seems to "just make sense." The amount of any one good bought during a sale, for example, depends on the **relative price** of the good on sale—the price in relation to the price of some other good or of goods as a whole. The actual money price of the good in isolation does not determine what we purchase. If the relative price of a particular pair of shoes declines—that is, the item is put "on sale"—the price has fallen relative to other shoes, shirts, or camcorders. Intuitively, we understand that more of these shoes will be purchased.

What determines how much of any good or service—camcorders, compact discs, or hair styling—consumers will purchase during some period of time? Econ-

FOCUS

Full Price and a New Orleans Restaurant

New Orleans is considered a restaurant town by gourmets. Restaurants such as Le Ruth's, Antoine's, Brennan's, and Commander's Palace consistently offer some of the best cuisine to be found anywhere. One of our favorite French Quarter restaurants, however, is Galatoire's. Galatoire's has earned a reputation for producing some of the highest-quality meals in the city. Menu prices, however, have remained low relative to other famous establishments over the past several decades.

Have both menu prices and full prices remained low at Galatoire's? If not, why not? Finally, what evidence might be offered for a real price increase? How would an economist view the matter?

The economist would focus on elements in the full price of a meal at Galatoire's. The restaurant has not enlarged its classic physical plant over the years but, over time, longer and longer lines form outside the door during the day and evening. Galatoire's, unlike most of its competition, does not take reservations and has only recently begun accepting credit cards. Moreover, Galatoire's enforces a dress code—ties or coats for men (evenings and all day on Sundays) and, until a few years ago, dresses (no pants) for women.

All these factors would tend to increase the full price of dining at Galatoire's. There are opportu-

nity costs to waiting for a table (time is a scarce resource); the time and resources spent dressing for dinner are also applicable to the full price. The length of the line at the restaurant can also make the real price higher or lower than anticipated, although diners can form hunches about when the line is apt to be shortest.

These additional costs mean that the full price exceeds the money price printed on the menu. However, the economist must calculate all benefits as well as all costs associated with purchasing products or services. Consider the possibility that some customers get positive benefits from dressing for dinner and from being surrounded by those similarly attired. Others may value the prestige or satisfaction of dining at the legendary restaurant. Such factors would tend to increase the benefits to these consumers. The full price paid for a meal at Galatoire's varies among consumers, depending on opportunity cost. However, all consumers marginally balance the perceived costs of buying products and services with the perceived benefits associated with consumption. When price or price formation is discussed in this book, it is therefore the full price, not the nominal or money price, that is being considered.

omists have answered that question for hundreds of years in the same manner—by formulating a general rule, or law, of demand. The **law of demand** states that, other things being equal or constant, the quantity demanded of any good or service increases as the price of the good or service declines. In other words, **quantity demanded** is inversely related to the price of the good or service in question.

The relation between price and quantity demanded is a fact of everyday experience. The reaction of individuals and groups to two-for-the-price-of-one sales, cut-rate airline tickets, and other bargains is common proof that quantities demanded increase as prices decrease. Likewise, gas price hikes will lower the quantity of gasoline demanded. The formalization of the inverse relation between price and quantity demanded is called a law because economists believe it is a general rule for all consumers in all markets. Imagine a graphical representation of the law of demand—called a **demand curve**—for two consumers.

The Individual's Demand Schedule and Demand Curve

Suppose that we observe the behavior of Dave and Marcia over one month. These two music lovers own compact disc players and are willing and able to purchase, or demand, CDs. To determine Dave's and Marcia's demand for CDs, we need only vary the price of discs over the month, assuming that all other factors affecting their decisions remain constant, and observe the quantities of CDs they would demand at the various prices. This information is summarized in Table 3.1.

Table 3.1 shows a range of CD prices available to Marcia and Dave over the one-month period and the quantities (numbers) of discs that each would purchase, all other things being equal. Given factors such as their income and the availability of other forms of entertainment, neither person would choose to purchase even a

Law of demand
The price of a product or service and the amount purchased are inversely related. If price rises, then quantity demanded falls; if price falls, quantity demanded increases, all other things held constant.

Quantity demanded
The amount of any good or service consumers are willing and able to purchase at all various prices.

Demand curve
A graphical representation of the quantities of a product that people are willing and able to purchase at all possible prices.

TABLE 3.1

Two Consumers' Demand Schedules
While individuals' demand schedules may differ, they do not violate the law of demand. For both people, the quantity demanded increases as the price falls.

Price of Compact Discs (dollars)	QUANTITY DEMANDED (PER MONTH)	
	Dave	Marcia
20	0	0
19	1	0
18	2	0
17	3	1
16	4	2
15	5	3
14	6	4
13	7	5
12	8	6
11	9	7
10	10	8

Fast-food restaurants reduce the full cost of meals by saving time for college students.

single CD at $20 per disc. Dave, however, would buy one CD per month at $19 and two at $18. Marcia would not buy her first CD until the price was $17. Each would purchase more discs as the price falls. Thus, Dave's and Marcia's CD-buying habits conform to the law of demand.

We obtain the individuals' demand curves by plotting or transferring the information from Table 3.1 to the graphs in Figure 3.2. The prices of CDs are given on the vertical axis of each graph, and the quantities of CDs demanded per month are given on the horizontal axis. The various combinations of price and quantity from Table 3.1 are plotted on the graphs. Each demand curve is then drawn as the line connecting those combinations of price and quantity. For both Dave and Marcia, the demand curve slopes downward and to the right (a negative slope), indicating an increase in quantity demanded as the price declines and a decrease in quantity demanded as the price rises.

Factors Affecting the Individual's Demand Curve

In addition to the price of a good or service, there are dozens, perhaps hundreds, of other factors and circumstances affecting a person's decision to buy or not to buy. These **factors affecting demand** include income, the price of related goods, price expectations, income expectations, tastes, the number of consumers, and time.

Factors affecting demand
Anything other than price, such as consumer income and preferences, that determines the amount of a product or service that consumers are willing and able to purchase.

Ceteris paribus
The Latin phrase for "all other things held constant."

Holding Factors Other Than Price Constant   To isolate the effect of price on quantity demanded, essential factors must be held constant. We want to know what quantity of CDs Dave and Marcia would choose to purchase in a month at various possible prices, given that other factors affecting their decision do not change. This condition is called *ceteris paribus* ("other things being equal") by economists. It is essential to the development of any economic theory or model dealing with real-world events since all events cannot be controlled. Economists hold factors such as income and the price of related goods constant when constructing a demand schedule or curve. This does not mean that these factors cannot change, but if they do change, the demand schedule or curve must be adjusted to account for them.

Change in quantity demanded
A change in the amount of a good a consumer is willing and able to purchase that is caused by a change in the price of the good or service.

Changes in Demand Versus Changes in Quantity Demanded   A simple but crucial distinction exists between a change in Dave's or Marcia's demand for CDs and a **change in quantity demanded** of CDs for Dave or Marcia. Other things being equal, a change in the price of CDs will change the quantity demanded of CDs, as we have seen. Figures 3.3 and 3.4 illustrate an increase and a decrease in quantity demanded, respectively. The graphs illustrate a movement along a single demand curve, indicating that factors like buyers' incomes and preferences are held constant. Figure 3.3 shows that a decrease in the price of discs leads to an increase in the quantity demanded. Figure 3.4 shows that an increase in the price of discs reduces the

FIGURE 3.2

Demand Curves for Two Consumers

A consumer's demand for a product is the quantity that he or she is willing to purchase at each price. The demand curve is downward sloping for both Dave (a) and Marcia (b). As the price falls, the quantity demanded increases; and as the price rises, the quantity demanded decreases.

Change in demand

A shift of the entire demand curve to the right or left

quantity demanded. A change in any factor other than the price will shift the entire demand curve to the right or left. Economists call this a **change in demand**. An increase in demand is shown as the rightward shift of the entire demand curve in Figure 3.5. A decrease in demand, shown in Figure 3.6, is a leftward shift of the entire demand curve.

Change in Income   Marcia's or Dave's income may change, and such a change would necessitate a redrawing of the entire demand curve for CDs. For most goods,

FIGURE 3.3

Increase in Quantity Demanded

Holding Marcia's demand constant, a decrease in the price of CDs from $14 to $13 will lead to an increase in the quantity of CDs demanded from 4 to 5 per month.

a rise in income means an increase in demand. For instance, if Marcia's income increases from $1500 to $2000 a month, she will demand more CDs at every price because she can afford more. Figure 3.5 shows that, given a new, higher income, Marcia's demand curve shifts to the right for every price of CDs. When demand increases, quantity demanded increases at every price.

Although the theory that rising income means greater demand for goods holds true for most goods, it does not apply to all goods. Economists distinguish between normal goods and inferior goods. **Normal goods** are those products and services for which demand increases (decreases) with increases (decreases) in income; the demand for **inferior goods** actually decreases (increases) with increases (decreases) in consumers' income. Joe's demand for Honda automobiles may decrease as his income increases; a Honda automobile is an inferior good to him. Beth purchases

Normal good

A good that a consumer chooses to purchase in smaller (larger) amounts as income falls (rises).

Inferior good

A good that a consumer chooses to purchase in smaller quantities as income rises or in larger amounts as income falls.

FIGURE 3.4

Decrease in Quantity Demanded

Holding Marcia's demand constant, an increase in the price of the CDs from $14 to $16 will cause Marcia to decrease the quantity of CDs demanded from 4 to 2 per month.

FIGURE 3.5

Increase in Demand

A change in any factors affecting demand causes a shift to the right or left in the demand curve. In this case, Marcia's income increases, causing an increase in her quantities demanded for CDs at every price. The demand curve shifts to the right. At a price of $14 per disc, Marcia previously would purchase 4 CDs, but given her increased income, she would now purchase 8 CDs.

less Haagen-Dazs vanilla ice cream as her income falls, indicating that Haagen-Dazs ice cream is a normal good for her.

The terms *normal* and *inferior* contain no implications about intrinsic quality or about absolute standards of goodness or badness. Indeed, a good or service that is normal for one consumer in a given income range may be inferior for another consumer in the same income range. It is even possible for a good to be normal for an individual consumer at certain levels of income and inferior at other levels. As one's income rises, for example, hamburgers or compact cars may change from normal to inferior. We will discuss this distinction in more detail later, but it is important for now to note that a change in income will produce a shift in the demand curve.

Prices of Related Goods   Suppose that the price of a good closely related to CDs—such as cassette tapes or CD players—changes during the month for which Dave's and Marcia's demand curves are drawn. What happens? Clearly, one of the assumptions about other things being equal has changed, and the demand curve will shift right or left depending on the direction of the price change and on whether the closely related good is a **substitute** for or a **complement** to the product under consideration.

Suppose that other forms of entertainment can substitute for CDs in Dave's or Marcia's budgets. If ticket prices for movies or tape prices decline during the month, the demand curve for CDs for both consumers would shift to the left; that is, the demand for CDs would decline. For every price of CDs, the quantity demanded would be lower. This shift is represented in Figure 3.6. If the price of a substitute good increased during the month, the demand for CDs would increase.

If the price of a good or service complementary to CDs rises or falls, the demand curve for CDs would shift. Such a complementary good or service might be compact disc players for home or auto. If the price of the complement increases, the demand for CDs would decrease (shift left). If the price of the complement decreases, demand for CDs would increase (shift right).

Other Factors Shifting the Demand Curve   A number of factors other than income and the price of related goods can cause a shift in the demand curve. Among

Substitutes

Products that are related such that an increase in the price of one will increase the demand for the other or a decrease in the price of one will decrease the demand for the other.

Complements

Products that are related such that an increase in the price of one will decrease the demand for the other or a decrease in the price of one will increase the demand for the other.

FIGURE 3.6

Decrease in Demand

A leftward shift of the demand curve indicates a decrease in demand. In this case, the price of a substitute good decreased, causing Dave to demand fewer discs at every price. The demand curve shifts to the left. Before the price change in the substitute good, Dave would purchase 5 CDs at $15 each, but given the change in the substitute good's price, he would purchase only 2 CDs at $15 each.

these are consumers' price and income expectations and consumers' tastes. If the price of CDs or the income of consumers is expected to change in the near future, the demand for CDs during the month will be altered. Marcia may discover during the month that she will receive an inheritance. The basis under which her original demand curve was derived changes because she anticipates a change in income. Or back-to-school CD sales might be announced for August during the middle of July, causing a decrease in demand during July. Likewise, any alteration in the time period under examination—changing from a month to a day, week, or year—will alter the construction of the demand curve. A purchase of four pizzas per month at a price of $6.95 each would be represented differently than a weekly consumption of one pizza. A change in the time period requires a redrawing of the demand curve. Also held constant is the quality of the good or service. Changing the amount of ice in a 10-ounce soft drink, for example, will alter the quality of the drink. The change in quality will alter quantity demanded at any price.

Reviewing the Law of Demand

The demand curve expresses an inverse relation between the price of a good and the quantity of the good demanded, assuming that a number of factors affecting demand are held constant. As price rises, quantity demanded falls; as price falls, quantity demanded rises. When any of the other factors affecting demand change, we must reevaluate the demand schedule and curve.

Economists predict that individuals (and collections of individuals), all things being equal, will purchase more of any commodity or service as its price falls. To verify this prediction, the individuals in question do not even have to be fully aware of their behavior; they need only act in the predicted manner. Individuals' response to sales of any kind—they buy more when price declines—is evidence that a general and predictable law of demand exists. That law is a fundamental tool of economists' analyses of real-world events.

From Individual to Market Demand

Market demand

The total amount consumers are willing and able to purchase of a product at all possible prices, obtained by summing the quantities demanded at each price over all buyers.

While an individual's demand curve is sometimes of interest, economists most often focus on the **market demand** for some product, service, or input such as automobiles, intercontinental transport, or farm labor. Market demand schedules are simply the summation of all individual demand schedules at alternative prices for any good or service. An increase in the number of consumers increases the market demand curve, and a reduction decreases market demand. The key is to add up the quantities demanded by all consumers at alternative prices for the good or service in question.

We can use the CD demand example to understand market demand. We constructed individual demand schedules for Dave and Marcia by varying the price and observing the quantities of discs that they would buy at those prices, other things being equal. To determine the market demand schedule, we simply observe the behavior of all other consumers in the same market situation.

Table 3.2 begins with the data on Dave's and Marcia's demand from Table 3.1. The table also contains a summary of quantity demanded for all other consumers at every price and, finally, the total quantity demanded for all consumers, or the total market demand. At a price of $20 no one, including Dave and Marcia, wants to buy CDs. At a slightly lower price, $19 per disc, Marcia does not choose to buy, but Dave and 39 other consumers buy 1 disc. The total market demand is, therefore, 40 discs at a price of $19. (Note that actual numbers of discs sold to all con-

TABLE 3.2

Market Demand Schedule
The total market demand for a product is found by summing the quantities demanded by all consumers at every price.

	QUANTITY DEMANDED (PER MONTH)			
Price of CDs (dollars)	Dave	Marcia	All Other Consumers	Total Market Quantity Demanded
20	0	0	0	0
19	1	0	39	40
18	2	0	78	80
17	3	1	116	120
16	4	2	154	160
15	5	3	192	200
14	6	4	230	240
13	7	5	268	280
12	8	6	306	320
11	9	7	344	360
10	10	8	382	400

sumers would be much higher. We use low numbers for simplicity. The important point is that the market demand schedule for CDs or any other privately produced product or service is constructed in precisely this manner.)

The market demand schedules can be represented graphically as market demand curves (see Figure 3.7). Dave's and Marcia's demand curves are repeated from Figure 3.2. The demand of all other consumers, taken from Table 3.2, is plotted in Figure 3.7c. The total market demand, shown in Figure 3.7d, is simply the horizontal addition of the demand curves of Figures 3.7a, 3.7b, and 3.7c.

As in the case of individual demand curves, the market demand curve is downward sloping (negatively sloped) and drawn under the assumption that all factors other than the price of CDs remain constant. If the incomes of consumers change, or the price of goods or services closely related to CDs is altered, the market demand would shift right or left, as in the case of individuals' demand curves. Economists must focus closely on these related factors in any real-world application. Changes in the demand for any product—compact cars, energy, crude oil—will be closely related to factors such as income changes and the price of substitutes and complements.

The important concept of market demand summarizes only half of the factors determining and affecting prices. Like the cutting blades of a pair of scissors, two sets of factors—demand and supply—simultaneously determine price.

Law of supply

The price of a product or service and the amount that producers are willing and able to offer for sale are positively related. If price rises, then quantity supplied rises; if price decreases, then quantity supplied decreases.

THE LAW OF SUPPLY AND FIRM SUPPLY

The **law of supply** states that, other things being equal, firms and industries will produce and offer to sell greater quantities of a product or service as the price of that product or service rises. There is a direct relationship between price and

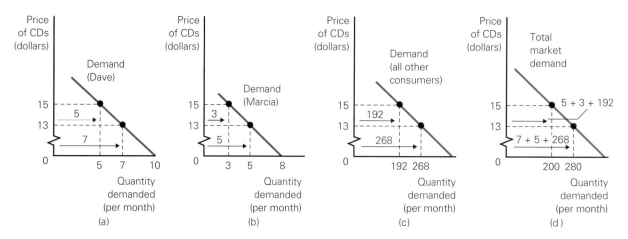

FIGURE 3.7

Market Demand Curve

The total market demand curve for a product is obtained by summing the points on all the individual demand curves horizontally. This is accomplished by selecting prices and summing the quantities demanded by all individuals to obtain the total quantity demanded at each price.

Quantity supplied

The amount of any good or service that producers are willing and able to produce and sell at some specific price.

Supply curve

A graphical representation of the quantities of a product or service that producers are willing and able to sell at all possible prices.

quantity supplied: As price rises, **quantity supplied** increases; as price falls, quantity supplied decreases. The assumption of other things being equal is invoked, as in the case of demand, so that the important relation between price and quantity supplied may be specified exactly. This relation, called a **supply curve**, shows the quantities of any good that firms would be willing and able to supply at alternative prices over a specified time period.

The method for constructing an individual firm's (and the market's) supply schedule is identical to the method we used for individual and market demand. All factors affecting supply except the price of the good or service are held constant. The price of the good or service is varied and the quantities that the firm or the industry will supply are specified.

To see how the supply curve is drawn, we turn to the supply side of CDs. Suppose that there are a number of firms supplying CDs in a given geographic area and that the output per month of two typical firms (Oranges Inc. and Joe's Audio) and all other firms combined is as shown in Table 3.3. The supply schedules of Oranges Inc. and Joe's Audio are given in the table by the combination of price and quantity supplied. That is, given alternative prices of CDs and the assumption that all other things are equal, Oranges Inc. and Joe's Audio specify the quantity of CDs that they would be willing to supply during a one-month period. At a price of $20 per disc, Oranges Inc. would be willing and able to supply 24 discs, but if the price falls to $13 per CD, Oranges Inc. will supply only 3 discs.

As in the case of demand schedules, the information from supply schedules can be graphically expressed as supply curves (see Figure 3.8). The individual supply curves for Oranges Inc. and Joe's Audio conform to the law of supply—other things being equal, as price rises, the quantity supplied increases and as price falls, quantity supplied decreases. Note that the supply curve for the individual firm slopes upward and to the right. This is because the marginal opportunity cost of

TABLE 3.3

Individual Firm and Market Supply Schedules

Individual firms' supply schedules follow the law of supply: As the price of the product increases, the quantity supplied increases. The total market supply is obtained by summing the quantities supplied by all firms at every price.

QUANTITY SUPPLIED (PER MONTH)

Price of CDs (dollars)	Oranges Inc.	Joe's Audio	All Other Firms	Total Market Quantity Supplied
20	24	16	410	450
19	21	14	365	400
18	18	12	320	350
17	15	10	275	300
16	12	8	230	250
15	9	6	185	200
14	6	4	140	150
13	3	2	95	100
12	0	0	50	50
11	0	0	0	0
10	0	0	0	0

resources used for increased CD production rises as more discs are produced. As more CDs are produced, less-adaptable resources are drawn into disc production. To increase the quantity of CDs supplied, a firm may have to enlarge its quarters by buying and converting buildings formerly used for other purposes, incur the costs of hiring and training workers who have never made CDs before, and perhaps redesign its product to use alternative materials as original materials become more scarce. These increases in marginal costs may make it unprofitable for the firm to supply more CDs unless the price of CDs rises.

Changes in Quantity Supplied and Shifts in the Supply Curve

Change in quantity supplied
A change in the amount of a good a producer is willing and able to produce and sell that is caused by a change in the price of the good or service.

As in the case of demand, a change in price will cause a **change in quantity supplied**, indicated by a movement along a given supply curve, and a change in any other factor will cause **a change in supply**, indicated by a shift in the supply curve either right or left. An increase in price will increase the quantity supplied, but a decrease in price will reduce the quantity supplied. The supply curve is positively sloped—upward and to the right—and, as we saw, the demand curve is negatively sloped—downward and to the right. When **factors affecting supply**—that is, factors other than the price of the good—change, the whole supply curve shifts.

Change in supply
A shift of the entire supply curve to the right or left.

Factors affecting supply
Anything other than price, such as technology or input costs, that determines the amount of a product or service that sellers are willing and able to offer for sale.

Changes in Cost of Production   The most important influence on the position of the supply curve is the cost of producing a good or service. The price of resources—labor, land, capital, managerial skills—may change, as may technology or production or marketing techniques peculiar to the product. Any improvement in

FIGURE 3.8

Market Supply Curves

The market supply curve of a product is obtained by summing the quantities that will be supplied by the two individual firms and by all other firms at every price. For example, at a price of $17 the total quantity supplied is 300 (15 + 10 + 275).

technology or any reduction in input prices would increase supply; that is, it would shift the supply curve to the right. More is supplied at each price.

Suppose that the price of plastic materials used in compact disc construction falls or that the wages of salespeople available to CD stores decline. As the production or sales costs to firms producing and selling CDs decline, the quantity supplied increases and the supply curve shifts to the right for every price of CDs. An increase in supply is shown in Figure 3.9a. At price P_0, the firm was willing to sup-

FIGURE 3.9

A Shift in the Supply Curve

As factors other than price change, the supply curve shifts. When input costs fall, the quantity supplied increases from Q_0 to Q_1 at the price P_0, shifting the supply curve to the right from S_0 to S_1. An increase in input costs causes a decrease in quantity supplied from Q_O to Q_2 and the supply curve shifts to the left, from S_O to S_2.

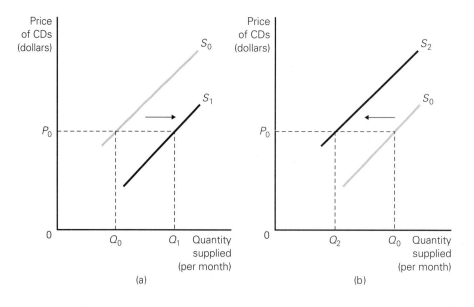

ply quantity Q_0 of discs when the supply curve was S_0. After the firm (and all other firms) experiences a reduction in costs, the supply curve shifts rightward to S_1, indicating a willingness to supply a quantity Q_1 at price P_0. An improvement in production or sales techniques or a reduction in the price of some resource shifts the supply curve to the right. An increase in any input cost shifts the supply curve to the left, as shown in Figure 3.9b.

Other Determinants of Supply   Factors other than cost of production changes can affect the location of the supply curve. One such factor is changes in producer-seller price expectations. The supply curve, like the demand curve, is drawn for a certain time period. If expectations of future prices change drastically in a market—for example, prices of the good or service are expected to rise suddenly—suppliers would withhold current production from the market in anticipation of higher prices. The current supply would be reduced, causing the supply curve to shift to the left, as in Figure 3.9b.

One other factor deserves mention. The supply curve is drawn for a given time period. A change in the time period (from one month to one week or one year) will alter the dimensions of the supply curve; it must be redrawn if the time period changes.

Market Supply

Market supply

The total amount producers are willing and able to offer for sale of a product at all possible prices, obtained by summing the quantities supplied at each price over all producers.

Market supply is the addition of all firms' quantities supplied for every price. If the number of firms in a given market increases or decreases, the supply curve would increase or decrease accordingly because the market supply curve is constructed by adding all the supply curves of individual firms. The market supply of CDs represented by the price-quantity combinations of the first and last columns of Table 3.3 is plotted in Figure 3.8d. The market supply curve is obtained by plotting the total quantities of CDs that would be produced and sold at every price during the time period. Note that market supply is simply the horizontal summation of all of the individual supply curves. For example, at a price of $14, quantity supplied would be 6, 4, and 140 units of CDs, respectively, from the three suppliers depicted in Table 3.3 and Figure 3.8. Thus the market supply of CDs at a price of $14 is $6 + 4 + 140 = 150$.

The market supply curve is positively sloped—that is, total quantity supplied increases with increases in price—because the real marginal opportunity cost of CD production rises as more discs are produced. Resources become more costly as more and more inputs are diverted from other activities into CD production.

MARKET EQUILIBRIUM PRICE AND OUTPUT

Market

The interaction of buyers and sellers producing and buying goods and services. Prices tend toward equality in a market through the continuous exchange between suppliers and demanders.

We now put the concepts of supply and demand together to understand how market forces work to establish a particular price and output. A **market** is any area in which demand and supply prices of products or services tend toward equality through the continuous interactions of buyers and sellers. Competitive (self-interested) forces of both buyers and sellers guarantee this result. All other things being equal, a buyer of dog food will always choose the seller with the lowest price, whereas a seller will choose if possible to sell at higher prices. Buyers will not pay more than price plus transportation costs, and sellers will not take less. There will always be a tendency to one price.

Perfect market

A market in which there are enough buyers and sellers that no single buyer or seller can influence price.

In a **perfect market**, both buyers and sellers are numerous enough that no single buyer or seller can influence price. In addition, buyers and sellers are free to enter or exit the market at any time. In this case of perfect competition, no single seller sells enough of the commodity and no buyer buys enough of the product or service to influence price or quantity. Each party to exchange has complete information. In a perfect market the **law of one price** holds: After the market forces of supply and demand, of buyers and sellers, are at rest or in equilibrium, a single price for a commodity (accounting for transportation and other costs) will prevail. If a single price did not prevail, someone could get rich by buying low and selling at a higher price, thereby driving prices to equality. The self-interested, competitive forces of buyers and sellers acting through supply and demand guarantee this important result.

Law of one price
In perfect markets, the market forces of supply and demand produce a single, equilibrium price for a good or service.

The Mechanics of Price Determination

Price and output are determined in a market by the simple combination of the concepts of supply and demand already developed in this chapter.

Tabular Analysis of Supply and Demand   Table 3.4 combines the data on the market supply and demand for compact discs and contrasts the quantities supplied and quantities demanded at various prices. The numbers used in Table 3.4 come from Tables 3.2 (market demand for CDs) and 3.3 (market supply of CDs). The principles discussed here apply to supply and demand functions in any market.

Consider a price of $20 for CDs in Table 3.4. At the relatively high price of $20, the quantity of discs supplied would be 450 while quantity demanded would be zero. That is, suppliers would be encouraged to supply a large number of CDs at $20, but consumers would be discouraged from buying CDs at that high price. If a price of $20 prevailed in this market, even momentarily, a **surplus** of 450 CDs would exist and would remain unsold on the sellers' shelves.

Surplus
The amount by which quantity supplied exceeds quantity demanded at a price above the equilibrium price.

TABLE 3.4

Market Supply and Demand
The equilibrium price is established when quantity supplied and quantity demanded are equal. Prices above equilibrium result in surpluses; prices below equilibrium result in shortages.

Price (dollars)	Quantity of CDs Supplied (per month)	Quantity of CDs Demanded (per month)	Surplus (+) or Shortage (−)
20	450	0	450 (+)
19	400	40	360 (+)
18	350	80	270 (+)
17	300	120	180 (+)
16	250	160	90 (+)
15	200	200	0
14	150	240	90 (−)
13	100	280	180 (−)
12	50	320	270 (−)
11	0	360	360 (−)
10	0	400	400 (−)

These unsold inventories of CDs would create a competition among sellers to rid themselves of the unsold discs. In this competition sellers would progressively lower the price. Consider Table 3.4 and assume that the price is lowered to $17. At $17 the quantity supplied of discs is 300, while the quantity demanded is 120—a surplus of 180. Only when the price falls to $15 per CD is there no surplus in the market.

Now consider a relatively low price: $13 per CD. As the hypothetical data of Table 3.4 tell us, the quantity demanded of CDs at $13 would far exceed the quantity that sellers would willingly sell or produce. There would be a **shortage** of 180 CDs—that is, 280 minus 100. Clearly some potential buyers would be unable to buy CDs if CD prices remained at $13. However, some buyers would be willing to pay more than $13 per CD rather than go without music. These buyers would bid CD prices up—offer to pay higher prices—in an attempt to obtain the product.

As the price bid by buyers rises toward $15, sellers will be encouraged to offer more CDs for sale; simultaneously, some buyers will be discouraged (will buy fewer CDs) or drop out of the market. For instance, at a price of $14 per disc, sellers would sell 150 CDs while buyers would demand 240, creating a shortage of 90 CDs. The shortage would not be eliminated until the price reached $15.

Equilibrium price in this market is $15; equilibrium quantity is 200 compact discs supplied and demanded. At this price, there is neither a shortage nor a surplus. A price of $15 and a quantity of 200 is the only price–output combination that can prevail when this market is in equilibrium—that is, where quantity demanded equals quantity supplied. The very existence of shortages or surpluses in markets means prices have not adjusted to the self-interest of buyers and sellers. Equilibrium means "at rest." In economic terms, equilibrium is that price–output combination in a market from which there is no tendency on the part of buyers and sellers to change. It is the price–output combination that clears the market. The free competition of buyers and sellers leads to this result.

Graphical Representation of Supply and Demand   The most common and useful method of analyzing the interaction of supply and demand is with graphs. Figure 3.10 displays the information of Table 3.4 in a graph that combines the market demand curve of Figure 3.7d with the market supply curve of Figure 3.8d.

The interpretation of Figure 3.10 is identical to the interpretation of Table 3.4, but the point of equilibrium is pictured graphically. Equilibrium price and quantity for CDs is established at the intersection of the market supply and demand curves. The point where they cross is labeled *E* for *equilibrium*. At equilibrium, both demanders and suppliers of CDs are mutually satisfied. Any price higher than $15 causes a surplus of CDs; that is, a higher price eliminates some demanders and includes more suppliers. Any price below $15 eliminates some suppliers and includes more demanders, resulting in a shortage of CDs.

The theory of supply and demand is one of the most useful abstractions from the world of events that is available to economists. Here we will discuss a few of the implications of supply and demand for society and for public policy.

Price Rationing

Prices, which are formed through the interaction of supply and demand, are **rationing** devices. Scarce resources are channeled to those who can produce a desired product in the least costly fashion for the demanders who most desire the product. Another way of saying this is that resources flow to their most highly

Shortage
The amount by which quantity demanded exceeds quantity supplied at a price below the equilibrium price.

Equilibrium price
The price at which quantity demanded is equal to quantity supplied; other things being equal, there is no tendency for this price to change.

Rationing
The allocation of goods among consumers with the use of prices. The equilibrium price rations the limited amount of a good produced by the most willing and able suppliers, or sellers, to the most willing and able demanders, or buyers.

FIGURE 3.10

Equilibrium Price and Quantity

The equilibrium price is established at the point where the demand and supply curves intersect. At this price, quantity demanded equals quantity supplied. At prices below equilibrium, the quantity demanded exceeds the quantity supplied, and the price is bid upward. At prices above equilibrium, the quantity supplied exceeds the quantity demanded, and the price is bid downward.

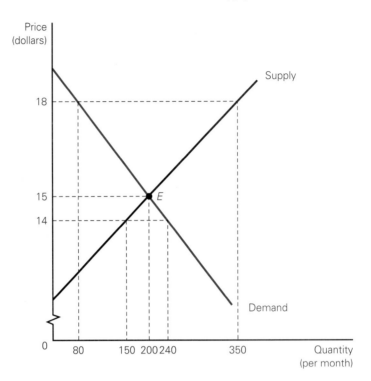

valued uses. Consider our hypothetical market for compact discs again. Suppliers who are able and willing to produce or sell CDs at a cost below $15 (including a profit) are "successful" in that their discs will be purchased. Demanders who are willing and able to purchase CDs at a price at or above $15 are the successful buyers of CDs. Only the most able sellers and buyers of CDs are successful in this market. High-cost producers (above $15) and buyers with a low preference for CDs (below $15) are eliminated from the market. CDs and all other goods are rationed by a price system—by the free interplay of supply and demand. In such a theoretical system no conscious attempt is made by any organization (such as government) to allocate scarce resources on the basis of factors such as presumed need, eye color, morals, skin color, or ideas of justice. As such, the market system plays no favorites. A price-rationing system ensures that only the most able suppliers and demanders participate in markets. All consumption decisions are made by individuals themselves.

Effects on Price and Quantity of Shifts in Supply or Demand

Both individual and market supply and demand functions are constructed by assuming that other things are equal. What happens if other things do not remain equal?

Demand Shifts　Any change in a factor other than the price of a good will shift the curve left or right. (Remember the difference between a change in demand, which is caused by a change in other factors, and a change in quantity demanded, which is caused by a change in price.) When demand changes, equilibrium price and quantity move in the same direction.

FIGURE 3.11

Shifts in the Demand Curve

(a) An increase in demand from D_0 to D_1 will increase equilibrium price and equilibrium quantity. (b) A decrease in demand from D_0 to D_1 will decrease both equilibrium price and quantity.

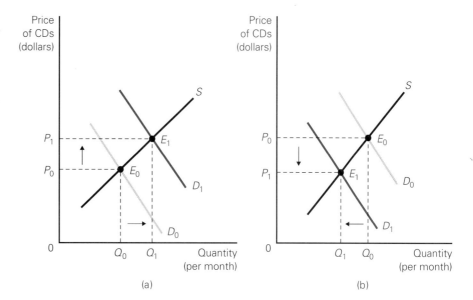

(a)   (b)

These facts can be seen graphically in Figure 3.11. Factors causing an increase in demand will have the effects on price and quantity shown in Figure 3.11a. An increase in demand shifts the whole demand curve rightward from D_0 to D_1. A shortage appears at price P_0. All the self-interested market forces that we discussed earlier now come into play. Demanders bid price up to P_1, where additional quantities are supplied by firms and where a new equilibrium, E_1, is established. Thus, an increase in demand has the effect of increasing the equilibrium price and the quantity of the product demanded and supplied. A decrease in demand causes the demand curve to shift leftward (Figure 3.11b). This has the effect of reducing equilibrium price and quantity demanded.

Supply Shifts Any increase or decrease in a factor such as resource prices or price expectations will cause increases or decreases in the whole supply schedule. Effects of such changes are shown graphically in Figure 3.12.

Figure 3.12a shows the effects on price and quantity of an increase (rightward shift) in the supply schedule. At price P_0 a surplus is created and self-interested competitive firms and buyers bid price down to P_1. Note, however, that while equilibrium price decreases, equilibrium quantity increases from Q_0 to Q_1. A price decline from P_0 to P_1 means that an additional quantity of the product or service will be demanded by consumers. Figure 3.12b shows the effects on price and quantity of a factor that decreases the supply curve (shifts it leftward). A decrease in supply has quantity-decreasing (from Q_0 to Q_1) but price-increasing (P_0 to P_1) effects, as Figure 3.12b shows. With supply shifts, unlike demand shifts, equilibrium price and quantity change in opposite directions.

Shifts in Both Supply and Demand In the previous two sections, we have examined the effects of shifts in either the demand curve or the supply curve. We now consider the effects of simultaneous shifts in both curves. If both curves shift simultaneously, changes in both equilibrium price and quantity are possible, but the direction of

FIGURE 3.12

Shifts in the Supply Curve

(a) An increase in supply from S_0 to S_1 will lower the equilibrium price and increase the equilibrium quantity. (b) A decrease in supply from S_0 to S_1 will increase the equilibrium price and lower the equilibrium quantity.

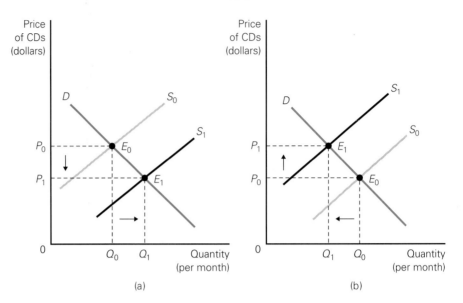

(a)   (b)

change for only one of the two can be predicted. To see why this is true, we turn to a new example. Each of the three parts of Figure 3.13 shows the initial positions of demand (D_0) and supply (S_0) of U.S. wheat. The initial equilibrium price in each part is P_0. An increase in the number of U.S. farmers who grow wheat would cause the supply curve in each part to shift from S_0 to S_1. If demand for wheat remained unchanged, the increase in supply would unambiguously lead to a decline in the equi-

(a)   (b)   (c)

FIGURE 3.13

Simultaneous Demand and Supply Increases
An increase in demand and supply will result in an increase in equilibrium quantity, but could cause an increase, a decrease, or no change in equilibrium price. Thus, the price change is said to be indeterminate.

librium price to some level below P_0. Suppose, however, that during the same time period that supply increases, Russia arranges to purchase a large amount of U.S. wheat, which leads to increased demand. In each part of Figure 3.13, the increase in demand is depicted as a shift from D_0 to D_1. The new equilibrium points occur where D_1 intersects S_1. Comparing each new equilibrium with each old one reveals that the equilibrium quantity has increased in each case. Since both increases in demand and increases in supply lead to higher equilibrium quantities, simultaneous increases in supply and demand also lead to higher equilibrium quantities. However, it is impossible to predict what will happen to the equilibrium price when both supply and demand increase. The increase in demand will raise the equilibrium price, but the increase in supply will lower it. The final result depends on the relative size of the change. As shown in Figure 3.13b, the equilibrium price will increase if the increase in demand is greater than the increase in supply. The equilibrium price will decrease, however, if the increase in demand is smaller than the increase in supply (see Figure 3.13c). Figure 3.13a shows that no change at all in the equilibrium price occurs when supply and demand increase by the same amount.

Because both decreases in demand and decreases in supply tend to lower equilibrium quantities, simultaneous decreases in supply and demand will also lead to lower equilibrium quantities. As is true with simultaneous increases in supply and demand, the effect of simultaneous decreases in supply and demand on equilibrium price depends on the sizes of the changes.

Suppose an increased demand for U.S. wheat occurs simultaneously with a decreased supply of U.S. wheat—perhaps due to a drought in the Midwest or a rise in the price of inputs used in wheat production. The decrease in supply is shown in each part of Figure 3.14 as a shift from S_0 to S_1; the increase in demand is shown

FIGURE 3.14

A Simultaneous Increase in Demand and Decrease in Supply

An increase in demand and a decrease in supply will always produce an increase in equilibrium price. Quantity change, however, will depend on the relative sizes of the shifts.

as a shift from D_0 to D_1. Since an increase in demand (with no change in supply) will always have a price-increasing effect and a decrease in supply (with no change in demand) will always have a price-increasing effect, equilibrium price will always rise with increased demand and decreased supply. However, the equilibrium quantity may remain constant (Figure 3.14a), rise (Figure 3.14b), or fall (Figure 3.14c), depending on the relative sizes of the shifts. If the decrease in supply is large relative to the increase in demand, equilibrium output declines; if the decrease in supply is small relative to the demand increase, equilibrium output increases.[1]

SIMPLE SUPPLY AND DEMAND ANALYSIS: OTHER CONSIDERATIONS

Many real-world events—new entrants into markets, oil price increases, new computer technology—can be analyzed using the simple laws of supply and demand. Some seemingly unrelated events also affect supply and demand. The theory of supply and demand is one of the most powerful tools the economist has to analyze the real world. It is important to understand some limitations and some possible applications and extensions of the simple mechanics described in this chapter.

Price Controls and Public Choice

As we have seen, a major effect of the free interplay of supply and demand is the rationing of scarce goods by a system of prices. One of the best ways to understand price rationing and its usefulness is to examine what happens when government intervenes with regulation in freely functioning markets. One such intervention into the natural functioning of supply and demand is called a **price control**. Rent controls, price controls, agricultural price supports, usury laws (controls on interest rates), and numerous other policies are examples of such tinkering in free markets. Simple supply and demand analysis provides the basis for an initial discussion of the rationing of goods and services by non-price means. For an example relating shortages, full price and supply and demand see the Application entitled "Opportunity Cost, 'Scalping,' and Full Price: Waiting for Van Gogh" at the conclusion to this chapter.

Price Ceilings and Price Floors   Imagine a hypothetical market for wheat. The market demand and supply curves are depicted in Figure 3.15. Without government interference, the equilibrium price of $7 per bushel would be reached with 12 million bushels of wheat being bought and sold each month. Government officials could become concerned about the high price of food and impose a **price ceiling** of, say, $5 per bushel. The government is declaring that wheat can be sold only at prices of $5 per bushel or less. While the intent of the legislation is to enable buyers to obtain all the wheat they want at a lower price, Figure 3.15 shows that at the ceiling price of $5 per bushel, the number of bushels that buyers would like to buy (14 million bushels) exceeds the quantity that sellers are willing to sell (9 million bushels) by 5 million bushels. In other words, at the $5 price, there will be a shortage of wheat equal to 5 million bushels. Clearly, the desires of buyers and sellers are not synchronized at that price. Wheat buyers who cannot obtain desired quantities of wheat will offer to pay more than $5 per bushel (in some cases even more than $7 per bushel) rather than go without.

Price control

The setting, by government, of a price in a market different from the equilibrium price.

Price ceiling

A form of regulation in which a maximum legal price is established by government above which exchange between buyers and sellers is illegal.

[1]Note that it is also possible for demand decreases to be accompanied by supply increases. In such cases, the equilibrium price declines. The change in the equilibrium quantity, if any, will be determined by the relative sizes of the supply and demand shifts.

To prevent the price from rising above legal levels, the government must engage in potentially costly enforcement activities. If the government succeeds in preventing illegal price increases, some other means will be used to determine which buyers get wheat. Any number of allocation plans could be used. Sellers could make the wheat available on a first-come, first-served basis, in which case long lines of consumers would form. Consumers could buy wheat at a reduced dollar price, but they would also pay with their time. Alternatively, the government could impose rationing so that each consumer is restricted to buying a fraction (nine-fourteenths) of their desired quantity of wheat. Other possibilities would be for government to establish priority schemes, with some consumers being permitted to buy and others being denied that opportunity. At any price below the equilibrium level there is an insufficient amount of wheat to meet demand, and some non-price rationing scheme must be used to determine who does and does not obtain wheat.

Alternatively, given the same circumstances, government officials might decide that the equilibrium price of $7 per bushel is too low to assure prosperity to wheat growers. They might decide to keep the price of wheat up by imposing a **price floor**— a minimum legal price of perhaps $9 per bushel—on the sale of wheat. Figure 3.16 shows that at $9 per bushel, the quantity supplied of wheat (16 million bushels)

Price floor

A form of regulation in which a minimum legal price is established by government below which exchange between buyers and sellers is illegal.

FIGURE 3.15

A Shortage Caused by a Price Ceiling

When the price of wheat is not allowed to rise above $5 per bushel, quantity demanded exceeds quantity supplied, creating a shortage of wheat.

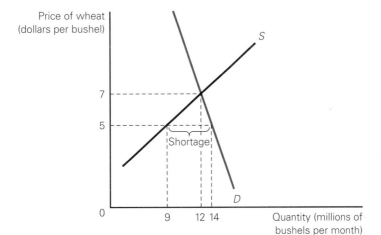

FIGURE 3.16

A Surplus Caused by a Price Floor

When a price floor above equilibrium price is placed on any commodity, quantity supplied exceeds quantity demanded, creating a surplus of wheat.

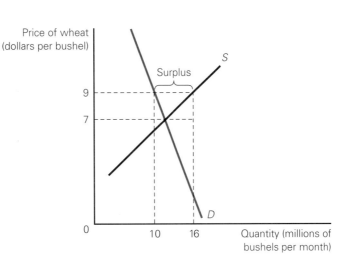

Milk price floors and subsidies established by dairy
interests in Congress have
long kept the price of milk
above its equilibrium level
in the United States.

exceeds the quantity demanded (10 million bushels) by 6 million bushels. In this case, a surplus of wheat of 6 million bushels exists. Wheat producers would find it diffi-cult to locate buyers at the legal price, and they would have an incentive to reduce the price (in the absence of government enforcement). With effective enforcement, only 10 million bushels will be purchased at $9 per bushel; the government would be forced to use taxpayers' money to buy the surplus and put it into storage. At any price above the equilibrium level, government must have a program to deal with the predicted surplus of product. Price floors are also costly for consumers; for an exam-ple, see Focus "Price Floors Cost You More Than Peanuts."

Price Controls and Quality Changes   An additional implication of price controls is interesting and relevant to understanding the competitive market process. We have assumed in the foregoing that the quality of goods and services produced remains the same when price controls are established. This is not generally the case.

Price ceilings also may be avoided through quality changes. New York, Washington, D.C., Los Angeles, and a host of other U.S. cities impose rent con-trols on apartments and other rental housing. This means that the rental price of these apartments is fixed by law. While such price controls are often enacted to "protect" low-income families, quality changes may often mean lower quality to these groups over time. In some cases, available housing goes to upper-income and well-connected individuals rather than to the poor. When landlord-owners cannot by law raise rents as the demand for housing increases or as the cost of supplying housing rises, equilibrium rents rise above the controlled ones. If these rates are adequately enforced, the available housing will be rationed to housing demanders as a result of the shortage. Since some of the demanders will be willing to pay higher prices than the controlled rate for the lower available quantity of housing, black markets (extralegal markets) may develop. Illegal side payments to land-lords, known as "key money," are common in rent-controlled cities.

Another possibility exists, however. If controls are effectively enforced and illegal side payments to landlords are prohibited, landlords have little incentive to

FOCUS

Price Floors Cost You More than Peanuts

Price floors have undoubtedly affected you. The U.S. government has supported prices of products such as milk, cheese, and peanuts for many years, and the purchase and storage programs (supported by your tax dollars) have been costly. Other nations have done the same. Trade disputes or "wars" have often broken out for these reasons. But more directly, you, the consumer, are paying more for milk and peanut butter than if quantity demanded were allowed to equal quantity supplied (see Figure 3.16).

As a taxpayer you pay for these subsidies, but as a consumer you pay as well. Suppose, for example, that the price floors on only three subsidized commodities—dairy products, sugar, and peanuts—costs you $5 per week. (Note that you also pay higher prices for all commodities and foodstuffs

that *use* these ingredients.) This price floor "tax" may seem a relatively small amount, but small amounts add up. The addition to the prices of the goods you buy is approximately $250 *per year* and over a seventy-year lifetime, $17,500. If you were able to save this money each year over a lifetime, beginning at birth and ending at seventy years old, you would have some real money. Given a real (or inflation adjusted) interest rate of 10 percent, you would have $2,000,000 (almost exactly) for retirement.[a] That ain't peanuts!

[a]Introductory business math texts demonstrate that the sum (S) of an annuity of R dollars per period at interest rate i for n years is $S = R\{1/i[1 + i)^n - 1]\}$. Using $R = \$250$, $i = 0.10$, and $n = 70$ in the above example yields the almost unbelievable figure of $2,000,000. Of course, a real or inflation adjusted rate of 10 percent may be high, but a real rate of only 5 percent would provide you with about half a million dollars at seventy years old.

FIGURE 3.16

A Surplus Caused by a Price Floor

When a price floor above equilibrium price is placed on any commodity, quantity supplied exceeds quantity demanded, creating a surplus of wheat.

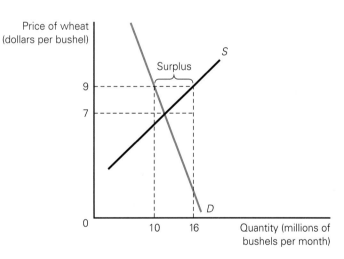

maintain rental property. Excess demand for apartments at the controlled price makes it possible to obtain tenants even if the unit deteriorates. Regulations that prevent prices from adjusting to equilibrium levels cause predictable changes in quality. Experience with rent controls in cities as diverse as New York City; Lisbon, Portugal; and Berkeley, California, shows that such programs produce low prices, substandard housing, and the allocation of rent-controlled housing to the well connected and well-to-do. Markets can clear at very low prices if quality can be reduced to a sufficiently low level. This type of nonprice competition has thwarted the best intentions of many regulators to provide better housing to low-income renters.

APPLICATION

Opportunity Cost, "Scalping," and Full Price: Waiting for Van Gogh

Matters relating to opportunity cost, full price, and supply and demand fill our daily lives, although we seldom stop to think of the mechanics of these central principles of economics. Our time is, as the French say, "money" and we have this scarce resource only twenty-four hours a day. Standing in line—at the grocery, at the movie theater, or waiting at the doctor's office—carries an opportunity cost. The opportunity cost of standing in line is our highest-valued alternative to, for example, working, sleeping later, or playing tennis. (Note that the highest-valued alternative does not have to be lost income from missed work time.) In general, however, the lower our income, the lower our opportunity cost of time. The fact that line-standing turns into a profession in many big cities is proof positive that such time has value. We can (and many do) pay individuals to stand in line for some items. In many cases, such transactions between people who have high value of time and those who will stand in line for a fee are perfectly legal.

In other cases, line-standing to obtain tickets for some event and the reselling of the ticket (called scalping) is restricted by law. Ticket scalping is often declared illegal by cities or other entities (if they catch you, that is). Football tickets, tickets to rock concerts, and passes to major art exhibits are all examples. Why, do you think, opportunities for scalping arise? Scalping arises from the policy of agencies or governments to keep the prices of goods or services low *despite the conditions of supply and demand*.

Consider a real-world example. Every year in major cities of the world, so-called blockbuster art exhibits come to city museums. Rembrandt, Vermeer, Cezanne, Degas, and many others are regularly represented in the great museums of the United States. In late 1998 a great exhibit of the works of Vincent Van Gogh hit the United States, first appearing at the National Gallery in Washington, D.C. That exhibit, lent from the Van Gogh Museum in Amsterdam, was provided "free" to the public. That is to say that tickets were free in nominal terms as described by Figure 3.17.

Consider Figure 3.17. Demanders, as described in this chapter, desire tickets depending on their price. At a money nominal or price of zero, Van Gogh lovers

FIGURE 3.17

Excess Demand at "Zero Price"

When quantity demanded (*OA*) exceeds quantity supplied (*OB*) and tickets are distributed "free," "scalping" often results.

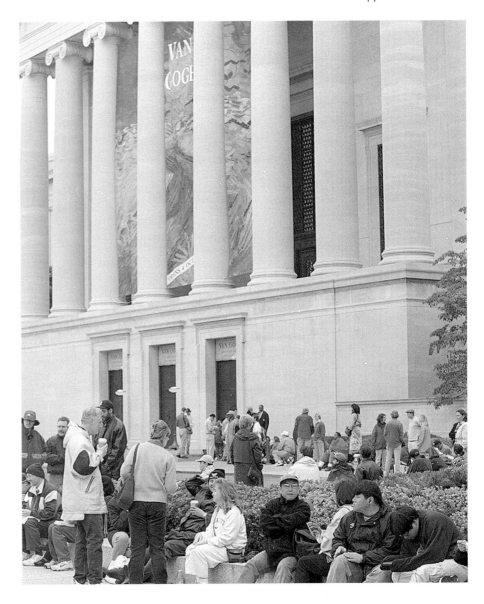

Lines form and full costs rise for tickets to see the Van Gogh exhibit at the National Gallery in Washington, D.C.

would demand an average quantity *A* of tickets to the exhibit per day. Unfortunately, the gallery can only accommodate *B* patrons per day (2050 same-day tickets). This means that at a zero money price, quantity demanded of tickets exceeds quantity supplied by some amount *AB*.

Fans may initially have favored the policy of free tickets, but lines got much longer, at times forming at midnight for the next day's tickets. Clearly, the full price, that includes time cost, was not zero. To those Van Gogh fans who valued time highly, the price of a ticket to see the exhibit was high indeed.

Enter the scalper. As you can see from the demand curve in Figure 3.17, there are Van Gogh lovers who would be willing to pay high prices for the exhibit. Some would be willing to pay—dearly—to avoid the long wait in line. Scalpers with lower time values were therefore able to sell tickets for prices ranging from $75 to $100 (and more). Clearly, there are winners and losers from this policy. We might sympathize with the losing Van Gogh fans who either must stand in line or pay high nominal prices for tickets of scalpers who were also willing to stand in line. Further, there are those who simply do not approve of the practice of scalping. But there are clear winners as well. Those paying scalped prices reveal that they value a Van Gogh ticket more than they value the dollars they pay. Scalpers obviously value the money more than the ticket.

It is the failure to price tickets to accommodate limited space that almost guarantees scalping in the first place. In other words, there are important effects when the laws of supply and demand are ignored. The National Gallery, by forgoing an entrance fee, misses out on millions of dollars in revenue. Such revenue could be used to expand facilities, among other projects. Laws, moreover, are costly to enforce, and private or semisecret transactions are seldom capable of being monitored to any degree. Finally, it is unclear why laws against scalping should be used to profit one group while hurting another.

QUESTION

Suppose your football, basketball, or baseball team makes it to the finals and that the final game is played at your school's field or stadium. Further, assume that tickets are sold out well in advance. What evidence could be gathered to show that quantity demanded exceeded quantity supplied at the ticket price charged by your school's athletic department?

Source: Some of the material for this discussion was drawn from "Perspective: Waiting for Van Gogh," *Investor's Business Daily* (October 30, 1998), p. A7.

SUMMARY

1. The extension of specialization from earlier societies is the modern market society, where individuals and collections of individuals buy and sell—demand and supply—millions of products and services.

2. Demand can be expressed as a schedule or curve showing the quantities of goods or services that individuals are willing and able to purchase at various prices over some period of time, all other factors remaining constant.

3. Supply can be expressed as a schedule or curve showing the quantities that individuals or businesses are willing and able to sell at different prices over a period of time, other factors remaining constant.

4. Equilibrium prices and quantities are established for any good or service when quantity supplied equals quantity demanded. In equilibrium, there is no tendency for price to change.

5. A change in the price of a good or service changes the quantity demanded or quantity supplied along a given demand or supply curve. A change in demand or supply occurs when some factor other than price is altered. When these factors change, the demand or the supply curve shifts to the right or left, either raising or lowering equilibrium price and quantity.

6. Simultaneous shifts of the supply and demand curves have predictable effects on either equilibrium price or equilibrium quantity, but not on both.

7. The market system, through supply and demand, rations scarce resources and limited quantities of

goods and services among those most willing and able to pay for them. Products and services, moreover, appear and disappear in response to the market system of supply and demand.

8. Price controls instituted by governments tend to create shortages or surpluses of products. Market forces usually result in some form of rationing other than price rationing under such circumstances.

KEY TERMS

products market
resources market
money price
full price
relative price
law of demand
quantity demanded
demand curve
factors affecting demand
ceteris paribus
change in quantity demanded
change in demand

normal good
inferior good
substitutes
complements
market demand
law of supply
quantity supplied
supply curve
change in quantity supplied
change in supply
factors affecting supply
market supply

market
perfect market
law of one price
surplus
shortage
equilibrium price
rationing
price control
price ceiling
price floor

QUESTIONS FOR REVIEW AND DISCUSSION

1. What happens to demand for a product if the price of that product falls? What happens to the quantity demanded?

2. What happens to the supply of coal if the wages of coal miners increase?

3. If income falls, what happens to the demand for potatoes? Are potatoes inferior goods?

4. If price is above equilibrium, what forces it down? If it is below equilibrium, what forces it up?

5. What is a shortage? What causes a shortage? How is a shortage eliminated?

6. If the demand for compact disc players increases, explain the process by which the market increases the production of CD players. What are the costs of CD players?

7. A price ceiling on crude oil has an effect on the amount of crude oil produced. With this in mind,

explain what happens to the supply of gasoline if there is a price ceiling on crude oil.

8. What happens to the supply of hamburgers at fast-food restaurants if the minimum wage is increased?

9. What is the full price of seeing a movie? Is it the same for everyone?

10. "Lately the price of gold keeps going up and up, and people keep buying more and more. The demand for gold must be upward sloping." Does this statement contain an analytical error?

11. What are price controls? When is a price floor imposed? What are some of the consequences of price controls?

12. Do the actions of self-interested coalitions of voters working through the political process help explain price controls? How? Can you think of an example?

13. What happens to the demand for pizza if the price of hamburgers increases? What happens to the demand curve for pizza? What are the effects on the equilibrium price and quantity of pizza?

14. If the price of sugar doubles, what will happen to the supply of regular (nondiet) colas? How will this affect the equilibrium price and quantity of regular colas?

15. Given the scenario in question 14, what will happen to the demand for diet colas? (Hint: Diet

and regular colas are substitutes. What effect will this have on equilibrium price and quantity of diet colas?)

16. Suppose that a big football or basketball game or a rock concert is a sellout on your campus at some given ticket price and that the quantity demanded far exceeds the quantity of tickets supplied at that price. "Scalping" results. Explain it on the basis of supply and demand.

PROBLEMS

1. Use the data in the table to answer the following.
   a. Graph the supply and demand curves.
   b. What is the equilibrium price?
   c. What is the equilibrium quantity?
   d. At what price does a shortage of 280 exist?
   e. At a price of $19, how much of a surplus exists?

Price	Quantity Demanded (per month)	Quantity Supplied (per month)
$0	400	0
3	340	60
5	300	100
8	240	160
10	200	200
13	140	260
16	80	320
19	20	380

2. Disasters have a way of highlighting economic problems. Consider the hurricane that devastated South Florida in 1992. As Hurricane Andrew approached, the people of South Florida rushed to buy batteries, canned food, and other provi-

sions. Afterward, a number of commodities, including ice, became extremely scarce. Assume that the price of ice was $50 per bag on the day after the storm and answer the following questions given the supply and demand schedule.
   a. What is the result of a price ceiling on ice at $30 per bag? Does $30 represent the full price of ice?
   b. If the mayor of Homestead, Florida, sets the minimum price of ice at $60 per bag, what type of price control is this?
   c. What is the impact on quantities traded at a controlled price of $60 per bag?
   d. Draw a graph of the price ceiling at $30 and indicate the shortage.

Price	Quantity Demanded (per month)	Quantity Supplied (per month)
$20	1600	250
30	1400	500
40	1200	750
50	1000	1000
60	800	1250
70	600	1500

WORKING WITH THE WEB

1. Suppose you decide it is time to buy a new polo shirt, and you are trying to decide whether to buy the interlock polo from L. L. Bean or Land's End. First, go to www.llbean.com and click on the "Product Guide." Next, click on Casual Clothing (Men's). Scroll down to "Shirts" and then find the interlock polo shirt. As of this writing, the current price for the L. L. Bean all cotton solid shirt is $18.50.

    Now go to www.landsend.com and under "Shop Our Store" select "Men's Casual." Next, find Interlock Polos and select solid short–sleeve. Here you see that the price of the regular short sleeve polo is $23.50.

    a. Assuming the shirts at L. L. Bean and Land's End are substitutes, if the price of the L. L. Bean polo rises, what do you expect to happen to both L. L. Bean's and Land's End's demand curves?

    b. What is the "demand shifter" at work here?

2. Everyone consumes water, and some consume more than others. We typically have tap water in our homes, yet bottled water has moved from being a fad to a staple for many consumers; it has become a multibillion dollar industry. To find out why so many people are consuming bottled water, go to http://www.bottledwaterweb.com/indus.html.

    a. In 1981, what was the level of bottled water consumption relative to all U.S. Liquid Consumption Trends?

    b. What was the level of consumption in 1997, and what was the growth rate of bottled water consumption in 1997?

    c. What do the statistics reveal about changes in the demand for bottled water?

    d. What factors are contributing to the change in demand?

4

Demand And Supply: Property, Markets, and Public Choice

The present chapter extends your knowledge of supply and demand to show how government or "the public sector" interacts with and affects private markets. Clearly, a role for government is critical in such areas as protecting property and establishing a rule of law. These institutions provide the very framework for free market functioning. Yet another concept—the idea of why economists believe free and competitive markets to be "efficient"—should be mastered before turning to the possible reasons that markets might "fail" or, alternatively, that additional roles might be provided for government. The political context of how decisions get made in the public sector will also help you understand the role and functions of government.

There are obviously many ramifications of government actions in the private economy and we will consider many examples later in this book. But after mastering this chapter you should understand:

- the basic institutions that facilitate a market system.
- the nature and efficiency of competitive markets.
- why markets might not function in a competitive fashion, thereby providing a role for government.
- some reasons that public choices (through voting and politics) differ from market choices in affecting the supply of goods and services to people.
- how efficiency might be affected by transfers and regulations granted in political markets.

INSTITUTIONS ARE "RULES OF THE GAME" THAT FACILITATE MARKETS

Economic system

The part of the social system determining what, how, and for whom goods and services are produced.

All exchange takes place within the context of some economic system. An **economic system** is the particular form of social arrangements through which the "what to produce," "how to produce" and "for whom to produce" questions are answered. The economic system of any given country is based on the institutions surrounding property ownership, incentives, and decision making that underlie all economic activity in that country.

Pure capitalism

An economic system in which most resources are owned, and most relevant decisions are made, by private individuals.

Pure communism

An economic system in which most productive resources, both human and nonhuman, are publicly owned.

Socialism

An economic system in which most nonhuman productive resources are owned by the state.

Systems differ among countries. The extremes are **pure capitalism** and **pure communism**, with **socialism** in between. A society organized along the lines of pure capitalism is one in which government economic control is minimal. Under pure capitalism, most resources are privately owned and government's role in the economy is pretty much limited to protecting and enforcing private property rights and to providing national defense and other public goods. Common ownership of both human and nonhuman resources, at the other extreme, typifies pure communism. Socialism, in between these two extremes, is a system in which the state owns most nonhuman productive resources and makes production decisions by planning the economy's output. In reality, of course, all systems that we observe in the world today are "mixed" with elements of each other. The initial "rush to capitalism" in the Russian Republics (after the breakup of the Soviet Union) and in Eastern European countries such as Poland is being rethought, with some communist politicians (if not the system) making a resurgence. Institutions—such as enforceable property rights—must exist to support capitalism, and such institutions have been lacking in many parts of Eastern Europe and Russia.

Economic efficiency

The allocation of resources that allows maximum benefit to be achieved at minimum cost.

Institutions are therefore the key to understanding the conditions and incentives under which exchange takes place. **Economic efficiency**—producing goods and services at lowest cost and exchanging goods so as to maximize the advantage of all traders—can be discussed only under some given set of institutions. The basic economic "questions" of every society are answerable only under the legal rules that determine rights, ownership, and obligations. The forms of legal institutions regarding contracts, property rights, and their enforcement are central to the attainment of high or low economic efficiency. They guide production, exchange, and consumption in all economies.

Different societies, in past and present, have created different institutions for the *ownership* and *use* of property, including goods and money. A capitalist economy relies primarily on market forces and the profit motive for production, distribution, and consumption of goods and services. Capitalism is characterized by individual ownership of property, free enterprise, open competition, and (ideally) a minimal role for government. Let us consider each of these features briefly.

Property Rights and Contracts

We exchange property every day. Billions of exchanges—contracts between exchanging parties—take place in the United States alone. Explicitly or implicitly, we make a contract when we supply or demand labor. On the New York Stock Exchange, an average of 700 million shares of stock are traded daily. A purchase of cat food at the supermarket is as much a contract as the agreement by a New Jersey electrical utility to buy a five-year supply of coal from a Montana mine. Throughout the world, in stock and commodity markets, bazaars, shopping centers, and resource markets, literally trillions of contracts are made every day. Property, a bundle of rights, is transferred through contracts in all cases.

Private property

Property that an individual (as opposed to a government) holds the right to control.

In the U.S. economy the individual's right to own and dispose of property is regarded as basic. In a system of **private property**, the individual (as opposed to government) holds the right to control property. The individual receives the benefits and must pay the costs associated with the use of her property. Property here takes on a wide definition. It includes both physical property (such as houses and computers) and intellectual or intangible property. For example, the ownership of poems, songs, and books by their authors is protected by copyright laws. Inventions are protected by patents. The formal legal apparatus set up to protect such rights may even make a distinction between property and property rights. Rental of a carpet cleaner from U-Rent-Um gives the renter certain property rights over the cleaner but not ownership of the property itself. In all societies, rights to use property are limited. For example, the Environmental Protection Agency has used its legislatively derived power to limit the rights of businesses to pollute air and water and has established worker protection standards (such as those limiting the use of asbestos) that restrict individuals' free use of property. The real key to understanding the importance of property rights is their link to economic incentives.

Property Rights and Economic Incentives

When we consider the operation of large economies like those of the United States, Japan, Poland, or Russia, we can see how overwhelmingly complex it is to solve basic economic problems. To attain efficiency, decision makers must have the incentive to make correct economic decisions. That incentive is governed by the legal institutions surrounding property rights. To put the matter more clearly, the assignment of property rights is the key to economic efficiency. The manner in which property rights are assigned, moreover, often has enormous implications for economic and social incentives and the ultimate welfare of people. (For a good example, see the Focus: "Shipping *Live* Prisoners to Australia.")

Individuals, such as reggae artist Ziggy Marley, have rights to their own intellectual property, such as songs, in a market system.

FOCUS

Shipping *Live* Prisoners to Australia

Legal changes, legislation and administration of rules and regulation may all be used to direct and channel incentives to achieve economic and social ends. In other words, given the costs and benefits of doing so, buyers and sellers in markets will find it profitable to make contracts and contract terms ever more perfect in terms of incentives and outcomes. A famous historical example drives this point home. One of the greatest reformers of nineteenth-century England (akin to modern-day consumer activist Ralph Nader) was Sir Edwin Chadwick (1800–1890).[a] Chadwick once devised a plan for reducing the mortality of British criminals transported to Australia. He noted that the British government paid a flat fee to a ship's captain for each convict who boarded from a British port. The captains quickly discovered that they could maximize their profits by packing on as many prisoners as could be carried without endangering the ship and by minimizing expenditures on prisoner food, drink, and hygiene en route to the colony. The survival rates stood at 40 percent under this incentive system. Humanitarians were outraged at the state of affairs. After a quick assess-

ment of the program, Chadwick changed the payment system so that the ship's captain received a fee for each *live* convict that *disembarked* in Australia. Soon the survival rate increased to 98 percent. The rule change gave ship's captains incentives to protect the health of the convicts. A new contract arrangement rearranged incentives and created an identity of interest between the public interest (that is, the health and safety of the prisoners) and private interests (that is, the profit of the shipper). Similarly, the design of modern-day contracts in the purely private sector to transfer property rights works toward ever more efficient results—that is, toward more efficient use of scarce resources in producing goods and services of highest value to consumers and society.

---

[a] See Edwin Chadwick, "Opening Address," *Journal of the Royal Statistical Society of London* 25 (1862), p. 12. Chadwick was also a pioneer contributor to the economics of crime, the courts, sanitation, and the public supply of utilities and other services. These and a number of other examples are discussed in Robert B. Ekelund, Jr., and Robert F. Hebert, *A History of Economic Theory and Method*, 4th ed. (New York: McGraw-Hill, 1997).

The basic point concerning property and incentives is simple: When property, such as a meadow or whales or owls, is communally owned, no one can exclude others from its use. All members of the community regard the use of the meadow, whales, or owls as "free" and of zero opportunity cost. A rush will be on to exploit the resource, because the marginal opportunity cost and the price of using it is virtually zero. Maximum demand (at a zero price) leads to overutilization and ultimately ruination of the resources. Here private incentives (to get there first and to get as much as one can) conflict with socially desirable incentives (to conserve the resource). This so-called "tragedy of the commons," that is to say, of common property, exists today in the problems generated by common property resources such as fisheries, endangered species, and ill-defined water rights (see the discussion of "externalities" later in the chapter).

Private property, on the other hand, where each individual is permitted to own or exchange property rights as she sees fit, is the key to economic efficiency. You bear the full costs of your decision to use or trade property, but you also receive the full benefits that might result from your decision. Without some guarantees that property rights will be protected, there would be little incentive to accumulate capital stock and, therefore, to grow economically. Without government guarantees of rights to property, individuals would have to protect their own property at high personal cost. Indeed, the higher opportunity costs of individual protection as one's property accumulates makes the collective enforcement of property rights through police, courts, and prisons less costly than the total costs of such enforcement to individuals acting separately (such as through the use of mercenaries or posses). In other words, the protection of property rights of citizens is naturally (in economic efficiency terms) a major function of government.

Private Competitive Markets

Free enterprise
Economic freedom to produce and sell or purchase and consume goods without government intervention.

Contracting and the exchange of property rights takes place within private competitive markets. American capitalism approximates these conditions. Free competition or **free enterprise** is a primary feature of this world. It is the freedom to pursue one's economic self-interest, with few or no governmental restraints or subsidies and where resources may be combined by businesspeople to produce goods and services for profit. Businesses, consumers, laborers and input owners of all types are free to produce, purchase, and exchange property rights to any good or service provided that their activity does not infringe on others' rights. Individuals are of course constrained by the rule of law concerning the use of property—you cannot drive your auto on the sidewalk, for example. (Bear in mind that participants are also not free of the constraints of limited resources and unlimited wants.)

Competition
A market which functions under two conditions—no collusion among sellers or buyers (which occurs with a large number of buyers and sellers) and freedom to enter and exit the market. Competition results in prices equal to the costs of production plus a normal profit for sellers.

Within these limits, however, the American economic system is characterized by free competitive markets. This means that, as implied above, property rights are well-defined, enforceable, and tradable. But **competition** implies two other important conditions: There is no collusion among consumers or any other market participants (such as laborers), and all transactors are able to freely enter or exit the market. The self-interested behavior of buyers and sellers will tend to keep the prices of goods and services at a competitive level—that is, at the costs of producing the good or service plus a normal profit for the entrepreneur—when these conditions are met.

Under the discipline of private competitive markets, noncollusion means that each seller and each buyer makes decisions about their willingness and ability to sell or buy that are completely independent of the decisions of other sellers or consumers. While this condition does not require large numbers of buyers and sellers, the existence of large numbers virtually guarantees that no individual buyer or seller can affect the market price of a product or service. Many millions of individuals purchase canned soup, for example, but not one buyer purchases enough to affect the market price of the soup. Likewise, the existence of competing suppliers means that no individual seller can acquire enough power to alter the market for his or her gain. Sellers of canned soup are numerous enough that no one seller can affect the price of soup by altering the market.

Firms must also be free to enter and leave markets in response to profit opportunities or actual losses. But bankruptcies and business failures are expected consequences of a competitive system (yes, failure of some is an essential feature of competition). New fast-food restaurants open every day in anticipation of profits. Airlines declare bankruptcy and leave the industry—a sure sign of losses. Competition requires that entry and exit into business be free and unregulated.

Actually, coordination of the billions of individual decisions involved in competition is an interconnected system of prices for inputs and outputs that is so complex that no individual or computer can fully comprehend it. We began to study the intricacies of the price system in Chapter 3. Supply and demand explains much about how resources are "efficiently" allocated between the production of CDs, chiropractic services, and home computers. However, we must be able to explain exactly what is meant by economic efficiency.

WHY ARE PRIVATE COMPETITIVE MARKETS EFFICIENT?

Clearly, the protection of private property and a legal system that protects the assignment of property rights are key factors in permitting markets to function. Noncollusive behavior and freedom of entry and exit from the market are two others. Other institutions, some of them provided by government, are critical as well. As we have seen, the provision of a stable money supply and the freedom to use resources in any way we please underlies free competitive markets. These and other factors define what we mean by competitive markets, but why should economists (or anyone else) champion private competitive markets? We must return to the principles of supply and demand learned in Chapter 3 in order to understand why private markets are considered "efficient" by economists.

Demanders Value Goods

Markets are the means through which individuals—self-interested demanders and suppliers—help relieve the problems brought on by the scarcity of resources. Economic efficiency means that total value is, in general, maximized in that goods are produced at least cost. And those who "want" the goods the "most" get them. Let us see how "value" is calculated and recorded by demanders.

Any demand curve—for an individual or for a whole market—may be given two different but equivalent interpretations. As you learned in Chapter 3, the demand curve indicates the specific amount of some good or service that consumers are both willing and able to purchase *at a given price* per unit of time (of course, holding all other factors affecting demand constant). Market demand is

FIGURE 4.1

Demand and Marginal Private Benefit Curve

The market demand curve represents the value consumers as a whole place on marginal units of the good. The total value of any quantity produced is the area under the demand or marginal private benefit curve from zero up to that quantity. The difference between what consumers would be willing to pay for the good or service and what they actually pay is called *consumers' surplus*.

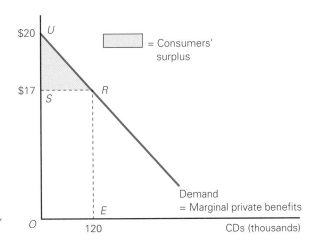

Marginal private benefit curve

A curve, equivalent to a demand curve, which represents the value that consumers place on marginal units of the good or service.

simply the summation of the quantities demanded by all consumers of the good or service at each price.

A demand curve, under certain conditions, may also measure the value that consumers place on a good because it expresses what they are willing and able to sacrifice to obtain it.[1] Consider Figure 4.1, which shows the market demand (taken from Table 3.4) for a competitively produced product—compact discs (CDs). The amount in terms of price that CD demanders are willing to sacrifice in order to obtain discs in Figure 4.1 is a measure of value. Specifically, the demand curve is equivalent to a **marginal private benefit curve**—which represents the value consumers place on the last (marginal) disc under consideration.

Continuing the numerical example from Chapter 3 (see Table 3.4), we may say that the value consumers place on the marginal disc—the 120th disc per month—is $17. The value that consumers would place on fewer discs per month, say the 40th, is $19. Looking at the areas under the demand curve, it is clear that the total expenditure is the quantity purchased times the price of discs (when each unit of discs is purchased at the same price). If the price of a disc, in Figure 4.1, was actually $17, consumers would buy 120 of them. Their total expenditure would be $17 times 120 or $2040. (In our example, we are keeping numbers simple—a more realistic demand would simply multiply consumers and expenditure by 1000.)

Clearly the figure—$2040—represents consumer expenditures on discs. But does it represent value to consumers? The answer is no! The total valuation of the 120 discs is higher than the $2040 that disc consumers must pay to get them. In fact, consumers are willing and able to pay a good deal more for a given quantity of most goods and services rather than not get these goods or services at all.

---

[1]This interpretation holds if we assume that consumers are buying a good or service that does not have any external or "third-party" effects, such as would take place if, for example, secondhand smoke had to be accounted for in the consumption of cigarettes. We consider the relevance of these external effects later in the chapter.

Total consumer valuation
The total amount that consumers are willing to pay for a given quantity of a good or service rather than go without it.

Total consumer valuation is the total amount consumers in the market are willing and able to pay for a given quantity of a good or service rather than go without it. This total value may be shown graphically as the area under the demand/marginal valuation curve from zero quantity (0) out to the quantity under consideration (in this case 120 discs).

In effect, most consumers get a real bargain because they are willing and able to pay more for discs than they must pay for discs. This is *value received but not paid for* by consumers in association with a purchase. For more than a century and a half, economists have known about this surplus and by consensus call it *consumers' surplus*. **Consumers' surplus** is defined as the total valuation consumers place on a given quantity of a good or service minus the total cost or expenditure of obtaining the good or service in exchange. If the market demand curve for discs is the one identified in Chapter 3 (in Table 3.3), total expenditures on discs at a price of $17 is $2040, but consumers get a surplus of the shaded area when they consume 120 of them—this is, the amount they would have spent less what they actually had to spend for 120 discs. The actual value of the surplus going to consumers may also be calculated—it is $180.[2] It is also equal to the shaded area of Figure 4.1 (triangle *SUR*). In general these surpluses exist in all markets for all goods and services— for airline travel, for broccoli, and for school tuition. Thus, the total valuation of consumers (area *OURE* in Figure 4.1) consists of two parts—total expenditures on the good or service (area *OSRE*) and consumers' surplus (area *SUR*). It is the total that consumers would be willing and able to pay for any good or service.

Consumers' surplus
The difference between what consumers are willing to pay for a given quantity of a good or service (the total consumer valuation) and what they have to pay (their total expenditure).

Supply, Costs, and Value

Recall now our definition of *supply* from Chapter 3. A so-called "law of supply" is the assumption we make concerning the behavior of producers or sellers of some good or service. A seller will be willing and able to sell or produce a larger quantity of a good or service at a higher rather than at a lower price, given all other factors that influence his decision (the *ceteris paribus* assumption). Conversely, any producer or seller would be willing and able to produce and sell smaller quantities of a good or service at a lower price than at a higher price, given all other factors affecting the decision (the *ceteris paribus* assumption again). Other things being equal, as price rises, the quantity supplied of a good or service increases and, as price declines, the quantity supplied decreases. A supply curve, recall, is obtained by summing up the quantities supplied at each price over all producers. A market supply curve, such as the one for compact discs in Figure 4.2, can be thought of as a collection of price and quantity supplied combinations of many individual suppliers. At a price of $13 dollars per disc, suppliers will be willing to put 100 discs per month on the market.

There are other ways to view the supply curve that are correct and equivalent to that above. The market supply curve indicates the minimum price (per unit or per disc in our case) that sellers will be willing and able to receive in order to get them to produce and sell the units of the good or service under consideration. Sell-

---

[2]The actual amount of consumers' surplus in dollars may be calculated in the following manner. Note from Table 3.4 that all consumers of discs disappear at a price of $20 per disc. The (shaded) area of Figure 4.1—consumers' surplus— is half a rectangle (that is, a triangle). The rectangle is calculated by the difference between the price consumers must pay ($17) and the price that eliminates consumption of discs altogether ($20) or $3 multiplied by the quantity consumed at a price of $17 or 120 discs. That value is $360 (the rectangle) and half of that—the consumers' surplus—is $180.

FIGURE 4.2

Supply and Marginal Private Costs

Market supply represents the marginal private cost curve showing the opportunity cost of producing additional units of the good or service. The total cost of producing any quantity of the good is equal to the area under the supply curve up to that point (that is, the alternative uses of opportunity cost in terms of resources forgone). Total receipts of sellers less this total cost results in a "producers' surplus" associated with the production of many goods.

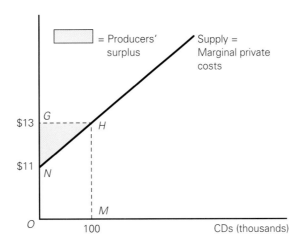

Marginal private cost curve

A curve showing the marginal or additional cost to society— the opportunity cost of scarce resources—of producing additional units of a good or service.

ers must receive $13 at a minimum in order to get them to sell 100 discs per month in the example above. We must now recall *why* this is so. Under competitive conditions, the supply curve (for any individual seller) is also the marginal cost of the inputs or resources used to produce the discs. These costs are, as we noted in Chapter 3, the marginal opportunity costs associated with any given amount of discs produced. As the quantities of discs produced rises, resources that are less and less adaptable to disc production must be drawn into use, producers must enlarge facilities and hire and train workers who have not produced CDs before, and marginal costs may be expected to rise. The opportunity cost of using resources in disc production rises and the rising supply curve reflects this fact. The production of more discs by sellers may become unprofitable if the market price of discs does not rise. When the production of a good or service (discs) does not create third-party or external effects (discussed below), the marginal or additional cost to society is the opportunity cost of the scarce resources used to produce discs. We may call the supply curve the **marginal private cost** curve of producing discs for society.

These points about supply may be illustrated with Figure 4.2. Consider again the price of $13 for discs. At this price 100 discs are produced. The total revenue of all disc sellers is simply the quantity sold times the price, and when the price of discs is $13, total revenue is $1,300 or area *OGHM* in Figure 4.2. But these total revenues are not equivalent to total cost. Total costs are the opportunity costs of all of the productive resources used up in the production process. The total opportunity cost is the sum of all of the marginal opportunity costs of producing 100 discs. Graphically, it is the area under the supply or marginal private cost curve from 0 quantity up to the quantity under consideration. It is, in Figure 4.2, equal to $1,200 or to area *ONHM*.[3]

---

[3]Note that in Figure 4.2, the total cost of producing 100 discs can be calculated by dividing up the area under the supply curve into two portions—a rectangle with a height of $11 and base of 100 units plus a right triangle with a height of $2 ($13 minus $11) and base of 100. The money amount of producers' surplus is the area formed by the triangle *GHN* in Figure 4.2. Since the area of the triangle is one-half the area of the rectangle found by multiplying the base (100 units) times the height ($2), the amount of producers' surplus in the example shown in Figure 4.2 is $100.

Producers' surplus

The difference between the total revenue to producers from selling a given quantity of a good or service and the total cost to them and to society of using the scarce resources in that particular production.

The difference between total revenue of the producers and the total cost to them (and to society) is called **producers' surplus**. (In dollar terms, producer surplus is $100 in Figure 4.2.) The concept, analogous in some respects to consumers' surplus, is expressed from the point of view of the factors of production that are employed in producing and supplying a good or service (discs in our case). It is the payment received by a factor of production over and above the minimum payment just necessary to induce the factor into the particular use (producing discs). The producers' surplus is equal to the total revenue of the disc sellers minus the total opportunity cost of all of the scarce resources used in producing 100 discs. Through the exchange process, the total revenue of disc sellers is distributed among all of the factors used in making discs. The total revenue of the disc sellers thus represents the total payments to the factors of production in association with producing and selling 100 discs.

Just like consumers, then, most producers receive a surplus from supplying production in the marketplace. The marginal producer who produces the last CD in Figure 4.2 just covers his or her opportunity cost of production, which is obviously $13. Every other producer along the supply curve form N to H earns a producer surplus given by the difference that they are actually paid, $13, and their opportunity cost as read off the supply curve. The first resources committed to the production of CDs are the most adaptable or lowest cost, and they therefore earn large producer surpluses. These lower-cost producers earn a producer surplus up to GN, or $2, in Figure 4.2.

And it should be kept in mind that both consumers' and producers' surplus represents wealth and wealth creation in the price system. Consumers' surplus in Figure 4.1 was $180, and producers' surplus in Figure 4.2 is $100. *This represents wealth that accrues to consumers and producers as a result of their market interactions.* The market system works to maximize the total of these surpluses and, what is the same thing, produces what economists call economic efficiency.

Competitive Equilibrium and Economic Efficiency

The efficiency of competitive markets may be analyzed with these simple tools. Recall from earlier in this chapter that competitive markets required certain conditions. They were that property rights were well defined, enforced, and tradable; that sellers or buyers were not able to collude or to have an effect on the market-clearing price (large numbers of buyers and sellers tend to guarantee this); and that any firm willing and able to become a seller can enter the market without entry barriers. Under these conditions, which we assume hold in the production, sale, and purchase of compact discs, the market will be efficient! Figure 4.3 tells us what is meant by this concept.

Figure 4.3 (as in Figure 3.10) shows the market-clearing price for compact discs. At $15 the market clears—that is, the quantity supplied (per month) of discs is 200 and the quantity demanded (per month) is 200. Alternatively, the quantity exchanged in the market is the amount that sellers produce (200 discs) and the amount that consumers buy at the market clearing price (200 discs). This is what is meant when we say "the market clears." In the case described in Figure 4.3, market equilibrium under competitive conditions means that just the right amount of

FIGURE 4.3

Allocative Economic Efficiency

The "market clears" where supply and demand (or marginal private benefit curve and marginal private cost curve) intersect. This means that the total net value of the good or service is maximized. At this point, the *sum* of consumers' and producers' surplus is maximized.

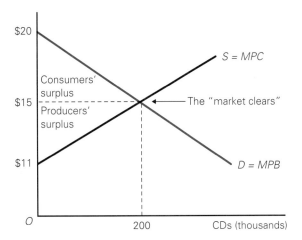

discs—not too many or too few—are produced. Competitive markets, under the conditions described, are said to result in *allocative efficiency*. Those individuals who most demand the product get it at a price that exactly represents society's opportunity cost of resources in producing it. All but the very last consumers value discs higher than the equilibrium price of $15, and only the very last consumer(s) pay the marginal opportunity cost of producing discs in terms of resources given up by society to produce discs.

The market clearance of Figure 4.3 is also critical to understanding economic efficiency. *Economic efficiency* means that, under competitive conditions, the net value of society's scarce resources is maximized. The *total value* produced by 200 discs to society (with reference to Figure 4.3) is equal to the area under the demand curve from 0 discs produced to 200. We may call that area the *total social value of consuming the scarce resources*. After subtracting the *total social cost* of using the scarce resource to produce discs—equal to the area under the supply curve from 0 to 200 discs—we arrive at the net social value of the scarce resource. If there are no third party effects, that is, if consuming or producing discs does not produce costs or benefits that are not borne by consumers or producers—a competitive market creates a maximum of *net* social value. This means that society's resources have been allocated in efficient fashion. The sum of consumers' surplus and factor or producers' surplus is maximized when net social value is maximized under competition.[4] Any attempt by producers or consumers to get a greater share of the surplus—such as through the political process—may result in a reduction in the sum of the total surplus produced (i.e., less consumers' + producers' surplus). We will soon see how this might well happen in the context of a democratic political system.

---

[4]In numerical terms, the net social value may be found by combining the procedures discussed in notes 2 and 3. You may verify that consumers actually pay $3,000 for discs, but that they would have been willing to pay $3,500 so that consumer surplus is $500. Sellers of discs receive $3,000 for 200 units (what the consumers actually pay), but of this $400 is producer surplus. Therefore, the total net value of disc production to society is $900.

THE ROLE OF GOVERNMENT

Government has always played a critical role in the economies of all nations current and historical. We have seen, at the beginning of this chapter, how one fundamental and essential role of government is to set the "rules of the game" for the economy. This means that, through government, a legal framework for the definition and enforcement of private property rights is established. Competitive markets function within these rules. But what if competitive markets fail to provide a maximum of total value to society; that is, what if society's assumed goal of maximizing the net social value of resources (described above) is not achieved? How might this **market failure** happen and what, if anything, can be done about it? Consider some possible market failures.

Market failure
A situation in which the socially optimal (most economically efficient) amount of a good or service does not get produced by the private market; usually stems from unclear property rights assignment.

The Environment, Externalities, and Market Failure

The failure of markets to provide maximum economic efficiency is most often related to problems with property and the definition of rights over property. Owners of private property are free to hold, trade, or exchange rights, and they bear the full costs and benefits of their actions. Market failure most often occurs when the rights over resources are either ill-defined or not defined at all. These so-called common property resources, such as air, whales, underground pools of oil, and the atmosphere belong in specific quantities to no one. But when they belong to no one, no individual has an interest in conserving them. Indeed, self-interest and the goals of society often conflict, so that individuals in the pursuit of their own self-interest damage the resource, sometimes irreparably, for society as a whole. You do not have to reach far to understand these cases—the "save the whale" and other endangered species campaigns or the "global warming problem" arising from the burning of fossil fuels are well known. For obvious reasons, these are called environmental problems.

Markets may fail for other reasons, but these failures are most often related to ill-defined or nonexistent property rights. The active pursuit of self-interest by one person may impose costs or benefits on others. There might be, in other words, third-party effects from consuming or producing particular products. **Externalities**, therefore, are the costs and benefits of somebody's behavior or activity that that particular individual does not bear. Well-known examples come to mind. Secondhand smoke might injure people who do not do the smoking. A factory emits smoke or waste products to the detriment of the population in the area or downstream. Automobile exhaust creates smog for the population generally, especially in congested urban areas. Other examples are your roommate's loud stereo, airport noise, or obnoxious perfume or cologne worn by the student sitting next to you.

Externalities
Benefits or costs of an individual's activity that the individual does not receive or bear.

But externalities may be positive as well as negative. Your neighbor may maintain a beautiful yard or garden, all of which pleases you and improves the value of your own property. This benefit—a positive externality—is (ordinarily) not compensated for by paying the neighbor for the benefits you receive. Smallpox vaccinations or flu shots provide other examples. The presence of externalities means that the marginal private costs or benefits of actions do not always

Vaccinations against communicable disease constitute a positive externality—others are protected when you protect yourself.

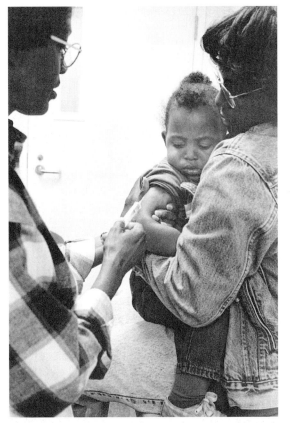

equal the marginal social costs or benefits of consumer or producer behavior on the part of the whole society. This divergence between self-interest and society's overall welfare would have the effect of causing adjustments in the "efficiency" arguments developed in the preceding discussion in this chapter. When marginal social costs exceed marginal private costs, unfettered private competitive markets produce too much of a good or service. When, however, marginal social benefits from some consumption (a beautiful garden or a polio vaccination) exceed marginal private benefits, too little of a good or service is produced. Economic efficiency might be achieved in these cases, but some nonmarket adjustments might be necessary.

Obviously, a wise and efficient government would identify and address each of these situations. But there are enormous problems involved in identifying and addressing externalities on the part of government. Not all problems should be addressed. If the cost of adding noise control devices on airplanes landing at some specific airport exceeds the collective value that homeowners around the airport place on noise reduction or elimination, the costs of eliminating the externality would exceed the benefit and it would be "uneconomic" to proceed. Determining just what these costs and benefits are is, of course, a very difficult problem to begin with in particular situations.

Once relevant externalities have been identified, there are a number of approaches that might be taken, some of them involving government, some not. In general, when the costs of bargaining and transacting between the parties to an externality are low, simply assigning property rights to one or the other parties to the externality may do the trick. If smokers and "relevant" nonsmokers are able to freely transact with one another, a private solution may be possible. Other cases are far more difficult to handle and demand other solutions. Water rights or rights to whales can hardly be assigned to individuals. Governments therefore often resort to taxing or subsidizing externalities in order to "correct" "inefficient" markets. Another well-known solution is to use administrative regulations of all kinds to address negative externalities. The Environmental Protection Agency, administered by the federal government, is an example of a regulatory approach to externalities. Indeed, many kinds of policies, including the sale of "rights to pollute" with proceeds going to reducing the effects of pollution, have been and are being tried. All of these solutions are partial in effect and, sometimes to the detriment of all parties, must be filtered through a political process. We will have more to say concerning this critical matter later in this book. For now, however, it is useful to remember that there is a positive role for government in addressing externalities, be it through the definition and enforcement of property rights or through more direct means.

Public Goods and Market Failure

Public good

A good such that, once produced, one individual's consumption of the good does not reduce or exclude the ability of other individuals to consume the good.

The failure or inability to assign property rights has led to specie endangerment, inlcuding certain members of the wolf family.

Another and somewhat more obvious role for government is in the provision of public goods—goods that would not or could not be provided through free competitive markets. Public goods are another kind of "market failure." What economists call **public goods** are those which, once produced, cannot reduce or impede the ability of others to consume the good regardless of whether consumers are willing to pay or not. The most widely acknowledged public good is national defense. Why should I provide national defense (in the right amounts) if you and everybody else in society can "free ride" on my provision? If I could exclude you from receiving the benefits of my provision, I could charge you for "units" of defense (missile protection, jet carriers). But I cannot exclude you from protection and you have no incentive to reveal how much national defense you "demand." So, it is not in a private individual's self-interest to pay for defense. More specifically, your consumption of national defense does not compete with mine; we both "consume" each unit of defense that is provided. Since defense is necessary to protect the property of all individuals in society, a role for government is created.

Conceptually, the case of national defense is easily understood. Not so for many other candidates. Are lighthouses public goods? Would they not be produced at all or in the right numbers if not provided by governments? (It is a historical fact that many were created and maintained privately.) What about circuses or outdoor rock performances? Does one individual's consumption compete with or complement another's consumption at an outdoor Lauryn Hill concert? These are difficult questions that await some answers later in this book.

One issue concerning the provision of public goods is worth noting at the outset. Just as it is difficult to determine costs and benefits in assessing the extent of "externalities," it is just as perplexing to determine, through a political process, how much of a public good would be "value maximizing" for society. Many smaller countries of the world have, for example, been "free riders" on U.S. investments in national defense. Further, certain features of the political process to be discussed later in this chapter bring into question the efficiency of national defense expenditures. What is indisputable, however, is that the government's provision of public goods, especially national defense, is a justifiable role for government.

Antitrust and Monopoly Regulation

Several other important problems in markets, in addition to externalities and public goods, have been put forward as justifying a role for government in markets. All of these reasons collapse into one—the existence of significant monopoly power. Monopoly (a single firm's control of a market) or oligopoly (the control of a market by a small number of firms) has justified government control over property rights through direct regulation of the activities of firms (over, for example, electric, water, or communications utilities) or by enforcing a set of "rules" with which firms must comply at the risk of civil and criminal penalties (antitrust regulations).

Antitrust policies

Regulations established by laws and government agencies that attempt to preserve business competition.

Industry regulation has included, since the early decades of this century, **antitrust policies** prohibiting price discrimination, collusion among producers, and deceptive advertising practices all passed in an attempt to restore competition where it no longer existed. Even earlier, however, economists and politicians believed that government had a role whenever competition could not exist, perhaps because of economies of large-scale production, or what economists call natural monopolies. Such monopolies are created when each seller can produce more and more output at lower and lower costs. Eventually it becomes profitable for only one seller to supply the total quantity demanded of a good, thereby creating a monopoly. Federal, state, and local governments undertook the regulation—not the ownership or operation—of transportation, communications, energy, and many other industries that were regarded as natural monopolies. Government regulation, in this view, was regarded as a substitute for competition or state ownership where viable competition could not exist because of industry production and cost conditions.

Some economists have strongly disputed this view and question the existence of large-scale economies (natural monopoly) in many of these regulated industries. Some economists believe, with some justification, that regulation of prices and profits must fail, either because regulation has been ineffective or because these industries are more competitive than previously thought. For example, since the early 1980s there has been significant deregulation affecting airlines, long-distance communications, and trucking. Questions have been raised concerning the self-interested supply of regulation by politicians combined with the self-interested demand for regulation by firms and industries. Do industries and other interest groups use the government regulatory apparatus for their own benefit? Should broad new areas of industry regulation, such as in telecommunications and public utilities, be reduced or eliminated? These and many other questions concerning the expanded role of government are in hot debate, and a firm foundation in economic theory will help you in providing answers to them.

PUBLIC CHOICE—THE RELATION BETWEEN POLITICS AND ECONOMIC EFFICIENCY

We live in a democracy with a particular set of political institutions. These include majority voting, the existence of political parties, a federal system or a hierarchy of representative governments, a huge administrative bureaucracy, and organized interests of all kinds. Public choice, as noted in Chapter 1, is the analysis of the political sector based on the economic notion that self-interest guides public decision makers (voters, politicians, bureaucrats) as well as private decision makers (consumers, sellers, and market intermediaries). Obviously, the individual who buys a new automobile is the same individual who votes, so that political and economic decision makers are often one and the same person. Importantly, however, there are different institutions and constraints facing economic markets—the decision to buy a car—and political markets—the decision to vote or the decision to sponsor legislation as a politician.

A fundamental question that we answer later in this book is whether political processes are themselves efficient at reflecting the true preferences of voters. But political decisions also have enormous implications for the efficiency of private markets. Environmental regulations may benefit some firms at the expense of others. Entry restrictions in certain professions may be designed to benefit a few workers at the expense of many. Tariffs on imported sugar or peanuts may raise their price to consumers in order to benefit a few favored domestic producers. We must therefore understand a few basic reasons (a) why political markets do not work the same way that economic markets do, and (b) how special interests tend to dominate the political process, often reducing economic efficiency in the process.

Political Versus Economic Markets

There are numerous differences between political and economic markets, although both are guided by *self-interested* behavior. Individuals make decisions in private markets in which *all* costs and benefits are borne by the decision maker. Suppose you decide to make an investment in a high-tech stock or in some rental property. If the stock or property fails to earn a competitive return, *you* will bear the full costs of your actions. Likewise, if the investment proves to be a bonanza, *you* receive the full benefits.

This complete internalization of costs and benefits does not take place in political markets. The politician does not bear the full economic consequences of his decisions and has poor incentives to control costs. Politicians cannot personally recoup any savings they make for the public and they are only weakly controlled by voters when high costs are incurred.

The self-interest of politicians also explains an enormous amount of activity within legislatures. The phenomenon of vote-trading or **logrolling**, where you vote for my courthouse and I'll vote for your water reclamation project, is clearly understood by most of the voting public. (*Why* voters let it go on is a question we pose presently.) While economists generally regard exchange as efficient, logrolling in a political context may not be efficient behavior. Since politicians represent particular geographic areas and since politicians face a re-election con-

Logrolling
The exchange of votes by legislators, usually in order to gain support for particular legislation.

straint (two years for U.S. House of Representatives, six years for U.S. Senate), bringing the "pork" back home improves reelection prospects. The problem is that logrolling is not generally efficient in reflecting the preferences of voters on national issues. Rather, it redistributes income toward certain regions and industries and generally does not lead to a more productive economy. We, as collective Americans, get more dams, military bases, and special-interest tax "reform" bills than we want. The political system, in short, tends to produce economic inefficiency. This occurs, even though politicians are in a "market" not unlike IBM stock, computer chips, or diapers—see the Focus, "Politicians Are Demanded and Supplied."

Why Are Voters "Myopic"?

Clearly, the electorate is not made up only of fools or idiots. Why do they "let" politicians pursue their own self-interest at the expense of the common good expressed as the will and preferences of the people? It is because there are substantial and critical differences in the private market and the political market that facilitate logrolling and other nonefficiency producing political behavior.

When you buy a second car, you buy only a second car. When you vote for your local congressional representative, you vote not for a single issue, but for a whole package of issues or a platform that she represents. We say that the consumer

FOCUS

Politicians are Demanded and Supplied

People who pursue (supply) a career in politics must, if they are rational, expect to achieve a higher level of satisfaction from a political career than from their alternatives. The rewards from supplying a political career include (but are not limited to) salary and benefits, the perks of office, the utility from being in a position of power, and the satisfaction of helping others. Those who seek the rewards of a life in politics must first be elected and then reelected to maintain this career path. Election (and then reelection) will be uppermost in their minds.

In a democracy such as ours, the individual citizen's role is indirect, with the voter usually restricted to selecting who will make the final decision on the many questions that come before the government. The problem is to determine which politicians to support (demand). The self-interest

of voters implies that they will select the candidates who support legislation that promotes their interests (both financial and nonfinancial). Individuals vote for the candidates who are closest to their own position on the "issues." An issue that is near and dear to the hearts of everyone is their source of income. Those earning their income in an industry (for example, defense, agriculture, housing, or automobile) will tend to vote for politicians who support that industry.

This process by which politicians seek and attain elective office bears a striking resemblance to the model of supply and demand. Politicians demand votes and need a majority of the votes to ensure election or reelection. Voters supply votes to the politicians who meet their "price," where the voter's price is a position on the issues.

makes marginal choices in the private market, but only all-or-none decisions in the political market. Another point is that voting is irregular when compared to shopping in the marketplace. That feature of political markets makes it difficult to alter your "consumption" of policies and candidates. You can fairly quickly change grocery stores when you find inferior vegetables at one of your local markets, but it is more difficult to change elected officials.

Perhaps the greatest problems occurring in political markets stem from the fact that voters have weak incentives to inform themselves on the particular political choices their representatives are making. Do you really know or care how your representative feels about or votes on providing a new federally sponsored park in northern Oregon? Voters have few incentives to gather information concerning their public choices, whereas they have strong incentives to acquire information concerning market choices. The costs of staying informed on the hundreds (even thousands) of decisions made by all of your representatives is enormous. Therefore, as a rational voter—one calculating the direct costs and benefits of your representative's decisions—you stay rationally uninformed or rationally ignorant. This does not mean that voters are stupid or that they "don't care about government." Rational ignorance simply means that the costs of being fully informed on each and every decision made are prohibitively high. The pro rata share of the costs and benefits of so many of these decisions—the new Oregon park—are so low to individual voters that they are not concerned with how politicians vote in such cases. When you decide to buy some private good, such as a health club membership, a new swimsuit or a plate of Asian food, you do so with direct "dollar votes." Whether or not a formal contract exists—it might for the membership but might not for the dinner or the swimsuit—property rights are directly traded in your purchase. You give rights over a certain amount of money, and you obtain property rights over the good or service you have purchased. You incur the costs of the exchange and obtain all the benefits of the new property rights.

This is not the case for public choices. Public choices, like private choices, are self-interested, but differ in important aspects. Political decision makers do not bear the full costs of their decision, nor do they reap all of the benefits. They cannot capitalize on decisions and have no incentives to control costs. Such is the case for many student governments at colleges and universities across the country. You pay a fee for student government activities—akin to a tax—and you vote for representatives. How do the results of student government activities differ from your private market participation?

First, allocations for funding student groups are made by your representatives and committees composed thereof, but there is no reason to believe that such funding will accurately or even closely reflect your preferences. Who gets the money will depend on who can muster the strongest coalitions within the student government. On some campuses, Panhellenic (fraternity and sorority) interests will dominate. On others, athletic interests or the Society of Student Engineers or even minority group clubs will win larger allocations. Allocations, in other words, will be made on the basis of interest groups and the coalitions they form. You may want to add new journals to the school library or to expand aerobics classes in the student union with the fees collected, but your preferences might not be recognized.

Then there is the familiar problem of voter or student apathy. You may be so busy with classes, activities, or a job that you remain rationally ignorant of exactly what the student government is actually doing or what the candidates are like in the first place. Even if you were *acutely* interested in the outcomes of the political process at your university, it would be exceedingly costly to monitor your representatives once they are elected. And, since most office holders in student governments are only around for one or two years, it is highly unlikely that "turning the rascals out" would be a viable or effective option. You cannot change student representatives as you can brands of fast-food hamburgers. In these senses, therefore, you are a captive (at least temporarily) of a political process not unlike that established for democratically elected officials at all levels of government.

Interest Groups Tend to Dominate

Since voters are rationally uninformed, they present serious difficulties for politicians. Naturally, elections do tend to generate some information for representatives, but that information is seldom direct. Inasmuch as individual voters are rationally ignorant of voting on particular issues, politicians are uncertain about voter preferences. But some individuals and, particularly, blocs of voters—called **interest groups**—are clearly interested in particular outcomes.

Interest groups
Collections of individuals with one or more common characteristics, such as occupation, who seek collectively to affect legislation or government policy so as to benefit members of the group.

Coalitions of particular interests—businesses surrounding the proposed Oregon park—are in a prime position to put pressure on politicians to vote their way. Politicians, ever mindful of promised votes, campaign contributions, and other perks, are all too eager to supply legislation. (See the Application at the end of this chapter: "Why Are There So Many Restaurants and Golf Courses in State Capital Cities?" for some insight into this issue.) Special-interest legislation at all levels of government—local, state, and federal—is therefore explained as the result of rational self interest on the part of voters at large (who are rationally ignorant), coalitions of particular interest groups directly affected by legislation, and by politicians who, in *their* own self-interest, want to be reelected. The problem, and it is a big problem, is that the demand and supply of such legislation within the political process reduces the economic efficiency of markets and thwarts the general will and preferences of the electorate. Let us see how with an example.

INTEREST GROUPS AND WEALTH TRANSFERS: THE CASE OF BARBERS AND COSMETOLOGISTS

The behavior of interest groups explains much in the political arena. Concentrated interests on the part of particular groups of individuals—as against the wider public interest—are represented by lobbyists in all political venues. Lobbyists and political action committees (PACs) for particular groups cover every conceivable interest at one level of government or another. Examples include real estate, physicians (the American Medical Association), defense industries, teachers, postal workers, banking and financial institutions, textiles, petroleum, labor unions, and virtually any other interest for which legislation or regulation can affect economic benefits or costs in a positive or negative fashion. To see how interest groups affect government policy, consider the process by which a statewide group of barbers might organize to advance their interests. (We conclude this discussion with some real-world data on how hair styling fees are affected by state regulations.)

The most fundamental problem that barbers (or hair stylists or health professionals) face is how to get organized. Specifically, each barber has incentives to stay outside the interest group, for if the interest group is successful in, say, obtaining higher prices for haircuts, a free-riding barber—one who does not pay dues to the barbers' association—can benefit without incurring any costs. Free-riding behavior makes the formation of interest groups difficult, but by no means impossible. For such reasons, interest groups seek ways to limit the benefits of their activities to members only.

Assume that the barbers organize. The group's representatives go to the state legislature and seek a legally sanctioned barbers' monopoly. The purpose of this monopoly (actually a cartel or interest group) is to protect barbers from new competition by erecting barriers to entry into barbering, thereby allowing barbers to raise the price of a haircut above competitive levels—that is, above costs in terms of resources used in providing a haircut. In other words, the barbers petition the state government to raise their wealth at the expense of haircut consumers. Put another way, they are demanders of a wealth transfer from the state.

Who are the potential suppliers of wealth transfers? The "suppliers" are those—in this case, consumers of the barbers' product—who do not find it worthwhile to organize and to resist having their wealth taken away by the barbers. This is an unusual concept of supply, but it is a supply curve nonetheless. The attitude that will prevail among suppliers of a wealth transfer is that it would cost them more to protest the barbers' proposal than any benefits they would derive from protesting. For example, the average consumer might spend $100 to defeat the barbers' proposal, the net result of which would save $10 in haircut costs. Why spend $100 to save $10?

This example describes a "demand" and a "supply" of wealth transfers in the case of barbers. How does the market for wealth transfers work? Politicians are brokers in this market and in the market for legislation generally. The politician's job is to pair demanders and suppliers of wealth transfers. If they transfer too much or too little wealth, they will be replaced at the next election by more efficient politician-brokers.

The outcome for the barbers may be shown (in Figure 4.4) as an extension of our discussion on the meaning of competitive economic efficiency earlier in the chapter. The barbers start out as a purely competitive industry, producing Q_c haircuts per year at a price of P_c. When their interest group forms, they persuade the legislature to grant them special cartel status. This persuasion is not very difficult because the consumers who are harmed by the cartel do not find it worthwhile to protest to the legislators. The barbers are the only ones to be heard, and perhaps by putting their arguments for a cartel in public-interest terms ("higher prices mean higher quality," "barbers must be licensed to ensure an orderly marketplace," and so on), they carry the day with the legislature.

Legislators, for their part, assess the costs and benefits of creating a barber cartel. In Figure 4.4, the barbers seek P_mABP_c in cartel profits at the expense of

FIGURE 4.4

How an Interest Group's Demands Are Met

P_c is the competitive price that the barbering industry charges per haircut, and P_m is the price established by the group after it is granted protected (cartel) status through the political process. After the cartel is formed, it stands to gain P_mABP_c in profit from consumers of haircuts. This transfer is from consumer surplus to profits, but society also loses a net amount ACB in welfare.

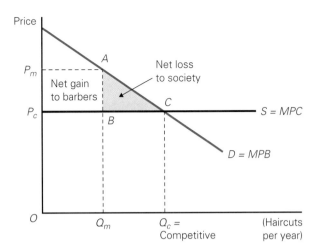

consumers' welfare. (We assume, for simplicity and not unreasonably, that barbering services are produced at constant opportunity cost of resources and that the supply curve lies flat at the competitive price.) This means that an amount of consumer surplus (P_mABP_c) is transferred to barbers as profits. Area ACB represents a net welfare loss to consumers due to the legal monopoly supplied by legislators. The per capita gains to barbers, who are a relatively small number of producers, exceed the per capita costs to the more numerous haircut consumers. The result: The legislature passes a law giving the barbers a cartel (and, perhaps, the barbers make campaign contributions to the legislators who supported their cartel bill). *The net value of society's resources is not maximized because of the transfer.*

There is actual evidence that state regulation of hair stylists has produced this result. A recent study of cosmetology regulation in the fifty states has shown that a variety of restrictions, on entry into the market, including educational, age, and training restrictions have had the effect of increasing the price of hair style services across the United States.[5] The greater the degree to which the cosmetology profession in a particular state has attained political power and influence, the greater the benefit to the profession in the state and the greater the cost to consumers of these services. Even a modest average increase in price due to restrictions—say 50 to 75 cents per hair style—will reduce consumer surplus by an enormous amount—possibly by several billion dollars per year—over all consumers. *The moral:* An industry does not have to be vital to health or national defense to seek transfers in this case from consumers to suppliers of barbering and cosmetological services—through the political process.

---

[5]See A. Frank Adams, III, Robert B. Ekelund, Jr., and John D. Jackson, "Occupational Licensing of a Competitive Industry: The Case of Cosmetology" (Manuscript: Auburn University, 1999).

Legal licensing granted through the political process transfers gains to barbers and cosmetologists from consumers along with a net loss to society.

Our discussion of barbers concerns a particular kind of restriction. Interest groups do not always work as producers versus consumers. Technically, any group can organize and act as an interest group, and we find that interest groups represent many overlapping segments of society. There are labor unions; women's rights groups; religious groups; trade associations; and organizations for doctors, nurses, and all health professionals, for lawyers, hunters, environmentalists, and farmers. Moreover, not all of these groups are small. Many large groups, such as farmers, are effectively organized as an interest group. The fundamental point is that you can begin to explain why a certain law is passed if you try to answer two questions: Who wins? and Who loses?

Another critical point is that the particular features of political markets—at least in a representative democracy—permit sanctioned and legal transfers of wealth from one group to another. Almost every policy you can think of has this effect. While transfers are not so important to the economists, overall economic efficiency—the maximization of the net value of all of society's resources—is of great concern. The differences between private markets and public choice practically guarantees that overall economic efficiency will not be attained.

Clearly, markets are excellent institutions through which to allocate resources. Markets, along with institutions such as private property and free contracting described in this chapter, give people in society the goods they value most. Indeed, they do this most of the time. When market activity creates third-party effects such as pollution or other externalities, government may step in to attempt to alleviate problems. In general, however, markets underlie wealth creation and wealth creation is about making society better off.

Market functioning, however, takes place in the context of democratic political institutions in a world of "public choice." When left alone, markets are unconcerned with "welfare triangles." But when politics and interest groups enter the picture, as we have seen in this chapter, society's wealth may be redistributed and the triangles under supply and demand curves become important. They showed, for example, how the barbers were able to increase their wealth at the general expense of the net wealth of society. When political participation in the economy is considered, the economist's emphasis turns from efficiency to distribution. Our discussion of public choices revealed that democracy and its institutions create the possibilities for losses through redistributions. This does not mean that democracy must be done away with or significantly altered, however. Democracy remains the best conceivable system in a world of imperfections.

APPLICATION

Why Are There So Many Restaurants and Golf Courses in State Capital Cities?

It is obvious that a lot of effective lobbying takes place. It would be difficult otherwise to explain many local, state, or federal allocations and subsidies, such as water subsidies in the West or inland waterways in the South. How much activity takes place is another question. If politicians are self-interested, as modern public-choice economists believe, they will always make policy with an eye to reelection and enrichment. Because the direct transfer of money for votes is fairly easy to detect, politicians must rely on other kinds of transfers and perquisites. Interest groups are often able to deliver blocs of votes, as mentioned in the text, or to finance campaigns by a variety of means. Most proposed reform focuses on changing methods of campaign finance.

But there are numerous other ways to pay off politicians for economic interventions that benefit special interests. For example, it would be a rare representative or senator specializing in banking or transportation legislation who did not have opportunities to work for the industry he or she regulated after retiring from politics. Family members or business partners and associates of the politician, moreover, may be in a position to accept payoffs.

Distortions (payoffs?) may take many other forms. Although most of the attention has been fixed on cash and other bribes, many forms of in-kind transfers (that is, not in money) are in fact used. Overt cash bribes attract attention and invite regulation, but lobbying efforts may be indirect, as when trips, fancy (or not-so-fancy) meals, transportation or limo services, employment of relatives or business associates, or golf rounds are provided for legislators.

Recent research into in-kind perquisites of state politicians has produced convincing results. When allowance is made for per capita income and other key variables, state capital cities have been shown to contain a larger per-capita percentage of sit-down (non–fast food) restaurants than paired, randomly chosen same-state cities with similar income characteristics.[a] The bigger the budget of the state (the more opportunities for profit-seeking transfers by special interests) and the more full-time lobbyists in the state, other things equal, the more restaurants the city has. The same goes for golf courses.

What are the costs of such lobbying by special interests? First, there is the cost to society of skewing regulations and goods toward concentrated interests and not to the public interest as discussed in this chapter. But there is a direct cost as well. In the sample of forty-seven state capitals, there are a total of 9,635 additional restaurants for the capital cities solely because of their political status as capital cities. A lower-bound estimate of resource distortion from restaurant payoffs is suggested by multiplying 9,635 times the average start-up cost per restaurant. Then there are also 286 additional golf courses to consider.

There are many forms of political payoffs from special interests. More hidden in-kind payoffs may be expected where functions and funding are shifted away from the federal level and to cities and states. Cruder, lower-cost forms of payoffs may be expected where the gains from special treatment are lower. In smaller communities, lunch at McDonald's or Wendy's or a weekend fishing vacation may do the trick. Whatever the case, such special-interest legislation and regulation will likely have negative benefits for voter-consumer-taxpayers at large.

---

[a]See Franklin G. Mixon, Jr., David N. Laband and Robert B. Ekelund, Jr., "Rent Seeking and Hidden In-Kind Resource Distortion: Some Empirical Evidence," *Public Choice* 78 (1994), pp. 171–185.

These negative benefits from lobbying may of course be resisted by the electorate at large. Voters at any level of government might demand lobbying restrictions by special interests, limits to campaign spending, and so on. In 1996, for example, the U.S. Congress placed a "gift ban" on its own members in response to criticisms from the media and the electorate. The "exemptions" that Congress passed along with the ban were interesting, however. Free meals are OK, it seems, if interest groups invite a "large group" to dine. And both major parties supported a total exemption on gift and party giving at the Republican and Democratic National Conventions held in August of 1996! At the federal level, moreover, "payoffs" continue to entail far more restaurant meals and golf games. Attempts to pass legislation that would curb campaign contributions at the federal level have not been successful. Despite a number of initiatives on the part of federal legislators and in spite of demands of consumer and other groups, the momentum for change has not enflamed voters. Without voter activism, self-interested U.S. Representatives and Senators, along with their state counterparts, have little incentive to limit campaign contributions and other payoffs that affect votes on critical economic and social issues. Those politicians who favor limits to campaign contributions have not been particularly successful in convincing their parties of the wisdom of that policy, and voter apathy continues into the new millennium.

QUESTION

How can you explain the proliferation of sit-down restaurants and golf courses in state capitals?

SUMMARY

1. All economies are characterized by institutions—the "rules of the game"—that shape and guide economic activity.

2. A key capitalist institution is private property. Private property, protected and enforced by government, permits and facilitates efficient contracting between individuals. It also encourages private incentives for long-term planning and investment, which promotes economic growth.

3. Private competitive markets exist when individuals are free to buy and sell resources, enter or exit business, and produce and consume goods and services with little or no government intervention.

4. Free and private competitive markets, in which there are no third-party effects to exchange, produce allocative efficiency. Such economic efficiency occurs at quantities where the demand curve or (what is the same thing) the marginal private benefit curve intersects the supply or marginal private cost curve. In different terms, maximum economic efficiency occurs where total net benefits are maximized, that is, where the difference between total value and total cost for producing some good or service is the greatest. Allocative efficiency is also (and equivalently) achieved when the sum of producer and consumer surplus is maximized.

5. Government's role in the economy, besides setting the institutional "rules of the game," is to address problems when markets and private exchange fails to produce allocative economic efficiency. Failures might occur when third-party effects, such as externalities, are created through market exchange or when property rights are difficult or impossible to define. Water pollution, factory smoke, and noise around airports are possible examples of this phenomenon.

6. The provision of public goods such as national defense provide another rationale for the role of government. Once produced, a public good is provided at little or no cost to all.

7. The government also institutes industry regulation through the regulation of business practices and through anti-monopoly regulation (called *antitrust laws*).

8. Public choice is the study of political markets—how self-interested individuals and groups of voters, politicians, and bureaucrats guide public decision making. Organized interest groups are often able to use the political process to transfer wealth. Unorganized and myopic voters permit transfers as they remain "rationally uninformed" or "rationally ignorant" when the cost of being informed is high and the *pro rata* cost of the political decision is low.

KEY TERMS

economic system
pure capitalism
pure communism
socialism
economic efficiency
private property
free enterprise

competition
marginal private benefit curve
total consumer valuation
consumers' surplus
marginal private cost curve
producers' surplus
market failure

externalities
public good
antitrust policies
logrolling
interest groups

QUESTIONS FOR REVIEW AND DISCUSSION

1. What is *capitalism* and what does it have to do with property rights and economic freedom?

2. What, exactly, is an *institution?* How do institutions help solve the basic economic "questions" in capitalist societies?

3. What is private property? What is common property? How do incentives differ under such systems?

4. What are the conditions underlying private competitive markets? Why is "noncollusion" a necessary condition for the existence of free competition in markets?

5. What is a marginal private benefit curve, and why is it equivalent to a demand curve for a good or service? What is a marginal private cost curve, and why is it equivalent to a supply curve for a good or service?

6. Explain clearly why economic efficiency (without third-party effects) occurs when the marginal private benefits from producing a good equal the marginal private costs of producing that good. Is this equivalent to saying that economic efficiency occurs when the *sum* of producer and consumer surplus is maximized? Why?

7. What are some of the roles of government in the U.S. economy?

8. What is an "externality"? Does cigar smoking on a crowded bus create an externality? Explain.

9. What is a public good? Explain whether or not the following items fit the definition of a public good: national defense, education, cable television.

10. Explain some of the differences between private choices and public choices. Why is a "vote" for a hamburger different from your vote for your congressional representative or city councilmember?

11. Are voters "myopic" or shortsighted in permitting politicians to pursue their own interests? What does it mean to be "rationally uninformed" or "rationally ignorant"?

12. Explain the process by which special interests might be able to take over the political apparatus for their own gain and against economic efficiency or the "general welfare."

13. How might you explain the desires for "campaign finance reform" on the part of the voters and the (successful) resistance on the part of the politicians to such reforms?

WORKING WITH THE WEB

1. As explained in this chapter of the text, economic efficiency in a market system depends on the assignment of property rights. There is some debate surrounding the question of who holds the property rights of Leonardo Da Vinci's famous painting, *The Last Supper*. Go to www.mises.org and select "Daily Articles." Next, select June 1999 and select the article "Who Owns Art?" Read the article. What is the nature of the property rights dispute, and what is Machan's point?

2. The dominance of interest groups is pervasive in contemporary society. Ekelund and Tollison discuss the role of interest groups and their attempts to influence legislation as well as the role of lobbyists and PACs. Go to http://www.opensecrets.org/lobbyists/98lookup.htm. Select "Agriculture" in the industry overview search box. For January–June 1998 (or the current year), what was the level of spending on lobbying in the agriculture industry? Return to the search page and select "Health." For the same period, what was the total lobbyist spending for the health industry? Return to the search page once more and select "Other" for the industry. Here, note the level of spending on education for the same six-month period in 1998 is $14,007,762. Using the theory of interest groups presented in the text, why do you think the level of spending in both the agriculture and health industries far outweighs the level of lobbyist spending in education? Is such spending efficient from a market perspective?

POINT

Karl Marx

Adam Smith

COUNTERPOINT

A dam Smith, one of the most important figures in the history of economics, actually began his career as a lecturer in moral philosophy at Scotland's Glasgow College in 1751. Moral philosophy in Smith's time encompassed a wide range of topics, including natural theology, ethics, jurisprudence, and economics. In 1776, Smith published *An Inquiry into the Nature and Causes of the Wealth of Nations,* known usually by the shorter title *Wealth of Nations.* The book won much attention from scholars of the day, and it brought together most of what was then known about the workings of the market system.

Smith was born in Kirkcaldy on the east coast of Scotland in 1723 and lived most of his life in his native country. Although known for his brilliant lectures (and for his many eccentricities), Smith did not devote his entire career to teaching. In 1778, he accepted a well-paying job as commissioner of Scottish customs, a post at which he remained until his death in 1790.

Karl Marx "looked like a revolutionary," writes Robert Heilbroner in *The Worldly Philosophers.* "He was stocky and powerfully built and rather glowering in expression with a formidable beard. He was not an orderly man; his home was a dusty mass of papers piled in careless disarray in the midst of which Marx himself, slovenly dressed, padded about in an eye-stinging haze of tobacco smoke."[a]

Marx wrote in response to the miseries of the European working class during the Industrial Revolution of the late eighteenth and nineteenth centuries. Coauthor with Friedrich Engels of the *Communist Manifesto,* which predicted the inevitable downfall of capitalism and the triumph of communism, Marx spent most of his life in difficult circumstances. His activities as a radical in the communist movement caused his exile from his native Germany as well as from Belgium and France. In 1849, a year after the publication of the *Manifesto,* he settled in London, where he and his family survived through the benevolence of Engels and where Marx researched and wrote *Das Kapital,* a theory and history of capitalism and its ills. Marx died in 1883 in London.

The "Invisible Hand"

Smith's views of the free-market system are summarized in a passage from the *Wealth of Nations,* in which

---

[a]Robert L. Heilbroner, *The Wordly Philosophers* (New York: Simon and Schuster, 1953), p. 131.

109

he writes that individuals pursuing their own self-interest are "led by an invisible hand to promote an end which was no part of [their] intention."[b] Smith believed that by freely exchanging goods and services across markets, individuals contribute to the public good—the aggregate wealth of society—even though they act from purely self-interested motives. In other words, markets cause individuals to benefit others when they intend only to benefit themselves.

To Smith, voluntary market exchange coordinated the decisions of consumers and producers and generated economic progress. Producers compete with one another to satisfy consumers with the most appropriate and cheapest goods and services, simply because they maximize their profits by doing so. Markets coordinate supply and demand by way of the price system. Consumers express their preferences in their decisions about what to buy; producers attract customers by producing goods at the least cost. In this system of coordination without command, individuals pursuing their own interests are led "as if by an invisible hand" to mesh their interests with those of other individuals trading across markets.

Smith was not opposed to government, but argued that its proper role in society was to provide a legal framework—police and courts—within which the market could operate, as well as to provide certain other services (including national defense, highways, and education) that the market itself would either not supply or would tend to supply in inadequate amounts. Smith also felt that government should provide welfare services for the poor. But he strongly believed that government could best assist the market economy achieve growth by stepping out of the way—that is, by not regulating and by not granting monopoly privileges to favored groups.

In Smith's view, income was distributed in a market economy by the production of wealth. An individual's income was a strict function of the value of his or her output. Smith did not feel that income inequality by itself was unfair, because he believed that anyone can increase his or her income in a free market by serving the consumers in a new, better, or faster way.

The "Anarchy of Production"

In *Das Kapital,* Karl Marx argued that Smith's writing represented merely the interests of the ruling capitalist class. To Marx, the market process was a system of exploitation by which owners of capital robbed their employees by paying them wages less than the worth of their labor (a situation he termed the *alienation of labor*).

The alternative social system that Marx thought would eliminate this exploitation and at the same time greatly increase the efficiency of production was a "general organization of the labor of society. . .[that] would turn all society into one immense factory."[c] He viewed the market economy as one of general disorganization. Its main feature was "the anarchy of production," where producers overproduced and consumers were forced to accept goods they neither wanted nor needed.

In Marx's view, Smith's "invisible hand" was a euphemism for describing the economic system in which "chance and caprice have full play in distributing the producers and their means of production among the various branches of industry...[T]he division of labour within the society [the theme of much of Smith's *Wealth of Nations*] brings into contact independent commodity-producers, who acknowledge no other authority but that of competition, of the coercion exerted by the pressure of their mutual interests...[T]he same bourgeois mind which praises division of labour in the workshop [as a conscious organization that increases productivity] denounces with equal vigour every conscious attempt to socially control and regulate the process of production."[d] Only the central planning of economic activity by society (government), which owned all means of production, could coordinate the needs of consumers and producers and eliminate the wastefulness of capitalism. To Marx, it was nonsense to describe the market as organized economic activity, because there was no organizer. Coordination of economic activity requires conscious, centralized control.

---

[b]Adam Smith, *An Inquiry into the Nature and Causes of the Wealth of Nations,* ed. Edwin Cannan (1776; reprint, New York: Modern Library, 1937), p. 423.

[c]Karl Marx, *Das Kapital,* ed. Max Eastman (1867; reprint, New York: Modern Library, 1932), p. 83.

[d]Marx, *Das Kapital,* p. 83.

While Smith described the emerging market economy of his day and offered reforms, Marx offered a vision of economic organization that did not exist at the time he wrote but that he maintained was the inevitable wave of the future. In a sense he was proven correct. Followers of the teachings of Marx and his admirer Lenin (who filled in many details of what a central planning system would look like in practice) imposed avowedly Marxist-socialist, centrally planned economies on many countries, including Russia and China, in the first half of the twentieth century. However, without exception, the centrally planned economies seemed to function poorly—providing low per capita income and poor rates of economic growth—relative to the modern versions of the capitalist economies whose central principle of market organization was so clearly seen by Smith.

PART TWO

The Architecture of Private Markets

2

Elasticity

S tudying the laws of supply and demand helps economists organize their thoughts about real-world problems. But it is not enough to understand that an inverse relation exists between price and quantity demanded or that a decrease in supply causes price to rise in a market. For supply and demand theory to explain and predict economic events, economists must be able to say how much the quantity demanded or supplied of a product will change after a price change. The laws of supply and demand tell us nothing about how responsive quantity demanded or quantity supplied is to a price change. But if, for example, you owned a fast-food restaurant, you would be very interested to know how responsive your customers would be to a hamburger price discount. The law of demand tells you that you would sell more hamburgers, but it does not tell you how many more. Or, if you worked for a legislator and she asked you how an excise tax increase would affect cigarette smoking (and how much revenue the tax would raise), you would have to find out how responsive cigarette sales would be to the proposed tax.

Economics does provide a means of determining how many more (or less) goods and services will be bought when prices or other factors change: the application of the concept of **elasticity**. When you finish Chapter 5 you should understand

- the idea of elasticity and how elasticity is measured.
- how to apply the idea of elasticity to economic events.
- what factors determine elasticity of demand and supply.
- how time affects the elasticity of demand.

Elasticity
A measure of the relative responsiveness of one variable to a change in another variable; the percentage change in a dependent variable divided by the percentage change in the independent variable.

THE CONCEPT OF ELASTICITY

You are contemplating two business alternatives: buying a gourmet delicatessen or opening a new travel agency. Best estimates tell you that consumers' incomes are expected to rise by 5 percent per year over the next eight years. On these grounds, which business should you enter? By what percent will an increase in consumers' incomes increase the amounts of gourmet foods purchased compared with the amounts of travel and leisure services consumed?

To answer these questions we must gauge the relative responsiveness of decision makers—consumers—to changes in price or income, or the elasticity. Elasticity is calculated as the ratio of the percent change in some effect (quantity demanded of a good or service) to the percent change in the cause (price change, income change, or any other change). You should keep in mind that while elasticity most often relates changes in demand to changes in price or income, the calculation may be applied to *any* cause-and-effect relationship. Elasticity is *always* a percent change divided by a percent change, resulting in a number that is independent of any absolute change in a cause or an effect.

PRICE ELASTICITY OF DEMAND

Elasticity, as the examples of fast food or excise taxes suggest, is a general and wide-ranging concept with many applications. The most common and important applications relate to the demand curve.

Formulation of Price Elasticity of Demand

The formal measurement of demand elasticity, like the generalized concept itself, is simple and straightforward. **Price elasticity of demand** is the percent change in quantity demanded divided by the percent change in price:

Price elasticity of demand
A measure of buyers' relative responsiveness to a price change; the percentage change in quantity demanded divided by the percentage change in price.

$$\varepsilon_d = \text{price elasticity of demand coefficient} = \frac{\%\ \text{change in quantity demanded}}{\%\ \text{change in price}}.$$

Price elasticity of demand is expressed as a number. In actual calculation, the demand elasticity coefficient will always be negative, owing to the inverse relation between price and quantity demanded (the law of demand). If price goes up, quantity demanded for a good or service goes down, and vice versa. Unless otherwise noted, this point is irrelevant to the interpretation of elasticity. We will accordingly eliminate use of a negative sign before the demand elasticity coefficient. If, for example, a 10 percent reduction in the price of jogging shoes causes a 15 percent increase in the quantity of jogging shoes demanded, then the ratio, called the **demand elasticity coefficient**, ε_d, is

Demand elasticity coefficient
The numerical representation of the price elasticity of demand:
$\varepsilon_d = (\Delta Q/Q) \div (\Delta P/P)$.

$$\frac{15\%}{10\%} = 1.5.$$

This elasticity coefficient or ratio, 1.5, and the percent changes in price and quantity demanded from which it was calculated are independent of the absolute prices and quantities of jogging shoes. If a 10 percent rise in the price of jogging shoes causes a 2 percent decline in sales, the price elasticity coefficient is calculated in the same way:

$$\frac{2\%}{10\%} = 0.2.$$

The price elasticity of demand coefficient (or, more simply put, the demand elasticity coefficient) always measures consumers' responsiveness, in terms of purchases, to a percent change in price.

Elastic, Inelastic, and Unit Elastic Demand

Elastic demand

A situation in which buyers are relatively responsive to price changes; the percent change in quantity demanded is greater than the percent change in price: $\varepsilon_d > 1$.

Unit elasticity of demand

A condition where the percent change in quantity demanded is equal to the percent change in price: $\varepsilon_d = 1$.

Inelastic demand

A situation in which buyers are relatively unresponsive to price changes; the percent change in quantity demanded is less than the percent change in price: $\varepsilon_d < 1$.

The size of the elasticity coefficient is important because it measures the relative consumer responsiveness to price changes. If the number obtained from the elasticity calculation is greater than 1.0, we say that demand is **elastic**; the percent change in quantity demanded is greater than the percent change in price. The larger the demand elasticity coefficient is above 1.0, the more elastic demand is said to be. (*Remember*: Price elasticity of demand measures the *relative* response of quantity demanded to a price change, the percent change in quantity demanded caused by some percent change in price.)

Unit elasticity of demand means that the elasticity coefficient equals 1. In this case, a given percent change in price is exactly matched by the percent change in quantity demanded. If, for example, a 2 percent increase in the price of candy bars causes a 2 percent reduction in purchases, demand would be of unit elasticity. The same would be said if an 8 percent decrease in the price of Volkswagens caused an 8 percent increase in quantity demanded.

An **inelastic demand** coefficient is a number less than 1, meaning that a percent change in quantity demanded is less than the percent change in price that caused the change in quantity. If the price of salt increases by 5 percent and the quantity demanded decreases by 2.5 percent, the demand elasticity coefficient would be 0.5, placing it in the inelastic category.

The various categories of price elasticity of demand can be shown with demand curves. Figure 5.1 depicts three responses to a 20 percent increase in pizza prices over a given time period in a small college town. In Figure 5.1a, a 20 percent increase in price causes a 5 percent reduction in quantity demanded. This means that pizza consumers are not very responsive to a change in price; since $\varepsilon_d = 0.25$, which is less than 1, demand is inelastic. In Figure 5.1b, a 20 percent increase in pizza price reduces pizza consumption by exactly 20 percent, meaning that demand is of unit elasticity: $\varepsilon_d = 1$. Figure 5.1c shows an elastic demand—a 20 percent price increase causes a 50 percent reduction in the quantity of pizzas demanded, so $\varepsilon_d = 2.5$ (greater than 1).

The elasticity of two special forms of the demand curve is also of interest in analyzing economic problems. Figure 5.2 shows a completely inelastic curve and a completely elastic demand curve. Total or complete price inelasticity means that consumers are not responsive at all to price changes, a condition that is seldom met in the real world. Increases or decreases in price leave quantity demanded unchanged—the demand curve is vertical, as in Figure 5.2a. One might think of the demand for addictive drugs—at least for certain price ranges and certain levels of use—as being completely inelastic. The price elasticity of demand coefficient is zero along such a curve: $\varepsilon_d = 0$.

A completely elastic demand curve is shown in Figure 5.2b. Individual businesses in competitive markets view the demand for their products as totally elastic. In a competitive market, producers are so numerous that they are unable

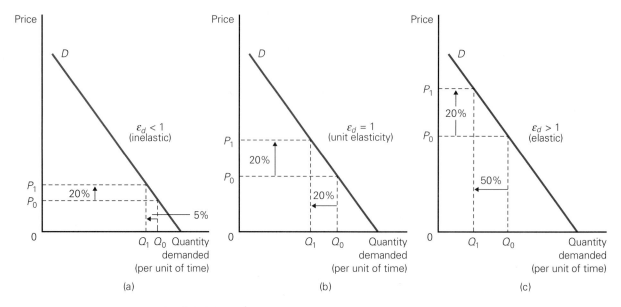

FIGURE 5.1

Price Elasticity of Demand

(a) The percent reduction in quantity demanded (from Q_0 to Q_1, 5%) is less than the percent increase in price (from P_0 to P_1, 20%). Demand is inelastic: $\varepsilon_d < 1$. (b) The percent reduction in quantity demanded equals the percent increase in price. Demand is unit elastic: $\varepsilon_d = 1$. (c) The percent reduction in quantity demanded is larger than the percent increase in price. Demand is elastic: $\varepsilon_d > 1$. The same relations hold for reductions in price or increases in quantity demanded.

to affect prices. The huge number of wheat farmers in the United States, for example, prohibits a single small producer from affecting the market price by altering production. If the wheat farmer raises his or her price by even a small amount, buyers will not purchase any of the farmer's production. Buyers can get all the wheat they want at the (lower) prevailing market price. In these competitive circumstances, a single wheat farmer faces an infinitely elastic demand curve ($\varepsilon_d = \varepsilon$). Quantity demanded is supersensitive to price increases. The farmer can sell as much or as little as he or she desires at the market price, but none at any higher price.

Elasticity Along the Demand Curve

Every negatively sloped demand curve will, in general, contain portions that are elastic, unit elastic, and inelastic. The elasticity coefficient will vary along straight (linear) and curving (nonlinear) demand curves. To verify this fact, consider the simple elasticity equation once more:

$$\varepsilon_d = \frac{\% \text{ change in quantity demanded}}{\% \text{ change in price}}.$$

FIGURE 5.2

Demand Curves May Be Totally Inelastic or Totally Elastic
(a) Quantity demanded is unresponsive to price changes (totally inelastic). (b) Quantity demanded is completely responsive to price changes (totally elastic); a small increase in price will cause quantity demanded to disappear. Perfectly competitive suppliers view the demand for their output as totally elastic.

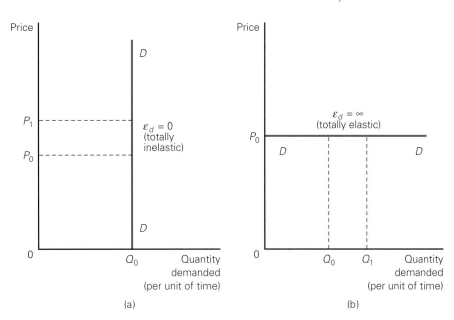

(a)   (b)

In the numerator, the percent change in quantity demanded is determined by dividing the change in quantity demanded by the initial quantity demanded. In the denominator, the percent change in price is determined by dividing the change in price by the initial price. This can be represented algebraically as follows:

$$\varepsilon_d = \frac{\Delta Q/Q}{\Delta P/P},$$

where Q stands for quantity and P stands for price. (The symbol Δ means "the change in.") The simple elasticity equation can also be written this way:

$$\varepsilon_d = \frac{\Delta Q}{Q} \times \frac{P}{\Delta P}.$$

The change in quantity demanded (ΔQ) can be written $Q_2 - Q_1$, where Q_2 is the new quantity demanded and Q_1 is the initial quantity demanded. Similarly, the change in price can be written $P_2 - P_1$, where P_2 is the new price and P_1 is the initial price. Therefore, substituting $Q_2 - Q_1$ for ΔQ and $P_2 - P_1$ for ΔP in the last equation yields

$$\varepsilon_d = \frac{Q_2 - Q_1}{Q_1} \times \frac{P_1}{P_2 - P_1}.$$

This is the form of the simple elasticity equation that we will use to make actual calculations.

Table 5.1 and Figure 5.3 show the market demand function—or price-quantity pairs—that constitutes the demand schedule for paperback books. Suppose that the price of paperbacks declines from $7 to $6. Quantity demanded would increase from 120 to 160 paperbacks. How would elasticity be calculated?

TABLE 5.1

Market Demand Schedule for Paperback Books

Price of Paperback Books (dollars)	Quantity Demanded (per month)
10	0
9	40
8	80
7	120
6	160
5	200
4	240
3	280
2	320
1	360

Returning to our simple formula, we can calculate the elasticity across this price range as follows:

$$\varepsilon_d = \frac{Q_2 - Q_1}{Q_1} \times \frac{P_1}{P_2 - P_1}$$

$$= \frac{160 - 120}{120} \times \frac{\$7.00}{\$6.00 - \$7.00}$$

$$= \frac{40}{120} \times \frac{7.00}{-1.00}$$

$$= -2.33.$$

The elasticity coefficient is −2.33, which means that demand is elastic over this range of prices. Consumers are responsive to a price reduction from $7 to $6.

Now assume that paperbacks are selling at $4 and that the price is reduced to $3:

$$\varepsilon_d = \frac{Q_2 - Q_1}{Q_1} \times \frac{P_1}{P_2 - P_1}$$

$$= \frac{280 - 240}{240} \times \frac{\$4.00}{\$3.00 - \$4.00}$$

$$= -0.67.$$

The coefficient indicates that demand is inelastic for a decline in price over the price range from $4 to $3. Consumers are far more responsive to a one-dollar price reduction from $7 to $6 than they are to a one-dollar price reduction from $4 to $3.[1]

The fact that elasticity changes at different points along demand curves suggests another important difficulty in accurately calculating elasticity. Since elasticity varies at all points along the demand curve, it also varies along the arc—for

---

[1] Note that the elasticity coefficient is always a negative number. In subsequent calculations we drop the negative sign as being understood.

FIGURE 5.3

Differing Elasticities Along a Market Demand Curve

The elasticity of demand is different between various points along a downward-sloping demand curve. If prices fall by $1 between *A* and *B*, demand is elastic. If prices fall by $1 between *C* and *D*, demand is inelastic.

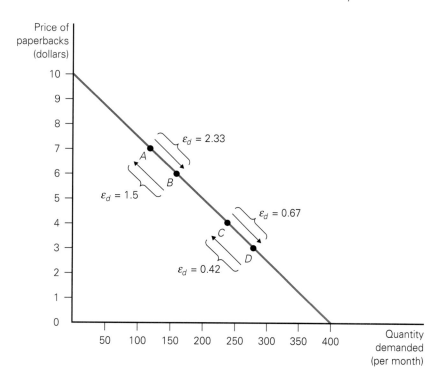

example, along length *AB* or *CD* in Figure 5.3. As shown in Figure 5.3, we will even get a different elasticity coefficient for a price *increase* from $3 to $4 (0.42) than we will get for a price *decrease* from $4 to $3 (0.67).

One compromise solution to the problem of determining the exact elasticity of demand over such a price range is to find the **arc elasticity**, or the average elasticity within the arc between two price–quantity combinations. To calculate the arc elasticity in the $3 to $4 price range for paperbacks, the prices $3 and $4 and the quantities 240 and 280 are given equal weight. To express the formula algebraically, we can let Q_0 represent one quantity and Q_1 represent the other quantity. The price at Q_1 is P_1; the price at Q_0 is P_0. The average elasticity of their relation can then be calculated as follows:

Arc elasticity

A measure of the average elasticity between two points on the demand curve.

$$\varepsilon_d = \frac{Q_1 - Q_0}{(Q_1 + Q_0)/2} \div \frac{P_1 - P_0}{(P_1 + P_0)/2}$$

$$= \frac{Q_1 - Q_0}{Q_1 + Q_0} \times \frac{P_1 + P_0}{P_1 - P_0}$$

$$= \frac{280 - 240}{280 + 240} \times \frac{\$3.00 + \$4.00}{\$3.00 - \$4.00}$$

$$= 0.53.$$

The average elasticity coefficient is *naturally* between the coefficients calculated for a price increase and for a price decrease.

Relation of Demand Elasticity to Expenditures and Receipts

It is often necessary to estimate the effect of a proposed increase or decrease in price on total revenue—how much, for instance, a fast-food chain will make (or lose) by offering a half-price sale on hamburgers. Estimates of elasticity from previous experience can make such projections possible. Or, if the price change and consumer response have already occurred, we can look at what happened to determine the elasticity of demand by examining either what customers have spent for a good or what businesses have received for it.

Common sense tells us that an industry's revenues are the same as consumers' expenditures for the industry's product. The number of items bought by all consumers multiplied by the price paid for each item is the same as the number of items sold by all producers multiplied by the average price charged for the items. Elasticity, therefore, is related both to **total expenditures** of customers and to **total revenues**, or receipts, of businesses.

To understand how elasticity is related to consumer expenditures, we consider the case of a single customer's purchases of paperback books. Let's call our consumer Anna. Table 5.2 shows Anna's demand and total expenditures (quantity times price) for paperbacks, and Figure 5.4 displays her demand curve with the associated elasticities. Anna's total expenditures on paperbacks begin to rise as the price of paperbacks falls below $10. As the price falls to $9, $7, and $5, Anna's quantity demanded *and* total expenditures on paperbacks rise. For decreases in price, if elasticity is greater than 1, total expenditures will increase. Why? When demand is elas-

Total expenditures

The total amount spent by consumers on a good or service; calculated as equilibrium price times equilibrium quantity.

Total revenues

Total receipts of businesses; always equal to total expenditures by consumers.

TABLE 5.2

Elasticity and Consumer Expenditures

The average elasticity of demand is greater at higher prices and falls as price falls. At the midpoint (near $5), the elasticity is equal to 1 and total expenditures are at a maximum.

Price of Paperbacks (dollars)	Quantity Demanded (per month)	Total Expenditure	Average Elasticity of Demand
10	0	0	
			} ·············· 19
9	1	9	
			} ·············· 5.66
8	2	16	
			} ·············· 3
7	3	21	
			} ·············· 1.85
6	4	24	
			} ·············· 1.22
5	5	25	
			} ·············· 0.81
4	6	24	
			} ·············· 0.53
3	7	21	
			} ·············· 0.33
2	8	16	
			} ·············· 0.17
1	9	9	
			} ·············· 0.05
0	10	0	

FIGURE 5.4

An Individual's Elasticity of Demand

The elasticity of demand varies along a downward-sloping demand curve. As price falls, the elasticity falls.

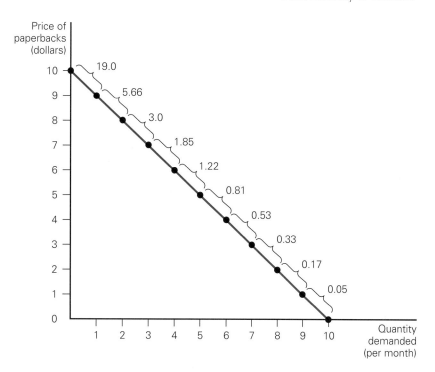

tic, the percent change in quantity demanded dominates (is larger than) the percent change in price. But as price is reduced below $5, Anna's total expenditures begin to decline, even though her consumption of paperbacks continues to increase. In the price range in which demand is inelastic (a coefficient of less than 1), total expenditures decrease as price falls. Here the percent decline in price dominates the percent increase in quantity, and total expenditures fall. *In other words, prices and total expenditures change in the same direction if demand is inelastic.*

The same relation between price and total expenditures is found when prices increase. If demand is inelastic, expenditures rise as prices increase from some low level, say $2, to a new level or over a range. If demand is elastic for that price range, total expenditures actually fall as prices increase. At some price–quantity combination, demand is unit elastic ($\varepsilon_d = 1$). For Anna in Figure 5.4, unit elasticity of demand occurs around $5, when her total expenditures for paperbacks will remain constant whether price is increasing or decreasing by some miniscule amount. At this point Anna's expenditures are at a maximum, as shown in Table 5.2.

If total expenditures are known, the relations between the direction of the price changes and total expenditures can be used as an informal method for determining elasticity, though not of calculating elasticity coefficients. The relations between the direction of the price change, the elasticity, and total expenditures (or revenues) are summarized in Figure 5.5. As the price falls from P_1, where consumption of the good is zero, to P_2, the midpoint on the demand curve, demand is elastic; total expenditures and, therefore, total receipts are rising. At P_2, price elasticity of demand is unitary, and total receipts and expenditures remain constant as the price rises or falls around this price. As the price falls below price P_2 (where quantity Q_2 is demanded), the demand elasticity coefficient falls below 1. Below P_2, total expenditures and receipts fall and demand is inelastic, becoming more inelastic as the price approaches zero.

FIGURE 5.5

Total Expenditures and Total Receipts Along a Demand Curve

As the price falls (P↓) along the demand curve, both total receipts (TR) and total expenditures (TE) rise, indicating that elasticity is greater than 1. At the point of unit elasticity, TE and TR remain constant. As the price falls from the midpoint, TE and TR decline owing to inelasticity of demand. Rising price (P↑) has the opposite effects on expenditures and receipts.

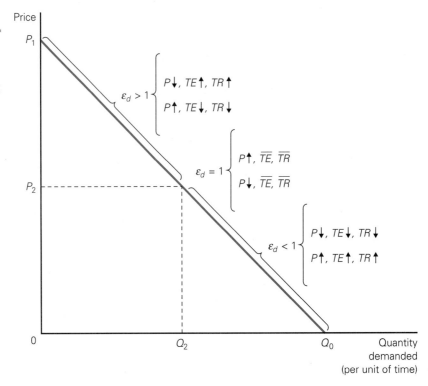

Armed only with this information, you are now in a position to teach yourself a simple economic lesson. Suppose you owned the business or product represented by the demand curve in Figure 5.5. Assuming you have no costs of production, what price would you set? Clearly, if you are interested in maximizing your revenues, you would set price at P_2, because that is the point where total expenditures on the product are greatest. In this simple case, elasticity is a useful guide to rational behavior.

The major point to remember is that elasticity varies along any ordinary demand curve. It makes no sense to say, for instance, that salt is an inelastically demanded commodity without reference to some price range. The demand for salt may be elastic over some price range and inelastic over another. In the next section we consider what makes the demand elasticity coefficient greater than, equal to, or less than 1 and what factors determine consumer responses to price changes. (See the Focus "How to Tell Who Your Friends Are" for an application of elasticity.)

DETERMINANTS OF PRICE ELASTICITY OF DEMAND

There are three major determinants of price elasticity: (1) the number and availability of substitutes, (2) the size and importance of the item in the consumer's budget, and (3) the time period involved. Since all three factors interact, the condition of other things being equal must be invoked to determine the specific effect of any one factor.

FOCUS

How to Tell Who Your Friends Are

Elasticity is a general measure of the responsiveness of one thing relative to another. The concept of elasticity is more than an intellectual device to examine strictly economic data, however. It has many practical applications, including, among others, providing a means of classifying relationships.

Friendship can be interpreted from an economic perspective. A "good friend" is someone who has a low price elasticity of demand for your companionship. In other words, the person in question desires your company pretty much independently of what it costs him or her. You can raise the "price" of your friendship to a friend by behaving badly—being late for dates, being loud and obnoxious, grinding your teeth, not keeping your word, lying, and so on. But your friend will not desert you at the higher "price." The demand for your friendship is inelastic; consumption of your friendship does not change much when its price rises.

Other people will not pass the friendship test. Their demand for your companionship will be very elastic. If things get even slightly more difficult, they will desert you. Perhaps there are larger numbers of substitutes for your friendship available.

Figure 5.6 illustrates this phenomenon. The "price of friendship" on the vertical axis is what it costs an individual to be your friend—Are you easy to get along with? Are you fun? Are you a good conversationalist? Are you trustworthy? Higher or rising prices mean that being your friend becomes more costly in terms of your behavior. The quantity of friendship on the horizontal axis may be thought of as the amount of time you spend with a friend. The two demand curves in Figure 5.6 illustrate two types of behavior. The steeper demand curve D_F is relatively less elastic than D_{NF} (NF = no friend). Demand curve D_F represents the behavior of someone who is a "true friend." At high prices or low, that person has a fairly constant desire to be around you. Demand curve D_{NF} proxies a "fickle friend." At a slightly higher price (suppose you get sick), the demand for your company is radically reduced. Friendship is an inelastic demand curve for you; a relatively higher elasticity of demand implies a weaker concern.

Think of your own personal relationships. Do you know of people who have a high elasticity of demand for you? How does their behavior indicate this—missed phone calls, only call when they need something, always insisting on doing what they want to do? And what about your good friends? Need we say more? Indeed, is not "love" a relatively inelastic demand curve?

FIGURE 5.6

Demand Curves for Friendship

Good friends express demand curves of relatively lesser elasticity for your friendship. Poorer friends show more elasticity of demand.

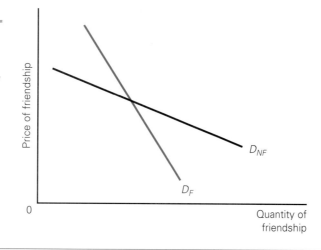

Number and Availability of Substitutes

By far the most important predictor of demand elasticity is the ability of consumers to find good substitute products. If the price of one brand of toothpaste rises, many consumers may respond by switching to a different brand. This substitution will happen only when alternatives are available.

Food is a vital commodity—everyone must eat. Elasticity of demand for nutrients in general is probably very low over relevant price ranges. For most of us, there is no substitute for food. But it is possible to substitute between kinds of food. While the demand for food as a whole tends to be inelastic, the consumer may substitute between broad food groups such as meat and seafood and also between foods within the broad groups. Consumers of meat, for instance, have a wide choice of substitutes, such as chicken, beef, pork, duck, quail, or alligator. Consumers are far more sensitive to changes in the price of beef when other substitutes are available. Elasticity of demand for meat itself is lower than that for *kinds* of meat over the same price ranges.

What about the elasticity of demand for beef versus beef products such as hamburger, sirloin steak, oxtails, and so on? The consumer can substitute among beef products. When the price of sirloin rises relative to that for hamburger, the consumer can substitute hamburger for sirloin. The elasticity of demand for hamburger is therefore higher than the elasticity of demand for meat. By now, the general rule should be apparent: The broader the product or service group, the lower the elasticity, because there are fewer possibilities for substitution. We expect the elasticity of demand for Budweiser beer to be more elastic than the demand for beer, just as the demand for a Ford or Mercedes-Benz is more elastic than the demand for automobiles. Ordinarily, the wider the selection and substitutability of similar products and services, the larger the elasticity of demand for those products.

The Importance of Being Unimportant

The size of the total expenditure within the consumer's budget is another determinant of elasticity. Ordinarily, the smaller the item in the consumer's budget, the less elastic the consumer's demand for the item will be over some price ranges. A salt user may be insensitive to price increases in salt simply because expenses for salt are a small part of his or her budget. If the price of salt were to rise too high, the user might substitute alternatives, such as artificial salt or lemon juice. Thus, in calculating elasticity it is important to analyze both substitutability and the size of the item in the consumer's budget.

The condition of other things being equal aids our understanding of elasticity determinants. Given some constant degree of substitutability, the more unimportant the commodity is to a consumer—that is, the smaller the item in the consumer's budget—the lower demand elasticity will be. This indicates that tastes, substitutability, and importance of the commodity in the consumer's budget must all be examined in gauging the demand elasticity of products over given price ranges.

Time and Elasticity of Demand

Time is the final factor affecting the elasticity of demand. We alluded to this at the beginning of the chapter, but now we expand on the effects of time.

Let's assume a local market for tennis rackets is represented in Figure 5.7. (For simplicity, we may neglect the supply function.) Assume that the initial price is P_0

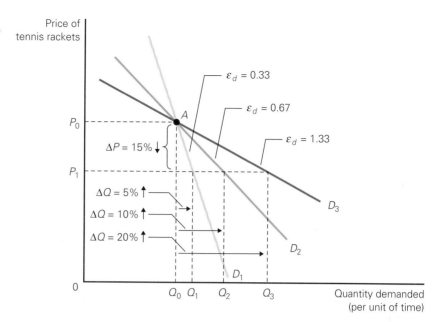

FIGURE 5.7

Elasticity of Demand over Time

As time goes by, a given price change (ΔP) may be associated with larger and larger changes in quantity demanded (ΔQ). Since the percent change in quantity demanded grows over time, the elasticity of demand grows as well.

and the initial quantity demanded is Q_0. What happens to elasticity of demand over time if tennis rackets go on sale—that is, if the price falls to P_1 per unit, a 15 percent decline?

The answer depends on how long it takes for consumers and potential consumers to adjust to the new price. If the sale is totally unpublicized, there may be no immediate reaction to the new price. As consumers gain information, however, demand increases. Thus, we may think of the demand curve as rotating around a point (A in Figure 5.7) as news of the sale becomes more widespread. Greater quantities (Q_1, Q_2, and so on) will be sold *through time* at the new lower price. For the given price change, the elasticity of demand will be different at different times—that is, it will depend on whether it is calculated on the first day of the sale ($\varepsilon_d = 0.33$) or one week ($\varepsilon_d = 0.67$) or one month later ($\varepsilon_d = 1.33$). Percent changes in quantity demanded are greater as time passes, meaning that the demand elasticity coefficient is larger and larger (up to some limit). The general rule holds: Given quality and consumer preferences, elasticity of demand increases the longer any given price change is in effect.

The time period of adjustment is a crucial factor in calculating or estimating all types of actual elasticities. Not only do tastes, substitutability, and size within the consumer's budget affect elasticity, but the ability of consumers to recognize and adjust to changes also plays an important part.

OTHER APPLICATIONS OF ELASTICITY OF DEMAND

The concept of elasticity is not restricted to price elasticity of demand. In general, we can calculate an elasticity of any dependent variable (effect) to a change in any independent variable (cause). We will briefly consider two other important applications of this versatile and useful economic concept: income elasticity of demand and cross elasticity of demand.

Income Elasticity of Demand

As you will recall from Chapter 3, a consumer's income is an important determinant of the demand for goods and services. It is often very informative to inquire about consumers' **income elasticity of demand**. Producers of all kinds are interested in the magnitude of consumption changes as incomes rise or in consumption habits within various income groups. Budget data compiled by the government and other sources can be used to calculate recent and historical trends in changing consumption patterns as incomes change.

Income elasticity of demand

A measure of consumers' relative responsiveness to income changes; the percent change in quantity demanded divided by the percent change in income, holding price constant.

The mechanics of income elasticity of demand are identical to those involved in the calculation of price elasticity; only the independent variable changes. With price held constant, income elasticity is the percent change in quantity demanded resulting from (divided by) a given percent change in income. It is expressed as ε_y, with Y representing income:

$$\varepsilon_y = \frac{\%\ \text{change in consumption of a good}}{\%\ \text{change in income}} = \frac{\Delta Q}{Q} \div \frac{\Delta Y}{Y}$$

or

$$\varepsilon_y = \frac{Q_2 - Q_1}{Q_1} \div \frac{Y_2 - Y_1}{Y_1}.$$

The income elasticity coefficient, ε_y, may be positive or negative, depending on whether the good is normal or inferior. (Recall from Chapter 3 that a good is normal if an increase in income results in greater consumption and inferior if an increase in income results in a reduction in product consumption.) When applying the income elasticity formula, if ε_y is greater than zero, the good is normal; if ε_y is less than zero, the good is inferior.

If the elasticity coefficient ε_y is greater than 1, demand (or consumption) is said to be income elastic; if ε_y is less than 1, the product is income inelastic; and if ε_y equals 1, the good is unit elastic. Suppose that income in the United States rose by 10 percent in 2000 and that the quantity of new automobiles consumed over the year increased by 8 percent. (New automobiles are a normal good; their consumption increases along with the increase in income.) The simple computation for income elasticity is

$$\varepsilon_y = \frac{8\%}{10\%} = 0.8.$$

The income elasticity of demand for automobiles in this hypothetical calculation is less than 1 but greater than zero. What does this mean for the auto industry? Other things being equal (such as price and tastes), the demand for automobiles will rise, but at a slower pace than income. In this example, cars are a normal good, but are income inelastic. This fact is important to groups such as auto manufacturers, investors, boat dealers, and airlines.

Income elasticity for a particular good may be determined for any individual consumer or for consumers as a group. The practical importance of this calculation is undeniable. An individual deciding between opening a gourmet food shop and a travel agency during a period of rapidly rising income would be very interested to know, for example, that income elasticity for gourmet foods is perhaps 0.2, while the same coefficient for Mediterranean vacations is 6.2. However, to achieve accuracy in actual use, all other factors, such as substitutability and the price of the product, must be kept constant. If these factors vary, as they often do in the real

FOCUS

Elasticity and Your World

The concept of elasticity is critically important in everyday decisions taken by businesses, politicians, and you. Elasticity is not some abstract issue. It becomes important almost every time the question of "how much" is asked. Consider the following examples:

Politicians acting through some state or federal legislature decide to crack down on teen smoking. The law of supply, which we developed in Chapters 3 and 4, tells us that new taxes will raise the price of cigarettes, and the law of demand tells us that this increase in prices causes a reduction in all smoking, including teen smoking. If the purpose of the tax is to reduce teen smoking, it is important to know whether teen smoking will fall by a large or a small amount from the tax. (Since cigarette smoking competes with other goods, including illegal substances like marijuana, it would also be interesting to know whether such other items will be substituted for cigarettes.) If demand is highly elastic with respect to an increase in price, the policy goal of reduced teen smoking will be achieved. If not, the tax might raise revenue, but it will not achieve the desired objective.

Or consider this; you are contemplating two business alternatives: buying a gourmet deli-

catessen or opening a new travel agency. Best estimates tell you that consumers' incomes are expected to rise by 5 percent per year over the next eight years. On these grounds, which business should you enter? By what percent will an increase in consumers' incomes increase the amounts of gourmet foods purchased compared with the amounts of travel and leisure services consumed?

To answer these questions, the relative responsiveness of decision makers and consumers to changes in prices or income must be gauged. *Exact* measurements are not possible when estimating the *future* effects of price or income changes. Economists can, however, make calculations based on past experience in particular markets. If such estimates remain reliable, that is, if conditions do not change significantly, these calculations may be used to predict quantity changes caused by changes in price or income in the future. Large firms that develop pricing strategies often employ economists to do just that. The success of given policies of politicians and businesses thus depend on elasticity—on "how much" of a change may be expected, given some particular change in price or income.

---

world, their impact on consumption must be determined and integrated into the analysis. Some real world applications of elasticity concepts are discussed in the Focus "Elasticity and Your World."

Cross elasticity of demand
Measures buyers' relative responsiveness to a change in the price of one good in terms of the change in the quantity demanded of another good; the percent change in the quantity demanded of one good divided by the percent change in the price of another good.

Cross Elasticity of Demand

Cross elasticity of demand reveals the responsiveness of the quantity demanded of one good to a change in the price of another good. As such, a cross elasticity coefficient can define either substitute or complementary products or services. In more general terms, cross elasticity is an extremely useful economic tool for identifying groups of products whose demand functions are related. Cross elasticity is calculated as the ratio of the percentage change in the quantity demanded of one good, A, to the percentage change in the price of another good, B, or

$$\varepsilon_c = \frac{\Delta Q_A}{Q_A} \div \frac{\Delta P_B}{P_B}.$$

Substitutes

Two goods whose cross elasticity of demand is positive; $\varepsilon_c > 0$.

If the price of one good rises and, other things being equal, the quantity demanded of another good increases, those products are **substitutes**. If Dorothy's demand for Bayer aspirin rises 85 percent following a 10 percent rise in the price of Bufferin, her cross elasticity of demand for aspirin is +8.5. The coefficient of cross elasticity of demand is calculated thus:

$$\varepsilon_c = \frac{\% \text{ change in the quantity demanded for Bayer}}{\% \text{ change in the price of Bufferin}} = \frac{85\%}{10\%} = 8.5.$$

For substitute commodities, the cross elasticity coefficient is positive because an increase in the price of one good causes an increase in the quantity demanded of the other. The larger the elasticity coefficient (in absolute terms), the more substitutable the products or services are.

Complements

Two goods whose cross elasticity of demand is negative; $\varepsilon_c < 0$.

Some items are complements in consumption—bacon and eggs; gasoline and automobiles; light bulbs, lamps, and electricity. Two goods are **complements** when an increase in the price of one results in a decrease in the quantity demanded of the other. A negative number is obtained for the cross elasticity coefficient for complementary goods because the increase in the price of one is always associated with a decrease in the quantity demanded for the other.

In calculating cross elasticity, therefore, a positive sign indicates that goods are substitutes and a negative sign indicates that they are complements. The absolute size of the coefficient, moreover, tells us the degree of substitutability or complementarity. A coefficient of −28.0 indicates a greater degree of complementarity than one of −4.0, for example.

ELASTICITY OF SUPPLY

Elasticity of supply

A measure of producers' or workers' relative responsiveness to price or wage changes; the percent change in quantity supplied divided by the percent change in the price or wage rate.

The versatile concept of elasticity, applied thus far only to demand, can also be applied to problems related to supply. **Elasticity of supply** is the degree of responsiveness of a supplier of goods or services to changes in the price the supplier receives for those goods or services.

A price elasticity of supply coefficient can be mechanically calculated in the same manner as all other elasticities. To determine the relation between a change in quantity supplied and a change in price, the following simple formula, which we studied earlier in the chapter in the discussion of price elasticity of demand, can be applied:

$$\varepsilon_s = \frac{\% \text{ change in the quantity supplied}}{\% \text{ change in price}}$$

$$= \frac{\Delta Q_s}{Q_s} \div \frac{\Delta P}{P},$$

$$= \frac{\Delta Q_s}{Q_s} \times \frac{P}{\Delta P},$$

or

$$\varepsilon_s = \frac{Q_2 - Q_1}{Q_1} \times \frac{P_1}{P_2 - P_1}.$$

Such a simple coefficient or some more elaborate "average elasticity" can be calculated for any supply curve at any instant in time, just as it can be for the elasticity of demand.

Time and Elasticity of Supply: Maryland Crab Fishing

An extremely important issue concerns the time dimension over which the economist calculates supply elasticities. To illustrate, consider a crab fisherman from Chesapeake Bay who daily brings in a catch and offers it for sale. The supply curve for crabs on any given day would be totally inelastic. On any given day, the quantity supplied of crabs would be completely unresponsive to price changes.

How, then, does the market establish a price? Price is determined by the interaction of supply and demand. If the demand for crabs on some particular day happens to be D_0 in Figure 5.8, price will settle at P_e and the entire quantity of crabs (a commodity that we assume, unrealistically, is not storable) will be sold.

Now suppose there is a change in consumers' taste. Maryland crabs become more desirable, and the demand curve shifts permanently to D_1. The fisherman's good fortune is revealed when his usual catch of Q_0 crabs brings a higher price P_0. How will the fisherman respond? If the price P_0 is higher than his average production costs, meaning a higher-than-normal profit, the fisherman will adjust by shifting available resources into crab fishing as soon as possible. If he has idle boats or nets and if there is plenty of labor available, all will be put to use. The act of producing more crabs takes time because resources are not instantly adaptable to crab fishing.

During ensuing days, weeks, or months, more crabs will be offered for sale per day, resulting in a more elastic supply curve for crabs. Such a supply curve over the initial adjustment period may look like S_1 in Figure 5.8. The price may temporarily fall to P_1 given that the demand for crabs remains stationary at D_1. Comparing the quantity Q_1 sold at price P_1 with the previous quantity of crabs sold, Q_0, shows us that over some adjustment period the supply curve for crabs is not completely inelastic but that quantity supplied is responsive to the initial price change.

If price P_1 is still abnormally profitable, the fisherman will continue to shift resources into crab production by purchasing new boats and equipment and by training new workers. Again, such activity takes time, but the effect will be to increase crab supply (perhaps to S_2). The end result in the crab market will depend on the adaptability and availability of resources for crab fishing and on the cost of producing new inputs. But the general rule is that elasticity of supply will tend to increase over time. The full impact of economic policy changes—levying taxes on industries, for example—often hinges on the elasticity of supply over time.

The concept of elasticity is not just related to the private choices of individuals; it is

The elasticity of supply increases through time with an increase in the demand for crabs.

FIGURE 5.8

Time and Elasticity of Supply

If the demand for crabs shifts from D_0 to D_1, then price rises quickly to P_0. As time goes by and crab fishermen are able to adjust inputs, the price begins to fall to P_1. After a long period of time and all adjustments are made to the increased demand, price falls to P_2. Over time, elasticity of supply increases.

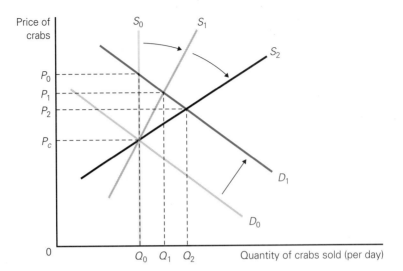

related to important public choices that individuals must make as well. Should we raise taxes or lower taxes, should we charge higher fees to go to public parks and museums, should we subsidize the arts and agriculture? These are but a few of the public choices that we must make that can be better understood by application of the concept of elasticity. In the Application, "Cigarettes, Elasticity, and Public Choice: The Effects of an Excise Tax," we provide an example of just such a situation.

APPLICATION

Cigarettes, Elasticity, and Public Choice: The Effects of an Excise Tax

An excise tax is a simple per-unit tax on the sale of a particular item. Tax collectors determine the amount of the taxable good sold by a retail or wholesale firm and require that the firm pay the amount of the tax times the quantity sold. Whatever the object taxed, an excise tax will have important effects on both demanders and suppliers, depending on elasticities of demand and supply. Consider a well-known excise or "sin" tax—the tax on cigarettes. For many years, particular interest groups within the voting public have found such a tax extremely appealing both as a revenue device and as a means of restricting "sinful" or undesirable behavior.

The equilibrium effects of an excise tax on cigarettes are shown in Figure 5.9. The hypothetical supply and demand curves for cigarettes before the excise tax are S_1 and D. The equilibrium price, E_1, is \$1.75 per pack and the quantity is 50 million packs per day. The effect of a 30-cent-per-pack excise tax can be shown by shifting the supply curve vertically upward by 30 cents to S_2. For each quantity along S_2, the price at which producers were willing to offer that quantity has now increased by 30 cents.

The new equilibrium quantity, E_2, is lower, at 40 million. This change occurs because buyers respond to price changes; their elasticity of demand for cigarettes is greater than zero. As the excise tax puts upward pressure on the price, a smaller quantity is demanded. The posttax equilibrium price to consumers, P_c, is \$1.90.

FIGURE 5.9

Effect of an Excise Tax on Cigarettes

When a 30-cent excise tax is added to the price of a pack of cigarettes, the entire supply curve for cigarettes shifts from S_1 to S_2. At the new equilibrium price, $1.90, the elasticity of demand is greater than zero; specifically, consumers will reduce their consumption of cigarettes by 10 million packs, and total tax revenues will equal 40 million times the tax. The shaded area represents government tax revenues, the 30-cent excise tax per pack multiplied by the number of packs of cigarettes sold after the tax is imposed.

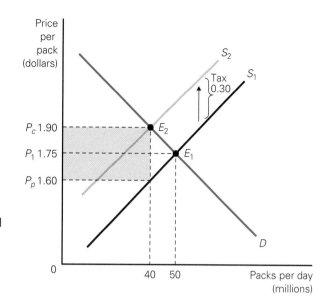

From this price, producers must pay the 30-cent excise tax and receive the net price, P_p, of $1.60 per pack.

The total revenues received by the government from the tax may not be as great as some politicians expected. Before the tax was instituted, the quantity bought was 50 million. A simple multiplication of 30 cents times 50 million would yield an overestimate of tax revenues. The actual tax revenues were 30 cents times 40 million, the new equilibrium quantity. For any excise tax the elasticity of supply and demand must be taken into account before a projection is made for tax revenues.

The elasticities of supply and demand also determine the relative burden of the excise tax. Who actually pays the tax—producers or consumers—is shown by the change in price to the buyers and sellers. In this example, the price to consumers increased 15 cents and the net price to producers fell 15 cents. Here the burden is shared equally by consumers and producers, but this is not necessarily the case.

If demand had been relatively less elastic, then price would have increased more to consumers than it fell to producers. If supply had been less elastic, more of the burden would have shifted back to the producers.

To summarize the effects of an excise tax: The lower the elasticity of demand, the greater the price increase or tax burden to consumers. The lower the elasticity of supply, the greater the net price decrease or burden to the producers.

QUESTION

Why are federal and state taxes on alcoholic beverages so prevalent? If "moral objections" to such beverages are the reason for raising excise taxes, do you believe that the taxes have had the desired effects? Why or why not?

SUMMARY

1. Elasticity is the ratio of the percent change in effect to the percent change in some cause. If changes in quantity demanded (the effect) are caused by changes in price, elasticity of demand is the percent change in quantity demanded divided by the percent change in price. This ratio is called the demand elasticity coefficient (ε_d).

2. A demand elasticity coefficient greater than 1 means that consumers are responsive to price changes; demand is elastic. When $\varepsilon_d = 1$, demand is unit elastic. When ε_d is less than 1, consumers are not very responsive to price changes; demand is said to be inelastic.

3. Elasticity can also be derived (in a general, short-hand manner) by examining total expenditures (or total revenues) as price rises or falls. If total expenditures rise (fall) as price rises (falls), ε_d is less than 1. If total expenditures remain constant as price rises or falls, $\varepsilon_d = 1$. If total expenditures fall (rise) as price rises (falls), the demand elasticity coefficient is greater than 1—that is, it is elastic.

4. There are three major determinants of demand elasticity: (1) the number and availability of substitutes; (2) the size and importance of the item in the consumer's budget; and (3) the time period over which the coefficient is calculated.

5. Other applications of the elasticity concept are the relation between income changes and changes in quantity demanded (income elasticity of demand) and between price changes for one good and changes in quantity demanded for another complementary or substitute good (cross elasticity of demand between two goods).

6. Time is at the center of most important economic calculations, including elasticity. A general rule regarding time and elasticity is that the elasticity of demand and supply increases with the time that a change (in price, for instance) is in effect.

KEY TERMS

elasticity	inelastic demand	cross elasticity of demand
price elasticity of demand	arc elasticity	substitutes
demand elasticity coefficient	total expenditures	complements
elastic demand	total revenues	elasticity of supply
unit elasticity of demand	income elasticity of demand	

QUESTIONS FOR REVIEW AND DISCUSSION

1. The formula for elasticity is

$$\frac{\%\Delta Q_d}{\%\Delta P} = \frac{\Delta Q_d/Q}{\Delta P/P} = \frac{\Delta Q_d}{Q} \times \frac{P}{\Delta P}.$$

Using this formula, calculate the elasticity of demand for a product when the price changes from $1 to $1.50, $2 to $2.50, $3 to $3.75, and the change in quantity demanded is 15 to 10, 25 to 5, 50 to 30, respectively. (Hint: Remember that ΔQ is equal to $Q_2 - Q_1$ and that ΔP is equal to $P_2 - P_1$.)

2. What are the three determinants of consumers' sensitivity to a change in price? Do these always work in the same direction?

3. Is it feasible to talk about *an* elasticity all along a single demand or supply curve? Why or why not?

4. Given that a price change remains in effect over a period of time, will elasticity increase or decrease? Why?

5. What is meant by cross elasticity? How is it algebraically different from elasticity of supply and elasticity of demand, which we calculated earlier?

6. What do cross elasticities indicate about relations between two goods?

7. What might reports about a link between aspirin consumption and heart attacks do to the elasticity of demand for aspirin?

8. Is the demand elasticity coefficient for large industrial consumers of electricity larger or smaller than that for residential users? If electric companies lower the price to both groups, would total revenues from each group change in the same direction?

9. Suppose a friend has an allowance of $25 per week. She spends all of her weekly income on banana splits. What is her income elasticity of demand for banana splits?

10. A college town pizza parlor decides to offer a back-to-school two-for-one special, in effect cutting the price of pizza in half. More pizzas will be sold according to the law of demand. Will the total receipts of the parlor increase, decrease, or remain the same if pizza consumption increases by 30 percent? By 80 percent?

11. What type of price elasticity of demand is likely for a casual user of drugs such as cocaine or heroin as opposed to a dependent user? If the enforcement of prohibitions on these drugs is increased, what will happen to the extent of the changes in price and quantity demanded for the casual user?

12. What would you expect to be more price elastic—a year's membership at a fitness club or a month's membership at the same club?

PROBLEMS

1. Consider the following figure.

a. Compute the price elasticity of demand for a change in price from $5 to $3.
b. Is the resulting value elastic, inelastic, or unit elastic?

c. Will the firm's total revenue rise or fall from such a price change?

2. The Sunrise Pet Store sells cats and dogs. During July, the price of each cat was $15. In August, the price increased to $20. The store sold 23 dogs in July and 35 dogs in August. Calculate the cross elasticity of demand. Are cats and dogs substitutes? Explain.

3. Sometimes societal problems are attacked without full considerations of elasticity. Politicians and sociologists often argue, for example, that the price of cigarettes should be raised through taxation to reduce or prevent teen smoking. Suppose cigarette taxes increase and that demand is found to be elastic, i.e., smoking is reduced among teens. Given that substitutes clearly exist for ordinary cigarettes among teens, comment on the possible effects of the tax as social policy.

WORKING WITH THE WEB

1. Suppose you are in the market to buy a new car and are considering your options. Go to www.autobytel.com and select "new cars." Next, click on the link for Sport Utility Vehicles and take a look at the number of vehicles available under this heading (there are several!). For a typical consumer (i.e., not brand loyal), do you expect the price elasticity of demand to be more or less elastic for a Ford Expedition or for a Sport Utility Vehicle in general? Why?

2. Go to ftp://ftp.bls.gov/pub/special.requests/ce/-msa/y9697/norteast.txt. This will bring you to Table 21, "Selected northeastern metropolitan statistical areas: Average annual expenditures and characteristics, Consumer Expenditure Survey, 1996–1997." Compare the income before taxes for consumers in Boston and Pittsburgh.

   a. What are these incomes in these two cities for this year?

   b. Now, find the average annual expenditure on alcoholic beverages in the two cities.

   Now go to ftp://ftp.bls.gov/pub/special.-requests/ce/msa/y9495/norteast.txt and find the same information for 1994–1995.

   c. What was the income before taxes in Boston and Pittsburgh in this year?

   d. Now find the average annual expenditure on alcoholic beverages in the two cities for 1994–1995.

   For simplicity, assume the level of expenditure represents units (quantity) rather than dollars. For example, in 1994–1995, alcoholic beverage expenditure in Boston was $487. Assume that this is 487 units of alcohol (where units could be tons, crates, etc.).

   e. Calculate the (point) income elasticity of demand for alcoholic beverages in each city, assuming the initial level of income and quantity of alcoholic beverage consumption is reported in 1994–1995.

   f. What type of good is alcohol to the average consumer in each city?

The Logic Of Consumer Choice And Demand

W e have seen in Chapters 3, 4, and 5 that the law of demand is an accurate and useful generalization about human behavior. Other things being equal, individuals will consume more of a good when its price is lower. In this chapter we examine why individuals increase their purchases of a good or service when its price falls. The heart of the analysis involves how consumers deal with the problem of scarcity. In other words, given that a consumer has a fixed budget or income, how does he or she allocate the budget among goods and services to obtain the most satisfaction from consumption? When you finish Chapter 6 you should understand

- how consumers affix value to goods and services in the marketplace.
- how scarcity affects individual behavior.
- how the economic theory of consumer behavior explains the law of demand.
- how marginal utility explains consumer behavior.

This chapter analyzes consumer choice in terms of marginal utility; in an appendix at the end of the chapter, the same analysis is cast in terms of indifference curves. Both approaches to the analysis of individual choice-making behavior are useful and introduce new tools and insights with which to study economic behavior.

UTILITY AND MARGINAL UTILITY

Why do we demand anything at all? The obvious answer is that we get satisfaction or pleasure from consuming goods and services. A vacation at the beach, a ticket to the big game,

Utility
A measure of the satisfaction that the consumption of goods or services yields an individual.

dinner at a fine restaurant—all give us pleasure. Economists call this pleasure or satisfaction **utility**. Economics, unlike psychology, does not provide any answers to questions such as why some people prefer red shirts to blue shirts or why so many people like chocolate. Economics analyzes the results of people's preferences—the observations that people will demand or pay for those things that give them utility.

Although economics cannot offer an answer to questions such as why people like chocolate, economics is interested in the intensity of consumer desires for goods. Why will individuals pay $3.50 for a magazine and $1000 for a vacation at the beach? In other words, why is the intensity of demand, as reflected in the prices people are willing to pay, greater for some goods than for others? Economists address questions like these with the aid of the **principle of diminishing marginal utility**. This principle is a simple proposition: As people consume a good in greater and greater quantities, eventually they get less and less extra utility from that good.

Principle of diminishing marginal utility
The more of a good or service being consumed, the smaller is the marginal utility obtained by consuming one additional unit of the good or service, all other factors equal.

Although the utility derived by a consumer from some good—shoes, books, raspberries—depends on many factors, such as past experience, education, and psychological traits that we may not be able to explain, the principle of diminishing marginal utility allows us to predict certain bounds for consumption behavior. Other things being equal, an individual will not be willing to pay more for an additional unit of good than what was paid for the last unit. Sooner or later, as the amount consumed increases, the consumer will be willing to pay even less for an additional unit because of diminishing marginal utility.

The principle of diminishing marginal utility is based on common sense. At lunch you might be ravenously hungry as a result of having skipped breakfast. The satisfaction, or utility, you get from eating the first hamburger in the cafeteria would likely be great. But after one burger, or certainly after two or three, the additional satisfaction you experience from an additional hamburger must decline. The amount of money that you would be willing to pay for additional burgers—amounts that reflect their **marginal utility** for you—would also decline.

Marginal utility
The amount by which total utility changes when consumption of a good or service changes by one unit; calculated by dividing the change in total utility by the change in quantity consumed.

Some given time period of consumption also must be specified in order for the principle of diminishing marginal utility to be relevant to behavior. Why, for example, do vending machine sellers of soft drinks and foods use costly and elaborate procedures to prevent buyers from stealing, while newspaper sellers usually permit the purchaser to take as many papers as he or she wants after the first is purchased?[1] It is because the marginal utility of the second or third candy bar, sandwich, or soft drink does not diminish much or at all after the first is consumed if the consumer paces his or her consumption of them through time. The additional utility you get from the fifth soft drink or prepackaged sandwich is clearly less if all are consumed over the period of an hour. However, packages of peanuts and diet drinks can be saved for later consumption. The utility of a daily newspaper, once read, is ordinarily used up immediately. The marginal utility of a second daily paper is low or zero, and vendors do not ordinarily use up costly resources in order to prevent you from taking three or four papers after paying for one. More "honesty" is therefore expected among paper buyers than would be expected from consumers of other products from vending machines, and the theory of diminishing marginal utility explains why.

---

[1]The example is suggested by the delightful mystery novel by Marshall Jevons (the nom de plume of economists William Briet and Kenneth Elzinga) in *The Fatal Equilibrium* (Cambridge, Mass.: MIT Press, 1985), pp. 113–114. We highly recommend this book and the latest in the series titled *A Deadly Indifference* (New York: Carrol & Graf Publishers, Inc., 1995). These mysteries, featuring economist-sleuth Henry Spearman, use marginal utility and a variety of other basic economic concepts to solve a series of murders.

TABLE 6.1

Total Utility and Marginal Utility

The umbrella consumer buys and uses between 1 and 5 umbrellas. The satisfaction the consumer gains from the umbrellas is measured in imaginary units called *utils*. Total utility increases as the consumer adds more umbrellas to his or her stock, but marginal utility—the satisfaction associated with each additional umbrella—decreases.

Umbrellas Acquired	Total Utility (utils)	Marginal Utility (extra utils per umbrella)
1	6	6
2	11	5
3	15	4
4	18	3
5	20	2

The principle of diminishing marginal utility can be numerically and graphically illustrated. Most people use umbrellas as shields from rain and sun. Unfortunately, umbrellas are items that are easily misplaced or lost; in addition, they are sometimes not available when we need them. Many of us, therefore, own more than one umbrella, although the first umbrella we own obviously yields us the most satisfaction, since, without it, we would go unprotected from the elements. Consider the data in Table 6.1 and Figure 6.1. Table 6.1 indicates the relation between the number of umbrellas a consumer owns, the **total utility** the consumer derives from umbrellas, and the marginal utility of each additional umbrella to the consumer. For convenience, economists construct imaginary units called *utils* with which to measure quantities of utility derived by the umbrella consumer. Note that as the number of umbrellas owned increases, total utility—a measure of the total satisfaction gained from the entire amount consumed—increases, but at a decreasing rate. Marginal utility—the satisfaction gained by the consumer from each additional umbrella—declines as the consumer acquires additional umbrellas.

In Figure 6.1a, the dotted step lines measure the total utility generated by the consumption of umbrellas. A smooth curve has been drawn through the steps to show that a positive relation exists between units of consumption and total utility. Notice that as consumption increases, total utility increases—but at a decreasing rate. The downward-sloping curve in Figure 6.1b shows the corresponding marginal utility associated with each umbrella acquired. As more umbrellas are consumed, the marginal utility of each additional umbrella declines.

Total utility

The total amount of satisfaction derived from consuming any given quantity of a good or service.

CONSUMER EQUILIBRIUM: DIMINISHING MARGINAL UTILITY AT WORK

If the principle of diminishing marginal utility applies only to a consumer's choices regarding umbrellas, then it is not very useful. To be useful, the concept of diminishing marginal utility must help us explain behavior in a world in which many different goods are consumed.

FIGURE 6.1

Total Utility and Marginal Utility

(a) Total utility increases, but at a decreasing rate, as more and more umbrellas are added to the consumer's stock.

(b) Marginal utility declines with each additional umbrella.

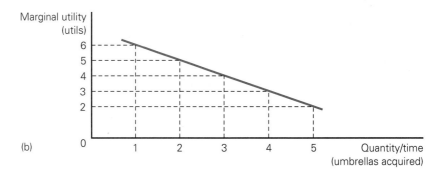

Basic Assumptions

To use diminishing marginal utility to understand consumer behavior, four concepts of consumer behavior need to hold.

1. Each consumer desires many goods, and no one good is so precious that it will be consumed to the exclusion of all other goods. Moreover, goods can be substituted for one another as alternative means of yielding satisfaction. For example, the consumer good of exercise can be satisfied by jogging, playing basketball, hiking, swimming, or a number of other activities. Dinner offers a variety of choices—steak, chicken, pizza, and so on.

2. Consumers pay prices for the things they want. For the purposes of the following analysis, it is convenient to assume that consumers pay fixed, constant prices for the things they choose to buy. Each good carries a given price, no matter how much is bought or where it is bought.

3. Consumers cannot afford everything they want. They have a budget or income constraint that forces them to limit their consumption and to make choices about what they will consume.

4. Consumers seek the most satisfaction they can get from spending their limited funds for consumption. Consumers are not irrational. They make conscious, purposeful choices designed to increase their well-being. This does not mean that consumers do not make mistakes or sometimes make impulsive purchases that they later regret. By gaining experience over time as they deal in goods and services, consumers try to get the most possible satisfaction from their limited budgets given their past experience. (See the Focus "Menus and

Marginal utility explains why college students will pay a bundle for a beach vacation and much less for a magazine or a soft drink.

Marginal Utility: 'Save Room for Dessert!'" for an explanation of how restaurant menus help increase your total utility from dining.)

Balancing Choices Among Goods

Armed with these concepts, we can better understand the behavior of consumers in the real world. To see how diminishing marginal utility works in a practical setting, assume that you—a consumer—are deciding how much of two goods to choose: movies and concerts. For each additional dollar you spend on movies, you experience an increase in utility. Simultaneously, you forgo the utility you could have experienced by spending the dollar on concerts. Because you seek to maximize the satisfaction you get from your consumption expenditures (concept number 4), you will spend your additional dollar on the good that yields you the largest increase in utility—that is, the good with the greatest marginal utility for you.

According to the principle of diminishing marginal utility, whether the utility of one good is greater than the other depends on the amount of each good consumed. If, during a month, you have already attended a large number of concerts but have seen relatively few movies, the marginal utility of concerts will tend to be low and that of movies high for you. You are therefore more likely to spend an additional dollar on movies than on concerts.

In this simple world of two goods, you will continue to spend additional dollars on movies until the marginal utility you receive from an additional dollar spent on movies is equal to the marginal utility of an additional dollar spent on concerts. This process of reaching equality in the two marginal utilities per dollar occurs naturally because the marginal utility of movies declines relative to the marginal utility

FOCUS

Menus and Marginal Utility: "Save Room for Dessert!"

Individuals make choices of all kinds every day. Consumers will demand, and suppliers have profit incentives to supply, choices in the forms that increase total utility.

Consider the typical restaurant menu, which is usually posted or presented individually to customers. However they are used, one function of menus is to serve as a device that limits diminishing marginal utility and increases the total utility *of any given meal*.[a] The typical menu is divided into appetizers, soups, salads, entrees (often subdivided into more specific categories of meat, seafood, pasta, vegetarian delights, and the like), and desserts. We all pick and choose the kind and variety of foods we eat so that excesses among the early courses do not diminish the marginal utility of later courses and so that the total utility of the whole meal is as great as possible. A huge quantity of onion soup will ordinarily provide less total utility than a cup of soup combined with a small salad and a modest entree.

[a]Another important function of menus is to convey information regarding the prices of each offering. The prices do affect the choice process, but our concern here is with other dimensions of the diner's choice.

Many variations and extensions of the menu exist. In some French and American restaurants, a *de gustation* menu is offered. This menu typically offers very small quantities of many dishes to thrill the palate of diners seeking higher total and less diminishing marginal utility. Cafeterias post the entire menu at the beginning of the queue and (for reasons related to diminishing marginal utility) usually present desserts early in the line. To say that "you haven't saved room for dessert" usually refers less to the capacity of your stomach than to the total utility-maximizing choices made about the range of offerings on a menu. How many times have we "regretted" total consumption levels at a menuless meal when our favorite dessert arrives, its identity previously unannounced?

Menus are devices that provide information to consumers about the availability of specific items. But a menu also enables an individual diner to plan his or her meal so as to maximize total utility from eating at any particular time. It also reminds us that the expression "variety is the spice of life" applies to the principle of diminishing marginal utility.

---

of concerts as you attend more movies. When the marginal utility per dollar of consuming the two goods is equal, you have maximized the total utility of your purchases, subject to the resources you have to spend. In other words, at the point of equality of marginal utility per last dollar spent, you will have no incentive to alter the pattern of your choices between concerts and movies. This condition of balance in consumer purchases, from which there is no tendency to change, is called **consumer equilibrium**.

Consumer equilibrium

A situation in which a consumer chooses quantities of goods that maximize total utility given a budget constraint; equilibrium implies that the per dollar marginal utility obtained from the last unit of each good consumed is equal for all goods.

How do economists take the differing goods—as well as their differing marginal utilities—into account? Note that consumer equilibrium occurs where the marginal utility of a dollar's worth of concerts is equal to the marginal utility of a dollar's worth of movies. To accommodate the differing goods, the following equation is used to describe the condition of consumer equilibrium:

$$\frac{\text{Marginal utility of concerts}}{\text{Price of concerts}} = \frac{\text{Marginal utility of movies}}{\text{Price of movies}}.$$

Equilibrium is reached when the marginal utility of the last concert attended divided by the price of a concert is equal to the marginal utility of the last movie seen divided by the price of a movie.

This equation is just a representation of consumer equilibrium. To see what it means, assume that concerts cost $12 and movies cost $6, and that you, the consumer, are initially not in equilibrium. This means that the above equation does not hold for you—that is,

$$\frac{\text{Marginal utility of concerts}}{\$12} \neq \frac{\text{Marginal utility of movies}}{\$6}.$$

Suppose that you begin by buying a movie ticket because its marginal utility per dollar to you is initially higher than that of concerts.

$$\frac{\text{Marginal utility of movies}}{\$6} > \frac{\text{Marginal utility of concerts}}{\$12}.$$

As you attend more movies, the marginal utility of an additional movie seen declines relative to the marginal utility of an additional concert attended. At each point you are trying to get the most possible satisfaction from your expenditures on the two goods—you are balancing the marginal utility of spending a dollar toward an additional movie against the marginal utility of spending a dollar on another concert.

At the end of the process, as the ratio of the marginal utility of movies to the price of movies declines relative to the ratio of the marginal utility of concerts to the price of concerts, equality between the two ratios is reached. Consumer equilibrium is restored at the point where additional movies seen add 2 times as much utility as a concert. Put another way, you will adjust your consumption of the two goods until the marginal utility of a dollar's worth of movies is equal to the marginal utility of a dollar's worth of concerts. This is what the equation of consumer equilibrium means and how it is reached by a consumer.

The Budget Constraint and Consumer Equilibrium

Consider a more specific example of how a consumer maximizes utility in the everyday world. Assume that a student consumer, Keith, is trying to allocate his (hypothetical) food budget on two goods—macaroni and cheese, and pizza—over some given time period. Call macaroni and cheese product X, pizza product Y, and Keith's relative preferences for macaroni and cheese versus pizza MU_x and MU_y, respectively. It is clear from Table 6.2 that Keith prefers pizza to macaroni and cheese. The marginal utility of the first unit of pizza consumed brings Keith 80 utils, whereas the first box of macaroni and cheese yields only 50. Likewise, for every successive unit from the first to the sixth of the two meals consumed, Keith's utility preference is for pizza over macaroni and cheese. How, then, do we explain why individuals always buy combinations of goods in order to maximize their utility? What rule do we apply to Keith's consumer behavior to explain how choices are actually made? The rule is simple: *Consumers will always balance the consumption of all of the various goods purchased so as to maximize utility given their respective budget constraints.*

Knowing that Keith prefers pizza to macaroni and cheese is not enough to explain the decisions he makes. Many of us would say that we would prefer (have a higher preference for) a Maserati or a Porsche to a Ford or a Hyundai. Most of us do not buy high-priced sports cars, however, when our utilities are adjusted for the relative prices of these two categories of automobiles and when our incomes

TABLE 6.2

A Consumer's Utility Maximization

Keith, a consumer with preferences for two goods, chooses a utility-maximizing combination of macaroni and cheese and pizzas by equating the "adjusted" marginal utilities of the two goods under an income constraint. When his income is $34, he buys 2 boxes of macaroni and cheese and 3 pizzas.

Units of Product	PRODUCT X: MACARONI AND CHEESE (BOXES) PRICE: $2 PER BOX		PRODUCT Y: PIZZAS (12-INCH) PRICE: $10 PER PIZZA	
	(1) Marginal Utility (utils)	(2) Marginal Utility (per dollar's worth)	(3) Marginal Utility (utils)	(4) Marginal Utility (per dollar's worth)
First	50	25	80	8
Second	8	4	50	5
Third	4	2	40	4
Fourth	2	1	20	2
Fifth	0	0	10	1
Sixth	−2	−1	0	0
Seventh	−10	−5	−40	−4

are considered. Thus, the marginal utilities of *all* goods consumed must be adjusted by the prices of those goods before we can explain the choices consumers make.

Price adjustments are made to the marginal utilities of macaroni and cheese and pizza in columns (2) and (4) of Table 6.2. If we assume that the price of macaroni and cheese is $2 per box and pizzas are $10 each, the marginal utilities per dollar's worth of the two goods may be readily calculated. For the first unit of macaroni and cheese, for example, the marginal utility per dollar's worth, or MU_x/P_x, is equal to 25 (50/$2). For the first unit of pizza, the marginal utility per dollar's worth, or MU_y/P_y, is equal to 8, or 80 divided by $10. Just as in the case of movies and concerts, consumers will attempt to balance these "adjusted" marginal utilities to maximize satisfaction given their income or budget constraint. Consider Keith's choices. As soon as he has an income of $2 per time period, he will buy a box of macaroni and cheese. Why? Because the marginal utility per dollar's worth of this item is greater than that of the first unit of pizza.

As Keith's budget or income constraint becomes less stringent, his consumption pattern changes, as Table 6.2 shows. Suppose that his budget rises to $12 over the time period. Table 6.2 tells us that he will buy the first unit of pizza in preference to more macaroni and cheese. The first unit of pizza would add 8 utils per dollar to his total utility, whereas the second unit of macaroni and cheese would add only 4 utils per dollar to his satisfaction. To maximize satisfaction, Keith will buy the first pizza with the additional $10 in income.

When his budget rises to $34 for these two products, Keith is in equilibrium when he buys 2 units of product X (macaroni and cheese) and 3 units of product Y (pizza). To see why, let Keith simply shop for the highest marginal utility per dollar. He first buys X (25), then Y (8), then another X (5), and then another X (4) and another Y (4). At this point, Keith has spent all his money ($34) on 3 pizzas ($30) and 2 boxes of macaroni and cheese ($4).

To look at Keith's behavior in another way, simply calculate the total utility that Keith receives. His total satisfaction on good X will be 58 utils (50 + 8), and the total utility obtained from good Y will be 170 (80 + 50 + 40), for a total of 228 utils of satisfaction. With $34 Keith could buy other possible combinations of products, such as 7 boxes of macaroni and cheese and 2 pizzas, but this purchase would yield a lower total satisfaction (52 utils on X and 130 on Y, for a total of 182 utils). Keith is looking for the *utility-maximizing combination*, and that is always found where the marginal utilities per dollar's worth of the two (or more) goods or services are equal. In terms of the simple problem considered in Table 6.2, equilibrium occurs when the dollar-adjusted marginal utilities of the items purchased are equal:

$$\frac{MU_{\text{Macaroni and cheese}}}{P_{\text{Macaroni and cheese}}} = \frac{MU_{\text{Pizza}}}{P_{\text{Pizza}}},$$

or

$$\frac{8}{\$2} = \frac{40}{\$10}.$$

All of us, moreover, are subject to a budget constraint. In Keith's case, the income constraint is assumed to be $34; the sum of the total expenditures for both items must equal that amount.

$$P_{\text{Mac}} \times Q_{\text{Mac}} + P_{\text{Pizza}} \times Q_{\text{Pizza}} = \$34,$$

$$\$2 \times 2 + \$10 \times 3 = \$34.$$

Here we assume that Keith, the consumer, expends all of his income on macaroni and cheese and pizza. This assumption is a simplification, since any consumer typically purchases hundreds or even thousands of goods and saves and borrows, as well. Some of these complications are treated below, but the same principles of utility maximization always apply. Symbolically, the equilibrium conditions for maximum consumer satisfaction may be stated

$$\frac{MU_X}{P_X} = \frac{MU_Y}{P_Y}.$$

This equilibrium condition for maximum consumer satisfaction is always subject to a budget constraint, or

$$P_X X + P_Y Y = \text{Income}.$$

Another interesting aspect of the consumer equilibrium described above is that Keith or any consumer will never knowingly consume a unit of any good or service that brings him or her *negative* marginal utility. Even if Keith's budget constraint permitted him to purchase 7 boxes of macaroni and cheese and 7 pizzas over the time period, he would never do so. Even if both of the commodities were *free*, Keith would never consume more than 5 boxes of macaroni and cheese and 6 pizzas. The purchase of units of goods giving negative marginal utilities will reduce the total utility produced by these consumptions. The last two boxes of macaroni and cheese would reduce total utility by 12 utils, and the last pizza would cause it to decline by 40 utils. No rational consumer would spend scarce resources to reduce utility.

Consumers Maximize Satisfaction Among Thousands of Goods

The two-good examples for entertainment and for food consumption are simplifications of consumers' actual choices among thousands of goods and services. We consume not only food and entertainment, but such items as electricity, medical services, music lessons, and cable television. To express the general condition of consumer equilibrium, the two-good equation may be expanded, with N denoting the total number of goods and services consumed. If $X, Y, Z,\ldots,N$ are goods in the consumer's budget; $MU_X, MU_Y, MU_Z,\ldots,MU_N$ are the marginal utilities of these goods and services; and $P_X, P_Y, P_Z,\ldots,P_N$ represent the corresponding prices of these goods and services, then the equilibrium equation for maximum consumer satisfaction is

$$\frac{MU_X}{P_X} = \frac{MU_Y}{P_Y} = \frac{MU_Z}{P_Z} = \cdots = \frac{MU_N}{P_N}.$$

The only numbers we have to put in the consumer equilibrium equation are the prices of the goods. We do not know—or need to know—what the subjective marginal utilities of the consumer are. The important point about the equation is that it is a proposition about individual behavior. It outlines how consumers will achieve balance or equilibrium in allocating their incomes among goods and services. In a sense, consumers assign their own utility numbers and arrange their patterns of consumption to achieve equilibrium; that is, they buy less of one good in order to buy more of another. Consumers solve the equation for themselves as an expression of their rational choices.

Consumers will equate the "adjusted" marginal utilities in the consumer equilibrium equation subject to an income constraint; in other words, the sum of all expenditures made on each item in the budget equals total income:

$$P_X X + P_Y Y + P_Z Z + \cdots + P_N N = \text{Income}.$$

In the budget constraint equation, prices of all the various goods and services as well as the consumer's income must be supplied, reminding us that utility is maximized only under an individual's budget limitations. The individual can only maximize satisfaction subject to given prices (of macaroni and cheese and pizzas, in Keith's case) and to income. The explanation given here of the rational consumer's behavior states that the individual always acts to maximize his or her satisfaction or utility—whatever that may be to any individual—given the economic environment. That environment always includes the prices of individual goods and services and the consumer's income.

Consumer Rationality and a Famous Riddle: Marginal Utility and Smith's Diamond–Water Paradox

Diamond–Water paradox
Adam Smith's belief that water and diamonds did not follow the same theory of value—a paradox confusing total and marginal utility that is unlocked by the principle of diminishing marginal utility.

Is consumer choice always rational? In describing the famous **diamond–water paradox**, Adam Smith pondered what seemed to be an irrational willingness of consumers to spend vast sums of money on "useless" goods like diamonds:

> Things which have the greatest value in use frequently have little or no value in exchange; and on the contrary, those which have the greatest value in exchange have frequently little or no value in use. Nothing is more useful than water; but it will scarce purchase anything, scarce anything can be had in exchange for it. A

diamond, on the contrary, has scarce any value in use; but a very great quantity of other goods may frequently be had in exchange for it.[2]

Water is useful but cheap; diamonds are not useful but expensive. This seems paradoxical. But using the principle of diminishing marginal utility, what errors can we find in Smith's reasoning about the paradox?

First, Smith failed to grasp the importance of the relative scarcity of a commodity in determining its value in use, or marginal utility. He compared a single diamond with the total supply of water. Had he compared the marginal utility of a single diamond with a single gallon of water, no other water being available, the paradox would have disappeared, for the scarce water would be considered quite valuable. As economic theorists later discovered, water commands little in exchange because its supply is so abundant relative to the intensity of consumer desire for it. Diamonds are scarce relative to consumer desires and therefore command much in exchange. There is no diamond–water paradox when one focuses on the value of the marginal unit of supply to the consumer. Water is plentiful and cheap; diamonds are scarce and expensive.

Second, Smith makes a personal judgment of utility when he suggests that diamonds have no value in use. Many wearers and investors in diamonds would disagree on this point. Within reason, modern utility theory does not allow judgments to be made that some preferences are good and others are bad.

A third point, related to the first, is that Smith's value paradox failed to distinguish between marginal and total utility. Assume for a moment that the marginal utilities of water and diamonds are identical, as in Figure 6.2. Figure 6.2 shows that the marginal utility of each good declines as units of each increase. For any given number of units (numbers of diamonds or gallons of water), the marginal

---

[2]Adam Smith, *An Inquiry into the Nature and Causes of the Wealth of Nations,* ed. Edwin Cannan (1776; reprint, New York: Modern Library, 1937), p. 28.

FIGURE 6.2

The Diamond–Water Paradox

When relative scarcity is considered, the marginal utility of diamonds is greater (when supply is given) than the marginal utility of water. This valuation is not incompatible with the total utility of water being greater than the total utility of diamonds.

and total utility would be the same. Under ordinary circumstances, diamonds are more scarce than water, which means that the supply curve for water is to the right of the supply curve for diamonds. Thus the marginal utility of diamonds is greater than the marginal utility of water. However, the total utility of water—represented by the area up to Q_{water} under the marginal utility curve in Figure 6.2—is greater than that of diamonds. (Return to Figure 6.1 and the related discussion earlier in this chapter for further explanation of this point.)

Of course, Adam Smith did not have modern utility theory available to him when he wrote his statement. Indeed, it was in trying to resolve this simple paradox that modern utility theory was developed by economists in the nineteenth century in France. The principle of diminishing marginal utility, developed many years after Smith's writings, helps us understand the rationality behind such choices. Intuitively, a rational consumer will always equate the marginal benefits to the marginal cost of his or her actions. This rationality applies to all kinds of human behavior, including various public choices the individual has to make. (For an example related to public choice, see the Application "Is It Rational to Vote?" at the conclusion of this chapter.)

FROM DIMINISHING MARGINAL UTILITY TO THE LAW OF DEMAND

The marginal utility equation helps us understand the relation between diminishing marginal utility and the law of demand. Assume that you, the consumer, are in equilibrium with movies priced at $6 and concerts priced at $12. The equation of consumer equilibrium then looks like this:

$$\frac{MU_{movies}}{\$6} = \frac{MU_{concerts}}{\$12}.$$

If the price of concerts falls to $6, this equality will be upset. The resulting disequilibrium will be temporary, however, for you will act to restore equality by attending more concerts. As you attend more concerts, the principle of diminishing marginal utility tells us that the marginal utility of concerts for you will fall. When the marginal utility of concerts has fallen by the same proportion that their price has fallen, consumer equilibrium will be restored.

Note the relation of this behavior to the law of demand. Because the price has been reduced, you will attend more concerts until a dollar's worth of concerts generates no more utility for you than a dollar's worth of movies—or anything else. The law of demand says that consumers will respond to a fall in the relative price of a good by purchasing more of that good. Diminishing marginal utility thus provides a behavioral basis for the law of demand. When price falls, consumption increases until consumer equilibrium is again established. Indeed, the marginal utility curve may, under certain circumstances, be associated with the demand curve. For such an example and for an understanding of how different pricing arrangements on the part of entrepreneurs could alter your consumption, see the Focus "'All You Can Eat' Pizza."

Substitution effect

The change in the quantity demanded of a good that results only from a change in the relative price of the good.

The Substitution Effect and Income Effect

Consumers' tendency to buy more of a good when its price drops in relation to the price of other goods is called the **substitution effect**. The relatively cheaper good is

FOCUS

"All You Can Eat" Pizza

One of the most popular foods served on and off campus at colleges and universities is that wonderful American invention, pizza. (It is actually a variation on traditional Italian cuisine, but only an American could invent taco pizza on pita bread.) There are a number of ways to order pizza other than a whole pie—by the slice or "all you can eat" are common. However it is ordered, the laws of marginal utility and costs apply. Consider the marginal utility–demand curve for pizza shown in Figure 6.3. Each person's curve will differ, of course, but assume that the one depicted in the graph is yours. The number of slices of pizza is depicted on the quantity axis (horizontal) and the price per slice on the vertical axis in Figure 6.3.

All other things equal, how much pizza will you consume at one time (dinner today)? A look at the figure shows that the answer will depend on your utility for pizza versus the cost to you. In particular, you will equate the marginal utility of pizza consumed (which diminishes with quantity like all other goods) and the cost to you of the pizza. Clearly, that cost will vary depending on *how* pizza is offered.

Suppose there are two pizzerias in your town, one offering pizza by the slice and the other "all you can eat." Assume that the pizza is of the same quality at both restaurants. At the first restaurant, pizza is offered at $1 a slice. From the figure, you will buy four pieces by the slice. Why? Because that is where your marginal utility for pizza equals the (marginal) cost of $1 to you. As the figure shows, the fifth slice has marginal utility (value), but it is not worth the extra dollar you would have to pay.

Now consider the "all-you-can-eat" restaurant. When you pay a fixed sum for the "all-you-

---

FIGURE 6.3

Marginal Utility and Demand for Pizza

At a price of $1 per slice, this consumer buys 4 slices. At an all-you-can-eat buffet, however, the consumer drives her marginal utility to zero by consuming five slices.

continued

continued

can-eat" dining alternative, the additional or marginal cost of an additional slice is, in effect, zero to you. Note that from Figure 6.3, you will eat 5 pieces of pizza in equilibrium. Small wonder that at such restaurants, sharing food and doggie bags are not allowed and that you have the strong temptation to eat "too much." Naturally the restaurant that you will choose will be the one giving you the greatest overall utility (consumer) surplus.

substituted for other now relatively more expensive goods. Concerts are substituted for movies when the price of concerts drops. To be precise, the substitution effect refers to that portion of the increase or decrease in quantity demanded of a good that is the direct result of its change in price relative to the price of other goods.

Price, however, is not the only relevant factor affecting the quantity demanded of a good. Changes in income will also tend to shift the demand curve for goods, as we saw in Chapter 3. The larger an individual's income, the more he or she will demand of most goods.[3] Other things being equal (primarily the prices of other goods remaining the same), the fall in price of a particular good will raise the **real income**, or buying power, of the individual consumer even where nominal income remains constant. This change in real income means that the consumer can buy more of all goods under the same budget constraint as before. This **income effect** can be stated more technically: It is that portion of the change in the quantity demanded of a good that occurs because of the change in the individual's real income that resulted from a price change.

Real income

The buying power of a consumer's budget; determined by the consumer's money income and the prices of goods and services.

Income effect

The change in the quantity demanded of a good that results from a change in real income.

Marginal Utility and the Law of Demand

The principle of diminishing marginal utility and the law of demand are thus closely related. A price change leads to a change in quantity demanded, which is composed of a substitution effect and an income effect. When the price of a good falls relative to the prices of other goods, the principle of diminishing marginal utility, acting by means of the substitution effect, tends to increase the quantity of the good that the consumer demands. The income effect is a separate and distinct influence that generally reinforces the substitution effect; that is, the income effect tends to increase the quantity demanded of the good whose price has fallen. Though there are cases where the income effect can pull in the opposite direction from the substitution effect, economists generally predict that the strength of the substitution effect will outweigh the strength of the income effect, leading to an increase in the quantity demanded of a good whose relative price has fallen.

Sometimes people claim that they have found exceptions to the law of demand, but the exceptions turn out, on close examination, to be based on simple mistakes in reasoning. For example, sometimes a fall in price of a good seems to result in a decline in the quantity demanded of that good. A department store may actually

---

[3]Increases or decreases in quantity demanded as a result of an increase in income will depend upon whether the good in question is normal or inferior. Goods for which consumption increases as the consumer's income rises, such as medical care, are called normal goods. When the consumption of a good falls with increases in income, we say that such goods are inferior goods. Used cars may be an example of an inferior good. See Chapter 3 for a discussion of these terms.

sell less furniture after it lowers furniture prices. If we look more closely at such cases, we may find that, in the calculations of consumers, the relative price of furniture has not fallen. Consumers may judge that the store is phasing out its furniture department and, as a result, expect that furniture prices will soon be even lower. Often what appears to be an exception to the law of demand is actually a confusion between a change in demand and a change in quantity demanded (see Chapter 3). This is the law of demand in action—relative and not absolute prices matter to consumers.

One more of the many possible examples of an apparent, but not real, exception of the law of demand is the case of a "prestige" good. The demand for caviar, for example, is sometimes said to be much higher as an expensive item than it would be if its price per pound were comparable to, say, tuna fish. The high price of caviar is said to actually increase the quantity demanded of caviar, contrary to the law of demand. But this notion is confused. Would the quantity demanded of caviar continue to increase as the price rose to $1000, $10,000, or $1 million per pound? It would not. Although prestige goods are usually expensive goods, they do not defy the law of demand. If they did, we would see their prices rise without limit, which does not happen.

SOME PITFALLS TO AVOID

The principles of diminishing marginal utility and marginal utility analysis are useful constructs for analyzing individual behavior. As we have seen, they help explain individual choice behavior and offer a richer understanding of the law of demand. In using this analysis, however, some fairly common misunderstandings must be avoided.

1. The individual wishing to maximize utility is motivated by personal self-interests, but the principle says nothing about what those interests may be. They may be based on purely selfish, greedy goals or on humanitarian concern for others. Marginal utility analysis does not specify the goals or desires of individuals; it is useful only in understanding and analyzing individual behavior once those goals have been specified.

2. Only individuals make economic decisions. When we refer to a government agency, a corporation, or a snorkeling club as making a decision, we are only using a figure of speech. Take away the individual members who make up these organizations, and nothing is left to make a decision.

3. Economics is concerned with the effects of scarcity on the lives of people. It does not address the issue of human needs. A need is not an object that can be measured in a way that everyone can agree on (like the size of a desk or the height of a building). Needs are subjective, just like love, justice, and honor. Economics is neutral with respect to subjective judgments.

4. Marginal utility analysis is an explanation, not a description, of individual choice behavior. Economists do not claim that individual consumers actually calculate marginal utility trade-offs before they go shopping. Indeed, most consumers, if asked, would probably deny that they behave in the way that marginal utility analysis suggests they do. The proof is obviously in the pudding. Individuals behave so as to generate the same outcomes they would produce if they actually did calculate and equate marginal utilities. Marginal utility analysis explains the outcomes we observe rather than describing the mental process involved.

APPLICATION

Is It Rational to Vote?

You decide to vote in a presidential election. Typically, you will be joined by more than 60 million other people. Your vote therefore has only 1/60,000,000 worth of influence on the outcome of the election, and it is, of course, filtered through the Electoral College process in the United States.

We also know that voting is not costless. To make a trip to the polling place, voters must pay for transportation, take time off from work or leisure, and so forth. Moreover, prior registration often means another trip to the voter registration office. Thus, voting is not free—it clearly places opportunity costs on the voter.

Suppose, in a radical simplification, that all these opportunity costs equal $1; that is, it costs you $1 to vote. Given that you are 1 out of 60 million voters who vote and that it costs you $1 to vote, what must your vote be worth to you to make it rational for you to go to the polls on election day? Since you have only a tiny effect on the election, the outcome would have to have an enormous impact on you to make it worth your while to vote. This concept can be represented algebraically by the formula

$$\frac{1}{60,000,000} \times \text{benefits} = \$1,$$

which gives the large value of $60 million in benefits to you to justify the cost of voting. In terms of this analysis, it is hardly reasonable to expect the outcome of any given election to be worth $60 million to the average voter. Therefore, no one should vote, and democracy should fall on its face.

Yet herein lies a paradox. A great number of people do vote, and the question is, why? Economics provides a simple explanation for the conditions under which it is rational to vote. Obviously, voters are smarter than to view themselves as only 1 vote out of 60 million. They have identified—before the election and during the campaign—with parties (Democratic, Republican, Socialist, Libertarian, and so forth) and individual candidates, and they will make their own estimates of the prospects of the candidates in the election.

Marginal benefits (broadly construed to include *all* benefits) and marginal costs explain why individuals vote in all elections, including campus elections.

Economics says that voters will behave in terms of the marginal utility and marginal cost of voting. Notice that the above example was stated in terms of the average influence of a voter on the election. The fact that the average influence of any one voter is low does not tell us anything about his or her marginal influence on the election. (As we stress repeatedly, the distinction between *average* and *marginal* is a crucial one in economics.) While we cannot directly measure the marginal influence of a voter in an election, we can indirectly gauge the marginal benefit from voting. The marginal influence of a vote will be greater the closer the election is predicted to be. Your vote counts for more in a close election than in a lopsided election. Therefore, economic theory leads to the following prediction: Voting turnout will be positively related to the expected closeness of the election. In other words, voter turnout will be heavier the closer the election is expected to be.

So the simple economic proposition that individuals behave according to marginal cost and marginal benefit provides an explanation for the conditions under which voting is rational. This is not to argue that the only reason people vote is to obtain narrow personal benefits. Benefits can be construed in a wide variety of ways, such as patriotic duty, citizenship, support for an ideological cause, voting for a friend, and so forth. The point is not what the benefits are but that, depending on the closeness of the election, these benefits are likely to be higher or lower relative to costs. Thus, if your friend is running for Congress, you are more likely to vote if he or she is in a tight contest than if your friend is a shoo-in.

QUESTION

Logically, how should each of the following situations affect voter turnout on election day?

a. Rain

b. An international crisis

c. A close race

d. Television coverage

SUMMARY

1. As individuals, we demand goods and services because the consumption of such things gives us utility, or satisfaction.

2. The principle of diminishing marginal utility says that the more we consume of a good, the less utility we get from consuming additional amounts of that good.

3. Consumer equilibrium occurs when individuals obtain the most possible utility from their limited budgets. Their respective consumption patterns are in balance, and they cannot increase total utility by altering the way they allocate their given budgets among goods.

4. In equation form, consumer equilibrium for N goods (the total number of goods and services that a consumer chooses from) is

$$\frac{MU_X}{P_X} = \frac{MU_Y}{P_Y} = \frac{MU_Z}{P_Z} = \cdots = \frac{MU_N}{P_N}.$$

In other words, the ratios of marginal utility to price are equal among all the goods a consumer purchases. The consumer's purchases, however, are always limited by a budget constraint:

$$P_X X + P_Y Y + P_Z Z + \cdots + P_N N = \text{Income}.$$

5. The principle of diminishing marginal utility underlies the law of demand. In the first equation in number 4, if the price of good X falls, the equality of the marginal utility ratios is upset. To restore equality, the consumer will consume more of the good that has fallen in price, driving its marginal utility down proportionately to its fall in price. This is equivalent to the type of behavior predicted by the law of demand. Other things being equal, more of a good is consumed when its price falls.

6. The increase in consumption of a good when its price falls is caused by two effects. More is consumed because the price of the good has fallen relative to the prices of other goods. This is called the *substitution effect*. In addition, more is consumed because the consumer has more real income owing to the fall in price. This is called the *income effect*.

7. Generally, the substitution and income effects taken together lead to increased consumption of a good when its price falls.

8. The law of demand is a widespread empirical regularity. We observe its action everywhere. Supposed exceptions to the law are usually misapplications or misunderstandings of basic economic principles.

9. Marginal utility analysis explains the observed patterns of consumers in making their consumption choices.

KEY TERMS

utility	total utility	real income
principle of diminishing marginal utility	consumer equilibrium	income effect
marginal utility	diamond-water paradox	
	substitution effect	

QUESTIONS FOR REVIEW AND DISCUSSION

1. What is meant by *utility*? How do you measure utility?

2. Define *marginal utility*.

3. What are the four basic assumptions about consumer preference?

4. Express consumer equilibrium algebraically in terms of marginal utility. Explain what your expression means in words.

5. "I love seafood so much that I could never get enough of it." Why would an economist disagree with this statement? Could there ever be a time when the person making this statement might actually receive negative utility from consuming more seafood? Give your answer in a graph and in words.

6. Explain the difference between substitution effects and income effects.

7. Oil is essential to the economic life of the nation. Our machines and homes cannot run without it. Yet a quart of oil is cheaper than a ticket to the Super Bowl. How can oil be so precious and yet so cheap? Resolve this oil–Super Bowl paradox.

8. Two economists are walking past the local Porsche dealer's showroom. One says, "I really want one of those Porsche 968s." The other says, "Obviously not." Who is right, and why?

9. In order to maximize total utility, the following must be true: $MU_X/P_X = MU_Y/P_Y = \ldots = MU_N/P_N$, where $X, Y, \ldots, N$ denote different goods and services consumed. Explain.

10. If Juan likes eclairs better than doughnuts, then for any given level of income, he will always purchase fewer doughnuts than eclairs. Do you agree or disagree? Explain.

11. Ocean cruises are becoming cheaper and more popular as vacation choices. The price of a cruise typically includes all food but not drinks (including colas but excluding water and tea) for the voyage. Analyze this practice from the standpoint of marginal utility.

PROBLEMS

1. Let the following table represent the total utility you receive from consuming chocolate chip cookies and glasses of milk. Calculate the marginal utilities.

Number of Cookies	Total Utility	Marginal Utility	Number of Glasses of Milk	Total Utility	Marginal Utility
1	14	——	1	10	——
2	26	——	2	18	——
3	36	——	3	24	——
4	44	——	4	28	——
5	48	——	5	28	——
6	48	——	6	27	——
7	44	——	7	24	——

2. Suppose you visit a friend's house whose family's policy is "all-you-can-eat-and-drink." According to the table, how many cookies and how many glasses of milk will you consume?

3. Suppose the price of cookies at a cookie shop in the mall is 25 cents each, and the price of milk is 50 cents per glass. Using your answers in problem 1, calculate the marginal utility per dollar to you at these prices.

Cookies	*MU*/$	Glasses	*MU*/$
1	——	1	——
2	——	2	——
3	——	3	——
4	——	4	——
5	——	5	——
6	——	6	——
7	——	7	——

4. If you only had $2.25 to spend, would you buy 4 cookies and 2 glasses of milk at the prices charged? Why or why not?

5. If you had $4, how many cookies and glasses of milk would you buy? If you had $7.25, how many of each would you buy?

WORKING WITH THE WEB

1. Suppose you love fine chocolates, especially Godiva chocolates. Go to the Godiva web site's chocolate guide at http://www.godiva.com/godiva/store/chocguide.asp and click the link for Truffles. After looking over the selection of truffles, you realize that ordering the 12 ounce deluxe assortment of truffles, which can be viewed with its description at http://www.godiva.com/godiva/store/product.asp?id=9, will give you 81 utils of satisfaction. This box of truffles has a price of $27. You are also considering buying some assortment of milk chocolates, and the 11 ounce All Milk Assortment box, described at http://www.godiva.com/godiva/store/product.asp?id=5, seems like it will satisfy your chocolate craving and will provide 48 utils of satisfaction. This box of chocolates is priced at $24.

Suppose you buy and consume a box of each selection of chocolates given the information above.
   a. Are you in equilibrium? If yes, how do you know? If not, why not and what should you do to move toward equilibrium?
   b. Why does your decision move you toward equilibrium?

2. Assume your uncle Bob has told you he will buy you a new car for your graduation present, so you decide to start shopping now. Return once again to www.autobytel.com and select the "research" link. Assume the car of your dreams is a Porsche 911. Select the "Porsche" link on the research page. The 1999 Cabriolet Convertible 2 door has a base MSRP of $74,460. Since this is the car of your dreams, let us assume that this car will allow you to achieve the highest level of satisfaction subject to your budget constraint. Now, let's assume you've told your uncle Bob what your choice in cars actually is; he tells you it is out of the question due to the high price tag and limits you to a car priced at $35,000 or less.

a. Graphically, what happens when your uncle Bob reduces your spending limit?

b. If you select an alternative automobile at the lower spending level, what does this suggest about your level of satisfaction subject to your budget constraint?

c. Are you in consumer equilibrium?

Indifference Curve Analysis[a]

APPENDIX

Suppose that we want to determine how a consumer feels about consuming various combinations of two goods, such as mystery and science fiction (SF) novels. One approach would be to ask the person how much utility she gets from consuming 4 mystery novels and 9 SF novels per year. She would perhaps answer, "50 utils." This would not be a very helpful answer because we do not know how much 50 utils represents to this person.

A second approach would be to observe how the individual chooses among various combinations of mysteries and SF books over a specified period of time, such as a year. We could then see, through her **revealed preferences**, how she ranks the various combinations. For example, does she prefer a combination of 4 mysteries and 9 SFs to a combination of 9 mysteries and 4 SFs? That is, when offered a choice of the two combinations, does she choose one over the other? Proceeding in this way, we are more likely to derive useful information about preferences. This type of approach yields the concept of an indifference curve.

INDIFFERENCE CURVES

Indifference curves are based on the concept of **indifference sets**. Indifference sets can be easily illustrated.

Suppose that four possible combinations of two goods confront an individual—say, four possible combinations of quantities per year of mystery and science fiction novels. Four combinations are given in Table 6.3. Assume that the consumer, through her revealed behavior, obtains the same total utility from consuming 10 mysteries and 3 SFs as she would from consuming 7 mystery novels and 5 science fiction novels, and so on through the table. Each combination is equivalent to the others in terms of the total utility yielded to the consumer. For example, if we compare combinations C and D, an additional mystery in

TABLE 6.3

Combinations of Novels Yielding Equal Total Utility
The data represent the consumer's observed behavior. The consumer derives as much satisfaction from consuming combination A, 10 mystery novels and 3 SF novels per year, as she does from consuming combination D, 4 mystery novels and 9 SF novels. The total utility of each combination, A, B, C, and D, is the same.

	NOVELS PER YEAR	
Combination	Mystery	Science Fiction
A	10	3
B	7	5
C	5	7
D	4	9

---

[a]We present indifference curve analysis in an appendix because it is not necessary to know the technique to understand any of the basic points about economics presented in this book. Indifference curve analysis is, however, an integral part of more advanced courses in economics, and many students who plan to do more work in economics will want to learn the technique.

combination *C* exactly makes up for the utility lost by consuming 2 fewer science fiction novels. The consumer reveals herself to be indifferent among these various combinations of the two goods; each combination yields the same level of total utility to her. An indifference set, then, is all combinations of the two goods among which the consumer is indifferent.

With this information about the individual's evaluation of the combinations, we can draw an indifference curve, as in Figure 6.4. Each point on the graph represents a combination of mystery and science fiction novels per year. The points representing combinations *A* through *D* are shown on the graph. These points and points in between them are joined by a smooth curve because they are members of an indifference set. The curve is the indifference curve, a curve made up of points that are all members of a particular indifference set. Any point on the indifference curve is equally preferred to any other by the consumer; all yield the same level of total utility.

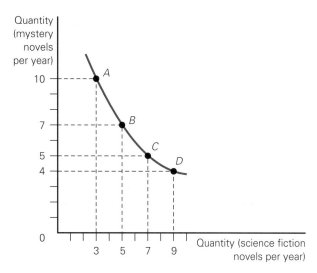

FIGURE 6.4

An Indifference Curve

This indifference curve is based on the data in Table 6.3. The curve shows the various combinations of mystery and science fiction novels among which the consumer is indifferent. The marginal rate of substitution of one good for the other is given by the slope of the indifference curve. The indifference curve is usually convex, which means that its slope decreases from left to right along the curve. The decreasing marginal rate of substitution is due to the principle of diminishing marginal utility.

CHARACTERISTICS OF INDIFFERENCE CURVES

Indifference curves have certain characteristics designed to show established regularities in the patterns of consumer preferences. Five of these characteristics are of interest to us.

1. Indifference curves slope downward from left to right. This negative slope is the only one possible if the principles of consumer choice are not to be violated. An upward-sloping curve would imply that the consumer was indifferent over the choice between a combination with less of both goods and another with more of both goods. The assumption that consumers always prefer more of a good to less requires that indifference curves slope downward from left to right.

2. The absolute value of the slope of the indifference curve at any point is equal to the ratio of the marginal utility of the good on the horizontal axis to the marginal utility of the good on the vertical axis. In Figure 6.4, the slope of the indifference curve between A and B is about −1.5, or simply 1.5 in absolute value. This absolute value tells us that in the area of combinations A and B, the marginal utility of SF novels is approximately one and one-half times that of mysteries. In this region, about 3 mysteries can be substituted for 2 SFs without lowering the consumer's total utility. For this reason, the slope of the indifference curve is called the **marginal rate of substitution**—in this case, substitution of science fiction for mystery novels. The marginal rate of substitution tells us the rate at which one good can be substituted for another without gain or loss in utility.

3. Indifference curves are drawn to be convex: The slope of an indifference curve decreases as one moves downward to the right along the curve. This convexity reflects diminishing marginal utility. As the quantity consumed of one of the goods increases, the marginal utility of that good declines. Hence, the ratio of the marginal utilities—the slope of the indifference curve—cannot be the same all along the curve. The slope must decrease as we move farther down and to the right because the quantity of science fiction novels consumed is increasing and their marginal utility is

therefore decreasing, whereas the quantity of mystery novels is decreasing and the marginal utility of mysteries is therefore increasing.

In Figure 6.4, the marginal rate of substitution of SFs for mysteries falls from 1.5 between points A and B to 0.5 between points C and D. As more science fiction novels are consumed, their marginal utility (measured by how many mystery novels the consumer is willing to give up per year in order to get an additional science fiction novel while remaining on the same indifference curve) falls. Fewer mysteries are consumed, and their marginal utility rises. Between A and B, the consumer is indifferent between 3 more mysteries and 2 less science fiction novels per year. Between C and D, fortified with more SFs, the consumer is indifferent between 1 additional mystery and 2 fewer SFs. With the consumption of more SFs, the marginal utility of mystery novels has risen and the marginal utility of science fiction novels has declined.

4. A point representing any assortment of consumption alternatives will always be on some indifference curve. Figure 6.5 presents a graph of combinations of bacon and eggs. We can select a point on the graph—such as A, representing 10 eggs and 1 bacon strip, or D, representing 9 bacon strips and 1 egg—and that point will have a corresponding indifference curve through it showing other bacon and egg combinations that generate the same level of total utility for the consumer. We can see from the graph that this particular consumer is indifferent among 10 eggs and 1 bacon strip (A), 5 eggs and 4 bacon strips (B), and 3 eggs and 8 bacon strips (C) per week.

Moreover, we know that the consumer will prefer any point on the ABC indifference curve, I_1, to any point on the FED indifference curve, I_2, because points on I_1 contain more of both goods than do points on I_2. The farther from the origin the indifference curve lies, the higher the level of utility the individual will experience.

We can draw as many indifference curves on the graph as there are indifference sets confronting the consumer. However many we draw—two or two hundred—the resulting graph is termed an **indifference map**.

5. Indifference curves never cross. The reason for this is **transitivity of preferences**, which simply

FIGURE 6.5

An Indifference Map

This consumer indifference map illustrates combinations of bacon and eggs. Any point on the graph will be associated with an indifference curve. Since a large number of indifference curves can be placed on the graph, it is called an indifference map. Indifference curves that are farther from the origin, such as I_1, represent higher levels of utility for the consumer because greater quantities of both goods are consumed.

means that if an individual prefers carrots to squash and squash to artichokes, he or she will also prefer carrots to artichokes. Indifference curves that cross would violate this assumption. Figure 6.6 illustrates this point.

In this graph two indifference curves do cross. The point where they cross (point A) lies on both indifference curves, I_1 and I_2. Since, by definition, all points along one indifference curve are equally preferred by the individual, the consumer will be indifferent among choices A, B, and C on I_1 and A, D, and E on I_2. This implies that the consumer is indifferent among all these points. But we see that this is impossible—if the consumer were indifferent between point B on I_1 and point D on I_2, this would mean that having more of both bacon and eggs (point B) made him or her no better off than having less of both (point D). Other things being equal, consumers always prefer more to less, so indifference curves cannot intersect

FIGURE 6.6

Indifference Curves Cannot Cross

Because preferences are transitive, point A cannot lie on two different indifference curves. If it did, the consumer would be indifferent among the combinations of bacon and eggs at point B with higher quantities of both, and point D with lower quantities of both.

without implying a type of irrationality that we do not observe in the real world.

THE BUDGET CONSTRAINT

Although we know that an individual consumer prefers a point on an indifference curve that is farther from the origin to a point on an indifference curve that is closer to the origin, this knowledge does not enable us to establish which indifference curve represents the best an individual can achieve with a limited budget. We can solve this problem by introducing a budget constraint, represented on the graph by a budget line.

In Figure 6.7a, we have assumed that the prices of two goods—apples and oranges—are the same: $1 per pound. If the consumer has a weekly budget of $10, the budget line will be a straight line running from the $10 level of apples (on the vertical axis) to the $10 level of oranges (on the horizontal axis). This line simply reflects the fact that the consumer can allocate his budget between apples and oranges in any way he sees

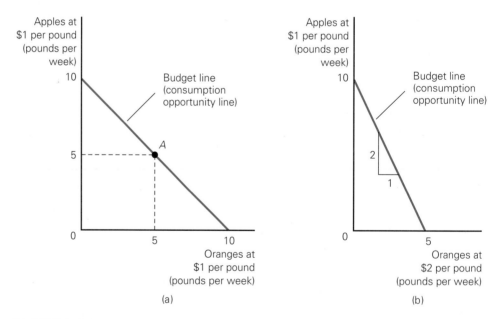

FIGURE 6.7

Budget Constraint

The budget line, or consumption opportunity line, depends on the relative prices of the two goods. The absolute value of the slope of the budget line is the ratio of the price of the good on the horizontal axis to the price of the good on the vertical axis. (a) The budget line represents all possible combinations of apples and oranges at $1 per pound each within a budget constraint of $10 per week. The absolute value of the slope of the line is 1. (b) The budget line, still with the budget constraint of $10 per week, has changed to reflect an increase in the price of oranges to $2 per pound. The absolute value of the slope of the line is 2.

fit—$10 on apples and zero on oranges, $10 on oranges and zero on apples, or any other combination that adds up to $10, such as point A: $5 for each.

How does a change in price affect the budget line? Figure 6.7b shows that the individual's budget remains the same ($10) but that the relative prices of the two goods have changed. While the price of apples remains at $1 a pound, the price of oranges has risen to $2 a pound. Although the consumer can still allocate his entire income to the purchase of either apples or oranges, $10 spent on apples would purchase 10 pounds of apples, while the same amount spent on oranges would yield only 5 pounds of oranges.

The budget line is thus drawn to reflect any combination of prices for the two goods. The absolute value of the slope of the budget line is equal to the ratio of the price of the good on the horizontal axis to the price of the good on the vertical axis. As illustrated in Figure 6.7b, where the price of oranges is $2 a pound and the price of apples $1 a pound, the absolute value of the slope is 2.

CONSUMER EQUILIBRIUM WITH INDIFFERENCE CURVES

The combination of an individual's indifference curves and budget line allows us to represent consumer equilibrium in a way that is equivalent to the method of marginal utility analysis. This alternative method is illustrated in Figure 6.8, which combines the budget line from Figure 6.7b with a set of indifference curves.

We can see that the consumer represented here will prefer point C to point F, because C lies on a higher indifference curve. She will also prefer point A to point C. All three of these points are actual opportunities confronting the consumer; she can afford them, given her budget constraint. Other things being equal, she would prefer point G to point A. However, point G is beyond the limit of her budget line. The best point she can achieve—the point on the highest indifference curve that can be reached within her budget constraint—is point A. This point represents consumer equilibrium—the combination yielding maximum utility from a given budget.

At A, the relevant indifference curve is exactly tangent to the budget line. This means that the slope of the budget line is equal to the slope of the indifference curve. We therefore know that in equilibrium the ratio of the marginal utility of the good on the horizontal axis (oranges) to the marginal utility of the good on the vertical axis (apples), indicated by the slope of the indifference curve, is equal to the ratio of the price of oranges to the price of apples, indicated by the slope of the budget line. Or, expressed somewhat differently,

$$\frac{\text{Marginal utility of oranges}}{\text{Marginal utility of apples}} = \frac{\text{Price of oranges}}{\text{Price of apples}}.$$

With terms rearranged, this formula is exactly the same result we arrived at earlier in the chapter when

FIGURE 6.8

Determining Consumer Equilibrium with Indifference Curves

The consumer attains maximum satisfaction at point A, where the budget, or consumption opportunity, line is tangent to the highest possible indifference curve. At A the slope of the indifference curve, or the ratio of the marginal utilities of the two goods, is equal to the slope of the budget line, or the ratio of the prices of the two goods. This relation reflects the same condition for consumer equilibrium as that suggested by marginal utility analysis.

FIGURE 6.9

Indifference Curves and the Law of Demand

As the price of oranges falls from $2 a pound to $1 a pound, the budget line rotates to the right from B_1 to B_2. The consumer reaches a higher level of utility by attaining the highest indifference curve, I_2 rather than I_1, possible. As the price of oranges falls, the consumer purchases a larger quantity; O_2 is larger than O_1. This is precisely what the law of demand predicts—that, other things being equal, quantity demanded varies inversely with price.

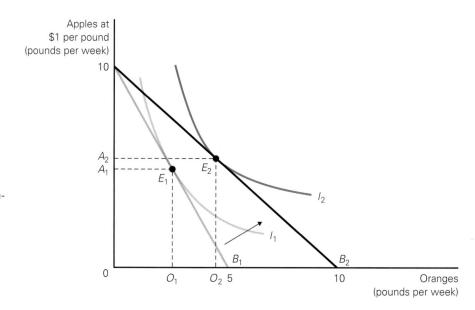

we discussed consumer equilibrium in marginal utility terms without the aid of indifference curves; that is, the preceding equation is equivalent to

$$\frac{\text{Marginal utility of oranges}}{\text{Price of oranges}} = \frac{\text{Marginal utility of apples}}{\text{Price of apples}}.$$

The two approaches thus yield the same predictions about consumer behavior.

INDIFFERENCE CURVES AND THE LAW OF DEMAND

Indifference curve analysis also can be used to demonstrate the law of demand. A demand curve can be derived by first allowing the price of a good to change, then finding the new equilibrium quantity of the good, and, finally, graphing the new and old price/equilibrium quantity combinations. Figures 6.9 and 6.10 together show how this is accomplished. Budget line B_1 is drawn by assuming that the price of oranges is $2 per pound and the price of apples is $1 per pound. Given these prices, and the consumer's income, the equilibrium quantity of oranges and apples for this consumer is shown as E_1 in Figure 6.8. Point E_1 is where indifference curve I_1 is tangent to budget line B_1. The consumer buys quantity O_1 of oranges per week when the price of oranges is $2 per pound.

If we allow the price of oranges to fall from $2 per pound to $1 per pound, the budget line rotates outward to line B_2. Indifference curve I_2, which is tangent to the new budget line at point E_2, lies farther from the origin than indifference curve I_1. This indicates that the lower price of one good leads to an increase in total utility. As Figure 6.9 shows, the lower price of oranges results in a larger quantity of oranges purchased, O_2.

By taking some of the information from Figure 6.9 and transferring it to Figure 6.10, the consumer's demand curve for oranges can be plotted. Figure 6.10 shows that at a price of oranges equal to $2 per pound, the consumer will purchase quantity O_1 of oranges per week. This information has come from the beginning situation in Figure 6.9, where the initial price of oranges was $2 per pound, the budget line was B_1, and the equilibrium quantity of apples and oranges consumed was E_1.

Figure 6.9 also shows that when oranges are priced at $1 per pound, the consumer will buy quantity O_2 of oranges per week. This information came from budget line B_2, where the price of oranges is $1 per pound and equilibrium quantity is E_2. The smooth line connecting the two points in Figure 6.10, labeled D_{oranges}, is the consumer's demand curve for oranges. It is downward sloping, indicating that the lower the price of oranges, other things being equal, the larger will be the amount of oranges purchased per week. The consumer equilibrium obtained through

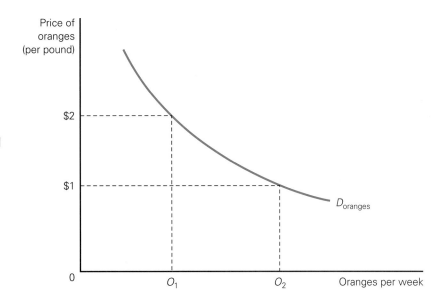

FIGURE 6.10

The Demand Curve for Oranges

The consumer's equilibrium quantity of oranges consumed increases from O_1 to O_2 if the price of oranges falls from \$2 to \$1 per pound. The demand curve for oranges is downward sloping.

indifference curve analysis thus yields the type of demand curve predicted by the law of demand.

SUBSTITUTION AND INCOME EFFECTS

This chapter discussed the two reasons that consumers buy more of a good when its price falls, or that demand curves are downward sloping. When a good's price falls, the good becomes relatively less expensive in comparison with other goods. Other goods become relatively more expensive when this happens. As a result, consumers tend to substitute relatively less expensive goods for relatively more expensive goods in their purchases. This is what we referred to as the substitution effect.

However, when the price of only one good falls, the total buying power of the consumer's budget increases. This rise in what economists call real income induces the consumer to buy more of any given good. The increase in consumption of a good due to the consumer's increased buying power (which, in turn, is due to a drop in some good's price) was called the income effect.

The substitution and income effects of a change in the price of oranges can be depicted graphically by using a graph similar to Figure 6.9. Parts of Figure 6.9 have been reproduced in Figure 6.11. Combination

E_1 on indifference curve I_1 is the initial combination of apples and oranges consumed when apples are \$1 per pound and oranges are \$2 per pound. Combination E_2 and budget line B_2 are also the same in both figures. Figure 6.11 ignores the effects on apple consumption in order to concentrate on the two effects on orange consumption.

Both Figures 6.9 and 6.11 show that when the price of oranges falls from \$2 to \$1 per pound, the equilibrium quantity of oranges consumed rises from O_1 to O_2. However, Figure 6.11 shows how much of this increased orange consumption is due to the substitution effect (the amount O_S minus O_1) and how much to the income effect (O_2 minus O_S). To see why these amounts are the substitution and income effects, we need to apply the formula for consumer equilibrium.

Consider point E_1 in both Figures 6.9 and 6.11. Combination E_1 is the initial amounts of the goods consumed. For this to be a point of consumer equilibrium, we know that

$$\frac{\text{Marginal utility of oranges}}{\text{Marginal utility of apples}} = \frac{\$2}{\$1} = \frac{\text{Price of oranges}}{\text{Price of apples}}.$$

At point E_1 in each figure, the ratio of the marginal utilities, given by the slope of I_1 at point E_1, equals the ratio of prices, given by the slope of the budget line. The substitution effect conceptually measures by how

FIGURE 6.11

Substitution and Income Effects

When the price of oranges is $2 per pound, O_1 pounds of oranges are consumed per week. When the price of oranges falls to $1 per pound, two things happen. The consumer substitutes oranges for apples because oranges have become relatively cheaper. Orange consumption changes from O_1 to O_S due to the substitution effect. The buying power of the fixed budget also rises. Orange consumption rises from O_S to O_2 due to the income effect.

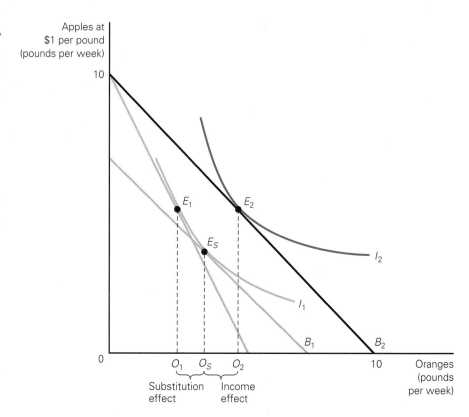

much consumption of a good would change if the consumer's real income remained unchanged when a price changes. This is accomplished by finding a combination of goods on the *original indifference curve I_1* that would be chosen by the consumer if the ratio of the prices were $1/$1 instead of $2/$1. This combination of goods, E_S in Figure 6.11, yields the consumer the same level of total utility as does combination E_1. Keeping total utility constant is the economist's way of hypothetically preventing a change in real income when a price changes. At combination E_S in Figure 6.11, the ratio of the marginal utilities (the slope of the indifference curve) is equal to the new price ratio, $1/$1. Conceptually holding real income, or total utility, constant, this consumer would buy amount O_S pounds of oranges if the price of oranges were to fall to $1 per pound. The substitution effect of a drop in the price of oranges is then measured as O_S minus O_1 pounds of oranges.

We know, however, that when one price decreases, the buying power of the consumer's budget increases. Figures 6.9 and 6.11 both show the consumer buying combination E_2 (O_2 pounds of oranges) after all is said and done. Both figures also indicate that the consumer's total utility has increased as a result of the

price decrease. This increased total utility results from the increased buying power of the budget, which in turn is caused by the price decrease. The change in orange consumption per week due to the budget's larger buying power is measured as O_2 minus O_S pounds of oranges in Figure 6.11. This is the income effect of the decrease in the price of oranges. It is that part of the increased consumption of oranges that is not explained by the substitution effect.

The sum of the substitution effect (O_S minus O_1) and the income effect (O_2 minus O_S) equals the total effect (O_2 minus O_1) on orange consumption of a fall in the price of oranges. This is so because the single price change affects the consumer's environment in two ways. It alters the relative price of one good compared to another. This induces the consumer to substitute one good for another in consumption—the substitution effect. It also changes the budget's purchasing power, allowing the consumer to buy more (in the case of a price decrease) of the good and thus increasing the consumer's total utility. While we could never actually see these two effects separately (we can only observe the total effect in the real world), they nonetheless exist and are important in explaining consumer behavior.

SUMMARY

1. The method of indifference curves is an alternative way to study the process of individual choice and consumer equilibrium. It is based on the idea of observing how an individual chooses among consumption alternatives.

2. An indifference set is a group of consumption alternatives that yield the same total utility to the consumer.

3. An indifference curve is a graphical representation of an indifference set. Each point on the curve represents the same total utility to the consumer.

4. Indifference curves have negative slopes, are convex, and do not intersect.

5. The slope of an indifference curve is called the marginal rate of substitution of one good for another.

6. There is an indifference curve associated with any combination of goods selected by the consumer. An indifference map consists of a set of possible indifference curves of the consumer.

7. The budget line shows the relative prices of the goods an individual consumes and the amounts of the goods that he or she can consume without spending beyond the budget constraint.

8. In the indifference curve approach, consumer equilibrium occurs at the point where the consumer's budget line is tangent to the highest possible indifference curve. This condition is the same as that derived for consumer equilibrium using marginal utility analysis—namely, $MU_x/P_x = MU_Y/P_Y$.

9. The indifference curve technique can be used to show that the quantity consumed of a good is inversely related to its price—in other words, the law of demand.

10. In terms of indifference curves, the substitution effect shows how a change in a good's relative price affects consumption of the good. The income effect shows the impact on consumption of a change in the consumer's real purchasing power.

KEY TERMS

revealed preference
indifference map
indifference set

transitivity of preferences
indifference curve
budget constraint

marginal rate of
substitution

QUESTIONS FOR REVIEW AND DISCUSSION

1. Explain why indifference curves cannot intersect.

2. What is the relation between the principle of diminishing marginal utility and the marginal rate of substitution?

3. Suppose that the consumer feels that each combination of X and Y in the following table yields the same total utility. What comment would you make about the individual's choice process?

GOODS		
Combinations	X	Y
A	10	7
B	15	8
C	20	9
D	25	10
E	30	11

4. What are the characteristics of indifference curves? What is the rationale for each characteristic? What would be the consequences of violating each of these characteristics?

5. How does the indifference curve approach show that consumer demand curves are negatively sloped? Explain.

6. Suppose that the price of oranges increases rather than decreases in Figure 6.10. Using indifference curve analysis, show the income and substitution effects of this price increase.

PROBLEM

Figure 6.12 shows three hypothetical indifference curves for Jill. Points A, B, C, and D represent different combinations of compact discs and movies.

1. Which combination represents the lowest level of satisfaction for Jill?

2. Which combination represents the highest level?

3. Is Jill indifferent about any of the combinations? If so, which combinations?

FIGURE 6.12

The Firm
and Costs
of Production

All profit-oriented business firms are alike in one basic sense: Firms purchase inputs in resource markets and use these inputs to produce a product or service, which is then sold to consumers. The fact that inputs to a production process are not free—that they carry an opportunity cost—leads to the concept of production costs.

In this chapter we develop the concept of production costs from the perspective of the economist. When you complete Chapter 7 you should understand

- The nature of product in a firm.
- How production costs are actually a form of opportunity costs.
- How an accountant's out-of-pocket costs may sometimes differ from an economist's measure of opportunity cost.
- How costs of production influence a firm's behavior.
- How the various types of costs relate to both business decision making and to the function of the market.

THE NATURE OF THE FIRM

We are now at the point in our study of microeconomics where the concept of the business **firm** comes into play. We will discuss the cost curves of a firm, and we will discuss competitive firms and monopoly firms. Before we do so, however, we briefly present an economic depiction of a firm.

Firm
An economic institution that purchases, organizes, and assembles resources to produce goods and services.

Firms occupy a critical role in a market economy. In fact, there are over 17 million business firms in the United States, ranging in size from the small corner grocery store owned by one individual to the immense multinational corporations owned by millions of stockholders.

In broad terms, the economic function of a business firm is to combine scarce resources (factors of production) to produce goods and services demanded by consumers. Firms that perform this function well make profits and survive; firms that perform this function poorly experience losses and fail. This brief definition of a firm, however, touches only the surface of the matter. To understand the role of firms in a market economy, we need to explore how a firm organizes resources.

HOW MARKETS AND FIRMS COORDINATE RESOURCES

Market coordination
The process that directs the flow of resources into the production of goods and services through the price signaling mechanism.

Basically, there are two methods of economic coordination in a market economy: market coordination and firm coordination. **Market coordination** is what we have studied so far in this book. It is the use of the price system to provide incentives to suppliers and demanders, to produce and consume goods and services in the appropriate amounts. Market coordination refers to the myriad daily economic activities that are guided by the "invisible hand" of the market. Our study of demand and supply is the study of how the market coordinates activities.

Not all activities in a modern economy are coordinated by the market, however. Part of the division of labor is carried out within firms. Automobile assembly-line workers do not sell their output directly in a market. Rather, they supply labor to the auto company, which employs managers to direct and coordinate the uses of their labor within the firm. **Firm coordination** is a productive process that depends on managerial rather than market direction.

Firm coordination
The process that directs the flow of resources into the production of a particular good or service through the forces of management organization within the firm.

Manager
An individual who organizes and monitors resources within a firm to produce a good or service.

The distinction between market and firm coordination is not absolute. Resource allocation within the firm is not really outside the price system, although it might superficially look that way. Decision making in the firm is centralized and performed by **managers**. Managers transfer and allocate resources within the firm in ways that are efficient given the prices for equivalent resources on the market. The manager's decision to transfer a quantity of a particular resource within the firm is based on prices, even though resources are not actually bought and sold within the firm.

If market and firm coordination are so similar, what accounts for the existence of firms? In actuality, much production is undertaken by independent individuals, and it is common for individual demanders to contract with individual suppliers for particular goods and services. For example, Saks Fifth Avenue, Tiffany's, and Neiman-Marcus contract with individual artists and artisans for many of their wares. Many publishers hire work out to freelance editors and artists rather than having all editorial services performed by in-house staff. It is often cheaper or more efficient to do so. Economic coordination between contracting individuals in such cases is achieved directly through the operation of the price system. So an interesting question arises: Why is all production not undertaken by freelance individual operators? In other words, why will an owner of capital goods hire employees for long periods of time instead of contracting out for the performance of specific tasks as they arise?

Ronald H. Coase was the first economist to pose and answer this important question. His answer was simple and profound: Firms exist when they are the least costly form of economic coordination; their size is determined by what is most efficient (least costly) for production.[1] (Coase won the Nobel Prize in economics in 1991, partly for his work on the theory of the firm.) We do not use the market to organize all production because it is not costless to use markets. Using the market necessitates finding out what prices are, negotiating and enforcing contractual agreements with suppliers, going to court when promises are not kept, paying transaction costs, and engaging in various other costly and resource-using activities. For these reasons, not all production in a market economy is coordinated through market exchange. It costs less in many cases to organize production in a firm where resource allocation is directed and coordinated by managers.

In firm production, the inside of the firm will be run by managerial coordination; the firm will deal with the outside world through market coordination. Which activities the firm chooses to organize internally will be related to the cost of organizing the same activities through market exchange. Automobile manufacturers can buy tires in a contractual arrangement with tire companies, or they can make their own tires. The relative costs of these alternatives will determine how the auto company gets its tires.

Firms exist in a market economy because they represent a least-cost means of organizing production. However, firms will not grow without limit, because at some point the marginal cost of organizing a task within the firm will exceed the marginal cost of organizing the same task through market contracting. This limit on firm size will evolve naturally because the managerial cost of organizing and keeping track of inside production rises along with the number of tasks the firm undertakes. There will be a natural division of production in an economy between firms and markets, determined by the relative costs of producing goods and services in each way. Limits on firm size have created a variety of types of business in our economy. The three Focus boxes within this chapter provide discussion of the principal kinds of firms that have emerged, from the most popular type, the single proprietorship (see the Focus "Going Into Business for Yourself" on p. 170), to the partnership ("Going Into Business With Others" on p. 178) to the type of organization that supports the very largest firms in our economy ("Big Business—The Corporation" on p. 185).

COSTS IN A BUSINESS FIRM

Consumers have unlimited wants, but resources to satisfy their wants are limited. Costs of production in a firm arise from the fact that resources have alternative uses. The same resources that are used to produce a good to satisfy consumers' demands can also be used to produce other goods. For resources to be drawn into the production of a particular good, they must be bid away from other uses. Production of a newspaper might require, among other things, that wood pulp be turned into newsprint rather than notebook paper, that photographers be enticed to work as photojournalists rather than as portrait photographers, and that youngsters be hired to distribute newspapers rather than earn money by babysitting or mowing lawns. The expenditures representing the opportunity costs necessary to do all of these things are called **opportunity costs of production**. Costs of production are therefore the value of resources in their next-best uses.

Opportunity costs of production
The opportunity costs of resources used to produce goods and services.

---

[1]Ronald H. Coase, "The Nature of the Firm," *Economics* (November 1937), pp. 386–405.

FOCUS

Going into Business for Yourself

Most people dream of going into business at one time or another in their lives. Hundreds of thousands of individuals go into (and out of) business every year. That form of business organization is called a proprietorship. A proprietorship is a firm that has a single owner who is liable—or legally responsible—for all the debts of the firm—a condition termed unlimited liability. The sole proprietor has unlimited liability in the legal sense that if the firm goes bankrupt, the proprietor's personal as well as business property can be used to settle the firm's outstanding debts.

More often than not, the sole proprietor also works in the firm as a manager and a laborer. Thus, most single-owner firms are small. Many small retail establishments, such as restaurants and men's clothing, dress, or antique shops, are organized as proprietorships.

The primary advantage of the proprietorship is that it allows the small businessperson to have direct control of the firm and its activities. It is up to the sole proprietor to decide how much effort to

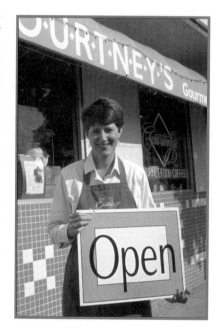

expend in producing output. In other words, the sole proprietor can be his or her own boss.

The primary disadvantage of the proprietorship is that the welfare of the firm and the liabiltiy for its activities largely rests on one person. The typical sole proprietor is the chief stockholder, chief executive officer, and chief cook and bottle washer for the firm. Since there are only twenty-four hours in a day, the sole proprietor faces problems in attending to the many different aspects of the business. Some say that the happiest two days in your life are the day you go into business "for yourself" and the day you get out!

Nevertheless, proprietorships are the dominant form of business organization in the American economy. They accounted for more than 75 percent of all businesses in 1998, but generated only 7 percent or so in revenues. But individual inventiveness sometimes pays off, and dreams of success do come true. It seems safe to conclude that this form of business enterprise will continue to be popular in the twenty-first century.

Explicit and Implicit Costs

Accounting costs
Payments a firm actually makes to resource suppliers; out-of-pocket costs or explicit costs.

Implicit costs
The opportunity costs of resources used in production for which no explicit payments are made.

The opportunity costs of production include both explicit and implicit costs. Take, for example, a small, owner-operated dry cleaning firm organized as a sole proprietorship. The dry cleaner has to purchase labor, cleaning fluids, hat blocks, bagging machines, insurance, accounting and legal services, advertising, and so on to produce dry cleaning services. The costs of these resources are called **accounting costs**, or explicit costs. They are so named because they are quite visible; they are the wages and bills the sole proprietor must pay to conduct business.

The firm does not make explicit payments for all the resources it uses to produce dry cleaning services. The owner of the firm may not include a wage for his own services. Omitting his salary from calculations, however, does not mean that the owner's services are free. They carry an **implicit cost**, valued by what the owner could have done with his time instead of working in the firm. Implicit costs are the opportunity costs of resources owned by the firm. They are called *implicit costs* because they do not involve contractual payments.

Opportunity cost of capital

The return that could be received from the next-best alternative investment.

The main implicit cost is the **opportunity cost of capital**. Individuals who invest in firms expect to earn a normal rate of return on their investment. For instance, they could have placed their capital in money market certificates and earned perhaps a 6 percent rate of return. In this case, the 6 percent rate of return represents the opportunity cost of capital invested in business ventures. Unless investors earn at least the opportunity cost of capital, they will not continue to invest in a business.

Total cost of production

The total opportunity cost of all resources used in production; the sum of all explicit and implicit production costs.

The **total cost of production** is the sum of explicit and implicit costs. Total cost is the value of all the alternative opportunities forgone as a result of production of a particular good or service.

The Nature of Economic Costs

Opportunity cost is a forward-looking concept. Opportunity costs are incurred when the decision maker decides about the future use of resources; they are the expected costs of possible alternatives available to an owner.

Historical costs

Costs measured by the cost of a resource at the time the resource was purchased.

Sunk costs

Previously incurred, irretrievable costs of a currently owned resource.

In contrast, accounting costs are **historical costs**, or costs that have been incurred in the past. While historical costs can be useful in estimating economic costs, historical costs look backward; opportunity costs look forward. Historical costs are poor guides to opportunity costs. Consider the case of **sunk costs**, which are closely related to historical costs. Current sunk costs are the difference between the initial cost—which exists prior to a commitment to a given investment or project—and the value that can be recovered after commitment to the given investment or project. Sunk costs are the irretrievable part of any fixed or historical investment.

For better or worse, certain portions of earlier decisions cannot be reversed. Economists consider certain of the costs of previous decisions—the sunk costs—to be irrelevant to current decisions. Suppose that you buy a farm in Vermont for $300,000 and spend an additional $200,000 refurbishing the old farmhouse, which you plan to operate as a bed and breakfast. After a year you realize that your location prevents you from profitably remaining in business. If you decide to sell, should your asking price be dictated by your having spent $500,000 on the property?

The answer is no. A portion of the $500,000 in costs you have already incurred is a sunk cost. Some of the alterations you made may have no value if the property is to be put to a use other than serving as a bed and breakfast—in fact, some changes may actually reduce the property's value for other uses. You must realize that some of your costs cannot be recaptured. Some of the money you invested is gone forever. It may be that we have to learn this the hard way—from experience. However, viewed rationally, current decisions should be based on current or expected costs and benefits of future actions, not on sunk costs and past benefits.

The general irrelevance of sunk costs is critically important for many economic decisions—some of them personal decisions. Indeed, the old adage "never cry over spilt milk" has a firm foundation in economic logic. A college athlete may skip her senior year to turn professional. Three years of studying, attending class, and other costs should be ignored when deciding whether to choose the degree or a million-dollar salary. Opportunity costs of all kinds affect our lives. Government policies, such as the draft, serving on juries, or being required to provide "public service," often have a direct effect on individuals' opportunity costs. (See the Application at the end of this chapter, "The Draft, Jury Duty, and Conscripted 'Public Service': Opportunity Cost and You" for a discussion of how these policies might affect you.)

Economic Profits Versus Accounting Profits

Economic profit

The amount by which total revenues exceed total opportunity cost.

Businesspeople must compare their total costs with their total revenues (all the money they take in) to determine whether they are making a profit. **Economic profit** is the difference between total revenue and total opportunity cost. It exists when the revenue of the firm more than covers all of its costs, explicit and implicit. Economic loss results when revenue does not cover the total opportunity cost. A firm's economic profit is said to be zero when its total revenue equals its total cost. Zero economic profit does not mean that the firm is not viable or about to cease operating. It means that the firm is covering all the costs of its operations and that the owners and investors are making a normal rate of return on their investment.

Accounting profit

The amount by which total revenues exceed total accounting, or explicit, costs.

Since accounting costs do not usually include implicit costs—such as the value of the sole proprietor's time or the opportunity cost of capital invested in the firm— accounting costs are an understatement of the opportunity costs of production. **Accounting profits** will generally be higher than economic profits because economic profits are calculated after taking both explicit and implicit costs into account.

Private Costs and Social Costs

Private costs

The opportunity costs of production that are borne, or paid, by producers.

We have so far discussed a world of **private costs**, in which the firm pays a market price for the resources it uses in production. The dry cleaner's costs of production were private costs, equal to the sum of explicit and implicit costs. The key aspect of the concept of private costs is that someone is responsible for them; that is, someone pays for the use of the resources. The owner of the dry cleaning firm incurs both explicit and implicit costs in business, and he incurred these costs to engage in business.

But what if the dry cleaner dumps used cleaning fluid into the town lake adjacent to his plant? In doing so, he is using the lake as a resource in his dry cleaning business—as a place to dispose of a by-product of his production process—but he pays nothing for the use of the lake as a dumping site. No one owns the lake for purposes of dumping, and it is therefore unpriced for this use. The private costs of the dry cleaner thus do not reflect the full costs of his operation. The cost of the use of the lake is not reflected in the dry cleaner's costs of production. Such a cost is called an **external cost** because the cost is borne by someone other than the owner of the firm.

External costs

The opportunity costs of production that are not borne, or paid, by producers.

Social costs

The opportunity costs of all resources used in the production of goods and services; the sum of private and external costs.

When external costs arise from a firm's activities—such as polluting the air or water—the private costs of the firm are lower than its **social costs**. The total cost to society of the firm's production includes the firm's input costs and the costs of using common property or other resources not owned by the firm, such as the town lake.

In Chapter 17 we further analyze external costs, including ways in which society can make public choices about problems arising from external costs. The important point here is that private costs of production do not always reflect the full opportunity costs of production; the use of unpriced resources, such as the environment, may also carry a hidden cost to society.

ECONOMIC TIME

Variable input
A factor of production whose level of usage may be changed in the short run.

Fixed input
A factor of production whose level of usage cannot be changed in the short run.

Short run
An amount of time insufficient to allow the usage of all inputs to vary.

Long run
An amount of time sufficiently long that all input usage levels can be varied.

The passage of time is fundamental to the theory of costs. Economic time is not the same thing as calendar time. To the economist analyzing costs, the firm's time constraints are defined by its ability to adjust its operations in light of a changing marketplace. If the demand for the firm's product decreases, for example, the firm must adjust production to the lower level of demand. Perhaps some of its resources can be immediately and easily varied to adapt to the changed circumstances. In the face of declining or increasing sales, an automobile firm can reduce or increase its orders of steel and fabric. Inputs whose purchase and use can be altered quickly are called **variable inputs**. The auto firm with declining sales cannot immediately sell its excess plants and equipment or its inventory. Such resources are called **fixed inputs**; a reduction or increase in their use takes considerably more time to arrange.

There are two primary categories of economic time: the short run and the long run. The **short run** is a period in which some inputs remain fixed. In the long run, all inputs can be varied. In the **long run**, the auto firm can make fewer cars not only by buying less steel but also by reducing the number of plants and the amount of equipment and labor it uses for car production. The time it takes to vary all inputs is different for different industries. In some cases, it may take only a month, in others a year, and in still others ten years.

SHORT-RUN COSTS: AN INTRODUCTION

In the short run, some of the firm's inputs are fixed and others are variable. Building on this distinction, the short-run theory of costs emphasizes two categories of costs—fixed and variable.

Fixed Costs and Variable Costs

Fixed costs
The costs of inputs that cannot be varied in the short run.

A **fixed cost** does not change as the firm's output level changes. Whether the firm produces more or less, it will pay the same for such things as fire insurance, local property taxes, and other costs that are independent of its output level. Fixed costs exist even at a zero rate of output. Perhaps the most important fixed cost is the opportunity cost of the firm's capital equipment and plant—that is, the next-best alternative use of these resources. This cost exists even when the plant is not operating. The only way to avoid fixed costs is to shut down and go out of business, an event that can occur only in the long run. Total fixed costs (TFC) equal the price of fixed inputs multiplied by the quantity of fixed inputs employed.

Variable costs
The costs of inputs whose usage levels can be changed in the short run. Variable costs change as output changes.

Variable costs are costs that change as the output level of a firm changes. When the firm reduces its level of production, it will use fewer raw materials and perhaps will lay off workers. Consequently, its variable costs of production will decline. Variable costs are expenditures on inputs that can be varied in short-run use. Total variable costs (TVC) equal the price of variable inputs multiplied by the quantity of variable inputs employed. **Total cost** (TC) is the sum of total fixed and total variable costs.

Total costs
All the costs of a firm's operations; total variable costs plus total fixed costs.

It is useful to determine how the cost of producing output changes in the short run as the level of output is increased or decreased. The fixed cost per unit is called **average fixed cost** (AFC) and is found by dividing the total fixed cost (TFC) by

Average fixed cost
Total fixed costs divided by the level of output.

TABLE 7.1

Short-Run Cost Relations

Terms	Symbols	Definition
Average fixed cost = Total fixed cost ÷ Output	$AFC = TFC/q$	A fixed cost does not vary with output. Average fixed cost per unit declines as output rises.
Average variable cost = Total variable cost ÷ Output	$AVC = TVC/q$	Average variable cost exhibits a U-shaped pattern as output increases.
Average total cost = Total cost ÷ Output = Average fixed cost + Average variable cost	$ATC = TC/q$ $ATC = AFC + AVC$	Total cost is the sum of fixed and variable costs. Average total cost also forms a U-shaped curve when graphed from very low to very high output levels.
Marginal cost = Change in total cost ÷ Change in output	$MC = \Delta TC/\Delta q$	Marginal cost first falls and then rises as the short-run capacity of a firm's fixed plant is approached.

the firm's total output of the good (referred to as q throughout this chapter). Since total fixed costs are the same at all levels of output, AFC will decline continuously as output increases. This relation is defined in Table 7.1 and shown graphically in Figure 7.1a. Symbolically, average fixed cost is expressed

$$AFC = \frac{TFC}{q}.$$

Average variable cost
Total variable costs divided by the level of output.

Average variable cost *(AVC)* is found by dividing total variable cost *(TVC)* by the firm's output. It is also drawn in Figure 7.1a and defined in Table 7.1. Average variable cost ordinarily has a U shape and may be expressed in the formula

$$AVC = \frac{TVC}{q}.$$

Average total cost
Total costs divided by the level of output.

Average total cost *(ATC)* is total cost divided by total output. Average total cost also can be found by adding average fixed costs and average variable costs. Thus, in Figure 7.1a, the ATC curve is shown as the vertical sum of the AFC and AVC curves. Average total cost is sometimes referred to as unit cost, and it is total cost (fixed plus variable) divided by the firm's output:

$$ATC = \frac{TC}{q}.$$

Although the average total cost curve provides useful information, economic decisions are made at the margin. In considering a change in the level of production, firms must determine the marginal cost of the change.

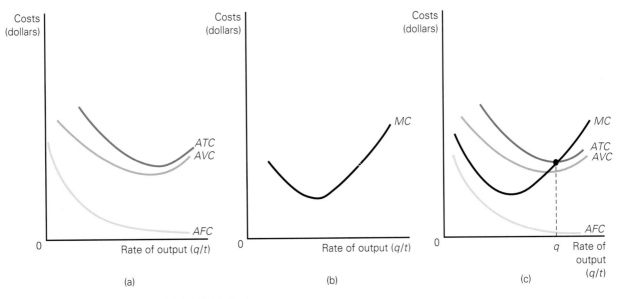

FIGURE 7.1

Short-Run Cost Curves of the Firm

(a) The behavior of average fixed cost *(AFC)*, average variable cost *(AVC)*, and average total cost *(ATC)* as output changes. *ATC* is the vertical sum of *AVC* and *AFC*. (b) The behavior of the firm's marginal costs *(MC)* as output increases. *MC* ultimately rises as the short-run capacity limit of the firm is approached. (c) All the short-run cost curves. Notice in particular the U shape of the *ATC* curve. *ATC* is high where the firm's plant is underutilized at low rates of output or overutilized at high rates of output. The rate of output is measured per unit of time.

Marginal cost

The additional cost of producing one more unit of output; the change in total cost divided by the change in output.

Marginal cost *(MC)* is the cost of producing each additional unit of output; it is found by dividing the change in total cost by the change in output. Symbolically, marginal cost may be expressed

$$MC = \frac{\Delta TC}{\Delta q}.$$

The result of such calculations is a marginal cost curve, shown in Figure 7.1b. As output rises, marginal cost declines, reaches a minimum, then rises—because it becomes increasingly hard to produce additional output in a **fixed plant**. Extra workers needed to produce additional output begin to get in each other's way; inefficiencies proliferate as workers must take turns using machines; storage room becomes filled; and so on.

Fixed plant

A given amount of equipment and size of production facilities with which the firm can use variable inputs in the short run.

Figure 7.1c brings all the short-run cost curves together. Notice that the *ATC* curve is U-shaped. At low levels of output a firm does not utilize its fixed plant and equipment very effectively. The firm does not produce enough relative to the fixed costs for its plant, causing the average total cost to be high. At high levels of output the inefficiencies of overloading the existing operation cause marginal costs to rise, raising the average total cost. These two effects combine to yield a U-shaped average total cost curve. Either low or high utilization of a fixed plant leads to high average total cost. The minimum point on the *ATC* curve, *q*, represents the lowest average total cost—the lowest cost per unit for producing the good. The *MC* curve crosses both the *AVC* and the *ATC* at their minimum. Table 7.1 provides a shorthand reference to all these concepts. We will return to these concepts below and explain them in more detail.

Diminishing Returns

Law of diminishing marginal returns

A situation in which adding more and more of a variable input to a fixed plant results in smaller and smaller amounts of additional output produced.

The behavior and shape of the short-run marginal cost and average total cost curves can be understood more completely with the **law of diminishing marginal returns**. The law of diminishing marginal returns states that as additional units of a variable input are combined with a fixed amount of other resources, the amount of additional output produced will start to decline beyond some point. The returns—additional output—that result from using more and more of the variable input will ultimately diminish.

Though the language sounds formidable, the law of diminishing marginal returns is little more than formalized common sense. Suppose that the dry cleaner in our previous example has a plant of a given size that we will view as his fixed input. He begins operations by adding workers one at a time and observes what happens to the resulting output of dry cleaning. The first few additional workers are very useful. One specializes in cleaning, another in pressing, another in bagging, and so on. The output of dry cleaning increases as the laborers are added. But the process cannot go on forever. At some point the output provided by one additional laborer will begin to diminish because capacity of the existing physical plant will be reached.

The law of diminishing marginal returns is a fact of nature. Imagine how the world would work if it were not true: All of the world's dry cleaning could be done in a single plant. And if diminishing returns did not exist in agriculture, all of the world's food could be grown on a fixed plot of land, say an acre.

The law of diminishing marginal returns can be illustrated numerically and graphically. A standard example comes from agriculture; we experiment by adding laborers to a fixed plot of land and observe what happens to output. To isolate the effect of adding additional workers (the variable input), we keep all inputs except labor fixed and assume that agricultural technology does not change.

Table 7.2 is a numerical analysis of the results of such an experiment. The first column shows the amount of the variable input—labor—that is used in combination with the fixed input—land. The simplified numbers for **total product** and **marginal product** represent real measures of output, such as tons of soybeans grown per year.

Total product

The total amount of output produced.

Marginal product

The additional output produced by employing one additional unit of a variable input.

Marginal product is the change in total product caused by the addition of each additional worker, or

$$MP = \frac{\text{change in output}}{\text{change in quantity of variable input}}.$$

At first, as workers (the variable input) are added, total product, or output, expands rapidly. The first three workers show increasing marginal products (10, 12, and 14 extra tons of soybeans with the addition of each worker). Diminishing marginal returns set in, however, with the addition of the fourth worker. That is, the marginal product of the fourth worker is 13 tons, down from the 14-ton marginal prod-

TABLE 7.2

Law of Diminishing Marginal Returns

If units of a variable input (labor) are added one at a time to a production process with a fixed plant (growing soybeans with no change in technology on a fixed plot of land), the total product, marginal product, and average product all increase at first. But as more workers are added, they begin to get in each other's way. Total output gained by adding more workers begins to decline, as predicted by the law of diminishing marginal returns.

Variable Input (units of labor)	Total Product (tons per year)	Marginal Product (tons per year)	Average Product (tons per year)
0	0		0
		} ·············· 10	
1	10		10.00
		} ·············· 12	
2	22		11.00
		} ·············· 14	
3	36		12.00
		} ·············· 13	
4	49		12.25
		} ·············· 11	
5	60		12.00
		} ·············· 10	
6	70		11.67
		} ·············· 5	
7	75		10.71
		} ·············· 3	
8	78		9.75
		} ·············· -2	
9	76		8.44
		} ·············· -6	
10	70		7.00

uct gained by adding the third worker. Marginal product continues to decline as additional workers are added to the plot of land. This agrees with our earlier definition of the law of diminishing marginal returns: As additional units of a variable input are added to a fixed amount of other resources, beyond some point the amount of additional output produced will start to decline. In fact, the addition of the ninth and tenth workers leads to reductions in total product. Marginal product in these cases is negative, meaning that the addition of these workers actually reduces output. It becomes more and more difficult to obtain increases in output from the fixed plot of land by adding workers. At some point the workers simply get in each other's way.

The last column in the table introduces the concept of **average product**, which is total product divided by the number of units of the variable input, or

Average product

Total output divided by the number of units of the variable input used to produce the total output; output produced per unit of variable input used.

$$AP = \frac{q}{\text{quantity of variable input}}.$$

The average product is the average output per worker. Average product increases as long as it is less than marginal product. Thus, average product increases through

FOCUS

"Going into Business with Others"—The Partnership

A partnership is an extended form of the proprietorship (see the Focus on "Going Into Business for Yourself" earlier in this chapter). Rather than actually "going into business for yourself," a partnership has two or more co-owners and so involves "going into business with others." The partners, who are team members, share financing of capital investments and, in return, residual claims to the firm's profits. Jointly, they manage the firm, organize team production, and monitor one another's behavior to control shirking. A partnership is a form well suited to lines of team production that involve creative or intellectual skills.

The partnership also has certain limitations. Individual partners cannot sell their share of the partnership without the approval of the other partners. Moreover, each partner is considered legally liable for all the debts incurred by the partnership up to the full extent of the individual partner's wealth—a condition called joint unlimited liability. Because of these limitations, partnerships are usually small and are found in businesses where monitoring of production by a manager is difficult.

A law firm is an example of team production in action. Most law firms are organized as legal partnerships. Each partner's liability does not end with the size of the partner's investment in the firm; it extends to the limit of each partner's personal assets. In the event of bankruptcy, creditors can attach the personal assets of the partners to settle claims against the firm.

What does this unlimited liability mean economically? Partners will be most careful about how they conduct their business. In particular, they will screen candidates for partners in the firm very carefully. A young lawyer is first given an associate status in the firm and must learn and compete with other young associates to become a partner after five or six years. This screening and training process is clearly motivated by the unlimited liability condition—the cost of making a mistake in the selection of a partner can be very high.

A law firm is a little society of profit sharers when organized as a partnership. A lawyer is engaged in what might be loosely called "artistic production." How do you know if your legal partner is working on a case when he or she is staring out the window or walking down the street? An external observer cannot tell whether the lawyer is goofing off or considering a new legal angle on a case. Making the lawyer a partner with shared responsibilities in the firm and a share of the firm's profits is a way to make sure that the lawyer devotes his or her time to cases and not to shirking. Thus, one rationale for the partnership is to promote efficient behavior by artistic producers such as lawyers, accountants, architects, and commercial artists. While partnerships constitute a small percentage of firms and business revenues in the U.S. economy, many important services are organized in this manner.

the addition of the fourth worker. The marginal product of the fifth worker is 11, which is less than the average product for five workers, and beyond this point the average product falls.

Figure 7.2 graphically illustrates the law of diminishing marginal returns with the data from Table 7.2. Figure 7.2a illustrates the total product curve. Total product increases rapidly at first, as the marginal product of the first three workers

FIGURE 7.2

Total, Average, and Marginal Product Curves

(a) Total product curve, plotting the data from Table 7.2. (b) Average product and marginal product curves. Marginal product is the rate of change of the total product curve. The area of diminishing marginal returns begins when marginal product starts to decline. Average product rises when marginal product is greater than average product, and it falls when marginal product is less than average product.

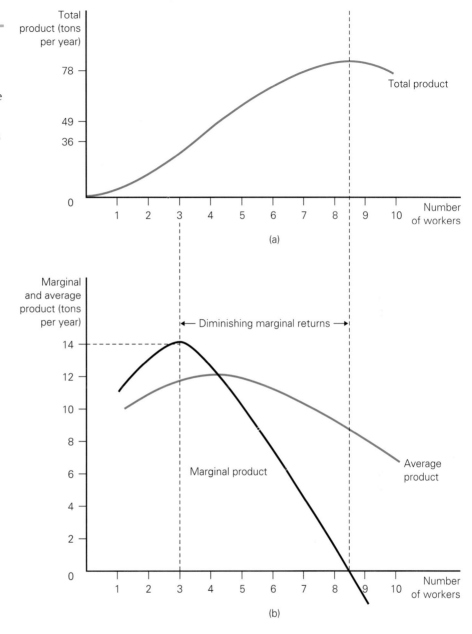

increases. Diminishing returns set in with the fourth worker, and thereafter the total product increases less rapidly. Beyond eight workers, the total product curve turns down and starts to decline. The maximum total product is reached with eight workers. The marginal product and average product curves are shown in Figure 7.2b. The marginal product curve is simply the slope of the total product curve. It rises to a maximum at three workers and then declines as diminishing returns set in. Eventually, it becomes negative past eight workers, indicating that total product is decreasing. The average product curve rises when marginal product is greater than average product, and it declines when marginal product is less than average product.

How can the law of diminishing marginal returns be applied to economic decision making? Consider the thinking of the farmer who owns the plot of land in this experiment. How many workers will he or she choose to hire? Before the area of diminishing marginal returns is reached, additional workers have an increasing marginal product. The farmer will add these workers and will go no further in hiring than the point where the marginal product falls to zero. Even if labor were free, the farmer would not go beyond this point because there would be so many workers on the land that the marginal product of an additional worker would be negative and the total product would decline. This implies that it is rational for the farmer to operate somewhere in the area of diminishing marginal returns.

Precisely how many workers will maximize profits? The answer depends on the cost of the workers (and on the productivity and prices of other inputs). Assume that each worker is paid a wage rate equivalent to 4 units of output. The farmer will compare the marginal product of each worker with the wage rate. The fourth worker adds 13 units of output and costs the farmer the equivalent of only 4 units. In fact, the marginal product of the first seven workers exceeds their wage rate. However, the marginal product of the eighth worker is 3 units of output, which is less than the wage rate. The rational farmer will therefore hire seven workers. This is the law of diminishing marginal returns in action. It points the farmer toward the rational utilization of factors of production.

Diminishing Marginal Returns and Short-Run Costs

What does the law of diminishing marginal returns imply about the behavior of the firm's short-run cost curves? Once diminishing marginal returns set in, more and more of the variable input—in our example, labor—is needed to expand output by an additional unit. If the price of the variable input is fixed, the firm's marginal costs will rise as a reflection of diminishing returns. Adding more workers to the plot of land at a fixed wage rate eventually leads to both diminishing returns and rising marginal costs. These are two ways of looking at the same thing. To argue that marginal returns are diminishing is to argue that marginal costs are rising: As the quantity of variable inputs increases, marginal product (and output) rises and then falls. This means that as output rises, marginal cost falls and then rises.

Table 7.3 presents a numerical illustration of how the law of diminishing marginal returns affects a firm's short-run costs. Columns (2), (3), and (4) show how total costs behave as output increases in the short run, and columns (5), (6), and (7) show the behavior of the corresponding average cost concepts.

In this example, we keep the numbers low for simplicity. Total fixed cost is constant at $10 per day; average fixed cost per unit is the total fixed cost divided by output. Fixed costs must be paid in the short run whether the firm operates or not. The level of average fixed cost falls continuously as output is increased. For the first unit produced, for example, both total fixed cost and average fixed cost are $10. Total fixed cost remains at $10 for the second unit, but average fixed cost falls to $5 per unit. As business grows, average fixed cost falls.

Remember, total variable cost is the sum of the firm's expenditures on variable inputs. As Table 7.3 shows, in order to produce more output, more must be spent on variable inputs. It takes an additional expenditure of $1.60 on variable inputs to expand output from 0 to 1 unit, but an additional expenditure of only $1.45 to expand output from 1 to 2 units. The increases in total variable cost get progressively smaller as output is expanded to 9 units; after 9 units the increases grow progressively larger. Since average variable cost is the total variable cost divided by output, it first declines and then rises at the tenth unit of output.

TABLE 7.3

Short-Run Cost Data for a Firm

The various concepts of short-run costs are expressed in both total and average terms.
Columns (1) through (4) present the firm's total cost data; columns (5) through (8) present
the cost data in marginal and average terms. Notice especially that short-run marginal
cost ultimately rises because of the law of diminishing marginal returns.

(1) Output (units)	(2) Total Fixed Cost	(3) Total Variable Cost	(4) Total Cost (2) + (3)	(5) Average Fixed Cost (2) ÷ (1)	(6) Average Variable Cost (3) ÷ (1)	(7) Average Total Cost (4) ÷ (1)	(8) Marginal Cost $\Delta(4) \div \Delta(1)$[a]
0	$10.00	$0.00	$10.00	$—	$—	$—	$—
1	10.00	1.60	11.60	10.00	1.60	11.60	1.60
2	10.00	3.05	13.05	5.00	1.53	6.53	1.45
3	10.00	4.40	14.40	3.33	1.47	4.80	1.35
4	10.00	5.70	15.70	2.50	1.43	3.93	1.30
5	10.00	6.90	16.90	2.00	1.38	3.38	1.20
6	10.00	8.00	18.00	1.67	1.33	3.00	1.10
7	10.00	9.00	19.00	1.43	1.29	2.71	1.00
8	10.00	9.90	19.90	1.25	1.24	2.49	0.90
9	10.00	10.20	20.20	1.11	1.13	2.24	0.30
10	10.00	10.85	20.85	1.00	1.09	2.09	0.65
11	10.00	12.15	22.15	0.91	1.10	2.01	1.30
12	10.00	13.65	23.65	0.83	1.14	1.97	1.50
13	10.00	15.40	25.40	0.77	1.18	1.95	1.75
14	10.00	17.80	27.80	0.71	1.27	1.99	2.40
15	10.00	21.05	31.05	0.67	1.40	2.07	3.25
16	10.00	25.30	35.30	0.63	1.58	2.21	4.25
17	10.00	30.65	40.65	0.59	1.80	2.39	5.35
18	10.00	37.20	47.20	0.56	2.07	2.62	6.55
19	10.00	45.00	55.00	0.53	2.37	2.89	7.80
20	10.00	54.30	64.30	0.50	2.72	3.22	9.30

[a]Δ means "the change in."

Total cost is the sum of total fixed and total variable costs. Average total cost
is the sum of average variable and average fixed costs, or total cost divided by output. Average total cost, like average variable cost, is U-shaped. Since the influence
of declining average fixed cost is less and less as output rises, the average total cost
curve takes on the U shape of the average variable cost curve.

Marginal cost, shown in column (8), is the change in total cost that results from
producing one additional unit of output. The behavior of marginal cost reflects the
law of diminishing marginal returns. In this example, marginal cost falls through
the production of the ninth unit of output and rises thereafter. The rising portion
of the marginal cost schedule reflects diminishing marginal returns from additions
of the variable input.

The data in Table 7.3 are plotted in Figure 7.3, which graphically demonstrates the behavior of short-run cost curves. Figure 7.3a illustrates the concepts of total cost, and Figure 7.3b presents the corresponding average and marginal cost concepts. In Figure 7.3b, *MC* intersects *AVC* and *ATC* at their minimum points; marginal cost bears a definite relation to average variable cost and average total cost. In the case of average total cost, marginal cost lies below average total cost when average total cost is falling and above average total cost when average total cost is rising. Marginal cost is equal to average total cost when average total cost is at a minimum. In Table 7.3, this occurs between the thirteenth and fourteenth units of output. At lower levels of output, the *MC* values in column (8) are less than the *ATC* values in column (7). *ATC* therefore declines. At higher levels of output—in this case, 14 and over—the *MC* values are greater than the *ATC* values, and *ATC* rises. The same analysis holds for the relationship between *MC* and *AVC*. Here, *MC* becomes greater than *AVC* at 11 units of output.

This type of relation holds for marginal-average series in general. If a baseball player is batting .400 and goes 3 for 4 today (.750), his batting average rises because the marginal figure (.750) lies above the average (.400). If he goes 1 for 4 today (.250), his average falls because the marginal figure (.250) lies below the average (.400). An example can be found closer to home. Suppose that your average grade in economics to date is 85. If you score 90 on your next exam, your average will rise. If you score 80, it will fall. When the marginal figure is above the average, it pulls the average figure up, and vice versa. This same relation holds for average total cost and marginal cost, which both Table 7.3 and Figure 7.3 verify.

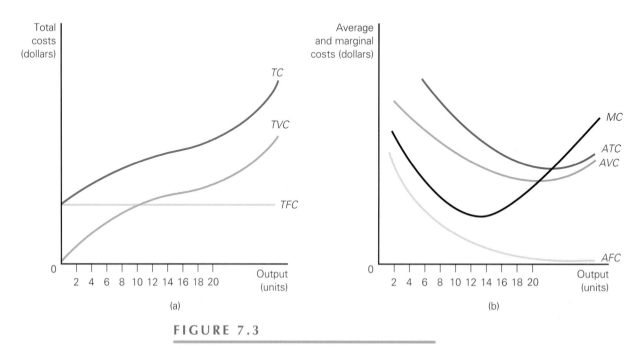

FIGURE 7.3

Short-Run Cost Curves

(a) Total cost data plotted from Table 7.3. (b) Average cost and marginal cost data. Notice the U-shaped average total cost curve. At low levels of output, *ATC* is high because *AFC* is high, and the firm does not utilize its fixed plant efficiently. At high levels of output, *ATC* is high because *MC* is high as the firm approaches the capacity limit of its plant.

In sum, the firm's short-run cost curves show the influence of the law of diminishing marginal returns. First, the firm has certain fixed costs that are independent of the level of output. These costs correspond to what the firm must pay for fixed inputs, and they must be paid whether or not the firm operates. Second, assuming the price of the variable inputs is constant, marginal costs reflect the behavior of the marginal product of the variable input. As output rises, marginal costs first decline because marginal product is increasing and it requires less and less of the variable input to produce additional units of output. At some point, however, diminishing marginal returns set in, and it takes more and more of the variable input to produce additional units of output. When this happens, marginal costs start to rise. Third, marginal cost will eventually rise above average variable cost and average total cost, causing these costs to rise as well, which results in U-shaped average variable and average total cost curves.

LONG-RUN COSTS

In the short run, some inputs are fixed and cannot be varied. These fixed inputs generally are characterized as a physical plant that cannot be altered in size in the short run. Short-run costs therefore show the relation of costs to output for a given plant. In the long run, however, all inputs are variable, including plant size. As economic time lengthens and the contracts that define fixed inputs can be renegotiated, a firm owner can adjust all parts of his or her operation. In fact, the scale of a firm's operations can be adjusted to best fit the economic circumstances that prevail in the long run; an owner can choose to arrange the organization in the best possible way to do business. Stated in terms of plant size, the owner will seek the plant size that minimizes long-run costs of producing the profit-maximizing output.

Adjusting Plant Size

Long-run average total cost
The lowest per unit cost of producing any level of output when the usage of all inputs can be varied.

The choice of plant size affects production costs. To determine the optimum long-run plant size, we introduce a new concept: **long-run average total cost** ($LRATC$). This measure shows the lowest-cost plant for producing each level of output when the firm can choose among all possible plant sizes. In fact, the number of possible plant sizes is unlimited. The owner sees the world of possibilities in terms of a long-run average total cost (or planning) curve such as that drawn in Figure 7.4. The long-run average total cost curve is smoothly continuous and allows us to see the full sweep of a firm owner's possibilities. On its downward course, the long-run average total cost curve is tangent to each short-run average total cost curve *before* the point of minimum cost for each given plant size. On its upward course it touches each short-run average total cost curve *past* the point of minimum cost. Only at the bottom of the long-run U shape do the minimum points of the long-run and short-run average total cost curves coincide. In effect, the long-run average total cost curve is an envelope of short-run average total cost curves.

Long-run marginal cost curve
The additional cost of producing an additional unit of output when all inputs, including plant size, can be varied.

Figure 7.4 also contains the firm's **long-run marginal cost curve**, *LRMC*. It is similar to the short-run marginal cost curve in that it shows the additional cost arising from producing an additional unit of output. However, the long-run marginal cost curve depicts the change in total cost associated with a one-unit expansion in output when all inputs can be varied. Expansions in output in the long run are accomplished not only by increases in labor (variable) inputs but also by changing the scale of operations, or the plant size. Thus long-run marginal cost measures *all* additional costs of changing output. Notice that the *LRMC* curve intersects the

FIGURE 7.4

Long-Run Average Total Cost and Marginal Cost Curves

LRATC is the planning curve of the firm owner. It shows how plant size can be adjusted in the long run when all inputs are variable. The plant size shown at *q* represents the lowest possible unit cost of production in the long run. Economies of scale prevail before *q* on the curve, and diseconomies of scale prevail past *q*. *LRMC* is the long-run marginal cost curve. It shows the additional cost of producing output under the condition that all inputs can be varied.

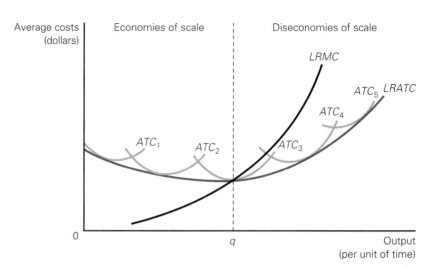

LRATC curve where the *LRATC* curve reaches a minimum. At output levels greater than *q* in Figure 7.5, *LRMC* is greater than *LRATC*, which implies that *LRATC* must be rising. Just the opposite is true at output levels less than *q* in Figure 7.4. The most preferred operating rate in Figure 7.4 is clearly at *q* when *LRATC* is at a minimum. Think of it this way — if you dropped a marble into the *LRATC* bowl, where would it come to rest?

Economies and Diseconomies of Scale

Why does long-run average total cost have a U shape, falling to *q* and rising thereafter? The answer involves two new concepts: economies and diseconomies of scale.

Economies of scale

A situation in which long-run unit costs *(LRATC)* decline as plant size increases.

    The initial falling portion of the *LRATC* curve is due to **economies of scale**. To a certain point, long-run unit costs of production fall as output increases and the firm gets larger. There are a number of reasons that a larger firm might have lower unit costs: (1) A larger operation means that more specialized processes are possible in the firm. Individual workers can concentrate on and become more proficient at more narrowly defined tasks, and machines can be specially tailored to individual processes. (2) As the firm grows larger and produces more, workers and managers gain valuable experience in production processes, learning by doing. Since workers and managers of a larger firm produce more output, they acquire more experience. Such experience can lead to lower unit costs. (3) Large firms can take advantage of mass production techniques, which require large setup costs. Setup costs are most economical when they are spread over a large amount of output. Production techniques such as the assembly line used by large automobile manufacturers would result in very high unit costs if used by a small producer of specialized cars.

Diseconomies of scale

A situation in which, beyond a point, the long-run average total cost of producing output increases as plant size increases.

    The fact that the *LRATC* curve rises after *q* is due to **diseconomies of scale**. In this range of outputs, the firm has become too large for its owner to control effectively. Managers do not have the monitoring technology to hold costs down in a very large firm, and bureaucratic inefficiencies creep in. If such bureaucratic problems did not exist, firms would be much larger. Large firms will reorganize, spin off component parts, hire new managers, and seek ways to avoid diseconomies of scale.

FOCUS

Big Business: The Corporation

Big businesses, such as Microsoft, General Motors, or Motorola, are all corporations. Although corporations are the smallest category of business organization in the United States (about 20 percent in 1998), they account for *90 percent* of buiness revenues. Thus, most businesses engaged in large-scale production and marketing are corporations.

There are enormous advantages to the corporate form. In a corporation, ownership is divided into equal parts called shares of stock. If any stockholder dies or sells out to a new owner, the existence of the business organization is not terminated or endangered as it is in a proprietorship or a partnership (see the previous Focus boxes in this chapter). For this reason, the corporation is said to possess the features of continuity and share transferability. Share transferability is the most economically important feature of the corporation; in fact, share transferability is one reason for the origin of the corporation. It allows owners and managers to specialize, thereby increasing efficiency and profitability in the firm. Large amounts of capital can be accumulated, because small investors can get into the act with a minimum of risk.

Another feature of the corporation that distinguishes it from other forms of business organization is limited liability. Corporate shareholders are responsible for the debts or liabilities of the corporation only to the extent that they have invested in it. This characteristic sharply contrasts with sole owners or partners, who are legally responsible for the firm's debts up to the amount of their entire personal wealth. The amount of direct investment in corporations is therefore increased as a result of the limited liability involved.

Not all observers see the corporation as the goose that lays the golden egg. Critics of the modern corporation often claim that it is inefficient because ownership and control are separated: Shareholders are the owners of the firm, but the control of the firm is vested in professional managers. While shareholders are interested in profits and higher stock values, managers *might* pursue different objectives. Managers may want to be "captains of industry," have job security, or occupy plush corporate headquarters. They may not be faithful agents of the stockholders, in other words.

This problem is not insurmountable, however. Corporate shareholders are not held in bondage by the corporation's management—the shareholder can sell shares at any time. When the corporation becomes inefficient due to bad management, stock values tend to fall, leaving the business ripe for corporate takeovers or stockholder rebellion (in which management is replaced). Further, the incentives for efficiency may be instilled in management by requirements that management own (or take as compensation) stock in the company. Self-interest, in this case as in all others, is a powerful motive for profit-maximizing behavior on the part of the manager.

Other Shapes of the Long-Run Average Total Cost Curve

The *LRATC* curve in Figure 7.4 shows a unique ideal plant size at q. There is only one minimum point on this U-shaped curve. This means that there is a small range of plant sizes that are efficient in a particular industry, and plant sizes in the industry will tend to cluster at the level of q. The fact that most discount department stores are approximately the same size illustrates this point.

Figure 7.5 shows two other possible shapes the *LRATC* curve can take. Figure 7.5a illustrates **constant returns to scale**. In certain industries an initial range of economies of scale prevails up to a minimum efficient size of q_1. Beyond q_1, a wide variation in firm size is possible without a discernible difference in unit costs. Small firms and large firms can operate with the same unit costs over this range of outputs. This flat portion of the *LRATC* curve shows constant returns, or the same unit costs, for a range of output levels from q_1 to q_2. Beyond q_2, diseconomies

Constant returns to scale

As plant size either increases or decreases, long-run average total cost does not change.

FIGURE 7.5

Alternative *LRATC* Curves

Not all *LRATC* curves are U-shaped. (a) Constant returns to scale. The lowest possible production costs per unit exist within a large range between output levels q_1 and q_2. Both small and large firms can have the same long-run unit costs between q_1 and q_2. (b) Increasing returns to scale. The more output the firm produces, the lower its long-run average total cost.

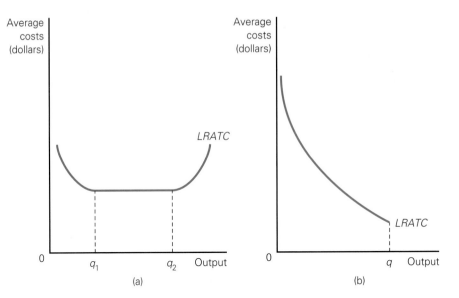

Increasing returns to scale

As plant size increases, long-run average total cost decreases.

of scale begin. This is apparently a very common *LRATC* curve in the real world because we observe both small and large firms surviving—even prospering—side by side in such industries as publishing and textiles.

Figure 7.5b shows an *LRATC* curve that exhibits economies of scale over its whole range; this is called **increasing returns to scale**. In such cases, the larger the firm, the lower its costs. This type of *LRATC* curve is perhaps representative of such industries as utilities and telephone service. Large firms may be more efficient in the provision of these services. Where one large firm prevails in a marketplace, some form of regulatory control over the pricing power of the firm may be required.

SHIFTS IN COST CURVES

Our analysis of cost curves has been based on the familiar *ceteris paribus*, or other things constant, assumption. In other words, we held certain factors constant in the discussion of short-run and long-run costs. What factors did we hold constant, and how do they affect cost curves?

Resource prices have been held constant. If resource prices rise or fall, the firm's cost curves will rise or fall by a corresponding amount. If the price of gasoline falls, the cost curves of a trucking firm fall; this is illustrated by the fall from ATC_1 and MC_1 to ATC_2 and MC_2 in Figure 7.6.

Taxes and government regulation have been held constant. If government increases the excise tax on gasoline, the trucking firm's cost curves will rise. In fact, the average and marginal costs of the trucking firm will rise by the amount of the tax. Similarly, if government imposes more stringent highway weight limits for trucks, the costs of trucking firms will increase.

Technological change has been held constant. Advances in technology make it possible to produce goods and services at lower costs. The invention of the diesel engine, which is more durable and less expensive to operate than the conventional gasoline engine, shifted the cost curves of trucking firms downward. Trucking services can now be produced with fewer resources because of this technological improvement. Such changes obviously affect the cost curves of firms.

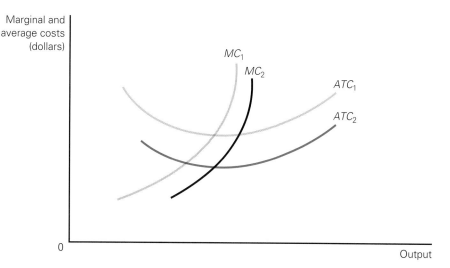

FIGURE 7.6

The Effect of a Decrease in Resource Prices on Costs

As resource prices decrease, the cost curves of the firm fall from ATC_1 and MC_1 to ATC_2 and MC_2. If resource prices increased, the cost curves of the firm would rise.

COSTS AND SUPPLY DECISIONS

Costs help explain the supply or output decisions of firms. Firms compare their expected costs and expected revenues in deciding how much output to produce. In the short run, the relevant comparison is between marginal cost and expected revenue. If the latter exceeds the former, the firm will supply additional units of output. In the long run the owner of a firm decides whether to enter an industry or to expand output within an industry by comparing long-run marginal cost with additional expected revenue. Again, if additional expected revenue exceeds long-run marginal cost, the firm enters or increases production, and industry output is expanded. There is a critical link between firm costs and the supply curve in a competitive industry; we examine this link in the next chapter.

APPLICATION

The Draft, Jury Duty, and Conscripted "Public Service": Opportunity Cost and You

The establishment of an all-volunteer army in the United States and in many other nations was based on the concept of opportunity costs. That is, to induce people (likely of your age) to volunteer for military service, the U.S. Government offered them benefits comparable to those they would receive in civilian careers.

Assume that you have a civilian job (before or after going to college) and that economics is your only consideration. If the government can offer you a package including salary, room and board, education (technical training or educational subsidies after serving) clothing, health care, and travel opportunities equal to or greater than your opportunity cost, then you would sign up. That very thing has happened in the post-Vietnam era.

If the opportunity cost to new recruits is not balanced by the army's offer, people will not volunteer in sufficient numbers. In this case, the government returns to the draft to meet its quota for national defense (as was argued for by some during the Kosovo-Albanian crisis). Such forced conscription can be viewed as a tax—"the draft tax." The draft tax is equal to what an individual could have earned as a civilian minus any compensation he or she gets from serving in the military. If

Much of the full costs of the jury system are borne by jurors themselves.

a man or woman earns $25,000 as a civilian but the military pays only $10,000 (including the value of benefits such as food and shelter), the draft tax is $15,000. This financial cost (where only money wages matter) would understate the real opportunity cost of a draft to you if you strongly prefer to work as a civilian no matter what the pay for military service is.

The draft is not the only example of "conscript labor." (A conscript is someone who is forced, by law and the threat of punishment, to provide labor services.) An American example (since the all-volunteer army) is the justice system's method of selecting jurors. Jurors are in fact paid a nominal sum, but this payment usually falls short of the costs of jury duty. Opportunity cost tells us why. If juror "pay" was more than the full costs of jury duty to individuals, people would volunteer their services and conscription would not be necessary.

Jurors are only one of a number of necessary inputs to the justice system of the United States. Judges, attorneys, court reporters, and courtrooms are also vital ingredients. Jurors (along with defendants and witnesses) are different in that they are not paid their opportunity costs. Other inputs participate voluntarily, however, indicating that their total compensation (money and nonmoney) is at least equal to their opportunity cost—that is, to their return in their next-best alternative.

An important thing to note about the draft and the jury system is that conscription does not reduce the cost or supply any product or service (national defense or justice): conscription merely shifts the costs of production from one group to another. Clearly, the economic costs of jury duty are the alternative value of jurors' time. These costs would be explicit under an all-volunteer system. An all-volunteer jury system, like an all-volunteer army, would attract participants by bidding them away from other activities. (Note that these would not have to be wage-earning activities—you might prefer to play tennis.) Under the conscript system, only part of the costs are explicit—the jury fees. You, the juror, pay the remainder of the costs. The conscription of jurors shifts some of the costs of the judicial system from taxpayers to conscripts. An all-volunteer jury would make all costs explicit. We would then know the exact cost of the U.S. system of justice.[a] Informed decisions are difficult when some of the costs of decisions are hidden.

Periodically, other forms of conscription are entertained. Compulsory public service by the youth of America has been proposed in one form or another. A popular proposal makes some form of public service, either military or civilian, a prerequisite for college aid programs. Others would make such service necessary for college admission, and other forms would make compulsory service universal. Instillation of "citizenship" is the rationale for most of these proposals. Missing in the arguments for mandatory public service, as in other forms of conscription such as the draft, is the fact that such programs represent a shift in taxation from older Americans to a "public service tax" on the young.

---

[a]Economists have attempted to estimate the full costs of the jury system; see, for example, D. L. Martin, "The Economics of Jury Conscription," *Journal of Political Economy,* 1972.

SUMMARY

1. Costs result from the fact that resources have alternative uses. An opportunity cost is the value of resources in their next-best use.

2. Explicit costs are like accounting costs; they are the bills that the firm must pay for the use of inputs. Implicit costs are the opportunity costs of resources owned by the firm. The total cost of production is the sum of explicit and implicit costs.

3. Economic or opportunity costs are the expected future costs of forgoing alternative uses of resources. Accounting or historical costs are costs that have been incurred in the past. Sunk costs are irretrievable historical costs and are not relevant to present decisions.

4. Private costs are payments by the firm for the use of inputs. External costs arise when the firm uses an input without paying for its services. The sum of private and external costs is social cost.

5. The short run is a period of economic time when some of the firm's inputs are fixed. The long run is a period over which all inputs, including the size of the firm's plant, can be varied.

6. The law of diminishing marginal returns states that when adding units of a variable input to a fixed amount of other resources, beyond some point the resulting additions to output will start to decline.

7. The law of diminishing marginal returns implies that the marginal cost curve of the firm will ultimately rise. As the firm adds more variable inputs to its fixed plant, diminishing marginal returns set in at some point, and marginal cost will start to rise as the firm approaches its short-run capacity.

8. Short-run costs are (a) fixed costs—costs that do not vary with the firm's output; (b) variable costs—the costs of purchasing variable inputs; (c) total costs—the sum of fixed and variable costs; and (d) marginal costs—the change in total cost with respect to a change in output. These costs can be expressed in total or average (unit) terms. The short-run average total cost curve is U-shaped. When marginal cost is below average total cost, the latter falls. When it is above average total cost, the latter rises.

9. Long-run average total cost shows the lowest-cost plant for producing output when the firm can choose among all possible plant sizes. It is the planning curve of the firm; it helps the firm pick the right plant size for long-run production.

10. Long-run marginal cost is the additional cost associated with producing an additional unit of output when all inputs can be varied. It measures additional costs arising from producing more output not only with more labor but also by altering plant size.

11. A U-shaped long-run average total cost curve results from economies and diseconomies of scale. Economies of scale cause long-run unit costs to fall, and diseconomies of scale cause long-run unit costs to rise as output is expanded.

12. Other shapes of the long-run average total cost curve are possible. Most important, the long-run average total cost curve can have a flat range with constant returns to scale, or it can be downward sloping over its entire range, reflecting a condition called increasing returns to scale.

KEY TERMS

opportunity costs of production
accounting costs
implicit costs
opportunity cost of capital
total cost of production
historical costs
sunk costs
economic profit

accounting profit
private costs
external costs
social costs
variable input
fixed input
short run
long run

fixed costs
variable costs
total costs
average fixed cost
average variable cost
average total cost
marginal cost
fixed plant

law of diminishing marginal
   returns
total product
marginal product
average product

long-run average total cost
long-run marginal cost
economies of scale
diseconomies of scale
constant returns to scale

increasing returns to scale
firm
market coordination
firm coordination

QUESTIONS FOR REVIEW AND DISCUSSION

1. Compare and contrast limited liability and unlimited liability. Which of them characterizes (a) a sole proprietorship, (b) a partnership, (c) a corporation?

2. What are the major advantages and disadvantages of the corporation as a form of business organization?

3. What is the difference between market coordination of resources and firm coordination?

4. Explain the difference between explicit and implicit costs.

5. State and explain the law of diminishing marginal returns.

6. What is the definition of marginal cost? How is it linked to the law of diminishing marginal returns?

7. Define economies and diseconomies of scale, and give an example of each.

8. How long is the long run? How does it compare to the short run?

9. When is the marginal cost curve below the average total cost curve? When is it above the average total cost curve?

10. An engineering student invests in obtaining an engineering degree. Let us say that the degree cost $50,000 in opportunity costs. Five years later, the engineer decides to become an artist. Is the $50,000 investment in the engineering degree relevant to the decision to become an artist?

11. Derive the long-run cost model using the short-run model. Be sure to include short-run average total cost *(ATC)*, marginal cost *(MC)*, and long-run average total cost *(LRATC)*. Where is the single most preferred operating position in the long-run model?

12. Suppose that the long-run average total cost curve in an industry exhibits increasing returns to scale. How will firms compete in such an industry? Will there be many suppliers in the industry in the long run?

13. Having spent $145,000 opening an exclusive dress shop, Judy realizes that her location is poor, causing her to lose money. In deciding whether to close the store or continue doing business at a loss, should she take the $145,000 into consideration? What term do economists use for this sum?

14. A business spends $20,000 on land, $50,000 on equipment, and $312,000 on salaries. What is the total cost of production for this business?

PROBLEMS

1. Use the table to answer the questions.
   a. What is the average total cost of producing 4 units of output?
   b. What is the total cost of producing 3 units of output?
   c. What is the marginal cost of producing the third unit?

Units of Output	Total Fixed Cost	Total Variable Cost
1	$1000	$300
2	1000	550
3	1000	900
4	1000	1400
5	1000	2050

2. Complete the following table.

Q	FC	VC	TC	MC	AFC	AVC	ATC
1	240	50	290	50	240	50	290
2	240	—	330	—	—	45	—
3	—	110	—	20	—	—	—
4	—	—	—	—	60	—	100
5	—	—	480	—	—	—	—

WORKING WITH THE WEB

1. First, be sure you have read the Application: "The Draft, Jury Duty, and Conscripted 'Public Service': Opportunity Cost and You" in this chapter. After reading it, go to www.mises.org and select (on the left-hand side) the link "daily articles." Next, select the link June 1999 and scroll down until you see the article "Jury Duty." In this article, Armentano reinforces the position described in your text regarding jury duty as a form of conscripted labor.
   a. What does Armentano advocate as a solution to mandatory jury duty and on what grounds? Explain.
   b. What are the potential objections to Armentano's free market system for jury duty? What are Armentano's solutions to the objections? Explain.

2. By now you should recognize that labor is a significant cost of production for most firms. In the short run, typically the firm will vary labor to increase output when capital is fixed. Eventually, this will create diminishing marginal returns for the firm. Consider some broad (by sector) measures of productivity in the U.S. economy.
   Go to http://www.bls.gov/news.release/prod2.-t01.htm and look at Table 1, "Business Sector: Productivity, hourly compensation, unit labor costs, and prices, seasonally adjusted."
   a. Which column measures the productivity of workers?
   b. What is the level of productivity for workers for the year 1997?
   Next, go to http://www.bls.gov/news.release/-prod2.t03.htm and look at Table 3, "Manufacturing Sector: Productivity, hourly compensation, unit labor costs, and prices, seasonally adjusted."
   c. What is the level of productivity for workers for the year 1997?
   d. Which sector (Business or Manufacturing) reports a higher level of productivity per worker in 1997?
   e. Assume that the difference in productivity in the two sectors is attributable to the fact that diminishing returns begins with fewer workers employed in the business sector than in the manufacturing sector. *Ceteris paribus* (including wages held constant in each sector), how will the marginal product and marginal cost curves in the Business and Manufacturing sectors differ?

Competitive Markets

C ompetition exists in virtually every aspect of life. Students compete for grades, animals compete for habitat, sports teams compete for championships, government agencies compete for budget appropriations, firms compete for customers. In each case, scarcity causes the competition. Funds available to support government agencies are limited; defense and social agencies therefore compete for scarce budget dollars. Likewise, there can be only one World Series champion; major league baseball teams therefore compete for this scarce distinction. If resources were freely available, there would be no competition. Everyone could have all they wanted of whatever they wanted.

This chapter introduces the economist's model of firm and industry behavior under pure competition (a market with many buyers and sellers, with sellers producing nearly identical products). It is the first of five chapters that analyze the impact of industry structure on price and output. Four chapters look at models of industry behavior: pure competition, monopoly, monopolistic competition, oligopoly, and cartels. The fifth relates industry structure to government policies. In this chapter we discuss the usefulness of the abstract model of pure competition and its relevance for real-world problems. After reading Chapter 8 you should understand

- the difference between competition as a dynamic process and the economist's static model of a competitive market.
- the principles underlying the behavior of competitive firms in both the short run and the long run.
- the nature of the supply curve of a perfectly competitive firm.
- how economic profits (or losses) motivate competitive firms to expand, contract, or go out of business.

THE PROCESS OF COMPETITION

Naturally, most people think of competition as the process of competition or the conduct of competitors. Seen in this way, the important question in determining whether firms are competing with one another is whether they are exhibiting rivalrous, competitive behavior. Do they compete hard for customers? Do they try to outperform one another? Do they use a variety of methods—persuasive advertising, a carefully chosen location, and attractive price—to win and keep customers? Do they seek the best managerial talent available? Are they forward-looking and innovative? Do they seek to eliminate waste and inefficiency? The list could go on, but the point is clear: Competition is normally thought of as a process of rivalry among firms.

This process of rivalry leads to better and less expensive products for consumers. Business firms compete to make profits, but the competitive process actually forces firms to meet consumer demands at the lowest possible level of profit. As Adam Smith observed more than 200 years ago, firms' self-interest is harnessed by the competitive process to promote the general well-being of society:

> It is not from the benevolence of the butcher, the brewer, or the baker, that we expect our dinner, but from their regard for their own interest. We address ourselves, not to their humanity but to their self-love, and never talk to them of our own necessities but of their advantages.[1]

The process of competition channels the pursuit of individual self-interest to socially beneficial outcomes, and for this reason economists put the study of the competitive process at the heart of their science.

The process of competition takes place in an uncertain world. Individuals have to make conjectures as they make resource commitments for the future. Some conjectures will turn out to be correct, and individuals who forecast correctly will prosper. Individuals whose conjectures turn out not to be correct will not fare so well in the future. The concept of competition as a process of rivalry under uncertain conditions is especially important for understanding entrepreneurial behavior in the economy.

PURE COMPETITION

Pure competition is an abstract model of the competitive process that emphasizes the importance of industry structure. In particular, it stresses the number of independent producers in an industry. The model of pure competition is a useful abstraction that, interpreted carefully, can help us understand the competitive behavior of producers in real-world industries.

Market
The interaction of buyers and sellers for the purpose of making transactions.

The model of pure competition is based on the concept of a **market**. As you will recall, market prices are subject to the laws of demand and supply, and within a market the price of a good or service will tend toward a single value. Buyers at point *x* will not pay more for a commodity than the price at point *y* plus transportation costs. Buyers at point *y* will not pay more for a commodity than the price at point *x* plus transportation costs. Price deviations will quickly be spotted by buyers, restoring the market's tendency to one price. Suppose that the price at point *y*

---

[1]Adam Smith, *An Inquiry in the Nature and Causes of the Wealth of Nations,* ed. Edwin Cannan (1776; reprint, New York: Modern Library, 1937), p. 14.

fell below the price at point x plus transportation costs. What would happen? Buyers would shift their purchases from point x to point y, decreasing demand and lowering price at point x and increasing demand and raising price at point y. This shift of buyers would restore the tendency to a single price.

The behavior of sellers in a market is equally predictable. In fact, one way to determine if two commodities are in the same market is to find out whether price reductions or increases for the commodity in one area are matched by price reductions or increases in other areas, after accounting for transportation costs. If the price of gasoline goes down in Atlanta because of a gas war, does it also go down in Savannah? In Chicago? In Seattle? In other words, do sellers in other areas of the country respond with competitive price reductions? To the extent that they do, we can delineate the market for gasoline from the tendency of all sellers to adjust prices in the same direction. Perhaps there is an Atlanta–Savannah gasoline market, but there is not an Atlanta–Seattle market.

Building on this concept of a market, we can define four conditions that characterize a **purely competitive market**.

Purely competitive market
The interaction of a large number of buyers and sellers under the condition that entry and exit are not restricted.

Homogeneous product
A good or service for which the consumer is indifferent as to which firm produces it; each firm's product is a perfect substitute for other firms' products in the eyes of the consumer.

1. Firms in a purely competitive market sell a **homogeneous product;** that is, they sell identical or nearly identical products that are perfectly substitutable for one another and all have access to the same level of productive technology. This means that advertising does not exist in a purely competitive market. Why would one firm want to advertise the advantages of its product if it cannot be distinguished by consumers from the products produced by a large number of competing firms?

2. A large number of independent buyers and sellers exists in a purely competitive market. Moreover, the large number of buyers and sellers ensures that the purchases or sales of any one buyer or seller will not affect the market price. Each buyer and seller is small relative to the total market for the commodity and exerts no perceptible influence on the market.

3. There are no barriers to entry or exit in a purely competitive market. Features of economic life such as control of an essential raw material by one or a few firms do not exist under pure competition.

Perfect information
A situation that arises when information about prices and products is costless to obtain; complete knowledge about the market.

4. A perfectly competitive market also offers **perfect information** to buyers and sellers. Everybody in the market has equal, free access to information about the location and price of a product. This assumption provides the basis for a single price to prevail in a perfectly competitive market. Buyers and sellers are constantly informed about price differences and act in turn to drive industry price to a single value. (The Focus "The Economics of Information: Searching for the Best Deal" shows how economists think about the process of acquiring information when it is not free.)

These four conditions are the assumptions on which the theory of pure or perfect competition is based. The assumptions may seem unrealistic. Products, for example, are rarely homogeneous. But the strict realism of the assumptions is not the point of this model. The point is the empirical relevance of the model. Does it explain behavior in real-world markets? As we will see, the purely competitive model helps us analyze important actual markets and industries such as the stock market and agriculture. Moreover, the purely competitive model gives us an analytical framework for what might be loosely described as the ideal working of an economy. In this sense the model provides a benchmark against which other industry models, such as pure monopoly, can be compared.

FOCUS

The Economics of Information: Searching for the Best Deal

The model of perfect competition is based on several key assumptions. One is that information about the price of products and services is free. Consumers are immediately aware at zero cost of any price differences in a given market for a given product. By acting to buy low and sell high, they will drive price in the market to a single value. One price for a product will prevail when a perfectly competitive market is in equilibrium.

We live, of course, in a more complex world. Information—about prices, quality, or anything else—is rarely free. It is an economic good that is costly to produce and to obtain.

Figure 8.1 illustrates the economics of information. The *MC* curve represents the marginal cost to the consumer of searching for a lower price for some product or service. Additional search is typically more and more costly, so *MC* rises to the right. If you are in the market for a used car, for example, the marginal cost of search might be the costs of visiting and negotiating with one or more used car dealers. Moreover, the level of the *MC* curve will vary across goods. It will be low, for example, when shopping for clothes by mail-order catalogue. It will be high, for example, when searching for a wedding dress.

The *MB* curve represents the marginal benefit to the consumer of searching for a lower price. As you check the prices of more and more sellers, the prospect of finding a lower price from the next seller declines, and so *MB* declines to the right. The marginal benefits of additional search also will vary across markets. When the value of the product is large (for example, consumer durables—houses, refrigerators, cars), it will pay the consumer to search more for a lower price. However, it will not pay the consumer to search widely for a lower price of toothpicks. Ordinarily, the larger proportion that the item is in the consumer's budget, the greater is the benefit of longer search.

The consumer will search until the *MC* of search equals the *MB* of search. This is the point of optimal or efficient search, depicted by point *E* in Figure 8.1. At levels of marginal cost and benefit before point *E*, the extra benefits of more search exceed the extra costs. After point *E*, marginal costs of search exceed the marginal benefits. Point *E* represents the correct or equilibrium amount of search for a given consumer (for a particular good). Consumers will employ such search procedures in an intuitive, instinctive manner. Since point *E* will not be the same for all consumers (for all products), the fact that information about prices is costly to produce and to obtain means that in most markets there will be a dispersion of final transaction prices and not a single price for a product at all locations.

FIGURE 8.1

Marginal Costs and Marginal Benefits from Search

Consumers, without free information about the prices or qualities of products or services, will spend resources to discover these attributes until the marginal benefit just equals the marginal cost of search.

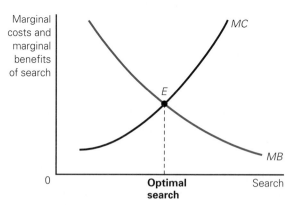

THE PURELY COMPETITIVE FIRM AND INDUSTRY IN THE SHORT RUN

How do firms behave within a purely competitive industry? We focus first on the purely competitive firm's decisions about how much output to supply in the short run—that is, over a period of time when it cannot adjust its plant size.

The Purely Competitive Firm as a Price Taker

Price taker
An individual seller who faces a single market price and is able to sell as much as desired at that price.

In a purely competitive market, an individual firm cannot influence the market price for its good or service by increasing or decreasing its output. Because each seller is only a small part of the total market, its actions have no perceptible influence on the market. The competitive firm is called a **price taker**: It must accept the going market price for its product. The farmer, for example, does not negotiate over the price of his wheat with the operator of the grain elevator. He either sells at the posted price or stores his wheat for a future sale.

The Demand Curve of the Competitive Firm

Figure 8.2a shows the demand curve (*d*) facing a Virginia peanut producer, and Figure 8.2b shows the world market demand (*D*) and supply (*S*) curves for peanuts. The demand curve of the Virginia producer is perfectly elastic with respect to the price of peanuts; it is drawn as a flat line at the level of market price (*P*). A perfectly elastic demand curve means that the firm can sell all it wants to sell at the prevailing market price. If it tried to sell its output at a slightly higher price, demand for its product would vanish because buyers can purchase peanuts at the lower price in whatever quantities they choose. If the firm is trying to maximize its profits, it has no reason to sell its product for less than the market price.

The scale for price is the same in both parts of Figure 8.2. They obviously are not the same for quantity because of the Virginia producer's minuscule proportion of world output. Keep this in mind as you interpret the diagrams in this chapter. Always check to see whether the horizontal axis represents *firm* or *industry* quantity. Capital *Q* will be used to represent industry output; small *q* will represent individual firm output.

To summarize: Every firm in a purely competitive industry is a price taker and faces a demand curve such as that of the Virginia peanuts producer in Figure 8.2a. And every purely competitive firm produces a tiny proportion of industry output.

Short-Run Profit Maximization by the Purely Competitive Firm

Profits
The amount by which total revenue exceeds total opportunity cost of production.

The purely competitive firm is a price taker and faces a given price represented by a perfectly elastic demand curve. Under these circumstances how does the firm decide how much to produce? The simple answer is that the firm compares the costs and benefits of producing additional units of output. As long as the added revenues from producing another unit of output exceed the added costs, the firm will expand its output. By following this rule, the firm is led to maximize its **profits** in the short run.

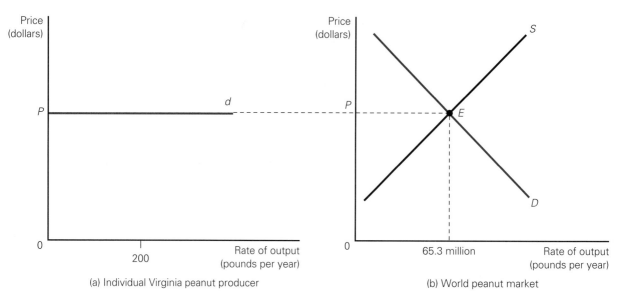

FIGURE 8.2

Firm and Industry Demand in a Purely Competitive Market

In a purely competitive industry, demand for an individual firm's product is perfectly elastic. The perfectly elastic demand curve facing the individual Virginia peanut producer is shown in (a) at the level of P, which is also the equilibrium price for the world market in (b) at an output of 65.3 million pounds per year. Note that the scale for price is the same for both the individual producer and the world market but that the scale for quantity is much different for the two.

Marginal revenue

The change in total revenue resulting from the sale of one additional unit of output; the change in total revenue divided by the change in output.

The added cost of producing an additional unit of output is the marginal cost. We know from our analysis in Chapter 7 that the short-run marginal cost curve of a firm will eventually rise. This is due to the law of diminishing marginal returns, which comes into play as the firm uses its fixed plant more intensively in the short run.

The extra revenue from producing an additional unit of output is **marginal revenue** *(MR)*. Simply, marginal revenue is the addition to total revenue from the production of one more unit of output, or

$$MR = \frac{\text{change in total revenue}}{\text{change in output}}.$$

In a purely competitive market, the denominator is 1—a one-unit increase in output—and the numerator is always the market price (*P*) because the demand curve facing the competitive firm is perfectly elastic. Therefore, marginal revenue equals market price, *MR* = *P*, for the purely competitive firm.

The purely competitive firm will decide how much to produce in the short run by comparing marginal cost with marginal revenue. To maximize its profits, the firm will produce additional units of output until marginal cost and marginal revenue are equal. Figure 8.3 illustrates this process.

The firm's perfectly elastic demand curve (*d*) in Figure 8.3a is drawn at the level of market price (*P*) from Figure 8.3b. As we have just seen, *d* is also the marginal revenue curve for the firm. Revenue will increase by the market price each time output increases by one unit. In other words, *MR* = *P*. We have also drawn the marginal cost (*MC*) and average total cost (*ATC*) curves of the firm.

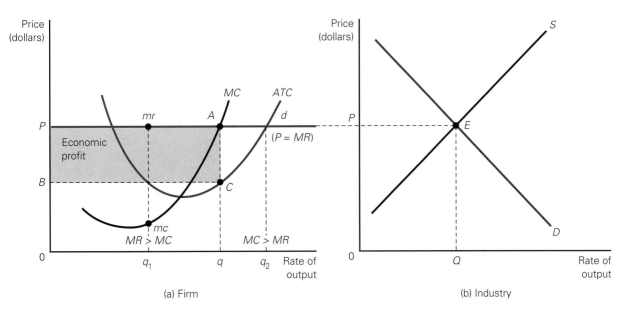

(a) Firm   (b) Industry

FIGURE 8.3

Short-Run Output Choice and Profit Maximization

(a) The short-run choice of output confronting the individual firm. At rates of output less than q, additional production adds more to revenue than to cost. Beyond q, additional production addes more to cost than to revenue. Therefore, the purely competitive firm will produce at q. At this rate of output the firm earns an economic profit equal to the difference between total revenues and total costs: $PAq0 - BCq0 = PACB$. (b) Prevailing market conditions in the industry.

The owners of the firm want to make as much money as possible, so their problem is to find the level of production or output that yields the largest profit. Suppose that the firm is producing peanuts by the pound. The firm presently produces a certain quantity q_1. Should the owners expand their level of production? The answer is yes because additional pounds of peanuts add more to revenue than to costs. In other words, marginal revenue exceeds marginal cost at q_1, as you can see by comparing points mr and mc at quantity q_1. Since the owners want to maximize their profits, they will expand output beyond q_1 as far as q.

Suppose instead that the owners are operating at an output q_2. What will their profit-maximizing reaction be in this case? At this level of production, an additional unit of output adds more to cost than it adds to revenue. That is, marginal cost exceeds marginal revenue. The rational profit-maximizing response of the owners will be to lower production. Through a process of trial and error, they find that their best level of output is q. At a market price of P, they can do no better for profits than to produce q pounds of peanuts. The short-run equilibrium level of production for the purely competitive firm is therefore defined by the condition $P = MC$. Since we know that price and marginal revenue are the same for the purely competitive firm, we can also write $P = MR = MC$.

Using the average total cost curve in Figure 8.3, we can see exactly how well the peanut firm fares by producing at level q. The total revenue of the firm equals its sales, which are the level of output q, times the price P for the output. **Total revenue** at q therefore equals Pq, represented by the rectangular area $PAq0$ in Figure 8.3a. Total cost is the level of average total cost (C) times the level of output q. Total cost

Total revenue
The total money receipts of a firm from selling its product; calculated as market price multiplied by the amount of output sold; the dollar value of sales.

Peanut farmers must adjust to the many conditions that affect the demand and supply of their products, including weather.

at output q thus equals Cq, represented by $BCq0$. Total revenue exceeds total cost in this case: $PAq0 - BCq0 = PACB$. This firm's short-run economic profit is shown by area $PACB$, the return in excess of the total opportunity cost of production.

In the real world, businesspeople do not spend a lot of time trying to draw marginal cost and marginal revenue curves for their firms. Moreover, they operate in an uncertain environment where future costs and prices cannot be known with certainty. Despite these considerations, however, the $P = MR = MC$ rule for profit maximization has predictive power. It is a rule based on common sense. If additional production promises to add more to revenue than to cost, most businesses will try to increase their production. If additional units will probably add more to cost than to revenue, most businesses will cut back production. Such behavior leads to the $P = MR = MC$ result even when businesspeople may know nothing about the economic rule involved.

A Numerical Illustration of Profit Maximization

Another way to understand how the choice of output levels allows a competitive firm to maximize profits is to examine the specific costs and revenues at each level of production. Table 8.1 presents a numerical schedule for the peanut firm. The

TABLE 8.1

Profit Maximization for a Purely Competitive Firm
This numerical schedule of the costs and revenues the peanut firm faces at each level of output provides data for determining the profit-maximizing rate of output. Marginal revenue equals marginal cost when the firm produces 14 pounds per day, and profit is maximized at $5.80 per day.

(1) Rate of Output (pounds/day)	(2) Price = Marginal Revenue	(3) Marginal Cost	(4) Total Revenue (1) × (2)	(5) Total Cost	(6) Profit (4) − (5)
6	$2.40	$1.10	$14.40	$18.00	$−3.60
7	2.40	1.00	16.80	19.00	−2.20
8	2.40	0.90	19.20	19.90	−0.70
9	2.40	0.30	21.60	20.20	1.40
10	2.40	0.65	24.00	20.85	3.15
11	2.40	1.30	26.40	22.15	4.25
12	2.40	1.50	28.80	23.65	5.15
13	2.40	1.75	31.20	25.40	5.80
14	2.40	2.40	33.60	27.80	5.80
15	2.40	3.25	36.00	31.05	4.95
16	2.40	4.25	38.40	35.30	3.10
17	2.40	5.35	40.80	40.65	0.15
18	2.40	6.55	43.20	47.20	−4.00

firm's output level is given in column (1). Column (2) shows that the firm confronts an unvarying market price of $2.40 per pound for its output. Price equals marginal revenue ($P = MR$) because this is a purely competitive firm. The marginal cost and total cost data in columns (3) and (5) are taken from Table 7.3, where these cost concepts were introduced and discussed. Total revenue in column (4) is the sales of the firm, or price times output: column (1) × column (2). Profit, in column (6), is the difference between total revenue and total cost, or column (4) − column (5)

There are two methods by which the firm will choose a rate of output to maximize profits. Suppose, with reference to Table 8.1, that managers do not actually draw the cost curves of the firm, as most real businesses do not. Instead, they operate the firm under a simple rule: Produce and sell output until profits begin to decrease. Examine column (6) in Table 8.1, which measures the firm's profits (total revenue minus total cost) from producing and selling various amounts of output. At a low rate of output, 8 units per day and under, profits are negative; that is, the firm is suffering losses. But as the firm expands output beyond 8 units, losses decline. This is the same thing as saying that profits are rising in this range.

When the firm produces the ninth unit of output, profits become positive ($1.40 per day). Profits continue to rise as the firm expands output up to 13 units per day, at which point profits are $5.80 per day. When the firm produces the fourteenth unit of output, profits level off at $5.80. With the firm's production rule of producing and selling output as long as profits do not fall, we know that at least 14 units of output will be produced.

If the firm were to continue to expand output, profits would decrease. The production of 15 pounds instead of 14 would yield the firm a profit of $4.95 rather than $5.80. If the firm produced 18 pounds of peanuts, it would again suffer a loss, this time equal to $4. As output expands beyond 14 units, profits decline and eventually turn to losses.

The simple decision to stop production when profits begin to decrease leads the firm to produce a rate of output, 14 units per day in Table 8.1, that maximizes profits for the firm. By comparing the total revenue and the total cost of producing and selling additional amounts of output, the firm will choose to produce that rate of output that maximizes profits.[2]

Figure 8.4a illustrates the total revenue–total cost approach to maximizing profits. The figure graphs columns (4) and (5) with respect to the output of the firm. The maximum profits possible in the short run occur where the total revenue line (*TR*) exceeds the total cost curve (*TC*) by the largest vertical difference. As Table 8.1 indicates, this takes place at a sale of 14 pounds of peanuts per day.

The second way to find the profit-maximizing rate of output using the numerical schedule in Table 8.1 is to compare marginal revenue and marginal cost,

---

[2]Even though profits are maximum ($5.80) at both 13 and 14 units of output, the marginal condition for maximum profit *MC* = *MR* is true only at 14 units of production.

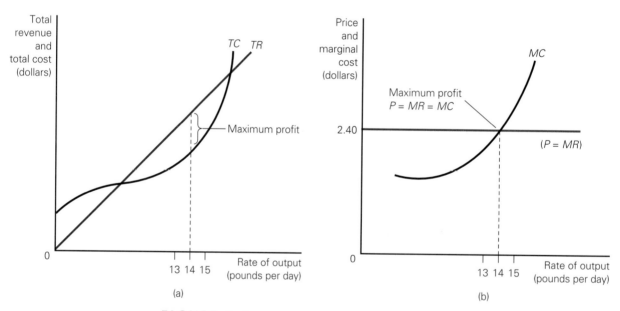

(a)   (b)

FIGURE 8.4

Profit-Maximizing Output for a Purely Competitive Firm

(a) Total revenue–total cost approach to profit maximization. The profit-maximizing rate of output occurs when the vertical distance between total revenue and total cost is greatest. (b) Marginal revenue–marginal cost approach. Profit maximization occurs where price, or marginal revenue (which are identical for the purely competitive firm), equals marginal cost (*P* = *MR* = *MC*). Both approaches result in the same profit-maximizing rate of output.

columns (2) and (3). As long as marginal revenue is greater than marginal cost, it pays to produce additional units of output. Clearly, marginal revenue ($2.40) is greater than marginal cost up to and including an output of 14 pounds of peanuts. This means that the point of maximum profit occurs at 14 pounds per day. The firm will cease producing additional peanuts after 14 pounds, since the marginal cost of producing the next pound is $3.25 and the marginal revenue is only $2.40. Units of output beyond 14 add more to costs than to revenue; that is, they cause profits to decline. Both the total revenue–total cost and the marginal revenue–marginal cost approaches yield the same answer for the profit-maximizing rate of output.

Figure 8.4b illustrates the marginal revenue–marginal cost approach. Again, note the equivalence of the two approaches by comparing the optimal rate of output, at 14 pounds of peanuts per day, in both graphs.

Economic Losses and Shutdowns

What will the firm do if the short-run situation changes for the worse? What if, for example, demand for peanuts declines because the government publishes an adverse report on the health consequences of eating too many peanuts? In this case, the market demand curve for peanuts will decrease, as shown in Figure 8.5b, shifting to the left from D_0 to D_1. This results in a price reduction in the peanuts market, causing

(a) Firm   (b) Industry

FIGURE 8.5

Short-Run Loss Minimization

(a) Firm's response to economic losses caused by (b) decreased industry demand from D_0 to D_1 and a price drop from P_0 to P_1. At P_1, the firm will minimize losses by continuing to operate in the short run because it covers all of its variable costs and some of its fixed costs by operating. At P_2, the firm may either operate, covering its variable costs, or shut down, eliminating its variable costs. At P_3, the firm will shut down in the short run because the price is too low to cover even its variable costs. It minimizes losses by shutting down and paying only its fixed costs, which must be paid whether the firm operates or not.

the market price confronting the firm to fall from P_0 to P_1. The firm's situation is shown in Figure 8.5a. Note that the average variable cost curve (AVC) has been added because it is now an important consideration.

We see in Figure 8.5a that the firm incurs an economic loss because the new market price, P_1, is below its average total cost curve. The firm's revenues are not sufficient to cover its total costs, and it therefore loses money on its operations. What will the firm do in the face of an economic loss? The firm has two options in the short run.

If it expects the adverse effect on sales to be short-lived, the firm can continue to operate in the face of short-run losses. While the price remains depressed at P_1, the firm can minimize losses by following the same rule it followed to maximize profits: It determines the output level at which price is equal to marginal cost and lowers production to that level, q_1 in the figure. Total cost at an output of q_1 is ABq_10, and total revenue is P_1Cq_10. The firm therefore incurs an economic loss equal to the difference between the two: $ABCP_1$. Why might the firm continue to operate in this case while making a loss? It covers all of its variable costs and some of its fixed costs at a price of P_1. If the firm stopped operating, it would still have to pay its fixed costs. These payments must be made whether or not the firm operates. By continuing to operate at price P_1, the firm earns *something* toward the payment of its fixed costs and pays all of its variable costs. Another way to understand this point is to compare the average fixed and average variable costs of producing q_1 rate of output. At q_1, the vertical distance between the average total cost curve and the average variable cost curve is average fixed cost. Figure 8.5a shows that the losses per unit of output incurred by producing q_1, the vertical distance BC, are less than average fixed cost. If the firm shuts down, its losses would equal fixed costs. It therefore "pays" the firm to stay in business in that its losses are lower than if the firm were to shut down.

Suppose, however, that the market price for peanuts continues to fall in the industry, say to P_3. At P_3, the firm does not take in enough revenue to cover even its variable costs of production. The loss-minimizing policy for the firm at this point is to cease operations. By shutting down, the firm is ensured of having to pay only its fixed costs. If it tried to operate at a price below its average variable cost, such as P_3, it would not only have to pay its fixed costs but also would incur a deficit in its average variable cost account. The loss-minimizing policy for the firm is to proceed with a **shutdown** when the price falls below its AVC curve.

Shutdown

A loss-minimizing procedure in which the firm stops production to eliminate all variable costs, although it must still pay fixed costs.

Suppose that the market price falls to point P_2, where it is just equal to the minimum AVC. What can the firm do in this case? Either operating or shutting down is a reasonable option. If it operates, it can cover its variable costs but none of its fixed costs. If it shuts down, it still must pay its fixed costs. Other things being equal, the firm should be indifferent about whether it operates in the short run under these conditions.

Keep in mind that we are discussing *short-run* policies for the firm. The short run is a period of time in which fixed inputs cannot be varied. Given that fixed costs must be paid, the firm's objective in the short run, when price falls below ATC and losses begin, is to minimize its losses. The firm's long-run adjustment will depend on what it expects to happen to prices and costs in the industry. If it expects prices to rise, the firm may shut down temporarily, keep its plant intact, and plan to reopen at some time in the future. Indeed, the firm may use the shutdown period to reorganize in an effort to have lower costs when production begins again. If the firm expects price to remain so depressed in the industry that losses are likely to continue into the future, it may act to sell off its plant and equipment and go out of business.

Supply Curve of a Purely Competitive Firm

The previous considerations help us understand a competitive firm's willingness to supply product as the market price changes, even when it declines. We saw in Chapter 3 that a supply curve shows the relation between the quantity supplied of a good and its price, other things being equal. What is the supply curve of a purely competitive firm in the short run? We answer the question in Figure 8.6.

We have drawn the firm's marginal cost curve and average variable cost curve and a series of different price levels that the firm faces from a competitive market. We know that the general profit-maximizing rule for the competitive firm is to operate at the level of output at which $P = MR = MC$. We also know that the loss-minimizing rule for the firm is to shut down when price falls below the minimum average variable cost. With these two facts, we can derive a supply curve for the competitive firm.

We know that the firm will not produce at a price such as P_0 in Figure 8.6. Since P_0 is below the minimum AVC, the firm will shut down and produce no output at that price. (Notice that no output corresponding to P_0 is given along the horizontal axis.) This decision of the firm applies at any price below P_1, which is the point of minimum AVC. At P_1, the firm will just cover its variable costs and will be economically indifferent about whether it operates. We show the firm producing q_1 units of output at the price P_1. At prices above P_1, the firm will operate in the short run and produce at the output level at which $P = MR = MC$. We show two such cases, at P_2 and P_3. In other words, the firm responds to changes in price above P_1 by producing output along its marginal cost curve. The marginal cost curve of the purely competitive firm above the point of minimum average variable cost is its **short-run firm supply curve**; it shows the relation between price and quantity supplied in a period of time when the firm's plant size is fixed.

Short-run firm supply curve

That portion of a firm's marginal cost curve above the minimum point on the average variable cost curve.

FIGURE 8.6

Short-Run Supply Curve of the Purely Competitive Firm

The short-run supply curve of the purely competitive firm is its marginal cost curve (MC) above the point of minimum average variable cost. The firm will not operate below P_1 because it cannot cover its variable costs of production. Above P_1, the firm produces where $P = MR = MC$.

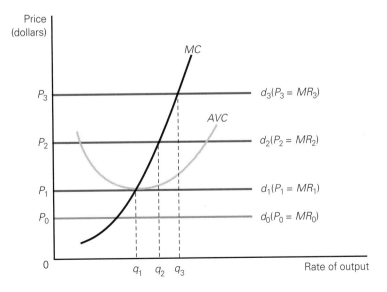

From Firm to Industry Supply

It is a simple step from the competitive firm's short-run supply curve to the short-run industry supply curve. The **short-run industry supply curve** is the horizontal sum of the individual firms' marginal cost schedules above their points of minimum average variable cost. This process is illustrated in Figure 8.7.

For simplicity, assume that the industry consists of two firms producing peanuts. At a price of P_0, firm A produces 3 pounds of peanuts per day and firm B produces 2 pounds; at these outputs, $P = MR = MC$ for each firm. In each case, P_0 is above the firm's minimum AVC. This point on the industry supply curve is 5 pounds per day at a price of P_0. That is, 5 pounds is the horizontal sum of 3 and 2 pounds of peanuts produced by the two firms. If price rises to P_1, the firms expand production, to 5 and 4 pounds, respectively, along their MC curves. The corresponding point for the industry is at 9 pounds of peanuts. Other points on the short-run industry supply curve (S_{SR}) are obtained in the same manner. The short-run supply curve of a competitive industry is the horizontal sum of all the individual firms' marginal cost curves above their respective points of minimum average variable cost.

Three points should be kept in mind about this discussion. First, a purely competitive industry encompasses many independent producers; the two-firm model used to illustrate the derivation of the industry supply schedule is an abstraction. In a real case of pure competition, thousands of marginal cost curves would have to be summed horizontally. Second, our analysis is conducted in the economic time

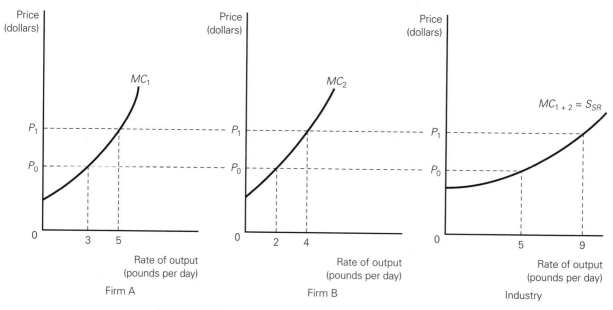

FIGURE 8.7

From Firm to Industry Supply Curves

The short-run supply curve of a competitive industry is the horizontal sum of individual firms' marginal cost curves above their respective points of minimum average variable cost. At price P_0, firm A supplies 3 units (pounds of peanuts) of output, and firm B supplies 2 units. Market supply is 5 units at P_0. Other points on the industry supply curve, such as $5 + 4 = 9$ units at P_1 are derived in the same way.

frame of the short run, in which firms adjust to price changes within the limits imposed by their fixed plant sizes. Third, the intersection of the industry demand curve and the short-run market supply curve determines the market price for the industry. Both firm and industry are in short-run equilibrium. The firm produces at a level where $P = MR = MC$ for its fixed plant, and industry demand equals industry supply. These two conditions define a short-run equilibrium for the purely competitive model.

THE PURELY COMPETITIVE FIRM AND INDUSTRY IN THE LONG RUN

The long run is a period of economic time during which firms can select the lowest-cost plant to produce their output and firms can enter and exit the industry. The result of these adjustments by firms in the face of economic profits and losses is to move the industry toward long-run equilibrium.

Equilibrium in the Long Run

Long-run competitive equilibrium

A market situation in which economic profits are zero for all firms; each firm produces output at minimum average total cost.

Zero economic profits

A condition in which total revenue equals total opportunity cost of production. Firms earn a normal rate of return and $P = MR = LRMC = LRATC$.

Long-run competitive equilibrium occurs when two conditions are met: (1) quantity demanded equals quantity supplied in the market and (2) firms in the industry are making a normal rate of return on their investments, a situation called **zero economic profits.**

Positive economic profits are returns above and beyond the total (explicit plus implicit) costs to the owner of or investor in a firm. They are returns above the opportunity cost of the owner's capital investment in the firm; that is, they are above the normal return that an owner could expect to make on an investment of some other form, such as a money market certificate. Positive economic profits therefore attract the notice of other investors. They are a signal that prods others to try to capture above-normal returns by entering the industry. Economic profits also lead firms already in the industry to seek to expand their scale of operations. Both cases will result in an increase in output in the industry. This causes the short-run industry supply curve to increase and the market price to fall, erasing economic profits and returning the rate of return in the industry to a normal level. This level is referred to as zero economic profits; investors do make an accounting profit, but they make no more than what their money would have earned through the prevailing rate of return on any other investment.

If firms in the industry are making economic losses, the opposite situation holds. Firms will cut back operations, and some firms will leave the industry. The short-run industry supply curve decreases, causing the market price to rise and restoring a normal rate of return to surviving firms.

A long-run equilibrium state for a purely competitive industry is depicted in Figure 8.8. The two conditions for this equilibrium are illustrated in the diagram: (1) quantity demanded equals quantity supplied at the industry level of output, and (2) price just equals the minimum average total cost of the firm. In other words, each firm earns a normal rate of return on its investment in the industry. Notice also that in a long-run equilibrium situation, the market price of output equals long-run marginal cost. Thus the price consumers pay for the good or service just equals the additional cost of producing the good or service.

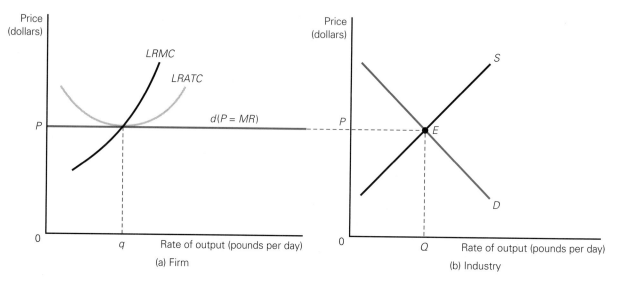

FIGURE 8.8

The Purely Competitive Industry in Long-Run Equilibrium

In a long-run equilibrium, two conditions are met: (a) the competitive firm earns zero economic profit, or a normal rate of return, and (b) at the equilibrium market price, industry quantity demanded equals industry quantity supplied. Market price is exactly equal to minimum long-run average total cost. The market price of the good also equals the long-run marginal cost of producing the good.

The Adjustment Process: Establishing Equilibrium

Establishment of equilibrium is a continual process in the purely competitive industry. (The Appendix to this chapter discusses how this process of adjustment takes place in agriculture.) To see how the position of long-run equilibrium is reached, consider a condition of long-run equilibrium in the peanut industry, which is depicted in Figure 8.9.

Increase In Demand   Now imagine that peanuts are not only given a clean bill of health by government researchers but also are praised as a cure for the common cold by a prominent scientist. The industry demand curve for peanuts suddenly shifts to the right, as shown in Figure 8.9b, raising the market price to P_1 from the previous equilibrium price P_0.

At first, individual firms in the industry (Figure 8.9a) adjust to the higher price P_1 by expanding output from q_0 to q_1 within their fixed plant sizes—that is, along their *SRMC* curves. This increase in firms' output is reflected at the industry level (Figure 8.9b) by the movement along S_0 as price rises from P_0 to P_1. Industry output thus initially rises from Q_0 to Q_1. However, P_1 is above the firm's *SRATC*, so firms in the industry are earning positive economic profits. Other firms will therefore be attracted to the industry. The effect of this adjustment will be to shift the market supply curve to the right, from S_0 to S_1. Eventually, long-run equilibrium is restored at the original price P_0, where firms again earn a normal rate of return. In the process, industry output has further expanded, from Q_1 to Q_2. The economy now produces and consumes more peanuts. In this case, larger industry production is accomplished with a larger number of firms, each operating at the plant size depicted by *SRATC* in Figure 8.9a.

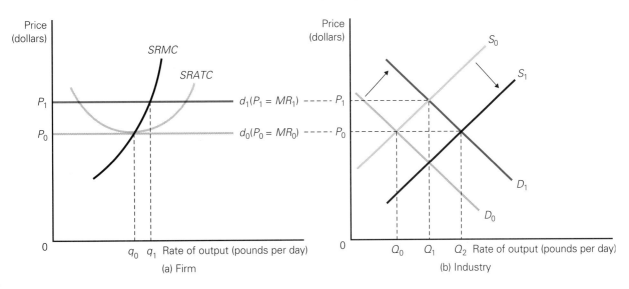

FIGURE 8.9

Industry Adjustments to Long-Run Equilibrium: An Increase in Market Demand

Demand increases from D_0 to D_1 in the industry, and price rises from P_0 to P_1 (b). As demand and price rise, firms now earn profits in excess of their average total costs (a). The opportunity for higher-than-normal profits induces entry by new firms. As this expansion of output takes place, the industry supply curve shifts to the right until a normal rate of return and the original price P_0 are restored in the industry.

Two points should be noted about this process. First, the long-run adjustment process in this example returned price to the original level of minimum average total cost—that is, to the previously prevailing price P_0. This is a special case of long-run adjustment in an industry in which the prices of resources used in the industry do not change when industry output is expanded.

Second, entry can take place from both without and within the industry. Entry from without is the entry of new firms. Entry from within is the expansion of old firms. Entry from within can take place only if there is a range of long-run firm sizes consistent with minimum-cost production. If the long-run average total cost curve of firms in the industry were U-shaped, only one firm size would offer lowest cost in the long run. When this is the case, entry takes place entirely by new firms. The existing firms will not expand their scale of operations because they are already operating with the lowest-cost plant size.

Decrease In Demand   Whereas economic profits lead to the expansion of output in an industry, economic losses lead to a contraction of industry output. Figure 8.10b illustrates a reduction in industry demand from D_0 to D_1. At the resulting lower price of P_1, firms incur economic losses because P_1 is less than firms' average total cost (Figure 8.10a). In the short run, the output of individual firms is reduced, depicted by movement down the $SRMC$ curve, or firms shut down if P_1 is less than their minimum average variable cost. The short-run drop in production by individual firms causes quantity supplied in the industry to fall to Q_1 along S_0. In the long run, some firms will leave the industry by going out of business. The decrease in the number of firms in the industry causes the industry supply curve to shift to the left, from S_0 to S_1. This causes a decrease in total market output from

FIGURE 8.10

Industry Adjustments to Long-Run Equilibrium: A Decrease in Market Demand
Industry demand declines from D_0 to D_1, and market price falls from P_0 to P_1 (b). At P_1 firms incur economic losses and cut back production to $q1$ (a). Industry output falls to Q_1. Losses cause some firms to leave the industry. The overall decline in production shifts the industry supply curve to the left, from S_0 to S_1, thus restoring the original price P_0 and a normal rate of return to firms that remain in the industry.

Q_1 to Q_2 and puts pressure on the industry price to rise. Ultimately, price will rise enough to restore the original price P_0 and a normal rate of return to firms in the industry. Here again, the size of each firm producing output is the same initially and after the long-run industry adjustments to the decrease in demand have taken place. Lower industry output is produced by a smaller number of firms, each operating a plant size represented by $SRATC$ in Figure 8.10a.

What are some of the uses of these analyses? First, they depict the desirable effects of competition on the use and allocation of resources. Signals to producers about what consumers want are sent through the market system, and producers respond by adjusting and supplying what consumers want in a way that minimizes the cost of production. (For an application of the competitive model, see the Application "Do You Have a 'Hunting License?': The Full Price of Parking on Campus" at the end of this chapter.) Second, the model generates testable propositions, such as the assertion that excess returns should promote entry in a competitive market, from both without and within. An indirect way to test for the presence of a competitive market is to see if excess returns or the presence of positive economic profits leads to an expansion of output in the industry, or if a decline in output follows economic losses.

Long-run industry supply

The quantities of a product that all firms in an industry are willing and able to offer for sale at various prices when the number of firms and the scale of operations of each firm are allowed to adjust.

The Long-Run Industry Supply Curve

The **long-run industry supply** curve represents the quantities of a product that all firms in the industry will be willing to supply at alternative prices in the long run—that is, during a period long enough for entry into and exit out of the industry to occur and for firms to adjust their plant sizes to the lowest-cost level. The long-run supply curve reflects what happens to the prices of inputs as the output of an industry is increased or decreased. In our example of long-run equilibrium, depicted in Figures 8.9 and 8.10, price returned to its original level after first rising or falling with a rise or fall in demand. As we noted, this is a special case that does not always apply because the costs of inputs may change as industry output changes. There are three possibilities related to input costs: They may remain constant, increase, or decrease, depending on the nature of the industry.

Constant Cost   In Figures 8.9 and 8.10, long-run adjustments led to the restoration of the original price in the industry (P_0). In the first case, the size of the industry expanded, and in the second case, the size of the industry contracted. In both cases, price returned to the level of P_0 as entry and exit and adjustments by firms in the industry took place.

Figures 8.9 and 8.10 are examples of a **constant-cost industry**, an industry in which expansions or contractions of industry output have no impact on input prices or costs of production. The long-run industry supply (*LRS*) curve in this case is perfectly elastic—a flat, straight line at the level of the long-run equilibrium price in the industry, as shown in Figure 8.11. Notice that the curve is derived by connecting points E_0 and E_1, the points where long-run industry demand intersects supply—that is, points of long-run equilibrium.

Constant cost is most likely to occur in industries where the resources used in industry production are a small proportion of the total demand for the resources in the economy. Take, for example, the toothpick industry. A major expansion, say a tripling, of the output of toothpicks would probably not have much impact on the price of wood used in the industry because far more wood is consumed in other uses, such as building materials, paper, and firewood. The cost of wood to toothpick producers would therefore remain the same as the industry expanded.

Increasing Cost   In an **increasing-cost industry**, expansions of industry output lead to higher input prices and therefore higher costs of production for individual firms. This type of industry exhibits the common slope of the long-run industry supply curve because the expansion of most industries puts upward pressure on costs in the industry. An increase in the demand for chicken meat will cause the

Constant-cost industry

An industry in which the minimum *LRATC* of production does not change as the number of firms in the industry changes; expansion (contraction) of the number of firms does not bid up (down) input prices; long-run industry supply is horizontal.

Increasing-cost industry

An industry in which the expansion (contraction) of the number of firms bids up (down) input prices; minimum *LRATC* of production changes as the number of firms in the industry changes; long-run industry supply is upward sloping to the right.

FIGURE 8.11

Long-Run Price in a Constant-Cost Industry

The long-run industry supply curve *(LRS)* for a constant-cost industry is horizontal at the level of the market price. Expansions in industry output do not change resource costs to individual firms.

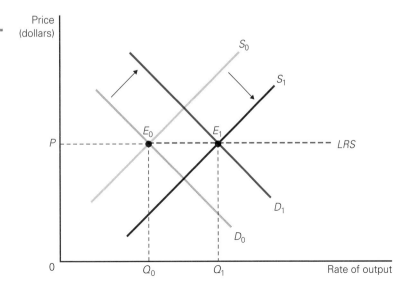

prices of chicken feed, farm land, and chicken coops to rise. An increase in the demand for newspapers will lead to higher prices for paper, printers, reporters, and so on. These increases in cost lead to a higher long-run price for the goods produced. To obtain more of these goods, consumers must pay higher prices in the long run in order to attract additional resources into their production.

The effects of industry expansion on price and supply in an increasing-cost industry are shown in Figure 8.12. Initially, the firm and industry are in equilibrium at E_0, with a market price of P_0. Demand increases, the market demand curve shifts to the right from D_0 to D_1, and price rises initially to P_1. Entry into the industry and increased production are encouraged by the higher price, with the additional entry represented by a shift in the supply curve from S_0 to S_1. As production expands, however, resource costs to producers in the industry rise, causing the individual firms' cost curves to shift upward. Thus, as entry takes place, price falls from its height at P_1, and costs to producers rise until a new equilibrium is reached at E_1. This new equilibrium price is higher than the initial equilibrium price of P_0. Connecting the two equilibrium points at E_0 and E_1 yields the long-run industry supply curve. The long-run industry supply curve in an increasing-cost industry slopes upward to the right because additional resources needed to produce additional output in such an industry come at higher costs.

Decreasing-cost industry

An industry in which the long-run industry supply is downward-sloping; expansion (contraction) of the number of firms bids down (up) input prices; minimum *LRATC* of production falls as the number of firms in the industry increases.

Decreasing Cost   In a **decreasing-cost industry**, expansion of industry output leads to lower input prices and lower costs for individual firms and hence to a lower long-run market price for the product. This is an unusual type of long-run industry supply, but a decreasing-cost industry is logically possible. As the clothing industry expands, for example, the costs of certain inputs may fall. Producers of cutting and sewing machines may experience economies of scale, leading to lower prices for their machines. Hence, it is possible for the long-run supply curve of clothing producers to exhibit the decreasing-cost phenomenon.

FIGURE 8.12

Long-Run Price Changes in an Increasing-Cost Industry

Expansions of industry output in response to higher demand D_1 and resulting higher price P_1 lead to higher resource costs facing individual producers in the industry. Equilibrium is reached at P_2 as costs to producers rise and price falls from P_1 to P_2. The long-run industry supply curve (*LRS*) for an increasing-cost industry, determined by connecting equilibrium points E_0 and E_1, slopes upward to the right.

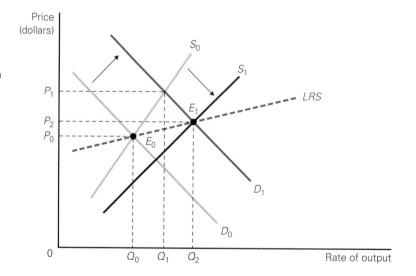

PURE COMPETITION AND ECONOMIC EFFICIENCY

The model of a purely competitive market is often used by economists as a bench-mark or ideal against which other models of market structure are compared. This point will be more obvious in Chapter 9, where we discuss the market structure of pure monopoly. But we first need to understand in what sense the operation of the purely competitive market represents an ideal outcome in the economy and in what sense the model is only an ideal.

The Competitive Market and Resource Allocation

Pure competition produces what most economists would agree is an ideal or opti-mal resource allocation. Purely competitive allocation of resources is optimal or best in two fundamental senses.

Productive efficiency

A condition in which total industry output is produced at the lowest possible opportunity cost of resources.

First, a competitive industry minimizes the resource costs of producing out-put. In effect, competition forces firms to produce their output at the minimum long-run average total cost and at a price just sufficient to cover that cost. This **productive efficiency** can be seen in long-run equilibrium in competitive firms, which produce at the point where $P = LRATC = LRMC$. It is the minimum possi-ble opportunity cost of producing the good or service. Consumers benefit because they get the goods they desire at the lowest possible cost. This is so because market equilibrium price equals minimum long-run average cost of production. Inefficient, high-cost firms will incur economic losses and will be driven from competitive mar-kets. Surviving will be firms who can provide industry output at the lowest cost.

Allocative efficiency

A situation in which the socially optimal amount of a good or service is produced in an industry; the socially optimal amount depends on the tastes and preferences of society and on the opportunity cost of the resources used to produce the good or service.

Second, a competitive market also results in **allocative efficiency**. Allocative efficiency exists when the price paid by consumers for one more, or the last, unit of a good or service just equals the cost of the resources that produce the addi-tional, or last, unit of the good or service. It is the socially optimal output of the good or service. In a competitive market, consumer demands are met as long as consumers are willing to pay a price for the production of an additional unit of output equal to the cost of the additional resources required to produce the addi-tional output. In competitive markets, resources flow to their most highly valued uses, resulting in allocative efficiency. As noted in Chapter 4, the equation of sup-ply and demand in competitive equilibrium produces a maximum net value to soci-ety of using scarce resources to produce a product. Competitive equilibrium also creates the maximization of the sum of consumer and producer surplus in the process of allocating resources to their most highly valued uses. Collectively, this means that market competition—in the absence of "third-party effects" in the use of resources—creates allocative efficiency and it is what economists mean when they say that "competition is efficient."

This situation is expressed in the now familiar condition $P = LRMC$. Price reflects the desire of consumers for additional units of a good. Long-run marginal cost represents the opportunity cost of the resources necessary to produce an addi-tional unit of the good. If P is greater than $LRMC$, consumers will pay more for additional units of production than the cost to produce them. When this is the case, resources in the economy will be reallocated from other uses considered less valu-able by consumers. If a chicken farmer, for instance, finds that consumers will now pay more for the relatively scarce rooster hackle feathers prized for fly-fishing than they will pay for relatively abundant chicken meat, the farmer will shift the use of some chicken coops, chicken feed, and farmhands from production of meat birds to production of roosters bred for hackle feathers.

If P is less than $LRMC$, consumers will pay less for additional units of production than the cost to produce them. Resources will be reallocated out of such production. If the price for hackle feathers is less than the cost, then fewer hackle feathers will be available for fly-fishing. If P equals $LRMC$, resource allocation is ideal in the sense that the things consumers want are produced by competitive firms in the exact quantities and combination (of feathers and food, for instance) that consumers desire and at the lowest cost.

This discussion should sound familiar. In Chapter 4 we pointed out why the intersection of supply and demand curves and the equilibrium price in a competitive market were so important in economics. We have now come full circle to establish this fact in greater detail. Long-run competitive equilibrium represents the best that society can do in producing and consuming goods and services. This condition ensures that products are produced at least cost and that individuals obtain the goods they want. As discussed in Chapter 4, such a process maximizes the sum of consumers' and producers' surplus in an economy. This is as good as it gets in economics.

The competitive model is really Adam Smith's concept of the "invisible hand" at work. Acting in their self-interest, consumers and producers create a mutually beneficial outcome. Looking out for their own interests, producers seek to maximize profits, and yet in a competitive market the result is that consumers' desires are met in the most efficient way possible. Consumers demand the goods and services they want, but competitive producers balance those demands against other demands for other goods and services. An incredibly complex process of consumer demand and producer response is put in motion by the behavior of each individual in heeding his or her own interest. No central planner is required, and yet a result emerges that is ideal.

Perfect competition may not be perfect in every sense, however. While a purely competitive world leads to an ideal resource allocation, it might not lead to an ideal distribution of income among people. Equity will conflict sometimes with the achievement of economic efficiency. In other words, competitive solutions will not always result in equitable solutions (or what is considered equitable in law or by society). Also, while pure competition accommodates consumers' preferences, these preferences themselves may not conform to anyone's image of the ideal state of human existence. Individuals are free to buy and sell as they see fit. If consumers want gadgets rather than great books, they are free to make this choice. Further, the model of perfect competition assumes that there are no "third-party" effects—social costs or externalities being inflicted on others by the competitive firms. This issue is addressed in more detail in Chapter 17. Finally, as we have noted earlier (see, for example, the Focus "The Economics of Information: Searching for the best Deal"), information is a costly "good" like running shoes or a steak. Information is seldom perfect, as the basic competitive model assumes it to be. Sometimes, the parties to an exchange have different information. This may cause problems in particular markets, such as those for used cars or other consumer durables. However, the competitive market provides some relief even in these cases (see, for example, the Focus "Don't Buy a 'Lemon': Information Problems and You").

FOCUS

Don't Buy a "Lemon": Information Problems and You

Suppose that you, a college student of somewhat limited means, are in the market for a used pickup truck. Your local newspaper runs the ad shown below, which catches your eye. This is exactly the kind of vehicle you want, so you call to inquire about the price. The price you are quoted over the phone is $2,000 lower than the price listed in a used car "bluebook." Instead of being ecstatic, however, you are suspicious.

> 1997 Ford Ranger, blk, 4WD, a/c,
> AM/FM/cass., showroom condition
> Call 555-1238 after 5 P.M.

Many products are sold in a used or "secondary" market under competitive conditions. When you manage to pay less than the going rate for many of these products, such as a bicycle or an exercise machine, you believe you are getting a great deal. This is not necessarily the case for used cars or other durable goods (washing machines and television sets, for example), because with "complicated" products of high replacement costs, you must be particularly careful about getting a "lemon," or a product of substandard quality.

In addition to asking price, the age of a car—or any other consumer durable such as a refrigerator or dryer—is a factor when you are trying to determine whether a seller is attempting to unload a lemon. While people have all sorts of reasons for wanting to sell their cars—even relatively new cars—most people hold off until they have put many thousands of miles on a car or until the car is

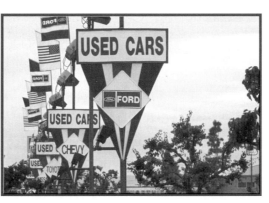

several years old. (Some would sell a year-old refrigerator because it is the wrong color, however.) You would probably be suspicious of a car that is "too new" as you would a car that is "too good" a deal. In fact, you are probably willing to pay a high price for a high-quality used car. While this price would certainly be acceptable to the seller, the competitive market might not facilitate such trades.

The problem is one of "asymmetric," or one-sided, information. Used car sellers tend to know the quality of the cars while buyers do not. If, for some given grade or model of car or refrigerator, there is an excess supply at an above-equilibrium price, price will tend to fall (some sellers will take less). But this very market mechanism that *lowers* price makes you even more suspicious that the car or other consumer durable is a lemon. Demand declines causing price to fall further, and you become even more suspicious, and so on….

Many transactions do in fact take place every day in used car and other secondary markets. Some buyers' and sellers' assessments will overlap. More importantly, the competitive market works at least partially to solve the information problems relating to such trades. Used car warranties offered by sellers, independent garages that will provide assessments, and reputations of new car dealers (who also sell used cars) are several ways to provide assurances of quality. Markets where "lemons" might exist may not function perfectly, but there are competitive forces at work to ensure that efficient, utility-producing trades will become more likely under such circumstances.

Competition in the Real World

Many critics argue that in the real world it is nearly impossible to find examples of perfectly competitive markets. To them, evidence that products sold by rival firms are not homogeneous, that prices charged by these firms are not identical, or that buyers are not perfectly informed proves the competitive model is not applicable.

Defenders of the competitive model, in turn, argue that the competitive model can explain real-world behavior in a variety of markets. To them, the assumption of homogeneous products is not essential.

The market for student apartments is one in which we can readily contrast the two conflicting points of view. As any student who has shopped for an apartment knows, the units are not homogeneous, and prices are not uniform. Should one infer from these real-world facts that the market for apartments is not competitive?

Advocates of free markets would argue that use of the competitive model in this case is quite appropriate. Instead of viewing apartment units as goods being bought and sold, imagine a market for some intangible good called housing services. Although a unit of housing services cannot be defined exactly, each apartment can be viewed as giving some quantity of services to its tenant. Luxury units in prime locations have a large number of units of housing services; substandard units in undesirable locations have a small quantity of housing services. In the rental housing market there are many students who are buyers of housing services, and many landlords who sell housing services.

From this perspective, the disparity in rental prices among apartment units is entirely consistent with the theory of perfect competition. If a particular apartment is perceived to be twice as good as another unit (yielding twice the quantity of housing services), we would expect the first apartment to rent for twice as much. The two units are physically quite different and have different locations, but the apartment owners still compete with each other. Although student tenants have imperfect information about apartment prices, students do have an incentive to acquire such information. The real-world alternative to perfect information is some information—not complete ignorance. The assumption of complete information is not totally unrealistic.

Price differences among auto dealers or among gasoline stations also can be reconciled with the competitive model. In each case, sellers are competing for the sale of services to buyers, so price differences may only reflect differences in the units of service provided to customers.

In the real world, owners of competitive firms are faced with constantly changing conditions: fluctuating prices for their products, new government regulations, natural disasters. To put it another way, entrepreneurs must operate in a world of risk and uncertainty.

The concept of risk involves aspects of the economic environment that, to some extent, can be predicted. The fact that risks are predictable implies that they are known. Fires and natural disasters, for example, are known risks involved in business ownership. When entrepreneurs take steps to protect themselves from known risks—for example, by purchasing insurance—they incur costs. These costs become a part of the firm's long-run marginal and average costs.

Uncertainty is distinct from risk in that uncertain events cannot be predicted. Pure uncertainty refers to events with no known probabilities—the announcement of an invention that will decrease (or increase) a firm's sales, for example. Therefore, competitive entrepreneurs cannot protect themselves from uncertainty by buying insurance. Entrepreneurs simply must live with uncertainty. The lucky ones will profit from uncertain events, and the unlucky ones will suffer a loss.

Neither risk nor uncertainty undermines the usefulness of the competitive model. As we have seen, risk can be treated as a cost of doing business in the competitive marketplace. And uncertainty brings out the best instincts in competitive entrepreneurs.

It should be obvious that the competitive model can be used to analyze markets even if all the underlying assumptions are not met. However, economists have developed alternatives to the competitive model to analyze the behavior of firms in industries comprising a single firm or only a few large firms. Economists have also developed useful models for examining forms of nonprice competition in markets that are not easily explained by the competitive model. The following three chapters develop several of the alternative models.

APPLICATION

Do You Have a "Hunting License?": The Full Price of Parking on Campus

A common problem at most universities—especially those in an urban setting—is parking. Universities, colleges, and public facilities must somehow allocate parking spaces among competing demanders. Space for parking, to the dismay of faculty and students, is grossly inadequate at most universities. Many devices are used to restrict campus parking to the available number of spaces. Parking stickers are commonly assigned with some kind of "pecking order" designed for faculty (chaired scholars, deans, assistant professors) and students (undergraduate students, graduate students). In many cases, however, without "reserved" spaces, stickers are no more than hunting licenses.

Problems are often compounded by universities who, often to please particular constituencies, invoke standards of "justice" in doling out the limited number of places. A popular standard that is usually devised by a faculty committee is to keep parking fees "low" in the interests of justice. A response to low prices and a means of reducing demand for spaces would be to schedule classes at all hours of the day and night, but this would run afoul of certain campus constituencies. Campus bureaucrats, faculty, and students would be up in arms. Another (and more

Valuable student and faculty time is spent "hunting" for a parking space on campus.

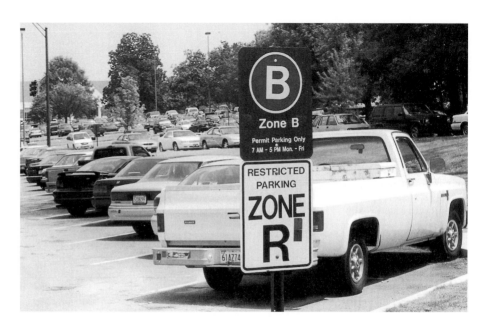

popular) means of allocating the spaces is to raise *implicit* prices of parking to faculty and students by imposing stiff fines for parking violations.

The typical problems may be viewed with the aid of Figure 8.13. In Figure 8.13 some homogeneous demand for campus parking is assumed (faculty, students, and administrators are lumped together in the demand curve). Full price, which includes not only the nominal sticker price of parking but the time spent in finding a parking space as well, is depicted on the vertical axis. The number of spaces is given on the horizontal axis. The supply of parking spaces is assumed to be limited to Q_s. The average price of stickers (hunting licenses) is P_s, a low nominal price set by the faculty committee in the interests of "fairness" or "justice." The result is an excess demand of $Q_d - Q_s$ or HG at price P_s.

What is the result of this low nominal or dollar price for parking? Clearly, ever-vigilant campus police, armed with tickets representing high fines, could reduce the demand to Q_s. This would, however, be at the cost of reduced utility and increased fine payments to those who require parking. This means that the implicit price of a parking sticker rises. If the system described in Figure 8.13 remains in place, students and faculty will be forced to hunt for a parking place at popular class times during the day. The costs to you will vary with the class time of day (how long you have to hunt) and with the value of time to you as an individual. Normally, this full price (the money or sticker price plus the value of time spent) will be greater for full professors (eminent scholars) than for assistant professors (they generally earn less income). For all individuals, however, these "hunting" costs form part of the full price of parking on campus. The result is that the full price rations the scarce number of spaces for students and faculty, but at higher costs—the time costs—not collected by anyone. The full price charged equals $P_s + t$, where t is the opportunity cost of search time for a parking space.

Competitive markets, even with spaces limited to Q_s in the short run, could come to the rescue. One solution would be to auction off spaces to faculty and students alike. Spaces would go to the highest bidders who may be well-heeled freshmen or wealthy sorority members. This would undoubtedly cause "outrage" among faculty, administrators, and less wealthy students. But the university would be richer (up to the amount of $0AFQ_s$) and would, in the long run, be able to build new parking facilities. Another solution is to randomly allocate the limited parking spaces at

FIGURE 8.13

The Campus Hunting License

The graph demonstrates some of the problems associated with campus parking when the nominal sticker price is P_s and quantity demanded of parking spaces (Q_d) exceeds the quantity supplied (Q_s).

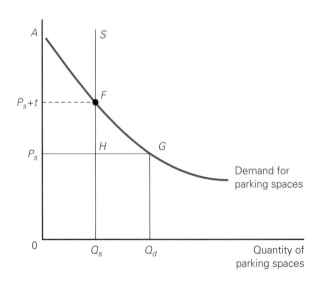

the sticker price (P_s in Figure 8.13) and to let faculty and students freely trade (buy and sell) their stickers. Those who valued them more would enrich those who valued stickers less. An amount P_sAG would be transferred. Thus, competition could be used to allocate the scarce spaces $0Q_s$. Mandatory imposition of "just" prices by the university, it must be noted, does not mean that a competitive market does not work. It does mean that more costly solutions are imposed on the market. Think about this the next time that you spend valuable time hunting for a parking space.

SUMMARY

1. Economists study competition in two basic senses: as a rivalrous, natural process among competitors and as an abstract concept described by the model of a purely competitive market.

2. A purely competitive market is characterized by many buyers and many sellers, a homogeneous product, no barriers to entry or exit by firms, and free information. Examples of this type of market include the stock market and agricultural markets.

3. The purely competitive firm is a price taker: the firm is so small in relation to the total market for its product that its output has no influence on the prevailing market price. The demand curve facing the purely competitive firm is perfectly elastic at the level of the prevailing market price.

4. Marginal revenue is the change in total revenue caused by an increase in output. Since the purely competitive firm faces a perfectly elastic demand curve, each unit is sold at the prevailing market price. Thus, marginal revenue is equal to market price for the pure competitor.

5. In the short run, the pure competitor decides how much output to produce by setting marginal cost equal to market price. If price is above the average total cost, the firm earns an economic profit in the short run. If price is below the minimum average variable cost, the firm will shut down in the short run to minimize its losses.

6. The supply curve of a purely competitive firm is its marginal cost curve above the point of minimum average variable cost. The supply curve of a purely competitive industry in the short run is the horizontal sum of individual firms' marginal cost curves above their respective points of minimum average variable cost.

7. Short-run equilibrium for the purely competitive firm and industry occurs when the quantity supplied and quantity demanded are equal in the market and each firm is producing at the level where $P = MR = SRMC$.

8. In the long run, firms in a purely competitive industry can enter and exit the industry and seek the optimal plant size in which to produce their output. The presence of positive economic profits leads to entry and expansion in the industry, and economic losses lead to the opposite.

9. Long-run equilibrium in a purely competitive industry results when firms in the industry earn zero economic profits and industry demand and supply are equal. In the long run, the purely competitive firm's position is such that price equals long-run marginal cost equals long-run average total cost: $P = LRMC = LRATC$.

10. The long-run industry supply curve in a purely competitive industry reflects what happens to firm costs as industry output expands or contracts. In a constant-cost industry, resource prices and firm costs are unchanged by industry expansion, and the long-run industry supply curve is perfectly elastic. An increasing-cost industry experiences rising costs as industry output expands; the long-run industry supply curve slopes upward to the right. In a decreasing-cost industry, resource prices fall as industry output expands, and the long-run industry supply curve slopes downward to the right.

11. The working of the purely competitive model represents a benchmark against which the working of the economy can be measured. In this model, resources flow to their most highly valued uses, and output is produced at the lowest cost in terms of resources used. In the real world, entrepreneurs face risk and uncertainty and the competitive model has useful applicability.

KEY TERMS

market
purely competitive market
homogeneous product
perfect information
price taker
profits
marginal revenue

total revenue
shutdown
short-run firm supply curve
short-run industry supply curve
long-run competitive equilibrium
zero economic profits
long-run industry supply

constant-cost industry
increasing-cost industry
decreasing-cost industry
productive efficiency
allocative efficiency

QUESTIONS FOR REVIEW AND DISCUSSION

1. What is a market? What is a purely competitive market?

2. Why are price and marginal revenue the same thing for a purely competitive firm?

3. What is the supply curve of a purely competitive firm? Of a purely competitive industry?

4. Describe the adjustment process between points of long-run equilibrium in an increasing-cost industry.

5. Suppose that the news media report the contamination of oyster fisheries in the coastal waters off the eastern United States. The news creates a decrease in demand for oysters. If oyster production is a constant-cost industry, describe the adjustment to the new equilibrium using graphical analysis.

6. Suppose that a competitive firm is earning economic profits because its owner has figured out a way to lower the costs of production. Since the source of the reduced costs is known only to the owner, how can entry take place? Should such information be proprietary (belong to the owner), or should the owner be required to tell potential competitors the reason for the lower costs?

7. Which of the following markets could be analyzed with the competitive model: (a) automobiles; (b) Swiss cheese; (c) blue jeans; (d) cheeseburgers; (e) trash collection; (f) television news; (g) janitorial services?

8. How long will a firm in a competitive industry endure economic losses before it leaves the industry? In your answer, assume that price is above minimum *SRAVC* but below *SRATC*.

9. Suppose that a perfectly competitive industry is in long-run equilibrium. In an effort to make a profit, could a firm in this industry raise the price of its product? Why or why not?

PROBLEMS

1. The following data and the graph at right pertain to a competitive firm.

Output	MC	MR	TR	TC	Profit
1	5.00	9.00	9.00	10.00	− 1.00
2	4.10	9.00	18.00	14.10	3.90
3	4.25	9.00	27.00	18.35	8.65
4	4.67	9.00	36.00	23.02	12.98
5	5.50	9.00	45.00	28.52	16.48
6	6.60	9.00	54.00	35.12	18.88
7	7.66	9.00	63.00	42.78	20.22
8	9.00	9.00	72.00	51.78	20.22
9	10.75	9.00	81.00	62.53	18.47
10	12.50	9.00	90.00	75.03	14.97

a. How much output should this competitive firm produce?

b. What will be the firm's profit at its profit-maximizing rate of output?

c. Why can't the firm charge a long-run price of $10?

2. Suppose that a cancer researcher finds that eating a large amount of turkey every day virtually eliminates your chances of getting a certain kind of cancer. Assuming that the market for turkey is perfectly competitive (for both inputs and outputs), construct figures and show what you would expect to occur in the short and long run for each of the following.

a. the industry demand for turkeys

b. profits of turkey producers

c. profits of beef producers

d. wages for experienced turkey science researchers

e. the price of turkey

3. Take any item of common consumption—for example, premium gasoline or a particular textbook that you require, and sample sellers' prices in your college town or campus area. You will likely find that prices are not homogeneous among sellers. How do you explain the differences in price? Does the variability in prices suggest that the market is not "competitive"?

WORKING WITH THE WEB

1. You have now learned about the problem of asymmetric information from the Focus "Don't Buy a 'Lemon': Information Problems and You." To consider how the problem of asymmetric information applies to you, go to www.ebay.com and select the link for "Collectibles." Scroll down and find the link for Lunchboxes and select "metal." Assuming you are a collector of metal lunchboxes, scroll through the available items up for auction. You will notice that some sellers provide pictures and descriptions, while other sellers do not provide pictures. For example, today there are two *Munsters* lunchboxes available—one for $20 and one for $12. The $20 item provides a picture while the $12 item does not. Look for a similar situation and click on the links to examine the lunchbox descriptions (and picture).

a. Assuming the descriptions are very similar and that the prices are comparable (as in the above example), which lunchbox would you select?

b. How does asymmetric information apply to your situation?

2. Parking on campus is typically a problem, as described in the Application "Do You Have a 'Hunting License': The Full Price of Parking on Campus" in this chapter. Some of the possible remedies suggested to help solve the parking problem were to have reserved spaces, auction the spaces to the highest bidder, or have a random distribution of spaces. Let's see if any of these remedies are put into action on a college campus. First, go to http://www.louisville.edu/admin/dps/parking/permit.htm and look at the permit options and fees.

A Red (reserved) space is available only to faculty and staff, and there are a limited number of reserved spaces. This is the most expensive permit and the permit holder is assigned a numbered, reserved space (until 5:00 P.M.). Since the University of Louisville is largely a commuter campus, the most common permit for students is the Green permit. Faculty, staff, and graduate assistants can also purchase a Blue permit. Holders of a Red permit are also permitted to park in the Blue or Green lots. Both the Green and Blue permits are "licenses to hunt." Blue parking lots tend to have closer proximity to campus buildings than Green lots. Red lots tend to be closest to campus buildings. Clearly, faculty and staff have the most choice, as they can select any of the three options. Students have the least choice, since they can only purchase the Green permit.

a. Has the University of Louisville done anything to remedy the problem of "hunting" for a space?

b. Why do faculty and staff have more options than students in choosing a permit? Is this fair from an economic perspective?

The Economics
of Agriculture
in the United States:
Toward a Market Approach

A P P E N D I X

When economists are asked to provide real-world examples of perfectly competitive markets, agricultural examples are usually among the first mentioned. There is a good reason for this. First, the total number of farms in the United States is huge—currently about 2.2 million. In addition, the number of competing producers within each segment is also quite large; for example, there are about 30,000 poultry producers and about 165,000 dairy farmers in this country. Therefore, the competitive model, which assumes a large number of competing producers of homogeneous products, is entirely appropriate for analyzing agricultural markets. Although economists consider competitive markets to be models of efficiency, agricultural markets continue to experience many economic difficulties. Year-to-year income instability has plagued the nation's farmers. Poverty on the farm continues, with many farmers forced out of business each year despite numerous government assistance programs.

Some indication of the farm problem may be seen in Table 8.2, which shows the number of farms, the acreage in farming, and the average (acre size) per farm between 1980 and 1996. (The annual change in the number of farms is from the immediate preceding year.) Clearly, the number of U.S. farms has declined precipitously—by almost 400,000 farms—with most of the reductions in the 1980s but with a reduction in almost 100,000 farms in the 1990s. Interestingly, the total number of acres farmed has

declined, while the average size of the American farm has undergone an upward trend. This means, in part, that a high rate of new technology is being experienced in U.S. agriculture, but technology is not the whole story. What is the underlying explanation for these phenomena? By applying some of the economic principles we have covered in the text to this point, we can gain insight into these problems. Further, the problems found in the U.S. farming sector help to explain the market-oriented approach of the new programs of the 1990s and the prospect for farming in the twenty-first century.

GOVERNMENT ATTEMPTS TO SOLVE BASIC AGRICULTURAL PROBLEMS

Since the 1930s, the federal government has implemented thousands of assistance programs aimed at reducing price instability or subsidizing the incomes of American farmers. Among them were programs to directly support agricultural prices, restrict production, promote consumption, and subsidize exports and restrict imports. All the programs fall into one of two categories. In the first category are programs that attempt to alter the demand or supply curves of farm products while allowing markets to clear at equilibrium prices. In the second type of program, the government regulates farm prices with direct price supports but does not attempt to manipulate demand or supply.

TABLE 8.2

Number and Acreage of U.S. Farms, 1980–1996

Year	FARMS Number (1,000)	Annual Change (1,000)	LAND IN FARMS Total (mil. acres)	Average per farm (acres)
1980	2,440	3	1,039	426
1985	2,293	−41	1,012	441
1987	2,213	−37	999	451
1988	2,201	−12	994	452
1989	2,175	−26	991	456
1990	2,146	−29	987	460
1991	2,117	−29	982	464
1992	2,108	−9	979	464
1993	2,083	−25	976	469
1994	2,065	−18	973	471
1995	2,072	7	972	469
1996	2,063	−9	968	469

Source: Statistical Abstract of the United States 1997 (Washington, D.C.: U.S. Government Printing Office), p.668.

Note: Over the past twenty years, the number of farms has declined steadily while the amount of land in farming has also declined. The steady increase in farm production has taken place on larger farms (on average).

Agricultural Programs That Manipulate Demand And Supply

Since both demand and supply of agricultural products tend to be inelastic with respect to price, relatively small shifts in either curve can affect incomes. Therefore, government policies that increase demand for farm products lead to large price increases and to huge increases in farmers' incomes. In Figure 8.14a, an increase in demand from D_0 to D_1 for apples causes the equilibrium price to rise from 10 cents per pound to 15 cents per pound and the equilibrium quantity to rise from 6 to 8 billion pounds per year. Such a shift would cause the receipts of apple producers to double from $600 million to $1.2 billion. Over the years, the federal government has implemented a number of policies that have affected demand in this way, including the school lunch and breakfast programs, food stamp programs, and export subsidy programs.

Programs that restrict the supply of agricultural products have similar effects on farmers' incomes.

Figure 8.14b shows that a decrease in supply from S_0 to S_1 will cause the price to rise from 10 cents per pound to 16 cents per pound and will increase the receipts of apple growers from $600 million to $880 million per year (5,500,000,000 × $0.16 = $880,000,000). Over the years, the federal government has implemented acreage restriction programs that limit the number of acres farmers can use for production of certain crops; land retirement programs that pay farmers to withdraw land from production; and conservation programs that subsidize farmers to plant cover crops in place of cash crops to improve soil fertility. The federal government has also, at times, restricted imports of agricultural products. Assuming that supply curve S_0 in Figure 8.14b includes apples produced by foreign growers, programs that restrict apple imports will also increase incomes of domestic apple growers.

Each of these programs has increased incomes of domestic farmers; however, the programs have done little to stabilize farm incomes. In fact, when programs

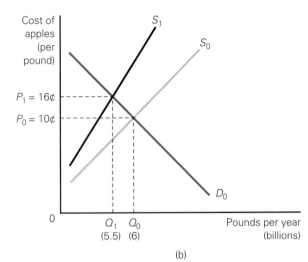

(a)   (b)

FIGURE 8.14

The Economic Consequences of Government Programs That Shift Demand or Supply

(a) Government subsidy programs that increase demand cause price and quantity to rise.
(b) Government programs that restrict supply cause price to rise but quantity to fall. If demand is inelastic, farmers' incomes will rise.

are changed from year to year, the effect can be a destabilization of farm prices.

Agricultural Programs That Regulate Prices

In addition to the various government programs designed to affect demand and supply of certain agricultural products, the government has also implemented two general types of programs that directly control prices. The first is a standard price support program. Under this program, the government sets a minimum price for a commodity and agrees to buy the commodity at that price.

Figure 8.15 shows the effect of setting a minimum price on wheat at $7.50 per bushel. When the government offers to buy wheat at $7.50 per bushel, growers will be unwilling to sell in private markets at any price below $7.50. As a consequence, growers will harvest 3.25 billion bushels but will sell only 2.25 billion bushels at $7.50 per bushel. The federal government must then buy the surplus 1 billion bushels of wheat at a price of $7.50 per bushel for a total cost of $7.5 billion. Farmers' incomes will go up, but consumers

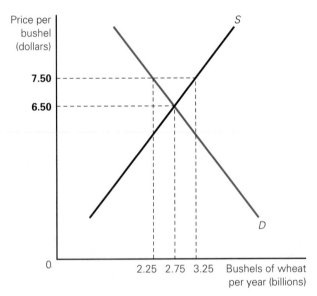

FIGURE 8.15

The Economic Effects of a Price Support Program

A government support price of $7.50 per bushel will lead to a wheat surplus of 1 billion bushels, which the government is forced to purchase.

FIGURE 8.16

The Economic Effects of a Target Price Program

A target price of $7.50 per bushel causes wheat farmers to harvest 3.25 billion bushels, which they sell for $5.50 per bushel. The government pays $2.00 per bushel to farmers to raise the price to the target level.

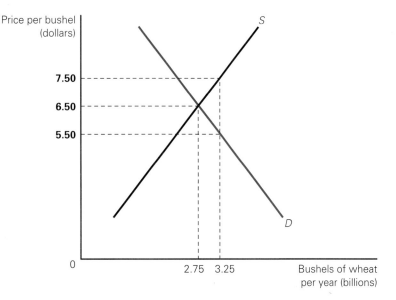

will pay higher food prices and higher taxes to provide the required subsidy. Having purchased the surplus wheat, the government must also determine what to do with it. It would do no good to sell the wheat—this would decrease the amount of wheat that could be sold privately at $7.50 per bushel and increase the surplus the government had to purchase. Instead, the alternatives are storing the wheat (and paying to do so), destroying it, or giving it away (to buyers who would not under any circumstances purchase American wheat).

Figure 8.15 illustrates how a direct price support program can become costly to finance. Increased supply due to improved technology leads to larger surpluses and greater government costs. Therefore, price support programs have usually been accompanied by programs to limit supply. In this way, the price can be kept at the support level without causing large surpluses.

In recent years the Department of Agriculture has phased out the simple price support system. Under the newer system, the government set a target price for affected commodities and agreed to make up the difference between the farmer's selling price and the target price. Figure 8.16 illustrates the operation of target prices, using demand and supply curves identical to those in Figure 8.15. If the government sets the target price at $7.50 per bushel, producers will supply 3.25 billion bushels. They would be willing to supply this

quantity because with the government subsidy included, the price they will receive is $7.50 per bushel. As the graph shows, producers will be able to sell that quantity at a price of $5.50 per bushel. Therefore, the government must pay a subsidy of $2 per bushel (the difference between $7.50 and $5.50) for each of the 3.25 billion bushels. The total subsidy cost of this program will be $6.5 billion.

The government, at least partially, has replaced traditional price supports with target prices for several reasons. One reason is that a given level of income can be generated with lower government subsidies. The subsidies in Figures 8.15 and 8.16 produce equal incomes to farmers, but the target price subsidy saves taxpayers $1 billion. In addition, the target price program keeps prices down for consumers and makes it easier for agricultural output to be sold abroad. And target prices require less expensive storage and wasteful destruction of surpluses.

THE MOVE TO MARKETS IN AGRICULTURE

Despite the use of target pricing in the subsidization of the farm sector, enormous problems and misallocations remained in the first half of the 1990s. Political pressures developed over the issues raised by subsidies and target pricing, with farmers often

Sales of farm equipment due to farm bankruptcies are common in some parts of the U.S.

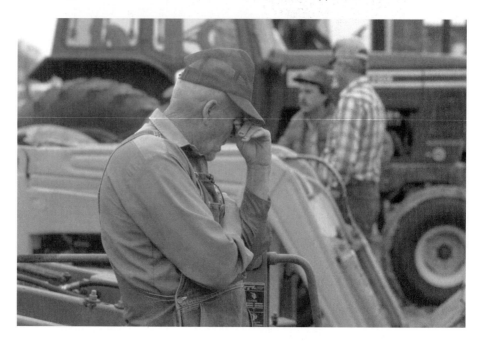

supporting different sides of the issues. The maintenance of grain and other large "reserve programs" and acreage allotments on particular crops were not eliminated under target pricing—only lessened. Political pressures developed on all sides of the issue as farm problems grew. The results of almost seventy years of government involvement in agriculture, when combined with the rate of technological change over that period, have been disastrous for many farmers. Consider some of the problems.

Government's Impact On Agriculture: An Assessment

Table 8.3 shows the extent of subsidy spending on various types of farms. Clearly, larger farms receive the lion's share of the farm subsidy. In real 1995 dollars, subsidies reached a high in 1988 of the years considered and, in recent years, they have declined on average. But the data are deceptive: Many government programs (particularly those that manipulate supply

TABLE 8.3

Government Payments to Farms of Various Sizes
Government subsidies for various size farms are shown below. The average dollar payment has been converted to 1995 dollars for easy comparison.

	AVERAGE PAYMENT PER FARM			
Amount of Farm Sales	**1975**	**1980**	**1988**	**1992**
Less than $20,000	$343	$190	$1,188	$383
$20,000 to $39,999	$1,261	$913	$7,378	$2,992
$40,000 to $99,999	$2,065	$2,050	$14,534	$6,425
$100,000 to $500,000	$3,555	$3,377	$30,941	$16,136
Greater than $500,000	$14,711	$6,749	$52,448	$26,764

Source: Statistical Abstract of the United States 1984, 1990, and 1994 (Washington, D.C.: U.S. Government Printing Office, 1997).

and demand and support the price of products) make no direct government payments to farmers. Despite massive government expenditures, the woes of American farmers continue. Farm debt has increased from $53 billion in 1970 to more than $140 billion today, and farm foreclosures and auctions have become weekly events in many regions.

Critics of U.S. farm policy argue that government subsidies are in fact responsible for many of these problems. With unrestricted competition, gains in productivity would create only short-run problems for farmers. As fewer farmers were needed, competitive forces would drive some out of business. In the long run, surviving farms would earn a normal profit. Government subsidy programs, however, have encouraged farmers to continue despite economic losses. While these programs have reduced the risks of farming and ensure an overabundance of agricultural products for consumers, they also contribute to long-run problems. For example, when drought conditions struck much of the United States in 1986 and again in 1988, the government provided emergency assistance even to farmers who had not purchased government-subsidized crop insurance. The same was true when the Mississippi River inundated huge quantities of midwestern farm land in the early 1990s. Rather than encouraging farmers to remain in an unprofitable industry, government reeducation and retraining programs could be instituted to encourage farmers to leave the industry. Such a policy would eliminate losses and the need for government income support programs.

The Freedom to Farm Act of 1996

The low income of farmers has been the legacy of improved productivity, low short-run elasticities of supply and demand, and, indirectly, government subsidy programs. Government support of farmers is very much a product of the social problems—hunger and malnourishment, in particular—of the 1930s. These conditions do not exist in the 1990s. This fact plus the huge cost of the farm program ($40 billion of taxpayers' money over five years prior to 1995) has led to attempted reforms. These reforms touch some, but certainly not all, commodities heretofore subsidized.

The Freedom to Farm Act, signed by President Clinton in April 1996, took a new and more "market-oriented" approach to the subsidization of American agriculture. At a price tag of $47 billion for seven years, the new approach eliminates target pricing and acreage allotments on many products. Over the seven years farmers have received a subsidy regardless of market prices. The bill covers rice, corn, soybeans, wheat, and other crops.

As usual, there are both winners and losers from the new legislation. Many farmers will welcome the flexibility of being able to plant what they want. Consumers may notice some small fluctuation in the price of groceries as the free market takes over (on average only about 20 percent of the price of farm products at the supermarket is the actual return to farmers). Taxpayers will, if all goes as planned, begin to find relief as the direct subsidy is phased out over time. But the truth is that

Floods and other natural disasters have profound impacts on agricultural production and prices.

political pressures mean that only *part* of agriculture will be opened up to market forces. The "Freedom to Farm" provision failed to eliminate price support programs for such items as tobacco, sugar, and peanuts. Huge (and unseen) subsidies in the form of import tariffs and quotas also protect many items, such as sugar, from foreign competition. Milk marketing regulations continue to add as much as 40 cents to the price of a gallon of milk. Lobbying efforts for some commodities appear to be too strong for many politicians to resist.

In the summer of 1999, drought conditions again plagued the eastern and midwestern farming areas of the United States. The plight of farmers became political fodder for politicians at the federal level, who got into a bidding war producing subsidies in the range of $8 billion. These subsidies, whatever their humanitarian value, will have the effect of maintaining and encouraging farm production and lowering farm prices over time.

Whether farm support programs will continue into the twenty-first century is debatable. Proponents argue that the loss of the small farmer would eliminate an American tradition and would create other social and economic problems, such as urban overcrowding and higher unemployment. Opponents believe that we have too many farmers and that this oversupply is and has long been an unnecessary burden on taxpayers. The fate of government subsidy programs, like other considerations of equity, will be dealt with through the political process.

Monopoly: The Firm As Industry

I n a purely competitive market, each firm's production is such a small proportion of industry output that a single firm has no influence on the market price. As we have seen, the competitive firm is a price taker. The opposite extreme to a purely competitive firm is a pure monopoly: a single seller in an industry. The pure monopoly, in fact, is an industry. It alone faces the industry demand curve for its output, and it can affect market price by changing the amount of output that it produces. For this reason, we refer to the pure monopoly firm as a **price searcher**: It must seek the price that maximizes its profits. The ability of the pure monopoly firm to affect market price is not absolute, however. Even a single seller in an industry is subject to competitive pressures from the makers of substitute products. When you finish Chapter 9 you should know

- how barriers to market entry can create monopoly power.
- the principles underlying the economist's (static) model of monopoly behavior, including how the monopolist makes profits or sustains losses.
- how, under specific circumstances, monopolists can charge different prices to different consumer groups for the same product or service.
- the costs of monopoly power to the economy.
- the pros and cons of monopoly as a market structure.

Price searcher
A firm that is able to choose a profit-maximizing price from a range of prices rather than have price imposed by market conditions and competition; such a firm faces a downward-sloping demand curve.

Pure monopoly
An industry in which a single firm produces a product that has no close substitutes and in which entry of new firms cannot occur.

WHAT IS A MONOPOLY?

A **pure monopoly** is an industry composed of a single seller of a product with no close substitutes and with high barriers to entry. This definition seems clear, but we must use some care in applying it.

Examples of pure monopoly in the sense of a single seller in an industry are rare. In sixteenth- through eighteenth-century Europe, monarchs granted monopoly rights to individuals for a variety of productive undertakings. These were pure monopolies because each was given the exclusive right to run an entire industry. For example, the king of England created only one English East India Company, which was empowered with a monopoly over the trade with India. This monopoly power was manifested in the high prices the East India Company charged for the goods it brought back from India and sold in England. (See the Focus "Mercantilism and the Sale of Monopoly Rights" for a more detailed discussion of such historical monopolies.)

Even in these historical cases of monopoly, the monopoly was usually granted to a group of merchants. These monopolies were therefore not technically a single seller; rather, they were a group of sellers acting as a single seller. This is a

FOCUS

Mercantilism and the Sale of Monopoly Rights

Mercantilism refers to the form of economic organization that dominated Western Europe from roughly 1500 to 1776. The English, French, and Spanish economies of the time were typical mercantile economies. They were characterized by monarchies in which a king or queen represented the central government. As practiced by these monarchs, mercantilism involved widespread and detailed regulation of the economy. More often than not, this regulation took the form of creating monopoly rights for favored individuals. The mercantile economies therefore came to be characterized by the existence of pure monopolies in such diverse areas as brewing, mining, trading, playing cards, and so on, endlessly.

The creation and protection of these monopoly rights had a clear purpose—to raise revenue for the "needs" of the sovereign. Such needs included the expenses of the king's court and the resources needed to fight foreign wars. In other words, the monarchies sold monopoly rights to raise revenues.

Why did sovereigns use monopolies rather than taxes for revenue? Fundamentally, tax collection was a relatively inefficient means to raise rev-

enue for the central state because the costs of monitoring and controlling tax evasion were high. Barter and nonmarket production were widespread in the agricultural economy of the times; moreover, commercial record keeping was not highly developed. Tax collection was therefore a difficult and unattractive alternative as a source of revenue.

The granting of monopoly rights as a means to raise revenue did not have the same deficiencies as taxation. Most important, competition among potential monopolists revealed to the state authorities the worth of such privileges. There were no problems of evasion or guessing at taxable values in this case. Those who wanted the monopoly right would come to the king or queen and make an offer for the right. The potential monopolists were buying the agreement of the ruler to protect and enforce the monopoly privileges that he or she granted.

Thus, pure monopoly had a prominent place in economic history because of its effectiveness at raising revenue for the state. As the state's power to tax has increased in modern times, this revenue-raising role of monopolies has diminished.

broader meaning of monopoly. In fact, we typically observe monopoly in the real world in groups of sellers acting together. Such associations of sellers are called cartels. The analysis of pure monopoly presented in this chapter is relevant to cartels, but pure monopolies and cartels are not the same. A group of sellers must somehow organize to form a cartel agreement; the single pure monopolist faces no such organizational problem. In this chapter, we discuss pure monopoly in the sense of a single seller facing the industry demand curve. In Chapter 11, we return to the cartel problem and see what extra elements have to be added to monopoly theory to account for cartel behavior.

A second problem in applying the definition of monopoly concerns the criterion that there be no close substitutes. All products exhibit some degree of substitutability. The monopolist's isolation from competition from substitute products is therefore a matter of degree. Consider electricity, usually sold by firms holding local monopolies on its distribution. Are there good substitutes for electricity? The answer depends on what the electricity is used for. If it is used for lighting services in residential homes, the few possible alternatives—such as candles and oil lamps—are not very good substitutes for the convenience of electric lighting. If it is used for heating, however, the range of substitute products is greater. The wood stove, oil, and natural gas industries are competitors with the electric utility company in the market for home heating. The degree of substitutability for the monopolist's product is an important determinant of monopoly behavior. Where there are close substitutes, the monopolist cannot substantially raise prices without losing sales. Where there are no close substitutes, the monopolist has more power to raise prices.

A third consideration in defining monopolies is high barriers to new entry by potential competitors, the basic source of a pure monopoly. There are several types of barriers to new competition: legal barriers, economies of scale, and control of an essential resource.

Legal Barriers to Entry

Legal barriers to entry
Government actions that prohibit other firms or individuals from producing particular products or entering particular occupations or industries; such barriers take the form of legal franchises, licenses, and patents.

Sometimes the power of government is used to determine which industry or firm is to produce certain goods and services. Such **legal barriers to entry** take several forms.

First, it may be necessary to obtain a **public franchise** to operate in an industry. Franchises are granted by government for a variety of undertakings. The U.S. Postal Service, for example, has an exclusive franchise to deliver first-class mail. (See the Application "Technology, Economics, and the Postal Monopoly" at the end of this chapter.) Similar arrangements for food and gasoline service are made along toll roads such as the New Jersey Turnpike. The essence of an exclusive public franchise is that a monopoly is created; competitors are legally prohibited from entering franchised markets.

Public franchise
A firm or industry's exclusive, government-granted right to produce and sell a good or service.

Second, in many industries and occupations a **government license** is required to operate. In most states a license is required to practice architecture, dentistry, embalming, law, nursing, medicine, or veterinary medicine; to dispense drugs; and to teach. At the federal level, a license is required from the Federal Communications Commission to operate a radio or television station. If you want to operate a trucking firm that carries goods across state lines, you must obtain a license from the Interstate Commerce Commission. Licensing therefore creates a type of monopoly right by restricting the ability of firms to enter certain industries and occupations.

Government license
A legal right granted by state, local, or federal governments to enter an occupation or industry.

Patent
A monopoly right granted by government to an inventor for a product or process; valid for twenty years in the United States.

Third, a **patent** grants an inventor a monopoly over a product or process for 20 years in the United States. The patent prohibits others from producing the patented product and thereby confers a limited-term monopoly on the inventor. The purpose of a patent is to encourage innovation by allowing inventors to reap the exclusive fruits of their inventions for a period of time. Yet a patent also establishes a legal monopoly right. In effect, the social benefit of innovation is traded off against the possible social costs of monopoly. (See the Focus "Patents: The Inventor's Monopoly" later in the chapter.)

Economies of Scale and Natural Monopoly

In some industries, low unit costs may be achieved only through large-scale production. Such economies of scale put potential entrants at a disadvantage. To be able to compete effectively in the industry, a new firm has to enter on a large scale, which can be costly and risky. The effect is to deter entry.

Natural monopoly
A monopoly in which the relation between industry demand and cost structure makes it possible for only one firm to exist in the industry.

In a **natural monopoly**, economies of scale are so pronounced that only a single firm can survive in the industry. In such a case, government enacts some sort of regulatory scheme to control the natural monopoly. Public utilities such as natural gas, water, and electricity distribution are examples of natural monopolies that are regulated. The regulation of natural monopoly is discussed in more detail in Chapter 16.

A firm may own all of an essential resource in an industry, in which case new entry is barred because potential entrants cannot gain access to the essential resource. The De Beers Company of South Africa, for example, controls 80 percent of the world's diamond supply. (For more on the De Beers cartel, see the Application at the end of Chapter 11.) This makes the company a virtual monopolist in the diamond market.

MONOPOLY PRICE AND OUTPUT IN THE SHORT RUN

The theory of monopoly can be applied to a large number of situations in the economy. These range from the behavior of government-created monopolies to natural monopolies, patent rights, and diamond companies. Moreover, virtually every firm has some control over the prices it charges. The degree of control varies with the type of market in which the firm sells, but the fact that the firm can choose its prices makes the concept of the monopoly firm as price searcher relevant to understanding firm behavior in general.

The monopoly firm, like the competitive firm, faces both long- and short-run production and pricing decisions. In this section we explore the concept of price searching, and we examine how the monopoly firm decides how much output to produce and what price to charge in the short run.

The Monopolist's Demand Curve

The demand curve of the pure monopolist is fundamentally different from that of the pure competitor. The purely competitive firm is a price taker; it accepts market price as given but can sell as much as it wants at the prevailing market price because demand for its product is perfectly elastic. The monopoly firm faces a downward-sloping market demand curve and must find the price that maximizes its profits. This means that to sell more, the monopolist must lower price. The monopoly firm therefore confronts the problem of finding the best price–output combination. For this reason, we say that the monopolist is a price searcher.

Figure 9.1 illustrates the difference in the demand curves facing price takers and price searchers: The former is perfectly elastic, while the latter slopes downward. How elastic is the price searcher's demand curve? Economic theory does not give us a single answer to this question. Recall from Chapter 5 that the degree of elasticity along a demand curve depends on a number of variables, including the price and the number of close substitutes for the monopolist's product. Even though monopolists are synonymous with the industries they occupy, they are not immune to competition from producers of substitute products. The cheaper and more numerous these substitutes are, the more elastic the monopolist's demand curve will be. And the more elastic a monopolist's demand curve, the less valuable is its monopoly position in setting prices. Figure 9.1b represents the demand curves for two monopoly industries. The demand curves for these two industries, D_1 and D_2, both slope downward, but D_1 is more inelastic than D_2 at price P_m because the latter monopoly faces stiffer competition from substitutes.

For this reason, a monopoly in tuna fishing, for example, would not be a tremendously valuable monopoly right. While tuna is a unique product, significant price increases for tuna would cause consumers to switch to other protein sources, such as chicken or beef. A monopoly over crude oil production, however, where consumers have few viable consumption alternatives in the short run, has proved to be tremendously valuable, as the price-raising success of OPEC in the 1970s testifies.

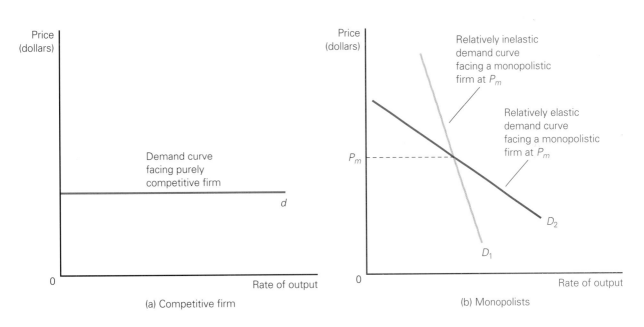

FIGURE 9.1

Demand Curves for Competitive and Monopoly Firms
(a) A perfectly elastic demand curve *d* facing a purely competitive firm. This firm is a price taker: It can sell all of its product that it wants at the prevailing market price.
(b) Two market demand curves facing different monopolists. The firm facing demand curve D_1 has more leeway than the firm facing curve D_2 in choosing price–output combinations because consumers cannot easily find substitutes for the former's product. But both monopolies are price searchers. They face downward-sloping demand curves; to sell more, they must lower price.

The basic point to remember about the demand curve facing the monopolist is that it is downward-sloping. The monopoly firm must lower price to sell more and must search for the best, or profit-maximizing, level of output. The concept of marginal revenue will help the monopolist to answer the question: Does the revenue gained by selling more at a lower price exceed the revenue lost by lowering the price?

The Monopolist's Revenues

Suppose that you are the owner of a monopoly. You have discovered a special kind of rock on your land that, when split, reveals a natural hologram. The mysterious beauty of these rocks is highly appealing to rock collectors and gift purchasers. If your aim is to earn the maximum profit from the production and sale of the rocks, how do you decide what price to charge for them?

Marginal revenue

The change in total revenue arising from a one-unit change in output; the change in total revenue divided by the change in output.

By trial and error—for you have no previous experience on which to base your pricing decision—you find that the revenues, costs, and profits you encounter at different prices vary considerably, as illustrated in Table 9.1. Columns (1) and (2) show the decreasing prices you must charge to sell increasing numbers of rocks. Together, columns (1) and (2) represent the market demand curve for hologram rocks, of which you are the sole seller. Your total revenue per day (also known as sales) is column (1) × column (2), or price × quantity.

Marginal revenue (*MR*) is the change in total revenue brought about by a change in output, or $\Delta TR/\Delta Q$. In Table 9.1, column (4) reflects the change in column (3) each time you lower price and produce an additional rock. In Chapter 8, we saw that for the purely competitive firm, *MR* was equal to price because the firm did not have to lower its price to sell additional units of output (see Table 8.1, p. 201). However, as Table 9.1 here shows, *MR* is not equal to price for you as a monopoly firm, except for the very first unit you sell, because you face a downward-sloping demand curve. When you cut your price, as for example from $22 to $21, two conflicting influences affect your total revenues. You gain additional revenue from the additional units you sell at the lower price. In this case, you sell one more rock for $21. But because the price reduction also applies to output that you were previously able to sell at a higher price, in effect you *lose* revenue on these units. In other words, the three rocks per day you could previously sell at $22 are now priced at $21, a reduction of $3 from your total revenues. Your marginal revenue is therefore $21 − $3 = $18 in this case.

When demand is downward-sloping, *MR* ($18) is less than price ($21) by the amount of the revenue lost on units that would have sold at the higher price. For price searchers, marginal revenue is less than price ($P > MR$) because of the need to lower price to sell additional units of output.

Figure 9.2 provides another way of looking at the fact that marginal revenue is always lower than price for the monopoly firm. At a price of P_1, total revenue is $P_1 \times Q_1$. At a price of P_2, total revenue is $P_2 \times Q_2$. Marginal revenue is the difference between these two total revenue rectangles. To see its components more clearly, consider what happens when price is cut from P_1 to P_2. First, additional revenue is generated by the sale of extra units at the lower price. This additional revenue is indicated by the shaded rectangular area CBQ_2Q_1. Second, there is a loss of revenue on units previously sold for P_1 but now sold for P_2. This loss is represented by the shaded area P_1ACP_2. Thus, the marginal revenue derived from a price reduction by the monopolist is less than the new price charged. Except for the first unit of output, the *MR* curve of the monopolist therefore lies below or

TABLE 9.1

Revenues, Costs, and Profits for the Pure Monopolist

These data are for the hologram rock monopolist. Columns (1) and (2) show the components of the demand curve facing the firm. Column (3) gives total revenue, or sales. Column (4) is the important concept of marginal revenue, which is the change in total revenue divided by the change in output. Columns (5) and (6) are the cost data. Maximum profits in column (7) occur where marginal cost equals marginal revenue, at 6 units of output per day.

(1) Rate of Output (units per day)	(2) Price (per unit)	(3) Total Revenue (per day) (1) × (2)	(4) Marginal Revenue $\Delta TR \div \Delta Q$	(5) Total Cost (per day)	(6) Marginal Cost	(7) Profit (per day) (3) − (5)
0	—	—		$40.00		−$40.00
			}······· $24.00		}······· $10.00	
1	$24.00	$24.00		50.00		−26.00
			}········· 22.00		}········· 8.00	
2	23.00	46.00		58.00		−12.00
			}········· 20.00		}········· 7.00	
3	22.00	66.00		65.00		1.00
			}········· 18.00		}········· 10.00	
4	21.00	84.00		75.00		9.00
			}········· 16.00		}········· 12.00	
5	20.00	100.00		87.00		13.00
			}········· 14.00		}········· 13.00	
6	19.00	114.00		100.00		14.00
			}········· 12.00		}········· 15.00	
7	18.00	126.00		115.00		11.00
			}········· 10.00		}········· 20.00	
8	17.00	136.00		135.00		1.00
			}········· 3.50		}········· 25.00	
9	15.50	139.50		160.00		−20.50
			}········· 0.50		}········· 30.00	
10	14.00	140.00		190.00		−50.00

FIGURE 9.2

The Dual Effects of a Price Reduction on Total Reveues

When the monopoly firm lowers price, it gains revenue from the additional output sold, Q_1 to Q_2, and loses revenue on the output previously sold at price P_1 and now sold at a lower price, P_2. The net effect is a marginal revenue curve that lies below and inside the demand curve.

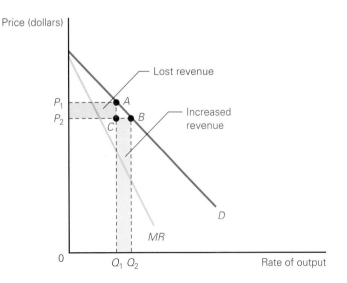

inside the demand curve. Even though the monopoly firm faces no direct competition, it still must search for its best price.

Total Revenue, Marginal Revenue, and Elasticity of Demand

The demand curve facing the monopoly firm shows the amount of output that can be sold at different prices. It also shows how the firm's revenues vary as price and output are changed. By observing this, we can learn something about the elasticity of the monopolist's demand curve over various ranges. Figure 9.3 illustrates the relation between total revenue, marginal revenue, and the elasticity of the monopolist's demand curve at various points. Suppose that we are joint owners of a firm with a monopoly on Gas-Saver, a unique additive that doubles gas mileage if one can is added to each tankful of gas. If we conduct a pricing experiment along our demand curve, we can observe its effects on our revenues. We start with a high price of $12 per can and lower it gradually to $6. At $12, we will not sell any of the stuff, for consumers know that a can will cost them more than the gas they save. As we lower the price toward $6, we sell more and more.

Figure 9.3b shows what happens to our total revenue as the price falls. Over the range of sales up to 30 cans per day, our total revenue rises. In Figure 9.3a, this rise is reflected by the positive marginal revenue. A demand curve is elastic when price reductions cause total revenue to rise. Thus, our demand curve is elastic up to the level of 30 units of output and a price of $6. Beyond 30 units of out-

FIGURE 9.3

Changes in Elasticity of Demand and Total Revenue as Price Changes

The elasticity of the monopolist's demand curve is linked to the behavior of total revenue as price changes. In the elastic ($\varepsilon_d > 1$) portion of the demand curve, price reductions cause total revenue to rise. When demand is unit elastic ($\varepsilon_d = 1$), price reductions leave total revenue unchanged. When demand is inelastic ($\varepsilon_d < 1$), price reductions lead to a fall in total revenue. The point of unit elasticity in part (a), beyond which marginal revenue becomes negative—30 cans per day—is also the point in part (b) at which total revenue stops rising and starts declining.

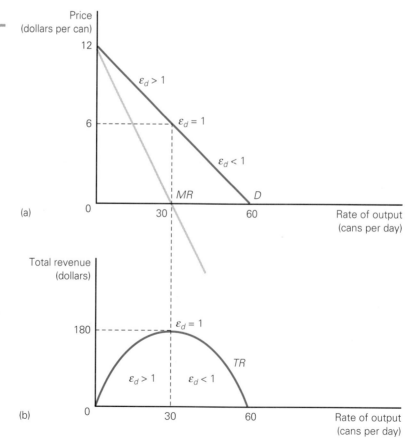

put, however, we observe that as we further lower our price, our total revenue falls, and our marginal revenue is negative. This drop means that we have reached the inelastic portion of our monopoly demand curve. Here, price reductions cause our sales to decline.

The regions of our Gas-Saver demand curve that are elastic and inelastic are labeled $\varepsilon_d > 1$ and $\varepsilon_d < 1$, respectively, in Figure 9.3. (ε_d is the symbol for price elasticity of demand.) The point labeled $\varepsilon_d = 1$ is where the demand curve is unit elastic. This point occurs where marginal revenue equals zero and where total revenue is at a maximum. It is the dividing line between the elastic and inelastic portions of the monopolist's demand curve. The link between *MR* and elasticity of demand can be stated thus: *MR* goes from positive to negative as demand goes from elastic to inelastic.

With this simple model, we can begin to discuss the rational pricing strategy of the monopolist. Suppose that our Gas-Saver monopoly firm has no costs of production so that profits are equal to total revenue. What price should we set to maximize our revenue? Figure 9.3b clearly illustrates that we can do no better than to be at the top of the total revenue curve. At this point, we reach our total maximum revenue: $180 per day. Reading vertically up to Figure 9.3a, you can see that to earn this maximum total revenue, we should produce 30 cans of Gas-Saver per day and sell them for $6 each. The profit-maximizing monopolist with no costs of production will set price along the demand curve where demand is unit elastic, or equal to 1. A monopoly firm will never operate along the inelastic portion of its demand curve because marginal revenue is negative along this portion. Increases in output and reductions in price actually cause total revenue to fall.

This simple analysis helps us understand the pricing behavior of any firm facing a downward-sloping demand curve. Such firms will not set price in the inelastic part of their demand curve because they can earn more revenue by raising price. This result and the discussion of this section are based on the properties of a straight-line, or linear, demand curve.

Short-Run Price and Output of the Monopolist

Although for simplicity we did not consider costs in the previous discussion, we introduce them now, because all firms incur costs of production. The fact that the monopolist possesses a monopoly in the output market says nothing about its position in input markets. In this respect the monopoly firm is like the competitive firm; it is one of many buyers of inputs. The cost curves of the monopolist therefore resemble those of the competitive firm.

By combining cost concepts with the revenue concepts of monopoly, we can analyze the choice of the best, or profit-maximizing, rate of output and price for the monopoly firm in the short run. To maximize profits, the monopolist follows the same rule that the competitive firm follows—it sets marginal cost equal to marginal revenue. The logic is identical in both cases. If *MR* is greater than *MC*, it pays to produce additional units of output because they add more to revenues than to costs. If *MR* is less than *MC*, it pays to reduce production because extra output adds more to costs than to revenues. The monopolist will therefore do best by producing at the output level where *MC* equals *MR*.

Look back at the cost and profit data in Table 9.1 for the hologram rock monopoly to check the viability of this rule for profit maximization. Comparing marginal revenue in column (4) with marginal cost in column (6), we see that the first 6 rocks produced per day add more to revenue than to costs; that is, $MR > MC$

over this range of outputs. The sixth unit of output adds $14 to revenues and $13 to costs. It pays to produce that sixth unit. Producing the seventh rock, however, has a marginal cost of $15 and a marginal revenue of $12. The firm would be losing money if it increased operations to 7 rocks a day. The maximum profit occurs at a rate of output of 6 rocks per day and a price of $19 for each. The profitability of this decision is recorded in column (7), which is the difference in total revenue from column (3) and total cost from column (5). The maximum daily profit of $14 occurs when 6 rocks are produced, the point at which MR equals MC.

The same point is illustrated graphically in Figure 9.4, where a monopoly's marginal cost curve is combined with its demand and marginal revenue curves. To determine the profit-maximizing rate of output, the monopolist would find the point along the horizontal axis where $MR = MC$—in this case Q_m. For outputs less than Q_m, $MR > MC$, and it pays the monopolist to expand production. In this area, extra units of output add more to revenue than to cost. For outputs greater than Q_m, it pays the firm to reduce output. At Q_m, $MR = MC$, and the firm can do no better than produce this output. Profits are maximized at Q_m.

The monopolist sets a price for Q_m units of output by reading the market value of this output off the demand curve at a point directly above the point where $MR = MC$. In other words, the price for this output is read off the demand curve by drawing a straight line from the intersection of MR and MC to the demand curve and over to the price axis, as shown by the dashed lines in the figure. Price is not set where $MR = MC$ on the marginal revenue curve; it is set by reference to the demand curve. In Figure 9.4, P_m is the **profit-maximizing price**.

Profit-maximizing price

The price associated with the quantity sold at which the difference between total revenue and total cost is greatest; the price associated with the quantity sold at which marginal revenue equals marginal cost.

Monopoly Profits

Figure 9.4 shows how the monopolist applies the $MR = MC$ rule and also depicts the level of profits the monopoly earns. To discuss monopoly profits we add the monopolist's average total cost curve to the analysis.

The monopolist sets $MR = MC$, selling Q_m units at a price of P_m. Just as in the case of the purely competitive firm, the monopolist's profits are determined with

FIGURE 9.4

Monopoly Profits

At point B, the monopoly firm would just cover its average total cost. But since it holds a monopoly, it can charge price P_m, creating economic profits equal to $AB \times Q_m$, represented by the area P_mABC. In other words, P_mABC is equal to total revenue, P_mAQ_m0, minus total costs, CBQ_m0.

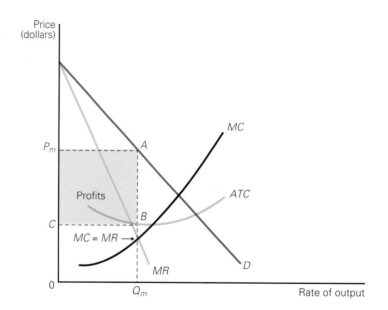

respect to the average total cost curve. At point B, the monopolist would just cover its average total cost. But its monopoly position and the demand for its product allow it to set price at P_m on its demand curve, creating economic profits in excess of its costs. In Figure 9.4, these profits are given by the shaded area $P_m ABC$, or the amount by which total revenue, the area $P_m AQ_m 0$, exceeds the total cost of producing Q_m, the area $CBQ_m 0$. Another way to look at monopoly profits in such a graph is to say that the monopolist makes AB profits per unit of output, where $AB \times Q_m = P_m ABC$.

This is a profitable monopoly. These returns are in excess of the total costs of the firm, which means that they are above the opportunity cost of the monopolist's capital investment. Were this a purely competitive firm, these excess returns would stimulate new entry and expansion in the industry. Remember, however, that this is a pure monopoly. Entry cannot occur here, by definition. So, unlike the profits of the competitive firm, which ultimately are restored to a normal rate of return by entry, the profits of the monopolist will persist in the long run.

Not all monopolies make monopoly profits. Some lose money. Such a case is graphed in Figure 9.5. In this case, demand is not sufficient to cover the average total cost of the monopolist at the level of output where $MR = MC$. Total revenue at Q_m is represented by $P_m CQ_m 0$; total cost is represented by the larger area $ABQ_m 0$. Total cost exceeds total revenue by the amount of the shaded area, $ABCP_m$. This monopolist makes an economic loss in the short run. As long as P_m is high enough to cover the monopolist's variable costs, the monopoly will continue to operate in the short run if it expects market conditions for its product to improve. Over time, however, if the losses depicted in Figure 9.5 persist, the monopolist will cease operations and go out of business. The investment in the monopoly firm is not earning a normal rate of return, and by closing down, the firm is free to move its investment where it can earn higher rates of return.

It may seem curious that monopolists should make losses, but this is a very real phenomenon. Many holders of patents, for example, never market their products because there is no demand for them. The fact that one has a monopoly does not automatically make it a valuable monopoly.

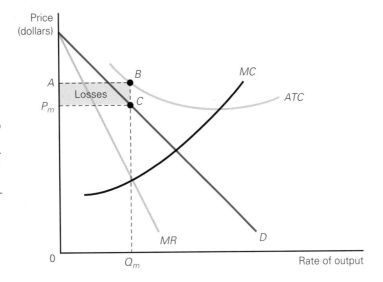

FIGURE 9.5

An Unprofitable Monopoly

Not all monopolies make profits. This monopoly makes BC losses per unit of output because demand for its product is not sufficient to cover its average total costs. Its total revenue at Q_m is represented by $P_m CQ_m 0$, and its total cost by $ABQ_m 0$. Therefore, its total losses are represented by the shaded area, $ABCP_m$. If the situation does not improve in the long run, this monopoly will go out of business.

Comparing the Monopoly Firm and the Purely Competitive Firm

Before we move on to long-run considerations for the monopolist, we note two important differences between the monopoly firm and the purely competitive firm. First, in a pure monopoly no distinction is made between the firm and industry. The pure monopoly is the industry, so there is no room for a separate theory of industry versus firm behavior, such as the one we presented for pure competition.

Second, recall that the marginal cost curve of a competitive firm (above the point of minimum average variable cost) is its supply curve because the firm sets marginal cost equal to price to maximize profits. Its pricing behavior traces out a relation between quantity supplied and price. No such relation exists for pure monopoly. The monopolist controls the quantity of output produced and sets $MR = MC$, but MR does not equal price for the monopolist. Because the monopolist does not set MC equal to price, no unique relation exists between MC and price in the case of pure monopoly. To know what the monopolist will produce at a given price, we need to know more than the firm's MC; we need to know the shape and position of its demand and marginal revenue curves as well. The lesson is simply that the monopolist does not have a supply curve—that is, a unique relation between the amount it produces and the price.

PURE MONOPOLY IN THE LONG RUN

Like all firms, the pure monopolist must face the long run, the period of economic time over which the firm can vary all of its inputs and enter or exit the industry. The long run for the pure monopolist is not analogous to the long run for a purely competitive firm and industry. Certain adjustments take place, but entry and other efficiency-enhancing adjustments do not occur. Monopoly and its effects persist in long-run equilibrium.

Entry and Exit

A pure monopoly may not be profitable and, hence, may leave the industry. Exit is a distinct possibility. Entry is not. By definition, high and prohibitive barriers to entry exist with monopoly; entry by new firms is barred. Long-run adjustments in the form of competitive entry do not take place in the case of the monopoly. Monopoly profits therefore persist in the long run.

Adjustments to Scale

The monopoly firm can adjust its scale of operations in the long run. Given that it makes a profit, the monopolist can seek to produce the profit-maximizing rate of output in the most efficient plant for that level of output. This plant size, however, will not generally be the most efficient plant size overall, as it was in the purely competitive model in long-run equilibrium. Typically, the monopoly will produce output in the long run with a higher-cost plant size than will a competitive industry.

PRICE DISCRIMINATION

In our discussion of monopoly theory so far, the profit-maximizing monopoly has charged a single price for its product. Each customer who buys the product pays the same price. Under certain conditions, however, a monopoly can make more money by charging different customers different prices for its product. For example, movie theaters and airlines often charge lower prices to children and senior citizens than to others, and utilities charge different rates for electricity to businesses and residences. This method of pricing is called **price discrimination**.

Price discrimination

The practice of charging one buyer or group of buyers a different price than that charged to others. The price difference is not due to differences in the cost of supplying the two groups.

Two points should be kept in mind as we discuss price discrimination. First, price differences that reflect cost differences do *not* constitute price discrimination. For example, large buyers (those purchasing more goods) are often charged less per unit for some goods than are small buyers. The general reason for this difference is that selling costs per unit are lower when dealing with the large buyer. Each sale may require the same paperwork, but the paperwork cost is lower per unit of sales for the large buyer. The lower price charged to the large buyer is not the result of price discrimination; it reflects the seller's different costs of serving the two customers. Second, equality of prices across buyers does not necessarily imply the absence of price discrimination because the costs of supplying the buyers may be different. Price discrimination is illegal under the Robinson–Patman Act (1936), which is enforced by the Federal Trade Commission.

When Can Price Discrimination Exist?

Price discrimination can occur only under certain conditions. First, the firm must have monopoly power and face a downward-sloping demand curve for its output. In other words, the firm must be a price setter, not a price taker. A price taker cannot charge different prices to different customers because the price it charges is determined by the prevailing market price, over which it has no influence. Second, the monopolist's buyers must fall into at least two clearly and easily identifiable groups of customers who have different elasticities of demand for the product. Third, the separation of buyers is crucial. Without the ability to separate buyers, the seller will not be able to keep buyers who are charged a low price from reselling the product to buyers who are charged a high price. Such behavior (normally called *arbitrage*) would undermine a price discrimination scheme and lead to a single price for the monopolist's product. The identification and separation of groups of consumers must be possible at low cost to make price discrimination worthwhile for the firm.

A Model of Price Discrimination

Figure 9.6 shows how a monopolist can gain from price discrimination. There are two groups of customers for the monopolist's product. The demand of buyers in market A is relatively more elastic than the demand of buyers in market B at a given price.

Two points are crucial in understanding the analysis in Figure 9.6. First, the marginal cost to the monopolist of supplying both markets is the same. The best way to think about this condition is to assume that the output sold to each market is produced in the same plant. MC is thus at the same level in both market A and market B. Second, to maximize profits, the monopolist sets marginal cost equal to marginal revenue in each market.

Following the $MC = MR$ rule in this case, the monopoly firm sets $MC = MR$ in both markets. In market A this leads to a price of P_1; in market B it leads to a price of P_2. The buyers in market B with the less elastic demand are charged a higher price than the buyers in market A ($P_2 > P_1$). These are the profit-maximizing prices in the two markets. The monopolist benefits from price discrimination to the degree

(a) Market A: Buyers with more elastic demand

(b) Market B: Buyers with less elastic demand

FIGURE 9.6

Price Discrimination

The figures demonstrate a case of price discrimination for the same product in two markets. Consumers in market A have a relatively more elastic demand than those in market B. The profit-maximizing monopolist confronts market A consumers with a lower price. That is, $P_1 < P_2$. For a price discrimination scheme to be viable, the monopolist must prevent buyers in market A from reselling its product to buyers in market B.

that its profits go up relative to what they would be if it sold its output at a single price to all buyers.

The monopolist must be able to keep the two markets separate to sustain a price discrimination scheme. Otherwise, buyers in market A could profitably resell the product to buyers in market B. In 1984 Apple Computer Inc. offered to sell all students at selected universities its then-new Macintosh computer for less than half of the full price being charged to other customers. Students and profiteers immediately saw the potential for profit in reselling the computers to nonstudents at marked-up but still below-retail prices. Newspaper ads hooked up students wishing to sell the cut-rate Macintoshes with nonstudents desiring to buy Macintoshes.

The seller who wants to practice price discrimination must therefore be able to distinguish and separate customers on the basis of their elasticity of demand. Moreover, the seller must be able to perform this feat without a large expenditure of resources. Thus, most real-world price discrimination schemes are based on general characteristics of customers, such as age, education, income, and sex. For example, children and older people are often charged lower prices for certain products because their age is thought to indicate that they have more elastic demand for these products.

A subtle factor that provides a basis for price discrimination is differences in the opportunity cost of time among customers. The practice of giving discount coupons for grocery purchases, for example, allows sellers to separate buyers into elastic and inelastic demand categories. Buyers in the inelastic demand category will not take the time and trouble to collect coupons and redeem them. These are customers who place a relatively high value on their time. They value other uses of their time and do not want to clip coupons. Buyers in the elastic demand group place a lower value on their time and will take the time to clip coupons and convert them into lower prices at the store. Sellers use coupons to separate buyers into classes and charge them different prices based on their different elasticities of demand.

A huge number of examples of ongoing cases of discrimination may be found in all areas of life. Many examples of price discrimination can be found on college and university campuses. Most publicly funded institutions charge different tuition rates to in-state and out-of-state students, even though the marginal cost of educating each type of student is the same. The students separate themselves into two groups when they complete the institution's application form and give their addresses. An in-state student cannot transfer registration in a class to an out-of-state student. Thus, no arbitrage can take place. Other things being equal, this pricing behavior will reap the institution larger tuition revenues than would the practice of charging one price to all students. For other examples, see the Focus "Are You a Victim of Price Discrimination on Campus?"

FOCUS

"Are You a Victim of Price Discrimination on Campus?"

Many examples of price discrimination can be found on college and university campuses. As mentioned in the text, most publicly funded schools charge different rates to in-state and out-of-state students. But there are a number of other methods of practicing price discrimination against students.

Consider the academic scholarship. Students with better academic credentials (high school GPA, SAT or ACT scores, and so on) generally find themselves with a larger number of schools to which they are accepted. The number of close substitutes they have for any particular institution is larger. This implies that their price elasticity of demand for a particular institution is relatively greater and that they will be charged a lower tuition than their less-adept fellow students. The college or university lowers price to them through the granting of a scholarship. Again, the institution of higher education is seen to be a practiced price discriminator.

Many university bookstores offer faculty members a small discount (usually 5 to 15 percent) on their purchases that is not given to students. This is

but another example of price discrimination. Resale of bookstore items from faculty to students is discouraged not only by college regulations, but also by the faculty member's opportunity cost of time. With such small discounts, most teachers find the profit from buying at a discount and reselling to students at a price below the student price not worth the time and effort. The two markets are separated at low cost in that faculty must usually present their ID cards to obtain the discount. In this market, faculty members are the relatively elastic demanders because of the number of alternative suppliers that are available to them. The students' relatively low elasticity is also probably due to the fact that many students live on campus, which makes substitutes for college-run bookstores more difficult to patronize. (Internet purchase of textbooks may disturb this relationship over time.) Whatever the reasons, price discrimination at the college bookstore implies larger bookstore revenues than if faculty and students both paid the same price for bookstore items.

Services of all kinds, in particular, are ripe areas for the practice of discrimination because services are ordinarily nontransferable from one consumer to another.[1] Whatever the source of discrimination, its desirability or lack thereof is closely related to the question of whether monopoly is good or bad for economic efficiency.

THE CASE AGAINST MONOPOLY

Monopoly is generally viewed as bad for the economy in comparison with the good expected from a competitive organization of markets. Critics base their indictment of monopoly on arguments that monopolies are lacking in both efficiency and equity, or fairness. After considering arguments against monopoly, we will examine the theory that monopolies provide certain social benefits that may offset their social costs.

The Welfare Loss Resulting from Monopoly Power

Contrived scarcity

A situation in which a monopoly produces an output below what a competitive industry would produce; the contrived scarcity results in price and profits above competitive levels.

The main efficiency argument against monopoly is that this market structure leads to **contrived scarcity**—that is, that a monopoly withholds output from the market to maximize its profits. The monopolist not only sets price where $MC = MR$, but where $P > MR$. At the profit-maximizing output for the monopolist, price therefore exceeds marginal cost. In the case of pure competition, price reflects the marginal benefit that consumers place on additional production, and marginal cost reflects the economic cost of the resources necessary for additional production. When price is greater than marginal cost, this is a signal to producers to increase output. The monopoly firm will not do so, because this approach is not consistent with maximizing its profits. Given market demand and the cost curves, the monopolist will produce a smaller quantity of output than would a competitive industry. So we say that the monopolist causes a contrived scarcity, a condition in which the monopoly's product is short in supply and high in price. For example, the gasoline crisis of the 1970s was a contrived scarcity put into effect by the OPEC cartel. The price of gasoline rose as the supply of oil was reduced.

A contrived scarcity is a social cost to the economy. Its nature and magnitude can be estimated with an economic model that contrasts the effects of monopoly and competition in a given market, as shown in Figure 9.7.

Figure 9.7 shows the industry demand and supply functions, D and S, for some commodity, say, cranberry juice. There are no economies of scale in this industry. The average total cost of producing cranberry juice is the same at all levels of output. This is a constant-cost industry with a flat long-run supply curve, along which $MC = ATC$.

Suppose that the industry is organized competitively, with many producers of cranberry juice. Long-run industry equilibrium is established at E, where industry demand and supply are equal. The juice output of the various firms is priced accord-

---

[1]Professional services such as those for physicians or lawyers are often used to illustrate the possibilities of discrimination between low and high income demanders. Organ transplants are an especially interesting and timely example: See Andy H. Barnett, T. Randolph Beard and David L. Kaserman, "The Medical Community's Opposition to Organ Markets: Ethics or Economics?" *The Review of Industrial Organization* (December 1993), pp. 669–678.

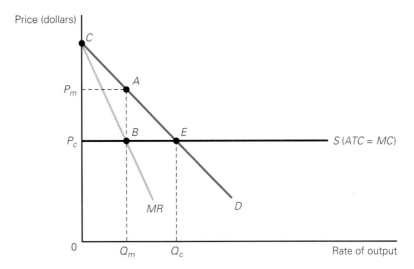

FIGURE 9.7

Welfare Loss Due to Monopoly Power

This graph illustrates the hypothetical case of converting a competitive industry into a monopoly. Consumer surplus at price P_c and output Q_c in a constant-cost industry is represented by CEP_c. When the industry becomes a monopoly, it cuts back output to Q_m, resulting in a decreased consumer surplus of CAP_m and monopoly profits of P_mABP_c. The welfare loss to the economy—that is, the amount of real income that does not reappear for anyone after the monopoly is formed—is represented by AEB. The area of monopoly profits can be considered a transfer from consumers to the monopolist.

ing to the marginal cost of producers along the industry supply curve and according to the wishes of the consumers along the demand curve. In other words, price is equal to the long-run marginal cost of production.

At the competitive price–output combination, P_c and Q_c, how much surplus do consumers receive? They are willing to pay the amounts given by the demand curve, but they pay only P_c. They thus receive a surplus of real income, in this case represented by the large area above the industry supply curve and below the industry demand curve, or CEP_c. This triangle represents the concept of consumer surplus: the amount that consumers would be willing to pay over what they actually pay for a commodity.

Now suppose that the cranberry juice industry is turned over to a single seller, a monopolist. As a result, the monopolist restricts juice output to Q_m (contrived scarcity) and raises price to P_m to maximize its monopoly profits. What has happened to the level of consumer surplus in this market? The consumer surplus before monopoly is given by CEP_c, but consumer surplus after monopoly is only CAP_m. The difference in these two areas is the trapezoid P_mAEP_c.

The area P_mAEP_c is made up of two components. First we consider the rectangle P_mABP_c, depicting monopoly profits, to represent a transfer from consumers to the monopolist. In other words, these dollars do not leave the economy: They are taken out of the pockets of consumers and put into the pocket of the monopolist. The triangle AEB is left over. Who gets the real

Welfare loss due to monopoly

The consumers' surplus lost by consumers and not gained by the monopolist that results from a monopoly producing a less-than-competitive amount of output and charging a greater-than-competitive price; also called deadweight cost.

income represented by this triangle? No one—it simply vanishes when the monopoly is formed. This triangle is therefore called the **welfare loss due to monopoly**, or the *deadweight loss*. It is a cost to the economy because it does not reappear as income to anyone.[2]

Production Costs of a Monopoly

Recall from our earlier discussion that the typical monopoly firm, after long-run adjustment, does not produce at the point of minimum long-run average total cost. In other words, the monopoly firm does not produce its output in the most efficient plant size in the long run. We learned in Chapter 8 that the competitive firm was compelled by competition to produce at the point of minimum long-run average total cost. By comparison, the monopoly produces its output inefficiently, resulting in another social cost of the monopoly relative to the competitive outcome.

Monopoly and the Distribution of Income

In addition to the potential efficiency cost arguments against monopoly—welfare loss and inefficient costs of production—there is an equity argument. The creation of a monopoly transfers wealth from consumers to the monopolist. In Figure 9.7, this transfer is represented by the area of monopoly profits, P_mABP_c. The average consumer gets poorer; the monopolist gets richer. Most people would regard this transfer to the monopolist as unfair.

In sum, pure monopoly compares unfavorably with pure or perfect competition. The pure monopolist ignores social costs by producing less output at a higher price and by producing that output inefficiently. Coupled with concerns about the fairness of monopoly profits, this is the case against monopoly.

THE CASE FOR MONOPOLY

Static inefficiency

A condition associated with the welfare loss due to the presence of a monopoly. The loss can be summarized as the production of too little output sold at too high a price.

Dynamic efficiency

A condition summarized in the idea that monopolies may, over time, be more innovative and efficient than competitive firms at developing new products and new production techniques.

We have seen that monopoly leads to economic inefficiency compared with a purely competitive organization of the economy. The monopolist essentially produces too little output at too high a price ($P > MC$). This type of inefficiency, called **static inefficiency**, can be seen as a social cost of monopoly given that other things are equal.

What if other things are not equal? Specifically, what if the monopoly produces more new ideas and products than the competitive firm? If this is the case, there may be an offsetting **dynamic efficiency** that makes monopoly a desirable form of market organization. One way to look at these counterforces is that the static inefficiency caused by monopoly pushes the economy inside its production possibilities frontier. This loss of production is the cost of monopoly power. But the dynamic efficiency of monopoly pushes the production possibilities curve out-

---

[2]Economist Gordon Tullock has argued that the monopoly profits rectangle, P_mAPB_c, can also represent a social cost of monopoly power if these profits are wasted in lobbying to procure a monopoly right or privilege. See Gordon Tullock, "The Welfare Costs of Tariffs, Monopolies, and Theft," *Western Economic Journal* 5 (June 1967), pp. 224–232.

ward over time, potentially swamping the short-run costs of monopoly power. In other words, monopoly has costs and benefits for the economy, and the benefits (dynamic efficiency) may outweigh the costs (static inefficiency).

This view of the potential efficiency of large-scale, monopolistic enterprise was put forth by Joseph Schumpeter.[3] He stressed the advantages of the ability of large firms to finance large research laboratories and hire thousands of scientists. While these firms with well-known, productive research labs—such as Du Pont, AT&T, and IBM—are not typically pure monopolies, they usually are large firms with dominant positions within their industries.

To Schumpeter, the traditional theory that competition spurred innovation seemed wrong. Small competitive firms were at a disadvantage in the innovation process because they could not afford large-scale research. Large firms were the key to innovation and success in the industrial order.

In Schumpeter's theory, the innovative monopolist did not possess a perennial advantage in the marketplace. He believed that innovation would proceed apace, and no one large firm would have more than a transitory monopoly in the face of a constant supply of new ideas and innovations by other large firms. The monopoly that any one large firm achieved by being creative was short-lived.

Studies of the source of major inventions indicate that a surprisingly large number of innovations have come from the backyard shops of independent inventors. John Jewkes, David Sawers, and Richard Stillerman found, for example, that more than half of sixty-nine important inventions were produced by individual academics or by individuals unaffiliated with any research organization.[4] Among these inventions were air conditioning, the Polaroid Land camera, the helicopter, and xerography. Much invention is individually inspired and created in small-scale, personal labs and workshops. Industrial creativity thus seems to stem from something other than firm size alone. (For more on the returns to invention, see the Focus "Patents: The Inventor's Monopoly.")

Evidence suggests that Schumpeter's vision of the economy is not entirely accurate. But, then, neither is the vision that pure competition is best for the economy. Innovation springs from many sources, from the backyard or basement lab of the inventor to the lab of the large industrial company. Diversity produces innovation—better yet, *individuals* produce innovation, whether they work in their own workshops or a large firm. Perhaps the most typical scenario is that an individual or small firm comes up with a new idea, and a large firm provides the vehicle by which the idea is realized.

Finally, what kind of balance is struck between the costs and benefits of monopoly? It is hard to generalize on this issue. In filling out a report card on firms, the best approach is to be pragmatic. Does the firm possess monopoly power? If so, can we judge how large this power is and how much it costs the economy? Does monopoly power carry with it some redeeming merit such as increased innovation? These are not easy questions to answer or to weigh in the balance, but they are the types of issues that must be confronted if the costs and benefits of monopoly are to be understood and its model applied intelligently.

---

[3]Joseph A. Schumpeter, *Capitalism, Socialism, and Democracy* (New York: Harper, 1942).
[4]John Jewkes, David Sawers, and Richard Stillerman, *The Sources of Invention* (New York: St. Martin's, 1959).

FOCUS

Patents: The Inventor's Monopoly

A patent is an exclusive right given to an inventor for his or her invention. In other words, a patent is a monopoly right given to the inventor for the invention. In general, economists complain about the costs of monopoly because they believe that the same industry could be organized competitively. A new patent monopoly grant for 20 years presents a different problem. That is, the purpose of the patent system is to encourage invention. The issue is not monopoly versus competition but, more fundamentally, invention versus no (or little) invention. Is the world better off with the invention, even though it is monopolized for 20 years? In other words, what are the costs and benefits of a patent?

Consider the simple case, depicted in Figure 9.8, of a new consumer product with a positive demand, such as a camera utilizing a new exposure process. The costs of the patent monopoly are simply the deadweight costs of monopoly as discussed in this chapter. These are measured by the area

BCD in Figure 9.8. Area BCD is the lost consumers' surplus from the 20-year patent monopoly. This cost must be assessed carefully in the context of an invention, however.

Obviously, the incentive to the inventor to reveal his or her new product and to market it resides in the monopoly profits that he or she hopes to capture as a result. These are given by the area P_mBDP_c. These profits are a transfer from consumers to the inventor, and as such, they represent neither a cost nor a benefit of the patent system.

What are the benefits of the patent system? First, there is the increase in consumer well-being brought about immediately by a desirable invention. This is measured by the area ABP_m. This area of consumers' surplus would not have existed without the new product. In 20 years, the patent monopoly ends, and a second source of benefits arises: The price of cameras will fall to a competitive level, such as P_c, and consumers will reap the

FIGURE 9.8

A Camera Patent Monopoly

An inventor's patent confers a temporary monopoly on the holder. Price of the patented good is P_m, in contrast to the competitive price P_c. Consumers' surplus of BCD is the temporary loss due to the patent.

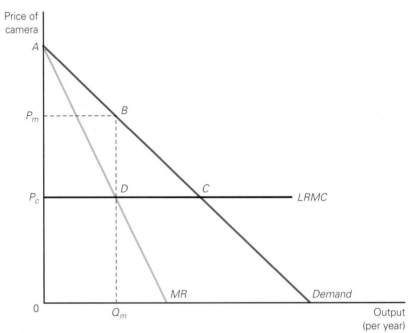

continued

continued

benefits of the camera at a lower price. Thus the patent system generates benefits in the amount ABP_m now and in the amount of an additional BCD in 20 years. Consumers also receive a transfer from the monopolist in 20 years in the amount of P_mBDP_c.

In sum, the theory of monopoly helps us to assess the costs and benefits of the patent system. The costs are BCD for 20 years. The benefits are ABP_m forever plus BCD forever after 20 years. P_mBDP_c is a trans-

fer to the inventor from consumers of his or her product, which he or she gives back to consumers after 20 years. In the end, the patent system creates goods and services and technologies that did not previously exist. It also underscores the importance of property rights to ideas as a source of economic growth and progress.[a]

---

[a]Readers interested in additional information on patents, trademarks and copyrights are directed to the U.S. Patent and Trademark Office web site at www.uspto.gov.

APPLICATION

Technology, Economics, and the Postal Monopoly

The postal monopoly has been criticized since it began operating under federal protection in 1775, but the criticism has intensified over the past two decades. The cost of mailing a one-ounce first-class letter has risen by 800 percent since 1958—twice as fast as the increase in the general price level (see Table 9.2). While the Constitution gives Congress the power to "establish post offices and post roads," it does not require postal service to be a monopoly or to be a government monopoly. Congress placed piecemeal restrictions on private carriage of mail throughout the nineteenth century. Since 1872, with the elimination of the Pony Express, only government employees can legally deliver a letter. The monopoly applies to first-class mail but not to second-class mail (newspapers and magazines), third-class mail (direct-mail advertising), or to parcels (fourth-class mail). The U.S. Post Office became the independent Postal Service in 1970 and retained the right to define a letter, which includes bills, receipts, and other business documents.

In this chapter's terms, the Postal Service is a nonprofit monopoly with the power to price-discriminate among customers. Since it is not permitted to retain profits, the Postal Service has little incentive to hold costs down or to improve the quality of service. Recall that price discrimination often accompanies monopoly

TABLE 9.2

Postal Rates, 1919–2000

Between 1958 and 1999, the cost of mailing a one-ounce first-class letter increased by 725 percent. Given technological changes, such as electronic banking and inexpensive facsimile transmitting (fax) machines, critics are questioning the necessity of a government monopoly on the delivery of first-class mail.

1919—2 cents	1981—18 cents
1958—4 cents	1981—20 cents
1963—5 cents	1985—22 cents
1968—6 cents	1988—25 cents
1971—8 cents	1991—29 cents
1975—10 cents	1995—32 cents
1975—13 cents	1999—33 cents
1978—15 cents	

and takes place when rates are not based on differences in costs of providing service. Equal rates are discriminatory when the costs of provision differ. This is the kind of price discrimination practiced when the Postal Service charges the same price to deliver a first-class letter from New York to Hawaii as it does to deliver the same letter across town, because costs are lower in the latter case. In effect, the price of a first-class stamp enables the Postal Service to internally subsidize distant customers and customers in small towns and isolated locales at the expense of urban, local, and business consumers.

The Postal Service also engages in price discrimination in pricing first-class mail compared with other classes. The Postal Service exploits its monopoly on first-class mail by pricing well above its marginal and average costs. It is then able to price lower classes of mail below cost by using profits from first-class mail to cover these losses. In this way it succeeds in extending its first-class monopoly to other classes of mail.

Criticism of the Postal Service is not limited to its rate structure. Despite rapid increases in postal rates since 1970, service has continued to deteriorate. Twice-a-day delivery has been halted, and most door-to-door delivery for businesses and multifamily dwellings has been abandoned. Many post offices have been closed, and many remaining offices no longer provide Saturday window service. Despite the adoption of ZIP codes, mail delivery is slower than it has been in years.

According to critics, privatization or repeal of the laws giving the Postal Service a monopoly is the only way to obtain rational, cost-based, and efficient service. Technological change poses threats to any monopoly, and the Postal Service is no exception. In 1974, the Postal Service's failure to develop an innovative way to transport parcels created the United Parcel Service (UPS). By introducing mechanization and containerization, UPS reduced both breakage and costs. Despite the Postal Service's attempts to learn from UPS's success, UPS remains a viable competitor in the area of parcel service. Other private commercial carriers developed in the 1960s and 1970s—these specializing in the rapid and reliable carriage of commercial documents. Despite past threats of legal action by the Postal Service, firms such as Federal Express and Emery Air Freight now openly and freely compete for overnight service. The Postal Service's "Express Mail" overnight service, despite a lower and subsidized price, has not been successful in eliminating private services. Lower-quality service—specifically, fewer cities covered and fewer services offered—is one reason for the lack of success.

Rapidly developing electronic and computer technology promises to offer serious competition for both the Postal Service and private overnight services. Banks, increasingly, are offering electronic bill-paying services. Offered at a price below that for stamps, envelopes, and checks, electronic bill-paying services provide stiff competition, especially for first-class mail. Yet more troubling to the Postal Service and overnight carriers is the remarkable increase in the use of facsimile transmitting (fax) machines and computer e-mail. Virtually unheard of when they sold for almost $4500 in the early 1980s, fax machines now cost, on average, less than $300 and are considered standard office technology, as are computers and e-mail.

Critics of the postal monopoly estimate that open competition for postal customers in all classes of mail could save $10 billion annually. While it is difficult to predict the exact form of the market with no postal monopoly, many economists, politicians, and observers argue that competition should be given a try.

Internet e-mail services, along with falling computer prices, are providing viable competition for traditional postal services.

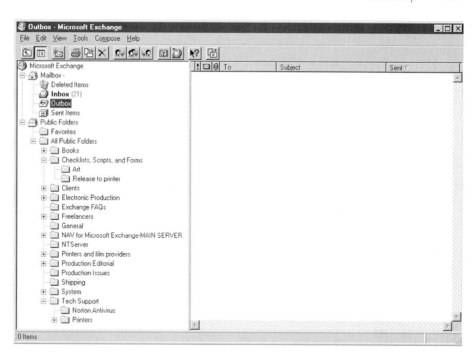

QUESTIONS

In what way does the Postal Service currently engage in price discrimination? How does the absence of competition facilitate slow mail delivery and high postal rates?

Sources: For more details, see James C. Miller III, "End the Postal Monopoly," *Cato Journal* (Spring/Summer 1985), pp. 149–155; James Bovard, "The Slow Death of the U.S. Postal Service," *Policy Analysis*, Cato Institute (April 3, 1988); and "Banks Hope to Stamp Out Paying by Check," *USA Today* (April 27, 1990).

SUMMARY

1. A pure monopoly is a single seller of a product for which there are no close substitutes in a market characterized by high barriers to new entry.

2. The monopoly firm faces the industry demand curve. When it lowers price, it must accept a lower price for all units previously sold for a higher price. The total revenue at the lower price minus the total revenue at the higher price is equal to the marginal revenue of the monopoly firm. For the monopoly, marginal revenue is less than price.

3. The monopoly selects an output to produce by setting marginal cost equal to marginal revenue. Since marginal revenue is less than price, the monopoly firm sets prices along its demand curve where price is greater than marginal cost.

4. Not all monopolies make profits. In the short run it is possible for the monopoly to incur a loss. If the loss persists in the long run, the monopoly will go out of business.

5. In the long run the monopoly firm can adjust its plant size. Normally, however, the monopoly does not operate at the point of minimum long-run average total cost.

6. Price discrimination requires that a seller be a monopoly firm, be able to separate buyers on the basis of their elasticities of demand, and be able to prevent buyers in the low-price market from reselling to buyers in the high-price market.

7. Where buyers can be separated into two classes, the monopoly firm will set marginal cost, which is

the same in both markets, equal to marginal revenue in each market. This is the definition of price discrimination—price differences that do not reflect cost differences.

8. There are two potential efficiency costs of monopoly: the welfare loss due to monopoly power—the deadweight cost—which is the lost consumer surplus caused by monopoly, and the degree to which the monopoly firm has higher costs of production than the competitive firm.

9. Monopoly affects the distribution of income. Monopoly transfers wealth from consumers to the monopolist.

10. A potential advantage of monopoly is that large firms may be more effective developers of new products. The monopoly or large firm might thus possess a dynamic advantage over a small, competitive firm.

KEY WORDS

price searcher
pure monopoly
legal barriers to entry
public franchise
government license

patent
natural monopoly
marginal revenue
profit-maximizing price
price discrimination

contrived scarcity
welfare loss due to monopoly
static inefficiency
dynamic efficiency

QUESTIONS FOR REVIEW AND DISCUSSION

1. What is a barrier to entry? Why is it important in the definition of monopoly?

2. Depict the short-run equilibrium of a pure monopolist. Can the monopoly firm make a loss? If so, diagram what the loss situation for the monopoly might look like.

3. What conditions need to be met before a monopolist can price-discriminate?

4. What are the efficiency costs of monopoly? What is a potential benefit of a monopoly firm?

5. Insurance companies offer lower rates for life insurance to individuals who do not smoke and who jog. Is this an example of price discrimination? Why or why not?

6. If entry is not possible with pure monopoly, how can the monopoly sell its monopoly right?

7. Monopolies and large firms are sometimes blamed for rising prices. Does the theory of monopoly presented in this chapter imply that prices under monopoly will rise quickly or will be high? Explain.

8. Would a license to operate a taxicab in your hometown constitute a monopoly restriction? Why or why not?

9. Suppose that you have invented a new and far more efficient means of converting salt water to drinkable water and that you have just received a patent on the process. As a student of economics, how would you justify such a restriction?

PROBLEMS

1. Use the figure to answer the following questions.

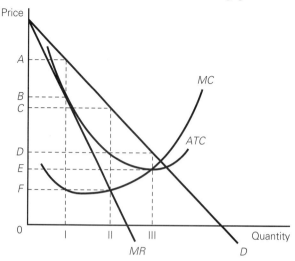

a. At what price and quantity will the monopolist operate?
b. Do monopolists produce more or less than competitive firms?
c. If the demand curve crosses the horizontal-axis when $Q = 500$, what does Q equal when the marginal revenue curve crosses the horizontal axis?

2. Owners of major league baseball teams are effectively monopolists in the sale of tickets in their franchise area (for example, Chicago or New York City). However, many of them price tickets such that there is excess capacity (unsold seats) for most games. Is it wise for them to pursue such a pricing policy? Use a figure to explain your answer.

WORKING WITH THE WEB

1. Patents are a source of monopoly power for many corporations in the United States. Because the holder of a patent holds a monopoly right for twenty years, patents are a great motivator for firms to invest in research and development. To get an idea of the impact of patents in U.S. business, go to http://www.uspto.gov/web/offices/ac/ido/oeip/taf/reports.htm#asgstc and scroll down to the section "By Patenting Organization," where single-year reports of the "Top 10 or 11 Patenting Organizations" are available for viewing. First, select 1998 and view the top 10 organizations in 1998 in terms of the number of patents awarded to the organization. The previous year is listed on the right-hand side and the current year on the left-hand side.
    a. Which organizations are newcomers to the top 10 list in 1998?
    b. Which public organization fell off the list in 1998, and how long had it been on the list?
    c. As of 1998, how long has IBM maintained the number one position in patents among the top 10 organizations?
    d. When IBM started its run in the top position, what organization did it displace from the number one spot? (You will have to look at other years to determine the answer to this question.)

2. This chapter introduces you to the economics of price discrimination. From the examples discussed in the text, you are probably aware of several instances of price discrimination, some of which might affect you. To examine price discrimination on campus, first go to http://www.bowdoin.edu/cwis/admissions/tuition.html and examine the tuition and fees charged per year at Bowdoin College. Next, take a look at Bowdoin's policy on financial aid at http://www.bowdoin.edu/cwis/admissions/finaid.html.
    a. Does Bowdoin engage in price discrimination between in–state and out–of–state students? Why or why not?
    b. If Bowdoin does not discriminate by residency, how might it practice price discrimination among its student body via the awarding of financial aid?
    c. How are the demanders of financial aid separated, and how do you think arbitrage is prevented?

CHAPTER 10

Monopolistic Competition and Advertising

Until the 1930s, microeconomic theory analyzed only two basic market structures: pure competition and pure monopoly. These structures are, of course, opposite extremes. With pure competition, prices tend to equal costs in the long run and consumers' economic welfare is theoretically maximized, whereas the pure monopolist may restrict output, raise prices, and capture economic profits. In the 1930s, two economists, E. H. Chamberlin of Harvard University and Joan Robinson of Cambridge University, wrote books developing models of market structures that did not fit the mold of either pure competition or pure monopoly. Both Robinson and Chamberlin emphasized that the real world was characterized by market structures that did not easily fit into existing economic theory.

All models of firms and markets other than the extremes of pure competition and pure monopoly are called theories of **imperfect competition**. The word *imperfect* means that not all the conditions for pure competition are met.

Some imperfectly competitive markets contain large numbers of sellers (as in pure competition) selling slightly different products (unlike pure competition). These are monopolistically competitive markets.

Other structures are composed of small numbers of competing sellers who recognize that their actions affect one another's sales, prices, and profits. Under these circumstances, firms may engage—or try to engage—in various forms of combination or collusion. Such associations are called oligopoly or cartel market structures. They are closer in economic results to pure monopoly than to pure competition. The spectrum of market structures, therefore, runs from pure competition to monopolistic competition to oligopoly and cartels to pure monopoly.

Imperfect competition
Market models, such as oligopoly, cartels, monopoly, and monopolistic competition, in which individual sellers' actions influence price.

Because real-world markets seldom fit into the neat categories of competition or monopoly, it is important to develop more realistic models. The economist, moreover, must assess the effects of these real-world market structures on consumers' and producers' welfare and on economic efficiency in general. We begin with monopolistic competition, the economic model closest to pure competition. After reading Chapter 10 you should understand

- the characteristics of monopolistic competition as a model of how firms behave when many sellers are selling different products or services.
- advertising's role in differentiating products.
- how economically efficient monopolistically competitive markets are when compared with pure competition and pure monopoly.
- how monopolistic competition can be useful as a model of a firm's behavior.

MONOPOLISTIC COMPETITION

In his search for more realistic models of firms and markets, E. H. Chamberlin developed a model close but not equivalent to pure competition. Since the model contained some monopolistic elements, Chamberlin labeled this theory "monopolistic competition."

Characteristics of Monopolistic Competition

Monopolistic competition
A market model with freedom of entry and exit and firms producing similar but differentiated products.

Monopolistic competition is a market structure in which a large number of sellers sell similar but slightly different products and in which no barriers to entry or exit exist. Advertising is a principal tool for differentiating products within monopolistic competition.

Large Number Of Sellers   Monopolistic competition, like pure competition, is characterized by a large number of competing sellers. The effect of large numbers is the same in both cases: Collusion to fix prices or other kinds of cooperation is costly—so costly that it ordinarily does not occur. The presence of many sellers is a competitive element in monopolistic competition. Unlike pure competitors, however, monopolistic competitors are not always price takers because of another characteristic—product differentiation.

Product Differentiation   Competitive sellers sell a homogeneous or identical product, such as corn. Monopolistic competitors sell products that are highly similar but not identical. Products may be distinguished by brand names, location, services, even differences merely perceived by the consumer. Because the monopolistic com-

Differentiated product
A product with features that make it distinct, in consumers' eyes, from close substitutes.

petitor is selling a slightly **differentiated product**, the firm will have a degree of control over price, unlike the competitive firm. Product differentiation is an example of **nonprice competition**, a term commonly used to refer to any action other than price cuts taken by a competitor to increase demand for its product.

Nonprice competition
Any means other than pricing decisions that firms use to sell output.

There are many varieties of nonprice competition. One is differences created in the products themselves. Consumers shopping for personal computers can choose among many firms' products, each differing slightly in hardware, software, styling, sturdiness, and user-friendly or state-of-the-art appeal. Sometimes, distinctions between brands are more illusory than real. Although aspirin is essentially a homogeneous product, monopolistically competitive firms produce it under many different brand names—Bayer, Excedrin, Bufferin, and so on—often at very different prices. The reason for the different prices for aspirin is that each brand is differentiated in consumers' minds, often through advertising or some other form of sales effort. Consumers who are convinced that brands actually differ will have some allegiance to a particular brand. This brand allegiance permits the seller to set price, within limits.

Location may also differentiate a seller's products. There may be ten Exxon gas stations within a city, alike in every respect, including the gasoline they sell. The gas stations each occupy a different location, however, and thus are free to set different prices. The Exxon station near the interstate might charge a higher price than the station downtown because travelers in a hurry are willing to pay more.

Service is another form of nonprice competition. Physically identical products may be offered for sale in supermarkets at identical money prices. However, one store may be untidy, another may employ rude cashiers, and still another may suffer chronically slow-moving checkout lines. Markets with well-swept aisles, neat shelves, automated checkout, and friendly clerks will have differentiated their products by the services they offer.

Subtle product differentiation, whether by packaging, service, location, or any other variable, is a common fact of life, but the degree of substitutability among such products is high. While demand is highly elastic under monopolistic competition, it is not infinitely elastic, as in perfect competition. A sudden tenfold increase in the price of one brand of aspirin would send buyers scurrying for substitutes. The monopolistically competitive firm, in other words, like the firm in pure competition, is primarily a price taker. It has a small and limited degree of control over price, however, stemming from its ability to differentiate its individual product from those of its many competitors. This limited control over price is the monopoly element in these markets.

No Barriers To Entry   Just as with competitive markets, entry into and exit from the monopolistically competitive market is open. Although monopolistic competition shares the free-entry conditions of perfectly competitive markets, entry is not costless in either market structure. Free entry means that there is no government regulation over entry and that essential raw materials are not controlled by one or a few firms. There are resource costs and commitments in opening any business: hiring labor, investing capital in fixed items such as buildings, training or hiring managers, and so forth.

In addition to the start-up costs of entering any new business, entry into monopolistically competitive markets entails the cost of introducing a new product. New product development and market entry through advertising and other sales efforts constitute a cost that the competitive firm does not face. A farmer's entry into the winter wheat market, for example, will not involve a sales or advertising campaign, whereas entry into the deodorant or restaurant market will. Product differentiation is simply part of the cost of entry under monopolistic competition. Entry is nonetheless assumed to be free, and in this characteristic, monopolistic competition is very much like perfect competition. Firms in this industry should expect to earn a normal rate of return in the long run.

Advertising and Monopolistic Competition

The keystone of monopolistic competition is product differentiation and advertising. Advertising, in fact, helps create product differentiation, giving individual firms some control over the product price. How does advertising affect the demand for products, and what is the economic assessment of such activity?

The Importance Of Advertising   With the general characteristics of the monopolistically competitive structure in mind, we examine a typical firm's demand curve
and assess the impact of **advertising** on it. The existence of nonprice competition
coupled with a high degree of substitutability means that the firm's demand curve,
while highly elastic, is downward sloping. Such a demand curve is drawn in Figure
10.1 for a hypothetical antacid product, Relief. The demand curve for Relief
approximates that of a competitive firm, but it is downward sloping because Relief
is not the same product as competitors Tums, Rolaids, Mylanta, and Maalox.

 As with the pure monopoly firm, the monopolistically competitive firm's marginal revenue curve lies below its demand curve, and for the same reason: Additional units can be sold only at a lower price. The main difference between a
monopoly firm and a monopolistic competitor is that the monopoly firm sells a
unique product—one with no close substitutes—while substitutes abound for the
monopolistic competitor's product.

 How elastic or inelastic will the demand curve be for Relief? The answer will
depend on the size and intensity of consumer preferences for Relief, given the
range and price of substitutes. Naturally, the firm will be interested in increasing
the size of its market and in intensifying consumers' preferences for its product.
The firm accomplishes these goals through product advertising. Advertising is
essential to the introduction of new products in monopolistic competition and to
the manipulation or management of demand for existing products.

 Advertising is a variable under the monopolistically competitive firm's control, within the limits imposed by its advertising budget. The firm in monopolistic
competition will seek, along with all firms who advertise, to equate the addition to
revenue from the final dollar spent on advertising to the marginal addition to cost
from the advertising. Firms seeking to enter markets will often spend large amounts
of money to introduce their products. But whether the firm is an established competitor or a new entrant, the purpose of advertising is the same: to increase demand
and lower the elasticity of demand for the firm's product.

 In Figure 10.2, demand curve d_0d_0 depicts a monopolistically competitive firm's
demand curve. The hoped-for effect of increased advertising is a shift rightward in
the position of the demand schedule d_1d_1 and a reduction in the elasticity of the

Advertising
Any communication or
information that firms offer
consumers to increase demand
for a product.

FIGURE 10.1

**Demand Curve Facing
Monopolistically
Competitive Firm**

The demand curve for the
monopolistic competitor
slopes downward because
the firm sells a product differentiated from its com-
petitors. The marginal
revenue curve lies below
the demand curve because
additional units can be sold
only at a lower price.

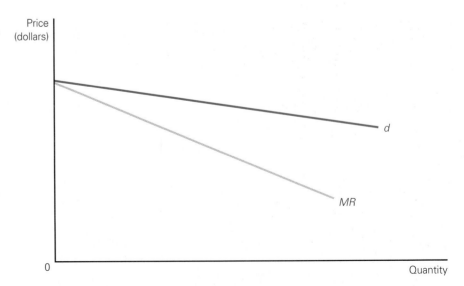

FIGURE 10.2

The Effects of Advertising on the Firm's Demand Curve

The firm advertising its product hopes to shift its demand curve to the right and to reduce its elasticity at a given price. In doing so, the firm tries to intensify demand for the product by distinguishing it in the minds of buyers.

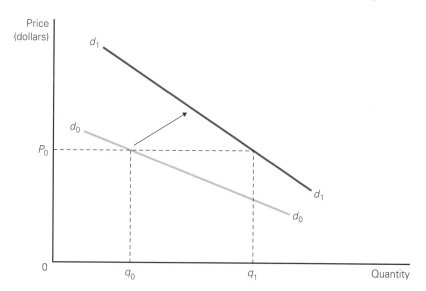

curve at a given price. Thus advertising is intended not only to increase demand but to intensify demand by differentiating the good or service in consumers' minds so that the firm can raise the product's price. If the advertisements for Relief are able to convince consumers that the product is "easier to swallow," "has no unwanted side effects," and the like, demand becomes more inelastic (less substitutable), and consumers are willing to pay more for it.

The Pros And Cons Of Advertising   Few subjects in economics have been debated as vigorously as advertising. Critics argue that ads are tasteless and wasteful assaults on consumers' senses. Since the products of monopolistically competitive firms are close substitutes, actual differences between the products of competing producers, if any, may be difficult to discern. Advertising creates perceived differences among similar goods and allocates demand among firms that produce products that are

Advertising takes on different forms in different media: it is often a blend of persuasion and information.

fundamentally alike. Some economists, then, view advertising as a squandering of society's resources on a costly exercise by which rival firms divide total sales.

Another criticism of advertising is that advertising expenditures raise both the costs of producing goods and services and the prices consumers pay. The resources used in advertising have opportunity costs, which means that the firm that advertises will bear higher costs and charge higher prices than the firm that does not advertise. And, of course, it should be kept in mind that there are various types of advertising. Some ads are designed to be persuasive, while others are designed to be informative. Generally, persuasive advertising has been the target of the critics of advertising.

Defenders of advertising deny that advertising is wasteful. They argue that advertising provides consumers with valuable information concerning the existence, characteristics, and location of goods and services. Such information reduces consumers' search costs and thereby reduces the full price that consumers pay. (See the Focus "Let Your Fingers Do the Walking: Information in Markets.")

Defenders of advertising also deny that advertising systematically leads to higher prices. While advertising is costly, it has two price-reducing effects. Since advertising can increase sales, advertising enables some firms to take advantage of economies of scale and produce output at a lower average total cost. Advertising also provides firms with a means of entry into markets and product lines. Without the ability to advertise, the process whereby new firms enter a market and compete away profits is short-circuited. The Focus "Advertising, Interest Groups, and the Price of Eyeglasses" examines the impact of advertising on prices in a specific market.

FOCUS

Let Your Fingers Do the Walking: Information in Markets

Entrepreneurs and sellers do not provide information willy-nilly. Market activity is rational, and sellers do not go to the expense of advertising their wares at random. Advertising, after all, is a key form of information provision. We would expect that advertising for high-value, infrequently purchased goods (for example, wedding dresses, travel agencies, carpet cleaning) would contain a higher proportion of information about quality than would advertising for low-value, frequently purchased goods (chewing gum, restaurants, photo finishing). The loss to us of making a mistake at a fast food restaurant is, after all, much lower than that resulting from the purchase of poor quality furniture. We will, therefore, demand more information about the latter kind of good.

Is this logic borne out in a traditional advertising outlet like the Yellow Pages? Two studies tested the proposition that the supply of product quality signals in advertisement increases with a rise in the expected marginal return to customers utilizing the Yellow Pages.[a] Sellers offering goods that were infrequently purchased (and/or of high value) placed ads that were far more informative (statistically) concerning quality (e.g., mention of certification or licensing) than were the ads placed by sellers of others kinds of goods. These studies found, further, that the proportions of informative ads rose in highly mobile cities (e.g., college or tourist towns) relative to cities with more sedentary populations. In short, advertising is both demanded and supplied as information connected to the purchase of goods and services of all types.

[a]See David N. Laband, "Advertising as Information: An Empirical Note," *Review of Economics and Statistics* 68 (1986), pp. 517–21; and Robert B. Ekelund, Jr., Frank G. Mixon, Jr., and Rand W. Ressler, "Advertising and Information: An Empirical Study of Search, Experience and Credence Goods," *Journal of Economic Studies* 22 (1995), pp. 33–43.

FOCUS

Advertising, Interest Groups, and the Price of Eyeglasses

The issue of advertising's effect on prices is an empirical (or statistical) issue. Economic theory suggests that two different effects on prices can exist. Since advertising requires scarce resources, it adds to the cost of producing output. In this sense, advertising would tend to cause prices to be higher than otherwise. But advertising also can be viewed as a tool of competition and as one vehicle businesses use to enter markets and product lines. From this perspective, advertising would exert price-lowering effects. Whether advertising raises or lowers price cannot be resolved through economic theory alone. The answer must be found by looking at actual markets and data.

In trying to gauge the effect of advertising on prices, economist Lee Benham considered the effect that a prohibition, or ban, on advertising has on prices. In the 1960s (and today still) a number of states had severe legal restrictions and outright prohibitions on the advertising of eyeglasses and eye examinations by physicians and optometrists. Other states had few or no restrictions on such advertising. Benham argued that the different states provided a good laboratory for the economic study of the relationship between advertising and prices. After adjusting for such factors as family income, sex, and customer age, any difference in prices paid in the two different types of states could be reasonably attributed to advertising (or the lack of it).

Some of Benham's findings are presented in Table 10.1. (Benham used prices during 1963. We have converted his results to 1998 dollars for easy comparison.) Table 10.1 contains average price differences for both glasses and glasses plus an eye exam between states with wide-ranging advertising restrictions and states with essentially no advertising prohibitions. The results suggest that the price-lowering effects of advertising dominate in the eyewear market.

Although Benham's study made no attempt to adjust for quality, it suggests empirical support for the proposition that advertising is a part of the competitive process. The prevention of advertising appears to have made prices higher than they would have been had advertising been allowed in the market.

State advertising restrictions are of course the product of interest group politics. Where groups (such as optometrists or physicians) are able to pass laws restricting advertising, returns as well as prices may be assumed to be higher than if advertising is not restricted. Rationales—such as ethics or consumer protection—are often used in order to quell opposition to price-increasing restrictions. But whatever the reason, such restrictions are price increasing and welfare diminishing in effect.

Source: Lee Benham, "The Effect of Advertising on the Price of Eyeglasses," *Journal of Law and Economics* 15 (October 1972), pp. 337–352.

TABLE 10.1

Advertising Restrictions and the Price of Eyeglasses

Average prices in states with severe advertising restrictions to prices in states with few, if any, legal advertising restraints. These prices, originally measured in 1963, have been converted to their 1998 equivalents.

	States With Restrictions	States Without Restrictions	Average Price Difference	Average Percentage Difference
Eyeglasses	$177.53	141.52	36.01	20%
Eyeglasses plus exam	$220.08	199.34	20.73	10%

Source: Lee Benham, "The Effect of Advertising on the Price of Eyeglasses," *Journal of Law and Economics* 15 (October 1972), p. 342, updated by authors.

Short-Run and Long-Run Equilibrium Under Monopolistic Competition

Now that we have defined the overall conditions for monopolistic competition, we can discuss how firms set prices. The firm in monopolistic competition has some control over price, but its control differs in the short and the long run.

Short-Run Equilibrium Monopolistically competitive firms, like firms in all other market structures, always equate marginal cost to marginal revenue to maximize profits. In the short run, the firm may enjoy economic profits or endure losses.

Figure 10.3 gives a firm's short-run cost curves, demand curve, and marginal revenue curve. MC intersects, or is equal to, MR at quantity q_0. The firm produces that quantity and sets price P_0 for q_0 units of output. At this price and quantity, the firm will earn economic profits. These profits are calculated by multiplying price times quantity sold ($P_0 \times q_0$) to get the firm's total receipts, and then subtracting the total cost of q_0 units, $ATC_0 \times q_0$. Profits to the firm are shown in the shaded area of the figure. Although the firm's demand curve is highly elastic (due to the large number of substitutes), it is still negatively sloped because, under monopolistic competition, products are differentiated through advertising and other forms of nonprice competition.[1] So far, this analysis is identical to that for the simple monopolist in Chapter 9.

The monopolistic competitor does have one advantage over the pure competitor in the short run: the ability to manipulate demand through advertising and intensified product differentiation. Optimum advertising outlay for the firm occurs when one dollar of additional selling costs adds exactly one dollar to the firm's receipts. In this sense, the cost of advertising is treated like the cost of any other input, such as capital or labor.

Long-Run Equilibrium: The Tangency Solution Long-run equilibrium for the firm in monopolistically competitive markets may take a number of forms. One of

---

[1]Like firms in all other markets structures, monopolistically competitive firms do not always make a profit.

FIGURE 10.3

Short-Run Profits for the Monopolistically Competitive Firm

The firm earns short-run profits. It sets price P_0 for q_0 units of output. Its profits are the difference between its revenue ($P_0 \times q_0$) and its costs ($ATC_0 \times q_0$).

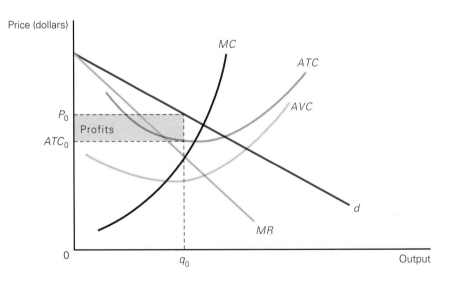

Tangency Solution

A long-run equilibrium situation in which the firm's downward-sloping demand curve is tangent to its *LRATC* curve; zero economic profits are earned.

them, described by E. H. Chamberlin, is the **tangency solution**, wherein the firm ends up making zero economic profits; that is, it simply breaks even.

Consider the situation of the firm in Figure 10.3. In short-run equilibrium, the firm is making economic profits. Just as in the case of pure competition, in the long-run entry and exit and other adjustments take place in the monopolistically competitive industry. In Figure 10.3 the economic profits of the monopolistic competitor send a signal that excess returns are present in this "industry." Hence, entrepreneurs will seek to enter the industry with similar but slightly differentiated products. As these entrepreneurs take away sales from the firm in Figure 10.3, its demand curve will shift to the left, reflecting the increased number of firms selling a similar product.

Figure 10.4 shows where the process comes to rest or equilibrium. Finally, demand curve d becomes tangent to the long-run average total cost function $LRATC$ (thus the term *tangency solution* to describe this case). At point E in Figure 10.4, all firms will produce q_2 units of output and charge price P_1 per unit. Quantities above this amount and prices below P_1 would force firms out of business. Quantities less than q_0 and prices higher than P_1 would provoke the entry of new rivals. Under these circumstances, a stable equilibrium characterized by zero economic profits for all firms is generated.

The model described in Figure 10.4 reflects but one set of behavioral assumptions among many possibilities. Its value is considerable, however, because it describes a tendency to zero economic profits. Additionally, the tangency model of monopolistic competition provides a convenient benchmark for a comparison of the attributes and economic effects of pure competition and those of monopolistic competition.

Does Monopolistic Competition Waste Resources?

A charge commonly leveled at monopolistic competition—unrelated to the alleged wastes of advertising—is that the tangency solution requires (1) underallocation of resources in production or (2) generation of excess capacity and prices higher than minimum long-run unit costs of production. This portrayal of monopolistic competition is possible when it is compared with the long-run competitive model.

FIGURE 10.4

The Tangency Solution

When all firms lower price from P_0 to P_1, the monopolistically competitive firm's demand curve shifts leftward. In final equilibrium E, the point of tangency with the *LRATC* curve, all firms break even.

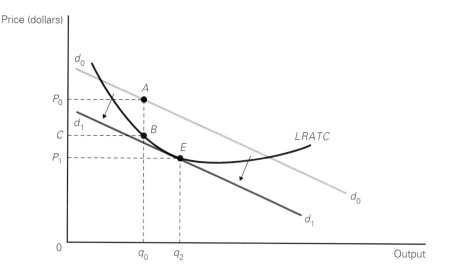

Monopolistic Competition Versus Pure Competition   Long-run equilibrium in the perfectly competitive model, discussed in Chapter 8, results in the following three conditions:

1. Price = long-run marginal costs;
2. Price = minimum long-run average total costs; and
3. Total revenue = total costs.

The first condition means that the consumer's marginal sacrifice (price) just equals the marginal opportunity cost of producing the last unit of a product or service consumed. The second condition means that consumers are getting the product at the lowest price at which the product can be produced. The third conclusion means that no competitive firm earns more than a normal profit in the long run. Firms are price takers under competition. Freedom of entry guarantees normal profits in the long run.

Consider, with the aid of Figure 10.5, how monopolistic competition compares to pure competition in these respects. Figure 10.5a shows the demand curve $P_c d_c$ and the short-run and long-run average cost curves for the typical firm in pure competition. Both long-run and short-run costs are tangent to the perfectly elastic demand curve for the firms in competition. Quantity q_c is produced at price P_c, which equals long-run (and short-run) marginal cost. Figure 10.5b shows the downward-sloping demand curve d_m of a monopolistically competitive firm in a tangency solution with the firm's long-run average cost curve. Given that the firms'

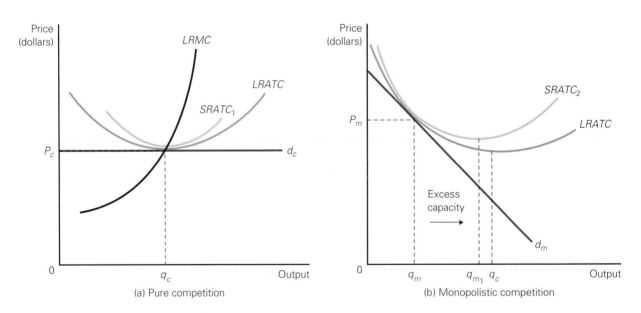

FIGURE 10.5

A Comparison of Pure Competition and Monopolistic Competition

In a technical sense, the monopolistically competitive firm (b) charges a higher price, P_m, than the purely competitive firm (a), P_c. The monopolistically competitive firm sets output at q_m to maximize profits, but the most efficient use of its plant would be an output of q_{m1}. The firm therefore produces with excess capacity, or underutilization of its scale of plant.

cost curves are identical under both market structures, how do they compare in terms of economic efficiency?

As Figure 10.5 shows, monopolistic competition has the following features:

1. Price > long-run marginal costs;
2. Price > minimum long-run average costs; and
3. Total revenue = total costs.

We can put the first point slightly differently: The additional sacrifice (price) that consumers are willing to make for an additional unit of the good is greater than the marginal opportunity cost of producing that additional unit. So resources are underallocated in the production of goods by monopolistically competitive firms, just as they usually are by pure monopolies.

Notice also that consumers pay more for goods produced under conditions of monopolistic competition than they do when goods are supplied by perfect competitors. The fact that P_m in Figure 10.5b is greater than P_c in Figure 10.5a means that price is higher and output is lower under monopolistic competition than under pure competition. Consumers are not paying the lowest possible unit cost. However, like perfect competitors, monopolistic competitors do not earn economic profits because a tangency solution means that total revenues equal total costs to the firm (or, alternatively, that the firm's average cost equals its average revenue).

Excess capacity

A situation in which industry output is not produced at minimum average total cost. The output actually produced is less than the output that would minimize average total cost.

Critics of monopolistic competition raise still another issue: **Excess capacity** is generated under the monopolistically competitive market structure. This criticism ordinarily holds for any less-than-perfectly competitive market. To understand what excess capacity means, consider Figure 10.5 again. The *LRATC* function is called an envelope curve because it is composed of a series of tangencies of points on the short-run average total cost curves (see Figure 7.5 on p. 186). The short-run curves $SRATC_1$ and $SRATC_2$ drawn in Figure 10.5 are two such curves. To utilize fully any scale of plant or to produce at an optimum rate of output in the short run, the existing scale of plant or existing resources invested must be used at the lowest average cost of production. For the monopolistically competitive firm depicted in Figure 10.5b, the output corresponding to that lowest short-run average total cost of production is q_{m_1}, not q_m, the profit-maximizing quantity the firm has chosen. From society's point of view, the firm producing at q_m is wasting, or underutilizing, resources. Excess capacity is the unused capacity of the scale of plant that the firm has built. From the firm's perspective, however, the scale of plant represented by $SRATC_2$ is perfect, or optimal, in that it produces the quantity q_m more cheaply than any other scale of plant could. Thus, critics argue that monopolistic competition creates excess capacity as well as the long-run resource inefficiencies outlined above.

Economic efficiency

The allocation of resources that allows maximum benefit to be achieved at minimum cost.

Economic welfare

The value society places on goods and services consumed.

A Defense Of Monopolistic Competition   Is monopolistic competition as inefficient as the critics say? In assessing this issue we must be careful to distinguish between pure **economic efficiency** and **economic welfare**. Economic efficiency means that resources are properly allocated (at minimum cost for a given output) from the firm's perspective. Pure economic welfare is the value that society places on goods and services consumed. Chamberlin argued that the monopolistically competitive market structure is not wasteful in either sense because product differentiation creates variety and extends the array of consumers' choices.

If price is established close to but not at minimum long-run average total cost, some inefficiency might exist with monopolistic competition, but consider what consumers get in return: varied products and a vastly expanded number of products and services from which to choose. If this variety is socially valued, advertising and product differentiation are not necessarily wasteful. Such differentiation, summed across all consumers, means that monopolistic competition may increase social welfare. A society that produces only white shirts may be efficient in a technical sense, but the repeated purchase of other colors of shirts at higher prices means that consumers are willing to pay for differentiation.

Depending on a given consumer's preferences, excess capacity may be either a cost or a benefit. Resource costs other than money are involved in the purchase of goods. Time, for example, is an important cost for some consumers. Since excess capacity reduces the time cost of making purchases, it reduces consumption costs. For consumers who place a high value on time, excess capacity is likely to be beneficial. For example, in cities where cab fares are relatively high, cabs typically line up in front of hotels and airports. Business executives who place a high value on their time are willing to pay a high dollar price rather than wait for a less expensive means of transportation. For them, excess capacity is clearly beneficial. In contrast, consumers who place a low value on their time will choose to pay lower money prices but higher time prices by taking public transportation or the hotel van.

How Useful Is the Theory of Monopolistic Competition?

When models of monopolistic competition and pure competition are subjected to real-world observation, is there a dime's worth of difference between them? How useful, in other words, is the model of monopolistic competition?

If the demand curve is very elastic when products are differentiated, the model of monopolistic competition is a close approximation of pure competition. Thus, a study of markets with differentiated products and rapid and free entry of substitutes is a study of what is usually called competition. Indeed, it is the rapid entry of new products and new brands that has often been the target of criticisms of competitive markets (see the Application "What's in a Brand Name? The Consumer Chooses"). With the ready emergence of substitutes, the adjective in *monopolistic competition* may be downplayed. Firms' ability to set prices is critically restricted by such entry and even by potential entry. Viewed in this light, the model of monopolistic competition, with its emphasis on product differentiation and other forms of nonprice competition, is of great value in helping us understand how dynamic real-world markets function, change, or thrive.

APPLICATION

What's in a Brand Name? The Consumer Chooses

Elaborate and seemingly bewildering displays of products greet the consumer at the modern American supermarket. And that is nothing compared with the new consumer goods we hear about daily on TV and in computer ads, newspapers, and magazines. Thousands of products are sold and thousands more are introduced every year. In any single year, massive quantities of new brands, new flavors, new sizes, new ways to sell products, or other variations on established brands are introduced by business entrepreneurs. How many new brands of chips or cold remedies came onto the market last year? The answer may be "hundreds."

Brand "variations" in type or quality are most common. You may now purchase spaghetti sauce plain, with green peppers, "Cajun style," with three different kinds of cheeses, with beef, with pepperoni, and in a host of other variations. Critics of the market system blast such product proliferation as unnecessary, costly, and of little value to the consumer or to the economy. This criticism is often primarily directed toward monopolistic competition. However, such criticism basically represents a misunderstanding of how the market system works to contribute to economic efficiency and to maximize the sum of producer and consumer surplus.

Big consumer-product-oriented companies such as Procter & Gamble, Johnson & Johnson, or Kraft Foods have every incentive to maintain "market share" and profitability for company stockholders by differentiating their products. The question is: Does such differentiation increase consumer welfare? The answer is (in the vast majority of cases) a resounding yes! This is especially so in markets characterized by repeat purchases and monopolistic competition.

Most product differentiation or quality variations do not come free to consumers and are offered only at added cost. Most often, the "plain" or "classic" variety remains available. The subjective evaluation of the consumer concerning the new product or variety will turn on whether the change (improvement?) in utility terms and in terms of how much "extra" the customer is willing to pay is sufficient to overcome the additional charge for the product or service. If it is, the consumer buys and her dollar votes encourage such variety. If not, the producer/seller discontinues the new brand (think of the Edsel automobile and the host of products that "don't make it" each year). Moreover, successful innovations in product or packaging—such as new computer software—are immediately imitated by other producers.

What critics of innovation and differentiation seem to misunderstand is that the market system, in responding to the particular demands of consumers and groups of consumers, is creating greater welfare for consumers. If there is no increase in utility, consumers will not buy a new product at a higher price. The ideal (perhaps) would be the ultimate in product differentiation—that each and every consumer gets exactly the product or service he or she wants. Because of resource scarcity and opportunity cost, this is not possible. The truth is, however, that the

A market system has provided an enormous range of choice for athletic shoes (of all kinds and descriptions), as it has for so many goods and services. This has led to a charge of "brand proliferation" from critics of free markets.

market system that allows trial, error, and fishing by producers and sellers for new variations or products to entice consumers comes closest to the ideal. Restrictions on this system are more likely to harm consumers than to help them.

QUESTION

Some politicians, economists, and media persons argue that brand proliferation by large corporations merely confuses people and is therefore not a benefit to the consumer. Do you agree? Why or why not?

SUMMARY

1. Monopolistic competition is a market structure that contains a large number of firms. Each firm sells a product that is similar to but slightly differentiated from the products of other firms in the industry. Freedom of entry and exit exists in this model.

2. Advertising is a means by which firms distinguish their products and attempt to increase demand for them. Advertising and other forms of nonprice competition characterize monopolistic competition.

3. In the long run, a tangency between the firm's demand curve and its long-run average cost exists under monopolistic competition. If this tangency occurs, then the firm produces a rate of output less than the rate associated with minimum average total cost—that is, excess capacity exists.

4. The excess capacity that exists in a monopolistically competitive market may have value. A large variety of differentiated products offers consumers a wider variety of choice than they have in a purely competitive market, where firms sell a homogeneous product.

5. The long-run equilibrium of the monopolistically competitive firm is similar to a competitive firm in that its price is equal to its average cost. It is similar to a monopolist in that its price is greater than its marginal cost.

KEY TERMS

imperfect competition	nonprice competition	excess capacity
monopolistic competition	advertising	economic efficiency
differentiated product	tangency solution	economic welfare

QUESTIONS FOR REVIEW AND DISCUSSION

1. Select two products or services that you regularly consume. Are these goods produced under monopolistically competitive conditions? What information must you have before giving a definite answer to this question?

2. What, exactly, is the role of product differentiation and advertising in monopolistic competition?

3. How many forms of competition can you name and analyze in addition to price competition? How is location a factor in competition?

4. Suppose that Pepsi is the best-selling soft drink in the market. Is it wasteful for Pepsi to continue to advertise on a large scale? Give reasons for your answer.

5. Suppose you are moving to a new town and must find an apartment. What benefits do you receive from apartment advertisements? What costs do you incur?

6. What is the tangency solution to the market model of monopolistic competition? Are half-empty airplanes on the New York–San Francisco route definite evidence of excess capacity and economic waste? Give reasons for your answer.

7. Compare the results of long-run equilibrium in pure competition and monopolistic competition from the standpoint of both economic efficiency and welfare.

8. Which of the following is more realistic, the model of perfect competition or the model of monopolistic competition?

WORKING WITH THE WEB

1. One of the characteristics of monopolistic competition is that firms differentiate their products in an attempt to capture more market share. An example of a monopolistically competitive industry is cereal. There are relatively few manufacturers, yet there are over one hundred different boxes of cereal on the shelves of your local supermarket. The two top manufacturers of ready-to-eat cereal are Kellogg's and General Mills.

   Go to http://www.kelloggs.com/corphq/products/index. html and look at the ready-to-eat cereals that Kellogg's sells. Next, do the same for General Mills by viewing its ready-to-eat cereals at http://www.generalmills.com/products/prodlist.asp?id=1.

   a. Which company is more diversified in terms of the number of different cereals it manufactures?

   b. Both Kellogg's and General Mills are publicly held corporations. To compare the dividend per share in each corporation, first go to http://www.kelloggs.com/corphq/financial/index.html and scroll down to the table titled "Per Common Share." Under the second column, cash dividends, what is the level of dividends per share in 1998? How does this compare with the dividends per share at General Mills in 1998? (Go to http://www.generalmills.com/financial/dividend and scroll down until you see the table containing the Fiscal Year and its associated dividend per share.)

   c. How might you explain the difference that exists in dividends per share in these two corporations in light of product differentiation?

2. The extent of advertising in monopolistically competitive industries is greater than in competitive industries. One source of advertising, as discussed in this chapter, is the Yellow Pages. Go to http://yellowpages.excite.com/bus and choose the option that allows you to search by category. In the search box, type "restaurants" (without the quotes). For "Search Area," select "City only" and in the search box, type in Auburn, AL.

   a. How many restaurant categories are there in Auburn (click on the "+" next to restaurants)?

   b. Enter a new search area—Washington, DC. How many restaurant categories are advertised in Washington? How do you explain the difference in the extent of Yellow Page advertisements in Washington relative to Auburn?

Few Competitors: Game Theory, Oligopoly, And Cartels

W here sellers of a particular product or service are few in number, the market is called an **oligopoly**. Beer, automobiles, cigarettes, steel, and aluminum are just some of the products of oligopoly markets. The key element in these markets composed of small numbers of competing sellers is that each seller recognizes that his or her actions have an impact on the other sellers' sales, prices, and profits. The fate of any one competitor is linked to the actions of each of the other competitors in the market; further, each competitor recognizes that this is the case. Economists call this condition **mutual interdependence**. Under such oligopoly conditions, firms may, for survival or profit, try to engage in various forms of combination or collusion.

A **cartel** is a formal or informal alliance among producers to restrict competition and to achieve some or all of the gains of monopoly. Such a structure may be closer in economic results to pure monopoly than to pure competition. While an oligopoly refers to an industry with a few sellers, a cartel can exist in any industry, depending on the difficulty of forming a collusive agreement among producers.

This chapter focuses on those market structures in which mutual interdependence is a factor in the functioning of the market and is recognized as such. When you finish reading Chapter 11 you should understand

- the implications of game theory for explaining mutual dependence and for the behavior of oligopoly firms and cartels.
- the conditions under which collusion may be expected when large competitors are few.
- how strategic behavior is important in understanding oligopoly market structures.
- the nature of legal and illegal cartels in U.S. and world markets.

Oligopoly
Market models characterized by a few firms producing either homogeneous or differentiated products, with entry of new firms very difficult or prevented.

Mutual interdependence
A relation among firms in which the decisions and actions of one firm have a significant impact on the decisions, actions, and profits of other firms.

Cartel
An alliance of firms that act collusively to reduce output and increase price in an industry in order to increase profits.

Game theory
A theory involving decision making in an atmosphere of mutual interdependence and imperfect information.

GAME THEORY AND MUTUAL INTERDEPENDENCE

Game theory is a tool that can be used in the analysis of strategic behavior between competing entities, such as the United States and the former Soviet Union.[1] In economics, game theory permits us to focus on the central feature of oligopoly—mutual interdependence—and the principles behind the strategies of firms in markets where the number of firms is small. First, we consider the matter of mutual interdependence more closely.

Mutual Interdependence in the Economic World

The key to the existence of oligopoly is that mutual interdependence develops among a small number of sellers. Mutual interdependence is a relation among firms such that what one firm does with its price, product, or advertising budget directly affects other firms in the market, and vice versa. For example, if Chrysler Corporation introduces two new types of automobiles or if the company increases its overall advertising budget by a significant percentage, sales of General Motors, Ford, and foreign automobile manufacturers will be directly affected. These oligopolistic competitors know that their sales and profits are affected by Chrysler's actions and are likely to react accordingly. Firms therefore devote resources to keeping track of their competitors' actions.

Recall that a firm under pure or perfect competition simply takes the market price as a given and produces accordingly and the pure monopoly has no direct competition to worry about. This is not the case with oligopolists. When competitors recognize mutual interdependence, each firm will base its market decisions (on price, product innovation, and advertising) at least partially on what it thinks its rivals will do. Because of the uncertainty facing sellers in oligopoly markets, mutual interdependence can lead to a variety of outcomes. The outcome of any action an oligopoly firm takes depends on the responses—both actual and assumed—of rival firms.

Game Theory: A Basis for Small-Numbers Behavior

The basic problem facing oligopolies should be familiar to everyone; we all find ourselves in situations of mutual interdependence every day. Anyone who has ever played competitive games of any sort—tennis, blackjack, bridge—will immediately recognize the problem. Our actions are interdependent when playing games because our actions affect other players' behavior, and our own behavior is conditioned by what we expect other players' reactions to our own behavior to be. Suppose that you and Joan have a weekly tennis match. Respectful of your powerful serve, Joan has learned to stand well behind the baseline when receiving. This position allows her to return an increasingly high percentage of your serves. Noticing this, you decide to surprise her with a shallow slicing serve. If you serve this way consistently, Joan will likely change her behavior. Joan's actions and yours are

---

[1]See John von Neumann and Oskar Morgenstern, *Theory of Games and Economic Behavior* (Princeton: Princeton University Press, 1944), the classic work applying game theory to economic analysis. Data for and discussion of several of the games considered in this chapter are taken, with permission, from Richard O. Beil, Jr., *Collusion in Experimental Oligopoly Markets* (Unpublished doctoral dissertation, Texas A&M University, 1988).

clearly interdependent—and recognized to be so. Game theory is the formalization of the effects of mutual interdependence on strategy.

Prisoner's dilemma

A scenario that illustrates the mutual interdependence of decision making; the basis for game theory.

The Prisoner's Dilemma As A Basis For Game Theory   An intriguing basis for game theory as applied to economic rivalry is called the prisoner's dilemma. The **prisoner's dilemma** originated in a story told by mathematician A. W. Tucker. It involves two criminals (here, Butch Cassidy and the Sundance Kid) and their likely behavior after capture. Suppose that the police have captured Butch and Sundance. Further, suppose that the police have sufficient evidence to convict both of lesser crimes but suspect that Butch and Sundance have committed more serious offenses that are punishable by lengthier stays in jail. The police separate the prisoners and attempt to obtain confessions. Butch and Sundance each know that (1) if one confesses, the confessor will receive a light sentence and the other will receive a more severe sentence; (2) if neither confesses, both will receive the modest penalty that goes with the lesser crime; (3) if both confess, both will receive a sentence that, while severe, is short of the sentence that would be given to each individual if he did not confess and the other did.

The decisions facing Butch and Sundance are organized in Figure 11.1, which represents the prisoner's dilemma by arranging the "payoffs" (in this case, punishments in years in jail) faced by the two decision makers. (Figure 11.1 is the *payoff table* for this situation.) The potential number of years of incarceration for Sundance is shown on the left side of each individual block, or quadrant, and the potential time served for Butch is shown on the right side. The police will try to get Butch and Sundance to testify against each other. If Butch confesses but Sundance does not confess, Sundance gets 12 years in prison to Butch's 1 year. Similarly, if Sundance confesses to the greater crime and Butch holds out, Sundance serves only 1 year in jail and Butch serves 12. If both refuse to confess, each receives 3 years, but if both confess, they each serve 7 years.

What is the most likely outcome of this "game" of strategy between Butch and Sundance? The outcome depends on the presumptions that each makes about the other's behavior. We may reasonably assume (1) that both Butch Cassidy and the Sundance Kid want to minimize their time in jail and (2) that neither is concerned about the cost his decision imposes on the other. Given these two assumptions, the

FIGURE 11.1

Butch Cassidy and the Sundance Kid Face the Prisoner's Dilemma

If Butch and Sundance want to minimize their time in jail, the prisoner's dilemma leads both of them to confess. Each receives a 7-year sentence.

The best choice for Butch Cassidy and the Sundance Kid is for neither to confess to wrongdoing.

Dominant solution

A situation in game theory in which each player has the same best choice no matter what course of action other players may choose.

solution to the game is for *both* Butch and Sundance to confess. Look at Figure 11.1 and consider the potential years served. What is Sundance's best strategy? If Butch confesses, Sundance gets 7 years if he confesses too, but *12 years if he doesn't*. If Butch does not confess, Sundance gets 1 year if he confesses and 3 years if he does not confess. Sundance is better off confessing. Given that Sundance cannot know Butch's decision, and can in no way influence that decision, a confession is the only way for Sundance to ensure a lesser jail term for himself. A look at Figure 11.1 will verify that the same is true for Butch; the best choice for each criminal is to confess and serve 7 years. (If the two could communicate, however, and if each could hold the other to his word, the best choice for both Butch and Sundance would be to not confess.) In the terminology of game theory, the choices offered to Butch and Sundance have a **dominant solution**: Each player has the same best choice, no matter what strategy the other player chooses. In the game represented by Figure 11.1, the dominant solution is to confess.

The Prisoner's Dilemma As Economic Game   The prisoner's dilemma can be directly related to economic behavior. Contests offered by fast-food chains can be viewed within the context of simple game theory. A contest increases the restaurants' production costs (prizes, promotion fees, and so on) and at the same time tends to reduce profits. Yet contests are often offered by firms acting in their own self-interest. Their reasoning is illustrated in Figure 11.2, in which profits to the restaurant chains replace the time in prison spent by Butch Cassidy and the Sundance Kid. Here, the two fast-food chains are trying to maximize their profits, represented by the dollar figures in the boxes.

From the industry's standpoint, the best decision for both firms is represented in box *A* of Figure 11.2. Industry profits total $120 million in box *A* ($65 million for Wendy's and $55 million for Burger King), as opposed to $100 million in boxes *B* and *C* and $90 million in box *D*. Yet box *A* does not represent the individual profit-maximizing choice for either firm separately. If Burger King offers a contest and Wendy's does not (box *B*), Burger King's profits are $70 million, up $15 million. If Burger King offers a contest and Wendy's does likewise, Burger King's profits will be only $40 million (box *D*). But if Burger King does not offer a contest and Wendy's does, Burger King's profits will drop to $30 million (box *C*). Wendy's management considers its own set of options and reaches a similar conclusion: namely, that acting independently, Wendy's will always be better off giving customers a contest to play. If each chain makes a decision that tends to maximize its individual profits, both will introduce contests and together earn smaller profits ($90 million) than they would have earned in the absence of contest offerings by both ($120 million).

The dilemma for Burger King and Wendy's is this: Both parties would be better off if they could communicate and stay in box *A*; but firms cannot legally com-

FIGURE 11.2

The Prisoner's Dilemma and Fast-Food Contests

Various possible combinations exist when Wendy's and Burger King try to maximize profits by deciding whether to offer contests. Profits for the firm's decisions are given in millions of dollars. The best choice for the industry as a whole is box *A*, where neither firm offers a contest. The best profit-maximizing option for each individually is to offer a contest.

Tacit collusive solution

A possible outcome in game theory when, given an indefinite time horizon and no formal communication, rivals recognize that it is in their best interest to act so that joint profits are maximized.

Backward induction

The incentive each player has to cheat in the last period of the game; exists because there are no future periods left to play in which possible consequences from cheating could occur.

Cheat

To violate a collusive agreement; cheating may result in an increase in short-run economic profits to the firm that cheats, followed by zero economic profits in the long run.

municate because of the fear that they might talk about more than contests—that is, that they would collude or cooperate to raise prices, an activity that would be a violation of federal antitrust laws. Therefore, the best option for each firm acting alone is box *D*.

One-Shot Versus Infinite-Series Games   Two keys to the actual outcome of such "games" in real-world situations are (1) the conjecture made about rivals' responses and (2) the time frame over which combatants work out their responses and strategies. The two games presented in Figures 11.1 and 11.2 are one-shot games; in each case, each party has just one chance to make the best decision. If these games were played repeatedly, perhaps both parties in each game—both Sundance *and* Butch and Wendy's *and* Burger King—would eventually decide to do what's best for both. Butch and Sundance might eventually get to box *A* in Figure 11.1, with each serving three years; Burger King and Wendy's might eventually get to box *A* in Figure 11.2, with neither offering contests. Such **tacit collusive solutions**—or outcomes without specific, formal agreement—exist when, over an indefinite period of time, firms recognize that their own interests will best be served when joint or combined profits are maximized.

When the time horizon facing two rivals is finite—that is, when the game has a known end point—the outcome is shaped by the principle of **backward induction**. Backward induction results from an incentive to cheat in the last period of the game.

Suppose Wendy's and Burger King's contest "game" will last three "periods." If the two firms have been in box *A* of Figure 11.2 for two periods, it would be in either Burger King's or Wendy's best interest to **cheat** in the third and final period. Why? To do so would mean bigger profits for the cheater—*but only if the other does not cheat.* If you think your rival will cheat in the third period, then you have an incentive to get there first—to cheat in the second period. If you think your rival will cheat in the second period, then you will cheat in the first period. The collusive, or joint profit-maximizing, solution tends to break down when the end period of the game is known. Each player has an incentive to cheat *before* the joint profit-maximizing solution has a chance to get off the ground; the outcome in such a case is identical to the outcome of a one-shot game.

OLIGOPOLY

As noted previously, industries with a few sellers or with a few large sellers and a large number of fringe competitors are characteristic of the modern marketplace. Oligopolies may sell homogeneous products such as steel or differentiated products such as automobiles or soft drinks. The simple principles of game theory tell us that pricing decisions by oligopolistic firms are much more complex than for firms in monopolistic or monopolistically competitive markets. Unlike other types of firms, oligopolistic firms find it extremely difficult to estimate their demand curves. If Ford is considering a 5 percent increase in prices, there is no reliable way of estimating sales at that higher price without knowing the price response of other firms like General Motors or Toyota. Before turning to some specific models of oligopoly, we consider another characteristic of all oligopolies: barriers to entry.

Barriers to Entry

Market power

A situation in which an established firm has influence over price and profit levels due to barriers impeding the entry of rival firms.

Oligopoly firms are normally thought to possess a large degree of **market power**. Subject to the reactions of competitors and to the ability of new competitors to enter the market, oligopoly firms are able to set prices and make economic profits, much like pure monopolists. But how does a firm achieve market power in the oligopoly market structure?

The source of the market power of oligopolists, as in any market structure, is barriers to entry. The pure monopolist is the sole supplier of a product because of barriers to entry into its industry. In any locality, for instance, there is ordinarily no close substitute for cable TV or residential power service, and there are legal barriers to firms wishing to enter these markets. If entry were free in these markets, new competitors would be attracted by higher-than-competitive prices, and excess profits would be eroded. Entry barriers are likewise essential to the maintenance of market power by oligopolists.

For an oligopoly, an entry barrier is a cost that confronts a potential entrant into the industry but does not affect the incumbent firms. There are both natural and artificial entry barriers in an oligopoly market.

Natural Barriers   Economies of scale are an example of a natural barrier to entry. The economies of large-scale production and distribution mean that long-run average costs decline as output grows. Minimum average cost is not reached until the firm is producing a huge proportion of the total industry output. Economies of scale in the U.S. automobile industry, for example, have promoted the presence of a few firms in the long run—far fewer than the hundreds of automobile manufacturers in existence at the beginning of the twentieth century. There are other natural entry barriers, including high fixed costs, high risk, scarce managerial talent, personal technological knowledge, and high capital costs.

Great care must be used in interpreting natural entry barriers, because most of these barriers reflect the different efficiencies of firms in producing output. Society benefits when firms achieve economies of scale, produce with the best technology, and allocate scarce managerial talent carefully. If a natural force like economies of scale leads to the possibility of market power, then the firm may be subject to antitrust prosecution. This means that the firm may be subject to laws enforced by the Federal Trade Commission and the Justice Department, which limit or eliminate anticompetitive practices.

Artificial Barriers   Government restrictions—patents, government regulations, licensing, tariffs, quotas, and other government actions—constitute artificial barriers to entry for oligopolists. Such restrictions are fairly self-evident, but consider some examples.

Government-sponsored import tariffs on foreign automobiles or steel are an example of government restrictions that encourage and protect oligopolies. Government-sponsored and -enforced cartels or legal agreements to collude—in such industries as railroads, ocean transportation, communications, TV, and radio—are another example of an artificial barrier to entry. Cartel arrangements legalized through regulation are probably the most important artificial barriers to entry established by government. The basic point is that oligopoly theory rests on the concept of barriers to entry, both natural and artificial.

Models of Oligopoly Pricing

Like other firms, oligopolies seek to maximize their profits. To do so, however, the oligopolist can pursue many different strategies because firms can compete on a number of bases—product development, prices, advertising budgets, and so on—and can form a whole spectrum of opinions about how rivals will react. Many theories of oligopoly based on price or nonprice competition have been developed. We present some of the standard models used by economists to analyze oligopolistic markets.

Game Theory And Oligopoly Behavior   While game theory becomes extremely complex in models involving more than two competitors or complicated strategies, simple models provide many insights into the problems of small-numbers competition. Unlike monopoly, where a firm's fortunes are largely dependent on the firm's behavior, game theory reveals an oligopoly firm's profits, prices, and output to be the result of mutually interdependent behavior. Further, game theory shows how mutual interdependence creates incentives to collude, as well as contradictory incentives to cheat on collusive agreements.

The Cournot–Nash Model   A slightly more complex model than those presented in Figures 11.1 and 11.2 can add to our understanding of strategic behavior in oligopolistic markets. The principles underlying our discussion were first put forth in 1838 by the French economist Augustin Cournot (1801–1877), and they were extended by mathematician John Nash in the 1950s. These principles are called the **Cournot–Nash solution** in game theory.[2]

Cournot–Nash solution
The likely outcome of a one-shot game or a game with a known end point; in this case, both firms cheat, thus bringing profits below the joint profit-maximizing level.

Suppose that two competitors—for example, Sony and Motorola—are considering three marketing or advertising strategies for the sale of high-resolution television sets. As shown in the payoff table in Figure 11.3, these three marketing strategies are labeled X, Y, and Z, giving Sony and Motorola nine possible combinations of choices, with the profits given in the nine individual boxes. If, for example, Sony chooses strategy Z and Motorola chooses X, profits to Sony are $544 million and Motorola's profits are $220 million.

The same basic solutions apply to the three-choice game as to the two-choice games described previously. The addition of an intermediate solution, however, helps us understand some other possible features of small-numbers behavior. As

[2]John Nash, along with two other developers of game theory John Harsanyi and Reinhard Selten, won the Nobel Prize in Economics for this work in 1994.

FIGURE 11.3

Sony and Motorola Caught in the Prisoner's Dilemma

In an "infinite" or many-period game, we expect Sony and Motorola to arrive at the joint profit-maximizing, or tacit collusive, solution (X, X). In a one-shot game or in one with a known end point, the Cournot–Nash solution (Z, Z) is most likely. (Payoffs are expressed in millions of dollars.)

		Sony			
		X	Y	Z
Motorola	**X**	Sony's profits $400 / $400 Motorola's profits	Sony's profits $481 / $310 Motorola's profits	Sony's profits $544 / $220 Motorola's profits
	Y	Sony's profits $310 / $481 Motorola's profits	Sony's profits $364 / $364 Motorola's profits	Sony's profits $400 / $247 Motorola's profits
	Z	Sony's profits $220 / $544 Motorola's profits	Sony's profits $247 / $400 Motorola's profits	Sony's profits $256 / $256 Motorola's profits

in simpler games, a one-shot or single play of the strategies open to Sony and Motorola will produce the prisoner's dilemma and result in the Cournot–Nash solution (Z, Z), where each earns profits of $256 million. When the time frame becomes infinite, we expect the tacit collusive arrangement (X, X) to emerge, where the rivals each earn $400 million in profits. The same is generally true when the competitive game is finite, provided that neither competitor knows the end point. Even when these competitive games are considered infinite or of unknown duration, there is still room for strategic behavior, due to the mutually interdependent nature of the competition.

Cheating appears as strategic behavior in most games. A close look at Figure 11.3 reveals that even if Sony and Motorola reach their joint profit-maximizing strategies (X, X), there is room for short-term profits from cheating by either party. Suppose that Sony continues "playing" the joint profit-maximizing marketing strategy, X, but that Motorola begins to employ strategy Y or Z. Sony's profits decline to $310 million or $220 million, while Motorola *raises* its returns from $400 million to $481 million or $544 million. Examination of Figure 11.3 tells us that Sony has a similar incentive to cheat on the tacit agreement with Motorola. In the real world, some cheating may be difficult to detect, but in this simple two-firm game any cheating is detected immediately by the victim's reduced profits.

One safeguard against cheating on the tacit collusive solution is to punish the offender. If Motorola moved to "cheating" strategy Y, Sony could immediately move to strategy Z, thereby restoring its returns to $400 million and reducing those of Motorola from $481 million to $247 million. Should Sony continue with strategy Z, Motorola could do no better than to also shift to strategy Z. We can easily verify that the Cournot–Nash solution (Z, Z) is the likely result once cheating begins.

Signals between game players are common in many games. As the dynamics of this game reveal, Motorola will be punished for cheating, but Sony's profits also fall with the movement to the Cournot–Nash solution. If the length of the game is infinite, or even just sufficiently long, cooperation and the re-establishment of the collusive solution is the most likely result. Either party, Sony or Motorola, *may* signal the other that it would like to return to collusion from the (Z, Z) level of profits.

Either may do so by moving to another strategy for a few periods, taking temporary losses, and giving its rival gains for those periods. Having been the first to cheat, if Motorola initiated this behavior, the move would be considered *repentance*. Such temporary losses may be a relatively small sacrifice if the joint profit-maximization, or collusive, solution can be maintained (or restored) over the long run.

These simple principles of games are more than just theory. They help explain a good deal of the maneuvering that actually occurs among firms. Clearly, it would be in the interests of businesses selling similar products to collude and to reach the joint profit-maximizing level of returns. But as the complexities of game theory tell us, such collusion is far less likely as the number of sellers increases. Successful collusion with little or no cheating is also less expected when firms compete in a large number of areas—for example, service, product qualities, and advertising. As games grow more complex—that is, accommodate a larger number of participants and items upon which competition is based—the possibilities for collusive behavior are drastically reduced. Simple game theory, including the prisoner's dilemma or Cournot–Nash game, is nevertheless of great value in helping economists understand the dynamics of competition and market processes.

Dominant-Firm Model   Many industries consist of one or a few large firms and many smaller rivals. Examples are the airlines, steel manufacturers, and the personal computer industry. Pricing in such a market is often characterized by **price leadership**, which means that there is an unwritten agreement that the largest firm sets pricing policy for the industry. When the largest firm announces that it is raising its price by 5 percent, the other firms in the industry follow suit (and usually on the same day!). This unwritten code of industry conduct is one way to solve problems of interdependent pricing.

The largest firm is not always the price leader; sometimes the price leader is the most respected firm in the industry or the firm, called a "barometric" firm, that best reflects average cost, demand, and other conditions in the industry. And sometimes the role of price leader shifts among firms. Jones-Laughlin, though not the

Price leadership

A market where a single firm sets industry price, with the remaining firms charging what the price leader charges. Industry price changes are initiated by the leader.

In many cases when competitors are in close proximity, the conditions for a competitive "game" (and for collusion) are set up. "Price wars" sometimes take place between competing gas stations that locate close to one another.

largest firm in the market, was for years the steel industry's price leader, whereas General Motors, clearly the dominant firm, provided a similar role for the automobile industry.

Oligopolists With Differentiated Products   Just as there are many cases of pure oligopoly, there are many cases in which few sellers supply differentiated products. Under such conditions, oligopolists may compete with each other and perhaps try to bar new entrants through nonprice means, such as advertising and quality variations, or through pricing strategies. Note that not all nonprice competition by oligopolists promotes efficiency in the economy. Our discussion of fast-food contests with regard to game theory illustrates how this sort of competition can lead to wasteful results.

Advertising   In oligopoly, as in monopolistic competition, advertising is used by rival firms to increase demand for their products (shift demand curves rightward and make them more inelastic) through the creation of brand loyalty and product identity. Heavy advertising by a few large firms is often held to be an entry barrier to new competition. The argument is that new firms cannot enter because they cannot afford the heavy advertising expenses necessary to establish a presence in the market.

Quality Variations   Quality variation and product development are other familiar methods of nonprice competition by oligopolists. Oligopolists, like monopolistic competitors, will alter products to increase their demand curves and to make demand more "intense" and inelastic in consumers' minds. Adding new colors to toothpaste, more or less chrome to automobiles, and more service to airline travel are familiar attempts to differentiate products and services.

Limit Pricing   In oligopoly industries with a differentiated product, incumbent firms may seek to deter potential competition by limit pricing. **Limit pricing** is the incumbent's practice of reducing price as much as necessary to limit entry.

Imagine a situation in which a new firm wants to enter an industry. Since other firms' products have already been differentiated, the new firm will have to incur heavy advertising expenses to become competitive with incumbent firms assumed to be earning positive economic profits. If a new entrant is successful in its bid for a share of the market, its sales will come at the expense of the incumbent firms. To block this challenge, an incumbent firm may lower price and increase output in response to the threat of entry, voluntarily (if temporarily) reducing its profits. In general, the incumbent firm could set a price (or threaten to set a price) at which entry would not be worthwhile for any potential rival.

We are talking about oligopolistic behavior. The potential entrant must make an estimate of what the incumbent firm will do in the face of entry. If the incumbent firm practices or even threatens limit pricing, entry may not be feasible. Indeed, the most rational thing for the incumbent firm to do is to keep price at profitable levels and at the same time make it clear to potential entrants that it will lower price and increase output if they enter.

Limit pricing
A pricing policy consisting of temporarily setting a price lower than the short-run profit-maximizing price in order to deter entry and maximize profits in the long run.

CARTEL MODELS

To this point in our discussion of oligopolies, we have assumed that competitor firms will not openly cooperate to set prices. But what if firms do openly cooperate? This question brings us to the topic of cartels.

Cartels and oligopolies are close cousins. The distinguishing feature of a cartel is an explicit (verbal or written) agreement among firms to restrict output in order to raise price and to achieve monopoly power over a market.

Characteristics of Cartels

Normally cartels are supported by agreements that restrict and segment output among markets. Cartel agreements may be legal or illegal. In countries with antitrust laws, including the United States, cartels are illegal, but they sometimes operate covertly. An illegal cartel rests on private, collusive agreements that are out of sight of the antitrust authorities. In the 1960s, certain U.S. firms made a secret agreement to fix the prices of electrical generators sold to municipalities; this illegal collusion was discovered and prosecuted under antitrust laws, with the guilty firms paying damages. (See the Focus "Bid Rigging: Cartels in Action.") Beyond the threat and reality of antitrust prosecution, such secret arrangements may tend to fall apart on their own. Reasons for the fragile nature of cartels will be discussed

FOCUS

Bid Rigging: Cartels in Action

All levels of government in the United States purchase many goods and services from private suppliers. At the federal level, the Department of Defense purchases cars, ammunition, and other products from private companies; state governments purchase paper, pencils, and road paving services from private contractors; and local governments buy milk for schoolchildren and services from water and sewer contractors. These are just a few of the many purchases that are made by government.

The process by which government typically purchases goods and services from private contractors is called sealed bidding. A road contractor, for example, will work up a bid or price for a road paving job, seal it, and submit it to the state highway department. Each road contractor submits his or her bid independently of other bidders. An official at the highway department then opens the sealed bids and awards the contract to the lowest bidder.

For the most part, the sealed bidding process works well, promoting the efficient, low-cost supply of services to government—as long as there is no bid rigging. Unfortunately, the provision of government services by private contractors has tended to encourage anti-competitive behavior. Bid rigging occurs when independent contractors get together and agree not to compete on their bids. Meeting at a restaurant, for example, the contractors might decide to "assign" job X to company A, job Y to company B, and so on. The contractors do not bid aggressively for jobs that have been assigned to someone else, guaranteeing that each company gets "its" job or a high bid. Since the bids are opened and read in public, all of the bidders can easily know if their bid conspiracy is being followed.

Obviously, bid rigging is a cartel or conspiracy in restraint of trade. By agreeing not to compete, firms earn cartel or monopoly profits. The result for taxpayers is higher prices for public services and, therefore, higher taxes.

During the 1980s and early 1990s, federal and state antitrust officials across the country uncovered numerous bid rigging schemes in such areas as road paving, water and sewer construction, and the sale of milk to school districts. The conspiracies were uncovered and the conspirators were prosecuted. Many executives of companies who participated in bid rigging were fined and sent to jail. The vigilance of the antitrust authorities thus served to save taxpayers money by ensuring the provision of basic government services at the lowest cost.

later in the chapter, but most are related to the incentives for some members to cheat on the agreement.

A legal cartel is supported by a law limiting entry and restricting competition among members. Such cartels may be made legitimate by the legal and political organization of an industry—communications, electrical distribution, and railroads, for example—under the umbrella of government regulation restricting competition and allowing price fixing. Or cartels may be made legitimate by legislation granting exceptions to antitrust statutes. Such is the case for some exporters, labor unions, and farm organizations.

Legal status does not protect such cartels from breaking down in the long run. Technology and competition have all but destroyed the railroad cartel in the United States enforced by the Interstate Commerce Commission since the late nineteenth century. OPEC (the Organization of Petroleum Exporting Countries) was unable to maintain its full cartel status, not because it was illegal within the participating countries, but because of the lack of adequate enforcement and the unwillingness of certain nations, notably Saudi Arabia, to meet the terms demanded by other members. The Colombian coffee cartel of the 1960s broke down for similar reasons, and the De Beers diamond cartel had some shaky times in the early 1980s. Thus, both legal and illegal cartels tend to be fragile, although cartel agreements enforced by law and the government are less so.

Cartel Formation

Assume for the sake of simplicity that cartels do not violate any law and that we are analyzing a case in which the cartel is to be privately enforced by the cartel members and not by government. The first problem facing any potential cartel or association of sellers is how to get organized. In this respect the cartel is no different from any other group. The usual problem in getting any group to do anything can be roughly summarized as "passing the buck." If somebody else forms the cartel or takes the lead in restricting output, other members can generally enjoy the benefits of the cartel without bearing any of the costs of organization. This behavior is called *free riding*.

Of course, if everybody in the cartel were a free rider, the cartel would never be formed. All potential members would hold back and expect to benefit from the organizational efforts of others. Suffice it to say that a cartel has to get organized. Someone has to get the individual suppliers in the industry together and hammer out an agreement to restrict output in order to raise price. The details of this feat are not simple. Which firms will reduce output and by how much? How will the resulting cartel profits be shared? How will deviations from cartel policies be monitored and enforced?

These and other questions are difficult for the cartel manager to answer and for cartel members to reach agreement on. The problem becomes more pronounced the more firms there are in the industry. As a rule, smaller groups are easier to organize than larger groups.

The Cartel in Action

Figure 11.4 illustrates how a cartel operates. Imagine that orange juice producers try to form a cartel. Initially, the orange juice industry is competitively organized. Orange juice industry demand and supply intersect to yield price P. Industry output is Q.

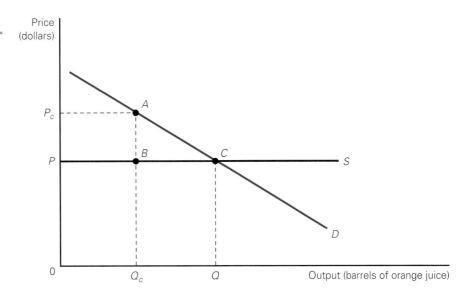

FIGURE 11.4

Organizing a Competitive Industry into a Cartel

Price rises from P to P_c as the cartel is formed and output is cut back from Q to Q_c. In the extreme case, the cartel price, P_c, is equivalent to the monopoly price.

A cartel manager emerges and strikes an agreement among the competitive producers to cut back production from the industry's Q to Q_c and to raise price from P to P_c. Cartel output Q_c will ordinarily not be equivalent to the output a pure monopolist would select. Why? In an industry such as orange juice production, with a relatively large number of suppliers, the costs of eliminating all competitive behavior—the costs of enforcing the cartel agreement against free riders—would be too high. Some competitive behavior will remain. Cartel price will therefore tend to be lower than the profit-maximizing price of a pure monopolist.

The incentive to form cartels is nevertheless clear. Cartel members who were previously earning a competitive rate of return in a competitive industry now earn an agreed-upon portion of $P_c ABP$—an equal share of cartel profits.

Cartel Enforcement

Holding the cartel together is not easy. Once the cartel has been organized, has restricted output, and has raised price to P_c, what is the position of the individual orange juice firm in the cartel? If an individual firm in the cartel lowers its price slightly below P_c, it will face a very elastic demand curve for its output. Buyers will prefer the lower price and will switch their purchases to the lower-priced firm. The fact that individual firms in a cartel can significantly increase their sales and profits by secretly lowering their price puts tremendous pressure on the cartel to fall apart. Given that individual firms have a large incentive to cheat on the agreement, cartels must give careful consideration to the matter of **cartel enforcement** from the outset.

Cartel enforcement

Attempts by members of the cartel to prevent other members from cheating and thus destroying economic profit potential.

Of course, to expect the price cutter's profits to hold up in the long run is unrealistic. Other firms would easily discover what was going on because they would suffer a drastic loss of sales. If they responded in kind with price reductions, the result would be that the initial price cutter would not experience an increase in sales and profits for long. Further spates of secret price cuts and price competition would lead to a return to competitive equilibrium.

Recognizing these possibilities, the individual firm in the cartel must form an estimate of what it can reasonably expect to gain from secret price reductions and compare this estimate with its share of cartel profits. A cartel will not be stable if the former amount is larger than the latter.

The general case in which a firm might expect to gain by secret price cutting is illustrated in Figure 11.5. Cartel equilibrium is at price P_c and output q_c, represented by E_c. D/n represents the prorated firm demand curve, where n is the number of firms in the industry. The gains to an individual cartel member from secretly cutting price are represented by d_i; d_i is more elastic than D/n. With the more elastic d_i curve, price increases would cause a sharp drop in sales, but price reductions cause a sharp gain in sales and profits at the expense of other cartel members. The gains of a secret price cut to P_s are traced out by d_i below P_c.

The key to cartel enforcement is now apparent. Means must be found to make d_i approximate D/n. Perfect cartel enforcement exists when each cartel member knows that secret price cuts are not possible and will be matched by other members. In this case, the prorated demand curve, D/n, is the relevant demand curve. If a firm cuts price, it will immediately be matched by other cartel members. There is thus no gain to cutting price. Movements will be along the prorated firm demand curve, D/n. Where it is costly to detect secret price cuts, a demand curve like d_i will confront each cartel member. Each firm's decision about whether or not to cheat will depend on the expected profits from cheating relative to the expected profits from staying in the cartel. In general, we can gauge the effectiveness of cartel enforcement by the degree to which the cartel is able to make the cheating demand curve d_i coincide with the prorated firm demand curve D/n. That is, how good is the cartel at detecting cheating?

Cartels will spend resources to control the incentive to cheat. Historically, many devices have been used. (See the Application "Diamonds, the De Beers Cartel, and the Russian Threat" at the conclusion of this chapter for a famous example.) Perhaps the most effective device is a common sales agency for the cartel. All production is sold through the agency, and individual producers do not negotiate sales for themselves. Cheating is not a viable strategy under such a condition. Producers pro-

FIGURE 11.5

Cheating in a Cartel

P_c is the agreed-upon cartel price at cartel output q_c. E_c is therefore the cartel equilibrium. If secret price cuts cannot be detected, the cheating firm will face the more elastic demand curve, d_i, and can gain from cheating on the agreement. If such behavior can be detected, movements will be along D/n, the prorated firm demand curve. The degree to which d_i diverges from D/n reflects the efficiency of the cartel enforcement system.

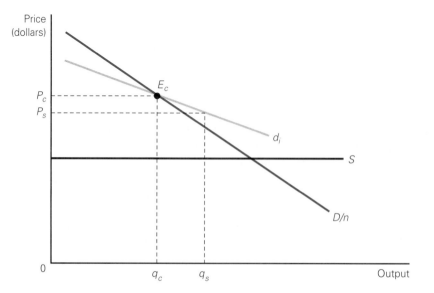

duce their allotted quotas, and the sales agency markets the agreed-upon cartel output (q_c). Exclusive sales territories and customer lists are other ways to control incentives to cheat on the cartel price. For example, exclusive territories are a way to divide markets, making intrusions by other cartel members easy to spot.

Why Cartels May or May Not Succeed

Collusive cartel agreements are more likely to occur under some circumstances than others. We offer now a menu of factors thought to be conducive to cartel-like behavior. Our list is not meant to be exhaustive—just illustrative of the types of economic conditions associated with a great likelihood of cartel activity.

1. A cartel is easier to form among a smaller number of sellers than a larger number.
2. It is easier to reach a cartel agreement when members produce a homogeneous product; sellers do not have to worry that their competitors will secure bigger market shares through advertising.
3. Collusion is more likely in stagnant or decaying industries. In this case low profits stimulate the demand for collusion.
4. The costs of collusion are reduced when there are many small buyers. Large buyers have a clear incentive and the power to seek to undermine collusion among sellers. In effect, large buyers make cheating on the cartel price very worthwhile to individual sellers.
5. Low turnover among buyers makes collusion easier. If sellers cheat on the cartel agreement, frequent turnover of buyers makes it difficult to detect who is cheating.

At this point, one fact should be clear: Private collusive agreements are hard to sustain. The incentive to cheat on such agreements is very strong, as game theory suggests, and cartels therefore tend to be unstable. Moreover, where antitrust law prevails, cartels must operate on the sly to avoid law enforcement; this secrecy further reduces their ability to control cheating.

FROM COMPETITION TO MONOPOLY: THE SPECTRUM REVISITED

We are now in a position to take an overview of the economic characteristics and welfare effects of market structures from pure competition (Chapter 8) to pure monopoly (Chapter 9) to those in between (Chapters 10 and 11). Table 11.1 organizes the long-run economic tendencies and conclusions of the various structures we have examined.

The table distinguishes the five market structures by number of sellers, barriers to entry, product characteristics, and long-run market tendencies. The number of sellers ranges from many under competition and monopolistic competition to one in the case of pure monopoly. Significant entry barriers characterize oligopolies, cartels, and monopolies. Oligopolies and cartels are characterized by the sale of *either* homogeneous or differentiated products, unlike the purely or monopolistically competitive structures. Pure monopolies sell unique products.

TABLE 11.1

Characteristics and Consequences of Market Structures

When static market structures are considered, only pure competition yields an efficient and welfare-maximizing allocation of resources. Resources are underallocated to the production of goods and services under all other structures from the consumers' perspective.

Type of Market Structure	Number of Sellers	Barriers to Entry	Type of Product	Long-Run Market Tendencies
Pure competition	Many	No	Homogeneous	$P = MC$ $P = ATC$
Monopolistic competition	Many	No	Differentiated	$P > MC$ $P = ATC$
Oligopoly	Few	Yes	Homogeneous or differentiated	$P > MC$ $P > ATC$
Cartels	Relatively few, acting as one	Yes	Homogeneous or differentiated	$P > MC$ $P > ATC$
Pure monopoly	One	Yes	Unique	$P > MC$ $P > ATC$

Most important, Table 11.1 provides a category—long-run market tendencies—that gives us some insight into the consumer and economic welfare created under these alternative structures. As the table reveals, price tends to equal long-run average total cost in only two of the structures—pure and monopolistic competition. Price, moreover, tends to equal long-run marginal cost only in the purely competitive market structure. What does this mean in terms of consumers' economic welfare?

An important concept introduced in Chapter 4 aids us in interpreting the effects of market structure on social welfare. In Chapter 4, we introduced the concept of consumers' surplus, defined as the difference between the amount of money that consumers would be willing to pay for a quantity of a good and the amount that they actually pay for the good.

Figure 11.6 shows what happens to consumers' surplus for a given hypothetical market—personal computer software—if the market is organized along monopolistic rather than competitive lines. The industry demand curve for this market has the usual negative slope, but the industry has a flat supply curve in this simplified conception. In other words, this is a constant-cost industry, in which additional output may be produced at a constant average cost that is also equal to marginal cost. The supply curve is simply a flat line.

To verify what happens to consumers' surplus under the different market structures represented in Figure 11.6, look again at the long-run market tendencies of the various models in Table 11.1. As we saw in Chapter 4 and Chapter 8, if the computer software industry is purely competitive, it will be producing an output of q_c at price P_c, which is the lowest possible price because it is equal to both the average cost and the marginal cost of production. In this situation, consumers enjoy a surplus represented by ACP_c. In contrast, price exceeds both average cost and marginal cost in the market models of oligopoly, cartels, and pure monopoly. Economic profits are therefore captured at the expense of consumers in these markets. In Figure 11.6, P_m and q_m represent the effects of a market structure on the monop-

FIGURE 11.6

The Effects of Competitive versus Monopolistic Markets

In contrasting the higher price and lower quantity (P_m and q_m) produced under a monopolistic market structure with the lower price and higher quantity (P_c and q_c) theoretically possible in a purely competitive situation, ACP_c represents the area of consumer surplus. This is real income available to anyone who can capture it. Under competition, it goes to consumers. Under monopoly, cartels, and oligopolies, part of it (P_mBFP_c) typically goes to producers and part (BCF) is lost to society.

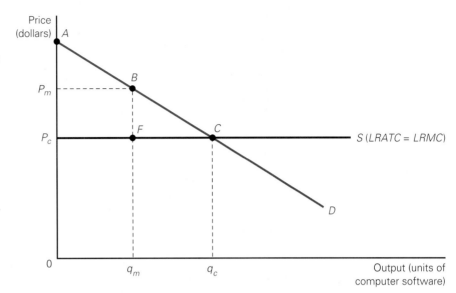

oly end of the spectrum; the area P_mBFP_c is redirected from consumers' surplus to producers' profits. In addition, society must also pay a deadweight loss (the area BCF in Figure 11.6) because price exceeds cost. This deadweight or social loss due to monopoly power or the power of cartels and oligopolies causes economists to criticize such structures.

As we have seen, monopolistic competition is something of a special case. Under monopolistic competition, there is a long-run tendency for price to equal average total cost, although price does not equal marginal cost when economies of scale are considered. The benefits of differentiated products—a greater range of choices—also exist in this structure. But the only unambiguously welfare-maximizing structure is that of pure competition. Only pure competition maximizes society's welfare by maximizing consumers' surplus.

This, of course, is a simple restatement of the discussion in Chapter 4. And it should be kept in mind that the model can fail to maximize economic welfare when monopoly power, externalities, and public goods are important aspects of market structure. In Part Four of this book we discuss each of these cases for the "failure" of the competitive model in detail.

APPLICATION

Diamonds, the De Beers Cartel, and the Russian Threat

De Beers Consolidated Mines markets more than 80 percent of the uncut diamonds sold yearly in the world. De Beers owns South African mines and acts as the marketing agent for virtually all other diamond-producing and supplying nations. De Beers pays royalties out of its retail sales to these nations for the exclusive rights to market their stones. Retailers must purchase wholesale boxes of diamonds from De Beers; if they refuse, they are not necessarily invited to purchase diamonds again. De Beers is, in short, one of the world's last great cartels.

The De Beers cartel system worked well until 1979, when a new diamond pipe was discovered in Australia and a worldwide recession created massive reductions in demand for diamonds. De Beers's earnings fell from $673 million in 1979 to $183

DeBeers leads the diamond cartel. Growing instability has characterized DeBeers' control over the last several decades.

million in 1982. Rather than reduce price in the face of declining demand, De Beers removed massive supplies of diamonds from the market by cutting production at its own mines to shore up the cartel price. De Beers also reduced purchases from participating nations in return for lump-sum payments. In all, De Beers added more than $1 billion worth of diamonds to its inventory between 1979 and 1982.

In 1981, Zaire pulled out of the cartel and entered into a five-year contract with three independent producers of industrial-quality diamonds, or boart. Although it was stockpiling diamonds in general, De Beers poured boart onto the market and encouraged illegal diamond smuggling by Zairian citizens. The result: Zaire's revenues and profits fell precipitously. The country was even refused loans from international agencies to upgrade its mines. In 1983, Zaire dropped the independent marketers in mid-contract. A cartel cheater was thus disciplined.

An important coup for De Beers was the securing of Australia as a member of the cartel. The two majority stockholders of Australia's huge Argyle mine had indirect ties to De Beers through a chain of stock ownership. Although there was opposition, De Beers's Australian friends helped bring Argyle within the cartel, but with some concessions: Australia is now free to market 25 percent of its industrial stones and 5 percent of its gemstones outside the cartel.

The worldwide recession of the early 1990s put new pressure on the cartel in the face of reduced demand and the desire to keep the cartel prices high.

As destructive as the threat of a global economic slowdown may appear, the event with the greatest potential for disrupting the cartel may be the dissolution of the Soviet Union. Large diamond deposits were found in Sakha, Russia's largest republic. In 1990, De Beers signed a five-year contract with Mikhail Gorbachev's government, agreeing to pay $5 billion for a mandatory sale of 95 percent of all of Russia's raw diamond production. Boris Yeltsin, however, has failed to honor the agreement and the future is (as always) uncertain.

De Beers has received uncut diamonds from Russia, but the Russians' failure to supply cut and polished stones suggests to some observers that Russia plans to establish new cutting and polishing plants in order to enter the more profitable market for "finished" diamonds. Further, it is known that the former Soviet Union stockpiled diamonds between the end of World War II and early 1990. The need for foreign exchange to aid the transition to markets and democracy in Russia is likely to prompt a sell-off of these valuable gems. De Beers continues to seek the cooperation of Moscow but has also—wisely—made deals with the regional and local governments in Sakha. De Beers is also establishing a diamond-cutting plant in Sakha.

By early 1996, the new contract was on hold due to the unwillingness of Russia to "toe the De Beers' line." While the Russian–De Beers agreement has maintained the cartel for over forty years, there has been evidence of cheating by Russia. Russian diamonds have appeared in increasing quantities at world cutting centers, in direct contravention of the cartel agreement. Though Russia's official "gem committee" (the State Committee on Precious Stones and Metals) denies it, Russia's own Interior Ministry admits that smuggling—as much as 748,000 carats of rough diamonds were sold between mid-1994 and January 1996—has been a much-used tactic. De Beers (predictably) matched the black-market price by reducing the charge on lower-quality stones by 15 percent in mid-1995. But how much cheating can the cartel take?

To make matters even worse, there are new threats from synthetic diamonds, both of industrial quality and of value in the gem market. Yellow-colored, gem-grade synthetic diamonds are being produced in and marketed by Russian interests even as De Beers is suspected of using strong-arm tactics to protect its market. Synthetics of industrial quality have been around since General Electric first "grew" synthetic diamond crystals in the 1950s. De Beers has also entered the synthetic market. But the Russians are the undisputed leaders, and the threat of Russian competition from high-quality synthetic stones, both of industrial and gem quality, is real.

De Beers apparently attempted both participation in Russian production and threats to accomplish the aims of the cartel in response to Russian competition in the later 1990s. De Beers wanted to mine diamonds in Siberia, but the deal fell through. (Russian interests must continue to be careful to avoid the flooding of the market by De Beers.) Another tactic considered by De Beers is to "brand" their diamonds by engraving a hallmark to designate quality.

De Beers is still in control of a huge segment of the diamond market, directing more than 80 percent of the $600 million industrial diamond business and 90 percent of the $5 billion annual market for jewelry-quality gems. But recessions, changing demand conditions, changing world political events, the technology and feasibility of synthetic gem production, and dissension within the diamond cartel will continue to challenge the successful operation of the De Beers cartel.

Sources: John R. Emshwiller and Neil Behrmann, "Restored Luster: How De Beers Revived World Diamond Cartel After Zaire's Pullout," *Wall Street Journal* (August 7, 1983); Vladimir Kvint, "Sorry, Mr. Oppenheimer," *Forbes* (February 15, 1993), pp. 42–43; Bill Gifford, "Pop Rocks," *The New Republic* (December 26, 1994), pp. 9–10; and Carol J. Williams, "Diamond Deal Not Forever, Russia Seems to Say," *Los Angeles Times* (December 29, 1995), p. A5.

QUESTION

Cartels are inherently unstable due to the profits that can be gained by cheating on the cartel agreement. What tactics have been used by De Beers to combat cheating by cartel members?

SUMMARY

1. Oligopoly is a market structure characterized by a few firms that recognize that their actions have an impact on one another's sales, prices, and profits. They may sell either homogeneous or differentiated products. Entry into the industry is difficult because of natural or artificial barriers.

2. When oligopolists recognize their mutual interdependence, they will engage in a variety of strategic behaviors, often trying to tacitly combine or collude. When these behaviors are successful, the market structure more closely resembles pure monopoly than pure competition, but tacit collusion does not result in all cases.

3. Game theory is an important tool for understanding oligopoly behavior because it focuses upon the variety of possible outcomes when mutual interdependence is recognized by a small number of firms selling competing products in the market.

4. The Cournot–Nash solution to the prisoner's dilemma in game theory is an important potential outcome in oligopoly markets. When the Cournot–Nash solution results from oligopoly behavior, it produces profits, outputs, and prices at levels midway between those produced under pure competition and pure monopoly.

5. Cheating appears as a dominant strategy in many games. Moreover, players may signal other players about their willingness to cooperate or to "repent" for earlier cheating. Such behavior, captured in games, helps explain a good deal of actual behavior that occurs among firms engaged in real-world competition and rivalry.

6. Cartels are formal or informal agreements among firms within an industry to restrict output or to segment the market in an effort to increase profits. The result may be similar to monopoly price and output in the industry.

7. There are potential profits for firms that cheat individually on a cartel. Cartels are therefore difficult to establish and maintain. The costs of enforcing the cartel agreement frequently jeopardize the cartel's survival.

8. Cartels can be legal or illegal. Those created and enforced by the government or those allowed to exist by government sanctions are legal. Cartels that form in the United States are illegal under antitrust laws.

KEY TERMS

oligopoly	dominant solution	Cournot–Nash solution
mutual interdependence	tacit collusive solution	price leadership
cartel	backward induction	limit pricing
game theory	cheat	cartel enforcement
prisoner's dilemma	market power	

QUESTIONS FOR REVIEW AND DISCUSSION

1. What are the general characteristics of the oligopolistic market model? Compare and contrast these to the characteristics of the monopolistic competition model discussed in Chapter 10.

2. Imagine a student cartel. If your professor promised to assign a fixed number of each letter grade, regardless of class performance, is there any type of agreement that you could make with classmates to exploit this grading system? Under what circumstances (for instance, class size) would your student cartel be most likely to succeed?

3. Although it is easy to draw a hypothetical demand curve, it is difficult to determine the position of real-world demand curves. In order to maximize profits, however, managers must accurately estimate the demand for their products. In which case is this estimation more difficult—when the good in question is sold in a monopolistic market or when it is sold in an oligopolistic market? Explain.

4. Cite three personal experiences you have had with free-riding behavior.

5. Suppose that firms forming a cartel have different marginal costs. Describe, both in words and in a graph, how this situation complicates the various problems that a cartel must solve to be effective in raising prices.

6. What effect on the likelihood of collusion do the following factors have: (a) the purchase of an input in the same market (such as pigs at the stockyard); (b) long-term contracts with buyers; (c) selling to governments; (d) salespeople staying in the same motel on the road; (e) an industry trade association and price list?

7. Explain the solution to the prisoner's dilemma commonly known as the Cournot–Nash solution.

8. What is a tacit collusive solution in game theory and when might it occur?

9. How might a former cheater (who has learned her lesson) signal a competitor in a game theory situation that she is repentant and wants to cooperate again?

PROBLEMS

1. Suppose that you are one of two people hired to sell ads for a local newspaper during the summer. Your employer agrees to pay $350 per week plus a $2000 bonus to be divided by the two of you in proportion to the number of ads you sell. For example, if you sell three-fourths of the total, you get three-fourths of the bonus. Construct a simple payoff table, like the ones in Figures 11.1 and 11.2 of this chapter, in which the options for both you and your co-worker are spending little time trying to sell ads, spending some time trying to sell ads, or spending a lot of time trying to sell ads. Are there incentives for you to form a cartel? To cheat on it?

2. Suppose that you own one of two lawn care businesses in a small town. Each firm has costs (salaries, equipment, lawn chemicals, and the like). The payoff table shows the average weekly profits that you and your competitor may earn under different pricing policies. If you both charge a high price for your services, for example, you earn $1000 profit while your competitor earns $1200 profit. Use the table to answer the following questions.
   a. Why would you earn more profit than your competitor if you charge a lower price for lawn services?

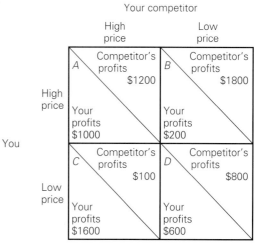

b. If you both engaged in price competition, what would be the outcome?
c. What would be the outcome if you both decided to maximize joint profits? What would be the risks?
d. If you formed a cartel, would there be an incentive to cheat? Explain.

WORKING WITH THE WEB

1. Strategic behavior becomes essential when the marketplace is not perfectly competitive. To try your hand at a game of strategy, go to http://serendip.brynmawr.edu/playground/pd.html, follow the instructions, and try your hand at some strategic behavior! Play the coin game repeatedly as instructed. Which strategy yields the best result in terms of the average number of coins you acquire? Why?

2. Licensing bodies such as the American Bar Association and the American Medical Association exist for many reasons. One of these is to create a barrier to entry into the profession. Without passing the Bar in a particular state and being licensed by the state, an individual cannot practice law. Go to www.mises.org, select "Daily Articles", and choose the link for June '98–October '98. Scroll through the list of articles until you find the article "Lawyer Cartels".
   a. According to Mr. Leef, why is the legal profession a cartel and how does it maintain its cartel status?
   b. What is the result of this cartel behavior for consumers of legal services?

POINT

Joan Robinson

Alfred Marshall

COUNTERPOINT

Alfred Marshall (1842–1924) was the strong-willed son of a harsh father, who early on tried to coerce young Alfred into the ministry. Much to his parents' dismay, Marshall rejected a theological scholarship to Oxford University and entered Cambridge, where he received his M.S. in mathematics in 1865. From mathematics, Marshall veered into metaphysics. He joined a philosophy discussion group at Cambridge and lectured for almost ten years in moral science. During this period Marshall became convinced of the overriding importance of economics to individual and social action. In 1877, Marshall married Mary Paley, a former student, and moved to Bristol, where they both lectured on political economy at University College. In 1885, they returned to Cambridge, where Marshall continued his illustrious career as a lecturer in political economy.

The most important of Marshall's books was the modern bible of microeconomics, *Principles of Economics* (1890),[a] which he revised through eight editions. Many of the concepts presented in today's introductory economics courses, including the principles of perfect competition among firms, were first set down systematically by Marshall. His mathematical precision and fondness for lucid examples made the text, and economics generally, accessible and popular.

In 1903, while his work on *Principles* continued, Marshall succeeded in establishing economics as a discipline separate from moral science. He is also credited with founding the neoclassical tradition in economics—the modern version of economic principles established by Adam Smith.

Joan Robinson (1903–1983), like Alfred Marshall, spent most of her academic career at the University of Cambridge. She completed her B.A. in economics at Cambridge in 1925, the year after Marshall's death. She began a teaching career at Cambridge in 1931, at a time when Marshall's influence over the principles and methods of economics study was still great. Robinson is perhaps best known for her book *The Economics of Imperfect Competition* (1933),[b] which expands upon many of Marshall's conclusions about business organization and his theory of perfect competition.

Robinson's contributions to economics reach well beyond her theory of imperfect competition. In the mid-1930s, she and a small group of Cambridge economists helped John Maynard Keynes write his monumental *General Theory of Employment, Interest, and Money*, which ushered in a new era of macroeconomic theory. She also wrote in the areas of economic development, international trade, capital theory, and Marxian economics.

---

[a]Alfred Marshall, *Principles of Economics*, 8th ed. (London: Macmillan, 1920).

[b]Joan Robinson, *The Economics of Imperfect Competition* (London: Macmillan, 1933).

Although Robinson later questioned her own analysis of imperfect competition, her critique of Marshall's assumptions of the way the economy operates presents an interesting chapter in the development of economic thought.

The World of Perfect Competition

Although Marshall acknowledged the existence of monopolies and oligopolies, he believed that these market structures were a special case. To Marshall, the microeconomic behavior of firms and individuals was kept in constant check by the competitive nature of markets. The dynamics of free enterprise, of limitless entry to and exit from markets, enforced the norm of perfect competition among buyers and sellers. By his terms, each market is made up of sufficiently large numbers of competing firms buying and selling virtually identical products and services. No single demander or supplier of goods can affect the market price because no single firm has a large enough stake in the market. Given these conditions, the market price for goods would always gravitate to a level equal to the firm's costs of production. As a result, economic profits could not persist. Under the rigors of perfect competition, no firm would be able to rise above its equals.

To demonstrate his model of perfect competition, Marshall chose a number of illustrations, including the market for fresh fish. Marshall noted that the ordinary daily price of fish depends on intensity of demand, weather, and luck, all of which affect the size of the catch. He then introduced into this illustration a cattle plague that permanently increased the demand for fresh fish over beef. How would the competitively organized fish market react? (Remember that cold storage facilities were not readily available in Marshall's day.)

Under competitive conditions, the price per pound of fish would immediately rise. Recognizing that the price rise was not a temporary phenomenon, fishermen would respond to the increased profits (since price would now be greater than costs of production) by using their boats, fishing crews, and nets more intensively. Supply would be increased by these activities, as it would by the entry into the market of new fishing firms attracted by profits. Supply increases would ultimately bring price down to the average cost of catching fish.

Marshall's vision of perfect competition comports well with Adam Smith's theory of "the invisible hand." In fact, Marshall's theory of perfect competition describes the invisible hand at work. In his illustration, new fishing firms enter the market and old firms expand not for the benefit of customers but in hopes of earning more profits. They act only in their own self-interest but in doing so promote the interest of society. The price of fish falls to the costs of production in the long run, and more fish are provided in the market.

Perfect Competition Turned on Its Head

"It is customary," Joan Robinson wrote in *The Economics of Imperfect Competition*,"…to open with the analysis of a perfectly competitive world, and to treat monopoly as a special case….It is more proper to set out the analysis of monopoly, treating perfect competition as a special case." Beginning with these words, Robinson set out to refute Marshall's theory of perfect competition.

Modern industrialized societies, she contended, were dominated by monopolies (a single firm in a market) or oligopolies (a few large firms in a market). To a greater or lesser degree, most markets were influenced by the power of monopoly control. In other words, individual firms in these markets were large enough to affect market prices on their own. (Modern examples of imperfect competition include the automobile industry, dominated by industrial giants such as General Motors, or the fast-food industry, dominated by firms such as McDonald's.) Given these assumptions, Robinson pointed out, the prices of goods and services would not gravitate to a level equal to the firm's costs of production. Economic profits could persist, enabling dominant firms to maintain or increase their dominance.

To further illustrate her point that imperfect, rather than perfect, competition was the norm, Robinson pointed to the pervasive evidence of price discrimination in markets. Whereas Marshall contended that only one market price could prevail under perfect competition, Robinson saw many instances in which a single good or service could command several different prices in the same market. Multiple prices for the same product are possible only in a world of imperfect competition.

Challenges to Marshall's system of perfect competition by Joan Robinson and other economists have led to alterations in the theory. Modern economists stress the manner in which information affects suppliers and demanders, the consequences of potential competition and rivalry on markets, and the impact on Marshall's model of interpreting price as "full price."

PART THREE

Input
Markets

3

Competitive Labor Markets

I n Chapter 3 we presented an overview of resource and product markets (see the circular flow model in Figure 3.1). We showed business firms as both suppliers of goods and services and demanders of inputs such as land, labor, capital, and entrepreneurship. Households were depicted both as demanders of goods and services and as suppliers of inputs. Up to this point in our study of microeconomics, we have focused on the upper part of the circular flow model and studied how the prices of final products such as psychiatric services, personal computers, and diapers are determined. We now turn to the lower part of the model to view firms as demanders or suppliers of inputs such as labor services, land, or capital. Specifically, we now inquire how input prices—wages of day laborers or engineers, lumber or machine prices—are determined. Once we know the economic process by which input values are determined, we will be able to understand better how and why people earn the incomes they do as owners of their own labor and other resources. After reading Chapter 12 you should understand

- how the demand for labor or any other input is related to its productivity and the demand for the product that the resource produces.
- the principles under which competitive firms demand labor and how income is generated by such demands.
- how human capital and its acquisition are related to individuals' wage rates and income-earning capacity.

FACTOR MARKETS: AN OVERVIEW

Factor market
A market in which the prices of productive resources (factors of production, or inputs) are determined by the interaction of firms acting as buyers with households and firms acting as suppliers of resources.

The markets in which input prices are determined are called **factor**, or resource, **markets**. The prices of factors such as wages, rent, and interest are determined through the interplay of supply and demand. Indeed, the theory of factor prices is just the familiar theory of demand and supply applied to factors of production.

We begin this chapter by presenting the marginal productivity theory of demand for one factor of production, labor. Although our example is labor, the marginal productivity theory is equally applicable to other factors of production, as we will see in Chapter 14, where we apply the theory to land and capital inputs. In the second part of this chapter, we present the theory of labor supply.

Derived Demand

Derived demand
The demand for factors of production that exists because of the demand for the products that the factors produce.

The demand for labor or any other factor of production is a **derived demand**. This term means that the demand for labor is directly related to the demand for the goods and services that the labor is used to produce. If the demand for computers increases, the derived demand for computer scientists and engineers will increase. If the demand for physical fitness increases, the derived demand for health foods and aerobics instructors will increase. If the demand for law and order increases, the derived demand for police officers will increase.

Derived demand also obeys the law of demand. All things being equal, if the price of health foods falls, more will be consumed; if the price of paper rises, fewer or shorter books will be published; if the rental prices on office space fall, more offices will be rented. So even though we call the demand for factors of production a derived demand, the law of demand applies to it in the same way that it applies to demand for final output.

Firms as Resource Price Takers

Just as there are different types of output market structures—such as competition, oligopoly, and monopoly—there are different types of resource markets. There can be perfectly competitive sellers and buyers of labor, for example. In such cases, there are large numbers of both buyers (employing firms) and sellers (workers) of a homogeneous type of labor. There can also be various types of imperfect competition in buying and selling labor, as we will learn in the next chapter. We limit the discussion in this chapter to a competitive labor market.

The following discussion of labor demand examines labor markets in which a large number of firms hire a single type of labor and a large number of people are willing to supply the labor. There are, of necessity, simplifications in our discussion. For example, we all know that labor comes in many alternative "qualities," depending on training, education, and other matters. To keep matters simple, however, we assume that labor is homogeneous. Another important simplification relates to the nature of the "wage rate." In reality, the wage that workers receive includes many factors other than the money wage. A full wage includes all non-money wage benefits, such as retirement plans, health insurance, vacation policy, and so on, in addition to the money wage payment. Although we mention only a wage rate in this chapter—without any elaboration of the nonwage benefits—we are referring to the full wage paid to workers.

Competitive labor market

A labor market in which the wage rate is determined by the interactions of a large number of sellers (suppliers) of labor and a large number of demanders (buyers) of labor. Neither group acts in a collusive manner.

Market demand for labor

The total quantity of labor demanded at various wage rates, other things constant. The sum of all individual firms' demands for a type of labor. The firms may or may not all be in the same industry.

Market supply of labor

The sum of all individuals' supplies of a type of labor. The total quantity of labor people will offer to the market at various wage rates, other things being equal.

In a **competitive labor market**, the wage rate is determined by the familiar forces of supply and demand. The **market demand for labor** is the sum of all firms' demand for the type of labor in question. All the firms may not be in the same industry—that is, they may not all produce the same product—but they all employ the same type of labor. For example, the demand curve in Figure 12.1a could represent the market demand for electricians. This overall demand would be found by summing the demand for electricians by all buyers of their labor, from AT&T and General Motors to construction companies, cable television companies, and even homeowners.

The **market supply of labor** is obtained by horizontally summing the supply of individual workers. As indicated by the supply curve S_m in Figure 12.1a, as the wage rate rises, a larger quantity of labor is supplied. The supply of labor to any particular occupation thus follows the familiar law of supply.

The interaction of supply and demand for labor results in an equilibrium wage W_0. Once this wage is established, the individual buyers of labor are price takers. That is, the firms must accept W_0 as the prevailing wage and may hire as many workers as they are willing and able to hire at that wage. Being perfectly competitive buyers of labor, employing firms face an infinitely elastic labor supply curve, as shown in Figure 12.1b. All buyers of any good or service who are price takers face an infinitely elastic supply curve.

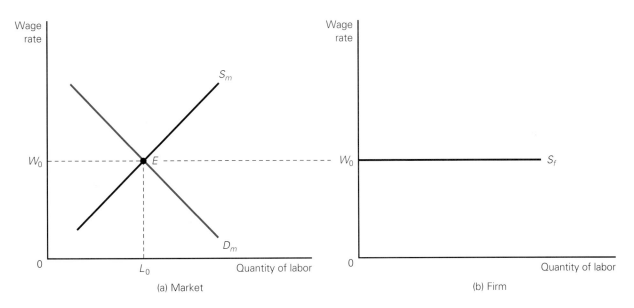

(a) Market

(b) Firm

FIGURE 12.1

The Firm as a Wage Price Taker

(a) The equilibrium wage, W_0, is determined in the competitive market by the market supply, S_m, and demand, D_m, for a particular type of labor. (b) The firm must pay wage rate W_0 for workers but is able to hire all it wants at that wage. The supply of labor to the competitive firm, S_f, is totally elastic at the prevailing wage. Note that while the scale for the wage rate is the same for both graphs, the scale for quantity of labor is smaller for the individual firm than for the market.

MARGINAL PRODUCTIVITY THEORY

We cannot say exactly how many electricians or computer programmers will be demanded within a given time period, but we can present some general rules about how the numbers of people demanded in these occupations might rise or fall. In this analysis, we reencounter many principles from earlier chapters. All apply equally to the demand for resource inputs, including labor.

The Profit-Maximizing Level of Employment

The firm hiring labor in a competitive market faces a market-determined wage. Since the equilibrium wage is established, the point of interest becomes the quantity of labor that an individual firm chooses to hire. If a firm is selling its product in a perfectly competitive product market, then how much labor will it hire at a particular wage rate?

To answer this question, let us say that the firm has many inputs, one of which is labor. Also, let the quantities of all inputs except labor be fixed. Labor, in other words, is the only variable input. (These circumstances, as you may recognize, describe a short-run situation for the firm.) To produce more output, the firm must hire more labor. The firm wishes to maximize profits and must therefore hire the profit-maximizing amount of labor.

Suppose the firm in this instance is a corn farmer who must decide whether to hire a worker to help pick and husk corn. How does the farmer make this decision? Hiring the worker will increase output, and the increase in production will be sold to obtain revenue. At the same time, hiring the worker will increase the cost of production because the farm worker must be paid. The farmer makes a profit-maximizing decision *at the margin*. If hiring the worker increases total revenue more than it increases total cost, then hiring the worker will increase profits. The farmer will always hire a worker if doing so increases profits.

Suppose the farmer is thinking about hiring a second worker. The same decision process is repeated. If the second worker adds more to revenue than to cost, then he or she will be hired. This process continues with every prospective worker. An important and familiar principle is in action: *the law of diminishing marginal returns*. As more and more of a variable input is added to a production process in which there is a fixed input, the marginal product of the variable input eventually declines. As more workers are hired, the extra output of each worker eventually falls. Since each additional worker adds less and less to total output, the additional revenues that each worker produces eventually fall below the additional cost of hiring. At some point, the farmer will stop hiring altogether. In short, the profit-maximizing farmer should hire all workers that add more to revenue than to cost but stop hiring at the point where the addition to revenue is just equal to the addition to cost.

The example of a corn farmer can also be expressed in economic terms. The extra output that each additional unit of labor adds to total output is called the **marginal product of labor** *(MP_L):*

Marginal product of labor (MP_L)

The additional output produced that results from hiring an additional unit of labor; change in total output divided by change in quantity of labor input used.

$$MP_L = \frac{\Delta TP}{\Delta L},$$

where MP_L is the marginal product of labor, ΔTP is the change in total product, and ΔL is a one-unit increase in labor. Adding units of the variable input to other fixed inputs will eventually lead to a decrease in the marginal product of the variable input in the short run.

Table 12.1 summarizes the hypothetical choices available to the corn farmer. The first column shows the units of labor, in number of worker-hours. The second column shows the marginal product of the workers—the amount by which total output increases as one more unit of labor is added to the production process. The first unit of labor adds 14 units of output (bushels of corn), the second adds 12 units of output, and so forth. MP_L decreases as the amount of labor increases, according to the law of diminishing marginal returns.

When the extra corn produced by each additional unit of labor is sold, the resulting increase in total revenue is called the **marginal revenue product of labor** (MRP_L):

Marginal revenue product of labor (MRP_L)

The additional revenue that results from selling the additional output produced by hiring an additional unit of labor; marginal revenue times marginal product of labor.

$$MRP_L = \frac{\Delta TR}{\Delta L},$$

where MRP_L is the mrginal revenue product of labor, ΔTR is the change in total revenue, and ΔL is the change in the amount of labor hired.

Another method of expressing MRP_L is

$$MRP_L = MR_C \times MP_L,$$

where MR_C is the marginal revenue under competitive conditions (the increase in total revenue resulting from selling one more unit of output) and MPL is the marginal product of labor.

For the firm that sells its product in a perfectly competitive market, marginal revenue is equal to the price of the product. Thus, the marginal revenue product (MRP) is simply the price (P) of the product times the marginal product (MP) of each unit. As shown in Table 12.1, the marginal revenue product of the first unit of labor is found by multiplying its marginal product, 14, by the price of the product, $2, to obtain $28. The MRP_L declines as more workers are hired because MP_L declines.

TABLE 12.1

A Marginal Revenue Product Schedule for Labor

The marginal revenue product of labor in column (4) falls as more units of labor are employed because the marginal product of labor in column (2) falls. The firm will hire additional units of labor up to the point where the extra revenue these units generate just equals the extra cost of paying for them. At this point, 6 units of labor, $MRP_L = MFC_L$.

(1) Units of Labor (worker-hours)	(2) Marginal Product of Labor MP_L (bushels of corn)	(3) Marginal Revenue $MR_C = P_C$ (dollars per bushel)	(4) Marginal Revenue Product $MRP_L = MR_C \times MP_L$	(5) Marginal Factor Cost (dollars per hour) $MFC_L = $ Wage
1	14	$2	$28	$8
2	12	2	24	8
3	10	2	20	8
4	8	2	16	8
5	6	2	12	8
6	4	2	8	8
7	2	2	4	8
8	0	2	0	8

Regardless of the economic shorthand used, the profit-maximizing firm will continue adding units of labor as long as the additional revenues the labor produces are greater than the additional costs of the labor. The firm will stop hiring when the additional revenues are less than the additional costs of hiring. The extra cost of hiring one more unit of labor is called the **marginal factor cost of labor** (MFC_L):

Marginal factor cost of labor (MFC_L)

The change in total costs associated with employing one additional unit of labor.

$$MFC_L = \frac{\Delta TC}{\Delta L},$$

where MFC_L is the marginal factor cost of labor and ΔTC is the change in total cost. Under competitive conditions, the firm may purchase all of the labor it wants at the prevailing wage rate. Each additional unit of labor in Table 12.1 has a marginal factor cost equal to the wage rate (shown as $8 on the schedule).

The profit-maximizing firm will hire labor up to the point where $MRP_L = MFC_L$. With the numbers in Table 12.1, this equation indicates that it will be most profitable for the farmer to hire 6 units of labor. Each unit from the first to the sixth adds more to revenue than to cost. By hiring 6 units, the farmer adds as much as possible to profit. However, the seventh unit adds more to cost than to revenue and therefore will not be hired.

This process should sound familiar: It is the mirror image of how the competitive firm determines its profit-maximizing output. The firm follows the same process to equate its marginal cost to marginal revenue in hiring inputs as it does in selling its output. In fact, when the firm hires the profit-maximizing quantity of labor, that amount of labor will produce the profit-maximizing level of output.

The numbers used in Table 12.1 are presented in graph form in Figure 12.2. The MP_L curve is drawn in Figure 12.2a by plotting the points from columns (1) and (2). The demand curve for the farmer's corn is shown in Figure 12.2b, where $P = \$2$. The MRP_L is found by multiplying marginal revenue by marginal product; the result is the marginal revenue product curve in Figure 12.2c.

The prevailing wage is $8, stated as MFC_L. The profit-maximizing quantity of labor is the point where the MFC_L curve crosses the MRP_L curve. At this point, the marginal revenue product of labor equals the marginal factor cost of labor.

Profit-Maximizing Rules for All Inputs

Firms employ many inputs other than labor. The profit-maximizing rule for the level of employment is the same for each resource. The corn farmer may be planning to use fertilizer, for example. If he applies 1 unit of fertilizer—a 100-pound bag—the amount of corn produced will increase. The extra corn is treated as the marginal product of the first bag of fertilizer. The extra revenue that results is the marginal revenue product, and the extra cost of the bag is the marginal factor cost. If the MRP of the fertilizer is greater than or equal to the MFC, then the farmer will purchase and use the fertilizer. The profit-maximizing amount of fertilizer is found at the point where the MRP of fertilizer is just equal to the MFC.

This rule applies to all inputs, such as tractors, seed, land, tractor drivers, and water. The profit-maximizing quantity of all inputs is the amount that makes the MRP of each input equal to the MFC of each input, or

$$\frac{MRP_1}{MFC_1} = \frac{MRP_2}{MFC_2} = \frac{MRP_3}{MFC_3} = \cdots = \frac{MRP_N}{MFC_N} = 1,$$

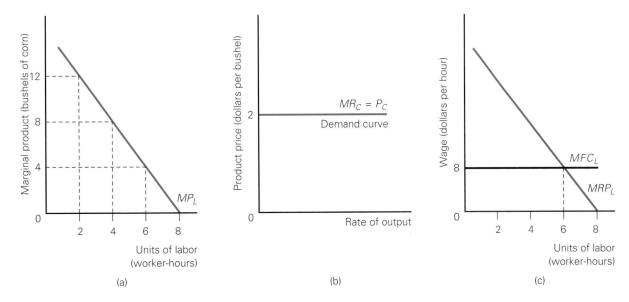

FIGURE 12.2

The Firm's Marginal Revenue Product Curve

(a) The farmer's marginal product of labor (MP_L) curve is plotted from columns (1) and (2) in Table 12.1. (b) The demand curve for the farmer's product is determined by the product price ($P_C = MR_C$ in this perfectly competitive market). (c) The marginal revenue product of labor (MRP_L) curve is found by multiplying MP_L by MR_C. The profit-maximizing firm hires labor up to the point where the marginal revenue product of labor equals marginal factor cost of labor (MFC_L). With a wage of $8 and a product price of $2, the firm will hire up to 6 units of labor.

where the subscripts 1, 2, and 3 indicate the MRP and MFC of the first, second, and third inputs, and N indicates the total number of inputs used. Each ratio of MRP to MFC is equal to 1 because the MRP of each is equal to the MFC of each. Under this condition, all inputs are employed in the profit-maximizing amounts.

THE DEMAND FOR LABOR

Marginal productivity theory gives insight into the purchasing behavior of firms. In the short run, when labor is the only variable input, the firm is willing to purchase or hire additional units up to the point at which $MRP = MFC$. The firm's marginal revenue product curve (Figure 12.2c) thus traces the relation between the price of labor (the wage rate) and the amount of labor a firm is willing to purchase. In other words, the marginal revenue product curve is also the firm's short-run demand curve for labor. Figure 12.3 illustrates this. At wage W_0 the firm chooses L_0 units of labor. A higher wage such as W_1 results in less labor hired. For each wage, the firm adjusts the level of employment to maintain the equation $MRP_L = MFC_L$. In the following sections we examine the demand for labor from several perspectives.

The Short-Run Market Demand for Labor

A single firm's demand for labor in the short run is equivalent to its marginal revenue product of labor. To obtain the overall market demand for labor in the short run, we must make some additional calculations.

Each firm will demand labor up to the point where $MRP_L = MFC_L$. Thus, at a particular wage, the market demand for labor may be shown as the sum of all the firms' MRP_L curves. Figure 12.4 shows such a curve, MRP_{L_0}. This curve represents the sum of all the firms' short-run demand curves for a particular type of labor. The curve

The Firm's Short-Run Demand for Labor

The firm hires labor up to the point where the wage is equal to the marginal revenue product of labor (MRP_L). The marginal revenue product curve shows the various quantities of labor the firm is willing to hire at all the different wage rates when labor is the only variable input.

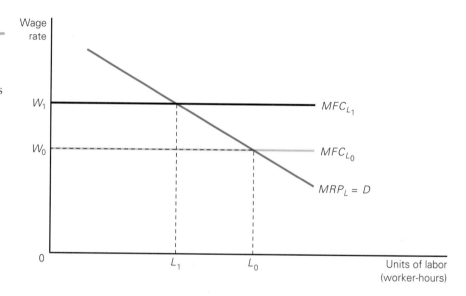

FIGURE 12.4

The Short-Run Market Demand for Labor

MRP_{L_0} represents the sum of all the firm's marginal revenue product curves for a particular occupation. When the wage for this occupation is W_0, the firms hire L_0 units of labor. If the wage rises to W_1, the firms initially hire the lower L_{0_1} units of labor. However, the increase in wages causes an increase in the price of the product. The higher product price shifts the sum of the firm's MRP_{L_0} to MRP_{L_1}. At W_1, when labor is the only variable input, the firms hire L_1 units of labor. D represents the short-run market demand curve for labor because it allows for changes in the wage rate.

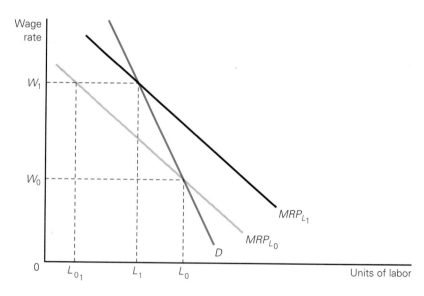

labeled MRP_{L_0}, however, is not the short-run market demand curve for this type of labor, although it does establish one point on the short-run market demand curve, D.

To establish the whole demand curve, we must examine what happens when the wage rate changes. Imagine the overall demand for cornhuskers. Many farmers employ huskers at wage W_0; the total number of cornhuskers employed at W_0 is L_0. Recall that the MRP_L curve is obtained by multiplying the price of corn by the marginal product of labor. If the wage rate rises to W_1, then each firm's costs of production will rise. Initially, the employment of labor is cut back to L_{0_1}, along the original MRP_{L_0} curve. However, the increased costs of production will decrease the supply of corn and increase the equilibrium price. To obtain the new MRP_L curve (MRP_{L_1}), we multiply the marginal product of labor by the new, higher price of corn, and we sum this quantity over all the firms. The new wage, W_1, and level of employment, L_1, establish a second point on the short-run market demand curve. The short-run market demand curve, D, differs from the sum of the MRP_L curves because it allows for increases in the price of the product that result from wage increases. Note, however, that the demand curve, D, obeys the law of demand. When the wage rate rises, given other factors, less labor is ultimately employed.

The Firm's Long-Run Demand for Labor

Firm's long-run demand for labor

The relationship between all possible wage rates and quantities demanded of labor at those wage rates, given that the firm has enough time to vary the usage of all inputs.

We have so far concentrated on the short-run demand for labor, in which labor is the only variable input. In the long run, many adjustments occur when wages change. Allowed enough time, firms may vary all inputs. Also, at the industry level, not only does the price of products change directly with wages, but the number of firms changes as well.

Suppose that the market wage rate for cornhuskers increases. What happens in the long run? First, farmers will adjust to the higher price of labor by hiring fewer cornhuskers; given enough time, they may turn to substitute inputs for this type of labor, perhaps by buying combines rather than hiring human huskers. Second, the increase in the price of labor increases the farmers' costs of production. With the increase in costs, the supply of the product decreases, and its price rises. Finally, the number of firms will adjust, establishing a new equilibrium. The number of firms, in the end, is likely to decrease. When wages rise, more workers lose their jobs in the long run than in the short run; when wages fall, more workers are hired in the long run than in the short run. In other words, long-run market demand is more elastic than short-run market demand.

Changes in the Demand for Labor

Change in the demand for labor

A shift of the entire labor demand curve; caused by a change in the marginal product of labor, by a change in the demand for the product produced by the type of labor in question, or by a change in the price of some other factor of production.

What causes an increase or decrease in the demand for a particular type of labor? Why would the demand for chemical engineers suddenly increase? Or why would a restaurant suddenly hire more waiters and cooks? Such questions may be answered by examining the origins of the demand for labor and the behavior of profit-maximizing firms.

The demand for labor is derived from the demand for the product the labor produces and the marginal product of the labor itself. If either of these increases or decreases, then the demand for labor will increase or decrease in the same direction. Understanding this relation simplifies things; however, further details are of value.

1. *If the demand for the product that labor produces changes, then the demand for labor will change in the same direction.* Remember that for a competitive firm, the marginal revenue product of an input is equal to marginal revenue (the output price) times marginal product. If the demand for the good increases, then its price increases and the demand for labor (*MRP*) and all other inputs also increases. The demands for electronics technicians and computer components have increased because the demand for personal computers has increased.

    The opposite situation occurs when the demand for a product decreases. If the price of a product falls, then the demand for inputs used to produce that product falls. When the demand for American-made cars decreases, the demand for domestic autoworkers decreases (along with the demand for tires and steel).

2. *If the marginal product of labor changes, then the demand for that labor will change in the same direction.* The productivity of a particular type of labor depends to a very large extent on the firm's employment of other inputs in the production process. Additional expenditures on other inputs often increase the productivity of labor. For example, the marginal product of farm workers is influenced by the amounts of other inputs that the farmer buys, such as land, equipment, seed, fertilizer, and water. If such inputs increase the workers' productivity, their use will also increase demand for the workers' labor.

The relation between the quantity of nonlabor inputs and the productivity of labor can be direct or inverse. In other words, increasing the amount of one input may either increase or decrease the productivity of labor. If increased usage of one input due to a decrease in that input's price increases the marginal product of labor and thus increases the amount of labor hired at any given wage, then this input and labor are **complementary inputs**. For example, if the farmer uses more fertilizer, then cornhuskers can produce more output; their marginal product increases. Increases in inputs that complement labor will increase the demand for labor.

Complementary inputs

Inputs with a relation such that increased usage of one input due to a fall in its price results in increased employment of the other(s).

If increased usage of one input decreases the marginal product of labor and thus decreases the amount of labor hired at any given wage, then that input is called a substitute input for labor. For cornpickers and huskers, a combine that picks and husks is a **substitute input**. If the farmer uses more combines, then the marginal product of human huskers and pickers will decrease, and so will the demand for them.

Substitute inputs

Inputs with a relation such that increased employment of one input due to a fall in its price results in decreased usage of the other(s).

Why would a farmer suddenly choose to purchase more fertilizer or combines? A firm makes decisions on the basis of expected profits. For example, if the price of fertilizer falls, then it is in the farmer's interest to purchase more fertilizer. If the price of combines falls, then the farmer will purchase more combines. Thus, if the price of a complementary input falls, the demand for labor rises. If the price of a substitute input falls, the demand for labor decreases.

In addition to changes in the quantity of inputs, technological advances may shift the demand for labor. New production techniques may increase or decrease the demand for labor in a particular occupation. In fact, technological change generally increases the marginal product of some workers and decreases that of others. Technological change can, for example, result in robots being more adept than factory workers at performing certain tasks. As a consequence, the marginal product of factory workers falls and the demand for their labor decreases. At the same time, the marginal revenue product of workers who make robots rises as the demand for and the price of robots increases. This produces an increase in the demand for workers who make robots.

Monopoly and the Demand for Labor

We have spoken so far of demand for labor only under conditions of competition. What if the firm demanding labor enjoyed a monopoly in its output market but was still a purely competitive buyer of labor? What would the farmer's demand for labor be if he were the only producer of corn? Recall from Chapter 8 that the demand curve for the monopolist's product is downward sloping. This suggests that as the firm hires more workers and increases output, the price of the product must fall for the firm to sell the extra output. As the firm hires more labor, not only is the marginal product of labor falling but the product price is falling as well.

Even though the price of the product is falling as more output is produced, marginal revenue product, MRP, still describes the change in total revenue that results from hiring one more unit of labor. As before, MRP is equal to marginal revenue times marginal product. The difference is that the marginal revenue of the competitive seller is equal to the market price, whereas the monopolist's marginal revenue is a downward-sloping curve, derived from its demand curve.

Table 12.2 is a numerical example showing the difference between the marginal revenue product of labor under competition (MRP_C) and under monopoly conditions (MRP_m). The MRP_C is calculated as shown in Table 12.1: marginal product of labor (MP_L) multiplied by the *constant* marginal revenue of the competitive firm (MR_C). *Remember*: Under competition, marginal revenue equals the price charged, since—being a price taker—the competitive firm can sell all of its units of output at the same competitive price. This means that $MR_C = P_C$.

The marginal revenue product of labor under monopoly is found by multiplying the marginal product of labor (MP_L) by monopoly marginal revenue (MR_m).

TABLE 12.2

Calculation of Marginal Revenue Product Under Competition and Monopoly

Since the marginal product of labor declines, the marginal revenue product falls with increases in labor input under both competition and monopoly in product markets. Under monopoly, MRP_m also declines because marginal revenue falls as the monopolist expands output.

(1) Units of Labor (worker-hours)	(2) Marginal Product of Labor MP_L (bushels of corn)	(3) Marginal Revenue (Competition) $MR_C = P_C$ (dollars per bushel)	(4) Marginal Revenue (Monopoly) $MR_m < P_m$	(5) Marginal Revenue Product (Competition) $MRP_C = MR_C \times MP_L$	(6) Marginal Revenue Product (Monopoly) $MRP_m = MR_m \times MP_L$
1	14	$2	$8	$28	$112
2	12	2	7	24	84
3	10	2	6	20	60
4	8	2	5	16	40
5	6	2	4	12	24
6	4	2	3	8	12
7	2	2	2	4	4
8	0	2	1	0	0

The marginal product of labor (MP_L) is the same under competition or monopoly conditions. What changes is the marginal revenue that the monopoly firm can obtain from selling more units of its product or service. The marginal revenue obtainable from selling additional units of output declines with each additional unit sold. As the monopolist sells more, he or she must reduce prices on the previous number of units sold, which means that the marginal revenue from additional sales declines more rapidly than price. In Table 12.2 this declining marginal revenue is shown in column (4). Since MR declines as more units of labor are hired (and more units of output are produced), the MRP falls more rapidly under monopoly conditions, shown in column (6), than in competitive conditions, shown in column (5).

A graphical comparison of the purely competitive firm's demand for labor and the monopolist's demand for labor is shown in Figure 12.5. The monopolist's MRP diminishes more quickly than the pure competitor's because not only is the marginal product of labor falling, but the monopolist's marginal revenue is falling as well, while the marginal revenue of the pure competitor remains constant.

A firm that enjoys a monopoly in its output market does not necessarily have any advantage in resource markets. For example, your local electric company may have exclusive rights as the only seller of electricity in your area. But this monopoly position does not imply that the electric company is the only employer of electricians, computer programmers, or bookkeepers. For these occupations, the monopoly is a purely competitive buyer of labor and must pay a competitive market wage for its labor. The marginal factor cost of labor is equal to the wage rate because the supply of labor to the firm is infinitely elastic.

In the end, the monopolist's decisions in hiring labor require the same marginal analysis as for any other firm. The firm will hire any unit of labor when its marginal revenue product is greater than its marginal factor cost and will continue to hire labor up to the point where the MRP_L is equal to MFC_L. The only difference for a monopoly firm is that its marginal revenue falls along with the labor's marginal product. The Focus "The Marginal Revenue Product of Professional Baseball Players" discusses these ideas as they relate to a special labor market.

FIGURE 12.5

The Monopolist's _MRP_ Versus the Competitive Firm's _MRP_

The marginal revenue product for each firm, obtained by multiplying marginal revenue by marginal product. The monopolist's marginal revenue curve is downward sloping, and the competitive firm's is equal to a given and constant product price; therefore, the monopolist's demand for labor, MRP_m, diminishes more rapidly than the competitive firm's, MRP_C.

FOCUS

The Marginal Revenue Product of Professional Baseball Players

The extra revenue that a firm obtains from hiring a worker is the marginal revenue product; if this is higher than the extra cost of the worker's wages, then the firm adds to its profits by employing the worker. Baseball players' salaries have increased sharply in the last few years, especially for superstars. Are they worth it? Are their *MRP*s greater than their wages?

Addressing this question in the 1970s, economist Gerald Scully calculated the extra revenues that team owners received from hitters and pitchers. He first found that a player's contribution to his team's win–loss record was best measured for pitchers by the percent each added to the team's strikeout-to-walk ratios and for batters by the contribution of each to the team's batting average. Using this information, Scully then estimated the total team revenue, where revenue is simply the number of tickets sold per season times the average ticket price. After adjusting for the size of the city in which the team played its home games, the age of the stadium, the team's league, and other factors affecting revenue, he calculated that every point added to the team batting average by a batter increased the team's revenue by $9504. Similarly,

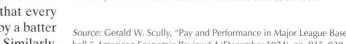

every .01 point added to the pitching staff's strikeout-to-walk ratio increased revenue $9297.

Once he estimated player *MRP*s, it was a straightforward calculation for Scully to determine whether the salary paid to a particular player was commensurate with the amount the player added to team revenue. For example, star hitters added from $250,000 to $383,700 to team revenues. Star pitchers contributed even more, from $321,700 to $479,000. However, during the 1968 and 1969 seasons, no player in Scully's sample was paid more than $125,000. He concluded, therefore, that players' salaries were well below their *MRP*s, with the greatest deficiency being the superstars' salaries. Scully's results help explain free agency and the huge increases in players' salaries in the 1970s, 1980s, and early 1990s. Today, numerous baseball players make more than $3 million per year. And, as salaries have grown, increasingly sophisticated attempts to measure players' marginal revenue value have been made, such as Bill James's *Baseball Abstract*.

Source: Gerald W. Scully, "Pay and Performance in Major League Baseball," *American Economic Review* 64 (December 1974), pp. 915–930.

THE SUPPLY OF LABOR

Now that we have some insight into the demand for labor, the next logical category is labor supply. We know that labor supply in competitive markets is highly elastic. But this fact does not answer two important questions: What determines the overall, or aggregate, supply of labor, and how are wage rates and labor supply interrelated?

Individual Labor Supply

Individuals in free markets are able to choose whether to offer their labor services in the market, and individuals' labor market decisions are based on the principle of utility maximization. The individual must choose between time spent in the market earning the wage that he or she may command and time spent in

Nonmarket activities

Anything an individual does while not working that directly or indirectly yields utility.

nonmarket activities, such as going to school, keeping house, tending a garden, or watching television.

Fortunately, the individual does not have to make an all-or-nothing choice. No one chooses to work twenty-four hours a day, seven days a week. People can divide their time between market and nonmarket activities. How many hours would one choose to work during an average week? This question cannot be easily answered, but we can speculate about the effect that the wage rate may have on an individual's labor supply choices.

A supply curve relates the quantity supplied of a commodity to its price. Applied to labor supply, it is a schedule that relates the quantity of work offered and different wage rates. The labor supply curve of an individual is given in Figure 12.6. The first thing to observe about this person's labor supply curve, S_i, is that below w_1 she would prefer not to work at all; she chooses all nonmarket activity. This cutoff occurs because wages below w_1 do not meet her opportunity cost; she receives more utility from nonmarket activities than she would from the income received from working. Wage w_1 may not be high enough to encourage her to forgo playing tennis, painting the house, or attending school, for example. At wages immediately above w_1, the hours of labor she supplies respond positively to increases in pay. As her wage rate rises from w_1 to w_2, the hours she is willing to supply increase accordingly, to q_2.

The value of one hour of market time (one hour spent working) is equal to the wage rate. This means that for each hour an individual chooses to enjoy nonmarket activities, he or she is forgoing an hour of pay. In other words, the opportunity cost or the price an individual must pay for an hour of leisure time is the wage rate. As the wage rate rises, the price of nonmarket time also rises. An individual's demand for nonmarket time is downward sloping, just as it is for any other good. If the wage rate rises, the individual is encouraged to opt for less nonmarket activity; that is, he or she is encouraged to substitute hours of work for hours of leisure.

FIGURE 12.6

Individual Labor Supply

The individual labor supply curve, the number of hours offered at various wages, may be positively or negatively sloped. If the substitution effect is greater than the income effect, the curve is upward sloping, as shown from w_1 to w_3. The individual substitutes hours of work for hours of nonmarket activities. As the individual's wage rises beyond w_3, his or her demand for nonmarket time increases. The income effect is greater than the substitution effect, and the curve is negatively sloped above wage rate w_3.

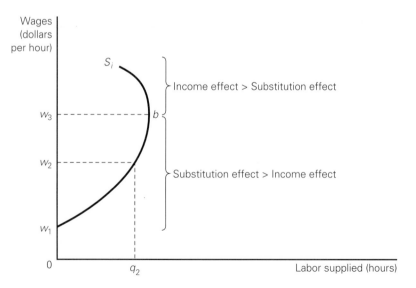

The substitution effect, however, may be offset by an income effect. As the wage rate rises, the individual's income rises. If nonmarket time is a normal good, as we might expect, then the demand for nonmarket time will increase as income rises. This type of income effect will encourage the individual to enjoy more non-market time and less work.

As the wage rate rises, the two effects pull the worker in opposite directions. The effect that dominates will determine whether higher wages encourage more or fewer hours of work and determine whether the labor supply curve is positively or negatively sloped. If the substitution effect is greater than the income effect, higher wages will bring more hours of labor. In Figure 12.6, the substitution effect is greater than the income effect from w_1 to w_3, so the slope is positive. However, the income effect is greater than the substitution effect at wages above w_3. In this range, higher wages bring fewer hours of labor, so the curve is negatively sloped. At point b, where the income and substitution effects are equal, the supply curve begins to bend backward.

The labor supply curves of different individuals would, in all likelihood, be shaped differently. Within a given range of wage rates, one person's labor supply curve may be positively sloped, while another person's may be negatively sloped. This could be due to differences in tastes and preferences for leisure time. The wage level that initially entices people to enter the labor market may vary across individuals for the same reason. Additionally, it would be theoretically difficult to say at which particular wage rate any one person's labor supply curve becomes backward-bending—that is, the wage rate at which the income effect becomes greater than the substitution effect.

Since the shapes of individual labor supply curves are difficult to determine, the slope of the total or aggregate labor supply curve is difficult to predict with accuracy. The aggregate labor supply curve is theoretically obtained by summing individuals' labor supply curves horizontally. The aggregate curve shows the total amount of labor supplied at all the different wages. Even though some individuals have backward-bending labor supply curves, we expect the aggregate labor supply curve to be positively sloped, as in Figure 12.7, for two reasons. First, as wages

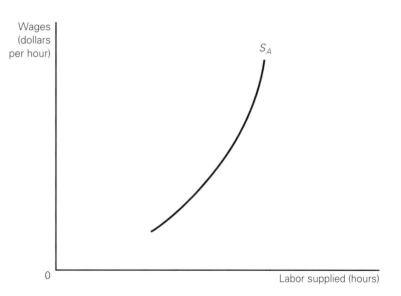

FIGURE 12.7

The Aggregate Supply of Labor

The aggregate labor supply curve, S_A, representing the number of hours of labor supplied by all individuals, is likely to be upward sloping. As wages rise, more people join the labor force, and many people work more hours.

rise, many workers will work more hours. Second, as wages rise, more people will enter the labor force.

Human Capital

Some occupations, such as medicine, law, and nuclear physics, require many years of training. The fact that the wages in these skilled professions are higher than the wages of unskilled labor is not coincidental. Before people are willing to endure the years of training to become highly skilled professionals, they must be reasonably sure that their investment of time and other resources will pay off in the long run. People frequently choose to invest in some form of training to make themselves more productive and to enhance their income-earning potential. While a person is going to college, attending trade school, or gaining on-the-job training, he or she is building **human capital**.

Human capital

Any quality, characteristic, or skill an individual has that enhances the individual's productivity, such as education and job experience.

Gaining human capital requires an investment period, such as four years in college. This investment involves a large opportunity cost. A college student loses the next-best alternative when attending college. For many students, the lost opportunity is the income they would have earned if working. Figure 12.8 portrays a simplified version of two alternative lifetime income streams for an individual.

After graduating from high school at age 18, individuals have a choice. They may enter the labor market immediately and earn income stream Y_N from that time until retirement at age 65 or so. This income stream could rise through the years as the individuals acquire job-related skills, but for simplicity we let it remain constant.

Some individuals go to college. From age 18 to age 22, they do not earn steady, full-time income. The opportunity cost of going to college—that is, the income the individuals forgo by choosing not to work—is represented by the shaded area above the horizontal-axis between ages 18 and 22. In addition, they must pay the direct costs of college—tuition, books, and so on. The shaded area below the horizontal-axis between ages 18 and 22 represents the direct costs of college, a nega-

FIGURE 12.8

The Economic Costs and Benefits of College

An individual may choose to earn income Y_N from age 18 to retirement age 65. Or an individual may attend college, lose income from age 18 to 22, pay the direct cost of college, and then earn income Y_C from age 22 to retirement. The total costs of college are represented by area C, the lost income and direct costs; the benefits of college are area B, the extra income earned with a college degree. In monetary terms it pays to go to college if B is greater than C.

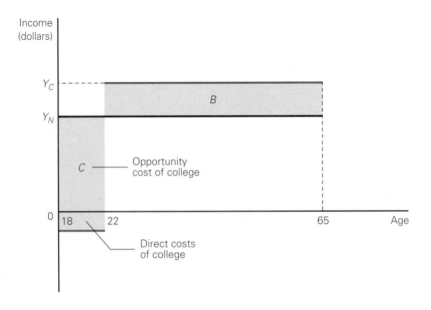

tive income. The total cost of going to college is the sum of both the opportunity cost and the direct costs of college, the entire shaded area C. After graduation, these individuals enter the labor market and begin earning positive income. Figure 12.8 indicates that their starting pay at age 22 after attending college is higher than it would have been had they not gone to college. They earn negative income for four years and then Y_C as a lifetime average from age 22 until retirement.

Which is the best choice? If the deciding factor is money, then the individual determines the relative values of the two income streams and chooses the higher one. One method of doing so is to compare area C (the investment period) with area B. Area C represents the total cost of going to college: the direct costs plus the lost income. Area B represents the benefits of going to college; it is the extra income earned with a college degree. If area B is greater than area C, then it pays to go to college.[1]

Some investments in human capital require more time than others and some require less time. Regardless of the length of the investment period (the number of years spent in school), if there is pure competition in the labor market and enough individuals choose the higher-income streams, then in the long run the sum total of the various income streams will be equal. That is, high school graduates will work at lower wage rates but for a greater total number of years than will college graduates. With a given retirement age for both groups, the lifetime earnings of high school graduates working more years but at a lower wage should just equal the lifetime earnings of college graduates working fewer years but at a higher wage. (This equilibrium requires that the wage rates for occupations with long investment periods be greater than the wage rates for occupations with short investment periods. The difference in wages is what equalizes the lifetime income streams.) And, of course, there may not be pure competition in the labor market. Some professions may attempt to limit entry, so as to keep their wages artificially high in the long run.

---

[1] It should be kept in mind that these values must be discounted for time, as discussed in Chapter 14.

College graduates forego income in order to add to their human capital. However, these additions, although costly, will likely pay future bonuses.

Other Equalizing Differences in Wages

A long investment period is not all that discourages individuals from entering a particular occupation. Other characteristics make it necessary for some occupations to offer higher wages to induce workers to enter. People will evaluate their alternative work possibilities in monetary and nonmonetary terms. Pay will be important, but so too will be working conditions, location, co-workers, risk, length of contract, personality of the boss, and myriad other factors. Although some of these factors are nonmonetary or psychological, this does not mean that they are not income. They are a part of workers' pay. The total compensation of a worker in a given occupation consists of the wage plus any nonmonetary aspects of the job.

The principle of equalizing differences in wages works in the following way. In a competitive labor market, laborers choose the occupation with the highest total compensation, other things equal. This brings the wage down until the total compensation for the occupation is on a par with that of other occupations. If total compensation is too low in some occupation, then people leave that occupation until the wage rises enough to equalize the total compensation. When total compensation is equalized across occupations, the competitive equilibrium is achieved. If this condition is not met, workers will move around and change jobs until it is met.

One student who spends the summer in an air-conditioned office may make a lower wage but more nonwage pay per hour than another student who spends the summer on a construction crew. As students compete for summer jobs, total pay between jobs will be equalized. This is the principle of equalizing differences at work in a competitive labor market.

The basic point is that observed wage differences across occupations may reflect differences in nonmonetary aspects of employment. Of course, labor markets may not always be competitive as we have assumed here. Some jobs may pay more and have more attractive working conditions if there are barriers to entry into the occupation. However, under competition, wage differences can exist. Forces fueled by interest groups have attempted to use the political process to impose what they regard as comparable worth in the workplace (see the Focus "Politics and 'Justice' in the Workplace: Comparable Worth" for a discussion of this phenomenon). The following are just a few of the many reasons for wage differences other than those caused by human capital differences.

- *Wages will vary directly with the disagreeableness of a job.* The more uncomfortable the job, the higher the pay will be. To induce workers to accept jobs that create discomfort—such as tarring roofs in the heat of summer—a higher monetary reward must be offered.

- *The more seasonal or irregular a job, the higher the pay will be.* To induce individuals to supply labor to irregular employments, the wage must compensate them for the likelihood of being laid off frequently. For example, construction workers often experience periods of unemployment between jobs. To have readily available workers, construction employers must pay a higher wage.

- *Jobs that require trustworthiness carry a higher wage.* Armored truck drivers, blackjack dealers, and some bank employees receive relatively high wages. One reason that such occupations pay more is that being trustworthy is both an extra burden and a form of human capital; employers must compensate such workers for their extra efforts.

FOCUS

Politics and "Justice" in the Workplace: Comparable Worth

The pay of various types of workers in a marketplace is typically assumed to be determined solely by the interaction of supply and demand. In recent years a movement has started that advocates an increased role for the government in ensuring greater equity in pay ("justice"). The aim of this movement is to ensure that the pay for different occupations reflects the comparable worth of the services provided by workers in various occupations. Advocates of comparable worth argue that the value of each type of worker can be objectively determined in terms of job qualifications and work conditions. Under their proposed system, impartial experts would rate each occupation and assign a number that reflects the worth of each particular job. A number of interest groups (women's, civil rights, and religious groups) seek the political means to end what they view as gender and racial discrimination in wages for equal skill, effort, responsibility, and working conditions—even with *different* job titles, work, or occupations.[a]

---

[a] A number of interest groups supported the introduction of the Fair Pay Act of 1996 in the U.S. Congress, which would have introduced the principle of comparable worth in government contracts. The legislation failed, although the demand for political solutions to labor market problems will continue.

Critics, including most economists, argue that it is impossible to assign points objectively to different occupations. The working conditions of a forest ranger are different from those of a registered nurse, but it is impossible to say which conditions are more demanding—it depends on preferences of particular workers. Physical and mental demands also differ across employments. Perhaps the most important objection is that the institution of comparable worth would rob the labor markets of signals that reflect changing demand, supply, and technological conditions in the economy. A crucial role played by labor markets is to attract new workers into growing occupations. Imposed wages could mean that, despite increases in demand, shortages in critical occupations could exist indefinitely. Comparable worth would severely restrict the ability of a market system to adjust to ever-changing conditions.

Few Americans, let alone economists, do not support the principle of "equal pay for equal work." Developing standards to make the principle operative, without creating other (sometimes unpredictable) adverse effects, is quite another matter.

- *Jobs with greater risk to health will have higher pay*. Occupations with higher than average probabilities of death or disability must compensate employees for taking a risk. People are not willing to risk lost future income because of injuries unless they can receive higher income in the present. Steelworkers who construct frames for skyscrapers must be paid more than those who work on the ground.

- *Jobs that carry the possibility of tremendous success will have a lower wage.* Acting is a good example of such a profession. Many young people aspire to be actors and are arguably attracted into acting by the sumptuous lifestyle of movie stars. Most never make it that big; the average salary of all actors is quite low. Yet some people are willing to take the plunge, feeling that they are good enough to be big winners. Attitudes toward risk are therefore important in determining relative wages. The wages for most actors will be lower because some successful actors make startlingly high pay, a possibility that induces many young people to enroll in acting school.

- *Wages will vary by region.* Wages in any region are determined by supply and demand. (For our purposes, a region may be an area within a particular country, an entire country, or several countries in close geographic proximity to each other.) However, if wages in market *A* exceed the wages in market *B*, then we expect to see labor flow from *B* to *A*. The shifting short-run supply brings wages into equilibrium. Wages fall in *A* and rise in *B*. (See the Application, "Where Do You Live? Regional Wage Differences," at the end of the chapter.)

MARGINAL PRODUCTIVITY THEORY AND INCOME DISTRIBUTION

The profit-maximizing tendency of competitive firms to set marginal revenue product (*MRP*) equal to marginal factor cost (*MFC*) leads to a wage that equals the value of a worker's marginal product. This result applies to the prices of all factors of production in competitive markets. Each resource—be it labor, land, or capital—is paid the value of its marginal product.

The marginal productivity theory of factor prices is a positive, not a normative, theory. It explains *how* factor prices are determined in markets, not how factor prices *should* be determined. It is not meant to be an ethical theory of income distribution, though it is sometimes attacked as such. It is meant as a demand and supply theory that explains the behavior of input prices and the allocation of factors of production to different employments.

It should now be clear that the theory of marginal productivity implies many things about income distribution. Where there is competitive voluntary contracting for labor services, labor's share of national income will be directly related to its marginal product. Of course, factor markets are not perfect, and various other forces affect income distribution in a society. These issues will be carefully addressed over the next several chapters. Our argument in this chapter is not that the marginal productivity theory is necessarily a good normative theory of how income should be distributed (although you might believe it is so), but rather that it provides an objective basis for understanding the economic behavior of demanders and suppliers of inputs.

APPLICATION

Where Do You Live? Regional Wage Differences

Does the "cost of living" where you live partially determine your wage rate? Why do we observe higher wages in the North than in the South or higher wages in San Francisco than in Oklahoma City? Can we expect these wage differences to persist in the long run?

Wages in any region are determined by supply and demand. However, if wages in market *A* exceed the wages in market *B*, then we expect to see labor flow from *B* to *A*. The shifting supply brings wages into equilibrium. Wages fall in *A* and rise in *B*.

The equality of wages is the result of individuals' actions. Furthermore, an individual's decision to move is based on the costs and benefits of doing so. Relocation requires resource expenditures that must be offset by extra income.

Suppose a worker could stay in location *B* and earn wage W_B or could move to location *A* and earn a higher wage W_A. The direct costs of moving are the expenses incurred in transporting the worker, her family members, and their personal belongings. There are also additional opportunity costs. The act of moving requires time, and so might finding a job in A. This is time that could have been spent earning income in B. The lost income is a cost of relocation, as shown in Figure 12.9.

At time 0 the individual must choose between earning wage W_B from T to retirement and spending time moving so as to earn wage W_A. The time T is the amount of time spent moving from B to A plus the amount of time spent seeking employment in A. The total cost of moving is the shaded area between 0 and T above and below the horizontal-axis, which represents the income forgone plus direct moving expenses. The benefit of moving—represented by the shaded area between T and retirement—is the extra income that may be earned after the move. It pays to move if the area of extra benefits is greater than the area of costs.[a]

If benefits outweigh costs, then many people will choose to move to A—the move is a good investment in human capital. However, the shifting labor supplies will increase wages in B, where workers are now scarcer, and decrease them in A. The maximum amount by which W_A can exceed W_B in the long run is the amount that forces the area of benefits to just equal the area of costs. Therefore, the lower the costs of moving, the smaller the difference in wages needs to be.

In fact, there are many reasons why we expect little variation in wages across the country within the same occupation in today's markets. First, the duration of lost income for most movers is very small. Indeed, it is quite possible to work until 5:00 p.m. on Friday in New York City and start work at 9:00 a.m. on Monday in Los Angeles. Many people will not move unless they have already found

[a]As in the earlier example of the economic costs and benefits of a college education, these values must be discounted for time, as explained in Chapter 14.

FIGURE 12.9

Wage Differences Across Regions

An individual must choose whether to remain in location B and earn wage W_B from time 0 to retirement or move to location A and earn wage W_A from time T to retirement. The decision to move to A necessitates costs in terms of the time T spent moving and income forgone while making the move, represented by the shaded area from 0 to T above and below the horizontal axis. After the move, the individual earns extra income represented by the shaded area from T to retirement. If this area of extra income is greater than the area of total costs of moving, the individual will choose to move.

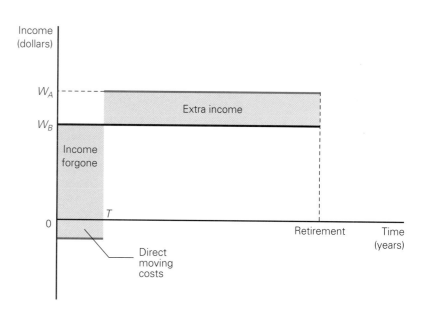

employment in the new location. If the amount of time it takes to travel across the country today were as great as it was two hundred years ago, then wage differences could be very large.

Another reason that regional differences in wages are small is that young workers have small costs and large benefits in moving. Young workers typically have small families or no families and few material possessions to move. Also, the years of receiving extra benefits are longer for young people. Thus, a smaller difference in wages can induce them to move.

Another important aspect of regional wage differences involves the demand side of the labor market. Firms will be encouraged to expand operations in areas where there are low costs of production and decrease operations where costs are high. Firms will invest more capital in low-wage area *B* and decrease investment in high-wage area *A*. Capital moves around the country just as labor does, and this movement tends to equalize wages. In fact, all resources that are mobile move to the locations that yield the resource owners the highest income.

In spite of this equalizing tendency, we observe that wages in the North are about 10 percent higher than in the South in the same occupation. Don Bellante suggests that the difference occurs only in money wages and not in real wages.[b] The cost of living in the South is about 10 percent lower than in the North. This difference in costs equalizes the real wage, just as we expect in the long run.

QUESTION

The city of Houston advertised for police men and women on Atlanta TV stations offering 30 percent (on average) higher wages than those paid by the Atlanta police department. Some personnel moved to Houston. What effect would this movement have on regional wage differences for police services between Texas and Georgia? What might we expect the average age of the migratory police workers to be?

---

[b]Don Bellante, "The North-South Differential and the Migration of Heterogeneous Labor," *American Economic Review* 69 (March 1979), pp. 166–175.

SUMMARY

1. The demand for labor is a derived demand; it is derived from the demand for the product that labor produces.

2. The demand curve for labor is a function of its marginal product and the demand for the product it produces. In the short run, demand is equivalent to marginal revenue product: $MRP_L = MP_L \times MR$.

3. The competitive firm hires the profit-maximizing amount of labor at the point where MRP equals the wage rate. The short-run market demand curve for labor shows the amount of labor that firms hire when labor is the only variable input and the number of firms is constant, but it allows for changes in product price as wages change.

4. The long-run market demand curve for labor shows the amount of labor hired at different wages when all inputs are allowed to vary and firms are in long-run competitive equilibrium.

5. The demand for labor changes when the demand for the product changes or when the marginal product of labor changes.

6. The relation between the wage rate and the number of hours of labor an individual supplies depends on the substitution and income effects. If the substitution effect is greater than the income effect, then the individual's labor supply curve is positively sloped; the curve is negatively sloped if the income effect is greater than the substitution effect. The aggregate labor supply curve is the sum of individual labor supply curves and is usually positively sloped.

7. Human capital is anything an individual acquires that increases his or her productivity. In an occupation that requires human capital, the longer and more costly the investment period, the higher the wages.

8. The total compensation in all occupations in competitive markets is equalized by differences in wages. The long-run supply of labor to each occupation ensures the equilibrium difference in wages.

9. Because of changes in either supply or demand, regional wage levels may vary. However, migration of workers will tend to eliminate regional wage differences.

10. In competitive markets, resources are paid a price that is equal to their marginal product. Labor's share of the overall income distribution is related to its marginal product.

KEY TERMS

factor market
derived demand
competitive labor market
market demand for labor
market supply of labor
marginal product of labor (MP_L)

marginal revenue product of
    labor (MRP_L)
marginal factor cost of labor
    (MFC_L)
firm's long-run demand for labor
change in the demand for labor

complementary inputs
substitute inputs
nonmarket activities
human capital

QUESTIONS FOR REVIEW AND DISCUSSION

1. What derived demands will result from increased demand for each of the following goods and services: (a) automobiles, (b) candy, (c) government regulation, (d) physical fitness, (e) education?

2. Explain why an individual's supply of labor curve may bend backward at some sufficiently high wage level.

3. What does the law of diminishing marginal productivity have to do with the demand curve for labor?

4. What is the difference between the demand curve for labor of a monopolist and of a perfectly competitive firm in the output market?

5. Apply the principle of equalizing differences to explain why the relative wage of the following occupations is high or low: (a) politicians, (b) schoolteachers, (c) morticians, (d) actors, (e) brain surgeons.

6. In what sense is the marginal productivity theory of wages a positive theory? In what sense is it a normative theory?

7. What activities will frustrate the equalization of total wages across jobs in the labor market? Does this mean that there is such a thing as nonequalizing wage differences?

8. Are tractor drivers substitutes for human cotton pickers? What happens to the demand for tractor drivers if cotton pickers' wages fall?

9. Is the demand for toothpicks elastic or inelastic? What about elasticity of demand for a machine that makes toothpicks?

10. Under what conditions are labor and some other input complementary inputs?

11. Explain how the firm's marginal revenue product curve is derived. Up to what point will the profit-maximizing firm hire labor?

12. "It is simply unjust that sanitation workers earn less than most stockbrokers. They work harder and longer hours." Comment on this quotation.

PROBLEMS

1. The data in the table apply to a competitive firm.

Units of Labor	Marginal Product	Marginal Revenue	Marginal Revenue Product	Hourly Wage Rate
1	21	$1.50	$31.50	$9.00
2	18	1.50	27.00	9.00
3	15	1.50	22.50	9.00
4	12	1.50	18.00	9.00
5	9	1.50	13.50	9.00
6	6	1.50	9.00	9.00
7	3	1.50	4.50	9.00
8	0	1.50	0.00	9.00

   a. What is the marginal factor cost of labor for this firm?
   b. If you are the personnel manager of this firm, how many units of labor will you hire?

2. Suppose that Zina, a skilled copy editor, owns her own freelance editorial business. Further assume that she wants to earn exactly $600 per week.
   a. What are the number of hours of labor that Zina is willing to supply at the (hourly) wage rates listed below?

Wage	Hours
$ 6	——
10	——
20	——
40	——
60	——
100	——

   b. Draw a graph showing Zina's supply curve based on the information in part a.
   c. Which is greater, Zina's substitution effect or her income effect? Why?

WORKING WITH THE WEB

1. The issue of equal pay, or comparable worth, as discussed in the Focus "Politics and 'Justice' in the Workplace: Comparable Worth," is a controversial issue and is not easily resolved. Go to www.mises.org, select "daily articles", and choose February '99. Scroll to the bottom of the list until you find the article "Women and Work". The article takes up the issue of pay equity across gender and analyzes the historical trends of men and women in the workplace.
   a. What percentage of the wage differential is unexplained by some factor?
   b. What is the situation for women employed in the marketing profession?

2. Regional wage differences are discussed in the Application "Where Do You Live?: Regional Wage Differences." The explanation given for regional variation in wage rates is the supply of and demand for labor. The application points out that wages tend to be higher in the North than the South, and higher in San Francisco than Oklahoma City. First, let's look at the North–South wage differential. Go to http://www.bls.gov/oes/msa/oes_5240m.htm#b20000 and select "Professional, Paraprofessional, and Technical Occupations".
   a. What is the mean annual income in Montgomery, AL, for Accountants and Auditors?
      Next, go to http://www.bls.gov/oes/msa/oes_1120m.htm and select the same category, "Professional, Paraprofessional, and Technical Occupations".
   b. What is the mean annual income in Boston, MA, for Accountants and Auditors?
   c. Does the data confirm that workers in the North earn more than their southern counterparts? Does the data confirm that workers in larger metropolitan areas earn more than workers in smaller areas?

Labor Unions

I n the previous chapter we discussed demand and supply conditions in a competitive labor market, where the wage rates tend toward equality. Although we do see wage discrepancies in competitive markets, many of these can be attributed to circumstances such as the amount of risk a particular job involves or the amount of training it requires. We naturally expect brain surgeons to make more than dishwashers in a competitive environment because of the human capital investment brain surgeons must make to perform their services.

All labor markets, of course, are not strictly competitive. In general, factor markets can assume the same kinds of imperfect market structures that we studied in Chapters 10 and 11. The imperfection in labor markets can occur on the supply side, the demand side, or both. On the supply side, labor unions account for the largest source of imperfect competition.

In this chapter we will look at how imperfectly competitive labor markets work. Specifically, we will look at the effects of labor unions. When you finish Chapter 13 you should understand

- the history and goals of labor unions in the United States.
- how unions achieve goals such as higher wages and better working conditions for their members.
- the impact of labor unions on consumers and nonunion labor.
- some of the effects on labor when a single employer exists in an individual market.

TYPES OF LABOR UNIONS

Labor union
A group of individual workers organized to act collectively in an attempt to affect labor market conditions.

A **labor union** is a group of workers who organize collectively in an effort to increase their market power. By acting as a collective unit, they are able to exert a greater influence over working conditions or wages. In this sense, a labor union is similar to a cartel (discussed in Chapter 11). In a union, the sellers of labor agree not to compete among themselves but to act as a single seller of labor.

The first labor unions in the United States started as workers' guilds in the late 1700s and early 1800s. These organizations of workers within the same trade—carpenters, cordwainers (shoemakers), hatters—began meeting to set standards and prices for their output. These loosely organized trade unions were typically short-lived but were the beginnings of the American labor movement.

The Industrial Revolution brought about new opportunities for labor unions. Large manufacturing plants employed many workers with similar skills and interests who could organize at relatively low costs to pursue their common goals. Today there are three major types of labor unions: craft unions, industrial unions, and public employees' unions.

Craft Unions

Craft union
Workers with a common skill who organize to restrict the supply of labor in their trade and obtain some market power; also called a trade union.

In 1886, the American Federation of Labor (AFL) was started in an effort to organize craftspeople into local unions. **Craft unions,** which flourished in the Middle Ages, organize workers according to particular skills, regardless of the industry in which they work. Thus, there are separate guilds for electricians, carpenters, and plumbers. The main function of the guilds is to advance their members' economic well-being. When workers act as a unit, their power in the market can limit competition and raise total compensation above the competitive level. In this sense, the American Medical Association (AMA) or the American Bar Association (ABA) may be viewed as effective unions because they restrict membership in the medical and legal professions, raising professional fees above competitive levels. (See the Focus "The American Medical Association as a Union" for more along these lines.)

Trade or craft unions increase members' total compensation by decreasing the supply of skilled workers. They do so by excluding potential workers from membership. Frequently, trade unions require high initiation fees, monthly dues, and long apprenticeship programs in an effort to discourage potential entrants. Existing members enjoy the higher wage brought about by the limited supply of workers in their trade.

Trade unions are very much like cartels in the sense that supply is artificially restricted so as to command a higher price. As such, craft unions face the same problems as cartels. Just as cartel members have an incentive to cheat on the cartel price, workers outside the union who offer their labor at a wage lower than the union wage can obtain jobs at the expense of union members.

Industrial Unions

Industrial union
Workers in a given industry organized independently of their skills in an effort to obtain market power.

Large manufacturing plants first appeared during the late 1800s and early 1900s. Rather than organize individual craft unions according to different skills, all workers within the same industry would organize a single industry-wide union. In 1938, John L. Lewis formally organized the Congress of Industrial Organizations (CIO), which unified workers first at the firm level and then at the level of the industry as a whole. Contemporary examples of these **industrial unions** include autoworkers' unions and steelworkers' unions.

FOCUS

The American Medical Association as a Union

A union must be able to restrict entry and increase fees and returns in order to function successfully. The American Medical Association (AMA) functions in this fashion while having the laudable (stated) goal of protecting the health care consumer by assuring the quality of care provided. The policies and practices of medical associations may well improve quality, but they have other effects as well: They protect the health care provider from the forces of competition. The AMA might not fit the public image of a union, but it is an unassailable fact that the association employs the tactics of a union to limit competition and raise wages.

The AMA (and its affiliated and often highly specialized unions) has been enormously successful in restricting entry into the health care profession. In part, the returns to doctors and other health care providers are due to the long and arduous path to success. Those wanting to be physicians must get into and through medical school and a residency program, accredited and, to some extent, controlled

by the AMA. A monopolist seeking to reduce the supply of labor would set high admission standards for those entering the market. You must have a license to practice medicine because you would face criminal sanctions if caught practicing medicine without one. Exams are given under the auspices of the AMA. All such policies are designed to reduce the supply of physicians.

"Codes of conduct" by national and state medical boards are designed to eliminate price competition among physicians. Advertising is not permitted—indeed it is designated as "unethical"—because advertising would make it possible for health care consumers to compare prices. Sanctions, such as denial of hospital privileges, are imposed on any physicians who attempt to advertise.

Government responded to this highly concentrated interest group long ago—in the nineteenth century, in most cases. This interest group (like the barbers and cosmetologists of Chapter 4) had criminal penalties installed for nonprescribed behavior. In addition, the government was used indirectly to support physicians. The laws regulating the market for prescription drugs effectively increase the demand for physicians. A licensed physician is necessary to write prescriptions—a necessary input in health care. Substitutes, such as midwives, nurses, or health care assistants, are heavily regulated by the states due to physician interest groups. All of these factors increase the demand for physician services.

A restriction in supply and an increase in demand lead to less competition and higher prices for health care services. However, the continuing debate over health care in the United States has not led to proposals for fostering competition among doctors. Indeed, in 1999 the AMA approved physician unions to counter the power of health maintenance organizations (HMOs). Such unions may be a step backwards. Establishing competition among physicians may be the prerequisite to solving what is called the health care crisis.

For an industrial union to be effective, it must unionize all firms in an industry. Otherwise, the lower-cost, nonunionized firms would prosper at the expense of the higher-cost, unionized firms. Thus, industrial unions often encourage membership rather than restrict it.

Public employees' union
Workers employed by federal, state, or local governments who organize in an effort to obtain market power.

Public Employees' Unions

Public employees' unions are organizations of government workers. Such unions cover a wide variety of jobs—such as fire fighting, police work, teaching, and clerical work—and include both blue-collar and white-collar workers. This sector of the union movement has been one of the fastest growing in recent years. The American Federation of State, County, and Municipal Employees (AFSCME) is now among the ten largest unions in the country. Indeed, membership in AFSCME tripled between 1968 and 1988.

The problems of public employees' unions have received a great deal of attention in recent years. Each fall finds teachers on strike for higher wages and benefits in cities across the country. The decertification of the Professional Air Traffic Controllers Union (PATCO) in the early 1980s resulted from a technically illegal strike by a public employees' union. Despite these much-publicized problems, public employees' unions continue to grow in membership relative to private sector unions. Figure 13.1 compares the percentage of union members in government with the percentage in private industries for years between 1973 and 1994.

The Decline of Union Membership in the United States

Membership in labor unions as a percentage of the total U.S. labor market grew steadily throughout the first half of the twentieth century; by 1953, about 26 percent of the workers in the United States were members of labor unions. Today, only 14 percent of all American workers belong to labor unions. Figure 13.1 shows the trends in unionization from 1973 to 1997. The composition of union member-

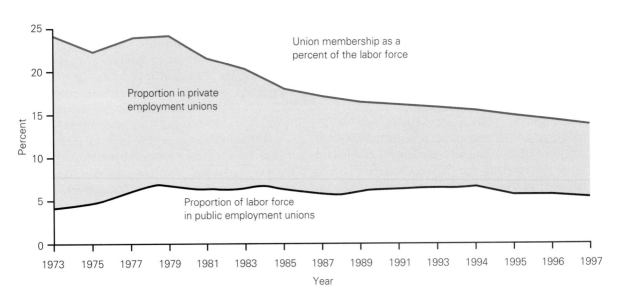

FIGURE 13.1

Trends in Union Membership

The number of workers belonging to unions as a percent of the labor force declined over the period 1973 to 1997. The percent decline was greatest in the private sector, where today only about 10 percent of private sector workers are union members. Union membership among public sector employees has remained constant at around 5 percent of the total labor force over the twenty-four-year period.

Sources: *Union Membership and Earnings Data Book* (Washington, D.C.: Bureau of National Affairs, Inc. 1995), p. 10; and *Statistical Abstract of the United States 1998* (Washington, D.C.: U.S. Government Printing Office, 1998), p. 414.

ship has changed dramatically. In 1953, less than 5 percent of union members were government employees. Today, almost half of all union members are employed by the government. These unionized government workers still represent only about 5 to 6 percent of the *total* labor force—a proportion that has remained constant over time. Such traditionally heavily unionized sectors of the economy as mining, construction, and manufacturing currently have a smaller percentage of workers represented by labor unions than does the government sector.

Several economic factors have contributed to the decline in union membership. Structural changes in the U.S. economy—brought about in part by the pressure of foreign competition—have resulted in a decline in the number of manufacturing and mining jobs relative to service sector jobs. Workers in the service sector have always been more difficult to organize because they tend to be dispersed over a large number of relatively small business firms. Another factor that has contributed to the decline in union membership is the increased participation of women in the labor force. While women have traditionally expressed stronger support for the labor union movement than have men, they have always participated in labor unions in smaller proportions than men; this reflects the concentration of women in the service sector.

UNION ACTIVITIES

Regardless of the means of organization, when workers successfully unite to act as a single seller of labor, the union gains monopoly power in its labor market. The union and its members are therefore no longer wage rate takers. There is a downward-sloping demand curve for the members' labor, and the union may seek any wage along this curve. However, the level of employment for union members is inversely related to the wage rate. Higher wages are gained at the expense of fewer jobs.

Union Goals

The ultimate goals of the union may depend on many competing objectives. Understandably, the union's elected, policy-making officials suggest that members want improved economic well-being: higher wages, more jobs, greater job security, safer jobs, more retirement pay, more fringe benefits, and so on. But relating union policy to a particular objective is difficult. For example, the union objective may be to maximize any number of options, some of which may be inconsistent—such as the utility of the union officials, the utility of members, the wage rate, the level of employment, the level of membership, the total wage income of members, the total wage income of senior members, and so on. The ramifications of pursuing three of these objectives are discussed below.

Employment For All Members   One objective of a union may be to achieve full employment—that is, a job for every member. To do so would require a wage rate that ensures that the quantity of labor demanded by firms is equal to the quantity of labor supplied by existing members. Suppose that the demand for the union's labor can be represented by curve D_L in Figure 13.2. If the amount of labor offered by the union is L_1, then wage W_1 will ensure full employment of union members.

Maximizing The Wage Bill   Although wage W_1 means that everyone in the union is working, full employment may not be the union's goal. Unions frequently have

FIGURE 13.2

The Union's Wage Goals

In setting its wage rate, a union must choose among many goals. If there is L_1 amount of laborers in a union, then wage W_1 must be chosen to achieve full employment of all members. If the elasticity of demand at W_1 is less than 1, then an increase in wages up to W_2 will increase the total wage bill while bringing about union unemployment in the amount $L_1 - L_2$. Still-higher wages such as W_3 will decrease total union income, although those union members who are working enjoy greater incomes. In trying to maximize total wages, the union may face some degree of unemployment according to this model.

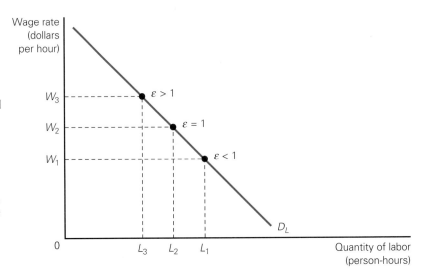

members sitting on the unemployment bench. Any wage higher than W_1 will leave some members unemployed, but there may also be some benefits to a higher wage. For example, it may increase the **total wage bill.** The total wage bill to firms hiring union workers is the wage rate times the total amount (in person-hours) of labor hired. This total wage bill is not only the total cost of labor to the firms; it is also the collective wage income of all the union members. Since workers prefer more income to less, all things being equal, the union may choose to maximize the wage bill. If the full employment wage occurs where the elasticity of demand is less than 1 (inelastic demand), then an increase in the wage will increase total union income ($W \times L$).

Total wage bill

The total cost of labor to firms; equal to wage rate times total quantity of labor employed.

To understand this possibility, recall from Chapter 5 how price, total revenue, and elasticity are related. Total revenue is maximized at the price where the elasticity of demand is equal to 1. If elasticity is less than 1, then an increase in price increases total revenue; if elasticity is greater than 1, it takes a price decrease to increase total revenue. In analyzing labor demand, the total wage bill, the wage rate, and the elasticity of demand have the same relation. If the union's objective is to maximize the total union income, then the wage is set where the elasticity of demand is equal to 1.

In Figure 13.2, wage W_2 maximizes the wage bill. However, with L_1 amount of labor in the union, unemployment in the amount $L_1 - L_2$ results. This may not be a problem because the total union income ($W_2 \times L_2$) is now higher than at W_1. All members can still be better off at a higher wage if the working members provide unemployment compensation to unemployed members. On the other hand, a trade union may choose to limit union membership to L_2.

In considering attempts by unions to maximize the wage bill, it is important to interpret the wage rate as a full wage. This includes both the hourly pay and the value of fringe benefits such as hospitalization insurance, retirement benefits, and paid vacation. For many union contracts, a large portion of the full pay takes the form of fringe benefits.

Maximizing Income for Limited Members   While wage W_2 would maximize income for the union as a whole, a higher wage such as W_3 in Figure 13.2 would increase income only for those who remain fully employed. L_3 workers would be hired, and their incomes would be higher as long as they are working the same number of hours. For example, senior members usually retain employment under a seniority system. Thus, wages above W_2 would probably increase senior members' incomes at the expense of younger members.

Union Objectives and the Elasticity of Demand

A union's ability to accomplish its goals is limited by the elasticity of demand for its members' labor. Increases in wages decrease the level of employment, but the percent decrease in employment is determined by the elasticity of demand. Unions would like to see large increases in wages with minor effects on employment; in other words, they would like the demand for their members' labor to be as inelastic as possible. The elasticity of demand for union labor is determined by many factors. Naturally changing patterns of demand and supply for the products of unions have a direct impact on elasticity and union success (see the Focus "'Services Pay' and the Restructuring of the American Economy" for an example). Unions themselves often engage in activities that decrease the elasticity of demand for union members. Such a change in elasticity of demand is shown in Figure 13.3 as a rotation of the demand curve from D_1 to D_2. Along D_2, increases in wages result in less unemployment than identical increases along D_1. The following are some familiar examples of this process.

Elasticity of Demand for the Product   The more inelastic the demand for the good or service that the unionized labor produces, the more inelastic the demand for the union's labor. While a union would like the demand for the good or service its workers produce to be inelastic, it cannot do much to decrease this elasticity. Union workers are mostly at the mercy of the market, although in some circumstances they can and do affect elasticity of demand. For example, an item's elasticity of demand is determined in part by the number and availability of substitutes. If a union can limit substitutes, then the elasticity of demand for the union workers' labor decreases. We see this happening in the automobile industry. Through the political process, U.S. autoworkers encourage import quotas, which have the effect of limiting the supply of foreign autos and decreasing the elasticity of demand for U.S.-made cars. With import quotas, increases in autoworkers' wages have less effect on employment than the same increases in wages if quotas are not imposed.

Availability of Substitute Inputs   The fewer substitute inputs for union labor, the lower the elasticity of demand for union labor. Unions would prefer no substitute inputs for their members' labor; then wage increases would have minimal effects on union employment. But there are almost always some inputs that may be substituted for union labor. Typically, nonunion labor is a good substitute. For this reason, labor unions try to form contracts with firms that maximize the use of union labor. (Closed shops—which legally bind firms to hire only union labor—are now illegal in the United States.) Unions also take direct actions to limit the amount of nonunion labor available. For example, unions support laws that restrict immigration to the United States because such laws decrease the availability of immigrant workers who could substitute for union members in the work force.

FOCUS

"Services Pay" and the Restructuring of the American Economy

Naysayers are around in all ages. When the great leap of the Industrial Revolution took hold in the eighteenth and nineteenth centuries, doom and gloom were predicted for workers in the factories as opposed to "wholesome" pursuits in farming. Agriculture and agricultural production most certainly survived, but amid ever-modernizing factories and assembly-line production. The modern "services revolution"—a technological movement of the latter part of the twentieth century— has had its critics. The deindustrialization of America, away from smoke-stack industries and assembly-line productions such as steel, was supposed to be replaced by low-paying, burger-flipping type jobs. Instead, high-tech positions and service jobs are paying as much as assembly-line work.

One reason for the decline in union membership (shown in Figure 13.1) is the decline in the smokestack-type production that has characterized the American economy. But this decline has been replaced by highly technical industries where unions have not made significant progress. (Public service unions, of course, have been very successful, as discussed in the text.) The critics had it that nonmanufacturing jobs created low pay and fewer fringe benefits for workers. But, for the first time in 1998, hourly earnings in services were higher than those in manufacturing (according to the Bureau of Labor Statistics). Manufacturing jobs (in 1998) were lost in the amount of 234,000 well-paying jobs, but more than one and one-half million jobs were created in high-tech industries such as computer services and telecommunications.[a]

Retailing and food-marketing jobs ("burger-flipping jobs") do not pay as well as assembly-line work, but high-tech jobs often pay workers better wages. Total returns to workers, of course, include benefits—particularly health benefits. While total (full) compensation in services is not as high as in manufacturing, it has begun to catch up. Benefits in the service industries are more flexible, however, offering employees more flexible forms of nonmonetary wages. In such industries, the competitive system, rather than labor unions, determines the provision of wages and benefits.

_____

[a]Data for this focus was obtained from John Berlau, "More than Just Flipping Burgers: Service-Sector Jobs Fuel U.S. Economic Boom," *Investor's Business Daily* (March 23, 1999), pp. 1–2.

Increasing the Demand for Union Labor

Regardless of the goals of unions, the members are always in favor of an increase in the demand for their labor. With increased demand, wages, employment, or both are increased. The curve representing demand for labor shifts to the right when one of two basic things happens: an increase in the demand for the product or an increase in the marginal product of workers.

Unions can and do engage in activities that affect the demand for their members. Some of this activity is unproductive—for example, the practice of *feath-*

FIGURE 13.3

Decreasing the Elasticity of Demand for Union Labor

Unions attempt to decrease the elasticity of demand for their members' labor. For example, unions support immigration laws that retard or block the flow of competitive foreign labor into this country. The effect of such activities is represented by a rotation of the demand curve from D_1 to D_2. This rotation of the demand curve indicates that future wage increases result in smaller employment decreases. If wages rise from W_1 to W_2, employment falls only to L_2 rather than to L'_2.

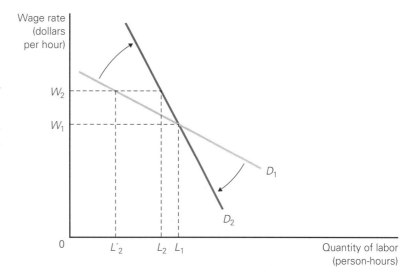

erbedding. Featherbedding is the attempt to increase demand for union labor through contractual obligations to hire what some would regard as unnecessary labor. When diesel locomotives replaced steam locomotives, firemen were no longer needed to shovel coal. Railway workers nevertheless required firemen to be hired. The union contracts of journeyman carpenters or electricians stipulate that each union member must be provided with an apprentice—regardless of need. Contracts negotiated by musicians' unions routinely require that a minimum number of players be hired—again, without regard to any reasonable expectation of need. Some of these demand-increasing activities also decrease elasticity of demand for labor.

Increasing Product Demand   Unions frequently attempt to increase the demand for the products they produce. Garment workers advertise the union label and encourage consumers, as well as union members, to buy union-made clothes. Autoworkers strongly encourage union members to buy domestically produced cars. As we have seen, unions sometimes try to influence lawmakers to decrease the supply of foreign products that are substitutes for union-made goods. Import tariffs or quotas also increase the demand for U.S. products.

Increasing Substitute Input Prices   If unions can increase the relative price of inputs that are substitutes for union labor, then the demand for union labor will increase. Unskilled nonunion workers can substitute for skilled union labor, for example. Unions have therefore supported increases in the minimum wage. As the relative price of unskilled nonunion labor rises, the demand for union labor increases.

Increasing Productivity of Members   Unions prefer that their members be very productive. If the marginal product of new members joining the union is relatively high, then the demand for all members increases. Apprenticeship programs offered by unions train new entrants in an effort to increase overall productivity. Unions also provide other services—for example, conflict resolution procedures to settle worker grievances—that may enhance worker productivity on the job.

MONOPSONY: A SINGLE EMPLOYER OF LABOR

Having examined unions' attempts to build the economic power of laborers, we now turn to the nature of the firms they face as employers. Before the Industrial Revolution, large manufacturing plants were not common. In most towns or regions there were several potential employers for most workers. As a matter of fact, most skilled craftspeople were self-employed. However, as technology changed, the benefits of mass production increased. Large manufacturing plants such as steel mills, textile mills, and coal mines became the principal employers of labor in some regions.

Monopsony

A single buyer of a resource or product; sometimes found in labor markets as the single buyer of labor.

A single buyer of a resource in a market is known as a **monopsony**. The monopsonist buyer has market power because rather than purchase all that it is willing and able to purchase at a market-determined price, the monopsony faces an upward-sloping supply curve. From along this curve it seeks the price that yields the profit-maximizing quantity of resource employment.

Consider Figure 13.4. The firm sells its product in a competitive market; its marginal revenue product or demand curve for labor is MRP_L. Since it is the only buyer of labor in the market, it faces an upward-sloping market supply curve of labor, S_L. To hire more labor, the firm must offer higher wages. Under these circumstances, the marginal factor cost of labor is no longer equal to the wage rate. The increase in total cost that results from hiring one more unit of labor is greater than the price paid for one more unit. And to attract one more unit of labor, the firm must offer a higher wage to all units of labor employed. This concept is summarized by the MFC_L curve in Figure 13.4, which lies to the left and above the supply curve of labor, S_L.

The firm will hire all units of labor that add more to revenue than to cost. Thus the monopsonist firm will maximize profit by hiring labor up to the point where MFC_L equals MRP_L. The monopsonist hires L_m amount of labor and must pay wage W_m to attract that amount of labor.

The monopsonist wage and level of employment may be compared with those of a competitive labor market under the same circumstances. If MRP_L in Figure 13.4 had been the summation of many firms' demand curves for labor, then competitive

FIGURE 13.4

Monopsony in the Labor Market

A monopsonist faces an upward-sloping supply curve of labor, S_L. It maximizes profit by hiring the amount of labor that equates its marginal factor cost (MFC_L) to its marginal revenue product for labor (MRP_L). The monopsonist's levels of employment and wage, L_m and W_m, fall below the competitive levels, L_c and W_c.

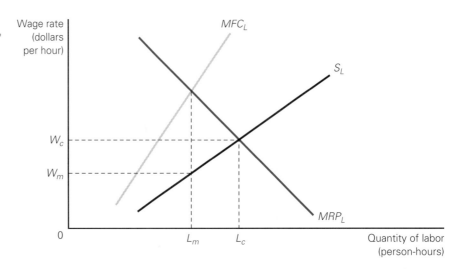

forces would have forced wages to W_c and employment to L_c. Under the same supply and MRP_L conditions, the presence of monopsony results in lower wages and lower employment.

The fact that the monopsonist pays a wage rate less than the MRP_L is known as **exploitation of labor.** If individuals are not being paid the value of their marginal product, then the monopsonist is extracting value from them. In the small regional markets of early days, monopsonists were actually exploiting the immobility of labor. As single employers, firms were able to pay lower-than-competitive wages in isolated areas because the cost of transportation was very high. It was very difficult for individuals to move around the country to work for other employers.

The more mobile an employee, the greater the number of potential employers and the more elastic the labor supply. Computers and the ability to work and transact globally from one's home are also affecting labor supply elasticity. Today, the costs of transportation are relatively low. The opportunity cost of moving from one side of the country to another or commuting to all firms within a 60-mile radius is lower today than it was a century ago, although the costs of moving may be rising along with the increase in dual-career households. It is extremely rare to find an individual who has only one potential employer. (However, see the Application "Should College Football Players Be Paid? The NCAA Monopsony" at the conclusion of this chapter for an exception.)

Exploitation of labor
A situation in which the wage rate paid to an input is less than the input's marginal revenue product.

Bilateral Monopoly and the Need for Bargaining

Bilateral monopoly
A market in which there is only one buyer and only one seller of a resource or product.

If there is a monopoly in a market, then the single seller has the power to determine the price of output. If there is monopsony in a market, then the single buyer has the power to determine the price of output. But in some markets, **bilateral monopoly**—a single seller and a single buyer—could exist. In such a case, what determines the price?

The price in a bilateral monopoly market cannot be determined theoretically. No competitive forces determine a single price, and the seller has a preferred price that is higher than the buyer's preferred price. However, if the maximum price the buyer is willing to pay is greater than the minimum price the seller is willing to accept, then a bargain can be reached. Bargaining between two parties is the process by which price is determined.

Consider a labor market with bilateral monopoly. Suppose a monopsony exists in an isolated mining town with only one employer, a mining firm. The firm must rely on the town's supply of labor. As Figure 13.5 illustrates, the mining firm maximizes profit by hiring L_m workers and by paying wage W_m. The workers, though, are unhappy with wage W_m and decide to form a union. They manage to sign up workers of all skill levels throughout the community to the union, maximizing their bargaining strength.

The wage most preferred by the union is not clear. If the union's goal is to maximize the total wage bill, then it will prefer a wage such as W_u.

There is a maximum wage that the union can obtain. Any wage above the maximum would result in no union employment at all because of the high production costs that would be imposed. If wages are too high, then the monopsony may actually go out of business, turn entirely to substitutes for the union labor, or relocate in a lower-cost area. The union's ability to extract value from the firm is limited by the mobility of the firm, just as the firm's ability to extract value from the workers is limited by the mobility of the workers.

FIGURE 13.5

Bilateral Monopoly

When a monopsonist employer chooses lower-than-competitive wage W_m and a monopoly union chooses higher-than-competitive wage W_u, the wage cannot be determined theoretically. But it can be determined by bargaining, and it will be between W_u and W_m. Although the wage is indeterminate, there is an incentive for the two parties to agree on employment level L_m because joint profits are maximized at that employment level.

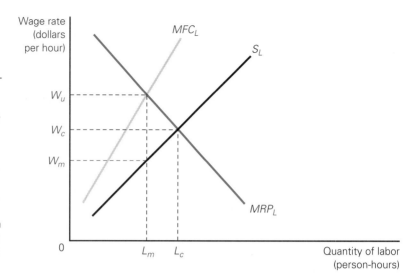

Collective Bargaining

When labor bargains collectively with a monopsonist, the final wage will be somewhere between the wage chosen by the monopsonist (W_m in Figure 13.5) and the wage most preferred by the union (W_u in the figure). The party that comes closest to establishing its goal is the one with the best bargaining strength. In **collective bargaining,** all buyers and all sellers of labor act as a unit to enhance their bargaining power.

Collective bargaining

The process whereby buyers and sellers negotiate, rather than compete individually, in order to determine a wage rate.

Bilateral monopoly brings forth the need to negotiate. The absence of competition on both sides of the market creates a situation in which neither employers nor workers are able to dictate a wage rate. Yet each year collective bargaining contracts are negotiated that cover the pay and working conditions for 6 to 9 million American workers. Unions definitely limit wage competition among their members in many markets, but are there that many monopsonies?

In some industrial unions, such as the autoworkers' union, the union representatives bargain with a single firm. Under these circumstances, a firm that employs a very large percentage of a union's members does have some monopsony power. Wages cannot be dictated by the union. On the other hand, craft unions' members are employed by many firms. Hundreds of firms in different sectors of the United States employ carpenters, for example. It might seem that a union would not have to negotiate with an employer that has no monopsony power. However, the potential employers of craft union members may form a coalition, a buyer's cartel, to negotiate with unions as a single buyer of labor. Thus, when labor bargains as a unit to gain market power, previously competitive employers would do the same. When wage contracts are determined by bargaining negotiations, there is, in effect, a bilateral monopoly in the market.

Strikes

The ability of a union to achieve higher wages depends on its bargaining strength, and its strongest weapon is the strike. When firms fail to meet labor's

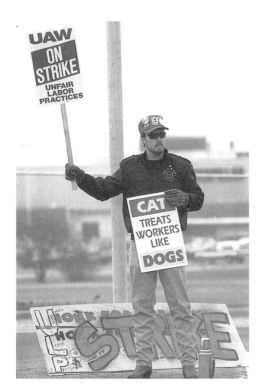

Caterpillar strikers demand benefits and job security.

Strike

A collective refusal to work at the current wage or under current working conditions.

Binding arbitration

An agreement between the buyers and sellers of labor to allow a third party to determine the conditions of a work contract.

demands for a higher wage or any other demand, the union can withhold the labor services of its members. Such a refusal to work, or **strike,** can severely limit or even eliminate the firm's ability to continue production. By striking, a union withholds not only its members' labor but also that of other unions who respect the picket line. Under some circumstances, members of nonnegotiating unions also withhold their labor from the negotiating firm. A firm's failure to concede to labor's demands can therefore be very costly. Of course, conceding to higher wages is costly as well.

Yet the strike is a double-edged sword. Not only does it cost firms income, but union members lose income as well. A strike is not attractive to either party, but it is the best weapon labor has to force firms to accept the union wage. The union must decide if the lost income is worth its members' increased future income.

Similarly, firms have the power to reject employment at the union's desired wage. By doing so, a firm in effect refuses to hire labor at a particular wage or any higher wage. In a sense, the firm strikes against employing labor at too high a wage rate.

The potential costliness of a strike leads to serious bargaining by both management and labor because both sides have significant incentives to arrive at a new labor contract without a strike. In fact, negotiation is the general pattern of collective bargaining in the United States. Each year, some 120,000 labor contracts are renegotiated in collective bargaining processes. In more than 96 percent of these cases, labor and management arrive at a new agreement without recourse to a strike.

Table 13.1 provides some data about strikes since 1950. Perhaps the most relevant statistic in the table is the percentage of working time lost to strikes. As the data make clear, this figure has fallen over time and generally constitutes less than 0.05 percent of total working time, a figure far less than the time lost to worker absenteeism each year. The fact that little working time is lost to strikes means that strikes are a powerful union weapon. The threat of a strike may be sufficient to make collective bargaining work smoothly.

Sometimes, if negotiations are not successful, both parties can agree to **binding arbitration.** Such an agreement brings in a third party acceptable to labor and management to make a decision that both sides must abide by. Binding arbitration is often used for public sector union disputes because public employees usually are forbidden by law to strike. Public sector strikes in basic service activities—such as commuter transportation, garbage collection, teaching, and fire and police protection—have the potential to bring the economy to a halt. If essential services provided by government cease to be performed because of a strike, much private economic activity will cease as well.

In private sector strikes, lost output can be made up to some extent if workers work overtime after the strike is settled. Moreover, substitute products and services are available to consumers during a private sector strike. Purchasers of new cars can buy used cars or drive their present cars until an autoworkers' strike is over, for example.

TABLE 13.1

Work Stoppages Involving 1000 Workers or More, 1960–1997

As these data for selected years since 1960 show, strikes have played a steadily declining role in the lives of American workers and the U.S. economy over the last four decades.

Year	Number	Workers Involved	Idle Days	Percentage of Work Time Lost
1960	222	896	13,260	0.09
1965	268	999	15,140	0.10
1970	381	2468	52,761	0.29
1975	235	965	17,563	0.09
1980	187	795	20,844	0.09
1985	54	324	7,079	0.03
1990	44	185	5,926	0.02
1991	40	392	4,584	0.02
1992	35	364	3,989	0.01
1993	35	182	3,981	0.01
1994	45	322	5,021	0.02
1995	31	192	5,771	0.02
1996	37	273	4,887	0.02
1997	29	339	4,497	0.01

Source: Statistical Abstract of the U.S. 1998, 115th edition (Washington D.C.: U.S. Government Printing Office, 1998), p. 443.

Public Choice and Union Bargaining

The bargaining power of unions and management is affected by legislation, which in turn is affected by the political environment. Legislation can favor either management or labor in the negotiating process. Until the 1930s, the struggle between management and labor in the United States was tilted toward management. The strike was not a strong labor weapon, because employers could obtain a court order against a strike. Employees suspected of having union sympathies could be fired or roughed up by company thugs. New employees could be required to sign a "yellow-dog" contract, which forbade the employees from joining the union.

The New Deal response to the Great Depression changed all of this. The Norris–La Guardia Act (1932) and Wagner Act (1935) denied management the use of antiunion tactics and granted labor the right to organize and engage in collective bargaining in a legal framework regulated by the National Labor Relations Board (NLRB). The NLRB has five members appointed by the president for five-year terms. Its functions include ruling on unfair labor practices, settling jurisdictional disputes among unions over bargaining rights, and calling for plant elections at the request of workers. These legal changes lent a tremendous impetus to the growth of the union movement and gave unions a favorable environment for pursuing their ends.

The post–World War II era was characterized by much industrial unrest. Unions showed little self-restraint or discipline, so Congress tilted the balance

Right-to-work law

A law that prevents unions from requiring that individual workers join the union as a condition of employment by a particular firm.

between labor and management back toward management. The Taft–Hartley Act, passed in 1947, allowed states to enact **right-to-work laws,** which forbid unions from coercing workers into their ranks. It added several other constraints on union behavior, such as outlawing strikes by government workers and secondary boycotts, by which the union would set up picket lines against other suppliers of the company being struck. After the Taft–Hartley Act, charges of union corruption and ties to organized crime led to further legislation to regulate union behavior. The Landrum–Griffin Act, passed in 1959, contained various provisions to ensure that unions were honestly managed. Among other things, this law required the filing of financial reports by union officers and the auditing of union finances.

Even in the face of such restraining legislation, the labor union has assumed a position of influence and power in the U.S. economy. No longer are unions viewed as weak associations of workers fighting for a better standard of living for their members. In some respects, unions are best thought of as strong special-interest groups that are proficient at obtaining legislative favors such as protective tariffs. On the other hand, union political power is sometimes used to promote general-interest legislation. Civil rights and welfare laws, Social Security, and similar programs have been strongly supported by organized labor.

The Union as a Political Interest Group

Unions are an ideal conduit for political activity in a number of respects. Once a union is formed, it is relatively inexpensive to use the organization to do more than simply engage in collective bargaining. For example, unions can expand their efforts into the political arena fairly cheaply. For this reason unions have long been a powerful political force in the United States. Unions support and lobby for public policies that directly or indirectly benefit their members. Two simple cases illustrate this point.

First, unions are typically against free international trade. Free trade inhibits the ability of unions and domestic firms to pass along union wage demands in the form of higher prices. Not surprisingly, then, unions have been among the most outspoken critics of the North American Free Trade Agreement with Mexico and Canada.

Second, labor unions always support minimum-wage laws and increases in the minimum wage. Although union officials often use terms such as justice and fairness in explaining their position on this issue, it is worth noting that minimum-wage laws effectively protect union members from competition with lower-priced labor. Such laws raise the legal wage required to employ workers, thereby lessening the ability of some workers to compete for jobs by offering their services at lower wages. One of the effects of minimum-wage laws, therefore, is to increase the power of labor unions by restricting labor market competition. For example, a minimum-wage law will reduce regional wage differentials, making it less attractive for firms to migrate to a lower-paying area and employ nonunion labor. In such a fashion, minimum-wage laws indirectly protect union labor. Unions were strongly behind the 1996 increase in the minimum wage from $4.25 to $5.15 per hour passed by Congress and signed by President Clinton. (There is fairly constant pressure on politicians to raise the minimum wage.)

These are only two examples of the politics of unionism. As with all groups able to organize and transfer wealth, unions' political efforts are designed to increase the well-being of union members.

THE IMPACT OF UNIONS ON LABOR'S SHARE OF TOTAL INCOME

Primarily, a general increase in wages requires an increase in the productivity of workers. An increase in productivity can occur in a variety of ways. The quality of tools and other physical capital used by workers can increase, workers' skill levels can be raised through education and experience, innovation or better management can increase worker productivity, and so on. Higher real wages for all workers can be realized only if the output of goods and services in the economy is increased. It would seem to follow that unions can increase the wages of all workers only if they increase the general level of productivity in the economy. While such an impact of unions is not out of the question, it is hard to imagine how it might happen.

Who pays for the benefits that unions obtain through bargaining power, legislation, and other means? The naive answer is that, of course, employers pay, but the evidence suggests otherwise. In fact, economic analysis indicates that consumers and nonunion employees pay for the benefits that unions obtain for their members.

Consumers pay because higher union wages mean higher costs for firms that employ union labor. If these firms produce in a competitive market for their output, output prices will rise to reflect the higher cost of union labor. Basically, the same result holds if the firm that hires union labor has monopoly power, although the monopolist may bargain with the union over the level of monopoly profits earned. In either case, higher costs caused by union wages lead to higher prices. Consumers thus pay part of the tab for higher union wages.

Nonunion employees pay because higher union wages lead firms to produce less output and to substitute nonhuman capital for union labor. Both of these effects cause the level of employment in unionized industries to fall. In other words, as we saw in the models of how unions increase the relative wages of their members, these are cases where union bargaining power leads to a lower employment level for labor in the unionized industry. The workers who do not make it into the union must seek employment elsewhere in the economy. This increases the supply of labor to alternative, nonunion employments and drives down nonunion wages. Thus, nonunion employees also pay part of the tab for higher union wages.

It can be argued on the basis of economic theory that employers do not generally pay for all union gains. Consumers and nonunion employees share the burden because the price of union-made goods rises and the wage rate for nonunion labor falls. Since this effect on nonunion labor covers about three-fourths of the labor force, the resource allocation effects of unions can be substantial in the aggregate.

As international trade increases, the ability of unions and firms to affect consumer prices becomes more limited. Free trade thus hampers the market power of unions and firms and, in general, protects consumers and nonunion workers. As noted above, unions are not supportive of free trade agreements.

Table 13.2 provides some data about the behavior over time of the share of national income that goes to labor. Two ways of measuring labor's share are shown. The second column measures total employee compensation (wage and salaries) plus the employer's share of the Social Security tax as a percentage of national income. This series shows a slight upward trend since World War II, a rise that has been attributed to a decline in the number of self-employed workers over this period, primarily in agriculture.

The third column in the table adds the income of self-employed persons—such as business proprietors, lawyers, and accountants—to employee compensation. Self-

TABLE 13.2

Labor's Share of National Income

The percentage of the nation's real output that labor receives has increased slightly since World War II. This increase is attributed to a decrease in small owner-managed firms rather than to union activities.

Year	Total Employee Compensation (Including Employer Contribution for Social Insurance) (percent of national income)	Total Employee Compensation plus Self-Employment Income (percent of national income)
1960	69.0	81.1
1965	67.5	77.9
1970	73.5	83.0
1975	72.8	82.1
1980	73.7	81.6
1985	71.7	79.6
1986	72.5	80.3
1987	72.3	80.3
1988	71.7	79.8
1989	71.7	79.8
1990	72.0	80.1
1991	72.6	80.5
1992	73.0	81.5
1993	72.4	80.1
1994	71.7	80.2
1995	71.0	79.2
1996	70.5	78.9
1997	70.5	78.8
1998	71.1	79.4

Sources: U.S. Department of Commerce, *Survey of Current Business,* various issues; Council of Economic Advisers, *Economic Report of the President* (Washington, D.C.: U.S. Government Printing Office, 1999), p. 358.

employment compensation is clearly income that goes to labor. When we look at this more inclusive concept of labor's share of national income, we see that it has been virtually constant for almost forty years. Thus, even when labor union strength grew in the United States, we do not find any evidence that labor's share of national income rose. While labor unions have increased the wages of their members relative to the wages of nonunion workers, there is no evidence to suggest that they have made all workers better off in terms of their share of national income.

The fact is that higher real wages for workers can come about only through increases in worker productivity. Workers in the United States earn high wages because their productivity is high. Their wages can rise only if the output of goods and services in the American economy is increased. All things being equal, it is the level of productivity that explains real wages.

CONCLUSION

The goals of unions are easy to understand. The members want more income, greater income security, and more pleasant working conditions than the market provides. Their ability to achieve these goals is limited by many factors, including the supplies of competing inputs, the monopsony power of employers, and the political power of unions. Unions have provided their members with higher wages and better job security, but they also provide something more.

The union's role extends beyond an economic wage and employment analysis to the plant, where the union provides workers with a set of rules and representation to settle disputes with employers. This presence of the union on the job cannot be discounted as a primary source of nonpecuniary benefits to union members. Such benefits accrue to workers in the form of greater job security, a feeling of power and dignity at work, and less alienation from their work. These are important aspects of work in modern factories and offices, and the union's role in providing workplace representation is a powerful force for creating greater worker satisfaction and thus greater productivity.

There is much concern today over the meaningfulness of work. Workers are said to be alienated and bored by assembly-line types of jobs. In this respect, the role of the union as an arbitrator of workplace rules and procedures will probably become increasingly important. Workers may be willing to trade off some wage gains to obtain changes in the way their work is done. If so, unions are certain to seek more meaningful jobs and factory arrangements for workers in future labor contracts.

APPLICATION

Should College Football Players Be Paid? The NCAA Monopsony

College athletics in the United States are governed by rules established by the National Collegiate Athletic Association (NCAA), a collection of colleges and universities that compete in intercollegiate athletics. The NCAA establishes and enforces the rules under which college players can be recruited and compensated for their play. The NCAA rules are very complicated and regulate all aspects of the player's relationship with the school. The bottom line, however, is that the NCAA regulations create a collusive agreement among colleges and universities to act as a monopsony in the purchase of high school athletes' services. In other words, the NCAA has established a buyers' cartel for athletic labor.

Colleges and universities are the only buyers of high school football and basketball players. (Baseball has minor professional leagues in which high school players can work and be paid for their services; many tennis players turn professional at a young age, skipping college competition altogether.) Even though a talented college football or basketball player may generate a lot of ticket sales and television revenues for the school, NCAA rules forbid the player from being paid a wage (beyond tuition, room, board, and incidentals) equal to the marginal revenue product of the player. (Marginal revenue product is the increase in school revenues realized by having the particular athlete playing for the school.) Marginal revenue product may be small for a benchwarmer, but it can run into the millions (TV revenue, sold-out stadiums, bowl and postseason tournament revenues, bumper stickers, and so on) for the services of an All-American basketball player or a Heisman Trophy–winning football star. Instead, the player can only be given a scholarship, room and board, and certain other min-

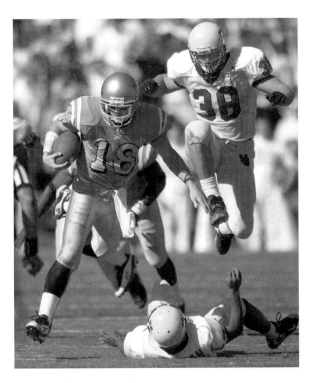

Payment of wages to college football players and other athletes, though much defended by college presidents, have a clear economic justification.

imal living allowances. Even the details of a player's summer or off-season employment are tightly regulated by the NCAA.

The NCAA system is a monopsony because (1) it is an agreement among schools to create a single system for compensating athletes, and (2) it functions so as to pay athletes less than they contribute to school athletic revenues.

Just like in an output or sellers' cartel, the NCAA agreement to hold down players' wages must be enforced. Individual schools will find it in their interest to cheat on the agreement by offering good players "illegal" inducements (cars, money) to play for them. Clearly, it is advantageous for any given school to behave in this way if all other schools follow the rules. Such a strategy will lead to the recruitment of better players, athletic success, and larger revenues. Cheaters must therefore be rooted out and punished by the NCAA. This is done in a variety of ways, such as taking away valuable bowl, tournament, and TV opportunities from violators or reducing the number of "legal" scholarships the cheating school can offer in the future.

There is no particular reason that college athletics could not be treated like any other form of student employment where the students are paid a wage for their work. What would be so bad about doing this with college football and basketball players? Colleges do not want to pay competitive market wages to their student-athletes, since this would erode their profits from athletic events. Of course, one should not downplay the ideals of amateur athletics and the amateur athlete. However, there is little economic justification for not paying the full value for the work done by student-athletes. A wage scale, for example, for college football players would bring into the open what are currently under-the-table practices, clean up the recruiting process considerably, and allow young college athletes to accrue savings.

In any event, the NCAA has established a monopsony that functions to benefit colleges and universities at the expense of student-athletes and their families (who are often from low-income and minority backgrounds). One would therefore predict that the most vocal defenders of the NCAA buyers' cartel will be college presidents. Students can easily check this prediction by soliciting the view of their president and administration on this matter; college officials will defend their position on the grounds that playing for pay would somehow corrupt the ideals of the amateur student-athlete. However, what is the difference between the basketball player and the student who works the graveyard shift at a local radio station to pay for school? Should all student jobs be banned? And what about graduate students, professors, and coaches?

QUESTIONS

Which type of schools, low-tuition or high-tuition, would you expect to violate the NCAA regulations more often? What will stadium size have to do with NCAA violations? What is the role of coaches in the NCAA cartel?

SUMMARY

1. A labor union is a group of workers in a craft, industry, or government job who organize to gain market power.

2. Labor unions attempt to improve the economic welfare of their members by increasing wages, decreasing the elasticity of demand for their services, and increasing the demand for their members' labor through a variety of activities.

3. Monopsony exists when there is a lack of competition in the employment of labor. A single buyer may force wages below the competitive level.

4. In a bilateral monopoly in a labor market, the wage is determined by the relative strength of the bargainers.

5. A union's ability to achieve its goals is in part determined by its bargaining strength. A union's ability to strike is its strongest negotiating tool.

6. It is estimated that unions have increased the wages of their members relative to nonunion workers in similar occupations.

7. Union activities have not increased all labor's share of total income. Gains made by union labor have generally been at the expense of employers, nonunion labor, and consumers.

KEY TERMS

labor union
craft union
industrial union
public employees' union

total wage bill
monopsony
exploitation of labor
bilateral monopoly

collective bargaining
strike
binding arbitration
right-to-work law

QUESTIONS FOR REVIEW AND DISCUSSION

1. How do craft unions increase wages for their members? What happens to the people who are not allowed into a craft union?

2. If industrial unions allow into the union anyone who wishes to enter, how can they increase wages? Could an industrial union in an isolated mining town increase both wages and employment?

3. Suppose the United States exports beef to Japan and imports cars from Japan. If autoworkers persuade Congress to impose a tariff on Japanese cars, what happens to the incomes of cattle ranchers and ranch hands?

4. Why do unions want to decrease the elasticity of demand for their members? How do they do so?

5. What is a monopsony? Does the existence of labor unions promote the existence of monopsonies?

6. It is frequently suggested that firms exploit women in the labor force. Monopsonists' power to exploit is based on the immobility of labor. Are women less mobile than men?

7. In the former Soviet Union, there was only one potential employer—the government. Did the former Soviet Union have the power to exploit workers? Could workers avoid exploitation?

8. Why are unions and union employers forced to negotiate wages while nonunion wages are determined without negotiation?

9. Are union wages closer to the monopsony wage or to the wage that maximizes the wage bill?

10. Suppose that a union is successful at organizing only part of the laborers in an industry. Do you predict that the union will be strong or weak? Why?

11. Why do you think unions favor minimum-wage laws?

12. How do the following affect the elasticity of demand for union labor: elasticity of demand for a product, the availability of substitutes, and union labor as a proportion of total costs?

13. What is bilateral monopoly? How is price determined in this model?

PROBLEMS

1. Suppose that all of the nurses in a particular state are employed in hospitals and nursing homes and that all earn equally competitive wages. Now suppose that some of the nurses in hospitals decide to form a union and to restrict membership in the union. Further assume that they have the legal authority of the state government to do so. As a result of these actions, nurses must be in the union to be employed in hospitals. Using supply and demand curves, show what happens to the wages in the union and nonunion nursing markets after unionization.

2. We tend to think of unions as those involving manufacturing or government services. Many professions, however, take on certain union characteristics. Consider the legal profession, for example. Entry is restricted and returns are raised. What sort of techniques and policies might lawyers and the legal profession use in order to establish and protect their "union"?

WORKING WITH THE WEB

1. Strikes are one of the most powerful tools used by unions. To get an idea of some strikes that have occurred in the past, go to http://www.igc.apc.org/strike/archive.html and scroll through the listed strikes that have been resolved. Are wages the only cause of the strikes?

2. Union membership spans a variety of occupations as well as a variety of demographic factors. Go to http://www.bls.gov/news.release/union2.nws.htm and read the summary on union statistics for 1998.
   a. What occupational group has the highest rate of union membership?
   b. Are men and women equally likely to be union members?
   c. By what percentage do union workers outpace their nonunion counterparts in terms of earnings when working full-time?
   d. What percentage of the private sector labor force is unionized? How does this compare with the unionization in the government sector?

3. Monopsony is said to exist when there is a single buyer of a resource, such as labor. A historical example of monopsony was the case of being the only employer in a town. If that was the case, workers who wished to offer their labor in exchange for a wage had no alternatives. As a result, they were paid less than the revenue they generated for the firm. A similar situation has been said to exist in Major League Baseball. To learn more, go to http://www.economicsamerica.org/econedlink/newsline/sports/app2.html.
   a. What is offered as evidence of the existence of a monopsonistic market in baseball?
   b. What is offered as an alternative system to the current draft and contract arrangement? In terms of salary, how would such a system benefit players?
   c. Does the salary data support the claim of Major League Baseball as a monopsony?

14

Capital,
Land,
and
Entrepreneurship

Thus far, we have looked at labor and its corresponding factor payment, wages. In this chapter we look at the other factors of production, and their corresponding factor payments, including capital and interest, land and economic rent, and entrepreneurship and economic profits. As we will see, the returns to these other factors of production can also be explained by the marginal productivity theory of input prices. After reading Chapter 14 you should understand

- that the choice between consuming and saving is a key factor in producing larger quantities of goods and services.
- how the rate of interest is determined.
- the concept of economic rent and the process by which land is priced.
- the nature of entrepreneurship, including the role of entrepreneurs in any economy and the rewards entrepreneurs get.

THE ROLE OF CAPITAL

Wealthy societies consume, or use, goods and services at an ever-increasing rate. Think, for instance, of the rate at which automobiles have become available in this country. Relatively few Americans owned cars sixty years ago, and most of those proud owners were happy to keep the same car for years. Today, many of us own more than one car, and most of us change cars at least every four or five years. Since consumption is possible only through production, the basis of a wealthy society is not its ability to consume but its ability to produce, to transform raw materials into more useful goods and services through the application of human skills and physical capital such as tools and factories. Societies that are better at this transformation are able to reach higher levels of wealth and to consume more.

Roundabout Production and Capital Formation

Economic behavior is forward-looking. The availability of the food we eat today is due to the foresight of farmers in the past who undertook the appropriate productive actions. The food we will eat tomorrow depends on actions farmers take now. A simple analogy illustrates this point.

Imagine Robinson Crusoe trying to survive alone on a windswept island in the middle of the ocean. Crusoe's economy is primitive. He lives by fishing with a simple wooden spear that he found on the beach. With his spear Crusoe can catch 5 pounds of fish in about 10 hours of fishing. Suppose that one day Crusoe decides to improve his fishing technique by weaving a fishing net.

Crusoe takes a day off to build the net. His opportunity cost of building the net is the fish that he would have caught during this day by fishing with his spear. Assuming that it takes 10 hours to build the net, the opportunity cost of the net to Crusoe is 5 pounds of fish.

Crusoe's purpose in building the net is to catch more fish in the future. That is, he hopes the net will enable him to catch more than 5 pounds in 10 hours. The anticipation of more production and therefore more consumption in the future drives Crusoe to a **roundabout production** of fish.

Of course, Crusoe must have some way to support himself during the period that he stops fishing to weave the net. He provides for his needs during this time by **saving.** If he consumes 5 pounds of fish every 10 hours and it takes 10 hours to make a net, Crusoe must set aside 5 pounds of fish to support himself while making the net. To do so, he could fish extra hours for several days, or he could eat only 4 pounds each day for 5 days. The hallmark of saving is some form of current sacrifice in anticipation of a higher level of future consumption. More hours worked means fewer hours for current leisure; fewer fish eaten in the present mean fewer calories consumed. However Crusoe manages to save fish, his planned one-day abstinence from spearfishing leads to saving and to a greater yield of fish.

What is Crusoe's incentive to abstain? Suppose that with the net he can catch 25 pounds of fish in 10 hours and that the net will last indefinitely. By abstaining from spearfishing for 10 hours, at a cost of 5 pounds of fish, Crusoe is able to raise his daily catch by 20 pounds. The increase is even more significant in the long run: For an investment of a mere 5 pounds of fish, Crusoe raises his weekly catch from 35 pounds to 175 pounds, an increase of 140 pounds per week. This particular act of saving and investment of resources to produce more capital is especially profitable. Indeed, even if the net wears out every so often, Crusoe will be able to afford to take 10 hours to make a new net in anticipation of similar rates of return in the future.

This simple example has relevance to a modern economy. In a modern economy individuals specialize in their activities. They don't spend part of the day fishing and part of the day making rods and reels. But this specialization does not change any of the essential features of what is called capital formation.

The term **capital formation** refers to the process of building capital goods and adding to the capital stock in the economy. Capital goods are things such as

Roundabout production
The current production of capital goods so that greater amounts of consumption goods can be produced in the future.

Saving
The act of forgoing present consumption in order to increase future consumption.

Capital formation
An increase in the stock of capital due to roundabout production.

machines and implements that are used to produce final goods and services. The **capital stock** of an economy is the amount of capital goods that exists at a given point in time. To increase capital stock, producers must resort to the use and production of capital goods as a means of achieving greater output in the future. Saving, or the abstinence from present consumption, is required for capital formation to take place.

Another important feature of capital is that it does not automatically reproduce itself. Instead, capital goods automatically decrease in productivity or value over time, a process known as **depreciation.** This wearing out of capital goods cannot be stopped. The capital goods or capital stock of a society must be repaired and replaced over time if the society is to continue to grow and experience high levels of consumption. This is one of the primary problems of economics: maintaining and increasing the ability to produce.

Capital consumption is the opposite of capital formation. Present consumption is increased temporarily at the cost of a reduction in the future rate of consumption. Suppose that a lumber company owns trees ranging in age from 1 to 25 years. Assume that it cuts down one thousand 25-year-old trees and plants one thousand seedlings each year. As long as external circumstances do not change, this forest can yield one thousand 25-year-old trees annually. For a while, however, the yield from the forest can be increased by harvesting some of the 24-year-old trees in addition to the regular harvest, then dipping into the stock of 23-year-old trees the next year, and so on. Cut in this manner, the amount of timber harvested will increase for a while. Still, the time will come when the total output of the forest will necessarily decline. Capital in the form of younger trees has been used up to increase current output, so the future output of timber must fall. This is capital consumption.

The Rate of Interest

Saving and capital formation depend on the willingness of individuals to pass up current consumption to achieve greater consumption in the future. In other words, individuals must abstain from current consumption to provide the flow of saving that is used to produce capital goods. Economists stress that an individual's willingness to abstain from current consumption is related to his or her **rate of time preference.** Time preference is the degree of patience that an individual has in forgoing present consumption in order to save. A person with a high rate of time preference has a strong preference for current rather than future consumption. Most individuals have positive rates of time preference; that is, they prefer present to future consumption. Since people prefer to consume now rather than later, they must be paid a price, or be rewarded, for waiting. This price is called **interest.**

The concept of interest has two related meanings. In the first sense, interest refers to returns on investments. A person who saves $100 in a passbook account earns 4 percent interest on saving. A firm that invests $1000 in a new piece of machinery earns $200 more in revenue annually because of the resulting improvement in productivity. The firm's investment thus yields 20 percent interest. In these terms, interest is the amount individuals are willing to *receive* in order to sacrifice current consumption; it is a payment for their abstinence, or waiting to consume.

Interest is also the price that individuals are willing to *pay* to obtain a good or service now rather than later. A consumer who wants a car today might pay 13 percent interest for a loan from the bank. A firm that wants a new plant might pay 10 percent interest to get the necessary financing.

Capital stock
The total amount of capital goods that exists in an economy at any point in time.

Depreciation
The wearing out of capital goods that occurs with usage over time.

Capital consumption
A decrease in the capital stock; occurs when the rate of depreciation is greater than the rate of capital formation.

Rate of time preference
The percent increase in future consumption over present consumption that is necessary to just induce an individual to be indifferent between present and future consumption.

Interest
The compensation to savers for the act of saving (forgoing present consumption) or the payment made by borrowers; when measured as a percent of the amount borrowed or lent, it is referred to as an interest rate.

Interest is not just a monetary phenomenon. Whether paid or received, interest is based on the fact that people prefer to consume and invest now rather than later. Moreover, the rate of interest reflects the rate of time preference in the economy. The more impatient people are, the higher the rate of interest must be to induce them to save and to create capital goods.

Demand and Supply of Loanable Funds

The rate of interest is determined in the market for loanable funds. It is, in effect, the price of loanable funds. Like other markets, the market for loanable funds has a demand side and a supply side. (For more on the market for loanable funds, see the Application "Trading Property Rights: Stocks and Bonds" at the conclusion of this chapter.)

Demand for loanable funds

A curve or schedule that shows the various amounts individuals are willing and able to borrow at different interest rates.

The **demand for loanable funds** arises from three sources. Consumers demand loanable funds because they want to consume more now than their current incomes will permit. Loans to these individuals are called consumption loans. They are made for myriad reasons. Individuals may want to take a vacation now and pay for it on time, borrow to tide themselves over a temporary decline in income, or borrow to buy cars or household appliances.

The second source of demand for loanable funds is desire for investment loans. Investors borrow to finance the construction and use of capital goods and methods of production that are expected to be productive. Firms borrow funds to build new plants and to purchase new equipment in the expectation that such investments will increase profits.

A third source of loanable funds demand is the government. Governments at all levels—local, state, and federal—demand funds to cover deficits (when tax receipts do not cover government expenditures), to finance road construction and schools, and to service debt. This demand is added to private demands for loanable funds for consumption and investing purposes.

The sum of the demand for consumption, investment, and government loans equals the total demand for loanable funds. The law of demand applies to the demand for loanable funds just as it does to any other commodity (see Figure 14.1). The price one must pay to borrow funds for consumption or investment loans is the interest rate. According to the law of demand, the amount of funds demanded is inversely related to the interest rate. As the interest rate falls, the cost of borrowing money to finance the earlier availability of consumption and capital goods falls. Other things being equal, we thus expect to see more borrowing when the interest rate falls. At a lower rate of interest, consumers will expand current consumption, and more investment projects will appear to be profitable.

Supply of loanable funds

A curve or schedule that shows the various amounts individuals are willing and able to lend or save at different rates.

In Figure 14.1, the **supply of loanable funds,** S, is provided by savers. These are individuals or firms who are willing to consume less than their present earnings in order to set aside something for the future. As the interest rate—in this case, the return on investment—rises, more and more individuals and firms will be enticed to save; that is, they will forgo current consumption in order to consume even more in the future. Thus, the quantity supplied of loanable funds varies positively with the interest rate offered to savers.

The intersection of the demand and supply curves for loanable funds in Figure 14.1 yields an equilibrium interest rate and the equilibrium level of loanable funds. At i and Q, the market for loanable funds is in equilibrium, and the plans of borrowers are compatible with the plans of lenders. At interest rates above i,

FIGURE 14.1

Determination of Interest Rates

D and *S* are the demand and supply curves for loanable funds. The market for loanable funds reaches equilibrium at *i* and *Q*, where the plans of borrowers and lenders are compatible. That is, for a given interest rate, the amount that borrowers want to borrow and the amount that lenders want to lend are equal.

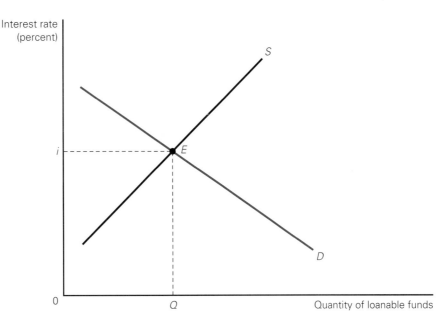

there will be an excess supply of savings, putting pressure on the interest rate to fall. Below *i*, there will be an excess demand for loanable funds, putting pressure on the interest rate to rise. (See the Focus "Should You Be Protected from High Interest Rates? Usury and Interest Groups" for an example of the effects of controlled interest rates.)

Variations Among Interest Rates   The discussion of the supply and demand for loanable funds might suggest that there is one interest rate in the economy. In reality there is a multiplicity of interest rates: the prime interest rate given to businesses with excellent credit ratings, mortgage rates offered to home buyers, credit card rates, consumer loan rates, and so on. These interest rates tend to be different. For instance, the interest rate on government bonds is generally lower than the interest rate on corporate bonds. What are some of the reasons that interest rates differ?

Risk

The chance that a borrower will default or fail to repay a loan.

Risk   The **risk** associated with particular borrowers—their likelihood to default on repaying a loan—in part accounts for the differences in interest rates. Creditors go to great lengths to ascertain the degree of this risk, and they adjust the interest rate they charge accordingly. Loans to a government agency will carry a low interest rate because the risk of default is very low. Government can use its power to tax to repay loans. On the other hand, loans to unemployed workers will carry high interest rates because the risk of default is high.

Cost of Making Loans   The cost of making loans differs. Large loans and small loans may require the same amount of accounting and bookkeeping work. The large loan will therefore be less costly to process per dollar loaned; for this reason it will carry a lower interest rate than the small loan. This distinction means, for example, that loans to large companies will carry a lower interest rate than loans to small companies.

Time   The length of time over which a loan is made will affect the rate of interest charged. The longer the term of the loan, the more things that can go wrong for the

FOCUS

Should You Be Protected from High Interest Rates? Usury and Interest Groups

Price controls have been known to all ages and all civilizations. The Roman Emperor Diocletian invoked general price and wage controls prior to the fall of the Roman Empire. During the Middle Ages, church doctrine combined with economic policy to create civil laws related to interest-taking. The laws, called usury laws, originated as early as Greek and Roman times in the belief that an uncontrolled market produced interest rates that were "too high." The laws consisted of a legal limit on the amount of interest that lenders could charge or borrowers pay. Such laws survive today in the enactments of certain U.S. state legislatures that protect borrowers with usury or "loan shark" laws and in federal regulations that establish the maximum interest rate allowable on small savings deposits.

The mechanics of the usury laws are simple; we demonstrate them in Figure 14.2. The figure shows the free-market supply and demand for loanable funds. Market equilibrium occurs at point E, where quantity demanded equals quantity supplied (Q_E) and where the equilibrium price—the market interest rate—is i_E.

What happens when the government declares that market rate i_E is too high for the poor and that henceforth the maximum rate will be i_C, a ceiling rate below i_E? At rate i_C the quantity of loanable funds demanded, Q_D (point C in Figure 14.2), exceeds the quantity supplied, Q_S (point B). A shortage of funds, BC, develops at the ceiling interest rate because banks are unwilling to lend the quantity of funds demanded at rate i_C. The available funds, Q_S, must be rationed because of the shortage. In the absence of price rationing, the process can take other forms. Unscrupulous lenders—"loan sharks"—may charge black market rates for the limited funds. Lenders may begin demanding additional collateral or better credit standing for loans at the ceiling rate, reducing their risk and making it more difficult for less creditworthy borrowers to obtain funds. Such borrowers are often the people whom the laws were designed to protect. The poor are often compelled to acquire funds from loan sharks in such circumstances. Usury laws, like all other forms of price controls, have built-in effects that often hurt those who are supposed to be the beneficiaries.

FIGURE 14.2

Interest Rate Ceiling

When a ceiling is placed on interest rates (i_C), a shortage (BC) develops, representing the difference between the quantity of funds that lending institutions are willing and able to supply (Q_S) and the quantity of funds that borrowers demand (Q_D). Without the ceiling, the forces of supply and demand interact to create equilibrium (E) between the plans of demanders and suppliers of loanable funds.

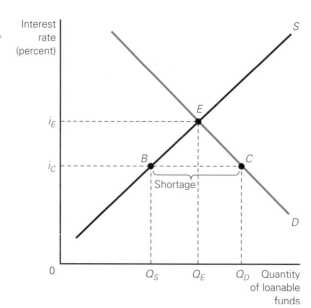

borrower. Because the risk of default rises with the length of the loan, longer-term borrowers must pay a premium for this rise. Long-term loans will carry higher interest rates than short-term loans, other things being equal. In addition to the risk factor, borrowers are willing to pay a premium for the longer availability of funds.

Nominal rate of interest

The market-determined rate of interest; usually expressed as a percentage per year of the dollar or nominal amount of the loan.

Inflation rate

The percent by which the average level of prices in an economy rises; usually expressed as a percent per year.

Real rate of interest

The nominal interest rate minus the rate of inflation; the interest measured in terms of real buying power.

Nominal and Real Rates of Interest   The **nominal rate of interest** is the interest rate set in the market for loanable funds. With inflation in the economy, the nominal rate of interest can be a misleading measure of how much borrowers pay for consumption and investment loans. Suppose that the **inflation rate,** which is the rate at which the average level of all prices in the economy rises, is 12 percent per year and that the nominal rate of interest is 17 percent. A borrower who borrows $100 will have to repay $117 in a year. However, during the year the average level of prices increases by 12 percent. The $117 paid to the lender at the end of the year will not buy the same amount of goods as the $100 made available to the borrower one year earlier. Since prices have risen by 12 percent, $100 a year ago is equivalent to $112 today. Therefore, the lender of the $100 effectively earns $5 on his or her loan ($117 minus $112), or a 5 percent real rate of return ($5 divided by $100). Thus, when the rate of inflation is factored out, the **real rate of interest** is 5 percent, or 17 percent minus 12 percent.

Lenders and borrowers will not generally be fooled by inflation. The nominal rate of interest will adjust to account for the expected inflation rate. The nominal rate of interest will include a premium to compensate lenders for the expected depreciation of the purchasing power of their principal and interest. Lenders will have to be compensated for expected inflation, or they will reduce the amount they are willing to lend. Borrowers will also recognize that they will be repaying loans with dollars of less purchasing power and will adjust the amount of interest they are willing to pay to obtain loans. In the above example, if both borrowers and lenders fully anticipate a 12 percent inflation rate, the nominal rate of interest will adjust to 17 percent. As the inflation rate changes, the nominal rate of interest will also change to reflect the level of expected inflation. The real rate of interest is the nominal rate of interest minus the expected inflation rate. In the late 1970s, the nominal rate of interest rose to over 20 percent on some types of loans, but the expected inflation rate was about 15 percent, so the real interest rate was only 5 percent.

Interest as the Return to Capital

So far we have considered interest to be the price of loanable funds. Interest may also be viewed as the return that goes to capital as a factor of production. The entrepreneur who buys a machine for $100 and makes $25 a year by using it in production earns 25 percent interest on the investment. Using this concept of interest, we can see how entrepreneurs make investment decisions.

The return earned on capital depends on the quantity of capital in use. In a world with only a few machines, the return on machines would be quite high. As the quantity of machines in use increased, the returns on the margin to each machine would decline. In Figure 14.3, the marginal return to capital is depicted as *MRC*. If a capital stock of Q_1 existed, the interest return to capital would be i_1. With a larger capital stock of Q_2, the return would fall to i_2.

To see how entrepreneurs decide how much capital to acquire, consider the marginal return to capital curve in Figure 14.3 as a demand curve. At an interest rate of i_1, entrepreneurs would prefer to hold Q_1 units of capital. If they initially had less than Q_1 units of capital, it would pay them to borrow funds at an interest

Return on Investment in Capital Goods

MRC shows the marginal return to capital. Because of diminishing returns, the return to capital declines as the capital stock increases. The *MRC* curve can also be viewed as the demand for capital curve, since it shows how large a capital stock entrepreneurs will want at each interest rate. If the interest rate falls from i_1 to i_2, entrepreneurs will undertake additional investment until the capital stock rises from Q_1 to Q_2.

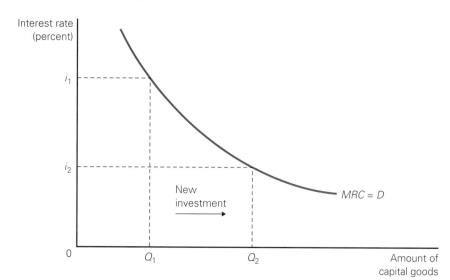

rate i_1 and use the money to obtain new capital that earned an interest rate above i_1. New capital would be acquired until the stock of capital rose to Q_1 and the return fell to i_1. Beyond that point, it no longer would be profitable to borrow money to obtain additional capital.

If the interest rate fell to i_2, firms would have an incentive to undertake new investment and increase their capital from Q_1 to Q_2 units. Other things remaining unchanged, a decline in the interest rate will lead to an increase in capital stock. A direct link exists between the market for loanable funds and the market for capital goods. An increase in the supply of loanable funds will cause the interest rate to fall, and this will lead to new investment. New investment will increase capital stock and lead to future increases in the productive capacity of the economy, causing living standards to rise.

The Nature of Returns to Owners of Capital

Individuals invest in capital goods because they expect to make a rate of return in excess of the cost of capital. The elements of this rate of return can be broken down into three categories: pure interest, risk, and profits and losses.

Pure interest

The interest associated with a risk-free loan. The interest rate that produces pure interest is called the risk-free interest rate.

Pure Interest   Capital investment yields a return called **pure interest,** the interest rate that must be paid to induce saving when the lender bears little or no risk. Think of pure interest this way: You have a sum of money, and you're trying to decide whether to invest in a piece of capital equipment or a savings account at the bank with a virtually guaranteed return of 5 percent. The 5 percent is a pure interest yield on your money; in a year you will have earned a 5 percent return on your investment in the savings account. Unless you are confident that the alternative investment in the equipment will yield at least 5 percent, there is no incentive for you to invest in it. Investments in capital equipment must pay at least the pure rate of interest, or investors will not provide funds for investments. Again, the pure rate of interest is the rate that must be paid to induce individuals to abstain from current consumption and to save.

Risk   Suppose that you are confronted with the following offer: You can have $100 for sure or you can have a 50–50 chance of receiving $200. The expected value of each alternative is the same. In the second alternative, the probability of receiving $200 is 0.50, and the probability of receiving no money is 0.50. Thus, $0.50(\$200) + 0.50(\$0) = \$100$. Yet the individual decision maker is not indifferent between these alternatives. The latter alternative involves risk, while the former does not. Individuals generally view the bearing of risk as a cost and have to be compensated to bear risk.

Risk has a lot to do with capital investment. There is no guarantee of a handsome rate of return on investments in capital goods. Market conditions can change, making the capital goods obsolete or making the things that the capital goods produce less popular with consumers. In other words, capital investments involve risks, so a premium must be paid to induce individual investors to bear risks on their investments. This risk premium is above and beyond the pure rate of interest.

Profits and Losses   Investors in capital goods can earn economic profits or losses. The opportunity cost of fixed capital is the price that must be paid to keep it committed to its present use. This cost consists of the pure interest and any risk premium. Yet something unexpected can happen in the economy to make the fixed capital more valuable. For example, the demand for the product produced by fixed capital may increase many times over what was expected. In such a case the owners of capital earn economic profits on their investment in addition to pure interest and a risk premium. In a competitive market, these returns will be eliminated by competition as other investors become aware of the excess returns and make capital investments of their own in the industry. Keep in mind, too, that economic profits can be negative; that is, investors in capital goods can incur large and unexpected losses.

These profits and losses are analogous to capital gains and losses to investors in the stock market. A capital gain, for example, derives from an unexpected increase in the value of a firm.

Summarizing, the rate of return to capital investment embodies three components: a pure interest return, a premium for bearing risk, and a residual component reflecting unexpected changes in the value of capital goods. Each of these components has an important allocative function in the economy. Pure interest induces people to save. The risk premium leads individuals to invest in risky but valuable ventures. Economic profits are the spur to entrepreneurship and innovation in the economy. We have more to say about profits and entrepreneurship later in this chapter.

The Present Value of Future Income

Investment in capital goods and saving balances the needs of tomorrow with the needs of today. Economists find it useful to look at this balancing act in a precise mathematical formula called *present value*. **Present value** refers to the value today of some payment that will be received in the future. This value depends on the current rate of interest and the length of time between the present and future.

How, for instance, would the prospect of making $100 in one year or in two years compare with the prospect of making $100 now, with an interest rate of 10 percent? The $100 made now would by definition have a present value of $100. But what about the $100 made in one year? What would be the equivalent amount of money made now? That is, what amount invested now at 10 percent would be

Present value

The value today of a payment to be made or received in the future; a future sum discounted by the current rate of interest.

able to generate a fund of $100 in one year? The answer is $90.91 with simple interest, computed by the formula

$$PV = \frac{\text{receipts in one year}}{1 + \text{interest rate}} = \frac{\$100}{(1 + 0.10)} = \$90.91.$$

What sum invested now at 10 percent and compounded annually would produce $100 after two years? Since we are interested in the amount that would yield $100 in *two* years, we *square* the denominator of the formula we used to calculate the present value of money invested for one year:

$$PV = \frac{\$100}{(1 + 0.10)^2} = \$82.64.$$

By extension of this procedure, the present value of any amount at any time in the future can be computed. The formula for doing this is

$$PV = \frac{A_n}{(1 + r)^n},$$

where A_n is the actual amount anticipated in a particular year in the future, r is the rate of interest, and n refers to the particular year in the future.

Note two aspects of present value computations. First, the lower the rate of interest used in making these computations, the higher will be the present value attributed to any given amount of income to be made in the future. Table 14.1 illustrates this point clearly. The present value of $100 one year from now is approximately $97.10 at a 3 percent interest rate and approximately $89.30 at a 12 percent interest rate. Second, the present value of a given amount to be received in the future declines as the date of receipt advances farther into the future. In Table 14.1, for any given interest rate the present value of $100 is less the farther it is to be received in the future. To see this relation, simply read down any column in the table. The point is that the present value of future revenues or costs is inversely related to the rate of interest and the distance of the date in the future when payment will be received.

The Benefits of Capital Formation

Saving means abstaining from consumption now in the expectation of being able to consume more in the future. Saving thus provides the resources needed to increase the stock of capital goods in the economy. A large stock of capital goods raises the rate of consumption that can be sustained in the future. Saving clearly benefits the saver, but it also benefits those who do not save. Indeed, the benefits from saving are diffused throughout the whole economy. Most of us benefit from advances in computer technology, though few of us contributed to the saving that made such advances possible.

Saving and capital formation also lead to higher wages and incomes for workers. In a competitive economy wages are a function of the productivity of workers, and this productivity is in turn a function of the amount and quality of the equip-

TABLE 14.1

The Present Value of $100 at Various Years in the Future

The farther in the future the $100 is received, reading vertically down the table at any interest rate, the less it is worth now. Reading horizontally across the table, the higher the interest rate, the less is the value of $100 at any year in the future.

Years in the Future	3%	5%	7%	10%	12%
1	$97.10	$92.50	$93.50	$90.90	$89.30
2	94.30	90.70	87.30	82.60	79.70
3	91.50	86.40	81.60	75.10	71.10
4	88.80	82.30	76.30	68.30	63.60
5	86.30	78.40	71.30	62.00	56.70
6	83.70	74.60	66.60	56.40	50.70
7	81.30	71.10	62.30	51.30	45.20
8	78.90	67.70	58.20	46.60	40.40
9	76.60	64.50	54.40	42.40	36.00
10	74.40	61.40	50.80	38.50	32.20
.	.	.	.	.	.
.	.	.	.	.	.
15	64.20	48.10	36.20	23.90	18.30
.	.	.	.	.	.
.	.	.	.	.	.
20	55.40	37.70	25.80	14.80	10.40
.	.	.	.	.	.
.	.	.	.	.	.
30	41.20	23.10	13.10	5.73	3.34
.	.	.	.	.	.
.	.	.	.	.	.
40	30.70	14.20	6.70	2.21	1.07
.	.	.	.	.	.
.	.	.	.	.	.
50	22.80	8.70	2.13	.85	.35

ment and tools that workers use. A worker with a tractor is far more productive than a worker with a mule-drawn plow. Since more productive workers are paid more, some of the benefits from capital formation are spread to workers who did not necessarily contribute to the saving that made the capital formation possible.

Indeed, those who save and who build capital goods are among the chief benefactors of society. The reverse is also true: Policies that reduce the incentive to save and to produce capital goods, while appearing to harm the suppliers of saving and the owners of capital goods, actually hurt all of us.

THE CONCEPT OF ECONOMIC RENT

A farmer pays rent to a landowner for the use of an acre of land. A student leases an apartment and pays rent to the landlord each month. A sales representative rents a car to call on customers in a distant city. These examples use the word *rent* in its most familiar sense—payment for the use of something. For the economist **rent** refers to the portion of the payment to any factor of production—land, labor, or capital—that is over and above the factor's opportunity cost. It is the amount a factor is paid that is greater than the forgone value of its next most productive use. Nearly every factor you can name has alternative uses. Farmland could be used as the site of an industrial park. An engineer could be put to use typing correspondence.

Economists originally introduced the concept of rent in discussing the nature of the returns to landowners. A **pure economic rent** is the payment to a factor of production that has a perfectly inelastic supply curve. In such a case the price of the resource is determined solely by the level of demand for its services because supply is fixed and does not change as price changes. Land in the aggregate is the classic example of a resource whose supply is given and whose return is characterized as a pure economic rent.

Rent
A payment to a factor of production in excess of the factor's opportunity cost.

Pure economic rent
The total payment to a factor of production whose supply curve is perfectly inelastic.

LAND RENTS

How is land priced? The obvious answer is that the price of land is determined where its demand and supply curves intersect. While this is correct, there are some special aspects of the price-determination process in the case of land. These aspects concern how the supply curve of land is defined. Although the focus of our discussion will be the supply of land, keep in mind the role of the demand curve for land. As you learned in Chapter 12, this demand curve is based on the marginal productivity of land. In this regard the demand curve for land is the same as the demand curve for any factor of production—it is based on the expected marginal revenue product of land as a factor of production. When land is rented, rent is paid to the landowner. The greater the demand for land, the larger the rent will be. In equilibrium, where the quantity demanded and the quantity supplied of land are equal, the rent to the landowner is equal to the marginal revenue product of the land to the renter.

A distinction must be made between the fixed supply of land and its potential allocation to varying uses. In Figure 14.4a the supply curve of land is drawn for all land, or the **aggregate supply of land.** The curve is drawn as a vertical line, indicating that land in the aggregate is in fixed supply. In general, the amount of land on earth is given by nature and cannot be changed. Actually, common sense tells us that the assumption of a perfectly inelastic supply of land is not completely true. The supply of usable land can be increased through reclamation of swamps and marshes or reduced through erosion. Nonetheless, it is a useful approximation to think of the aggregate supply curve of land as perfectly inelastic, as drawn in Figure 14.4a.

Aggregate supply of land
The total amount of land available for use by the entire economy.

What are the economic implications of this vertical supply curve for all land? First, the perfectly inelastic nature of the supply of land in the aggregate means that the quantity supplied of land is unresponsive to price. Whether land is priced at $1 per acre per year or $1 million per acre per year, the quantity supplied of land in the aggregate will not change. Because the quantity of land—Q in Figure 14.4a—is fixed, the rental price of land will be determined solely by the level of demand.

(a) Aggregate

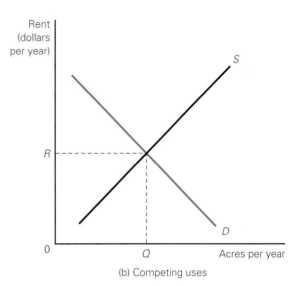

(b) Competing uses

FIGURE 14.4

Pure Economic Rent and the Supply of Land

(a) The supply curve for land in the aggregate is perfectly inelastic with respect to rent, which means that the return to land in the aggregate is a pure economic rent. (b) The supply curve of land to competing uses appears as it is normally drawn—sloping upward to the right. This slope reflects the fact that land has competing uses and hence that the price of using land or rent plays an important role in determining the uses to which land is put.

Thus, the equilibrium level of rent on the vertical axis depends on where the demand curve for land intersects the fixed supply curve.

The return to land in the aggregate is labeled a pure economic rent. To understand this concept, recall that economic rent is defined as a payment in excess of the opportunity cost of a factor of production. Recall also that a factor's opportunity cost is reflected in its supply schedule because a supply schedule indicates what it takes to bid resources away from their next-best alternative use. A vertical supply curve such as in Figure 14.4a means that land in the aggregate has no opportunity cost; nothing is given up for its supply, for it has no alternative uses. Very simply, this means that the whole return to land in the aggregate is a pure economic rent. In Figure 14.4a, land garners $REQ0$ in pure rent.

The concept of pure economic rent is normally associated with the supply curve of all land. However, it is possible that other resources will exhibit a range of their supply curve that is perfectly inelastic and that they therefore stand to earn pure economic rents. This characteristic may be true of uniquely talented performers (superstars) in the worlds of sport and art, for example.

The Supply of Land to Alternative Uses

Since the return to land in the aggregate is a pure economic rent, a price does not have to be paid to call forth a supply of land. If rent does not have to be paid to call forth a supply of land, then why pay it? Or why not tax all rents away as an unearned surplus to landowners? The attractiveness of such a tax is apparent—it raises the revenue without affecting the available supply of land. In Figure 14.4a, for example, a tax equal to the area of pure rents, $REQ0$, would leave the supply of land unaffected at Q.

In 1879, in his book *Progress and Poverty,* Henry George proposed a single tax of 10 percent on land rent on just these grounds. George argued for a single tax on land because he felt that landowners contributed nothing to the land's productivity. Rising land values were determined by general economic growth and by increases in the demand for land. Thus, a tax on land would not affect the amount of land available to the economy and would prevent landowners from getting rich from windfall profits while nonlandowners remained poor. (Windfall profits could occur to lucky landowners with favorable and unexpected changes in economic conditions.) Moreover, George thought a single tax on land rents could finance all the government of his day, eliminating the need for other types of taxes.

George's proposal rests on the assumption of a perfectly inelastic supply curve of land. He was essentially assuming that land has no alternative uses. But this assumption concerns land only in the aggregate. While land in the aggregate has a vertical supply curve, the supply of land to alternative uses does not. Consider what happens, for example, as a city expands. Farmland is converted to sites for houses and shopping centers, as people bid for the right to use the land in other ways. The market process reallocates the land from less valued to more highly valued uses, from farmland to city land.

The supply curve of land for particular uses slopes upward to the right, as shown in Figure 14.4b. To rent land for a particular use, one must bid it away from competing uses. As more desirable land is rented, the rental rate rises. With a normally sloped supply curve, the rental price paid for land serves to allocate land to competing uses. Those who value the use of a parcel of land more highly will offer higher rents than others. In this sense, rent functions like any other price in signaling the intentions of buyers and sellers in the market for land.

The proper distinction to keep in mind is that while the supply curve of land in the aggregate is approximately vertical, the supply curve of land to alternative uses is positively sloped. Since the latter concept of the supply of land is far more relevant to real-world situations than the former, a proposal such as Henry George's could do much damage to the economy. It was never implemented, although George was a popular politician and twice ran for mayor of New York City.

Whether land is viewed in the aggregate or as a resource of varying desirability and alternative uses, rent does serve a function: It rations land among available bidders.

PROFITS AND THE ALLOCATION OF RESOURCES

Profits are a residual return to those individuals in the economy who provide economic foresight and leadership in an uncertain environment. Profits play an instrumental role in the way the competitive price system works to allocate resources to their most highly valued uses.

Profit Data

For individual firms, industries, or the economy as a whole, profits are not computed directly but are determined by what is left over from revenues after payments have been made to land, labor, and capital. It is in this sense that the profit earner is referred to as the *residual claimant*. This view of profits as a residual contrasts sharply with the common but misguided notion that employees and other input suppliers are paid only after the entrepreneur has secured profits.

Have levels of profits earned in the economy as a whole grown over the years? Table 14.2 traces after-tax corporate profits and nonfarm proprietors' income for selected years between 1970 and 1998. Corporate profits as a percentage of national income (NI) ranged between 3.9 percent of NI in 1985 and 7.4 in 1997. In contrast, nonfarm proprietors' income exhibits a strong constant trend as a percent of NI, showing little change from year to year. Overall, the data in Table 14.2 fail to confirm the widely held perception that profits and proprietors' income have been rapidly growing over time, at least as a percentage of national income.

Rate of Return on Capital

**Rate of return
on invested capital**

Profits earned during a period of time divided by the value of invested capital; usually measured as a percent per year.

The profit data given in Table 14.2 are not directly relevant to the decisions of firms concerning investments in plant and equipment. What matters for such purposes is not the absolute level of profits but the economic **rate of return on invested capital.** That is, at the margin it will pay to buy an additional dollar's worth of equipment only if the firm expects to earn more than a dollar from the sale of the resulting output from the equipment.

TABLE 14.2

Corporate Profits and Nonfarm Proprietors' Income, 1970–1998

Corporate profits have remained quite steady as a percentage of NI (between 3.9 and 7.4 percent) since 1970. Nonfarm proprietors' income has exhibited steady growth but has remained fairly constant as a percentage of NI.

| Year | CORPORATE PROFITS | | NONFARM PROPRIETORS' INCOME | |
	After Tax (billions)	Percent of National Income	After Tax (billions)	Percent of National Income
1970	44	5.2	65.4	7.8
1975	89.5	6.9	97.7	7.5
1980	156.6	7.0	164.4	7.3
1985	133.4	3.9	245	7.2
1990	231.2	5.0	338.6	7.3
1991	240.8	5.0	347.2	7.3
1992	263.4	5.3	386.7	7.8
1993	300.2	5.7	418.4	7.9
1994	348.5	6.2	434.7	7.8
1995	424.6	7.2	465.6	7.9
1996	454.1	7.3	488.8	7.8
1997	488.3	7.4	515.8	7.7
1998*	479.4	6.9	543.9	7.8

*Average of first 3 quarters of 1998.

Source: Economic Report of the President (Washington, D.C.: U.S. Government Printing Office, 1999), p. 358.

The economic rate of return on capital may be approximated with accounting data by dividing the amount of stock or capital valued at its current replacement cost into profits earned during the year. Historical data indicate that after-tax rates of return on capital have fallen over time. The average annual rate of return between 1955 and 1969 was 10.1 percent, with the highest rates occurring during the 1960s. By contrast, the average annual rate of return on capital between 1970 and 1998 was approximately 8 percent. This decline in rates of return has two important implications. The first involves incentives to make capital investments. For investments in capital to be profitable, not only must the rate of return be positive, but the rate of return on capital must exceed the expected return on alternative investments. Since a larger number of competing uses of funds—buying bonds, for example—become attractive as the rate of return on capital falls, the available data suggest that incentives to invest in plants and equipment during the 1970s were lower than in earlier years. Second, the data provide further evidence that the popular view of large and ever-increasing corporate profitability is mistaken.

Accounting Versus Economic Profits

Accounting profit

Total revenue minus total explicit payments for inputs or out-of-pocket costs.

Economic profit

Total revenue minus total opportunity costs of production.

As noted in Chapter 7, **accounting profits** tend to overstate the level of **economic profits** because accountants by necessity take a less theoretical view of costs than do economists. Accountants count as costs only those business expenditures involving direct money outlays—wages and salaries, raw materials purchased, rental payments on land and buildings, borrowing costs, advertising expenses, and so forth. Economists identify costs as *all* opportunities forgone, explicit or implicit. If you are self-employed, for example, you must count what you could earn working for somebody else as a cost of your operation. Accounting profits thus generally overstate economic profits because they understate economic costs.

ENTREPRENEURSHIP

Entrepeneur

An individual who perceives profit opportunities, organizes resources into productive ventures, and bears the uncertain status of residual claimant of the resulting risky economic outcome.

Assuming that economic profits can be measured, what role do they play in the economic process? Economic profits are the return to a particular factor of production, entrepreneurship. As such, profits are the residual income accruing to the **entrepreneur** as a return on the services he or she brings to the productive process. These services include technical abilities in organizing the other factors of production into combinations appropriate for the efficient manufacture of goods. More important, though, is the entrepreneur's alertness to the existence of potential profit opportunities in the economy. In this sense, entrepreneurship consists of linking markets by perceiving the opportunity to buy resources at a lower total cost than the revenue obtainable from the sale of output, or by recognizing that sellers in one market are offering to sell output at a price lower than buyers in another market are willing to pay.

Put another way, entrepreneurship consists of offering the most attractive opportunities to other market participants—perceiving unfulfilled demands, offering higher prices to sellers or lower prices to buyers, improving existing goods or making them more cheaply, finding more effective means of communicating to consumers the availability and attributes of goods. In all of these activities, the entrepreneur takes advantage of opportunities that exist because of the initial ignorance of other market participants. But as a result of the entrepreneur's actions, markets move closer to the prices and quantities emerging in equilibrium, the plans of buyers and sellers more closely dovetail, and the knowledge of economic data held by market participants is increased.

In addition to alertness and organizational skills, the entrepreneur brings to the production process a willingness to act in the presence of uncertainty. (We distinguish risk from uncertainty in that risk involves events that occur with known probabilities—the toss of a coin, for example—while uncertainty entails outcomes whose probabilities cannot be specified with precision—for example, war or peace and long-run weather forecasts.) There is no guarantee that perceived profit opportunities will materialize. Because it takes time between the purchase of inputs and the sale of output—between the expenditures on resources and the receipt of revenue—intervening events may reveal the entrepreneur's plans to be either overambitious or underambitious when evaluated with the advantage of hindsight. Entrepreneurs, then, bear responsibility for incorrect anticipations. Profits can be viewed as a return for bearing both risk and uncertainty.

Entrepreneurs and Information: The Austrian View

Economists who work in the tradition of the Austrian economic theorists of the late 1800s are referred to as the modern Austrian school of economics. The modern Austrians include Friedrich A. von Hayek, who won the Nobel Prize in economics in 1974, and Israel Kirzner.

The traditional view of the entrepreneur as a person who discovers and bears the risks of profit opportunities has been expanded in the modern Austrian view.[1] In this view, the entrepreneur must also design and sell particular commodities or particular groups of commodities. Most products and services, such as dishwashing detergent and automobiles, are sold in a variety of qualities, locations, and with a variety of financial terms and warranties. For example, generic and brand name detergents are often found side by side in supermarkets. The entrepreneur not only must perceive profit opportunities in producing and selling such items but also must develop and fit the *characteristics* of each product or service to a targeted group of consumers. The entrepreneur must discover what consumers are willing to buy and inform them about the wares available for purchase.

One very important aspect of the modern Austrian view of competition is that it is a *rivalrous process,* which contrasts with the traditional view of competition as a static *situation* (as presented in Chapter 8). The traditional model, which often assumed homogeneous products with perfect knowledge of consumers' demand curves, gives the economist an exact account of the course of economic events with the aid of scientific generalizations. But the traditional model of competition has some limitations. Concentrating on some of these limitations, the modern Austrians view competition as the businessperson's rivalry against competitors for a prize. Assuming freedom of entry and *non*homogeneous products and services, the Austrian view is one of perpetual disequilibrium. Economic profits are created and destroyed perpetually, and products and product qualities change continually as an integral part of the process. In this view, entrepreneurs are constantly experimenting with different products and informing consumers about these differences.

---

[1] The Austrian view of the entrepreneur's role in the competitive process is detailed in Israel Kirzner, *Competition and Entrepreneurship* (Chicago: University of Chicago Press, 1973) and in Friedrich A. von Hayek (winner of the 1974 Nobel Prize), "The Nonsequitur of the Dependence Effect," in E. Mansfield, ed., *Microeconomics: Selected Readings* (New York: W. W. Norton and Co., 1979). See also Robert F. Hebert and Albert Link, *The Entrepreneur* (Boston: D. C. Heath, 1988).

If consumers received perfect information, there would be no reason to inform them about new products or services, let alone about different qualities of existing products or services. Having perfect information about products or services amounts to having innate wants for products or services. If tastes in music were innate, for example, no amount of advertising by an entrepreneurial promoter could convince someone predisposed to classical music to attend a country music concert. Economists such as Hayek argued that very few human wants, except for food, shelter, clothing, and sex, are innate. Human wants, personality, and opinions are shaped by a cultural environment, and one element in this environment is advertising. An entrepreneur may, in a free market, attempt to devise products and affect their consumption, but consumers will also be informed about competing products. The success of an individual entrepreneur will depend on the actions of other producers and many other factors that affect consumers of any particular product. The main point is that consumers cannot react without information. To argue that some tastes and desires are unimportant or irrelevant when compared with desires for food, shelter, and clothing would be to ignore much of cultural history, in Hayek's view.

One role of the entrepreneur, then, is to develop, design, and sell products in the market process. Part of this entrepreneurial role is the ability to advertise products and product qualities. The costs of *selling* output by informing customers of goods and services through advertising and other means are, in other words, part and parcel of entrepreneurship. When the entrepreneur successfully discovers consumer tastes and preferences, and when he or she molds products and services to meet these desires, consumer utility and welfare are enhanced.

The entrepreneur is a prime actor in the economic process. Entrepreneurs develop products, organize production, and provide necessary capital; they are alert to profit opportunities, willing to act in uncertain conditions, and can inform consumers and potential consumers about the product. Profits are simply a payment to another factor of production, but they are different from the other factors in that the entrepreneur is paid last, claiming the residual after the other factors have been compensated. Profits spur entrepreneurial activity in the economy and thereby encourage the whole competitive process.

This completes our discussion of factor pricing and the associated returns to each factor. Hopefully, at this point the unity of microeconomics is apparent. Demand and supply conditions determine prices and quantities in all markets, and the principles that guide individual behavior across these markets are the same. Opportunity cost matters, choices are made at the margin, and individual behavior is purposeful and rational. We started our study of microeconomics in Chapter 1 by emphasizing these points, and now the student is in a position to understand why they are so very important.

APPLICATION

Trading Property Rights: Stocks and Bonds

Most daily newspapers list the previous day's closing prices of stocks and bonds. These listings show how the market for loanable funds works, coordinating the supply of funds, primarily held by investors and investor groups, with the demand for funds, primarily the desire by corporations to raise capital for future production. Figure 14.5 explains how to read newspaper stock listings.

Corporations have two primary means of raising capital: selling shares of stock or issuing bonds. By selling shares of stock, a corporation is effectively selling prop-

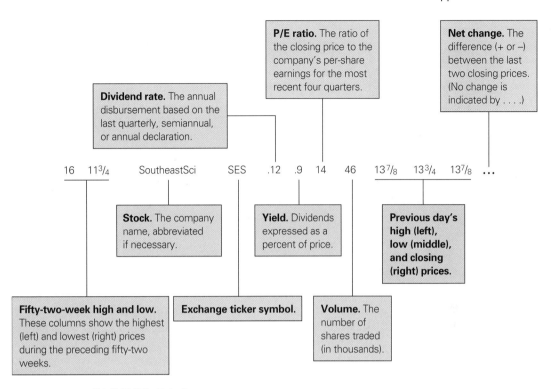

FIGURE 14.5

Sample New York Stock Exchange Listing

Most daily newspapers carry complete listings of transactions on the New York Stock Exchange. This sample listing for the stock of a hypothetical company, Southeast Scientific Company, is accompanied by explanatory notes.

erty rights to itself: When you buy a share of stock, you are trading property rights over one asset (money or other assets) and acquiring property rights over a portion of the firm. The shareholders of a corporation are its owners. Each share of stock permits its holder one vote at meetings that determine the firm's future management. In this way, corporate policy is directed by the will of the holders of the majority of the firm's shares—whether one or many individuals. Shareholders do not make operating decisions for the firm, but they are legally responsible for hiring the managers—the board of directors—who do. When shareholders are pleased with the existing management of the firm, they usually assign their votes to the management, which then acts as a proxy for the shareholders in voting on corporate policy.

The stock market is an organized exchange where corporate shares are bought and sold. In the stock market the prices of shares issued by different firms reflect the market's estimate of the future profitability of the firms in question. From the shareholders' standpoint, investing in the stock market means bearing the risk resulting from the uncertain prospects of any given firm. A share of the stock's future value is not guaranteed and can rise or fall with the firm's fortunes, or because of general market conditions such as interest rates.

Corporations and governments also issue another type of obligation—bonds. Unlike shares of stock, bonds do not confer ownership rights; they simply

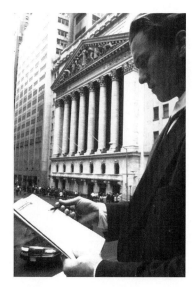

An investor considers his options with the New York Stock Exchange (on Wall Street in New York City) in the background.

represent IOUs. The firm or government body agrees to pay the bondholder a fixed sum (the principal that represents the loan to the firm) either on a specific date or in installments over a specified period. Most bonds pay, in addition, a fixed return per year, usually expressed as a percentage of the face value of the bond. For example, a corporation may issue a $10,000 bond (which, if sold, represents a $10,000 loan to the corporation for some specified period) at an interest rate of 5 percent. This bond would pay the holder $500 per year until maturity, when the entire $10,000 is returned to the investor.

Although bonds tend to be issued for long terms (thirty-eight years in the case of some U.S. Treasury bonds), bonds are commonly bought and sold prior to the date of maturity. The bond market is like the stock market; it represents an organized exchange specializing in the buying and selling of bonds.

Interest rates affect the prices of shares of stock indirectly by their impact on the activities and hence the profitability of firms, but interest rates bear a direct relation to the price of bonds. Take, for example, a bond issued with a face value of $10,000 that pays an annual rate of interest of 6 percent. Until maturity, whoever holds the bond is entitled to $600 annually. Suppose, however, that the market interest rate rises to 10 percent. Purchasers of newly issued $10,000 bonds can earn $1000 annually, other things equal. What happens to the price of the 6 percent bonds? Their market value must fall to reflect the new, higher interest rate. No one, in other words, would invest in a bond paying less than 10 percent, since they can earn 10 percent on newly issued bonds. The price of the 6 percent bond must fall to $6000 to reflect the new, higher rate of 10 percent. Individuals will not buy the original bonds unless their price falls so as to produce a 10 percent return on a given investment ($600/$6000). The bond will still pay $10,000 at maturity (the firm must pay back what it borrowed), but the sales value of the bond right now is $6000.

The general point to remember is that the price of a bond varies inversely with the interest rate. When the interest rate rises, the price of a bond falls; when the interest rate falls, the price of a bond rises.

It is worth noting that firms can hold back part of their earnings as an additional source of investment capital. Modern corporations routinely retain a part of their earnings rather than paying all of it out to stockholders.

QUESTIONS

What do you think would be the stock market's reaction to an unexpected rise in interest rates? What would your response be as an investor?

SUMMARY

1. Wealth can be defined as a high level of sustainable consumption in an economy. The elements of a wealthy society are production, resources, knowledge, capital, technology, and institutions.

2. Time preference is a measure of an individual's concern for present versus future consumption.

3. Interest is the price that individuals must be paid for waiting to consume later; it also is the price that individuals are willing to pay in order to consume now rather than later.

4. The rate of interest is determined in the market for loanable funds by the demand and supply of loanable funds.

5. In reality, there is a multiplicity of interest rates—such as prime rates, government rates, and credit card rates—determined by the degree of risk, cost, and time allowed for payment. Because it takes the rate of inflation into account, the real rate of interest is lower than the nominal rate of interest.

6. The returns to capital are composed of pure interest, a risk premium, and economic profits or losses.

7. An economic rent is a return in excess of the opportunity cost of an owner of a resource.

8. Land in the aggregate is fixed and has a perfectly inelastic supply curve. Its entire return is a pure economic rent determined by the level of demand for land as a factor of production.

9. The supply of land to competing uses is not fixed. Land must be bid away from competing uses, so the supply curve of land to a specific use is upward sloping.

10. Proposals to tax land rents away would be costly to the economy. Land is like any other factor of production. It has alternative uses, and it is used in the production process by entrepreneurs and firms up to the point where its marginal revenue product equals its marginal cost.

11. Economic profits are a residual that the entrepreneur receives after the other factors of production have been paid. Profits can be positive or negative (or zero). The receivers of profits are called residual claimants. Although the absolute level of profits in the economy has grown over time, the rate of return on capital has not. It has declined in recent years. The rate of return on capital is the crucial determinant of firm profitability.

12. Accounting profits differ from economic profits. Typically, accounting procedures understate economic costs and thus overstate economic profits.

13. Profits are the force in the economy that leads to entrepreneurship. They are a return to decision making under conditions of risk and uncertainty. The most basic characteristic of entrepreneurs is that they are alert to economic opportunities.

KEY TERMS

roundabout production
saving
capital formation
capital stock
depreciation
capital consumption
rate of time preference
interest

demand for loanable funds
supply of loanable funds
risk
nominal rate of interest
inflation rate
real rate of interest
pure interest
present value

rent
pure economic rent
aggregate supply of land
rate of return on invested capital
accounting profits
economic profits
entrepreneur

QUESTIONS FOR REVIEW AND DISCUSSION

1. Suppose that you are thinking about investing in a personal computer and laser printer. Your costs will be $2500 and the equipment will last four years. You expect to earn $900 a year typing papers part-time with the computer. The bank will lend you the money at 19 percent interest. Should you buy the computer and printer? What if the bank's interest rate was 12 percent?

2. Why is the concept of time preference important in the discussion of interest rates? Explain.

3. How would the following events affect the prime rate of interest in the United States?
   a. The threat of war in Central America
   b. An increase in the inflation rate
   c. The discovery of massive domestic oil resources
   d. Greater impatience in the general population
   e. Capricious government intervention in the economy

4. At what point in the production process do residual claimants receive their return? Can their return be negative?

5. What are the essential things that an entrepreneur does?

6. There is a fixed supply of oil in the world. Is the return to oil producers therefore a pure economic rent? Explain carefully.

7. Evaluate the following statement: Land rent should be completely taxed away.

8. Suppose that all of your earnings were a rent. What implications would this situation have for your behavior in the workplace? Would you be cantankerous with your superiors or docile and easy to get along with? Why?

9. Are you earning economic rents as a college student? (Hint: Suppose your college raises tuition.)

PROBLEMS

1. Identify the present value of a stream of payments of $150 per year for the next seven years if the interest rate is 10 percent. (Use Table 14.1 for this problem.)

2. Suppose that Enrique, an entrepreneur, has determined that land yields the following marginal revenue product per year:

Acres	MRP
1	21,000
2	16,400
3	10,600
4	8,400
5	6,200
6	3,600
7	1,720
8	480

If Enrique can employ as many acres as he chooses at a rent payment of $6200 per acre per year, how many will he employ? Why? Present your conclusion in graphical form.

WORKING WITH THE WEB

In this chapter, you have been introduced to the Austrian school of economics. To learn more about the Austrian school, go to www.mises.org, select "daily articles", and choose November '98. Scroll through the articles until you find "The Austrian Tradition". This is a bit lengthy but contains good information about the differences between the Austrian school and other schools of economic thought. Use this article to answer the first two questions that follow.

1. According to the Austrian school, how do entrepreneurship, private property, and government intervention fit into its view of the economy?

2. The "third virtue" of Austrian economics is the theory of entrepreneurship. According to Mises, why is everyone considered an entrepreneur?

3. One difference between the Austrian school and the neoclassical school of economics is that the former views competition as a process while the latter views competition as a static situation. Economist Thomas DiLorenzo maintains that the static view of competition has contributed to the attack on Microsoft. Go to , select "daily aricles", and choose June '98–October '98. Scroll through the articles until you find "Static Analysis". What is DiLorenzo's point regarding market dominance, given that Microsoft stands accused of being a monopolist?

Income
Distribution,
Poverty,
and
Health Care

I n studying income distribution, economists look at how personal or family earnings are measured and divided among members of society. They try to see how various factors such as individual choice and effort, education, experience, and
discrimination influence the distribution of income. Also, they pay close attention
to the effects of various government policies on income distribution. Economists generally have strong personal views concerning the equity of various income distributions.
However, recognizing that their views are value judgments, economists tend to focus on
other aspects of redistribution proposals. In particular, they pay much attention to efficiency aspects of various proposals to redistribute income. Although it is tempting to
imagine that programs such as tax reform simply transfer income from those who need
it less to those who need it more without side effects, redistribution never works so simply. Inevitably, some individuals will incur costs to avoid paying higher taxes, while others will adjust their circumstances to qualify for new subsidies. Due to such activity, it
almost always ends up costing some groups in society more than a dollar for each dollar that is transferred to other groups. Economists therefore are aware that any program
to redistribute income involves a trade-off between equity and efficiency.

Many contemporary public policy issues are distributional issues. Health care and
poverty are two examples. Health care costs in the United States are soaring, and many
Americans do not have health insurance. Poverty persists in many parts of the United States.
Any government program that attempts to reduce poverty or to reform the health care system will involve income distribution. After reading Chapter 15 you should understand

- some of the differences between economic efficiency and social equity as they
  relate to income distribution.

- the meaning of income inequality and how it is measured.
- patterns and characteristics of income distribution in the United States, especially those related to poverty and discrimination.
- modern policy programs and proposals relating to distribution, poverty, and health care in contemporary society.

THE INDIVIDUAL AND INCOME DISTRIBUTION

The economic question of why some individuals are rich and others are poor has many facets. Individuals accumulate income from their labor and entrepreneurial skills, from the ownership of assets such as stocks and bonds and land, or from the receipt of cash or government subsidies called transfer payments. At the same time, most individuals pay a certain portion of income through taxes. We will analyze each factor of **individual income** briefly.

Individual income
The earnings individuals receive from their labor, from their assets, and from government transfer payments, minus their tax payments.

Labor Income

Labor income—income received from supplying labor—is the wage rate received multiplied by the number of hours worked. The supply of labor is by far the largest source of individual income. The supply of labor ordinarily varies according to wage rates, but individuals also differ in their choice of work hours over leisure hours, and wages themselves vary for a number of reasons.

Labor income
The payments an individual receives from supplying work time; equal to the wage rate times the number of hours supplied.

Choices of Work Versus Leisure   Different people with the same skills will often supply different quantities of labor at identical wage rates. The same wage rate affects people differently because they can make choices about the trade-off between work and leisure. Harpo, who has the same skills as Gummo, chooses to play his harp six hours a day for no pay and to work two hours a day for pay. Gummo chooses work and income over leisure, working twelve or fourteen hours a day.

What else accounts for differences in attitudes toward work? No human being is a machine who can supply labor without limit. At higher and higher wage rates and longer and longer hours worked, we all become leisure lovers (see Chapter 12 on this point). As we choose more work, the costs of losing more and more leisure rise and the rewards of earning more income fall.

Differences in Wage Rates   Wage rates vary widely among occupations. The wage rate you earn is largely a function of the human capital you have built up through education and investments in other skills. Human capital has a lot to do with whether you are rich or poor. Level of schooling attained (a college degree, a high school diploma) is a ticket to enter some occupations. Given government-enforced regulations of the American Medical Association, entry into the physicians' market without a medical degree would almost certainly land you in jail.

Luck also plays a role in the wage rate. At the beginning of the energy crisis in the early 1970s, those entering the labor market with degrees in petroleum engineering received much higher wages than under previous conditions. (The situation was short-lived, since more and more college students were attracted to petroleum engineering by high wages, and, as usual, supply expanded and wages fell.)

Individuals' or families' incomes are also determined by their stage in the life cycle. Law students at Harvard, Stanford, or the University of Michigan may be poor now—students everywhere tend to be poor now—but they will not always be poor. Income or earnings tend to rise throughout the period of the active work life. Earnings increase at a fairly rapid pace in early to middle work life. In the latter portion of the work life, earnings still tend to increase, but at a slower pace. After retirement, earnings generally decrease. Other factors also influence the wage rate an individual receives. Without question, race and sex discrimination have historically affected wage rates. We look at this matter in more detail later in the chapter.

Income from Savings and Other Assets

The other major source of income is the return from savings or other assets one owns or has accumulated. Motives for the sacrifice of current consumption are numerous: security, expected future gaps in income, education, retirement, large consumer expenditures, and so forth. In any case, the sacrifice of current consumption for future consumption is rewarded by an interest return or **asset income.**

Asset income
Earnings from interest on savings, from capital investments, and from land; all result from forgone consumption in the past.

Many people save for future generations. Some current income earners set aside assets for their children's later use, which brings us to another major source of income. Inheritance of money or other assets is related to the luck of having had wealthy parents. Historically, free societies have permitted inheritance and protected the rights of income owners to bequeath gifts at death or while still alive. Most societies have nevertheless taxed the recipients of inheritance on the grounds that such wealth was not due to their own productivity.

The returns from both savings and other wealth and asset accumulations also depend on one's skill at investing. Returns on all sorts of investments—monetary, real capital, or land—are determined by the costs of investing and the incentives to maximize income from investments.

Taxes and Transfer Payments

***Ex ante* distribution**
The distribution of income before government transfer payments and taxes are accounted for.

***Ex post* distribution**
The distribution of income after government transfer payments and taxes are accounted for.

Transfer payment
A resource received by an individual from government that is not directly or explicitly paid for by that individual; it may be in the form of money or goods and services such as education or health care.

A final source of income is government tax collections and benefit distributions. Economists distinguish between the ***ex ante* distribution** of income, the before tax and transfer payments distribution, and the ***ex post* distribution,** or after tax and transfer payments distribution. We all receive benefits from government, and we all pay taxes in one form or another. National defense, roads, and the local public swimming pool are some of the benefits; property taxes, sales taxes, and income taxes are some of the costs.

Most individuals are either net taxpayers or net benefit receivers. In other words, the determination of how rich or poor we are *ex post* depends partly on our position with regard to taxes and benefits. The receipt of government services and **transfer payments**—such as direct welfare payments, food stamps, subsidized public housing, Social Security, and unemployment compensation—must be added to privately earned income. Transfer payments are money or real goods or services transferred by government from one group in society (taxpayers) to other groups (transfer recipients). Tax payments of all kinds must likewise be subtracted to help explain *ex post* why we, as individuals, are rich or poor. Most government statistics on income distribution reveal only *ex ante* money distributions of family or household income, but economists have attempted to make some *ex post* calculations as well.

HOW IS INCOME INEQUALITY MEASURED?

Family income
The total of all incomes from all sources except transfers received by members of a household.

The money income of families (often termed *households*), or **family income,** is calculated annually by the U.S. Bureau of the Census. Table 15.1 shows family income in the United States for selected years between 1970 and 1996. Total family income is broken down into the percentage received by each fifth of the total number of families over these years, ranked from the lowest, or poorest, fifth to the highest, or richest, fifth. (A fifth of a total distribution is called a quintile.) In addition, Table 15.1 gives the percentage of total money income earned by the top 5 percent of income earners between 1970 and 1996.

Interpretation of Money Distribution Data

The data in Table 15.1 reveal something very interesting: *the distribution of reported money income did not change significantly between 1970 and 1996,* although in recent years the disparity in income distribution appears to have widened. Reading horizontally across the table, we see that the shares for each quintile stayed roughly the same. The lowest quintile received about 5 percent

TABLE 15.1

Money Income of Families, Percent of Aggregate Income: 1970–1996
These data show an amazing uniformity in pretax income distribution over more than twenty-five years. Special care must be used in interpreting the data, however, since noncash transfers by government also affect income distribution.

PERCENT OF AGGREGATE INCOME

Families by Quintile	1970	1975	1979	1984	1987	1991	1996
1. Lowest fifth	5.4	5.4	5.3	4.7	4.6	4.5	4.2
2. Second fifth	12.2	11.8	11.6	11.0	10.8	10.7	10.0
3. Middle fifth	17.6	17.6	17.5	17.0	16.9	16.5	15.8
4. Fourth fifth	23.8	24.1	24.1	24.4	24.1	24.1	23.1
5. Highest fifth	40.9	41.1	41.6	42.9	43.7	44.2	46.8
Highest 5%	15.6	15.5	15.7	16.0	16.9	17.1	20.3

Sources: U.S. Department of Commerce, Bureau of the Census, Current Population Reports—Consumer Income, *Money Income of Households, Families, and Persons in the United States 1984* (Washington, D.C.: U.S. Government Printing Office, 1986), p. 37. 1998 Update, Department of Commerce, Bureau of Census Web Site.

of aggregate income, and its share is declining, while the highest quintile consistently got over 40 percent. Further, the share of the highest quintile has been rising, as has the share of the top 5 percent of income earners. Before accepting these figures at face value, we should note some limitations of the data in Table 15.1.

1. Money income statistics reported by the Bureau of the Census do not conform to the economist's definition of income. Income, in the economist's sense, is what an individual accumulates from labor, assets, or transfer payments minus what is paid in taxes. By contrast, the Census Bureau's statistics on income ignore transfer payments, all assets such as capital gains, and income and payroll taxes.

2. The government statistics report family, not individual, income. Therefore, an increase in the number of family units, income remaining the same, will alter the reported income distribution. In the period 1960–1998, the number of family units increased significantly through later marriages, high divorce rates, and the increasing independence of the elderly. The government's statistics do not take this increase into account.

Given these two deficiencies in the Census data, conclusions about the distribution of economic welfare should be deferred until the raw statistics are refined. Before actually making some of these refinements, we turn to the tools economists use to deal with income distribution.

The Lorenz Curve

Lorenz curve

A curve plotting the actual cumulative distribution of income in percentages; usually compared with a curve showing a perfectly even distribution of income.

Economists have developed a number of useful methods for describing and analyzing income distribution. The **Lorenz curve,** the primary tool for measuring income distribution, was developed in 1905 by M. O. Lorenz. A Lorenz curve plots the relation between the percentage of families receiving income and the cumulative percentage of aggregate family income. To gain an understanding of the Lorenz curve, consider a hypothetical income distribution for a hypothetical country in the year 2020, as shown in Table 15.2. Table 15.2 tells us that the lowest 20 percent of family income earners in this country receive only 5 percent of total income. The next 20 percent of families get 15 percent. Therefore, the lowest 40 percent receives a cumulative share of 20 percent. The middle 20 percent get 20 percent of total income, indicating that the lowest 60 percent of income earners receives only 40 percent of total income. Obviously, 100 percent of income recipients receive a cumulative total of 100 percent of income.

The data in Table 15.2 may be translated into graphical form. The vertical axis of Figure 15.1 represents the cumulative percentage of family income, and the horizontal axis shows the percentage of income-earning families. If all families earned equal incomes, the Lorenz curve would be a straight line. Ten percent of all families would earn 10 percent of income; 80 percent of families would earn 80 percent; and so on. Such a curve would actually be a diagonal cutting the square in half, as represented by the line of perfect equality in Figure 15.1.

A Lorenz curve may be constructed from the hypothetical data of Table 15.2. Point *A* in Figure 15.1 corresponds to point *A* in Table 15.2—it is the intersection

TABLE 15.2

Hypothetical Income Data for the Year 2020

The second column shows the percent share of total income received by each quintile of families in this hypothetical country; the third column adds these shares cumulatively. For instance, since the lowest fifth receives only 5 percent of total income and the second fifth receives 15 percent, together these lowest two-fifths receive a cumulative share of only 20 percent of total income. The lowest four-fifths receive a cumulative share of 65 percent. Data from the third column are plotted on a Lorenz curve in Figure 15.1.

	AGGREGATE INCOME	
All Families by Quintile	**Percent Share (year 2020)**	**Cumulative Percent Share (year 2020)**
A. Lowest fifth	5	5
B. Second fifth	15	20
C. Middle fifth	20	40
D. Fourth fifth	25	65
E. Highest fifth	35	100

FIGURE 15.1

A Hypothetical Lorenz Curve for the Year 2020

The Lorenz curve shows the cumulative percentage of family income earned by percentages of families. The Lorenz curve indicates that 40 percent of families earned only 20 percent of total income, while 80 percent earned a cumulative 65 percent. This distribution is unequal and falls short of the line of perfect equality. The shaded area in the diagram indicates the degree of income inequality. The farther the Lorenz curve moves away from the line of perfect equality, the less equal is the income distribution.

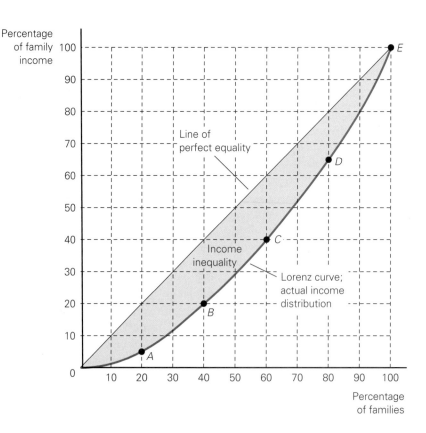

of the lowest 20 percent of families and their cumulative share of total income. Point *D* in Figure 15.1 shows that 80 percent of families (the fourth fifth in Table 15.2) received 65 percent of total income. The combination of points *A, B, C, D,* and *E* forms a Lorenz curve.

The distance of the Lorenz curve from the line of perfect equality is a measure of income inequality. The shaded area of Figure 15.1 is a measure of the degree of income inequality for our hypothetical society. Should the shaded area become larger, or more bowed, money income would be more unevenly distributed. A smaller area or a flatter curve would signal a more equal income distribution.

INCOME DISTRIBUTION IN THE UNITED STATES

We have already looked at family income distribution for selected years between 1970 and 1996. We now construct Lorenz curves with the data for the years 1970 and 1996. In Table 15.3, the cumulative percent share of all families by quintiles is calculated from the simple shares for 1970 and 1996. In 1970, for example, the lowest 60 percent of families received 35.2 percent of total income; their share had dropped to 30.0 percent in 1996.

Lorenz curves are calculated for these two years in Figure 15.2. Money income distribution has changed very little over the period, as shown by the differences between the Lorenz curves. For the lowest and the fourth quintiles of income

TABLE 15.3

**Share and Cumulative Share in Income Distribution
of All Families, 1970 and 1996**

The data show changes in income distribution. The second fifth lost about 2.2 percent of its share between these two years, while the highest 20 percent gained about 6 percent. The middle fifth lost about 1.8 percent.

Quintile	Percent Share 1970	Percent Cumulative Share 1970	Percent Share 1996	Percent Cumulative Share 1996
Lowest fifth	5.4	5.4	4.2	4.2
Second fifth	12.2	17.6	10.0	14.2
Middle fifth	17.6	35.2	15.8	30.0
Fourth fifth	23.8	59.0	23.1	53.1
Highest fifth	40.9	100.0	46.8	100.0

Sources: U.S. Department of Commerce, Bureau of the Census, Current Population Reports—Consumer Income, *Money Income of Households, Families, and Persons in the United States: 1991* (Washington D.C.: U.S. Government Printing Office, 1999), p. B-11. 1999 Statistical Update, U.S. Department of Commerce Web Site.

Note: Data do not sum due to rounding.

FIGURE 15.2

Lorenz Curves for 1970 and 1996

The Lorenz curves of income distribution for 1970 and 1996 show little change in before-tax income distribution in the United States.

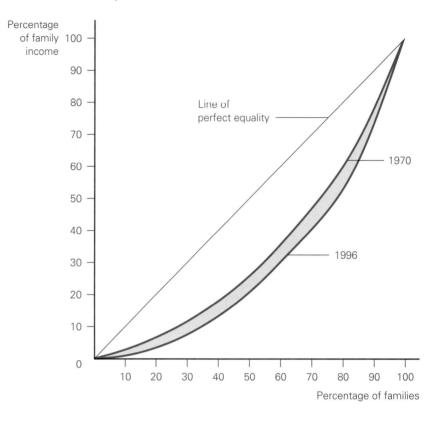

receivers, the distribution of income remained about the same. In between these two quintiles, income shares declined. The share of the highest quintile rose.

What can we conclude from this money income data? Has overall distribution become more unequal over the period 1970–1996? Have the lowest 60 percent of income recipients on balance become worse off? Have the rich gotten slightly richer?

The answers to these questions lie in the taxes and transfers that are not reported in the *ex ante* money income statistics from which the Lorenz curves of Figure 15.2 were constructed. Consider what happens to income distribution when adjustments are made for such things as income and payroll taxes, capital gains, in-kind transfers, money transfer or welfare payments, and other factors.

Adjustments to Money Income

Adjusted income

An individual's income after all taxes and all government transfer payments are accounted for.

Two important factors related to money income data must be considered before any conclusions are drawn about recent trends in income distribution in the United States. First, the data in Tables 15.1 and 15.3 do not account for payroll and income taxes. Since the U.S. income tax system is progressive, meaning that the higher-income recipients pay higher tax rates, the **adjusted income** distribution is affected in the direction of greater equality.

TABLE 15.4

Distribution of Adjusted Income in 1990

Adjusted income distribution statistics for any single year require the addition of such items as in-kind transfer benefits and the subtraction of income and payroll taxes. In a 1976 article Edgar K. Browning calculated the distribution resulting from these adjustments using data for 1972. Browning showed that when adjusted and unadjusted figures are compared, the adjusted distribution is considerably more equal. The following table compares the adjusted with the unadjusted income distribution for a more recent year.

HOUSEHOLDS BY QUINTILE (SHOWN IN BILLIONS OF DOLLARS)

Income Item	Lowest	Second	Third	Fourth	Highest	Total
Unadjusted money income	39.5	276.5	543.9	864.5	1772.4	3461.4
Plus						
Benefits in kind, capital gains, potential additional earnings, and other adjustments	167.4	104.7	55.0	33.7	30.3	391.1
Minus						
Income and payroll taxes	1.3	29.0	89.3	166.8	445.7	696.7
Equals						
Adjusted money income total	205.6	352.2	509.6	731.4	1357.0	3155.8
Adjusted percent distribution	6.5%	11.2%	16.1%	23.2%	43.0%	100%
Unadjusted percent distribution	1.1%	7.9%	15.5%	24.7%	50.7%	100%

Sources: Edgar K. Browning, "The Trend Toward Equality in the Distribution of Net Income," *Southern Economic Journal* 43 (July 1976), p. 914; Council of Economic Advisers, *Economic Report of the President* (Washington, D.C.: Government Printing Office, 1992); and Bureau of the Census, *Money Income of Households, Families, and Persons in the United States: 1991* (Washington, D.C.: U.S. Government Printing Office, 1992).

In-kind transfer payments

Transfer payments that take the form of goods and services such as public housing, veterans' hospitals, or a mass transit system.

A second important set of items that is not included in the raw money income statistics is transfer payments. These include **in-kind transfers** of benefits other than money—such as food stamps, public housing, Medicare, Medicaid, and other subsidies received largely by lower-income groups—in addition to money transfers or welfare payments. Such in-kind subsidies also tend to equalize income distribution across the various classes.

Economist Edgar K. Browning has attempted to develop a measure of income that conforms more closely to the definition of income used by economists. Browning estimated the effects of compensation for taxes, welfare transfers, transfers (benefits other than money), and other factors for the year 1972. In Table 15.4 we report similar calculations for a more recent year, 1990. The table shows the distribution of money income in 1990 in billions of dollars, with adjustments for in-kind transfers and other factors added in and with income and payroll taxes subtracted from the raw money income data.

Consider the additions to money income shown in Table 15.4. In-kind benefits are received largely by the poorest classes in society, whereas capital gains on stocks, bonds, and houses—which are not reflected in money income data—are six to seven times greater for the highest quintile of income recipients than for the lowest.

After these items are added to money income, taxes must be subtracted to obtain an estimate of net income. In the United States the largest burden of income tax—in both percent terms and total amount—falls on those in the highest quintile. In 1990, as the income and payroll taxes line in Table 15.4 shows, this group paid about $159.3 billion more in income taxes than all other income earners combined.

What is the net result of these adjustments to money income? Table 15.4 reports the results in terms of total income adjustment and in unadjusted and adjusted percent distribution. Total income rises for each class after additions to and subtractions from money income are made. But the important point is that the percent distribution among the quintiles is affected. The poorest 60 percent of income recipients all receive increased shares, with the lowest 20 percent receiving a 5.4 percent increase in adjusted income.

The effects indicated in the data of Table 15.4 are summarized in Figure 15.3 as Lorenz curves. Figure 15.3 shows a set of three Lorenz curves for 1990. The most bowed curve is the unadjusted distribution of money income. Figure 15.3 also shows a Lorenz curve that is adjusted for payroll and income taxes. The tax adjustment makes the curve less bowed and moves income distribution closer to the line of perfect equality. This shift indicates that a progressive tax system does effect greater

FIGURE 15.3

Lorenz Curve Including Income Adjustments

When taxes are subtracted from before-tax money income and in-kind transfers and other factors are added, the Lorenz curve moves closer to the line of perfect equality.

Source: Figure based on conclusions of Browning, "The Trend Toward Equality in the Distribution of Net Income." *Southern Economic Journal* 43 (July 1976), pp. 912–923 and Table 4.

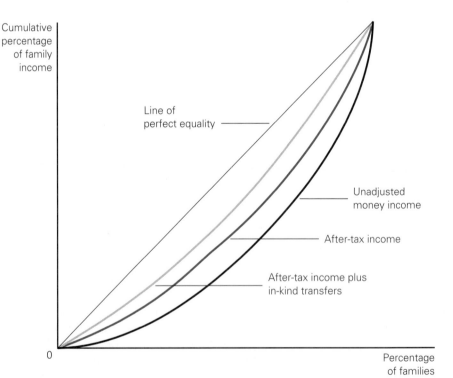

equality in income distribution. The inclusion of in-kind transfers and other adjustments pushes income distribution to still-greater equality, as the third Lorenz curve shows. These curves indicate the importance of social programs such as Medicare, food stamps, and public housing in creating greater income equality across the various segments of society.

Factors Affecting Income Distribution

Recently, considerable attention has been focused on data that indicate that the share of total unadjusted income earned by the poorest quintile of families has declined sharply since 1970. At that time, the poorest fifth of all families earned about 5.4 percent of *unadjusted* income. By 1996, this figure had fallen to about 4.2 percent. In attempting to explain the decline, a number of factors have been considered. Some observers attribute the decline to reductions in spending on government social programs. Others have placed the blame on foreign competition, which, in their view, has displaced American workers from high-paying jobs in manufacturing to low-paying jobs in the service sector. There are many reasons explaining low earnings, including the increase in single-parent families (see the Focus "Divorce, Single-Parent Families, and Income Distribution"), the age distribution of the population, and the degree of income mobility in the economy.

Age Distribution and Income

Another useful factor in understanding income distribution is the age structure of the income-receiving population. Take your own situation as an example. Perhaps you are a college student with a part-time job. If so, you are now probably part of the poorest quintile of the population in calculated annual income distribution. But you are not likely to be poor forever. Education and training alone will give you an edge in earning income later. At any point in time, the relative mean income of heads of households tends to peak between ages 45 and 55. Therefore, annual income figures will either overstate or understate multiyear inequality in income distribution, depending on the age structure of the population.

If the population is heavily populated by young people in the college age group, annual data will overstate actual lifetime or multiyear inequality in income distribution. There is in fact less inequality over multiyear distributions in the United States than there appears to be in any given year. Economists' estimates vary on how much more equal income distribution is over the long run, but all agree that there is more equality when age distribution is considered.

Rags to Riches Mobility

Economic mobility

The movement of individuals among income ranges.

Economic mobility—movements up or down in the quintiles of income distribution—also influences the question of how seriously annual data should be taken. How, for example, do we know that a family in the poorest quintile of income receivers in 1965 was not in the richest quintile in 2000, or vice versa? The answer

FOCUS

Divorce, Single-Parent Families, and Income Distribution

One factor that has received relatively little attention is the growing divorce rate and the resulting increase in the number of single-parent families. Families in the top quintile have always differed from those in the bottom quintile in terms of age, education, and the number of employed adults. In 1970, about 95 percent of families in the top quintile were husband–wife units, and this figure has changed little since then. What has changed is the percentage of high-income families with an employed wife—it has risen from 50 percent to about 70 percent. As a consequence, the total income of top quintile families has risen sharply. In contrast, the growing divorce rate has brought about a sharp decline in the percentage of husband–wife families in the lowest quintile—from 70 percent to about 50 percent today. Divorce transforms one family into two—usually

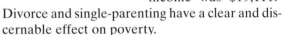

resulting in a drop in income for at least one of the two, if not both. If income statistics are reported on a per family basis, the increasing numbers of low-income single-parent families will lead to increases in income inequality. Data from the U.S. Department of the Census are indeed self-explanatory in this regard. In 1996 (the last year for which data are available), the median income of married couples was $49,707. For male-headed households, with wives not present, median income was $31,600, and for female-headed households, with husbands not present, median income was $19,111.[a]

Divorce and single-parenting have a clear and discernable effect on poverty.

[a]See *Statistical Abstract of the United States 1998* (Washington, D.C.: U.S. Government Printing Office, 1989), p. 473.

is that we do not know. To the extent that there is upward (and downward) mobility among income classes, greater equality is achieved over time.

Most studies indicate that there is a high degree of mobility in the United States, especially in the lower quintiles, but there are important statistical problems with identifying mobility over long-run periods. Such problems also extend to measuring age distribution factors and multiyear inequality. While it is safe to say that age distribution factors and economic mobility undoubtedly *reduce* income inequality over time, economists and policy-makers do not yet have the data or the wherewithal to judge the exact amount of the reduction.

CHARACTERISTICS OF INCOME DISTRIBUTION: POVERTY AND DISCRIMINATION

The data in population surveys and Census reports reveal a great deal about ourselves as a nation. Consider the total and average incomes of white, African Amer-

Mean income
A measure of average income; can be computed as per capita, per family, or per earner of income.

Per capita income
Average income per person; the total income of a population divided by the number of people in the population.

Poverty
A substandard level of income.

ican, and Hispanic families for 1997. The **mean**—or average—**income** of white families was about $18,000 greater than that of both African American and Hispanic families. (If **per capita income**—income per person—were compared for white, African American, and Hispanic families, the differences would be even more striking because white families are, on average, smaller than African American and Hispanic families.) Some of these differences are undoubtedly the consequence of differences in education, training, and experience, but some of the differences result from economic discrimination.

Although the numbers change from year to year, the pattern of income distribution continues to show that there are striking differences among the mean incomes of white, black, and Hispanic families, not all of which can be accounted for by differences in age, education, or family size.

Poverty

Poverty and economic discrimination are interrelated within our economic system. First we will define poverty; then we will examine various contributing factors to poverty in the United States.

Poverty can be defined as the condition of relatively lower incomes for some individuals or groups compared with others in a society. Defined this way, poverty will always be with us. As long as the Lorenz curve for unadjusted income is not diagonal—in other words, as long as there is not perfect income equality—some families will be better off than others.

Government measures of poverty are based on a poverty index devised by the Social Security Administration in 1964 and modified by a Federal Interagency Committee in 1969. (Indeed, Social Security was designed as a plan to protect the poor. See the Application "Does Social Security Protect the Poor?" at the end of this chapter.) This is an attempt to define poverty in absolute terms. The index delineates a poverty level according to such factors as size of family, rate of inflation, number of children under age 18, and place of residence. Accepting this official definition, we can observe changes in the incidence of poverty over time to different types of families.

Even when measured in absolute rather than relative terms, much poverty still exists in the United States. Many of the poorest families in our society are living in conditions below those that most Americans would deem to be acceptable. Table 15.5 provides an overall profile for various types of families for selected years between 1959 and 1996. In 1959, the number of persons living below the poverty line was almost 40 million, or more than 22 percent of all persons in this country. By 1996, the poor had fallen in number to below 37 million, or 13.7 percent of the population; but this progress is somewhat misleading: In 1979, the number of persons living below the poverty line was 26.1 million, or 11.7 percent of the population. Overall, then, there has been an increase in poverty since 1979.

Although the number of African Americans living in poverty fell more than 25 percent between 1959 and 1996, the incidence of poverty among African American families has remained high since 1979, falling only during the prosperous 1990s. Unemployment rates for Hispanic families have remained at about twice the national average. A third demographic group for which poverty rates have remained high is families headed by single women. In 1996, 40 percent of

TABLE 15.5

Poverty by Family Status, Race, and Sex of Householder, 1959–1996
While poverty has declined in absolute numbers and in percentage terms over time, the
relative positions of African Americans and female householders are still a matter of concern.

Family Status, Race, and Sex of Householder	NUMBER BELOW POVERTY LEVEL (MILLIONS)					PERCENT OF PERSONS BELOW POVERTY LEVEL				
	1959	1969	1979	1987	1996	1959	1969	1979	1987	1996
All persons	39.5	24.2	26.1	32.5	36.5	22.4	12.1	11.7	13.5	13.7
White	28.5	16.7	17.2	21.4	24.6	18.1	9.5	9.5	10.5	11.2
African American	9.9	7.1	8.1	9.7	9.7	55.1	32.2	31.0	33.1	28.4
Hispanic	(NA)	(NA)	2.9	5.5	8.7	(NA)	(NA)	21.6	28.2	29.4

Sources: U.S. Department of Commerce, Bureau of the Census, Current Population Records—Consumer Income, *Money Income and Poverty Status of Families and Persons in the United States: 1984* (Washington, D.C.: U.S. Government Printing Office.,1986), pp. 20–24: *Statistical Abstract of the United States* (Washington, D.C.: U.S. Government Printing Office, 1998). p. 447. (1998 Statistical Update, U.S. Department of Commerce Web Site.)

such families were living in poverty, and over one-half of all poor families were headed by women.

Race and Sex Discrimination in Wages

The overall statistics on poverty since the 1960s do show improvement, but the undeniable fact is that there are poor among us and that poverty is often related to race, sex, and family status. What are the reasons for the facts of poverty? Factors are many and often interwoven. Some people are unlucky. Others are not able-bodied; they are simply unable to work. But these factors cannot explain the existence of all poverty.

Lower incomes also exist for clearly identifiable economic reasons. The poor tend to have lower skills and lower stocks of human capital. These lower stocks of human capital are the result of less education and lower job-related training. Lower productivity means unemployment and lower wages, lower wages mean lower incomes, and lower incomes mean poverty. Environmental factors may make poverty a vicious cycle: Children of the poor often receive less education and training. Moreover, many wage and income differences are the result of outright race and sex discrimination. In particular, current differences in training and education may be related to past and present economic discrimination.

We must be careful to distinguish between social discrimination and economic discrimination that leads to significantly lower wages and income, although the two are often related. Groups such as Jews, gays, and the handicapped may meet with social discrimination in seeking housing and club memberships but be little affected by economic discrimination.

Economic wage discrimination

A situation in which individuals in the same occupation who have the same productive abilities are paid different wage rates by a given employer. The wage-rate differences are based on race, sex, religion, or national origin rather than on productive differences.

Economic wage discrimination exists when individuals of equal ability and productivity in the same occupation earn different wage rates. Thus, while the median income of African Americans is only 60 percent of that of whites (in all income classes), empirical studies show that about half of this difference is related to educational, productivity, and job-training differences. The remaining half is the apparent result of economic discrimination or other unidentified factors.

Economists do not pretend to know the causes of discrimination. Nonetheless, economic discrimination involves costs to those who discriminate as well as to those against whom discrimination is practiced. An employer who refuses to hire women or African Americans of equal productivity to men or whites is discriminating. If the wages of the preferred groups are driven up by these actions, employers must pay a premium for their labor services. In a competitive system, discriminating firms will be at a disadvantage in the marketplace. Employers who do not discriminate in hiring can acquire equally productive labor at lower wage rates, eventually driving discriminating competitors out of business.

Consumer-initiated discrimination

Wage discrimination arising from consumers' preferences for goods or services produced by individuals of a certain sex, race, religion, or national origin. Consumers must pay a premium in the form of higher prices or lower quality to exercise such discrimination.

Even if employers do not discriminate, consumers may. In a competitive system, **consumer-initiated discrimination** is costly to the discriminator as well as to those discriminated against. Consumers who will deal only with whites or men (avoiding, say, African American or female lawyers, doctors, or interior designers) must pay a premium for their prejudice. Prices of goods and services of favored sellers will be higher than prices for the same goods or services available to those who do not discriminate. In sum, the competitive system makes it costly for employers or consumers to discriminate. This economic deterrent has failed to eradicate discrimination in our economy, however, as have government regulations explicitly forbidding discrimination.

Alleviating Poverty: The 1996 Revolution in Welfare

Welfare programs center on the relative needs of the poor. In-kind benefits such as food stamps, Medicare, housing subsidies, and outright money transfers (such as Aid to Families with Dependent Children) have been, for more than six decades, allotted to the poor on the basis of a government agency's determination of need. Passed as a "safety net" during the Great Depression of the 1930s, federal guarantees of welfare benefits were supposed to be a temporary stopgap for those that found themselves in poverty. These programs became increasingly "federalized" with the federal government mandating benefits to the poor, although benefits did vary from state to state and among local governments.

Without questioning the need or the existence of poverty, economists have for many years analyzed the costs of fairly and accurately administering these programs. But more important, economists are concerned with the effects of such programs on the incentives of the poor. While there will always be those who for health or other reasons cannot work, the strongly federalized welfare system historically discriminated against most of the poor in one respect: It has tended to discourage any effort on the part of the poor to better themselves by earning income in addition to their subsidy and perhaps acquiring job training in the process. The specter of third and fourth generation (often fatherless) families on welfare payments mandated by the federal government created an enormous groundswell for change.

In November 1988, the first major welfare reform legislation in fifty-three years, the Family Support Act of 1988, was signed into law. As a major revision in the rules affecting the approximately 11 million people receiving Aid to Families with Dependent Children (AFDC), the program attempted to institute economic incentives into the welfare system. It was specifically addressed to the problem created by the tremendous increase in the number of households headed by women. In particular the Act created a system whereby working did not disqualify the welfare recipient from receiving assistance.

But this change in the Act was clearly not enough to have a significant effect on those on welfare and in poverty. In 1996, the government embraced one of the largest "social experiments" concerning poverty since federally mandated welfare assistance was passed during the presidency of Franklin D. Roosevelt. Congress passed and President Clinton signed the Personal Responsibility and Work Opportunity Act in August 1996, ending the sixty-one-year guarantee that families and poor children are entitled to federal benefits. This historic piece of legislation returns to states the authority to establish many of the rules and regulations concerning qualifications for welfare. Each state receives a set amount of money for welfare payments with the option of spending more out-of-state funds. Each state must maintain its welfare disbursements at 75 percent of the total amount spent in 1994, however.

In principle, the entire incentive structure will change for those in poverty and receiving welfare. In addition to the change in terms of responsibility for welfare, some of the major provisions of the bill:

- Require that states cut off welfare benefits after an individual has collected for five years;
- Provide no cash benefits to unmarried teenage parents unless states decide to provide benefits to teen mothers who remain in school and live with an adult;
- Mandate that all able-bodied adults work after two years on welfare. Refusal to work would mean a cut-off of benefits, although states could make "hardship" exemptions for 20 percent of the recipients;
- Allow nonworking, childless adults to qualify for food stamps for six months during a three-year period for only three months at a time. Students remain eligible for school lunch programs so long as they are legally eligible for free public education;
- Cut off those convicted of drug felonies from food stamps and cash assistance (pregnant women and those in drug treatment are excepted);
- Permit state officials to deny Medicaid benefits to adults who fail to work and who have lost benefits, although health benefits would be guaranteed to families on welfare, continuing for one year after individuals go to work;
- Exclude illegal immigrants from most benefits and future legal immigrants (noncitizens) for their first five years in the United States.

Economists, generally, have hailed these reforms as a step in the right direction of providing incentives for individuals and families to remove themselves from poverty. Although critics have complained that children are not adequately protected under this system, supporters see the new welfare rules as the only way to provide compassion for poor children and their families. The short-term preliminary evidence on welfare reform (between the 1996 Act and 1998) is quite posi-tive.[1] Welfare caseloads fell dramatically, with most states experiencing double-digit reductions. But we must be very careful in interpreting these stark reductions in the welfare rolls. Welfare rolls are known normally to fluctuate with the busi-ness cycle. As the unemployment rates goes down, so does the welfare participa-tion rate. We should expect fewer people and families to be on the rolls over the highly prosperous 1990s.

Surely, welfare reform at the federal and state levels has had a positive effect on poverty and labor force participation, but the real question is "how much?" When the (inevitable) business cycle turns downward, will families and individu-als continue to be employed in the economy or will they experience long-term unemployment, putting pressure on private charities? A number of years must pass before these important questions will be answered. Clearly, there was very little defense of the system as it existed, either from politicians or from society at large. The new system means that states, not the federal government, will compete and lead to the evolution of innovative policies to deal with the problems of poverty and welfare assistance.

HEALTH CARE: AN ONGOING PROBLEM

The provision of health care is closely related to the issues of income distribution and poverty. Consider the fact that infant mortality rates in the United States are higher among people living in poverty than among people in higher-income groups or the fact that people in higher-income groups tend to live longer than people in lower-income groups. Health care is thus intimately linked to issues of income distribution.

The U.S. Health Care System

Despite some obvious inequities in the provision of health care, surveys indicated that most Americans were generally satisfied with the level of health care bene-fits they were receiving during the 1990s. What conditions, then, led to the wide-spread belief among Americans around that time that an overhaul of the U.S. health care system had become essential? First, there was the matter of soaring health costs. Between 1985 and 1995, spending on health care grew at a faster rate than the overall economy. In fact, health costs grew faster than GDP in all but one of the 32 years prior to 1993, and there was every reason to believe that the trend would continue. Health care expenditures, which accounted for 6 percent of GDP in 1965, swallowed up more than 14 percent of GDP in 1995. Some experts sug-gested in the early 1990s that inaction on health care matters would cause health care's share of GDP to increase to 17 percent by the year 2000 and 37 percent by 2030, although the rise in health care costs moderated the second half of the 1990s.

---

[1] For additional information on this issue, see the *Economic Report of the President 1998* (Washington, D.C.: U.S. Gov-ernment Printing Office, 1998), pp. 117–120.

FOCUS

Should You Buy Health Insurance?

In 1996, by some estimates, approximately 15 percent of all persons in the United States (41 million) were without any form of health insurance *at any given time*. Access to health insurance is considered a major indicator of access to health care for individuals and families. Consequently, reducing the number of uninsured persons is a common goal of most proposals to reform the health care system in the United States.

By itself, however, the 41 million figure for the uninsured population may not be very helpful in understanding access to health care. Over time, there are changes in the composition of the uninsured population, a process called churning. In other words, most of the uninsured are uninsured for relatively brief periods of time—usually when they are between jobs.

The uninsured tend to use fewer health care services than the insured, and as a result may have a poorer health status than the insured population. However, while the uninsured may use fewer health care services, they nevertheless generally do receive some health care. Some of the uninsured pay for these services out of their own pockets; some receive care from clinics that receive public subsidies; and some get care from providers who are subsidizing their care through increased charges to their paying customers. By law, the condition of anyone who checks into a hospital emergency room must be at least stabilized. Much of hospitals'

uncompensated care was financed by shifting the cost to patients with insurance.

A sizeable portion of the uninsured population is not poor. Forty percent of uninsured households have incomes of $20,000 or more; 22 percent have incomes of $30,000 or more; and 13 percent have incomes of $40,000 or more. Most uninsured individuals are in the middle (and healthier) years of life (18–54). Many of these families choose to "self-insure." In other words, they plan to pay for necessary health care costs as they arise.

Does the purchase of some level of health insurance make sense for you? Economists can only guess at the incentives involved. If an individual is young, healthy, risk-loving, and earning a small income, no insurance or a minimum amount rationally may be chosen. Older, less healthy, risk-averse, and high-income individuals rationally would make other choices. Difficulties are introduced into the system when portability and the prospects of a catastrophe are considered. Basically, the purchase of insurance depends on a number of individual factors, not least of which is your attitude toward risk.

Sources: Madeleine Smith, *Health Insurance Coverage: Characteristics of the Insured and Uninsured Populations* (Washington, D.C.: Library of Congress, Congressional Research Service, August 19, 1991); Joseph L. Bast, Richard C. Rue, and Stuart A. Westbury, Jr., *Why We Spend Too Much on Health Care* (Chicago: The Heartland Institute, 1992); and *Statistical Abstract of the United States 1998* (Washington, D.C.: U.S. Government Printing Office, 1998), p. 125.

While expenditures on health care (as a percentage of total expenditures) have remained fairly constant over the 1990s, dissatisfaction with the state of the health insurance industry in the United States has prompted calls for change. As many as 41 million Americans—15 percent of the population—are uninsured, and another 37 million "underinsured." This number may be seriously misleading, however, and it may well be rational behavior for some Americans to remain uninsured (for more details, see the Focus "Should You Buy Health Insurance?"). The high cost of health insurance was a significant factor in the large size of the uninsured population in the 1990s, but many observers also pointed to the linkage of health insurance and employment and the virtually unlimited ability of insurers to "dump" people with serious illnesses or who pose serious risks.

Health Care Reform: Some Models

Bill Clinton's pledge to do something about reforming the U.S. health care system was partly responsible for his victory over George Bush in the 1992 presidential election. Indeed, shortly after taking office, Clinton appointed a health care task force (chaired by the First Lady, Hillary Rodham Clinton) and charged its members with developing a reform plan. Deciding how to fix the system proved to be an enormously complicated job, and the Clintons' efforts at reform were rebuffed by Congress in 1994. The issue is not over, however, and it is useful to reflect upon some of the things that we learned from this historic debate over health care reform. For one thing, there is more than one way to structure a health care system. One method is the Canadian system of universal health insurance. This single-paper system is what is termed "socialized medicine" in that all essential medical services are provided equally for everyone at government (that is, taxpayers') expense. Americans have apparently rejected this system. But the issue of rising health care costs remains on the minds of voters and politicians. Some reform, therefore, is to be expected. Some of the alternative systems and the means of financing them must be considered.

Managed Competition   Whereas the Canadian model provides a large role for government, most managed competition or "managed care" proposals are a hybrid of free market forces and government intervention. At the heart of all managed competition proposals are organizations called health insurance purchasing cooperatives (HIPCs) or health alliances. Some proposals envision the cooperatives as privately run consumer advocacy groups. Each HIPC would function as a kind of medical "farmer's market," where buyers and sellers of benefit packages that meet or exceed the federal government's standard package would be brought together to conduct transactions. The appeal of the HIPCs is that they provide a way for health providers to spread the costs and risks associated with universal coverage over a vast pool of individuals. In other words, the number of individuals in each pool would be large enough that providers could afford to charge everyone in the pool an average, or community, rate, thereby eliminating the need for cost adjustments based on individuals' medical histories. Additionally, the sheer size of the HIPCs—millions of individuals would belong to each cooperative—would give them tremendous bargaining strength with health providers. Each HIPC, therefore, would be able to negotiate for the highest-quality, lowest-cost medical services being offered.

The most extreme managed care proposals include some regulatory powers for the health alliances. Some reformers have advocated establishing a global health budget—or a cap on all health expenditures, public and private—in order to curb rising costs. There have also been calls for limiting the amount by which health insurance premiums can be increased each year. If these two proposals were enacted, the health alliances would be charged with enforcing the associated regulations. It is worth noting that a configuration in which the cooperatives have regulatory powers closely resembles the Canadian system.

Another wrinkle in health care policy concerns the role of health care providers such as health maintenance organizations (HMOs). These organizations substitute for insurance policies and offer the individual a range of medical services for a fee. However, HMOs employ a particular form of medicine. The patient,

FOCUS

Who Pays the Bill for Patients' Rights?

Can your insurance company deny you necessary medical treatment? What rights do you have as a patient, and how much do they cost? Health maintenance organizations (HMOs) now cover more than 60 percent of the American population and reduce costs by better organizing health care. They introduce new efficiencies and reduce the use of expensive medical treatments when less costly ones are available.

In response to outrage over the withholding of certain medical treatments and restrictions on consumers' choice of doctors, politicians of both stripes are promoting patients' bills of rights at both the state and federal levels. This legislation typically provides for independent arbitration between patients and their health plans, holds health plans accountable for injuries caused by the restriction of treatments, and protects doctors who report abuses of the health plan companies for which they work.

President Clinton's proposal contains rights such as access to accurate, easily understood information, choice of health care providers, access to

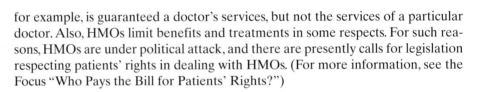

emergency services, participation in treatment decisions, and grievances and appeals processes. While many of the provisions are common sense and are already a part of standard medical services, mandating them across the board will have costly economic effects. By mandating that HMOs must cover a broader range of expensive treatments, these new rights will force all ratepayers to buy unwanted coverage like the mandates in some states that require coverage for such things as hair transplants and massage therapy. The bill of rights will therefore result in higher premiums, make health insurance less affordable, and enrich lawyers. It has been estimated that as many as 600,000 people would no longer be covered by health insurance if the patients' bill of rights is passed.

Rights are not for free. Scarcity still plays a role. Guaranteeing high-quality medical care comes at a price that consumers must pay and prices health insurance beyond the reach of more Americans. Alternative policies, or simply letting competition work in this new industry, may provide improvement in health plans at a lower cost.

for example, is guaranteed a doctor's services, but not the services of a particular doctor. Also, HMOs limit benefits and treatments in some respects. For such reasons, HMOs are under political attack, and there are presently calls for legislation respecting patients' rights in dealing with HMOs. (For more information, see the Focus "Who Pays the Bill for Patients' Rights?")

Tax-Code Changes   Some observers blame many of the problems that created the crisis in health care on the U.S. tax code. Medical care and health insurance provided by employers as part of an employee's wage package are exempt from federal taxes. Therefore, employees have an incentive to take a larger share of their total compensation in the form of health care than they would if health care were subject to federal taxes. Removing the exemption would create an incentive for employees to bargain with their employers for more take-home pay and less health care. (A similar idea—taxing benefits that go beyond some government-defined list of core benefits—is popular with people who doubt that any attempt to create a new health care system overnight will succeed.) With the proper incentives, employees might even decide to provide for their own health care by dealing directly with providers or by buying health insurance on their own. When employees rely on employers to finance their health care, they have little incentive to monitor costs. Because the recipients of health care are in the best position to monitor costs, tying health care to employment and one's compensation package is not the most efficient approach. Whether or not individuals know enough about health care to judge the best plan for their family's needs is a matter of debate. Some observers feel that most people would be better off letting a government agency make the choice for them. Others argue that individuals usually make well-informed choices when they are provided with strong economic incentives.

Deregulation   The provision of health care in the United States has always been influenced by government regulatory policies, tax subsidies, and various price and output policies. Government owns and operates medical facilities and purchases vast amounts of medical sector output at prices it helps to set. Virtually all aspects of the supply and demand of the health care market are affected by government. Some observers argue that government actions distort market price signals and that large government spending programs do a poor job of controlling rising medical costs. One possible reform, therefore, would eliminate existing government health insurance programs (Medicare and Medicaid) and require that every family have a major medical insurance policy, which the family would purchase in a competitive insurance market. In most cases, each family would pay for its own insurance coverage and would receive a reduction in taxes in return from the government. Special provisions might be made for lower-income families or for families unable to qualify for private insurance at reasonable rates.

Obviously, providing even a modest package of health benefits to every American is an enormously expensive—and complex—undertaking. Working out the details relating to the structure of a universal-coverage scheme may actually be easier than finding a formula for financing the program. Even among President Clinton's advisers there were numerous disagreements over alternative schemes for financing the administration's proposed reforms.

Health reforms relating to the "portability" of health insurance were passed in 1996. The Health Insurance Reform Act (also called the Kassebaum–Kennedy Act) aimed at making it easier for people to renew or acquire health insurance coverage despite "preexisting conditions" or health status, particularly when they lose or change their jobs. These new rules apply to all employment-based health plans and prohibits these plans from denying or limiting coverage for more than twelve months for most "preexisting" medical problems. Further, the Kassebaum–Kennedy legislation guarantees group-to-individual coverage portability for those individuals who leave group coverage. The bill also permits an "experiment" whereby a sample of 750,000 individuals may opt for "medical savings accounts" or voluntary purchasing pools offering insurance contracts (although Kassebaum–Kennedy puts rate restrictions on the latter).

Some economists are skeptical of the value of the Kassebaum–Kennedy "reforms." A number of economists point to one critical problem—the matter of insurance rates. Rates have been based on risk assessments for certain conditions—high-risk individuals have been "redlined" or charged higher rates to reflect the higher risk. Under the 1996 legislation, the government mandates that individuals be covered, but does not put rate restrictions on this coverage. Under such circumstances, rates will rise, and healthy people will subsidize the higher costs to those with higher health risks. It is not difficult, from a public choice–interest group perspective, to understand the popularity of such legislation.

The debate about health care reform is part of a larger debate about the proper role of government. Some people advocate more direct government involvement and finance to set things right, while others advocate the use of the tax system to provide individuals with the financial wherewithal to make their own decisions about health care. Time will tell which approach wins out.

THE JUSTICE OF INCOME DISTRIBUTION

Justice itself is not part of the positive economist's vocabulary, but the effects of concepts of justice are within the economist's purview. More than a century ago, the classical economist John Stuart Mill observed that two kinds of equality are involved in questions of distribution: *ex ante* equality and *ex post* equality. *Ex ante* equality is a situation where "all start fair"—where, through educational opportunities, the absence of discrimination, social and economic mobility, and so on, every individual is given an opportunity to maximize his or her potential. *Ex ante* equality is equivalent to equality of opportunity. *Ex post* equality is a guarantee that through redistributive policies all end up at the same place. While Mill championed *ex ante* equality, he believed that differing incentives, innate talents, luck, and so on meant there would be differences in income distribution in the end. To guarantee all citizens *ex post* equality would stultify incentives, which are the very core of economic progress. Enforced *ex post* equality would surely shrink the total economic pie.

Modern economists concerned with income distribution face the same problem. The trick is to evaluate the contemporary system and to propose means that provide that all start fair but that do not force redistributions that significantly reduce incentives to produce.

APPLICATION

Does Social Security Protect the Poor?

The Social Security Act was passed during the Great Depression era of the 1930s as part of President Franklin D. Roosevelt's New Deal policies. The central program of Social Security is government-guaranteed supplemental retirement benefits paid for by Social Security taxes (some of which come out of your paycheck under the heading F.I.C.A.). Protecting the poor against severe hardship is a primary justification for forcing virtually everyone into the Social Security system.

In order to help the poor and lower-income worker, Social Security was designed with a scale of "progressive benefits," where those with lower wage rates receive a higher percentage of their average monthly income in Social Security benefits than do average and high-wage earners. Low-wage workers get a Social Security retirement benefit check equal to approximately 58 percent of their pre-retirement income, while average income earners receive 43 percent and high-wage workers get back only about 25 percent. The system would seem to benefit the poor and lower-income groups.

Despite its bias toward helping the poor, there are many reasons that Social Security does not benefit low-wage workers or protect people from poverty. Today, more than 10 percent of senior citizens live in poverty, with nearly 20 percent of elderly widows and 30 percent of elderly African Americans living below the poverty line. It seems that there is little that can be done to increase these benefits, because the system is expecting a shortfall in revenues during the first half of the twenty-first century. Absent reform, this long-predicted crisis in Social Security could ultimately necessitate up to a 25 percent cut in benefits to close the gap between the system's revenues and its expenses. Such a big cut in benefits would be particularly painful to low-income groups that are already below or just above the poverty line.

The system of progressive benefits that is supposed to benefit low-wage workers is offset by the regressive nature of the Social Security tax. The total Social Security tax is now the equivalent of more than 15 percent of wages. This tax applies to the first $62,000 in annual income, so that the poor and middle-income workers pay the tax on all their income, but high-income earners stop paying the tax after they reach that limit. Social Security, therefore, not only takes a high percentage of income from the poor, it takes a higher proportion of income from low-wage earners.

Studies have also shown that the progressive scale of Social Security benefits may be completely offset, if not reversed, by differences in life expectancy. Low-wage individuals tend to die younger than high-wage individuals, and therefore they collect fewer retirement checks from Social Security. Men in the highest income bracket live three years longer than men in the lowest income bracket and therefore receive, on average, thirty-six more checks from Social Security.

Differences in income and longevity also result in different benefits for African Americans and whites. The life expectancy of a black man born today is 66 years—a fact that translates into only one year of benefits in exchange for decades of taxes. African American males who reach age sixty-five are expected to live an additional fourteen years, but this is two years and twenty-four checks less than the average white male. The Rand Corporation estimated that Social Security is a $10,000 per person transfer from blacks to whites.

Low-wage workers also tend to work more years than high-wage workers, who often attend college and graduate school. A high-school dropout would work and pay Social Security taxes for nearly fifty years before being eligible for full Social Security benefits, but someone who went to graduate school might work less than forty years. Because Social Security benefits are based on a maximum of thirty-five years of earnings, the additional years above thirty-five mean the individual pays more taxes that are not compensated for by higher benefits.

Finally, Social Security taxes are so high now that low-wage workers accumulate little or no private savings over their lifetime. Private savings help supplement Social Security income to raise individuals above the poverty level. Unlike Social Security, private savings can be passed down to future generations. For all these reasons, Social Security appears to be a bad deal for low-wage workers.

Private investing yields a much better return than Social Security. Consider private investment as an alternative to Social Security. If a couple who dropped out of high school both worked at full-time minimum-wage jobs, the total Social Security taxes on their labor (including Medicare taxes) would exceed 15 percent, or more than $250 per month. If they invested $250 per month in a tax-free mutual fund account that invested in conservative stocks and bonds with an average return of 7 percent, they would have a nest egg of more than $1.2 million when they retired at age sixty-five. If the money was invested in a more aggressive stock fund that averaged 11 percent, their nest egg would amount to more than $5 million dollars.

Without spending any of the principal, the couple would have an annual retirement income of $84,000 in the case of the conservative investment and $550,000 per year in the case of the aggressive investment. Not only would our couple live much better than if they had to live off of Social Security, but they would have a substantial inheritance to give to future generations. It may seem implausible that families would save 15 percent of their income, but the Japanese save at an even higher rate. Our government could provide tax incentives to encourage people to save more.

In addition to the poor returns that the current and future Social Security recipients receive, the two main economic problems with Social Security are that the taxes discourage work and employment and the benefits discourage savings. Reverting to a private system in which the government provided incentives to save and allowed people to keep all of their investment returns would permit individuals, especially low-income individuals, a way to accumulate wealth and break the cycle of poverty. Experiments in partial privatization of Social Security in the South American country of Chile and Galveston County, Texas, have thus far proven successful and popular with citizens.

QUESTIONS

Has Social Security fulfilled its promise? Why might low-income individuals oppose a return to private investing and other reforms of Social Security?

Source: A reference for the material in this Application is Carrie Lips, "The Working Poor and Social Security Privatization," (Washington, D.C.: Cato Institute), September 29, 1998.

SUMMARY

1. Economists deal with positive, not normative, aspects of income distribution. The economist does not normally deal with questions of justice or fairness, but focuses instead on the facts of income distribution and on the possible effects of alternative welfare programs.

2. Money income distributions differ for a number of reasons: Some persons choose leisure over work and income, while others earn lower incomes because of bad luck, poor health, lower educational opportunities and productivity, and race or sex discrimination.

3. A Lorenz curve is one measure of income inequality. Ordinarily, the more bowed the Lorenz curve, the more inequality there is in a society's income distribution.

4. Lorenz curves showing money income distribution for a given year overstate actual inequality when in-kind benefits, income and payroll taxes, and other factors are considered. Age distribution of the population and income mobility also create greater long-term equality in income distribution.

5. Poverty and economic discrimination are interrelated features of our economic system. Economic discrimination exists when individuals of equal productivity are paid different wages on the basis of sex or racial differences.

6. Economic discrimination exists against African Americans and women in our society; only half of the difference between African American–white and male–female earnings is related to productivity differences.

7. Economic discrimination cannot be practiced by employers or consumers without costs in a competitive environment. Government-sanctioned regulations and restrictions on competitors appear to account for a large amount of observed economic discrimination in the United States.

8. In 1996 Congress passed and President Clinton signed the Personal Responsibility and Work Opportunity Act. This legislation returns authority over welfare programs to the states and sets time limits and work requirements for welfare recipients.

9. Spending on health care has been growing faster than the overall economy for more than thirty years. Numerous reform measures have been proposed, most of which are designed to curb rising costs while guaranteeing every American a standard package of health benefits. In 1996 Congress passed and President Clinton signed legislation implementing health care reform, stressing the portability of insurance across jobs, access to health insurance for those with preexisting conditions, and medical savings accounts.

KEY TERMS

individual income
labor income
asset income
ex ante distribution
ex post distribution
transfer payment

family income
Lorenz curve
adjusted income
in-kind transfer payments
economic mobility
mean income

per capita income
poverty
economic wage discrimination
consumer-initiated discrimination

QUESTIONS FOR REVIEW AND DISCUSSION

1. What are the components of an individual's income? Which of these are matters of choice by the individual?

2. How does an individual obtain asset income?

3. What does a Lorenz curve show? What does it mean if the Lorenz curve moves closer through time to the line of perfect equality?

4. What is the difference between income as measured by government and adjusted income as reported by some economists?

5. What is economic wage discrimination? Give an example of wage discrimination that fits the description.

6. Why do young people have lower incomes than older people?

7. If every married couple in the United States obtained a divorce, would the Lorenz curve move away from the line of perfect equality? Would this alteration change the actual distribution of income?

8. Suppose all people were born with the same amount of natural abilities and the same amount of inherited money wealth. Under these circumstances, what would the sources of income differences be?

9. Is a perfectly equal distribution of income necessarily desirable? Why or why not?

10. What conditions led to the widespread dissatisfaction with the U.S. health care system that developed in the early 1990s? Discuss two possible solutions to the health care problem and indicate which you would prefer to see implemented. Explain your selection.

11. There are constraints to public solution of the retirement problem. Devise a possible solution to the problems posed by the Social Security crisis.

PROBLEM

The table shows the distribution of family income in the small nation of Microvia before taxes and transfer payments.

Quintile	Household Income	Adjusted Income
Lowest	$10,000	———
Second	$20,000	———
Third	$30,000	———
Fourth	$40,000	———
Highest	$50,000	———

a. Suppose that the Microvian government enacts a transfer payment that gives $5000 to every household that earns less than $20,000. Also suppose that it enacts a progressive income tax with no taxes for households that earn $20,000 or less, a 10 percent tax on household income of $30,000, a 15 percent tax on household income of $40,000, and a 20 percent tax on household income of $50,000. Fill in the blanks in the table to show household income after it is adjusted for the transfer payments and income taxes.

b. Complete the following table using the data provided for income and adjusted income in the first table.

Quintile	Percent of Income	Cumulative Percent	Percent of Adjusted Income	Cumulative Percent of Adjusted Income
Lowest	———	———	———	———
Second	———	———	———	———
Third	———	———	———	———
Fourth	———	———	———	———
Highest	———	———	———	———

c. Draw the Lorenz curves for the unadjusted and adjusted income distributions you have calculated.

WORKING WITH THE WEB

1. The Application "Does Social Security Protect the Poor?" discusses a variety of problems that exist with the current Social Security system as well as with proposed changes to the system, such as privatization. In San Diego, city employees are exempt from Social Security and instead are required to invest in a defined contribution plan. Go to http://www.socialsecurity.org and read the article "Social Security Differences" by J. T. Young, which was the "Daily Comment" for June 25, 1999.

   Analyze the case of the San Diego employee who invests 3.1% of their $32,000 salary compared with the expected returns if this individual participates in Social Security. Under which plan is this person better off?

2. To see the reality of the impact of privatization, return to http://www.socialsecurity.org and choose the link that allows you to calculate what you would gain from privatization. Or, if you prefer, the direct link is http://www.socialsecurity.org/calc/calculator.html. Click on the button "Estimate Social Security." Assume you were born in 1975 and that your current earnings are $50,000. Leave the other settings unchanged (i.e., they should read retirement age 67, Salary Scale 5%, Inflation 3%, Bond Return 6%, Bond/Stock 50%/50%, Stock Return 10%, Social Security Pct You Expect to Receive 100%).

   a. In nominal 2042 dollars, what is your annual retirement income under Social Security?

   b. In nominal 2042 dollars, what is your annual retirement income if you have invested aggressively in a stock fund?

   c. Is there any private investment alternative (i.e., bond fund, mixed fund, or stock fund) that leaves you worse off than the annual income expected under Social Security?

3. The Cato Institute offers a plan for an alternative to Social Security. Go to http://www.socialsecurity.org/alternative.html and read "Cato's Social Security Alternative."

   a. Does Cato advocate eliminating Social Security entirely?

   b. How does the level of investment differ between Social Security and Cato's proposed plan?

Thomas Malthus

Gary Becker

Thomas Malthus
and Gary Becker:
The Economics of
Population Growth

Thomas Malthus (1766–1834) was born in Surrey, England, during the Industrial Revolution. It was widely believed at the time that the effects of industrialization, such as increased trade and specialization of labor, would eventually improve the quality of human life. When anarchist and pamphleteer William Godwin published his utopian outlook for society in his book *Political Justice* in 1793, an argument developed between Malthus and his father. Malthus's father was inclined to agree with Godwin's views, but the younger Malthus believed that society was caught in a trap in which population would increase more rapidly than the food supply, leaving the standard of living at a subsistence level at best. In 1798, the same year he became a minister of the Church of England, Malthus published his views of population and the economy in his treatise *An Essay on the Principle of Population*. It was this pessimistic treatise on the future of humanity that led essayist Thomas Carlyle to label economics "the dismal science."

Malthus went on to become the first professor of political economy in England at the East India College in 1805. His work on population influenced his friend and critic David Ricardo as well as Charles Darwin.

Gary Becker (b. 1930), currently University Professor of Economics at the University of Chicago, gained international recognition for his work in applying microeconomic theory to areas such as marriage, crime, and prejudice. His book *The Economics of Discrimination* (1971) introduced prejudice and discrimination as forces that can be analyzed and measured in their effect on the economy. In *The Economics of Human Behavior* (1976), Becker argues that all human behavior, even selection of a marriage partner, is based on economics.

In 1965, Becker authored *Human Capital,* his famous treatise on the concept of human capital. In *Human Capital,* Becker treats the individual as a "firm" that makes investment decisions (such as education or on-the-job training) on the basis of rate of return. Soon after the book's publication, Becker was awarded the John Bates Clark medal by the American Economic Association for excellence in research by an economist under the age of 40. In 1992, Becker was awarded the Nobel Prize in economic science.

The Check of Misery

Malthus's theory of population growth is strongly pessimistic. In *An Essay on the Principle of Population,* Malthus wrote that the world's population will increase at a rate that will ultimately test the limits of our available food supply and other subsistence goods. As the supply of food increases through additional labor and agriculture, population will increase as well, with the result that per capita income—the fruits of labor—will never exceed bare subsistence standards for the population as a whole. The threat of widespread famine will persist indefinitely. Only the lucky will survive.

An alternative way of stating Malthus's proposition is that children are what economists call normal goods, demand for which rises and falls in response to changes in income. Any increase in income to parents will increase their demand for children, other things being equal. At the point when an additional child will actually reduce living standards below subsistence—a point Malthus called the "check of misery"—parents will cease reproducing.

Given this gloomy scenario, it is not surprising that Malthus, a parson, would urge "moral restraints" on parents. Such restraints included abstinence and postponing marriage. It is interesting to speculate about whether Malthus would urge modern forms of birth control. The morality of contraceptive use, forced sterilization, and abortion is one of the burning issues of our times.

Malthus's theory of population growth seems today most applicable to the exploding populations of China, Mexico, Bangladesh, and other developing countries. In the industrialized nations, including the United States, the last century has seen actual declines in average family size, while average family incomes have risen well above the level of bare subsistence. Many economists, including Gary Becker, have sought reasons that the theory has not, fortunately, held true.

The Price of Children

Becker's theory of human capital helps explain both the power and the limits of the Malthusian theory. For Becker, the choice of whether to reproduce has a second rationale, one beyond a simple change in income. Parents' demand for children will be influenced not only by changes in income but also by the relative "price" of children. This price is partly the direct costs of raising the child, but it also includes the opportunity costs that additional children represent. As the parents' income increases, the opportunity cost of children will also tend to increase. In other words, the sacrifices borne by increasing the size of a family will increase with income. To take one example, if an executive forsakes a high-paying job to stay home with the children so that his or her spouse can pursue a career, the cost of that decision is the wages and income the executive receives now and the higher income he or she could expect to receive in the future.

As the costs of children increase, the quantity demanded will decrease, other things being equal. As a result, parents may substitute quality for quantity in their decisions to raise children. Instead of feeding an additional child, parents might decide to spend additional income on housing, education, or any of a host of goods that improve living standards for the children they already have.

Becker's approach to the costs of children helps explain why parents in developed countries, with relatively high incomes, have fewer, better-educated children than parents in developing countries with relatively low incomes. In less-developed, largely subsistence agricultural countries, children represent direct labor inputs—even small children can do useful work on a subsistence farm—thus lowering the price of children. Where the price of children is lower, we expect to see more children produced, other things being equal. Thus we see the law of demand at work.

According to Becker, then, Malthus failed to take into account relative prices in his theory of population. While rats or horses may tend to breed up to the limit imposed by the available food supply, the behavior of human beings will also reflect the influence of opportunity costs and the rational choices such costs inspire.

PART FOUR

Applied Microeconomics and Public Choice

4

C H A P T E R 16

Antitrust,
Regulation,
and
Public Policy

O ur market economy has grown in ways that Adam Smith could never have imagined. Smith believed that market forces, operating under a laissez-faire form of government, would eventually bring us to a point of perfect competition among firms, what Smith termed "a nation of shopkeepers." Our economy, however, has followed a different path, and its market structures range from nearly pure competition to nearly complete monopoly

Public policy in the area of monopoly is two-pronged. Some policies are designed to restore and maintain competition where viable competition can exist. These **antitrust policies** control business practices such as anticompetitive mergers, cartels, price discrimination, and deceptive advertising. **Regulatory policies,** on the other hand, establish and manage the behavior of firms and industries where competition cannot exist or where positive goals—for example, health and safety—are pursued. Here, the government imposes on natural monopolies and other businesses rules and regulations that substitute for competition and undesirable behavior in markets. After you read Chapter 16 you should know

- how economists recognize and measure monopoly power in the economy.
- how government has dealt with monopoly and large-scale enterprise through antitrust and regulatory policies.
- how regulation may have *created* more monopoly power than it has dispersed.
- whether deregulation of natural monopolies helps economic efficiency and enhances consumer welfare.

Antitrust policies
Regulations established by laws and government agencies that attempt to preserve business competition.

Regulatory policies
Administrative or legal attempts to influence the behavior of firms or industries when competitive goals cannot be realized or when positive goals are to be pursued.

Concentration ratios
A measure of the degree to which the largest firms in an industry account for total industry assets, sales, or some other factor.

MEASURING INDUSTRIAL CONCENTRATION

Economists have devised several methods of detecting the existence of monopolies—all of which assumed that the number of firms in an industry indicates the degree of competition present. We examine a rough estimate of the degree of concentration of market power within an industry—industry concentration ratios.

Industry Concentration Ratios

A method of looking at business structure is to calculate **concentration ratios** (CR) for various industries. Concentration ratios are determined by ranking firms within an industry from largest to smallest and then calculating the share of some aggregate factor such as sales, employment, or assets held by the largest four or eight firms. Sales is the most common factor used in these calculations.

Figured by this method, the concentration ratio will lie between 0 and 100. If an industry is totally monopolized, one firm will have 100 percent of industry sales, or $CR = 100$. If an industry has several firms but the four largest have 50 percent of the market sales, then $CR = 50$. If a very large number of companies each have a very small market share, then CR will be close to zero, suggesting the existence of competition.

Table 16.1 displays four-firm and eight-firm concentration ratios for a small sample of manufacturing industries. Some industries are very highly concentrated. In 1992, for example, the top eight producers of electric lamps accounted for 94 percent of industry shipments, indicating that the remaining lamp manufacturers were very small businesses indeed. In contrast, the eight largest firms supplying ready-mix concrete had only an 11 percent share of total sales in 1992, suggesting that this industry is made up of a large number of relatively small companies. (The system for calculating ratios in particular industries has been undergoing significant change in the mid to late 1990s. Data later than 1992 is not directly comparable to that for 1992 or earlier.)

Table 16.1 also reveals trends in concentration. Concentration ratios that have risen over the years indicate that the leading firms have grown relative to other industry members, either by internal expansion, merger, or decreases in the number of other firms. Declining concentration ratios imply that more and more competitors have made successful inroads into the industry and thereby reduced the dominance by leading firms. While examples of each pattern appear in the table, in general concentration ratios remain fairly stable.

One problem with using concentration ratios to determine the degree of competition in an industry is that the data can obscure quite vigorous competition. Since the ratios do not identify individual firms, the concentration ratio can remain stable over time even though the leading firms rapidly turn over. For example, if the first and fourth companies in meat packing change places, the four-firm concentration ratio would remain unchanged. Additionally, concentration ratios usually ignore the impact of foreign firms that sell goods and services in a country on that country's industry structure. Concentration ratios calculated solely from the assets or sales of domestic firms will understate the degree of competition in an industry when domestic firms in the industry face stiff foreign competition. This understatement is clearest for such product categories as motor vehicles or radios and TVs (see Table 16.1).

A further difficulty with the concentration ratios in Table 16.1 is that they are based on the Commerce Department's Standard Industrial Classification (SIC) groups. The SIC codes group firms that produce similar products, but these codes

TABLE 16.1

Selected Concentration Ratios in Manufacturing

Concentration ratios measure the share of sales held by the largest four or eight firms in an industry. The data shown here represent a selected group of manufacturing industries for the years 1963, 1982, 1987, and 1992. In some industries—such as men's and boy's suits—the concentration ratio increased through the years, suggesting that the largest firms obtained a larger share of total industry output. In some cases—such as jewelry and precious metals—the ratio fell, suggesting a more competitive situation.

CONCENTRATION RATIOS

	1963		1982		1987		1992	
	Four-Firm	Eight-Firm	Four-Firm	Eight-Firm	Four-Firm	Eight-Firm	Four-Firm	Eight-Firm
Meat packing	31	42	29	43	32	50	50	66
Fluid milk	23	30	16	27	21	32	22	30
Cereal breakfast foods	86	96	86	97	87	99	85	98
Distilled liquor	58	74	46	68	53	75	62	82
Roasted coffee	52	68	65	76	66	78	66	75
Cigarettes	80	100	–	–	92	–	93	–
Men's and boy's suits and coats	14	23	25	37	34	47	39	50
Women's and misses' dresses	6	9	6	10	6	10	11	17
Mobile homes	–	–	24	39	30	44	35	50
Pulp mills	48	72	45	70	44	69	48	75
Book publishing	20	33	17	30	24	38	23	38
Pharmaceutical preparations	22	38	26	42	22	36	26	42
Petroleum refining	34	56	28	48	32	52	30	49
Flat glass	94	99+	85	97	82	–	81	–
Ready-mix concrete	4	7	6	9	8	11	6	11
Blast furnaces and steel mills	48	67	42	64	44	63	37	58
Metal cans	74	85	50	68	54	70	56	74
Electric lamps	92	96	91	96	91	94	86	94
Radio and TV receiving sets	41	62	49	70	39	59	41	53
Motor vehicles, car bodies	–	–	92	97	90	95	84	91
Jewelry, precious metals	26	33	16	22	12	18	16	21
Pens and mechanical pencils	48	60	41	62	49	65	49	73

Sources: U.S. Department of Commerce, Bureau of the Census, *Census of Manufacturers* (Washington, D.C.: U.S. Government Printing Office, 1977); U.S. Department of Commerce, Bureau of the Census, *Concentration Ratios in Manufacturing* (Washington, D.C.: U.S. Government Printing Office, 1982, 1987). Update by Census Bureau Website http://WWW.Census.GOV/, March 1996.

do not account for substitutability by buyers. For example, plastic panes may frequently be substituted for flat glass, but the SIC codes compare glass manufacturers only with other glass manufacturers. Thus, the concentration ratios do not show the competition among groups that results from actual market structures. Also, the SIC categories include sales data for the entire nation and therefore do not give information about concentration levels in different geographic regions; concentration in particular regions may be greater than that for the nation as a whole.

PUBLIC POLICY: ANTITRUST

Purely competitive industries represent the ideal in market performance. In industries characterized by imperfect competition, the ideal is not obtained—profits may be greater than normal, production costs are not necessarily minimized, and welfare losses can occur. If these losses to society are significant, then there is a call for social action in the form of government regulation of some businesses' activities.

Public solutions to the monopoly problem take four basic forms.

1. Antitrust laws basically designed to prevent the creation of monopolies.
2. Price regulations designed to allow the existence of monopolies but to control their prices and profits.
3. Government ownership that removes the firm from the private sector and thus places its performance directly in the hands of the public.
4. Laissez-faire policy that allows the market to determine the fate and performance of firms with no government interference.

Antitrust Law

Predatory pricing
The temporary pricing of goods or services below cost in order to reduce or eliminate competition.

The late 1800s was a time of great change in the American economy. A significant merger wave led to the creation of very large firms with nationwide operations—the first modern corporations. Some of these firms engaged in questionable business practices, such as **predatory pricing** (the act of selling goods below cost as a method of destroying competitors), price fixing, and collusion.

Antitrust policies are aimed at preventing firms from engaging in such anticompetitive activities. During the 1870s and 1880s, an antitrust movement sprang up, primarily among American farmers. Facing falling prices for their products and stable prices for the goods they bought, they became fearful that monopolies or trusts were wielding unwarranted economic power. Through organizations such as the National Grange and the National Anti-Monopoly Cheap Freight League, the farmers successfully influenced the two major political parties to add antimonopoly planks to their 1888 election platforms. Antitrust legislation was enacted soon after, with subsequent revisions to strengthen the government's ability to fight monopolistic practices in court.

Sherman Antitrust Act   The Sherman Antitrust Act of 1890, the first antimonopoly law passed by Congress, provided that "every contract, combination in the form of trust or otherwise, or conspiracy, in restraint of trade or commerce among the several states, or with foreign nations, is hereby declared to be illegal. . . ." The

Sherman Act also declared "every person who shall monopolize, or attempt to monopolize. . .[is] guilty of a misdemeanor, and subject to fine or imprisonment." The statute did not spell out what would constitute an illegal restraint of trade. Its main purpose was to place the antitrust issue under federal law and to provide a means of penalizing monopoly whenever it was discovered.

Clayton Antitrust Act   Believing that the Sherman act was ineffective in preventing monopoly, Congress passed the Clayton Act in 1914. The Clayton act enumerated some specific restraints of trade that could be challenged if their effects lessened competition substantially or created a monopoly. These included (1) price discrimination—selling the same product to different customers at different prices not related to cost differences; (2) tying arrangements—making the sale of one good contingent on the purchase of some other goods; (3) interlocking directorates—the same person's serving on the boards of competing companies; and (4) exclusive dealing—selling to a retailer only on the condition that the firm not carry rival products.

Federal Trade Commission Act   Section 5 of the Federal Trade Commission (FTC) Act, also passed by Congress in 1914, contains the broadest statutory language, declaring illegal "unfair methods of competition in commerce." The act established a five-member commission independent of the executive branch, with the idea that the FTC would be a repository of economic and antitrust expertise not available to the federal courts.

The Federal Trade Commission building, where mergers and "unfair" methods of competition in commerce are considered.

Other Antitrust Statutes   The Clayton Act has been amended twice. In 1936, the Robinson–Patman Act revised the provisions relating to price discrimination and added language prohibiting predatory pricing. In 1950, the Celler–Kefauver Act closed a Clayton Act loophole relating to mergers through the acquisition of physical assets.

The FTC Act has been revised even more often. First, in 1938 the Wheeler–Lea Act added "unfair or deceptive acts or practices in commerce" to the behavior declared illegal. In the late 1970s, the Hart–Scott–Rodino Antitrust Improvement Act established a premerger notification system by which firms contemplating a merger would notify the FTC and the Department of Justice prior to consummating the acquisition.

Antitrust Agencies

The United States has a dual system of antitrust enforcement whereby two government agencies—the Federal Trade Commission and the Justice Department's

Antitrust Division—share responsibility for policing the antitrust laws. Both agencies can enforce the Clayton Act, and, since 1948, the FTC has had the power to bring charges against behavior that violates the Sherman Act.

In addition to the two government agencies, complaints charging Sherman and Clayton antitrust violations can be brought by private parties. Private plaintiffs can sue for treble damages; that is, guilty defendants can be required to pay penalties of up to three times the value of the actual injury caused by their illegal conduct. Because private suits offer such potentially large rewards for successful plaintiffs, in any given year the number of private antitrust actions is many times greater than the number of cases brought by government.

Enforcement of Antitrust Policies

Antitrust policies are carried out in the courtroom. Antitrust officials, policymakers, and court officials face difficulties in distinguishing between behavior that is a conscious intent of firms to decrease competition and behavior that is the result of firms' responding to external changes. For this reason, the Justice Department and the FTC treat every market situation as unique. Before either agency takes action in altering market activities, it examines the individual firms and their activities. Firms judged to be in violation of antitrust laws may be ordered to stop their anticompetitive practices or to divest themselves of some of their assets by splitting a monopoly into several smaller competing firms. Sound economic theory is not always well represented in these court decisions. We will consider some specific cases that have been tried and the consequences of the decisions.

Cartel Policies   In 1927, the Supreme Court held that price-fixing conspiracies were per se illegal under the Sherman Act, even though the act did not specifically prohibit price fixing.[1] That is, attempts by competitors to fix prices would be found illegal regardless of the level of the fixed price.

The case involved the activities of the Sanitary Potters Association (SPA), a Trenton, New Jersey, trade association, whose twenty-three member firms produced 82 percent of the U.S. output of bathroom sinks, tubs, and commodes. The SPA published price lists that included suggested discounts and surcharges for six geographic regions; members following the SPA lists charged identical prices.

The question addressed by the Supreme Court was whether a lower court judge was correct in directing the jury not to consider the reasonableness of the particular prices charged. The Court held that "uniform price-fixing by those controlling in any substantial manner a trade or business in interstate commerce is prohibited by the Sherman Law, despite the reasonableness of the particular prices agreed upon."[2] Economic theory would support the Court's decision. If a large percentage of the firms in an industry agree on price, then it is likely that price competition has been abolished.

---

[1] *United States v. Trenton Potteries Co.*, 273 U.S. 395 (1927).
[2] See Phillip Areeda, *Antitrust Analysis: Problems, Text, Cases,* 3rd ed. (Boston: Little, Brown, 1981), p. 165.

Merger
The combining of the ownership of two firms' assets, which results in a single firm.

Merger Policy   One way that concentration ratios may rise is through **mergers.** If there are only a few firms in an industry, the combination of two or more firms into one may decrease the degree of competition. However, the types of mergers vary and thus their effect on the market varies. There are three basic types of mergers: horizontal, vertical, and conglomerate. Each type is distinguished by the relation between the products produced by the merging firms.

A horizontal merger occurs when the merger partners produce the same product. Examples include mergers between two beer producers, two manufacturers of glass containers, two retail grocery stores, and so forth. Horizontal mergers may decrease competition because they have the direct effect of raising industry concentration ratios and moving the affected market closer to monopoly.

Mergers are characterized as vertical if the product of one firm serves as an input for the other firm—that is, if the merging companies are at different stages of a production process. A vertical merger would occur if a company producing crude oil acquired a petroleum refinery, if a steel producer purchased iron ore deposits, or if an automobile manufacturer acquired a string of retail car dealerships. Vertical mergers do not raise industry concentration levels and are usually motivated by the prospect of lower costs. Accordingly, vertical mergers do not normally decrease competition.

Conglomerate mergers occur when the products of the firms are unrelated—when an insurance company buys a firm that produces bread or when a cigarette producer merges with a soft drink company. The usual explanation for such mergers is that they are motivated by a desire to spread the risks associated with economic ups and downs across products. However, spreading risks can be accomplished much more simply by, for example, purchasing shares of a variety of businesses. Rather, conglomerate mergers can better be explained by the desire to diffuse managerial expertise across firms. That is, if an efficient corporate management team believes that its executive talents can be profitably applied to some other firm, it will have an incentive to acquire another company regardless of the product produced by the other firm. Since conglomerate mergers do not raise industry concentration levels, they do not generally decrease competition.

As we noted earlier, the Clayton Act, as amended by the Celler–Kefauver Act, seeks to limit corporate acquisitions that "tend to create a monopoly." Under the Hart–Scott–Rodino premerger notification system, large firms contemplating a merger are required to apprise both the FTC and the Justice Department's Antitrust Division of their intentions. The agency chosen to handle the merger must decide whether to challenge it by seeking a preliminary injunction in federal court or to allow the merger to proceed without opposition.

An important aspect of merger law enforcement is the use of guidelines to establish which particular acquisitions will be challenged. For example, vertical and conglomerate mergers are not often challenged, but horizontal mergers that significantly decrease competition are. The merger guidelines issued by the Justice Department contain numerical standards that identify markets thought to be "unconcentrated" or "concentrated" prior to a merger. The guidelines set limits on the amount that concentration will be allowed to rise in each case before antitrust action is initiated. Concentration ratios were established for this purpose in 1968.

In 1966, before these measures were in use, the Supreme Court considered the legality of a merger between two Los Angeles retail grocery chains, Von's Grocery Company and Shopping Bag Food Stores.[3] At the time of the acquisition, 1960, Von's was the third largest grocery chain in Los Angeles; Shopping Bag was the sixth largest. Together, the two grocery retailers accounted for only 7.5 percent of sales in the Los Angeles area, however. Despite the relatively small market shares involved in the merger, the Court held that Von's had violated the Clayton Act. The decision placed great weight on the fact that the number of owners operating single grocery stores in Los Angeles had declined from 5365 in 1950 to 3818 in 1961. This decline, the Court alleged, indicated a trend toward concentration.

If the number of firms in an industry is declining because of technological changes, economic theory suggests that the optimal size of firms is increasing. This change will naturally lead to an increase in concentration. According to economic theory, therefore, the merger probably should not have been prevented, especially since the two firms constituted such a small percentage of the market.

Price Discrimination   Charges of price discrimination may also require subtle distinctions. In a private suit, the Utah Pie Company charged Continental Baking Company,[4] Carnation Company, and Pet Milk Company with price discrimination in the sale of frozen pies. Utah Pie, located in Salt Lake City, alleged that its three California-based competitors sold pies shipped to Salt Lake City at prices below those charged for pies sold nearer their own plants.

The evidence before the Supreme Court pointed to a highly competitive pie market in Salt Lake City. The price discrimination evidence appeared superficially correct in the sense that, given the cost of transportation, one would not expect the prices of the California firms to be lower in Salt Lake City. Accordingly, the Supreme Court found in favor of Utah Pie.

Some feel that the Court's decision does not square with some of the facts, however. For one thing, it can be argued that the prices charged by Utah Pie were consistently lower than the prices of its rivals throughout the price discrimination episode. Second, Pet Milk Company suffered substantial losses on its Salt Lake City sales. Third, Utah Pie consistently increased its sales volume and continued to make a profit while facing the alleged anticompetitive practices of its rivals. Finally, prior to the entry of Continental, Carnation, and Pet, Utah Pie enjoyed a 67 percent market share in Salt Lake City, and while the new competition cost Utah Pie a portion of its market, at the end of the price discrimination period the Salt Lake City firm still accounted for 45 percent of the pies sold in the area. It appears to some observers that Utah Pie could have been using the antitrust policy to eliminate price competition and to gain a larger share of the market.

---

[3]*United States* v. *Von's Grocery Co.*, 384 U.S. 270 (1966).
[4]*Utah Pie Co.* v. *Continental Baking Co.*, 386 U.S. 685, 699 (1967).

Pure Monopoly and Antitrust Cases   Antitrust policies have also been applied to pure monopolies. The Aluminum Company of America (Alcoa) was involved in antitrust litigation as early as 1912 on allegations that it had violated the Sherman Act by, among other charges, monopolizing deposits of bauxite (the crucial ore in aluminum production), conspiring with foreign aluminum firms to fix world prices, and entering into exclusive contracts with power companies guaranteeing that the power companies would not supply electricity to any other aluminum producers. In 1945, the U.S. Court of Appeals for the Second Circuit finally rendered its decision on charges brought by the government that Alcoa had monopolized the production and sale of virgin aluminum ingot.

The appeals court decision, written by Judge Learned Hand, is one of the most celebrated in American antitrust history.[5] Judge Hand, in overturning a lower court decision favoring Alcoa, wrote that even though Alcoa's monopoly was "thrust upon it" and the firm "stimulated demand and opened new uses for the metal," the firm would not increase production in anticipation of increases in demand. He contended that Alcoa prevented new firms from entering by increasing its capacity as demand increased and that because of Alcoa's lower cost, no new firms could effectively compete.

Although the court found Alcoa guilty, it refused to dissolve "an aggregation which has for so long demonstrated its efficiency." The "problem" of lack of competition in the aluminum industry was solved at the end of World War II, when the government sold to Reynolds Metals and Kaiser Aluminum the aluminum production plants it had set up for the war effort.

Multinational Firms

The economies of the world are becoming increasingly interdependent. Events outside our borders have an important impact on our economy—so much so that the U.S. economy should be viewed as but one component in the global economy. This global setting has important implications for U.S. antitrust and regulatory policies.

Many firms in the global economy operate as multinational corporations. These firms operate simultaneously in a number of countries. Many business arrangements fall under the heading of the multinational corporation. Firms may locate production facilities abroad to obtain lower labor and production costs; Ford Motor Company, for example, has production facilities in Mexico. Other firms, such as RCA, make arrangements with foreign suppliers to produce products abroad for sale in the United States under the American firms' respective brand names.

Globalization of business firms and increased international competition will make the U.S. economy more competitive. If U.S. producers have high costs, they

---

[5]*United States* v. *Aluminum Co. of America*, 148 F.2d (2nd Cir. 1945).

will lose market share to foreign competitors. The huge increase in the number of imported cars in the United States since the 1960s aptly illustrates this point. Similarly, the presence of excess profits in the U.S. economy will attract the entry of foreign competitors. To some extent, then, international competition is a substitute for U.S. antitrust policy.

The proliferation of multinational firms is not without its troubling aspects, however. Multinational firms owe allegiance to no particular country; they can operate wherever they please, holding out the prospect of jobs and incomes to competing countries for promises of a less strict regulatory and antitrust environment. Moreover, these large firms may find it easier to collude and to behave monopolistically across international markets. In short, multinational firms may be better equipped to undermine competition.

Multinational firms are a mixed economic blessing. Their impact on competition must be assessed on a case-by-case basis. However, one cannot adequately assess the role of competition and competitive policy in the U.S. economy without considering these firms.

An Economic View of Antitrust Cases

How well enforcement of the antitrust laws agrees with economic principles is a complex question with no simple answers. On the basis of our brief sketch of laws, agencies, and court interpretations, we can draw the rough conclusion that economic theory has not made a large impression on legal thinking.

In particular, the courts seem to equate the degree of competition with the number of firms in an industry and to seek to protect competition by protecting competitors. This focus on the number of firms in an industry ignores the other dimensions of competition (number of buyers, entry and exit conditions, degree of product homogeneity, number of close substitute goods, and so forth). More important, the numbers game neglects the possibility that firms can grow relative to their rivals not because they use unfair methods of competition or expand by buying out their competitors but because they can serve consumers better at lower cost. Modern technology has fostered similar antitrust cases—cases where monopolization might be the result of success (see the Focus "The Microsoft Case: Is It Monopoly, or Is It Envy?").

PUBLIC POLICY: REGULATION

Natural monopoly
A combination of market demand and cost conditions that results in only one firm in an industry being able to produce output profitably; occurs when decreasing long-run average costs exist up to the level of total industry demand.

Antitrust policies are basically designed to maintain competition when competition can exist. Therefore, the antitrust policies are not very effective when a natural monopoly exists. A **natural monopoly** occurs where conditions in the market lead to a situation when only one firm is able to produce profitably. How does the public avoid the potential problems of monopoly when only one firm can survive in an industry? Price regulation is offered as a solution to some of the problems that can arise under these circumstances. Governments may attempt to regulate prices to keep them low for consumers' sake or may even establish agencies controlling the activities of specific industries. Like

FOCUS

The Microsoft Case: Is It Monopoly, or Is It Envy?

No antitrust case in recent memory has generated as much interest as *United States* v. *Microsoft*. The Department of Justice (DOJ) filed the case on behalf of the "people," alleging that Bill Gates's company is a monopoly with the wherewithal to restrain trade. The issue is the bundling (selling together) of the Internet Explorer web browser with Microsoft's Windows operating system. The allegation is that such bundling—selling Windows packaged with the Explorer—gives Explorer an "unfair" advantage in the market.

This high-profile case has created (actually uncovered) a debate that will rage long after the case is (politically) settled in the courts. The case raises critical economic issues. How, for example, can we tell if high and/or growing market share is due to monopoly or simply to success in the market? No one debates the fact that Microsoft has been wildly successful. When Microsoft entered the combined Windows–Explorer market, Netscape was the chief competitor to the Explorer web browser. Netscape then had a high market share. Furthermore, prices for web browsers fell only *after* Microsoft introduced its Explorer.[a] That is, of course, not what one would expect if Microsoft were establishing a monopoly (remember that a monopolist will reduce output and raise price).

Other important issues are raised by the case. In industries such as high-tech PC development, there is a trade-off between standardization (such as bundling the net browser with the operating system) and technological innovation. There is, for example, every indication that the bundled product is the way consumers want to buy these products. (The DOJ, in July 1994, permitted the company to develop "integrated products" given, of course, that it did not force consumers to buy them.)

Most basically, perhaps, antitrust authorities are acting not on what *has* happened in the PC market, but on what *might* happen. The DOJ's case against Microsoft appears to revolve critically on what the company may do if and when it outcompetes its rivals. Many, but by no means all, economists are skeptical that technological innovation can be better run by the courts (government) than by the market. Competition is not comfortable. The DOJ appears to argue that Microsoft's success is "unfair" to the competition. History contains many examples of arbitrary punitive action against the successful and the "politically incorrect." Such may well be the case with the *United States* v. *Microsoft*.

[a]For additional insight, see Barry Fagin, "The Case Against the Case Against Microsoft" (Competitive Enterprise Institute, April 1999).

antitrust litigation, however, these regulatory efforts may have unwanted economic effects.

Regulatory Agencies

Broadly, regulation is any administrative or legal attempt to influence markets for goods and services. Government at any level can create regulation, which takes the form of subsidies to businesses, municipal zoning commissions, rate regulation of telephone and electricity services, legal support of occupational licensing, or any other attempt to intervene in markets.

TABLE 16.2

Major U.S. Regulatory Agencies

A great deal of industry regulation was passed in the 1930s, including that related to telephone service, pipelines, and broadcasting. More recent regulation has centered on health, safety, and the environment.

Agency	Year Established	Jurisdiction
	Economic Regulation	
Interstate Commerce Commission (ICC)	1887	Interstate railroads (1887)
		Interstate trucks (1935)
		Interstate water carriers (1940)
		Interstate telephone (1910–1934)
		Interstate oil pipelines (1906–1977)
State regulatory commissions	35 states 1907–1920; 50 states by 1973	Local electricity (46 states by 1973)
		Local gas (47 states in 1973)
		Local telephone (48 states in 1973)
Federal Communications Commission (FCC)	1934	Interstate telephone (1934)
		Broadcasting (1934)
		Cable television (1968)
		Cable television prices and services (1992)
Federal Power Commission (FPC)	1935	Interstate wholesale electricity (1935)
		Interstate natural gas pipelines (1938)
		Field price of natural gas sold in interstate commerce (1954)
Federal Energy Regulatory Commission (FERC)	1977	Oil pipelines (1977)
		Interstate gas and gas pipelines (1978)
Federal Maritime Commission (FMC)	1936	Ocean shipping (1936)
Civil Aeronautics Board (CAB)	1938	Interstate airlines (1938)
Postal Rate Commission	1970	Established classes of mail and rates for these classes; set fees for other services (1970)
Federal Energy Administration (FEA)	1973	Petroleum prices and allocation (1973)
Energy Regulatory Administration (ERA)	1974	
Copyright Royalty Tribunal	1976	Copyright material (1976)

In the United States, regulation by administrative tribunals, or commissions, is a compromise between outright government ownership and free market functioning. Since legislative bodies (Congress, state legislatures, city councils) are ill-equipped to directly regulate industries themselves, the regulatory commissions they set up deal with monopolistic imperfections such as natural monopoly. The first such commission at the federal level was the Interstate Commerce Commission, which was established to regulate the rates and practices of interstate railroads (see Table 16.2). The

TABLE 16.2 (*Continued*)

Agency	Year Established	Jurisdiction
Environmental, Safety, and Health Regulation		
Food and Drug Administration (FDA)	1906	Safety of food, drugs (1906), and cosmetics (1938) Effectiveness of drugs (1962)
Animal and Plant Health Inspection Service	1907	Meat and poultry packing plants (1907)
Federal Trade Commission (FTC)	1914	False and misleading advertising (mainly after 1938)
Securities and Exchange Commission (SEC)	1934	Public security issues and security exchanges (1934) Public utility holding companies (1935)
Civil Aeronautics Board (CAB)	1938	Airline safety (1938) (flight standards program only)
Federal Aviation Administration (FAA)	1958	
Atomic Energy Commission (AEC)	1947	Licensing of nuclear power plants (1947)
Nuclear Regulatory Commission (NRC)	1975	
National Highway Traffic Safety Administration (NHTSA)	1970	Automobile safety (1970), automobile fuel economy (1975)
Occupational Safety and Health Administration (OSHA)	1971	Industrial safety and health (1971)
Environmental Protection Agency (EPA)	1972	Air, water, and noise pollution (various environmental laws were enforced by several agencies 1963–1972)
Consumer Product Safety Commission	1972	Safety of consumer products (1972)
Mine Enforcement Safety Administration (MESA)	1973	Safety and health in mining, especially coal mines (1973)
Mine Safety and Health Administration	1978	

ICC (finally eliminated in 1995) and all other administrative commissions at all levels of government extend the legislative power of government with members appointed by the administrative branch (the president, governors, mayors, or city councils) and confirmed by the legislative branch.

Within the limits set forth by the respective legislative bodies that create them, commissions do a good deal of rule making and "quasi-judicial" decision making. On some major points of law, commission decisions may be brought before state or federal courts, but the regulatory commissions regulate industries or services for the most part autonomously.

What are the industries and services that have been subjected to commission regulation in the United States? As you can see from Table 16.2, electricity, gas, and telephone services followed the railroads into regulation early in this century. A surge of new federal regulations in the 1930s brought interstate commerce in electricity, natural gas, broadcasting, telephone, ocean shipping, airlines, and securities issuance under the regulatory umbrella. This period produced the

Securities and Exchange Commission (SEC), the Federal Communications Commission (FCC), and the Food and Drug Administration (FDA), among others. Recent federal regulatory activity has focused on such matters as industrial health and safety, automobile safety and fuel economy, air and water pollution, and the safety of consumer products. When state and municipal regulations—of occupations, zoning, rents, sanitation, highway safety, funeral homes, milk producers—are added to federal regulations, practically no area of the economy remains untouched by regulation.

The Purpose of Regulation

Economists hold varying interpretations of how and why regulatory policies emerge. In a natural monopoly, the market fails to provide goods and services in quantities and at prices that would prevail under competitive conditions. However, there are many regulations in businesses and professions where the market does seem to provide goods and services at competitive prices and quantities. Why, for example, are physicians, lawyers, nurses, and hairstylists subject to extensive regulations?

Public interest theory of regulation

Maintains that regulations are contrived so as to promote the public interest by correcting market failures and improving economic efficiency.

Capture, or interest group, theory of regulation

Argues that regulations are constructed so as to further the interests of the existing firms within a particular industry.

Some economists argue that regulation promotes the public interest by correcting market failures and improving economic efficiency. This is the **public interest theory of regulation.** Other groups of economists believe that in many cases regulatory agencies are captured by the industry or profession they are supposed to regulate. This is the **capture,** or **interest group, theory of regulation,** wherein groups interested in the suppression of competition lobby legislatures and press regulatory agencies to obtain particular goals. Electricians, carpenters, barbers, and construction firms typically lobby at local or municipal levels for "standards restrictions" that limit entry into their lines of work. Physicians, lawyers, veterinarians, nurses, and architects have engaged in similar efforts at the state and federal levels. Such occupational licensing has important economic effects—notably, to restrict entry into the profession and carefully limit competition. Unions, of course, have similar effects. On a larger scale, some economists argue that whole industries have at times "captured" the agencies that regulate them: namely, railroads, the trucking industry, television networks, airlines, and coastal water transportation.

Regulatory agencies are said to be captured when an industry or a subset of firms within an industry can influence agency activity to the benefit of the industry. This might be accomplished by agency employment of industry partisans or "experts," by hiring agency staff within the industry after their agency tenure, or by other means. Administrative bodies are appointed to balance the benefits and costs of imposing regulations. Regulations always benefit some industry members or some consumers and impose costs on others. Legislators frequently must weigh the benefits they receive from proponents of regulation (in terms of votes, money, and other perquisites) against the costs they incur from imposing regulation (also in terms of votes and support). Proponents of the capture theory argue that this process redistributes wealth based on politicians' self-interest. They argue, further, that consumers, who do not have a large *pro rata* stake in legislation and regulation, often get shortchanged. The stronger interests of industry tend to dominate.

Price Regulation   Public utilities—such as firms that provide local electricity, telephone, gas, and water services—are often considered natural monopolies because their provision is usually associated with economies of scale. Figure 16.1 illustrates the relation between demand for and cost of these services.

With no regulation, a firm holding a natural monopoly chooses the profit-maximizing price and output P_m and Q_m, which result in profits. If the local government chooses to regulate the firm to eliminate profits, it may force the firm to charge a price that just covers its average cost of production.

This price regulation is achieved through an agreement between the firm and the local government—the government allows the firm to exist as the sole provider of services, and in return, the firm agrees not to allow profits to rise above a normal rate of return and also agrees to meet the total demand for the product. The resulting price and output, P_{AC} and Q_{AC}, occur where the industry demand crosses the average cost curve. Economic profits are zero, since price equals average cost.

This **average cost pricing** is indeed a very popular form of price regulation. It seems to eliminate one of the problems of regulating a monopoly. However, it does not result in the optimal level of output. Many economists believe that price should instead be set equal to marginal cost, in what is called **marginal cost pricing.** The

Average cost pricing
A regulatory policy that causes a firm to charge a price equal to average cost, inducing the firm to produce an output such that economic profits are zero.

Marginal cost pricing
A regulatory policy that forces a firm to charge a price equal to marginal cost, resulting in a socially optimal allocation of resources.

FIGURE 16.1

Two Forms of Price Regulation

An unregulated natural monopoly might charge the profit-maximizing price P_m, at which it would sell the quantity Q_m. With average cost price regulation, the price would be set equal to the firm's average cost, P_{AC}, increasing the quantity sold to Q_{AC}. Marginal cost pricing would result in even lower price and higher quantity: Price P_{MC} and output Q_{MC} result where the demand curve intersects the marginal cost curve. But such a policy would force the firm to operate at a loss, for the marginal cost is lower than the firm's average cost of production.

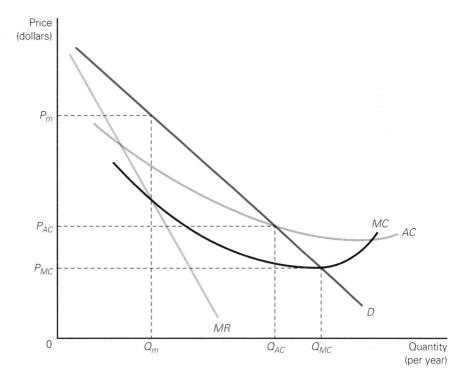

price and output that result from the intersection of the demand curve and the marginal cost curve, P_{MC} and Q_{MC}, are optimal. That is, when price equals marginal cost, the benefit to society of one more unit of output is just equal to the extra cost of that unit. However, as in the case shown in Figure 16.1, marginal cost pricing may result in losses for the firm. One of the basic problems of price regulation is that natural monopolies cannot be forced into the ideal competitive solution where $P = AC = MC$. Since marginal cost pricing may result in losses, average cost pricing may be the preferred form of price regulation.

Another problem with price regulation is that when firms are forced to earn only a normal rate of return, their incentive to achieve efficiency is diminished. Maintaining low costs of production is not rewarded with higher profits. For this reason we may see public utilities allowing costs to rise.

In spite of the potential problems of price regulation, direct control of industry prices became popular in the late nineteenth century. It was believed that government regulation beyond antitrust legislation could promote more efficient behavior than could market forces.

Problems with Price Regulation   Direct regulation of prices to achieve economic efficiency and to improve consumer welfare often proves to be self-defeating. When rates are inflexible over a period of time, surpluses or shortages are likely to occur with changes in demand or cost. The inability of a board of commissioners to accurately predict market forces can cause great inefficiencies in some regulated markets.

Rate of return regulation
A cap imposed by a regulatory commission on the allowable percentage that a utility can earn on its capital invested.

In an attempt to establish prices that reflect costs, state and federal regulatory agencies have resorted, with regard to telephone and electric rates especially, to **rate of return (*ROR*) regulation.** Instead of setting the prices charged by utilities, regulators attempt to control prices and output *indirectly,* by placing maximum allowable rates of return on capital and other investments. Rate of return regulation is a direct attempt by state and federal regulatory commissions to limit to competitive levels the aggregate return that a utility makes on its operations. In calculating the allowable rate of return for a utility firm, a commission must estimate what a "competitive" rate would be for a comparable firm in the marketplace. For example, if an electric utility is earning 14 percent on its investment in capital and the allowable rate (computed from returns to similar businesses) is 11 percent, the regulatory commission will order price reductions to increase the welfare of the utility's consumers. Calculations of an allowable or competitive return will differ among various commissions and jurisdictions for a number of reasons, including regional differences in costs and technology. Unfortunately, rate of return regulation may induce regulated firms to behave inefficiently. If the allowable rate of return exceeds the firm's cost of acquiring capital, the firm may overinvest in capital to increase the basis for its allowable return. Consumers might have to pay higher prices to support this overinvestment.

Product Quality and Price Regulation   To add to the problems of price regulation, it is impossible to regulate *all* dimensions of a market. For many years, the Civil Aeronautics Board regulated airline rates as well as entry into the airline services market, but the CAB did not regulate service quality. Since regulated airlines could not compete on the basis of nominal price, they competed by constantly changing and improving quality. Costs rose because of better meals, better in-flight service and more flights for more departure–arrival time choices, even though planes were seldom filled to capacity. Costs increased to equal (and sometimes exceed) the regulated rates imposed by the CAB. Deregulation of rigid rates—in this case, their elimination—was necessary for the survival of some airlines, and the policy was supported by many competing carriers. Presently, in the era of deregulation, airlines have better control over nominal rate schedules and are able to offer consumers many alternative price–quality "packages" of airline services. Deregulation, the relaxation or elimination of legal price or entry controls on firms or industries, is discussed later in this chapter.

What if the Monopoly Is Not "Natural"?   Many modern economists have questioned the usefulness of regulation. In part, doubts about regulation are related to concerns that many markets may be mislabeled "natural monopolies." That is, they may not experience the constantly downward-sloping average cost curve shown in Figure 16.1.

The important issue for public policy is whether and to what degree a firm can sustain its monopoly power. If a monopoly can completely forestall entry in the absence of regulation, it is a **sustainable monopoly.** Such a firm is able to restrict output and, therefore, to reduce economic welfare; the firm might properly be the subject of regulation. On the other hand, if entry into any of the firm's markets is viable, the market is said to be characterized by **contestability.** If the firm's cost curves are U-shaped over the range of demand, unlike those in Figure 16.1 which slope downward over the range of demand, the need for regulation does not exist; market forces will ultimately generate competitive results. With a U-shaped cost curve, the average or unit cost of producing the good or service does not decline over the entire range of demand. If one firm can satisfy all demanders at lower and lower unit costs, entry by other firms is, if not impossible, far less likely. (See the Focus "Airline Deregulation: Success Story or Consumer Nightmare?" later in this chapter for a discussion that relates this point to the airline industry.)

Sustainable monopoly
A monopoly that can forestall the entry of competitors in the absence of regulation.

Contestability
Characteristic of a market in which the entry of competitors is possible.

Health and Safety Regulation

As Table 16.2 reveals, much of the recent economic regulation deals with product safety and safety in the workplace. Here, we briefly consider the issue of safety in the workplace.

If employers are not liable to employees for accidents that result from unsafe work conditions, employers may have an incentive to scrimp on safety; safety equipment tends to be expensive. This does not mean, however, that employers will have no economic incentive to provide safety. The employer whose place of work is unusually dangerous will be at a competitive disadvantage in recruiting workers and must compensate by offering higher wages. The issue, then, is the degree of safety provided.

Theoretically, there are several ways employers could be induced to improve safety. The government could subsidize installation of safety procedures and equipment, but this would burden taxpayers. Alternatively, tax penalties could be imposed on employers with bad safety records. Or the liability for accidents due to negligence could be placed solely on the employer; this solution would require changes in current workers' compensation laws, which limit the employer's liability.

Most modern health and safety regulations do not employ any of these methods. The Occupational Safety and Health Administration (OSHA) instead relies on a system of standards for safe behavior, and the burden of maintaining these standards is on businesses. While health and safety standards have changed the behavior of business firms, they are costly to enforce because each place of business must be inspected regularly by an OSHA employee. In addition, there is reason to believe that there are much cheaper ways to provide equal levels of safety.

To comply with government standards, for example, employers might be required to provide hard hats for each employee—even though employees have little use for hard hats and generally refuse to wear them. If, instead, employers were provided with incentives to improve safety records (either by fines or by strict assignment of liability), they would have an incentive to spend money wisely to reduce accidents.

Government Ownership

Socialization

Government ownership and operation of a firm or industry.

An alternative to antitrust policy or regulation is government ownership, or **socialization,** of firms. When monopolies exist and their performance is less than socially optimal, government may choose to own and operate the firm in the interests of the public. We see this happen occasionally, more often at the state or local level than at the national level. For example, many public utilities such as electric services, water, and natural gas are owned and operated by local governments.

Socialization of firms is a solution to the monopoly problem, but is it an efficient solution? Ideally, the firm should approximate the competitive equilibrium. It should minimize its costs of production and charge a price equal to marginal cost. However, the performance of the firm depends on its managers. The managers must operate within the bounds allowed by the politicians who employ them, the voters, and the buyers of their services.

The efficiency of publicly owned firms is questioned by many economists. Many suggest that there is a lack of incentive for efficiency because there are no residual claimants. That is, no one may receive any profits acquired by the socialized firm, so managers have no reason to ensure low costs of operation or product quality.

To judge the efficiency of publicly owned firms, it is possible under some circumstances to compare their price, costs, and quality of service with those of privately owned firms in the same industry. For example, we can compare a locally owned electric firm's price and service to a privately owned electric firm's price and service. Many industries—such as education, medical care, telecommunications, television, garbage services, and employment agencies—have both privately owned and publicly owned firms. However, in most situations we must compare government-owned firms with government-regulated firms, as in the case of electricity.

The U.S. Postal Service is a socialized firm that we cannot compare directly with a private firm, for the government prohibits the delivery of first-class mail by anyone except the U.S. Postal Service. However, there are many firms wishing to enter the mail delivery market, and occasionally they do so illegally. The suggestion that private firms could make a profit at the same price whereas the U.S. Postal System does not is an indication that the Postal Service is run inefficiently. Indeed, many government-owned firms must be subsidized by tax dollars.

Despite its lack of incentives for efficiency, socialization is still considered by some supporters to be an appealing alternative to trust-busting or regulation in monopoly-prone industries. The price of medical services has been rising, and socialized medicine has been offered as a solution. AT&T (American Telephone and Telegraph) was divested through an antitrust case, but an alternative could have been to socialize telephone services. The possible consequences of such actions can be predicted by observing the prices and quality of services of similar industries that have been socialized in other countries.

When government seeks to improve the efficiency of certain businesses, it may not be necessary for the government to regulate or operate the facility itself. As a compromise, the government may acquire the property rights to supply the good or service and then franchise, or lease, the right out to private businesses. Cities as diverse as New York City and Scottsdale, Arizona, use this system of **franchise bidding** to provide garbage collection, fire protection, and other public services. The practice, first formalized by the utilitarian philosopher Jeremy Bentham and his associate Edwin Chadwick, has been employed in European cities for centuries. (See the Focus "Franchising Funerals in Nineteenth-Century London and Paris.")

Franchise bidding
The privatization of traditionally governmental responsibilities via a bidding process.

Laissez-Faire

Antitrust policies, regulations, and government ownership are not the only alternatives to the monopoly problem. Under many circumstances, the forces of the market are capable—given enough time—of eliminating the undesirable performances of monopolies, cartels, and trusts. Over a long enough period of time, for example, entry and new competition will emerge, perhaps through technological innovation, to challenge existing monopolies. Leaving an industry alone is called **laissez-faire** (allow to do) policy.

Laissez-faire
A public policy of not regulating to any degree or interfering with market activities (from the French, meaning, roughly, "allow to do").

THE MOVEMENT TO DEREGULATION

In addition to simply leaving monopolized industries alone, a laissez-faire policy might dictate removing previous regulations—a process called **deregulation.** Firms in regulated industries often attempt to use regulatory agencies to promote the firms' profits. Government regulation has often protected the very companies that antitrust laws and regulations are intended to suppress. In particular, regulatory limits on the entry

Deregulation
The removal of some or all government regulations from a previously regulated industry in an effort to improve the allocation of resources.

FOCUS

Franchising Funerals in Nineteenth-Century London and Paris

Franchising is often presented as an alternative both to government ownership or operation and to more traditional forms of regulation. The most ardent proponent of franchising was nineteenth-century English social reformer Sir Edwin Chadwick (1800–1890). Practically no industry escaped Chadwick's scrutiny. Chadwick wanted the government to take over property rights to sell the good or service (milk, beer, police services, prisons) and then auction the rights to private businesses as a franchise wherever waste or inefficiencies were found.

Consider Chadwick's case for franchising funerals in London. He estimated that between 600 and 700 undertakers in London performed over 100 funerals per day. Therefore, about six undertakers competed for each funeral. Though the market situation appeared to be noncollusive and roughly competitive, Chadwick alleged that the funeral suppliers acted as monopolies. They could charge exorbitant prices because demanders were faced with high information and search costs when shopping for a funeral supplier. Such high costs, moreover, encouraged home funerals, which led to health and sanitary hazards—all the more reason to make funeral supply a fit object of franchising.

Parliament ignored Chadwick's proposals, but Munich, Frankfurt, Berlin, and Paris implemented his principle. Chadwick estimated the total cost of 28,000 interments in Paris at £80,000 in 1843, while the estimated cost of 45,000 interments in London under open competition was £626,000. Under the Paris rate system, Chadwick estimated that London funerals would have cost £166,000, a savings of £460,000, which would be directly attributable to uniform rates within the various classes of services. Thus, in Chadwick's logic, monopoly power

created by high information costs could be eliminated by franchising.[a]

How good was Chadwick's case? In the first place, it is doubtful whether funeral service directors, then or now, have significant monopoly power. At the time of bereavement, most individuals rely on recommendations by friends and family when selecting a funeral home. (Most funeral homes today allow you to plan ahead.) Experience and reputation are important in the business, and long-standing firms represent high or acceptable quality levels.

Franchising funeral services by contract would entail—whenever implemented, even today—policing, enforcing, and contracting costs. If you lose the franchise, what happens to the "horses and carriages" and how would they be transferred? How long will the contract run? What happens if costs or demand change within the period of the contract, forcing losses on the funeral suppliers or abnormal profits? What happens to private property? Chadwick's proposals would apply whenever "waste" occurs in markets. It would apply not only in natural monopoly (or regular monopoly) situations, but also when *competitive markets* are in *disequilibrium,* as may have been the situation in the funeral example Chadwick describes. Chadwick failed to recognize that a real-world competitive system always operates with some friction.

---

[a]Edwin Chadwick, "Results of Different Principles of Legislation and Administration in Europe; of Competition for the Field, as Compared with Competition Within the Field of Service," *Royal Statistical Society Journal* 22 (1859), pp. 389–390; or see Robert B. Ekelund, Jr., and George S. Ford, "Nineteenth Century Urban Market Failure? Chadwick on Funeral Industry Regulation," *Journal of Regulatory Economics* 12 (July 1997), pp. 27–52.

of new firms into an industry and on the prices charged by existing companies can give the existing firms a degree of market power they could not otherwise achieve.

That regulation is more costly to society in many cases than the benefits it produces was first perceived by economists in the 1960s and early 1970s. Nobel Prize–winner George Stigler demonstrated that state electric utility regulation had done little to reduce prices and price discrimination and to suppress monopoly returns in that industry.[6] Glaring inefficiencies and misallocations of resources on railroads and airlines also brought the public's attention to the problem. During the Carter and Reagan administrations, portions of the transportation, banking, telecommunications, and natural gas industries were deregulated. Table 16.3 shows the major deregulation decisions since 1968.

Technology, moreover, erodes monopoly power created by the government, ultimately necessitating deregulation. Such has been the case with modern telecommunications. The simple fact is that the invention of coaxial cable and fiber optics, not to mention the establishment of the Internet (and net communications, advertising, entertainment, etc.) made competition more feasible in some communications markets. Thus, deregulation has ensued, often with mixed results. Monopolists will not willingly give up the monopolies created for them by prior government regulations. The Application at the conclusion of this chapter, "The Telecommunications Act of 1996: Good Intentions Meet Market Realities," delves at some length into this issue.

Two examples of deregulation have occurred in the interstate trucking and airline industries. Until 1980, the Interstate Commerce Commission severely restricted entry of new firms into the trucking industry, as well as price competition among firms. The Motor Carrier Act of 1980 decreased the ICC's ability to restrict new entry. Since that time, the number of firms has increased by several thousand, and prices have fallen 20 percent. (The ICC was finally eliminated in 1995.) In the airline industry, the Civil Aeronautics Board set passenger fares and restricted entry until the Airline Deregulation Act in 1978. From then until the CAB's demise in late 1984, the CAB's ability to restrict price competition and entry was severely limited. Deregulation results in the airline industry have been similar to those in trucking. The number of firms has increased and prices have fallen. Since deregulation, some trucking and airline firms have also gone bankrupt—exactly what one would expect of inefficient firms facing competition. (For an analysis of the successes and problems of airline deregulation, see the Focus "Airline Deregulation: Success Story or Consumer Nightmare?")

The negative impact of deregulation can be quite severe. When banks and savings and loan institutions (S&Ls) were deregulated in the 1980s, the system of federally insuring deposits up to $100,000 remained in effect. This encouraged the owners and directors of S&Ls to undertake very risky investments, many of which subsequently failed. The federal government has had to bail out many failed S&Ls by reimbursing depositors. The government bailout has been an extremely expensive program, but it would not have been necessary if S&Ls had been required to provide their own deposit insurance. The problem was not the deregulation of the banking industry; rather, it was the way the banking industry was deregulated.

Moreover, the privatization and deregulation of industry is a hallmark of economies across the world. The transitional economies in the former Soviet Union and Eastern Europe have been selling off state-run enterprises to private

---

[6]George J. Stigler and Claire Friedland, "What Can Regulators Regulate? The Case of Electricity," *Journal of Law and Economics* 5 (1962), pp. 1–15.

TABLE 16.3

Major Deregulation Decisions Since 1968

Deregulation of the communications, transportation, and financial services industries is an ongoing process and has taken place in both Democratic and Republican administrations.

1968	The Supreme Court permits non-AT&T equipment to be connected to the Bell system.
1969	MCI is permitted to connect its long-distance network with local phone systems.
1970	Interest rates are deregulated on bank deposits of $100,000 or more.
1972	The Federal Communications Commission (FCC) establishes a domestic satellite open skies policy.
1975	The Securities and Exchange Commission ends fixed brokerage fees for stock market transactions.
	Rate bureaus for railroads and trucking firms are prohibited from protesting independent rate filings.
1976	The Railroad Revitalization and Regulatory Reform Act of 1976 partially deregulates railroads and makes rate setting more cost-based.
1977	Deregulation of air cargo gives airlines more freedom in pricing.
1978	Congress partially decontrols natural gas.
	The Occupational Safety and Health Administration revokes 928 "nit-picking" rules.
	The Civil Aeronautics Board is phased out, eliminating controls over airline entry and prices.
	The Environmental Protection Agency permits emissions trading.
1980	The FCC removes most federal regulation of cable TV and of equipment in consumers' premises.
	The Motor Carrier Act eliminates barriers for new entries and permits operators to establish fares and routes with little oversight by the Interstate Commerce Commission.
	The Depository Institutions law phases out interest rate ceilings and permits savings and loans and banks to offer interest-bearing checking accounts.
	The Staggers Rail Act enables railroads to adjust rates without government approval and enter into contracts with shippers.
1981	President Reagan decontrols crude oil prices and petroleum allocations.
	The FCC removes many radio regulations.
1982	A new bus regulatory statute allows intercity bus companies to change routes and fares.
	The Garn-St. Germain Act allows savings and loans to make more commercial and consumer loans and removes interest rate differentials between banks and savings and loans.
1984	As part of an antitrust settlement, AT&T agrees to divest local operating companies.
	Individual ocean shipping companies are allowed to offer lower rates and better service than shipping "conferences."
1986	Trading of airport landing rights allowed.
1987	Sale of Conrail.
	The FCC eliminates fairness doctrine.
1989	Natural Gas Wellhead Decontrol Act.
1992	Energy Policy Act modified to allow for the creation of a new class of independent power producer free from corporate and geographic restrictions imposed by current law.
1995	Interstate Commerce Commission is dissolved.
1996	Telecommunications Act sets standards for the deregulation of local phone service, cable rates, radio and television provision, and many other features of telecommunications.
1999	Cable rates fully deregulated.
1999	Maritime agreements between shippers and ocean carriers deregulated, allowing short- and long-term contracts between parties to be held in private.

Sources: Dennis W. Carlton and Jeffrey M. Perloff, *Industrial Organization* (Glenview, Illinois: Scott, Foresman, 1990), Chapter 23; Murray Weidenbaum, *The Benefits of Deregulation* (Contemporary Issues Series 25, Center for the Study of American Business, Washington University, December 1987); Tenpao Lee, C. Phillip Baumel, and Patricia Harris, "Market Structure, Conduct and Performance of the Class I Railroad Industry, 1971–1984," *Transportation Journal* 26 (1987), pp. 54–66; and Robert N. Hahn, "Regulation: Past, Present, and Future," *Harvard Journal of Law and Public Policy* 13 (Winter 1990), p. 183, and author update.

FOCUS

Airline Deregulation: Success Story or Consumer Nightmare?

The airline industry has undergone enormous changes since the Airline Deregulation Act of 1978. Both fares and route patterns have been deregulated, determined by airline management and the marketplace. Most economists would argue that airline deregulation provided and continues to provide enormous generalized welfare benefits to consumers. However, deregulation has not been a total success. Problems include (possible) monopoly pricing in specific ("hub") markets,[a] a confusing fare structure, and crowding at airports. In order to gauge the benefits and costs of deregulation, it is necessary to understand the market structure of the industry before and after regulation.

When airfares were controlled, nonprice competition in the form of higher quality meals, better service, and greater frequency of flights caused costs to rise. Airline routes were established under regulation in north–south and east–west patterns, imitating railroad corridors established in the nineteenth century.

Since deregulation, many airline passengers have grown accustomed to the availability of relatively cheap restricted fares. Price discrimination does exist, however, with business travelers—who cannot always plan ahead or travel only on certain days—paying significantly higher fares than tourists. All travelers have had to adjust to a radically different route structure since deregulation. Most airlines have replaced their pre-deregulation linear routes with a hub and spoke system. This flexible system feeds traffic through medium and small cities (spokes) to one of several regional hubs. The implementation of this system has resulted in much bet-

ter coordination of flights, lower costs, and much less inconvenience to airline passengers (the necessity of changing airlines and making several intermediate stops having been sharply reduced for most travelers). New computer reservation systems—which also provide consumers with car rental and other services in addition to ticketing and boarding passes—and new marketing plans (for example, frequent-flier programs) have also increased consumer welfare and enhanced the cost efficiency and managerial effectiveness of airline operations.

In addition to changing fare and route structures, the airline industry has been characterized by mergers, bankruptcies, and price wars since the early 1980s. Those companies that were able to gain strategic advantages in the highly competitive market (companies such as American, Delta, and United) have prospered. Most of the other carriers have been punished by the market, and some, such as Eastern and Pan Am, were driven out of business.

When an airline establishes a hub, the airline usually comes to dominate service to the hub city. For example, Delta dominates the Atlanta market and American dominates the Dallas market. There is some evidence that travelers in hub cities pay fares that are slightly higher than fares elsewhere, but, on average, fares have fallen significantly since deregulation. (It appears that consumers do in fact prefer lower-priced, no-frills service.) Some travelers—especially business travelers—may complain about high unrestricted fares, but many of these same travelers have probably also benefited from "supersaver" fares or from frequent-flier programs. Overcrowding is an occasional problem at certain airports—particularly hub airports—but this is to be expected when airfares are as affordable as bus and train fares, as has often been the case in recent years. Overcrowding is also, for many people, a small price to pay for cheaper fares. All in all, consumers have enjoyed dramatic gains from deregulation.

[a]Some economists dispute the fact that monopoly is created at hub cities. See Andrew N. Kleit and Steward G. Maynes, "Airline Networks as Joint Goods: Implications for Competition Policy," *Journal of Regulatory Economics* 4 (June 1992), pp. 175–186.

bidders, with some success. Privatization and deregulation of industry are part and parcel of the same phenomenon. They represent a return to reliance on private "incentives" and markets to allocate resources and spark economic recovery and growth.

CONCLUSION

We have examined several forms of public policy that are aimed at preventing poor market performance. Each of these—antitrust, regulation, socialization, and laissez-faire—has its merits, but no public policy can achieve the efficiency generated by a competitive market. When imperfect competition exists, our best solutions are themselves imperfect.

Not only are our best solutions theoretically imperfect, but actual government policies appear to be schizophrenic. One action attempts to increase competition and reduce profits, while other actions promote monopolies and their profits. The reason for these contradictions is that public policies are formulated in a political arena and not by impartial economic theorists or forces. An understanding of public choice theory—to be explored in Chapter 18—can tell us more about public policy in monopolized industries.

APPLICATION

The Telecommunications Act of 1996: Good Intentions Meet Market Realities

Trumpets blared as President Clinton signed the new Telecommunications Act into law on February 12, 1996. The purposes of the Act were explicit—". . . to provide for a pro-competitive, de-regulatory national policy framework" to take into account the astonishingly rapid technological development in most areas of modern telecommunications. Bright promises of enhanced competition, lower prices, and expanded choices in the provision of all telecommunications services raised great expectations on the part of consumers everywhere.

But surprises were in store. Despite the best of stated intentions, the Telecom Act has done very little to establish market competition in many areas of modern telecommunications. How are consumers getting the short end of the stick? Here are only a few ways.

Local Phone Service

Local exchange companies (both Bell and non-Bell) retain their monopolies over local phone communications despite the Act's stated intention that competition prevail in these markets. The government effectively deregulated long-distance phone service fifteen years ago, and rates have fallen by half with the new competition. Why not the same for local rates? The problem is that the local companies are attached to their monopolies. With the help of state public service commissions (PSCs) around the country, they have maintained local monopoly control. Kicking and screaming and with lawyers in tow, they have kept competition out of local phone markets by effectively preventing potential competitors from gaining access to their local exchange operations (which the Telecom Act envisioned). These hold-ups have taken many forms, including the attempt to charge outrageous rates for renting facilities. Merely leasing resale facilities does not, moreover, amount to the establishment of viable competition.

Payphones

Used a pay phone lately? If so, you probably have noted that local pay phone providers, most prominently local Bells, have upped the rate to call for a cab. These rates were "deregulated" by the Act and are administered by your local PSC. The intention was to provide more pay phones at competitive rates. The problem is that the owner of the property on which the phone sits is free to charge "monopoly" rates for use of the location. Translated, that means that you, the consumer, are paying *higher* rates to property owners with the "deregulation."

Credit Card Calls

Use of credit cards from a pay phone is also costing you more. The FCC decided that local exchange carriers (again mostly local Bells) should be compensated for 800 and credit card calls made from payphones. The problem is that the rate that your long-distance carrier must pay to use the facilities is far higher than a competitive rate. Guess who pays for these monopoly-priced long-distance calls? These so-called "pass-throughs" are charges passed right on to you, the consumer.

Cable Rates

Noticed your cable bill rising lately? They have risen by about 21 percent across the country in 1997. "Deregulation" of cable meant that prices of cable were not to be regulated at the local level, but by the Federal Communications Commission. This is just what the cable companies wanted. Out of sight, out of mind. It is far harder for you to get a response from a Washington agency than from City Hall. The cable companies still have their local monopolies. The result: higher *and rising* cable rates for basic service despite threats to effectively re-regulate rates by Congress. Cable companies claim that costly new services have been added to the consumer's menu, although recent research shows that the welfare decrease caused by the increase in price is just matched by the additional welfare to consumers from a new channel.[a] Whether new and higher-quality cable services compensate for the higher prices may determine whether re-regulation of rates will occur.

---

[a]See T. Randolph Beard, Robert B. Ekelund, Jr., George S. Ford, and Richard S. Saba, "Price-Quality Tradeoffs and Welfare Effects in Cable Television Markets," (Manuscript, Auburn University, 1999).

Radio and TV Markets

The structure of radio and over-the-air TV markets, once forcefully fragmented to a great extent, is now characterized by increasing levels of concentration. The Telecommunications Act contained provisions that allowed greater concentration of ownership of broadcast media resources. This new concentration, created in recognition that new efficiencies might be had by additional local and national ownership concentration, has caused genuine concerns about the creation of market power—in, for example, the potential ability of communications firms to charge monopoly rates to local and national advertisers. The Department of Justice has disallowed some media mergers on such grounds. The evidence, however, is that efficiency rather than market power characterizes media mergers, at least in radio.[b] The hope is that emerging new information and entertainment technologies may create close substitutes for radio and television advertising outlets, such as those appearing on the Internet.

Has the Telecommunications Act of 1996 yet fulfilled its promises? In certain areas of telecommunications the answer is clearly "no." Competition has not materialized between local Bells and cable companies; between long-distance providers and local Bells; and among computer service providers, phone, and cable operations. At least a modicum of technology exists to accommodate myriad kinds of new competition. Local Bells are engaged in some serious foot-dragging with local competition. Delay benefits these companies because they want to enter the long-distance market without paying the dues of letting long-distance carriers into their local markets. Baby Bells want a piece of the lucrative long-distance trade rather than tinker with less remunerative local cable competition. Cable companies do not want to lose their local monopolies, either, and they have been fighting effective regulation tooth and nail. Meanwhile, consumers continue to pay unnecessarily high prices for service.

Despite the problems, it is probably not wise to engage in re-regulation in the many areas of telecommunications. Positive experience with deregulation and competition in other formerly regulated markets over the past two decades clearly argues against such a myopic interpretation. Huge consumer benefits realized in airlines, trucking, banking, long distance, and so on provide ample testimony to the general soundness of moving from a government-controlled monopoly to a market-controlled competitive environment. But competition was evolving in these markets *before* full deregulation.

In the case of telecommunications, technology should be given a chance to work through the stubborn actors in the monopoly play. In local exchange phone services, however, there is little or no actual competition in place, and the market-disciplining force of potential competition is weak at best. As a result, deregulation is premature and will only lead (as it already has) to monopoly pricing and preemptive practices that actually *delay* the advent of meaningful competition. In effect, the Telecommunications Act raises hopes that, in today's market

---

[b]See Robert B. Ekelund, Jr., George S. Ford, and Thomas Koutsky, "Market Power in Radio Markets: An Empirical Analysis of Local and National Concentration," *Journal of Law and Economics* (April 2000).

environment, simply cannot be met. *Government can encourage competition, but it cannot create it.*

The Act and its enforcers failed to recognize the important realities of the affected markets—the most important being the incentives of both regulators and regulatees to resist its implementation. Government *created* much of the monopoly in telecommunications. Reorienting markets of this magnitude takes time. Politicians and regulators should recognize, however, that consumers' patience is wearing thin. Technology may come to consumers' rescue, but technology must, of course, work through all-too-fallible human institutions.

QUESTIONS

To what extent do you believe the problems of telecommunications deregulation to be of a "short-term" nature? Do you believe re-regulation is the answer in such markets as cable television? Why or why not?

SUMMARY

1. Antitrust laws are basically designed to promote and maintain competition in the economy.

2. Industry concentration ratios change through time because the optimal number of firms changes as demand and cost conditions change.

3. The number of firms in an industry is determined by the number of firms of optimal size that industry demand is able to support. A natural monopoly exists when industry demand is sufficient to support only one firm of optimal size in an industry.

4. Mergers are the combination of two or more firms in an industry into a single firm. Mergers may decrease competition or enhance competitive efficiency. The latter effect may result from technological innovations that reduce the number of firms required in an industry for economic efficiency.

5. Price regulation allows the existence of monopoly but attempts to decrease the social loss by imposing a particular pricing policy. However, price regulation may decrease the firm's incentive to maintain efficiency. Regulation of competitive industries has resulted in government-managed cartels.

6. Government ownership as an alternative to monopoly can prevent higher-than-normal profits. However, a government-owned business is not forced by the market to maintain efficiency.

7. Franchise bidding is an attempt to assure that competitive prices will be charged without destroying incentives for efficiency.

8. Economic regulation has the potential to achieve results in the public interest. However, economic groups that are harmed by or that could benefit from regulation have an incentive to capture the regulatory process and frustrate regulations conceived in the public interest.

9. Since regulation is inevitably imperfect, the existence of a less-than-perfect unregulated market does not necessarily justify regulation.

10. A laissez-faire system is an alternative to active public policy. Under some circumstances this policy to leave the market alone is clearly preferable.

KEY TERMS

antitrust policies
regulatory policies
concentration ratios
predatory pricing
merger
natural monopoly

public interest theory of regulation
capture (interest group) theory
    of regulation
average cost pricing
marginal cost pricing
rate of return regulation

sustainable monopoly
contestability
socialization
franchise bidding
laissez-faire
deregulation

QUESTIONS FOR REVIEW AND DISCUSSION

1. Why does government sometimes act, through regulation, to enforce a cartel? Why do voters and consumers put up with such programs and policies? What effect would deregulation have on such an industry?

2. Blue laws outlaw Sunday sales in a given locality. From the point of view of economic regulation, explain who gains and who loses from such legislation.

3. How does rate of return, or profit, regulation affect firm behavior? Does this regulation promote production efficiency? Do we achieve the optimal output with average cost pricing?

4. Are local television companies natural monopolies? How could the answer be determined? If they are, would they want to be regulated?

5. Can public policy change an industry characterized as a natural monopoly into a competitive industry that results in competitive equilibrium?

6. Suppose that your university decided to have its cafeterias operated under a franchise bidding arrangement. Could the university assure that the franchisee maintained adequate standards in the food served? Might the franchisee actually improve the quality of food served? Explain.

7. States uniformly require teachers of primary and secondary schools to be licensed, but they do not require the licensure of college professors. Between students and professors, which group do you think would be more likely to make demands for the licensure of professors? What does your answer say about your confidence in the capture theory of regulation versus the public interest theory?

8. Businesses and workers often have conflicting interests about worker safety. Can you think of some safety standard that both workers and businesspersons would oppose? One that they both would support?

9. Some economists argue that there is a trade-off between safety regulations and employment in a particular industry. Is it likely that tighter safety standards in, say, the textile industry will lead to fewer textile jobs? Explain.

PROBLEMS

1. Look back at the concentration ratios for the jewelry and precious metals industry in Table 16.1. Has this industry become more or less concentrated through time? Does an increase in concentration always imply an increase in monopoly power? Why or why not? How might consumers actually benefit from an industry becoming more concentrated?

2. How do public choice and interest group politics affect regulation? Pick a particular area of business and explain the interests that might support or reject government regulation. Why might these interests be effective or ineffective in obtaining regulations?

WORKING WITH THE WEB

1. The Focus "The Microsoft Case: Is It Monopoly, or Is It Envy?" in this chapter reviews the Department of Justice's antitrust case against Microsoft. You learned earlier in the text that monopolists are price searchers; that is, they search for the price that maximizes profit. They also create artificial scarcity by restricting output. Hence, compared with a competitive market, monopolists offer less output for sale and do so at higher prices. Go to http://www.cei.org/MonoReader.asp?ID=702 and choose the link "Full Text Available in PDF."

   Read Fagin's paper on the Microsoft case, "The Case Against the Case Against Microsoft."

   a. Which antitrust Act is Microsoft accused of violating?

   b. The Focus article notes that web browser prices fell after the introduction of Microsoft's Internet Explorer. What price did Microsoft charge for Internet Explorer? Is this indicative of monopoly behavior?

   c. Typically, once a monopolist has "locked in" its consumers, it is likely to increase its price. Microsoft has many users, given that the Windows operating system is the most common system on computers today. In this respect, a large proportion of Microsoft customers can be considered locked in. Has Microsoft increased the prices of its software and operating system upgrades over time to take advantage of its captive customer base?

2. Another Focus in the chapter addresses the pros and cons of airline deregulation, noting that on balance, consumers have gained from deregulation. Recently, however, there has been a push for government regulation of airlines in the form of a "passenger bill of rights" as airlines increasingly overbook flights, cancel flights, or have delays without providing adequate information to passengers. For example, in January 1999, thousands of Northwest Airlines passengers were stranded due to a snowstorm and many were stuck on the runway for up to nine hours! Go to http://www.freep.com/news/airtravel/qair182.htm and read the article about the proposed changes offered by the airlines.

   a. Why did Congress feel pressured to act on behalf of consumers?

   b. What does the proposal promise passengers in the event their luggage is "mishandled"?

   c. Upon making a reservation, in the past some airlines required immediate payment. What does the new proposal suggest regarding payment terms?

   d. How will customers who searched the Internet for the lowest plane fares likely be affected by the proposed changes?

17

Natural Resources, the Environment, and Public Goods

oncerns about the use of scarce, perhaps even vanishing, natural resources and about environmental issues are commonplace in today's headlines. Global warming, the ozone layer, the rain forest, endangered species, urban pollution, soil erosion, and other natural resource and environmental topics raise concerns on every front. The costs of addressing such issues and who pays these costs are also of concern to the interested groups. User fees, higher automobile prices, bans on urban barbecuing, international competitiveness, and the like animate the activities of those who must pay for the use of environmental assets.

Natural resources and the environment represent challenging issues for the application of economic principles. Not the least of the reasons for this is that markets sometimes work well in pricing natural resources and environmental assets, and sometimes they fail miserably. As we shall see, markets are excellent devices for pricing renewable and nonrenewable resources and for ensuring a steady supply of these commodities when property rights are well defined among resource owners. However, in the case of the environment, markets sometimes fail to achieve desirable economic results. That is, markets can fail to provide goods and services in the right quantities at the right prices. Market failure with respect to environmental and natural resources often arises from problems of incomplete or nonexistent ownership rights to basic resources. Owners of private property bear directly the economic results of the use of property and are therefore motivated to use resources efficiently. In contrast, when property is held or used by everybody in common, users do not bear the full costs of its use. Common ownership creates a conflict between the pursuit of self-interest and the common good.

We also consider another role for government in this chapter as the provider of certain goods and services that markets would fail to produce in the correct amounts, if at all (e.g., national defense). These goods are called public goods, and their existence represents another potential role for government in a market economy.

In this chapter we review the economics of natural and environmental resources and the approach to market failures, including the failure of markets to provide certain public goods. To improve on situations of market failure, we must carefully weigh the costs and benefits of alternative policies. After reading Chapter 17 you should understand

- how the markets for nonrenewable (oil) and renewable (forests) resources work.
- how common ownership of property creates an incentive problem with respect to the management (or lack of it) of natural resources, and how the definition of property rights can overcome this problem.
- the nature of market failure and how market failures such as pollution and overfishing can be corrected.
- how market failure may have international implications through the creation of global problems.
- how the legal system—specifically, assignment of rights to use property—might be used in market failure situations.
- the nature of public goods and their relation to market failure.

Our analysis begins with a discussion of how the market for nonrenewable and renewable resources works in terms of the familiar concepts of demand and supply. We then present an analysis of the problem of commonly owned resources. We consider two concrete cases from the U.S. economy: the common stock of fish in international waters, and the oil pool. The discussion then turns to global environmental problems: acid rain and global warming.

NATURAL RESOURCES

Natural resources
All those renewable and nonrenewable resources that are given to an economy or society.

Natural resources are those resources that come to an economy or society from nature. Some societies are endowed with abundant natural resources, while others have few and have to trade for those that they desire to use. Natural resources fall into two broad groups.

Nonrenewable natural resources
Resources that exist in finite quantities.

First, there are **nonrenewable natural resources**. These are resources that exist in finite quantities. There is, for example, only so much oil, coal, bauxite, natural gas, and iron ore in the world. When we consume some of these resources today, there is automatically less available for consumption tomorrow.

Renewable natural resources
Those resources that may be reproduced through time if not exhausted by unwise policies.

There are also **renewable natural resources** which include plant and animal life such as forests and fish. Renewable resources can be used over and over again, provided that we do not exhaust them through unwise policies. A key problem with renewable resources, as we shall discuss in this chapter, is to provide the proper economic incentives to those who supply renewable resources so as to ensure that these resources are not depleted in the present at the expense of our future well-being.

The prices and quantities used of natural resources are determined in markets for these goods. By understanding how these markets work, we take the first step to a fuller appreciation of what the appropriate policies are for conserving both renewable and nonrenewable natural resources.

The Market for Nonrenewable Resources

We begin with the market for nonrenewable resources; we use oil as our example. The demand for oil is derived in the same way as that for any factor of production. The demander uses oil in production according to the marginal revenue product of oil. In other words, the demand for oil depends on its contribution to firm revenues (see the discussion in Chapter 12), and this is the basis on which the demand curve for oil (D_{market}) in Figure 17.1 is drawn.

The derivation of the supply curve of oil involves a couple of steps. There is a fixed (finite) supply of oil in the world. There is only so much oil, and no more. Thus the aggregate supply curve of oil is totally inelastic. The total supply of oil depends on the total amount in existence. If we use oil this year, there will automatically be less for use next year. This means that the relevant concept of supply in this case is how much oil do we extract and offer for sale *today* as opposed to *tomorrow*. This supply curve of oil (S_{today}) is given in Figure 17.1, and it shows the positive relationship between the price of oil and the amount that producers are willing to supply (discover, refine, and so on) today or this year. As price rises, producers are willing to extract and sell more of the fixed resource of oil today. As in any other market, the price and output of oil are determined by the intersection of the supply and demand curves in Figure 17.1, which represents a market equilibrium outcome in the oil market ($14 and 100 million barrels).

FIGURE 17.1

The Market for Nonrenewable Resources

The current price of a nonrenewable resource is set at $14, where the quantity demanded and quantity supplied of oil are equal. The supply curve of oil is the amount that producers are willing to sell at current prices, or S_{today}. The fact that we consume 100 million barrels of oil today means that there will be less oil available to consume in the future and that oil in the future will carry a higher price. These effects are represented by the shift to $S_{tomorrow}$ in the figure.

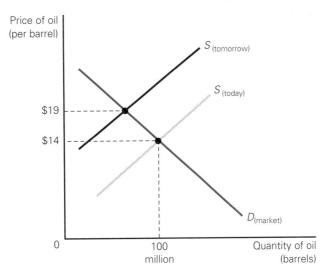

Remember that the oil we consume today cannot be consumed tomorrow. This effect is illustrated in Figure 17.1, where the supply curve of oil has shifted to the left (decreased) to $S_{tomorrow}$. Today's consumption means less oil is available for consumption tomorrow; moreover, the oil tomorrow will be more costly to find and extract for sale. This is why the supply curve of oil decreases. Producers have already discovered and produced the lowest-cost oil, and as we consume that oil, future oil becomes more costly to find and to produce. Over time, then, there will be a tendency for the price of this or any other nonrenewable resource to rise. The price of such resources should be higher tomorrow than today because of the forces of supply and demand depicted in Figure 17.1.

This rise in the price of oil means two things. First, the higher price means that, by the law of demand, users will be driven to reduce their consumption of oil and economize on its use. This helps society spread out the available stock of oil in the most effective way possible. Only those consumers who place the largest marginal values on the use of oil will bid for and use oil. Second, the higher price of this valuable input will spur entrepreneurs to seek new sources of oil and innovators to seek cheaper ways of extracting oil and alternative ways to power the world than oil. This is because the invention of an effective alternative power source to oil would make such individuals wealthy. There is, of course, no guarantee that innovation will help the world avoid the ultimate resource scarcity of oil dictated by nature, but history is replete with examples of such ingenuity. (See the Focus "The Economics of Doomsday.")

Oil field owners will decide what to do with their oil based on profit maximization, just as the owners of any other resource will do. If they make more money by pumping oil and selling it, then that is what they will do. If not, they will keep the oil in the ground. In general, if the returns to investments in the economy are high, they will pump and sell the oil and invest in these other high-yielding investments. Thus, the rate of oil supplied today will be a function of the interest rate. As interest rates rise, oil field owners will pump more oil because the return to holding oil in the ground has fallen.

Pumping more now, however, raises the future price of oil, counteracting the incentive to pump more now. Equilibrium is reached where the marginal return from pumping oil now is just offset by the marginal return to pumping oil tomorrow. In this way, private owners will conserve the fixed resource in just the right way over time, pumping and selling when it is in their interest and holding and selling tomorrow when it pays to do so. With private ownership, we get the optimal rate of extraction of a finite resource over time.

The Market for Renewable Resources

Renewable resources can reproduce themselves. The problem that an economy faces in this case is to be sure that the owner of a renewable resource, such as a forest, has an incentive to renew the resource at a rate that is coincident with what is best for the economy as a whole. In other words, what rate of replenishment do we want?

Forest owners could cut down and sell all their trees today, and then we would be without the products produced by trees (e.g., lumber to build homes) for a while. The increase in trees produced today means a decrease in trees produced tomor-

FOCUS

The Economics of Doomsday

Predictions of a global environmental collapse may be just the latest in a string of disaster scenarios relating to natural resources that now dates back more than 10,000 years. Below are some of the more prominent examples of important doomsday predictions:

- Global warming—1990s (the earth will heat up and be covered by water);
- Water crisis—1980 to 1982 (only 18 percent of America will have a drinkable water supply);
- New Ice Age—1970s (pollution brings about new Ice Age);
- The energy crisis—1970s (the world is running out of oil);
- The timber famine—1900 to 1930 (the world is running out of trees);
- The first oil crisis—mid-1800s (the world is running out of whale oil);
- The English energy crisis—1550–1650 (the world is running out of trees);
- Greek timber crisis—seventh century A.D. (the world is running out of wood);
- Greek Bronze crisis—1000 B.C. (bronze is becoming very expensive); and
- Early food crisis—8000 B.C. (there is a growing scarcity of food for hunter-gatherers).

History has shown that these doomsday predictions never come to pass. In the face of increased scarcity, people adapted, used substitutes, and invented new technology. In response to the early food crisis, for example, people switched from being hunter-gatherers to farming and domesticating animals; and they improved their diet and standard of living as a result. The scarcity of bronze encouraged people to switch to iron, which turned out to be more abundant and more useful. The scarcity of whale oil resulted in a switch to petroleum. Energy and wood crises encouraged people to conserve and to adopt new technologies.

Economists also have had their own doomsday predictions. For example, economist Robert Malthus's population theory held that population would outpace food production, and the world would be faced with an ongoing food shortage and famine. While this theory is still popular today, history has demonstrated that food production has grown with population and that famines are short-lived phenomena mostly due to war, not population growth.

Modern doomsday predictions about global warming and new Ice Ages should be put in the context that human beings have shown the ability to conserve, adapt, and invent new technologies and have in many cases emerged better as a result of the challenge.

Source: Charles Maurice and Charles W. Smithson, *The Doomsday Myth: 10,000 Years of Economic Crisis* (Stanford, Calif.: Hoover Institute Press, 1984).

row, so that the forest owner's decision lowers the price of wood products today and raises it tomorrow. The tree farmer's decision of what to do, just like the owner of the oil, depends on the interest rate. If the interest rate rises, the tree farmer will convert trees into cash in order to earn the higher interest rate. Thus, rising interest rates are associated with increased present consumption of renewable resources, and falling interest rates are associated with more future consumption.

Counteracting this tendency is the fact that as the tree farmer cuts down more trees today, the current price of trees falls and the future price of trees rises. Just like the nonrenewable case of oil, these adjustments go on until the market allocates trees to their highest-valued uses now and in the future.

So long as we depend on markets to produce and allocate nonrenewable and renewable natural resources, the result obtained will be that natural resources, even ones that are limited in supply, are properly allocated between present and future uses. This result, however, depends critically on the presence of clearly defined property rights among the owners of natural resources. If this condition does not hold, private production of natural resources can lead to problems, as we see in the next section.

THE ECONOMICS OF COMMON PROPERTY

Common ownership

An arrangement whereby the property rights to a resource are nonexistent or poorly defined; by default, anyone may use or consume the resource.

The fundamental economic disadvantage of **common ownership**—the right to the use of a resource by anyone or by competing users—is the lack of incentive to invest in the productivity of the common property. Rather, each person with access to the resource has an incentive to exploit it and neglect the effects of his or her actions on the resource's productivity. This principle applies both to renewable resources, such as fish, and nonrenewable resources, such as oil.

Fishing in International Waters

In international waters anyone may acquire exclusive ownership of a fish by catching it, and no one has rights to the fish until it is caught. This system causes each fisherman to ignore the effect of the well-known biological law that the cur-

Ocean fisheries present a common-pool problem whereby each individual has little incentive to conserve present stocks of fish.

rent stock of a species of fish determines its reproduction rate. Thus, fish harvested today reduce today's stock and thereby affect the size of tomorrow's stock and tomorrow's harvesting costs and revenues. Overfishing results because no single fisherman has an incentive to act on this bioeconomic relation. If all fishermen would cooperate to restrain themselves now, tomorrow's stock would be larger and future harvesting cheaper and more profitable. However, under competitive conditions, each individual knows that if he or she abstains now, rivals will not, and the effect of abstention is lost. Further, the reduction in future costs would accrue to everyone, not just to the abstainer. Hence each person has little reason to abstain, since the major effect is to lower others' future costs at some immediate present cost to the abstainer.

Sole ownership removes this dilemma. If only one person is fishing, he or she need not worry that rivals will not abstain. (Of course, groups such as tribes of indigenous people can also be sole owners, but the group must be able to control the behavior of its members with respect to the resource.) When there is more than one owner, all parties involved could negotiate an agreement to abstain, and all would benefit. The fact that such agreements are not usually successfully negotiated is due to the costs of dealing with all current and potential people who will fish and the difficulty of ensuring that all abstain as agreed.

Another method of dealing with this dilemma is government regulation. Such regulation usually sets an annual catch quota. To allocate the quota, regulators rely on restrictions on technology or simply close the season when the quota is taken. Both means create difficult enforcement problems and potential economic waste. If the season is closed when the quota is taken, for example, excess profits are dissipated in competition among fishermen to buy bigger, faster boats and thus get a larger share of the quota. The season progressively shrinks, and resources stand idle or are devoted to inferior employments.

Thus, fishing in international waters presents a devilish problem of negotiating international agreements, and there is widespread evidence of the depletion and possible extinction of a major source of food supply for the world.

Drilling for Oil

Oil presents another version of the same common ownership dilemma (see Figure 17.2). Unlike fish, oil is nonrenewable. However, oil does move about, so pumping one well lowers the entire reserve and affects the pressure below other wells. These characteristics create a problem when more than one person has rights to the same oil reserve. For example, if the land above a reserve of oil is owned by two people, each has the right to drill for oil. But the only way to own the oil is to pump it to the surface. Oil in the ground belongs to the landowner only when that person pumps it to the surface. Herein lies the crucial lack of private ownership rights to oil reserves.

It may be more economically efficient to exploit an oil reserve with a single well than with two wells—not only because it costs more to drill two wells than one, but also because the existence of one well interferes with the other's technical ability to pump. If one person owned the property rights to all the oil, he or she would probably use only a single well. Likewise, if two landowners with rights to

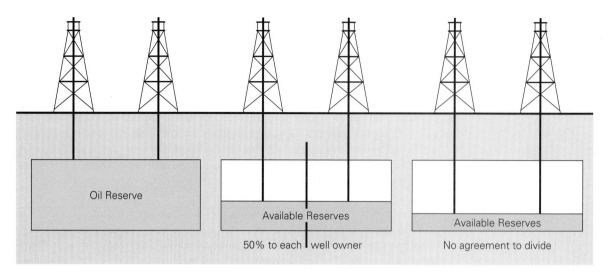

FIGURE 17.2

The Problem of Common Ownership in Oil Drilling

If a fixed reserve of oil is owned in common and the co-owners cannot agree to share the reserves, then each owner will likely try to pump as much oil as possible from the reserve. Doing so reduces the available reserves at a rate disadvantageous to both owners.

a common oil pool negotiate, both can be made better off by agreeing to split the proceeds of a single well rather than both drilling.

If they cannot negotiate, perhaps because of legal restrictions, or if a larger number of owners causes difficulties in communication, each may go ahead and drill. Once two wells are in production, there is an economically efficient rate of pumping for each well that a single owner would adopt to maximize his or her wealth. Nevertheless, if the two owners cannot agree on efficient exploitation, each will be tempted to pump oil at too high a rate, a tendency reinforced by the fear that the other is doing the same thing. In fact, even if negotiations are successful, it may be costly to monitor each other's pumping, and the agreement might dissolve in mutual cheating. The costs of negotiating and enforcement probably rise in proportion to the numbers of owners, as do the incentives for each to overpump because others are likely to do so.

The problems of market failure and common property resources encountered in modern society are not unique to contemporary modes of production, nor are they based on greed. There is evidence that overexploitation of resources was a common feature of primitive peoples. For example, the Anasazi Indians of the Southwest developed settlements in Chaco Canyon, Arizona, but failed to manage the forest product resources in the vicinity by replanting or employing conservation techniques. As a result, according to one account, the community's size and progress were limited and it was ultimately abandoned. The woolly mammoth disappeared from the North American continent as a result of rapid population growth and the absence of private property rights thousands of years ago.[1] In New Zealand, scientists have linked the disappearance of the moa, a huge flightless bird, to overzealous exploitation by natives in search of food. The problems of market failure are not the result of good or bad behavior, so blaming any population, ancient or modern, is unproductive. The lesson regarding common property resources is straightforward: What belongs to everyone belongs to no one; the deterioration and rapid exploitation of common property resources are clear implications of economic theory.

International Pollution Problems: Acid Rain and Global Warming

Market failure can occur on a global level. Pollution in many forms is a particularly persistent side effect of "progress." As more countries have become developed, the problems associated with pollution have grown in scope. Pollution stems from by-products of the production and consumption of goods and services. The problem, basically, is this: Gaseous by-products of industrial and agricultural production, such as carbon dioxide, methane, nitrous oxide, ozone, and chlorofluorocarbons, have collected in the atmosphere. At best, the collection of these gases has become undesirable; it may be, however, that our failure to control pollution in the past will have catastrophic effects now and in the future.

We know that the residue of the gaseous by-products of production returns to earth as acid rain. Acid rain kills trees, streams, even whole lakes. Besides damaging the ecosystem, acid rain speeds the deterioration of bridges and buildings. Even worse, many scientists warn of a "greenhouse effect," or global warming, which could have drastic effects on weather, food production, sea levels, and the environment. The warming effect could be an increase of between three and nine degrees Fahrenheit in mean temperature by the mid-twenty-first century. This seemingly minor temperature change would have dramatic effects. Melting glaciers would raise the level of the seas, causing whole islands to disappear and altering coastlines everywhere. Shifts in regional weather patterns, brought about in part by warmer sea water, would bring drought to some areas and greater than normal rainfall to others, with profound implications for agricultural production. The ozone layer in the upper atmosphere is also being depleted by gaseous by-products. Holes in the ozone layer caused by pollution let in rays of the sun that encourage skin cancer, eye diseases, and immune system deficiencies.

Naturally, these problems have caused a great deal of debate among scientists, politicians, producers, and consumers. While the extent of the problem is hotly disputed, no one denies that a market failure of some magnitude does exist. In other words, the socially optimal amount of some good—in this case, clean air—is not being produced. Incomplete or nonexistent property rights to air have resulted in the failure of individuals, acting in their own self-interest, to conserve this resource.

---

[1]On these fascinating issues see two articles by Jared Diamond, "The American Blitzkrieg: A Mammoth Undertaking," *Discover* (June 1987) and "The Golden Age That Never Was," *Discover* (December 1988).

FOCUS

The Kyoto Treaty: Who Benefits from Global Warming?

A conference on global warming was held in Kyoto, Japan, in December 1997; from this, the "Kyoto Treaty" was developed. It calls on thirty-eight developed countries to cut the emission of greenhouse gases to 95 percent of their 1990 level by the year 2010. Economists have examined important aspects of this treaty, which has yet to be ratified.

Will the Kyoto Treaty reduce pollution? Most nations are exempt from the restrictions, and these "developing" nations have done the least to clean up their environments and are predicted to greatly expand their pollution over time. Also, countries facing restrictions will be allowed to buy the right to pollute or could move their high-pollution activities to nonrestricted countries.

How much will the treaty cost, and who will pay? The treaty is potentially very expensive. The United States would have to reduce emissions by 7 percent of 1990 levels, but that will mean a 40 percent cut in 2010 levels. The price of energy and electricity would have to rise dramatically; coal prices and energy-intensive production processes would be hurt the most. The treaty is expected to be expensive to the United States relative to other countries and particularly harmful to poor, coal-producing states like West Virginia and Alabama.

Who will benefit from the treaty? Other than environmental groups, who are the moral crusaders for a cleaner environment, it is difficult to identify the true beneficiaries. However, economics does allow us to identify the nations, industries, and companies that expect to benefit from the treaty and push for its implementation.

Countries that are unrestricted by the treaty support it, because they will be able to sell their unused rights to pollute. Other countries hope the treaty will raise their competitors' costs and thus earn them a greater share in world markets. Certain industries, such as natural gas, also expect to benefit from higher prices as producers switch from coal to natural gas. Finally, firms in the alternative energy business such as Archer-Daniels-Midland already receive a $300 million subsidy for producing ethanol as a substitute for gasoline, and the treaty both protects and will probably increase the amount of the subsidy. Economics shows that an unusual coalition of nations, environmental groups, and major corporations expect to benefit from "global warming" and, more importantly, provides a more realistic view of the effects of regulations such as the Kyoto Treaty.

Information for this Focus was drawn from Bruce Yandle, "Bootleggers, Baptists, and Global Warming" (Political Economy Research Center, 1998).

Identifying the problem is simpler than solving it, however. (See the Focus "The Kyoto Treaty: Who Benefits from Global Warming?") Because pollution controls—such as automobile emissions standards or requirements that smokestacks be outfitted with scrubbers—are not free, resistance by producers and consumers to new and more severe regulations can be expected. Strong resistance is likely when the suggested solutions entail huge costs, particularly when the scientific evidence is in dispute. Further, the global nature of market failure and the potentially discriminatory effects of radical temperature change have not encouraged international cooperation. Some regions and countries may actually benefit from potential temperature changes. Countries whose pollution causes acid rain may not themselves bear the costs due to prevailing wind patterns in the atmosphere. Air pollution is a most complex common ownership problem. Everyone agrees that world governments should do something, but there is much disagreement on what should be done and on who should bear the costs.

EXTERNALITY THEORY

Under certain circumstances, an individual's pursuit of his or her self-interest results in costs or benefits to others. This kind of market failure is called an **externality**; the costs and benefits are external to the individual who caused them. Obviously, any economic entity can create an externality, including firms, government agencies, and individuals.

Negative and Positive Externalities

A common example of an externality is a factory's emission of smoke as a by-product of production. If the factory is able to avoid responsibility for the consequences of its smoke—such as the expenses for painting soot-covered buildings nearby or laundering sooty clothes—the output of the factory will be excessive, in that the value of additional output is less than the additional costs of the additional output plus the damage. If the factory were held responsible for the damage done by its smoke, its costs would rise, its product would become more expensive, and it would produce less. This example illustrates a **negative externality,** a situation in which production entails costs for others, such as those living near a factory. Other potential examples of negative externalities are the exhaust emissions of automobiles, a neighbor's excessively loud stereo, low-flying jet airplanes landing at an airport, drunk drivers, the contamination of underground water by toxic chemical dumps, and so on.

Positive externalities are benefits accruing without costs to the beneficiaries. Suppose a beekeeper and the owner of an apple orchard have adjoining land. The beekeeper's bees fly into the orchard and pollinate the apple blossoms, making the orchard more productive. If the beekeeper were to reap the consequences of the increased value of the orchard, the yield on his investment in bees would rise, and he would raise more bees. But as it is, his bees' social service is provided free. For both illustrations, the point is

Externality
Benefits or costs of an individual's activity that the individual does not receive or bear.

Negative externality
A situation that arises when an individual or other economic entity imposes costs on others without compensating them.

Positive externality
A situation that arises when an individual or other economic entity creates benefits for others without receiving any compensation in return.

A positive externality is created when beekeeper's bees pollinate the apple blossoms in an orchard, making the orchard more productive.

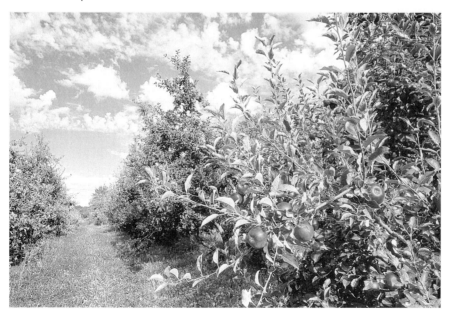

identical: Externalities arise when one person's activities affect the well-being of others, either positively or negatively. Some other examples of positive externalities are the reductions in contagious diseases that result from widespread inoculation and the clothes homeless people receive from charitable organizations.

Determining the Need for Government Intervention

To promote general economic well-being through a more socially efficient allocation of resources, an ideal government would intervene to encourage the production of goods that generate positive externalities and retard the production of goods that yield negative externalities. These inducements to alter production may be indirect in that they focus on the side effects of production, but they nonetheless work to change the amounts of output produced, which generated the externalities to begin with. Consider the externalities associated with the previously mentioned factory and bees. Government might intervene to reduce the amount of smoke emitted by the factory or to increase the number of bees kept by the beekeeper. Intervention is not always called for, however. Individuals might settle such matters privately.

To enhance the bees' contribution to the orchard's productivity, the orchard owner could contract with the beekeeper to supply more bees.[2] Alternatively, the orchard owner could raise his own bees. As long as the beekeeper's marginal costs of raising additional bees are less than the value the bees contribute to the orchard owner, it will be possible for both parties to reach an agreement that will leave each better off. Such private contracting in effect eliminates the apple–bee externality and makes public intervention unnecessary.

In addition to the possibility of private settlements, a second consideration when determining the need for government intervention in externalities is whether the externality is irrelevant or relevant. Externalities are trivial when the situation is not worth anybody's effort to do anything about it. The world is full of trivial externalities. You may not like the way a friend dresses, but not enough to say anything about it. Some people's unfailingly gracious and friendly behavior creates external benefits, and yet they are rarely complimented or rewarded for such behavior. The same goes for an attractive lawn. Neighbors reap external benefits from a well-kept lawn, but not so much that they would offer a subsidy to support the yard work.

Externalities are termed irrelevant when the externality generates insufficient demand by the affected party to change the situation. Your neighbor's messy yard may disturb your sense of propriety. You would be willing to pay her $50 a year to clean up the mess, but her price to clean it up is $600 a year. In this event her yard will not be cleaned up, and the externality will persist. The messy yard is a nuisance but not enough of a nuisance to cause sufficient demand to get the yard cleaned up. In principle, the best thing to do with an irrelevant externality is to leave it alone because it costs more than it is worth to correct the problem.

---

[2]See Steven N. S. Cheung, "The Fable of the Bees: An Economic Investigation," *Journal of Law and Economics* 16 (April 1973), pp. 35–52.

A relevant externality creates sufficient demand on the part of those affected by it to change the situation. Suppose that your neighbor is willing to clean up her messy yard for $10. You are willing to pay as much as $50. In this case you can make an effective offer to correct the externality and reach a deal with your neighbor. With relevant externalities, it is worthwhile to correct the situation because the benefits of correction exceed the costs.

Correcting Relevant Externalities

Economic theory suggests that correction of relevant externalities can be approached in a number of different ways. In general, these can be categorized as defining property rights, taxing negative externalities or subsidizing positive ones, selling rights to create an externality, and establishing regulatory controls.

Establishing Ownership Rights   Externality problems generally persist because of the presence of some element of common ownership. The beekeeper's and the apple grower's ownership rights are clearly established and easily transferable. In such a situation it will be in the interest of both parties to conclude an agreement that places resources in their most highly valued uses. But in the case of the polluting factory, does the factory have the right to use the air as it pleases, or do the people in the surrounding community have the right to clean air? Air-use rights are indefinite and nontransferable: It is generally impossible for people to buy and sell rights to the use of air. In this case, there is no reason to believe that the pursuit of individual interest will promote the use of air in its most highly valued manner.

The establishment of ownership, then, is one way of eliminating problems associated with externalities. Since nonownership is a source of market failure, the creation of ownership is a means of correcting market failure. (See the Application "Can Economic Incentives Save the Elephant and Other Endangered Species?" at the conclusion of this chapter.)

An important analysis of the economics of establishing ownership rights was first introduced by R. H. Coase, who was awarded the Nobel Prize in economics in 1991 for this work.[3] Coase posed the question: Does the legal assignment of property rights to one party or the other in an externality relationship make any difference to the observed market outcome? To keep the analysis simple, Coase assumed that the costs of bargaining and transacting among the parties were zero.

We will apply the Coase analysis to an example of air pollution—a factory belching smoke over a nearby community. Figure 17.3 illustrates the analysis. Firm output per unit of time is given along the horizontal axis. The marginal benefits (*MB*) to the firm of producing this output are given in dollar terms on the vertical axis. For the sake of this analysis, marginal benefits can be thought of as the net profits of producing additional units of output. The *MB* schedule therefore declines

---

[3]R. H. Coase, "The Problem of Social Cost," *Journal of Law and Economics* 3 (October 1960), pp. 1–44.

FIGURE 17.3

The Coase Theorem

In this graph depicting the Coase theorem, *MC* represents the externality imposed by the firm's pollution, and *MB* represents the profits to the firm from producing various levels of output (*Q*). The Coase theorem states that regardless of who is assigned ownership rights to the air, costless bargaining between the parties will result in the same market outcome at *Q*.

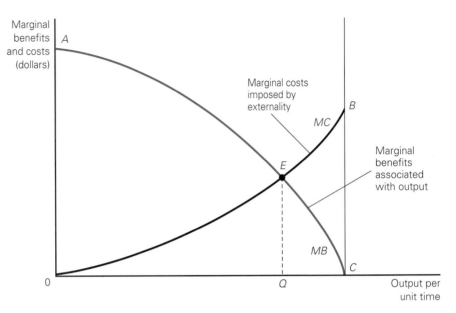

with increases in output because the rate of return on additional production generally declines (see Chapter 7). The marginal cost (*MC*) curve represents the externality caused by the firm's production and is also given in dollar terms along the vertical axis. The *MC* function measures the additional cost created at each output level by additional smoke. (Assuming that the amount of smoke the firm produces is directly related to its rate of output, more production will cause more smoke.) The *MC* curve rises as output increases.

Now we apply Coase's analysis. As an experiment, we give the ownership right to clean air to the homeowners in the surrounding neighborhood. Assuming that bargaining costs nothing, we can predict what will happen with the help of Figure 17.3. For rates of output up to *Q*, we observe that *MB* > *MC*. The firm's profits on additional units are greater than the additional pollution costs borne by the neighborhood; this means that the firm would be willing to buy and the neighborhood would be willing to sell the right of using the air to produce these units. Since the total cost of the externality caused by this output is represented by the area under the *MC* curve, 0*EQ*, a bargain can be struck between the firm and the neighborhood to produce *Q* by agreement on how to divide the surplus marginal benefit, *AE*0. Beyond *Q*, *MC* > *MB*. A bargain to produce these units cannot be reached between the firm and the neighborhood because the firm would not be willing to bid enough to obtain the right to produce these units. So *Q*, where *MB* = *MC*, is the equilibrium outcome when the neighborhood is given the transferable right to use of the air.

Suppose that a judge decided instead to award the firm the right to use the air as it chooses. What happens in this case? We go through the same analysis, but now we see that the neighborhood must pay the firm to produce less output. For up to *Q* units of output, *MB* > *MC*, which means that the neighborhood cannot offer a large enough sum of money to induce the firm to reduce its output and its smoke. Beyond Q, the situation is changed: The firm would be willing to accept an offer of money to reduce its output. Beyond Q, the smoke causes $EBCQ$ in damage to the neighborhood, and the benefits to the firm of this output are only ECQ. The neighborhood is therefore willing to make it worthwhile to the firm to reduce pollution to the point where $MB = MC$ at Q.

Provided that we have been logical, we have shown a simple but powerful result: No matter who has the legal right to the use of the air, the amount of pollution is the same. When the firm must pay to pollute, it produces Q. When the firm has the unfettered right to pollute, it produces Q. This is the central insight offered by the **Coase theorem**: In a world in which bargaining costs nothing, the assignment of legal liability *does not matter*. A certain equilibrium level of output and its resulting level of pollution will exist regardless of whether firms or consumers own the air.[4] Under the stated conditions of the Coase theorem, government intervention—in the form of pollution guidelines, tax penalties, and the like—cannot improve upon a settlement negotiated by those parties who are directly involved with the externality problem. Note also that the efficient solution in this case implies the presence of a positive amount of pollution. It is rarely going to be efficient to set pollution at zero.

The Coase theorem provides a benchmark for analyzing externality problems. It shows what would happen in a world of zero bargaining and transaction costs. Many real-world externality problems can be analyzed with the Coase theorem, as long as the bargaining and transaction costs are low.

Nevertheless, using the establishment of ownership to correct externalities cannot always be relied upon to eliminate the difficulties of market failure because it may be exceedingly difficult, if not impossible, to establish ownership in some instances. Many externality problems do not fit the assumption of zero or low transaction and bargaining costs. In the factory smoke example, the neighbors of the plant are likely to be numerous, difficult to organize, and diffuse in their interests with respect to the air pollution problem. The widely dispersed sufferers of the smoke damage would face insuperable costs if they had to organize to purchase the agreement of the factory to reduce its emissions. If the firm had the right to pollute, it is not likely that the neighborhood could overcome these problems, get organized, and offer the firm money to cut pollution back to Q in Figure 17.3. Looked at the other way around, if the neighborhood owned the air space, the firm would find it costly to track down all homeowners and arrange for the purchase of their consent to produce up to output Q.

No matter who held the right to use of the air, bargaining costs would be high, and the likelihood is that nothing would be done to correct the situation. If the neighborhood owned the property rights, for example, some homeowners would seek to hold out for a larger payment from the firm. This would jeopardize the

Coase theorem

States that the amount of an externality-generating activity will be the same regardless of the assignment of property rights if the bargaining costs are small.

---

[4]The Coase theorem also marked the beginning of a new field in economics called *law and economics,* which studies the impact of legal rules and institutions on the economy; the Coase theorem, for example, analyzes the role of legal liability assignment in an externality problem. Many law schools have specialized fields in law and economics, and much of the literature in this area is published by the *Journal of Law and Economics* and the *Journal of Legal Studies.*

possibility of a bargained agreement. The costs of defining and enforcing a system of ownership can be so high that some system of taxation or administrative control would be more effective than reliance on the definition of property rights and any contractual arrangements.

Taxing or Subsidizing Externalities   A seemingly simple way of dealing with externalities is to tax activities such as pollution that create negative externalities and to subsidize activities such as beekeeping that create positive externalities. Many complexities surround such a simple-sounding prescription, however. How could a negative externalities tax be levied? Against the product the factory produces? Against the amount of smoke it emits? Either solution might create burdens on the industry and on consumers that are not necessary in cleaning up the environment. Similarly, how would a subsidy for positive externalities be worked out? Based on the honey produced by the beekeeper? Based on the number of bees kept? Despite such complexities, the essential idea of taxing the negative externality and subsidizing the positive has a rich tradition in economic theory.[5]

To understand the effects of taxation, consider the pollution problem in terms of output decisions facing individual firms. In deciding what output to produce, the competitive firm compares marginal cost and marginal revenue. Marginal cost in this context means **marginal private costs** (MPC), the extra costs that the firm must pay to increase its output. These costs do not include externalities. By definition, an externality imposes costs on others that are not reflected in the private costs of the firm. The full costs to society of an increase in the firm's operations are summarized as **marginal social costs** (MSC). MSC are equal to MPC plus the externality costs (E): $MSC = MPC + E$. When there is no externality ($E = 0$), then $MSC = MPC$.

This analysis can be applied to the competitive industry. Consider the situation depicted in Figure 17.4. These are the same types of graphs that we used in Chapter 8. Figure 17.4b shows that an industry is initially in equilibrium at E_1, where industry demand (D) and supply (S_1) intersect. Under these conditions the firm (Figure 17.4a) reacts as a price taker to P_1 and sets its MPC curve equal to P_1 ($ = d_1 = MR_1$). The competitive firm, acting on the basis of marginal private costs, produces q_1 units of output.

Notice, however, that the firm's MSC curve lies above the MPC curve at all levels of output; for example, it exceeds MPC by ab at q_1 units of output. The MSC curve traces the externality that the firm's operations impose, such as the amount of damage that the firm's air pollution causes in the surrounding neighborhood.

What can government do to improve the situation? Basically, government must get the firm to behave as if its marginal cost curve is MSC, not MPC. In this way the competitive firm would equate MSC to price, and the externality would be "internalized" in the firm's output decision; that is, the firm will produce the output where $MSC = P$, which is the correct output from society's point of view. (As

Marginal private cost
The change in total costs that only the firm bears when output changes by one unit.

Marginal social cost
The change in total cost borne by the economy as a whole (the firm plus all others, or society) that results from a one-unit change in the firm's output.

---

[5]The tax-subsidy approach to externalities is often called Pigovian, after A. C. Pigou, author of the *Economics of Welfare* (London: Macmillan, 1920).

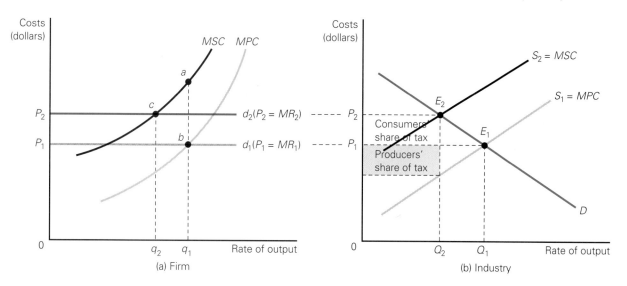

FIGURE 17.4

The Effects of a Tax on an Externality

(a) A pollution excise tax of *ab* per unit is placed on the output of the firm to correct the externality. The marginal private costs facing the firm are given by *MPC,* and marginal social costs are given by *MSC*. The tax raises the *MPC* curve to become identical with the *MSC* curve. In such a way the firm is made to account for the externality in its decision about how much output to produce. (b) At the industry level, the pollution tax reduces industry supply to S_2, and the pollution tax is paid by both consumers and producers, though the proportions need not be equal as depicted in Figure 17.4b.

we saw with the Coase theorem, the socially optimal level of pollution is not zero. At some point, clean air costs more than it is worth.)

This solution can be obtained by imposing a tax on the industry's output that reflects the degree to which *MSC* and *MPC* diverge. Such a tax is illustrated in Figure 17.4 as an excise tax imposed on the firm of *ab* per unit. The impact of the pollution tax is to shift the marginal cost curve of the firm from *MPC* to *MSC*. This change is reflected at the industry level by a shift in the industry supply curve from S_1 to S_2. The tax forces the competitive firm to account for the externality in choosing its output level. It thus chooses the socially efficient output level where $MSC = P_2$, or where marginal social costs are equal to marginal private benefits.

Who pays the pollution tax? Part of the tax will be paid by producers and part by consumers. Consumers will face a higher price for the industry's output, but the price will not rise by the amount of the tax. The producer thus absorbs some of the pollution tax. (See the earlier discussion of the incidence of an excise tax in Chapter 5.)

Selling Rights   A simple alternative to the tax example is to establish a market for externality rights such as the right to pollute. In this approach, government sets an allowable level of pollution and sells the right to pollute. In theory, this market works like any other market. Those who value the pollution rights most highly will buy and hold them. Firms will make decisions about whether it is less costly to install pollution-control equipment or to buy pollution rights. Government does not tell industry how to clean up the air. Instead, it sets the allowable level of pollution and lets firms decide how to control their pollution. This marketlike approach to pollution control has the virtue of ensuring that the acceptable level of pollution is reached at least cost. In fact, the Bush administration started such a program for the smokestack emissions of public utilities in 1990. Under this program, utilities are allowed to trade pollution rights.

Difficulties arise in such a scheme, however. Indeed, whether it chooses to tax pollution or sell pollution rights, government must somehow estimate what the "optimal" level of pollution is. The relevant knowledge in this case is economic rather than technical; the government's interest is less in determining the damage done by varying degrees of air pollution than it is in determining the values individuals attach to the different degrees of damage. Such knowledge is not easy to come by. Moreover, both a tax scheme and a pollution rights scheme must be monitored and enforced by government. Without such actions, tax evasion and pollution without permit will be serious problems.

Setting Regulations   In the past, government has most often not adopted an economic approach to control externalities such as pollution. More typically, government has sought to control pollution and other externality problems through direct regulation of industry. In the case of pollution, regulation generally consists of detailed rules about the technology that firms must adopt to control pollution. Firms in certain pollution-prone industries must install special pollution-control equipment as a condition of being able to stay in the industry. This is a practical way to control pollution. Each firm must clean up its emissions in the prescribed manner. In contrast to the pollution-rights approach, however, direct regulation does not allow firms to choose the most efficient means of staying below the allowable level of pollution. Firms cannot choose to pollute or not pollute or select among different types of pollution-control technologies. They must follow the rules laid down by government.

Each approach to the problem of externality control that we have discussed—the establishment of property rights, taxation or subsidy, selling of rights, and direct regulation—has costs and benefits in different applications. In some cases, the establishment of property rights may resolve the externality. Selling pollution permits may work to control air pollution by public utilities. In other cases, like automobile pollution, some form of government taxation or regulation may be used to control the externality of pollution. No approach will yield a perfect solution to these problems.

Public Choice, Politics, and Externalities   The attempted solution to real-world externality problems often directly involves the political process. Solutions dictated by political forces do not necessarily produce economic efficiency. Consider, for example, the attempt to save several species of Gulf Coast sea turtles, particularly the Kemps Ridley turtle. Some environmentalists—a clear "interest group"—claim a major reason for the disappearance of the turtles is that many are killed in shrimpers' nets. This alleged externality has been at the center of a protracted debate involving fishermen, environmental groups, state governments, federal agencies, and legislators. Over the years, environmentalists have supported a technological solution to the problem—the use of turtle exclusion devices to be attached to shrimpers' nets. Sewn into shrimp nets, the cagelike devices are designed to permit accidentally snagged turtles to escape. Fishermen—another interest group—charge that the devices are ineffective and, more important, that they reduce the shrimp catch by up to 20 percent.

The debate became politicized, with some U.S. senators and representatives from coastal states arguing that the proposed devices would put unnecessary financial hardship on shrimpers. Most state legislators and state fishery commissions opposed mandatory use of the devices. The National Marine Fisheries Service (an agency of the Department of Commerce) has enforced implementation of the device, although Congress initially disapproved of the agency's spending federal money to enforce the proposed regulations. High costs of government enforcement due to the large number of shrimpers has meant spotty implementation of the exclusionary devices. Meanwhile, the turtle population continues to decline.

PUBLIC GOODS THEORY

As we discussed in Chapter 4, government affects the economic well-being of a society in two essential ways. Government provides and maintains a system of laws to protect and enforce property rights and to permit the free flow of goods through markets. And government provides various goods and services that are not ordinarily provided through the free market system. Public goods thus represent another example of potential market failure.

Public good

A good such that, once produced, one individual's consumption of the good does not reduce or exclude the ability of other individuals to consume the good.

These government-provided goods and services fall into the broader category of **public goods** —goods such as national defense that, once provided to one person, are available to all on a noncompeting or nonrivalrous basis. It is difficult or impossible to exclude anyone from the use of a public good, and its use by one person does not prevent its use by another. A nuclear submarine, for example, provides national defense as a public good for all members of a society. One member's consumption of national defense does not preclude another's consumption. The use of a lighthouse beam by one ship does not stop other ships from using the same beam. The consumption of a public good by one consumer does not impose an opportunity cost on other consumers; all can consume the public good at the same time.

A private good is consumed exclusively by the person who buys it. Its consumption by one individual precludes consumption by others. When Benny eats a cheeseburger, Barbara cannot eat the same cheeseburger. The concern here is not with the fact that Benny bought the cheeseburger and owns it (in the sense that he has legal title to it). The concern is with a technical characteristic of consumption—that when one person is consuming a private good, it cannot be simultaneously consumed by other people. The consumption of a private good carries an opportunity cost: Consumption of the same good is denied to other consumers.

A mixed good embodies attributes of both private and public goods. A parade, for example, would seem to be a pure public good. Two people can watch it at the same time without interfering with each other's consumption. If the crowd gets large enough, however, the parade can become more of a private good because congestion detracts from each person's view. In other words, rather than being equally available to all, consumption becomes rivalrous; some people's consumption of the parade detracts and may even prevent other people's consumption. We say then that the parade is a mixed good. It has characteristics of both private and public goods.

Public Provision of Public Goods

How can a free market system provide national defense? Once a defense system is provided, it is equally available to all consumers or citizens. Since individuals cannot be excluded from the benefits of military defense, who would voluntarily contribute to its provision? Most individuals would hold back in the expectation that someone else would provide the necessary funds, and then they would reap the benefits of military defense for free.

Lighthouses provide another illustration of market failure to provide public goods. A lighthouse's beam is available to all ships passing by, regardless of whether a particular ship pays for the light. Since it is difficult or impossible to exclude non-payers from using the beam, individual shipowners probably will not contribute to the lighthouse, even though it provides an obviously valuable service for all ship-pers. To overcome this market failure, government assumes responsibility for the lighthouse. Through its power to tax, government can raise enough revenue to build and maintain the lighthouse.[6]

Public health services also illustrate the need for government to overcome market failure to provide a public good. At certain times when the public health seems in danger, such as the swine flu outbreak in the late 1970s, the government provides inoculations against disease. Individuals who are inoculated protect themselves against the disease. Their inoculation also protects those who are not inoculated. As more and more people are inoculated, the sources of contagion for the disease are reduced, so person A's inoculation reduces the odds that B and C, who have not been inoculated, will catch the disease. Persons B and C theo-retically owe A something for the protection, but would they pay for it? Obvi-ously not, since they cannot be excluded from A's protection. Government's providing such a public health service is a way of overcoming the market failure in this case.

Not all goods provided to a number of people at once require government provision. In some cases, the costs of excluding noncontributors are low enough that private firms will produce goods enjoyed cooperatively by many people. For

---

[6]While the lighthouse has long served as an archetype of a public good, the private provision of lighthouses is an historical fact. See R. H. Coase, "The Lighthouse in Economics," *Journal of Law and Economics* 17 (October 1974), pp. 357–376.

example, a movie, a football game, and a concert are goods that are jointly provided to many consumers at once. In this respect these goods are like the lighthouse and national defense. The difference is that it is feasible for the producers of these goods to exclude those who do not pay for their provision, and so they can be supplied by private producers within the free market.

Free Riders

Sellers of private goods can exclude nonpayers from using the goods by charging a price for their use. Once a public good is produced, however, it is equally available to all consumers, regardless of whether they contribute to its production or not. Individuals who do not contribute to production and yet enjoy the benefits of goods are called **free riders.**

Free rider
An individual who receives the benefit of consuming a public good or service without paying for it.

The problem facing producers of public goods is that free-riding behavior makes it difficult to discover the true preferences of consumers of a public good. Individuals will not reveal their true preferences for public goods because it is not in their self-interest to do so. For example, if a neighborhood tried to organize a crime-watch group, many neighbors might not contribute but would still appreciate any protection provided, thus concealing their true preferences for the service. On the other hand, some who do not contribute voluntarily might be totally disinterested in the service. The possibility of free riding makes it difficult to determine the true level of demand for the public good.

If everyone free rides and no one contributes to the production of public goods, then everyone will be worse off as a result. No public goods will be produced, even though each individual would like some provision of public goods. Herein lies a rationale for government provision of public goods. Government has the power of coercion and taxation, and it can force consumers to contribute to the production of public goods. Citizens cannot refuse to pay taxes and thus contribute to the costs of public sector output. When the cost of excluding nonpayers is high, government can produce public goods through tax finance.

Pricing Public Goods

Should a price be charged for use of public goods? In a sense, the correct price of a public good is zero. Take the example of a bridge. Once the bridge is built, the marginal cost of one more car going over it is approximately zero. If we follow the rule in Chapter 8 for optimal pricing, we should set price equal to marginal cost. Since the marginal cost of an additional bridge crossing is effectively zero, price should be zero according to the $P = MC$ rule. According to this logic, public goods should be free.

This rationale is fine as far as it goes, but it does not go far enough. In rationing the use of the good among demanders, zero is the correct price. Except for cases of congestion, a public good presents no rationing problem; by definition, additional individuals can consume a public good at zero marginal cost. But rationing is not the only function of price. A second important function of price is to achieve the right quantity of the public good by relating quantity to demand.

FIGURE 17.5

Sharing the Costs of Defense

MC is the marginal cost curve for production of military protection under an alliance. D_A and D_B are the individual country demand curves for national defense. The appropriate "prices" for national defense for each country are P_A and P_B. $D_A + D_B$ is the vertical sum of D_A and D_B. Optimal output for the alliance is QT where $D_A + D_B = MC$.

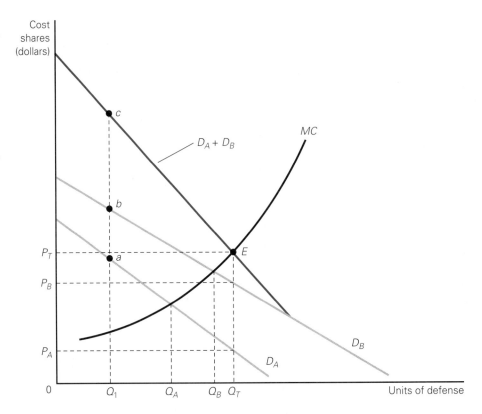

Without information about what people are willing to pay to cross the bridge, authorities are left in the dark about the desired amount of bridge construction to undertake. After all, public goods involve the expenditure of scarce resources, and prices for public goods help public officials develop information about the demand for these goods.

How then should a price be set for a public good? Suppose a defense alliance is formed by two countries, *A* and *B*.[7] The alliance provides for a common defense policy through a treaty agreement. National defense is a public good for the alliance, and the problem facing the two countries is how to reach an agreement on the amount of national defense to be produced by the alliance. Figure 17.5 illustrates the problem.

We assume that each country faces the same marginal cost curve (*MC*) for providing a common defense. *MC* rises because additional scarce resources devoted to defense come at an increasing cost to the two countries.

Each country has a demand curve for national defense, D_A and D_B. The consumption of private goods is mutually exclusive. When *A* gets a unit of a private

[7]See Mancur Olson and Richard Zeckhauser, "An Economic Theory of Alliances," *Review of Economics and Statistics* 47 (August 1966), pp. 266–279.

good, there is one less unit available for B to consume. In Chapter 3, this condition meant that to derive a market demand curve for a private good, the demand curves of individual consumers had to be summed horizontally. National defense, however, is not a private good. It is a public good, and this makes the nature of the "demand curves" in Figure 17.5 quite different.

Consumption of a public good is not mutually exclusive among consumers. All the units along the horizontal axis in Figure 17.5 are equally available to both demanders for simultaneous consumption. Both A and B receive benefits from, for example, Q_1 units of military protection. Thus, the total protection benefits offered by Q_1 to A and B are equal to the vertical sum of their demand prices for this quantity or output. At Q_1 the benefit that each country places on alliance protection is read vertically off its demand curve. A derives aQ_1, B derives bQ_1, and both countries together place a value of cQ_1 (equal to $aQ_1 + bQ_1$) on Q_1 units of alliance output.

Market demand curve for a public good

Obtained by summing vertically, instead of horizontally, all individuals' demands for the public good. Vertical summation is used because consumption is noncompeting.

This point applies to all public goods. The **market demand curve for a public good** is obtained by vertically summing all individuals' demand curves. The demand curves are summed vertically rather than horizontally because all demanders can consume any given unit of output along the horizontal axis at the same time. In Figure 17.5, then, market demand is given by $D_A + D_B$, which is the vertical sum of D_A and D_B.

At points along the horizontal axis less than Q_T, marginal benefit exceeds marginal cost $(D_A + D_B > MC)$, and production will be expanded. At points beyond Q_T, marginal benefit is less than marginal cost $(D_A + D_B < MC)$, and production will be cut back. Equilibrium output is at E, where $D_A + D_B = MC$. The equilibrium defense output in the alliance is Q_T, and the alliance defense budget is $P_T \times Q_T$.

How should this budget be divided between the two countries? One way to apportion the costs is in proportion to the benefits received. P_B represents the benefit that accrues to country B from consuming Q_T units of defense, and P_A is the benefit that country A receives from consuming the same amount. Country B pays more because it benefits more from alliance output. Country B, for example, may be larger, with more income, capital, and population to defend.

This is an idealized presentation of alliance behavior. For example, what happened to the concept of free riding? Basically, we ignored it to depict a perfect outcome for the alliance. But free riding will be a thorn in the alliance's side. Look at the individual equilibrium positions of the two countries in Figure 17.5. Given the marginal cost of providing defense, the small country prefers Q_A as its defense output; the large country prefers Q_B. When the treaty to form the alliance is signed, A gains access to the benefits of B's production. B's production more than satisfies A's demand for national defense. In group alliances, small countries like A will therefore have strong incentives to reduce their defense spending and to free ride on the defense expenditures of larger countries such as B. This tendency will lead to much bargaining and many debates about contributions to alliance output, with the large countries complaining about the efforts and contributions of the small countries. The problem of free riding will be more pronounced the more countries there are in the alliance.

A ROLE FOR GOVERNMENT

The presence of common-resource problems and other externalities and public goods means that government has an important and productive role to play in the economy. Externalities lead to a regulatory role for government. Public goods imply a role for government as a direct producer of some goods and services. If properly undertaken, government activities will serve to enhance the productivity of the private sector by providing police protection, a system of property rights and their enforcement, a court system, national defense, and other goods and services that might otherwise not be provided by purely private markets.

APPLICATION

Can Economic Incentives Save the Elephant and Other Endangered Species?

The property rights structure (common or private) that evolves or is chosen in an economy has much to do with the scarcity of a particular resource. Common ownership—the right of anyone to use resources in unrestricted quantities—has a powerful impact on the incentives of individuals to neglect conservation. Property rights systems begin to change at the point when increases in demand for a resource held in common begin to exceed the supply of that resource. In the case of renewable resources such as timber, lobsters, shrimp, or fish, overfishing or timber stripping can have negative effects on future harvests. In many cases, however, it is possible to save a resource by altering property rights. This has enormous implications for various endangered species. Consider the endangered African elephant.

Children of all ages love elephants, as any zookeeper will tell you. Unfortunately, an externality in the form of a common pool problem has created a growing (and justified) fear of extinction of the African species. Data suggest a continent-wide decrease in the number of elephants by 30 percent in only 8 years (from 1.2 million in 1981 to 760,000 in 1988). In particular countries the decline is indeed shocking. In the Sudan, the decline between 1979 and 1989 was from 134,000 to 40,000 animals. In Zaire, over the same period, the decline was from 377,700 elephants to 85,000.[a]

Biological characteristics of elephants (such as a long gestation period) are undoubtedly part of the problem. But there is an externality created by the common pool—that which belongs to no one will soon be gone. Besides much pleasure to the zoo visitor, the elephant produces hide, meat, and, most importantly, valuable ivory. Ivory poaching has become a way of life and a means to prosperity for many Africans. Good intentions and help from outside agencies have not been enough in most countries to protect the elephant on its way to extinction. An ivory ban, honored by most nations, has been implemented by world conservation organizations, again with every good intention. But an ivory ban may not do the trick when economic incentives are considered.

An ivory ban, if it is not totally enforced and honored around the world, may in fact hasten the demise of the elephant, at least according to some economists.[b] Although the ban may temporarily alleviate pressures on elephant populations, it will also (if not very effectively) drive the price of ivory up, encouraging more intense poaching and improved poaching technology. The total ban on ivory sales,

[a]See Phillip Shabecoff, "Seeing Disaster, Groups Ask Ban on Ivory Import," *New York Times* (June 2, 1989), p. 19.
[b]See Michelle McKeever, "The Economics of Conservation: African Elephants and the Ivory Trade" (Auburn University thesis, 1991).

although laudable in intent, does nothing to eliminate the poacher. Goodwill and enforcement monies, especially in poor Central and East African countries, may be at a premium insofar as the security of the elephant is concerned.

Southern African nations such as Zimbabwe and Botswana have launched innovative solutions that take economic factors and incentives into account. These countries have calculated the biologically optimal number of elephants in particular habitats, used property-rights assignments, and permitted the limited and scientific harvesting of elephant ivory to finance wildlife conservation programs. Hunting rights are given to farmers who harvest elephants themselves or sell the rights to others. (Elephants themselves create negative externalities by competing with farmers for land and crops in some regions.) Incentives to create picture safaris are also being implemented. Populations grew from 1981 to 1989 by 38,000 elephants in Botswana and by 2000 in Zimbabwe.[c] By 1999 elephant populations in southern Africa were burgeoning, reaching an estimated 200,000.[d] All these elephants have created an enormous debate between villagers, whose water supplies and crops are endangered by the animals, and wildlife preservation interests. (An average adult elephant eats 650 pounds of vegetation and drinks 40 gallons of water a day, reducing or endangering many other species in the process.) In 1989 the United Nations banned the ivory trade, but in a controversial decision, a UN panel gave permission for a one-time auction of ivory from Namibia, Zimbabwe, and Botswana to Japanese buyers. Tusks were those of elephants who died naturally or were culled from oversized herds, and funds were to go to conservation efforts in theses poor countries.

Outside of these Southern African countries, elephant populations have been in decline. Saving the elephant from a common-pool disaster may require a variety of solutions. One policy, currently in play, is to relocate elephants from areas of high population to those countries where they are endangered. In Zimbabwe, with a population of more than 70,000, elephants have become a problem for farmers and ranchers. Here they are captured and moved to areas such as Angola and Mozambique, where they are endangered. These practices and the use of economic incentives and biological considerations are surely part of any rational approach to such problems.

Of course, the application of economic and property-rights theory to endangered species will not work in all cases. There are special problems, for example, with migratory populations and with species for which an "economic value" is small or nonexistent. But the application of legal rights may work in many instances, as in the case of alligators, with economic and/or social benefits for all concerned interests.

QUESTIONS

The sidewalks, landscaped grounds, swimming pools, and social facilities typically found in condominium developments are common areas—that is, they belong to everyone in the development. How are such areas usually maintained? What do you predict would happen if the individual owners were responsible for the upkeep of common areas?

---

[c]Data from "Saving the Elephant," *Economist* (July 1, 1989), p. 16.
[d]Information from "Ivory Tusks Auction Gives Activists an Uneasy Feeling," *Orlando Sentinel* (April 4, 1999), p. A-11.

SUMMARY

1. Dependence on markets to produce and allocate nonrenewable and renewable natural resources will mean that such resources are properly allocated between present and future uses.

2. Market failure occurs when the private market system fails to allocate resources in an optimal or ideal fashion. Externalities and public goods are two categories of market failure.

3. Owners of private property bear the economic results of its use. When property is held in common, users do not bear the full costs of its use. Common or undefined ownership creates a conflict between the pursuit of self-interest and the common good. The implication is that common resources will be overused and exploited. Creating ownership is one way to correct market failure.

4. An externality occurs when an economic unit does not bear all the value consequences of its actions. Externalities can be positive or negative, trivial, irrelevant, or relevant. A relevant externality creates an effective demand to correct the externality.

5. The Coase theorem assumes that in a world of zero transactions and bargaining costs, the amount of an externality such as pollution will be the same no matter who has legal liability for it.

6. Where transaction and bargaining costs are high, other routes to externality control become feasible. A per-unit pollution tax would force a firm to act as if its marginal cost curve were identical to its marginal cost curve plus the cost of the externality, or the marginal social cost curve. Other approaches include establishment of a market for pollution rights and direct regulation of firm technology.

7. Public goods are goods that are nonrivalrous in consumption, with high costs of excluding non-payers. Whereas a private good is consumed exclusively by one individual, a public good can be simultaneously consumed by all consumers. A mixed good has characteristics of private and public goods.

8. To "free ride" means to reap the benefits of a public good without bearing its costs. If everyone free rides, no public good is produced by the private sector, even though each individual values its production. Such behavior means that public goods typically have to be produced by government through its power to tax.

9. Public goods are not free; they cost real resources. In terms of rationing a public good among consumers, a zero price is the correct price because additional consumers can consume a public good at near-zero marginal cost. However, a zero price for a public good offers no guidance for public officials about how much of a public good to produce. There is thus a trade-off regarding the pricing of public goods.

10. Individual demand curves for public goods are summed vertically to arrive at total demand for a public good. Optimal output of a public good occurs where the vertically summed individual demand curves intersect the marginal cost curve. Optimal prices for this output are read off the individual demand curves.

KEY TERMS

natural resources
nonrenewable natural resources
renewable natural resources
common ownership
externality

negative externality
positive externality
Coase theorem
marginal private cost
marginal social cost

public good
free rider
market demand curve for a
    public good

QUESTIONS FOR REVIEW AND DISCUSSION

1. Are whales an example of a common property resource? If so, what sort of behavior would you predict among whale hunters?

2. What is an externality? Name the various types of externalities. Why is an externality considered a type of market failure?

3. Suppose that pollution is controlled with a pollution tax on polluting firms. Who will pay the tax? Firms? Consumers?

4. Define a public good. What is the difference between a private good and a public good? How will individuals behave when asked how much they will contribute toward payment for a public good? What does this mean for the nature of the demand curves for public goods?

5. Evaluate the following statement: Museums should be free.

6. Are all public goods produced by government? If not, name some goods that fit the definition of a public good that are produced by private producers.

7. Explain the importance of private property rights in preventing the kinds of market failure that are typically associated with common ownership.

8. Explain the Coase theorem and tell how it could solve externality problems in a world with zero transaction and bargaining costs.

9. Because real-world transaction costs are not zero, taxes or subsidies are sometimes used to eliminate externalities. Explain how taxation eliminates an externality such as pollution.

10. Explain what is meant by noncompeting consumption for a public good.

PROBLEMS

1. Suppose that the government of a hypothetical city has decided to add ten new programs to local schools, each with a cost of $100,000. Each group of voting citizens must share equally in the tax to pay for the new programs. The table shows the dollar value of the benefits that each of eight citizen groups receives from the programs.

Group of Individuals	Benefits
A	$ 80,000
B	140,000
C	160,000
D	60,000
E	40,000
F	180,000
G	120,000
H	110,000

a. If each group gets only one vote and if each group votes on its *pro rata* net benefit from the public good, will the city schools get the new programs?

b. On the basis of the total benefits and total costs, should the programs be provided?

c. Why do most local governments provide primary and secondary education for "free" as public goods? Is such "free" provision necessarily optimal? Explain.

2. "The market and technology work in mysterious ways. The Internet, for example, may ultimately have profound effects on the environment." Explain briefly.

WORKING WITH THE WEB

1. As explained in the chapter, when common ownership of a resource exists, it typically is overutilized. The case of ocean fishing is one example of the common ownership problem, where in this case, overfishing results. As a result, many commercially important fish species have been depleted. Go to http://seawifs.gsfc.nasa.gov/OCEAN_PLANET/ HTML/peril_overfishing.html. There is a brief introduction to the problem of overfishing followed by an overview of the status of many fish species, ranging from depleted (the worst case) to abundant (the best case).
   a. Other than the damage to the fish population, what other perils exist as a consequence of overfishing?
   b. Who enforces fisheries law?
   c. According to the web site statistics, is it a good time to be a northern Atlantic (either northeast or northwest) fisherman? Explain.
   d. Go to http://www.wh.whoi.edu/sos/spsyn/pg/ cod.html and read a bit about the cod species. What are some of the regulations in effect to prevent elimination of the species?

2. The link between private property rights and environmental protection is demonstrated in South Carolina, where island property owners take it upon themselves to preserve beaches and other island attributes rather than rely on or promote government–sponsored beach erosion programs. Go to http://www.perc.org/june99.pdf and download the file to your hard drive. (This file is in Adobe Acrobat format. If you do not already have the Adobe Acrobat Reader, go to http://www.adobe.com and

find out how to download it for free.) Open the file and look for the article called "Preserving Beaches" on page 7.
   a. What is the value to oceanfront property owners of increasing the beach width from 322 to 472 feet? Is there any value to inland residents?
   b. As the article describes, the beach protection programs are short-lived and must be undertaken repeatedly to maintain the wider beaches that protect the island and the property on the island. How is it determined whether or not a protection program should be undertaken? Is the method efficient from an economic perspective?

3. The Coase theorem is one way to resolve an externality problem. An alternative solution might be obtained via a system of taxes and subsidies. The Coase theorem, however, relies on the assignment of property rights to achieve an efficient solution. Go to http://www.reason-mag.com/9701/int.coase.html to read an interview with Ronald Coase conducted by economist Thomas Hazlett in *Reason* magazine.
   a. In describing the Coase theorem in his own words, what determines the "best" use of a resource?
   b. Pollution is often used as an example of a negative externality, as in your text. According to Coase, why is pollution both a negative and a positive?
   c. What is Coase's opinion of government regulation? Does he have an example of a good regulation?

CHAPTER

18

Public
Choice

Democratic governments act through a unique set of institutional arrangements, such as majority voting, representative democracy, political parties, bureaucracies, and special-interest groups. The theory of **public choice** attempts to use economics to understand and to evaluate how governments operate. We have already discussed public choice issues in some detail in this book. We have examined why people vote, how government price controls affect markets, how politicians act to supply regulation to industries, the behavior of countries in defense alliances, along with other examples of public choice at work. In fact, this book is permeated with examples and discussions of public choice. In order to gain more perspective on public choice issues and to expand our consideration of the theory of public choice, this chapter discusses some of the key elements of public choice analysis.

The fundamental premise of public choice is that political decision makers (voters, politicians, bureaucrats) and private decision makers (consumers, market intermediaries, producers) behave similarly: They follow the dictates of rational self-interest. In fact, political and economic decision makers are often one and the same person—consumer and voter. The individual who buys the family groceries also votes in an election. If the premise of public choice is correct, we can learn a lot about such issues as why people take the time and trouble to vote by applying the same logic to the voting decision that we have applied to the grocery-buying decision. As we do so, keep in mind that the institutions and constraints facing political decision makers are different from those facing private decision makers. For example, the benefits of buying groceries are fairly obvious, but what are the benefits of voting? We will be careful to specify such differences between private and public choices throughout our analysis.

457

Public choice

The economic analysis of political decision making, politics, and the democratic process.

Normative public choice

Economic analysis that determines shortcomings and failures of the political process and suggests improvements.

Positive public choice

Economic analysis of political decision making and other political behavior that aims to understand, explain, and predict such behavior.

Public choice, like the rest of economics, has both a normative and a positive side. **Normative public choice** involves judgments about the desirability of certain political situations. In the design of voting procedures, for example, how does majority rule compare with other voting rules in reflecting the true preferences of voters? Is there a better voting rule or process through which to make political decisions? Normative public choice looks at the way political institutions work from the standpoint of how we might make them work better.

Positive public choice seeks to explain actual political behavior. Why do high-income individuals vote more often than low-income individuals? How do committees and legislatures work? What is the impact of special-interest groups on government? In this chapter we will examine both normative and positive aspects of public choice after first exploring how self-interest affects decision making. When you finish Chapter 18 you should understand

- some of the consequences of treating government decision makers as rationally self-interested individuals.
- how the process of voting may not lead to optimal choices by individual voters.
- how self-interested groups affect government.
- the nature of bureaucratic behavior and its relation to government growth.

SELF-INTEREST AND POLITICS

The public choice approach to politics is based on the idea that political actors are no different from anyone else: They behave in predictable ways and seek to obtain their goals efficiently.

Proprietary

Relating to private ownership and profit motivation; individuals directly bear the consequences of their decisions.

Nonproprietary

Relating to nonprivate ownership; entails motivations other than strictly profit motivations; individuals do not always or fully bear the consequences of their decisions.

Nevertheless, market behavior and political behavior differ in the constraints facing decision makers. The market is a **proprietary** setting—one in which individuals bear the economic consequences of their decisions, which either enhance or decrease their wealth. In the market economy, a firm that produces a new product stands to make profits or losses depending on the quality of its efforts. The political arena is a **nonproprietary** setting—one in which individuals do not always bear the full economic consequences of their decisions. For example, the political entrepreneur who comes up with a new political program does not bear the full costs of the program if it is a failure and does not reap all the benefits if it is a success. Behavior will therefore differ in market and in political settings, not so much because the goals of behavior are different but because the constraints on behavior are different.

We can distinguish the economic constraints at work in a market or proprietary setting and in a political or nonproprietary setting by analyzing the roles of agents and principals in each case. In both settings the agent, whether a firm or a politician, agrees to perform a service for the principal, whether a consumer or a voter. Because the agent and the principal are both self-interested, the agent will not always act in the interest of the principal, particularly if the agent's behavior is costly to monitor.

The agent–principal problem has been analyzed primarily in a private setting. For example, the corporate manager is an agent, and stockholders are principals.

How do the stockholders get the manager to act in their interest? They do so primarily through economic incentives. Managers of private firms have incentives to control costs in their firms because increased costs cause a decrease in the firm's profitability. Stockholders, through such mechanisms as stock options and takeover bids, can discipline managerial behavior toward maximizing wealth.

Managers of political "firms," or bureaucracies, do not face a similar incentive to control costs. They cannot personally recoup any cost savings that they achieve for their agencies, and the means available to voters to curtail poor performance by political managers are minimal and costly to implement. This does not mean that public officials can do anything that they want to do. Like any other economic actors, they are constrained by costs and rewards.

The main point about the agent–principal problem is that political agents face different constraints on their behavior than do private agents because political principals face different incentives to control the behavior of the agents. This difference is the focus of public choice analysis.

PUBLIC CHOICE ANALYSIS OF MAJORITY VOTING

Normative public choice theory analyzes the performance of political institutions in serving voters. In this section we illustrate the usefulness of this approach by examining the process of voting by majority rule.[1]

In a democracy, public choices are typically based on a majority vote: If candidate A wins even one vote more than candidate B, then candidate A is elected to office. Particularly when more than two choices are available, majority rule does not always accurately reflect voter preferences.

Imagine a three-person nominating committee that must choose from among three alternatives—Smith, Jones, and Tobin—the nominee for club president. Each committee member ranks the three candidates in order of preference (first, second, third), and the winner is to be selected by majority vote (two out of three committee members in favor). Table 18.1 shows the rankings of the three candidates by the committee members (A, B, and C). Member A, for example, prefers Smith to Jones and Jones to Tobin. Note that each member has consistent preferences; that is, each member is able to rank the three candidates in order of preference.

Now let the voting begin. To find the preferred nominee, the committee pairs each candidate against one of the other two until a winner is found. Suppose they start with Smith against Jones. Who wins? A votes for Smith, B votes for Smith (B prefers Tobin overall, but between Smith and Jones prefers Smith), and C votes for Jones. Smith wins by a majority vote of 2 to 1. Can Smith now beat Tobin? A votes for Smith, B votes for Tobin, and C votes for Tobin. Tobin wins that round.

---

[1] The origins of this analysis can be found in Kenneth Arrow's *Social Choice and Individual Values* (New York: Wiley, 1951) and in Duncan Black's *The Theory of Committees and Elections* (London: Cambridge University Press, 1958). Arrow won the Nobel Prize in economics in 1972.

TABLE 18.1

A Voting Problem

The committee must choose among Smith, Jones, and Tobin. The candidate receiving a simple majority (two votes) wins. When each candidate is paired against another (Smith versus Jones, Jones versus Tobin, Tobin versus Smith), no clear winner emerges. Smith beats Jones, Tobin beats Smith, but Jones beats Tobin. This is a problem of simple majority voting with two candidates at a time. Individual voters can clearly rank candidates, but majorities cannot. Majority voting in this case leads to a repetitive cycle of winners.

Committee Member	Smith	Jones	Tobin
A	1	2	3
B	2	3	1
C	3	1	2

Now, how does Tobin fare against Jones? Since Smith previously beat Jones, we would also expect Tobin to dominate Jones because Tobin dominated Smith. But notice what happens: A votes for Jones, B votes for Tobin, and C votes for Jones. This time, Jones wins! Thus in three rounds of voting, a different candidate wins each round.

The committee's stalemate points up a problem with majority voting. Under majority voting each individual voter can have consistent preferences among multiple candidates or issues, and yet voting on candidates two at a time can lead to inconsistent collective choices. In other words, individuals can make clear choices among Smith, Jones, and Tobin, but majorities cannot. Majorities will choose Smith over Jones, Tobin over Smith, Jones over Tobin, and on and on in a repetitive voting cycle until a way is found to stop the voting. Either Smith, Jones, or Tobin will win when the voting is stopped, but only because the voting stopped at a particular point, not because one candidate is a clear winner over the other two.

This simple proof strikes at the rationality of majority voting procedures. Although individual choices will be clear and rational, majority choices will be inconsistent and cyclical. Where does such a paradoxical result lead us? First, it leads us to look for a better voting procedure than simple majority rule when voting on two issues or candidates at a time. (See the Application "Registering Minority Votes," which discusses a proposal for "point" voting to protect minority interests, at the conclusion of this chapter.) Second, the problem of voting cycles is mitigated to some extent by the institutions of democracy. Our legislatures and committees do not cycle endlessly among alternative proposals without reaching a decision. Votes are taken and decisions are made. Attempts to reach agreement do not go on forever. Powerful committee chairpersons, for example, can call for votes on legislation and see to it that the legislature produces new laws. While such legislative procedures do not solve the problem of inconsistent choices in majority voting, they do keep the tendency toward voting cycles in check.

PUBLIC CHOICE ANALYSIS OF POLITICS

Positive public choice analysis is like positive economics: It consists of the development of models of political behavior that can be subjected to empirical testing. In this section, we present some positive propositions about government and political behavior that seem to be supported by evidence from the world around us.

Political Competition

Have you ever wondered why by election time the two major parties' candidates sound like Tweedledum and Tweedledee, and you cannot see any difference in the views espoused by either? Perhaps more important, why do we have only two major political parties in the United States? The following model helps us answer these and other questions about political competition in a democratic setting.

Assume that voter preferences on issues can be distributed along an imaginary spectrum running from radical left (perhaps the Socialist Workers) to radical right (perhaps the John Birch Society), as in Figure 18.1. Further assume that voters vote for the candidate closest to their ideological position. The normal distribution of voters holding different ideological positions is split down the middle by M. The total area under the curve in Figure 18.1 represents 100 percent of the voters. We call the voter at M the median voter. If either candidate in a two-party race adopts a middle-of-the-road position such as M's position, he or she is guaranteed at least a tie in the election; he or she will receive at least 50 percent of the vote, since 50 percent of the votes lie to the left of M and 50 percent lie to the right. If the other party's candidate adopts any other position, such as R, he or she will get less than 50 percent of the vote. Remember: Voters follow the rule of voting for the candidate closest to their ideological position;

FIGURE 18.1

Ideological Distribution of Voters

The distribution of voters in this example is single-peaked, ranging from radical left to radical right. M represents voters at the middle, or median, of the distribution. The total area under the curve represents 100 percent of the votes. Two-party political competition leads to middle-of-the-road positions, similar to those held by voters at M. Points a and b represent ideological positions midway between points L and M and points R and M, respectively.

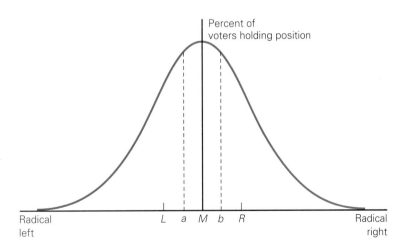

fewer than half the voters in Figure 18.1 are closest to *R*. With one candidate at *R* and one at *M*, the candidate at R receives the percentage of total votes to the right of the line at *b*, while the candidate at *M* receives the larger percentage equal to the area under the curve to the left of *b*. Point *b* represents the ideological stance midway between *M* and *R*. The best strategy for each candidate is to adopt position *M* and hope that random error (pulling the wrong lever) by voters will make him or her a winner. *M*, the median position, is the vote-maximizing position for both candidates; by election time, therefore, both candidates are virtual carbon copies of each other.

This model of political competition is oversimplified, but it does offer some insights into political behavior. Where the distribution of voter preferences is single-peaked, as at *M* in Figure 18.1, there are strong tendencies toward median outcomes. This holds true for virtually any type of collective decision process, from a committee consensus to a public election. Middle-of-the-road policies are vote-maximizing; therefore, we expect middle-of-the-road candidates and policies to be winners. In addition, the analysis underlying Figure 18.1 gives some clues as to why we have only two major parties in the United States. If parties can enter on either the left or right flank of parties at *M*, such entry jeopardizes control of government by the center parties. We can expect that the *M*-type parties will do their best to place barriers to entry in the way of noncenter parties, such as making it costly and difficult for a new party to get on the election ballot.

Finally, this discussion assumes that parties know what the distribution of voters is. If there is uncertainty or lack of information about what voters want, then political parties will have to spend resources and take risks to better understand voter desires. Individuals may also have that incentive (see the Focus "Can You Buy an Election?"). Uncertainty about the distribution of voters explains why political parties commission polls, spend money on campaigns and advertisements, and engage in a host of activities to try to attract voters.

Logrolling

Logrolling

The exchange of votes by legislators, usually in order to gain support for particular legislation.

Positive public choice also takes into account the behavior of officials once they are in office. A typical political behavior is **logrolling,** a term used to describe the process of vote trading. Representatives in a legislature are constantly making deals with one another. One wants a dam in his district; the other wants a new courthouse in hers. They agree to trade votes on issues: You vote for my dam; I'll vote for your courthouse.

There are many beneficial aspects of logrolling. Mainly, it enables representatives to register the intensity of their preferences across issues. For example, a minority representative who feels strongly about animal rights can trade his votes on issues about which he does not feel so intensely for support on the animal rights issue. Logrolling also helps mitigate the problem of indifferent majorities winning over intense minorities. In essence, logrolling, or vote trading, is a form of exchange, and economists usually view exchange as a productive and efficiency-enhancing process.

FOCUS

Can You Buy an Election?

Recent elections have seen billionaire candidates like Steve Forbes and Ross Perot entering national elections and a near-epidemic of abuses of campaign finance regulations, most notably allegations of Chinese influence on U.S. elections. As a result, campaign finance reform has been a hot topic in Washington, but little has been done.

Economists view campaign donations as a means to an end. You need money to carry on a modern political campaign, but victory goes to the candidate with the most voter support, not to the one with the biggest bucks. Donations help purchase election experts, pollsters, equipment, campaign literature, and television advertisements, but they are no guarantee of success.

Steve Forbes and Ross Perot, for example, spent millions of dollars but did not win; in fact, they did not even come close. Other wealthy candidates for Senate and House also have fared poorly in recent elections. It appears that rich people cannot purchase office. It is also the case that the candidate with the most money does not always win. Well-funded candidates can and do beat candidates with larger campaign war chests on a regular basis, and sometimes poorly funded candidates such as Jesse Ventura beat well-known and well-funded opponents.

Is too much money spent on politics? Spending by candidates in congressional races alone is approaching a total of $1 billion per election. How-

ever, even if you took spending by all candidates from local, state, and federal races during an election year, the total spending would only be around $10 per eligible voter. As a nation we spend much more on goods such as ice cream, lottery tickets, and Barbie dolls. These goods are in some sense trivial when compared with the impact of politics on our lives.

Another argument against most proposed campaign finance reforms is that campaign contributions are protected by the First Amendment to the Constitution as a form of political free speech. Donors are simply" voicing" their support for the candidate of their choice, just as campaign volunteers and those that write letters to the editor do.

Regulation of campaign finance is also a tricky constitutional and practical matter. Third-party candidates, who do not have the expert staffs and extensive donor lists of the major parties, consider current regulations unfair and burdensome. Recent elections have shown that major-party candidates can evade regulations by raising "soft money," which is donated to their political parties but used to support their campaign. Interest groups can avoid spending limits by producing their own "issue ads" that indirectly support their candidate. It seems that regulation produces a new set of problems for the electoral process.

We must be careful, though, in assessing logrolling. Its general efficiency depends on the political setting. Most legislatures, for example, are formed on the basis of geographic representation, under which a representative's constituents have one thing in common: They all reside in the same area. Any bill the representative can get through the legislature that benefits the members of her district should win votes at election time. In effect, a geographically based system provides the legislator with incentives to represent local interests in the national legislature at the expense of broader national issues.

Most individuals in a community share an interest in the vitality of the community's economy. In many instances, a bloc of voters from a single voting district may receive income from a single firm or industry, as in a company town or in geographically concentrated industries like the steel, automobile, lumber, defense, and regional agricultural industries. When economic activity is concentrated, representatives can win political support by serving the economic interests of their respective home districts. Tariffs, industry- and company-oriented tax concessions and subsidies, local public works projects, and defense contracts are all examples of issues that often are decided, in part, on the basis of their economic impact on certain regions.

Representatives therefore trade their support on national issues, such as air pollution control, for support on amendments or separate bills that serve their local interests. National legislation often becomes a vehicle for local support, and the result is pork-barrel legislation that carries rich rewards for specific locales. Logrolling, which attempts to redistribute income toward certain regions and industries, generally does not lead to a more productive economy. Rather, it leads to legislation such as individual industry tariffs, unnecessary and costly public works legislation, and special-interest tax "reform" bills. This form of logrolling at the national level is unproductive not because it reveals relative intensities of preferences on national issues, but because in its most blatant forms it reveals relative intensities of preference on essentially local issues. When restricted to national issues, however, logrolling can be a beneficial means for revealing voter preferences. For example, the voters of one senator's state may prefer more foreign aid for Latin America, while the voters in another's state may strongly favor increasing Social Security benefits to the elderly. The necessary legislation for both issues may be passed with the exchange of the senators' votes, thereby indirectly promoting voters' preferences.

Voting

In Chapter 6 we discussed whether voting was rational. Simply put, one voter out of many has very little impact on any election. Therefore, even if the marginal costs of voting—the time it takes to register and go to the polls—are very low, it may be too costly for the average voter to vote. The voter is rational; he or she will vote when the marginal benefits exceed the marginal costs of voting. If an election is predicted to be close, the marginal benefit of voting will rise, and voter turnout will rise.

In this section we examine the act of voting in more detail by discussing some of the relevant differences between the market and voting as means to allocate resources. We compare consumer behavior within market institutions and voter behavior within political institutions.

1. *In markets, consumers make marginal choices; in politics, voters must evaluate package deals.* When you buy carrots or hot dogs, you can buy one more or one less; that is, you engage in marginal decision making. When you vote for a politician or a party, you vote not for a single issue but for a package or a platform—a form of all-or-none decision making. Politicians do not offer voters a little more or a little less of this or that public program. They offer package deals.

Political decisions at the national level take place within the Congress of the United States.

This feature of voter choice makes voting complex and costly. Moreover, when people are forced to make package choices, they are likely to end up choosing a lot of items that they really do not want in order to get a few things that they do want.

2. *Elections generally involve the choice of numerous candidates and issues.* In addition to the packaged nature of political choice, the voter has to make a variety of choices at the same time; many candidates and issues are on the ballot. To some extent, this is efficient. It is better to vote on many things at once than to vote on a lot of individual matters in separate elections. Clearly, economies of scale accrue in voting. But having numerous candidates and issues on the ballot also leads to greater complexity and cost in voter choice.

3. *Consumption is frequent and repetitive; voting is infrequent and irregular.* The consumer goes grocery shopping weekly or daily; the voter votes every year or every two or four years. This infrequency makes it more difficult for the voter to find reliable policies and candidates. Imagine how the grocery-buying decision would be altered if you bought groceries once a year. Your ability to discard bad products and try new ones would be reduced dramatically.

4. *The primary difference between voting and the market, deriving from the preceding three factors, is that voters have little incentive to be informed.* Voting is

more complicated than market choice. This means that voters have little incentive to gather information about their public choices. In market choice, consumers have direct and strong incentives to gather information and to search for useful, reliable products. In public choice, voters have difficulty evaluating candidates and issues. The costs of being informed are high. How can the average voter hope to obtain the information needed to make rational decisions about proposals for dams, foreign aid, welfare, relations with China, the money supply, jobs, and so on? Voters are quite rationally uninformed about such matters; they estimate that the costs exceed the benefits of being fully informed. Indeed, they may free ride by not gathering information, not voting, and letting those who do vote make the choices for them. If the choices of other voters happen to be beneficial to nonvoters, the nonvoters benefit without bearing any of the costs. This behavior leads to a fifth and final implication.

5. *Since voters are not well informed, the information transmitted to politicians by elections is not very useful in helping politicians determine what voters want.* Politicians predictably have great difficulty assessing the implications of an election with respect to what voters want them to do. Politicians who are good at reading the public's pulse will survive and be reelected. Nevertheless, the transmission of information is not direct. In markets, if consumers want more carrots, they can effectively transmit this information to producers and get more carrots. In voting, if consumers want more domestic spending and less defense spending, it is costly and hard to make this preference known to politicians.

Interest Groups

Interest groups

Collections of individuals with one or more common characteristics, such as occupation, who seek collectively to affect legislation or government policy so as to benefit members of the group.

As we discussed in Chapter 4, the behavior of **interest groups** helps explain a significant amount of government activity. To see how interest groups affect government policy, consider the process by which a group of florists might organize to advance their interests.

Organization is the most fundamental difficulty facing the florists. The individual florist has every incentive to remain outside the interest group. Why? Because the success of the group at some objective—say, raising prices—will "spill over" to the florist who "free rides" and obtains benefits without paying a fee. Free-riding behavior makes the formation of interest groups difficult but by no means impossible. Interest groups seek ways to limit the benefits of their activities to members only for such reasons.

Assume that the florists organize. Representatives of the florist group go to the state legislature and use all means at their disposal to obtain a legally sanctioned florists' cartel. The cartel's primary purpose is protection; that is, to protect florists from new competition by creating entry barriers into the florist business. This entry control allows florists to price their wares above the costs of production. Government is petitioned to increase the wealth of florists, but at the expense of flower product demanders. The florists are, in effect, demanders of a wealth transfer from the state.

If the organized florists are the demanders of the wealth transfer, who are the potential suppliers? Flower consumers are the suppliers of the transfer. These consumers do not find it worthwhile to organize and to resist having their wealth taken away by the florist-demanders. Of course, this is a nontraditional concept of supply, but it is a clear supply concept. Consumers of flowers and florist services—the suppliers of wealth—do not find it in their interest to spend money to protest the florists' proposals. The cost would exceed the benefit. It may cost the individual (average) consumer $200 to defeat the florists' plan to bring about a $20 cost savings. Why spend $200 to save $20?

This example describes a "demand" and a "supply" of wealth transfers in the case of florists. (It is exactly analogous to the case described for barbers in Chapter 4.) What are the features of the market for wealth transfers? Politicians are

Market for legislation

The interaction between interest groups acting as demanders of legislation beneficial to the group and legislators acting as suppliers of legislation; legislation generally entails some type of wealth transfer.

brokers in this market and in the **market for legislation.** Politicians in effect pair up demanders and suppliers of wealth transfers. A miscalculation—a transfer of too much or too little wealth—will mean that they will be replaced at the next election by more efficient brokers.

Results for the florists are described in Figure 18.2. Assume that florists begin as a purely competitive industry, producing Q_c flower arrangements per year at a price of P_c. Due to the establishment of their interest group, the legislature is persuaded to grant them cartel status. Persuasion of the legislature is facilitated because the consumers who are harmed by the cartel do not find it worthwhile to protest to the legislators. Florists are the only ones to be heard, and perhaps by putting their arguments for a cartel in public-interest terms ("inferior flowers must be driven from the market," "there's chaos in the market for flowers," and so on), they carry the day with the legislature.

The legislators assess the costs and benefits of creating a flower cartel. In Figure 18.2, the florists seek P_gABP_c in cartel profits at the expense of consumers'

FIGURE 18.2

How an Interest Group's Demands Are Met

P_c is the competitive price that the industry charges, and P_g is the price established by the group after it is granted cartel status. After the cartel is formed, it stands to gain P_gABP_c in profit from consumers, and consumers stand to lose ACB in welfare. In some cases, the former wealth transfer dominates the latter welfare loss, and a law is passed sanctioning the cartel.

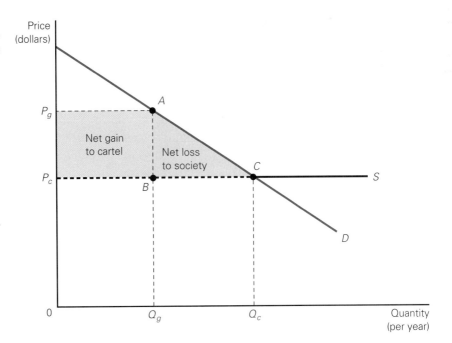

welfare; flower consumers also incur an additional loss equal to ACB. (Area ACB represents the welfare loss due to monopoly discussed in both Chapter 4 and Chapter 9. The per capita gains to florists, who are a relatively small number of producers, exceed the per capita costs to the more numerous flower consumers. The result: The legislature passes a law giving the florists a cartel (and, perhaps, the florists make campaign contributions to the legislators who supported their cartel bill).

However, this discussion is highly stylized. Interest groups do not always work as producers versus consumers. Technically, any group can organize and act as an interest group. There are labor unions; women's rights groups; religious groups; trade associations; and organizations for doctors, lawyers, hunters, environmentalists, and farmers. Moreover, not all of these groups are small. Many large groups, such as farmers, are effectively organized as an interest group. And not all interest groups seek money transfers from government; some seek increases in utility or satisfaction from the passage of a particular public policy. However, the basic point is that you can begin to explain why a certain law is passed if you try to answer two questions: Who wins? and Who loses? The Focus "Economics of the Birds and the Bees" presents an example of how the demands of interest groups result in government subsidies that are not justified on economic grounds.

Bureaucracy

Bureaus

The arms of government that serve to implement and enforce legislation and to administer programs created by legislation.

While legislatures enact laws and authorize levels of public spending, the actual implementation of those laws is delegated to a variety of agencies, commonly referred to as **bureaus.** Created by the legislature, bureaus are generally supportive of the legislature's interests. Bureau employees generally fare better as the bureaus' budgets expand because, among other things, opportunities for promotion expand and, with them, salaries. At the same time, legislators have strong interests in the enactment of legislation that will be implemented by bureaus. Consequently, bureaus and the legislative committees with which they deal generally have similar interests.

As organizations engaged in the supply of services, public bureaus differ from private firms in two important respects. These differences in turn lead to important differences between the conduct of bureaus and the conduct of firms.[2]

1. Bureaus derive revenue from legislative appropriations, which in turn come from tax collections. By contrast, firms derive revenue from the voluntary buying decisions of customers.

2. There are no transferable ownership rights in public bureaus. In bureaus, there is no status comparable to that of stockholders, the residual recipients of dif-

---

[2] See, for example, Ludwig von Mises, *Bureaucracy* (New Haven, Conn.: Yale University Press, 1944); Gordon Tullock, *The Politics of Bureaucracy* (Washington, D.C.: Public Affairs Press, 1965); Anthony Downs, *Inside Bureaucracy* (Boston: Little, Brown, 1967); and William A. Niskanen, *Bureaucracy and Representative Government* (Chicago: Aldine-Atherton, 1971).

FOCUS

Economics of the Birds and the Bees

Everyone knows that birds, bees, butterflies, and a host of other creatures are important for the pollination of plants, including an estimated $10 billion worth of crops per year. For example, bees pollinate fruit and nut trees and thus provide a positive externality to the owner of orchards.

The problem arises if not enough bees are available in nature. Fruit and nut production will be reduced. Economists used the example of the bees and apple orchards as a prime example of this type of market failure—low bee populations and reduced pollination. In 1952, the federal government responded to bee and orchard interest groups. An interest rate subsidy was established for beekeepers to increase the number of beekeepers and to foster the joint production of bees (honey) and fruit farming. The subsidy affects 3000 to 5000 beekeepers in about a half-dozen states.

Economist Steven Cheung examined the market for bees and found that the case for government subsidies was a "fable" and that elaborate and effective contracts between beekeepers and farmers were routine and effective in overcoming the supposed market failure.[a] Cheung found that some plants produce much nectar but did not require pollination, that other crops require bees for pollination but produce little surplus nectar for honey, and still other crops yield high amounts of nectar and require pollination. He found that the contracts and rental fees for bees reflected both pollination requirements and nectar production.

In 1990, the General Accounting Office of Congress agreed that the subsidy was unnecessary and that fruit and nut growers who needed bees could buy or rent them. There was no market failure; there was a failure to examine the market. In 1993, the $16 million subsidy to beekeepers was eliminated.

[a]Steven N. S. Cheung, "The Fable of the Bees: An Economic Investigation," *Journal of Law and Economics* 16 (1973), pp. 11–33.

ferences between revenues and expenses. Although there may be profits in the operation of bureaus, these profits do not show up as residual income to residual claimants or owners. Rather than being converted to personal use, any differences between revenue and expense disappear through added expenditures. For example, at the end of each fiscal year in Washington, bureaus with funds left over try to find ways to spend the funds—which helps explain why many large research grants are made at the end of the fiscal year.

The difference in incentives between private and public decision making yields many familiar results. It is often more difficult to register a car or get a passport than it is to buy an automobile or plane ticket. It is more difficult to buy alcoholic beverages from a state-franchised liquor store than from a private firm. Under government operation, a bureau's hours of operation are usually shorter than those of private businesses and, hence, less convenient to customers. There is also a reluctance on the part of bureaus to accept checks and credit cards.

Without the profit-maximizing incentives of private business, there are numerous ways that the indirect appropriation of excess funds through higher expenditures can take place within bureaus. Different public bureaus face different opportunities for appropriating profits. A public hospital, for instance, may overinvest in equipment that is underutilized. A highway department may award contracts without competitive bidding and pay higher prices than necessary. Since excess funds cannot be appropriated directly, they are appropriated indirectly, as these funds are dissipated through expenditures.

One main difference between a private firm and a public bureau lies in the identification of the customer. For private firms, the people who use the good or service are the customers whose continued favor is essential for the firm's success. The public bureau's customers, however, are not the people who queue up for space at a public campground or who try to get efficient service at the motor vehicle department. Although the bureau provides services to those people, the public bureau's customer actually is the legislature because it is responsible for the bureau's existence through legislation and funding. To remain in existence and to be successful, the bureau must please the legislature.

To some extent, of course, the legislature reflects the interests of citizens. But we must distinguish between the special interests of particular citizens and the interests of citizens in general. In cases where a bureau's performance pursues special interests, those special interests may represent a quite different set of people from those who use the bureau's service. For legislation to reward some special interests, it must penalize other, general interests. The often poor performance of public bureaus is another feature of a special-interest approach to government; this performance may not be so poor viewed from the perspective of the bureau's true customers—the special interests that benefit from the legislation.

CONSTITUTIONAL POLITICAL ECONOMY

A normative branch of public choice theory is called constitutional economics or political economy. This is an important area of analysis that takes us beyond the world of ordinary, everyday politics. That is, in a constitutional democracy there are two levels of political decision making: day-to-day decisions about running the government, which are made under given rules and procedures, and decisions about the rules and procedures themselves. The first level of decision making takes place under given political constraints. The second involves the choice of the constraints themselves, which amounts to selecting a constitution or the set of rules under which day-to-day government operates. For example, the choice of whether to employ simply majority voting or some other system would be a constitutional choice, while voting on current issues with the chosen voting system would be part of the day-to-day process of running the government.

Constitutional decision making

The process of choosing which set of rules (voting rules, for example) society will adopt for its use.

Public choice theory can be applied to an analysis of **constitutional decision making.**[3] As an illustration, we will analyze the choice of a voting rule for the legislature. We assume that the constitutional decision makers are unbiased and impartial (a large assumption). Figure 18.3 illustrates the analysis.

---

[3] This analysis was first developed by James M. Buchanan, the Nobel laureate in economics for 1986, and Gordon Tullock, *The Calculus of Consent* (Ann Arbor: University of Michigan Press, 1962).

FIGURE 18.3

Constitutional Choice

Curves *D* and *E* represent the expected costs facing the constitutional decision maker. *D* represents the costs of collective decision making; as the number of voters increases, *D* increases at an increasing rate. *E* is the cost of a decision rule requiring less than unanimity. Summing the two curves (*D* + *E*) and taking the minimum point gives the optimal voting rule chosen by the constitutional decision maker. N_1 represents the optimal number of individuals in the society of *N* persons who must agree before a collective decision is made. N_1 may be any number. Here it is a simple majority, (*N*/2) + 1.

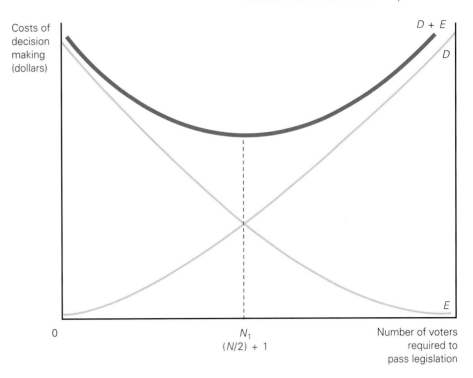

The horizontal axis measures a number of people *N*, all the members of a hypothetical society; *N* can also be thought of as all the voters in the society. The vertical axis is a measure in dollars of the expected costs of the various voting rules that could be selected for the society. Examples of these costs will be presented shortly.

Constitutional decision makers face the following problem: How do they choose the voting rule that minimizes the expected cost of collective decision making in this society? The answer to the question can be found by examining the *D* curve and the *E* curve in Figure 18.3. The *D* curve measures the costs of collective decision making. As the voting rule is made more inclusive—requiring, for example, a two-thirds vote rather than a simple majority for approval or defeat of an issue—the costs of reaching collective decisions increase. In fact, as more people are required for agreement, the *D* curve increases at an increasing rate. This is a logical result in any group decision process. More people require more discussion, larger meetings, more bargaining, and so on. Agreement is more costly to obtain in a larger group.

The *E* curve reflects the potential costs that a collective decision can impose on the individual affected by the decision. If very few people are required to agree on a measure, agreement will occur more frequently, and *E*-type costs will be high. In other words, a small number of people could get together and pass measures that benefit them at the expense of other voters. If a unanimity rule prevails, however, requiring that all members of the legislature must agree before a tax can be passed, then E-type costs to any individual will be zero. Under these conditions, no collective decision can be made unless every voter consents. Unanimity means that one person can block a collective decision.

We have, then, the two major categories of costs related to the choice of a voting rule by constitutional decision makers. The minimum of the two costs can be found by vertically summing the D and E functions and picking the minimum point on that curve. This occurs at N_1 in Figure 18.3. In this society, the two types of voting costs are minimized where N_1 persons are required to agree before a collective decision is made. N_1 may be any number. It may, for example, be a simple majority voting rule—$(N/2) + 1$ in Figure 18.3—or it may be a stricter voting rule in which more than a simple majority agreement is required before a collective decision is made. Though stricter voting rules involve higher D-type costs, the prospect of lower E-type costs could easily make stricter voting rules an important route to the improvement of collective decision procedures. What would happen, for example, if every proposal for a public expenditure had to carry with it a proposal for the taxes to finance it and, moreover, to pass the legislature with a majority of seven-eighths?

Constitutional political economy thus examines the rules and procedures of politics in an effort to improve the way societies make their public choices. As such, this type of work by economists and political scientists is critical and important.

The theory of public choice represents an expansion of normal economic analysis into the realm of politics. This area of research will undoubtedly attract the attention of economic researchers in the future. Hopefully, work in this area will enhance our understanding of how the political process works and how it can be made to better serve the interests of the average citizen.

APPLICATION

Registering Minority Votes

We explored the problems of *majority* voting in this chapter. What about the interests of *minorities*? How do they fare under majority rule?

Imagine the simplest of all democratic processes: a local referendum to increase the property tax by a relatively small amount and to use the funds to build a new school. This situation can easily lend itself to a problem of neglected minority interests. For example, a majority of voters may not have children and may be slightly opposed to the measure because of the small tax increase that accompanies it. The parents of school-age children may be intensely in favor of the tax–school package because of the poor condition of the existing school. Despite their strong concern, the parents lose to a relatively indifferent majority in the defeat of the referendum. Conversely, one could envisage a situation in which the parents are in the majority, the proposed tax increase is substantial, the present school is in good condition, and the nonparents feel tyrannized by the passage of the tax–school referendum because it promises more costs than benefits for them. In one person/one vote majority rule, unless all voters have an equal expected gain or loss from the outcome of an issue, voting may not accurately reflect the underlying intensities of voter preferences.

To clarify the example further, look at the distribution of potential gains for two voters over a set of issues, shown graphically in Figure 18.4. The height of each curve is a measure of the potential gain to a voter from a favorable outcome on a

FIGURE 18.4

The Minority Voting Problem

Utility curves *A* and *B* measure the intensity of preference of two voters or two groups of voters across issues. The *B* group feels more strongly about each issue than the *A* group. A one person/one vote majority rule does not register this different intensity of feeling in voting outcomes. Point voting, when each voter is given a certain number of votes to allocate among all issues, may be a solution to this problem.

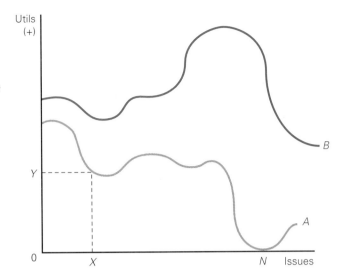

particular issue (a favorable outcome may represent either the passage of a desired bill or defeat of an undesired bill). To avoid the problem of minority interest under majority rule, each voter must have exactly the same utility curve. For example, all voters must experience a *Y* gain from the outcome on issue *X*. If 51 percent of the voters have a utility curve like *A* and 49 percent have a curve like *B*, the *A*'s will win on every issue even if the *B*'s feel more strongly in each case. Majority rule is disadvantageous to minorities in this case and does not lead to voting outcomes that reflect the preferences of all the voters.

The problem is that no mechanism exists by which minorities and majorities can vote according to their differing intensities of feelings on issues. When voters have only one vote per issue, this vote represents a different underlying amount of gain or loss to majority and minority voters.

Suppose, however, that instead of having one vote on each issue, each voter is given 1000 votes and is asked to allocate them in proportion to his or her preferences over a wide number of issues. If issue *J* provides 7 times as much benefit as issue *K*, the voter allocates 7 times as many votes to it. Voting would consist of each voter's filling out a form indicating how the 1000 votes are to be assigned to each issue and whether the voter casts them for or against each issue. The issues would be decided by totaling the votes over all voters and passing all the issues that receive more yes votes than no votes.

This *point voting system* gives accurate information about the relative intensities of each voter's preferences over the various issues and makes it unnecessary for all voters to have the same utility curve. Stated in economic terms, point voting reveals individuals' marginal rates of substitution among issues, analogous to marginal rates of substitution among private goods. In other words, point voting for public issues is like the process of consumer equilibrium discussed in Chapter 6. The consumer allocates his or her fixed number of dollar votes in such a way as to establish equal marginal rates of substitution across goods. Point voting provides the voter with the opportunity to do the same with public issues.

Point voting is a possible solution to the problem that minority interests are not registered under one person/one vote majority rule. No voting system is perfect, however. The voting scheme that accurately reflects the preferences of all voters in final voting outcomes has yet to be invented. One of the key jobs of the public choice analyst is therefore to analyze voting systems and seek improvements in them.

QUESTION

It is well known that different cities provide different levels of public goods such as education, street repair, police and fire services, and so on. Individual citizens, however, do not value different "packages" of public goods in the same manner. One response to the situation is to move to other cities when those other cities offer a more satisfactory package. Describe conditions of local public goods supply under which you might prefer one city over another.

Source: Dennis C. Mueller, Robert D. Tollison, and Thomas D. Willett, "Solving the Intensity Problem in Representative Democracy," in Ryan C. Amacher, Robert D. Tollison, and Thomas D. Willett, *The Economic Approach to Public Policy* (Ithaca, N.Y.: Cornell University Press, 1976), pp. 444–473.

SUMMARY

1. Public choice analysis is the study of government with the tools of economics. It treats government decision makers like private decision makers—as rationally self-interested actors.

2. Public choice theorists assume that government officials maximize their individual interests, not the "public interest." In the process, they face different constraints than private decision makers, and so they behave differently.

3. Normative public choice analysis evaluates the effectiveness with which political institutions represent the preferences of voters, focusing on the evaluation of voting rules.

4. Voting on issues two at a time by majority rule can lead to a voting cycle where there is no clear winner, even though each individual voter knows clearly which candidate he or she prefers.

5. Positive public choice analysis seeks to present testable theories of government behavior. It is analogous to positive economics applied to politics.

6. In political competition the median voter is the controlling force. Parties and candidates compete by taking middle-of-the-road positions.

7. Logrolling, or vote trading, reveals relative intensities of preference across issues. When combined with geographic representation, however, logrolling can lead to an overexpansion of local public projects.

8. Voting and the market are two different means of allocating resources. For a variety of reasons, voters have little incentive to be informed in making voting decisions. As a result, voting is an imperfect mechanism for allocating resources.

9. Interest groups seek wealth transfers from government. Successful interest groups win transfers at the expense of general efficiency in the economy.

10. Bureaucracy is the production and management side of government. Unlike private production, government production takes place in a not-for-profit environment. As a consequence, bureaucrats behave differently from private decision makers.

11. Constitutional political economy represents a branch of public choice that describes the process of choosing sets of rules, such as voting rules, that society adopts to use in making collective decisions.

KEY TERMS

public choice
normative public choice
positive public choice
proprietary

nonproprietary
logrolling
interest groups
market for legislation

bureaus
constitutional decision making

QUESTIONS FOR REVIEW AND DISCUSSION

1. What is a voting cycle? What conditions cause a voting cycle?

2. What is logrolling? What are the benefits and costs of logrolling?

3. Name three differences between voting and the market as mechanisms for allocating resources.

4. What is the difference between a public bureau and a private firm as a productive unit?

5. Discuss three experiences you have had in dealing with government that can be explained by the not-for-profit nature of government production.

6. Suppose that the size of government is declining relative to the size of the economy. Apply public choice theory to explain how this might happen.

7. Using the median voter model of voter preferences discussed in the chapter, explain why Democratic presidential candidates are more liberal in the primaries than in the general election.

8. Why do we not observe voting cycles in the U.S. House of Representatives?

9. In public choice theory, what is the fundamental assumption regarding the behavior of politicians and bureaucrats?

10. What is the primary problem with majority voting? Explain.

11. What role do interest groups play in the market for legislation? What do they hope to gain from the legislative process?

PROBLEM

Suppose that ten members of a large family jointly own a vacation home. The family is trying to decide whether to build a swimming pool on the property. Building and maintaining the pool will cost $3000 per year, and each family member must pay an equal amount to cover the expenses of the pool. The table shows the dollar value of the benefits that each family member would receive each year from the pool.

a. Find the annual cost per person of the pool and then determine the net benefits or costs of the pool per year for each family member.

b. If each family member's vote is determined by his or her net benefits or costs, which family members will vote for the pool and which family members will vote against the pool? Will the pool be built?

c. When the total costs and benefits are considered, does this project represent an efficient use of resources?

Family Member	Annual Benefits
A	$450
B	0
C	65
D	400
E	350
F	150
G	0
H	650
I	385
J	420

WORKING WITH THE WEB

1. The issue of campaign funding is a controversial one, as described in the Focus "Can You Buy an Election?" Go to http://www.pbs.org/wgbh/pages/frontline/president to read more about the issue and select the link "The Money Charts."
   a. Which candidate in the 1996 election raised the most money? Where did billionaire candidate Steve Forbes land on the money list?
   b. Which industries put most of their support behind Texas Senator Phil Gramm?
   c. Which industry had the largest amount of campaign contributions to a candidate? Which candidate was the recipient of this generosity?
   d. What special-interest group was the largest contributor to the Democratic National Committee? Which group was the largest contributor to the Republican National Committee?
   e. At this point, we all know Democratic candidate Bill Clinton won the election. Did the Democratic National Committee have a greater level of donations than the Republican National Committee? Does this imply the election was bought?
2. The impact of interest groups in politics is well known. Clearly, different interest groups seek different benefits from government, ranging from money transfers to favorable legislation. To see the influence of Political Action Committees

(PACs) in campaign funding in 1997–1998, go to http://www.opensecrets.org/pacs. At this site you will find a listing of the various PACs. Under each category, summary as well as complete statistics are listed.
   a. The tobacco industry was under heavy criticism in 1998. The link for the tobacco PACs can be found under "Agriculture." How did the level of contributions from tobacco PACs vary across Democrats and Republicans? Why do you think the tobacco PACs contributed in this manner?
   b. Another industry that has strong PACs on each side of the issue is the gun industry, where there are both gun control advocates and gun rights advocates. Review the statistics of the Gun Control PAC as well as the Gun Rights PAC (both appear under the heading "Ideological/Single Issue"). Which PAC contributed more to candidates in 1997–1998? What is the largest single PAC (in terms of total financial contribution) within both the Gun Control and Gun Rights PACs?
3. Which single PAC in the Computer Equipment & Services category was the largest contributor in 1997–1998? In light of what you learned in Chapter 16 as well as what you have learned in the current chapter about interest groups and the public choice approach to politics, is this surprising?

Ronald Coase

A. C. Pigou

A. C. Pigou
and
Ronald Coase:
Solving
the Problem
of Social Costs

COUNTERPOINT

Arthur Cecil Pigou (1877–1959), an English economist, succeeded Alfred Marshall in the chair of political economy at Cambridge University in 1908. Like Marshall, Pigou had been drawn to economics because of its social importance. Both men were deeply interested in improving the living standards of the poor. Both had great faith in the power of economics to improve the welfare of all members of society. Pigou and Marshall disagreed, however, on the proper role of government. Like his neoclassical peers, Marshall advocated laissez-faire policies, whereas Pigou felt that government's power to tax and redistribute wealth among all members of society was a crucial ingredient of general economic prosperity.

Pigou held his prestigious position at Cambridge for more than thirty-five years. During this period he wrote several books, including *Wealth and Welfare*, *The Economics of Welfare*, and *The Theory of Unemployment*. His students at Cambridge included Joan Robinson and John Maynard Keynes. Pigou continued to be productive after his retirement from Cambridge in 1943. For many, his death in 1959 marked the end of the English neoclassical tradition in economics, a tradition begun in the 1870s.

Ronald Coase (b. 1910) has earned international recognition for his papers "The Nature of the Firm"

(*Economica*, November 1937) and "The Problem of Social Cost" (*Journal of Law and Economics*, October 1960). Modern theories of the firm and of externalities owe much to the work of this English-born economist. Coase's novel economic analysis of institutions, particularly the law of business, has helped spawn a new area of economic inquiry, much of which has challenged traditional views of how government and government regulations affect the behavior of firms. Coase has written extensively on utilities, broadcasting, and other government-regulated monopolies. He is generally critical of the effects of regulatory law, believing that solutions to market failure can and do exist outside of government intervention. Coase was awarded the Nobel Prize in economics in 1991. He is professor emeritus of economics at the University of Chicago. He has held posts at the University of Buffalo and the University of Virginia.

Taxing the Smoke

Pigou pioneered the modern microeconomic theories of externalities and market failure. In *The Economics of Welfare* he distinguished between private costs of production—the operating and maintenance costs of producers—and social costs of production—the expense or damage to society that results from the producer's activity. There are many possible illustrations of social costs. A nuclear power plant's social costs include the potential danger of radiation to the surrounding community. A railroad's social costs might include the danger of fire caused by sparks from its wheels. Pigou's own example of private and social costs is a smoke-belching factory. The factory owner's private costs derive mainly from the people and machines that make up the factory. The social costs of the factory derive from the smoke the factory produces as a by-product of its operation. The smoke from the factory soils clothing and property nearby, creates a noxious odor, and poses a health risk to the community.

Pigou pointed out that there is nothing in the economic forces of market supply and demand to prevent the factory owner from continuing and even increasing the pollution. Since the market, in essence, permits the owner to shift part of the costs (the smoke) onto others, the owner will likely protect this advantage.

Pigou also sought to prove that market failure resulted in inefficient resource allocation. According to Pigou's theory, the factory owner will try to manage production so that the marginal private costs of the factory equal the price of the product. Pigou pointed out that by doing so, however, the owner is not responding to the true costs of production. Since the owner's private costs are less than the full (private plus social) costs of production, the owner will produce "too much" output. If, however, the owner managed production so that private plus social costs equaled price, the excess output would be eliminated, and all resources would be allocated according to their true opportunity cost.

To remedy the inequities and inefficiencies of market failure, Pigou proposed a tax on polluters and other sources of social costs. In the case of a smoke-belching factory, the tax would depend on the amount of smoke produced and would force the owner to restrict pollution to the point at which the benefits of production were equal to its true costs. Such a tax would also restrict output. In this way, both producers and consumers would share the costs of the tax.

Assigning Liability

In his 1960 article "The Problem of Social Cost," Ronald Coase challenged Pigou's major assumption that social costs always move in one direction—from producer to society. In fact, Coase argued, the issue of social costs poses potential harm to both parties. On the one hand, society may be harmed by the unwanted by-products of production, and on the other hand, producers may be harmed by society's attempt to correct the market failure through taxation. In terms of Pigou's example, should the factory owner be allowed to pollute the local community, or should the local community be allowed to drive up the factory's costs of production by forcing it to cease polluting? The issue is especially pertinent today in the debate over acid rain and toxic waste.

Coase argued that an efficient solution to the problem of social costs would involve negotiation between the polluter and those affected by the pollution. If it were possible for both sides to negotiate, then a market might be created between them. The two sides could "trade" for the right to the pollution: Either the factory would pay the local community for the right to pollute or the community would pay the factory not to pollute. Coase showed that the actual outcome of such negotiations would be the same regardless of which side had the "right" to use the atmosphere as it saw fit.

In the real world, such negotiations between parties help solve a variety of potential social cost problems. For example, restaurant customers have influenced restaurants to segregate smokers from nonsmokers, eliminating the social cost of tobacco smoke. Home buyers shopping for a house near an airport can negotiate for a lower price to offset the social cost of airplane noise.

Often, both sides in the dispute face enormous transaction costs to enter such negotiations. A community, for instance, might find it very costly to organize into a bargaining unit with a nearby factory. The millions of people affected by acid rain and the hundreds of producers responsible for the pollution could hardly transact freely. In such instances Coase suggested that the parties look to the courts, not the legislature, for a solution. Courts could determine the relative costs involved and could assign liability, or responsibility, to the party whose costs of adjusting to the social cost are lower.

For example, who should be responsible for injuries and death resulting from the use of defective products? For a long time, the rule of *caveat emptor,* or "let the buyer beware," prevailed in the courts, and the consumer was fully responsible for the safe use of products. Such a rule worked reasonably well in times when products were relatively simple in design and use. However, as products become more complex, consumers may not be able to judge their safety and reliability. As a result, the courts have gradually increased the range of cases in which producers are held liable for shoddy and dangerous merchandise. This shift in the legal posture of the courts is an illustration of the Coase idea at work: The legal system alters liability assignment in response to the relative costs of adjusting to social costs.

International Trade and the Global Economy

30

International Trade

We do not often stop to ponder all the ways in which imported goods enrich our lives and improve the material well-being of all nations of the world. On a typical day, for example, an American student's consumption patterns are clearly global. She awakes on sheets made in England and prepares breakfast on a hot plate made in Taiwan. Donning a cotton dress made in India and shoes made in Mexico, she catches the morning news on a TV with components manufactured in Japan. She drives to campus in a Japanese-made car.

The desirability of a diverse array of available goods and services and the interrelation of the U.S. economy with the economies of other nations present us with issues and problems we have left mostly unexamined until now. The issue of the competitiveness of U.S. firms in world markets may have directly affected you or your family. The large foreign trade deficit that arose in the 1980s and 1990s spawned much debate in business, labor, and government circles on the desirability of a new U.S. trade policy with countries such as Japan, Canada, and Mexico. Large swings in the value of the U.S. dollar overseas can alter not only vacation plans but consumption patterns and employment as well.

New technology has enabled nations to become more economically interdependent. In a sense, the whole world is now an economic system. Our entire study of economics has highlighted the role of global factors in U.S. economic functioning. In particular, we have emphasized the impact of free markets and trade on U.S. competitiveness and economic growth and on global development. In this chapter and the next, we focus closely

In many ways, importing automobiles from Japan into the U.S. economy in exchange for corn is no different from residents of Hawaii and California trading pineapples for oranges.

on international trade and finance in order to make clearer the role the United States plays in the global economy. We will demonstrate that the familiar concepts of supply and demand and production possibilities are extremely useful in discussing international trade (Chapter 30) and the financial system that supports it (Chapter 31).

International economics is composed of both microeconomic and macroeconomic elements. This chapter focuses on the microeconomics of trade. After reading Chapter 30 you should understand

- the reasons for and the advantages of specialization and trade.
- the factors that determine actual amounts and directions of trade between countries.
- how artificial interferences with trade, such as tariffs and quotas, affect the prices and quantities of goods and services sold in importing countries.
- how historical and contemporary trade policies and international integration, such as that contemplated by Western European nations, affect world trade.

THE IMPORTANCE OF INTERNATIONAL TRADE

Specialization
An economic entity's (an individual's or a nation's) producing only one good or service, or the performance of a single task in a production process by an individual.

All nations have particular talents and resources; like individuals, whole nations can specialize in one or many activities. For example, the islands of the Caribbean have abundant sunshine and good weather year round, and so these islands specialize in tourism. **Specialization** enables nations to emphasize the activities at which they are most efficient and at the same time gain certain advantages through trade.

Examples of international specialization and trade abound. France has a favorable climate and specialized land for wine growing, so it exports wine to Colombia and the United States and imports Colombian coffee and U.S. machinery. Likewise, both Colombia and the United States specialize and trade products that best utilize their qualities and quantities of resources.

National Involvement in International Trade

The overall magnitude of international trade and countries' shares in this trade can be measured in a variety of ways.

Table 30.1 lists the foreign trade of eleven nations as a percentage of gross domestic product for 1996/1997; the percentages vary widely. Exports accounted for 30 percent of Germany's total output but less than 10 percent of Argentina's output. Imports were about one-fourth to one-third of the real consumption of such countries as South Africa, Germany, Sweden, and Switzerland.

Percentage figures do not tell the whole story, of course. In absolute terms the United States was the world's largest trader in both exports and imports in 1997. The value of merchandise exports totaled $625 billion, and the value of merchandise imports was over $822 billion. (The values of both exports and imports have doubled in a generation.) The United States trades with virtually every nation of the world, the primary sources of imports being Canada and Japan (both with about 19 percent in 1997). The main destinations of U.S. exports in 1997 were Canada, Japan, and Western Europe. In terms of products, the three main U.S. imports are

TABLE 30.1

Exports and Imports as a Percentage of GDP in 1996/1997

Country	Exports as a Percentage of GDP	Imports as a Percentage of GDP
United States	7.7	10.2
United Kingdom	21.6	22.8
Switzerland	57.5	50.2
Sweden	48.0	38.0
Japan	13.7	11.0
Italy	20.2	15.3
Germany	30.0	26.2
Canada	31.7	30.0
Argentina	7.2	8.7
South Africa	11.6	10.4
Venezuela	11.2	6.0

Source: Central Intelligence Agency, *World Factbook* (1998) at www.odci.gov/cia/publications.

crude oil, motor vehicles, and food, and the three main exports are machinery, motor vehicles, and grain.

The United States is far and away the biggest exporter of products in the world, although exports were only 10.2 percent of GDP in 1996/1997. Some countries' economies—Venezuela, Germany, and Switzerland, to name just three—depend very heavily on exports; economic business cycles in other (importing) countries can have a dramatic effect on these countries' macroeconomies.

Why Trade Is Important: Comparative Advantage

The reason for all this trading is that all nations benefit from some degree of specialization and trade. Suppose two nations produce computer components and food with an equal expenditure of time and resources. Trade between the two countries will likely emerge because each can specialize at what it does better—emphasizing the production at which it is more efficient—and trade with the other country for the other good. As we will see, both countries will be better off because specialization and trade lead to increases in production and therefore to increases in the attainable consumption levels of both goods in both countries.

Comparative advantage
An economic entity's (an individual's or a nation's) ability to produce a good at a lower marginal opportunity cost than some other entity.

According to the principle of **comparative advantage,** countries will specialize in producing those goods and services in which they have relatively lower opportunity costs than their trading partners. For example, a hilly, rocky country will not be able to raise as many sheep per acre as a country with fertile grasslands, but the rocky land cannot support any production other than sheep raising, whereas the grassland will support more lucrative cattle production. Even though the grassland is absolutely more productive at raising both sheep and cattle, the rocky land has a comparative advantage in sheep growing because the opportunities forgone are very small. The rocky country will therefore tend to specialize in sheep; the grassy country, in cattle.

Consider the simplicity and power of the idea that each country produces those products that it can produce with relatively greater efficiency—that is, at a lower relative opportunity cost. Countries that have relatively lower opportunity costs of producing certain goods and services have a strong incentive to produce those goods and services. The large amounts of fertile U.S. farmland combined with advanced farm technology have made the American farmer the most productive in the world. America has a clear comparative advantage in certain farm products and raw materials. America's skilled labor force and high rate of technological advance through huge investments in private and public research and development have helped make the United States relatively efficient in producing highly sophisticated machinery and equipment. Trading partners of the United States, especially Japan, have specialized in routinized productions such as automobiles and steel. Energy regulations and increased demand have forced the United States to import immense quantities of petroleum. The pattern of U.S. imports and exports therefore shows the process of economic specialization and comparative advantage at work. (For an example of the idea of comparative advantage, see the Application "NAFTA: Free Trade or Free-for-All?" at the end of this chapter.)

Production Possibilities Before Specialization   To demonstrate more precisely how all trading partners benefit by exercising their comparative advantages, we must look at what happens in each country before and after specialization and trade. Suppose that both the United States and Japan, in isolation, produce just two goods: computer components and food. Further assume that the production possibilities schedules facing the United States and Japan are depicted in Table 30.2, which gives the alternative combinations of food and computer components that could be produced in the United States and Japan if resources are fully employed. The United States, for example, may choose to produce 60 units of food and no computer components, 40 units of food and 10 units of computer components, 20 units of each, or 30 units of computer components and no food. With fully employed resources, Japan may choose between 45 units of computer components and no food at one end of the production spectrum and no computer components with 30 units of food at the other, or combinations between these extremes, as shown in Table 30.2.

These production alternatives are merely the trade-offs that are implicit in the countries' production possibilities curves. For the United States, the extreme choice is between producing 60 units of food (F) or 30 units of computer components (CC). That is, if the United States produces 60F, it will have to forgo 30CC. Within the United States, then, the opportunity cost of producing 1F will be ½ a unit of CC. Alternatively, the cost to the United States of producing 30CC is 60F, or 1CC costs 2F. In summary, within the United States,

60F costs 30CC to produce, or

1F costs ½CC to produce, or

1CC costs 2F to produce.

TABLE 30.2

U.S. and Japanese Production Possibilities Schedules for Food and Computer Components

Within the United States, 2 units of food cost 1 unit of computer components. Within Japan, ⅔ unit of food costs 1 unit of computer components. The relative opportunity cost of food production is lower in the United States, and the relative opportunity cost of computer component production is lower in Japan.

PRODUCTION POSSIBILITIES (AT FULL EMPLOYMENT)

	1	2	3	4
United States				
Food	0	20	40	60
Computer components	30	20	10	0
Japan				
Food	0	10	20	30
Computer components	45	30	15	0

These costs measure how many units of food must be given up to obtain a unit of computer components, or how many units of computer components must be given up to get an additional unit of food. In either case, what is being measured is the relative opportunity cost of producing food or computer components in the United States—that is, what must be given up to increase the production of food or computer components.

Exactly the same analysis can be applied to Japan. For Japan, the production possibilities schedule indicates that, in the extreme, either 45 units of computer components and no food or 30 units of food and no computer components can be produced. The opportunity cost of producing 1F in Japan is then 1½CC. Likewise, 1CC costs ⅔ a unit of F. In Japan, the opportunity cost of production is summarized as

30F costs 45CC to produce, or

1F costs 1½CC to produce, or

1CC costs ⅔F to produce.

Therefore, in this example, the United States has a comparative advantage in producing food and Japan has a comparative advantage in producing computer components. Do you see why?

Gains from Specialization and Trade   The concepts of production possibilities and opportunity costs provide a perspective for understanding the benefits of trade. Continuing our example of trade between the United States and Japan, first look at the U.S. and Japanese production possibilities curves in Figure 30.1. Notice that these production possibilities curves are straight lines. In practical terms, this means that resources can be transformed from food production to computer component production at constant opportunity cost, that resources are perfectly adaptable to one production process or the other in both economies. The simplicity of this assumption does not compromise the argument for specialization and trade.

The important part of the argument for gains from specialization turns on the pretrade opportunity costs of producing the two goods that face Japan and the United States. Before trade, consumers in the United States must sacrifice 2 units of food to produce 1 unit of computer components, while Japanese consumers must sacrifice only ⅔ unit of food to produce the same amount of computer components. Or American consumers must sacrifice ½ unit of computer components to obtain 1 unit of food, while their Japanese counterparts must give up 1½ units of computer components to get 1 unit of food. Thus, Japan is the least-cost producer of CC, and the United States is the least-cost producer of F. This is not the end of the story, however!

Both countries can gain from trade. Since the United States produces food at an opportunity cost of ½CC and Japan produces computer components at an opportunity cost of ⅔F, we know that the Americans would gain if trade gave them more than ½CC for 1 unit of food, and the Japanese would gain from more than ⅔F for a single unit of computer components. These differences in relative opportunity costs of producing food and computer components yield a basis for specialization and trade between the two countries.

Terms of trade

The number of units of one good that exchange in the market for one unit of some other good; a relative price.

At what price will trade take place? The **terms of trade**—the ratio at which two goods can be traded for each other—will settle somewhere between the relative opportunity cost ratios for each country. For example, terms acceptable to

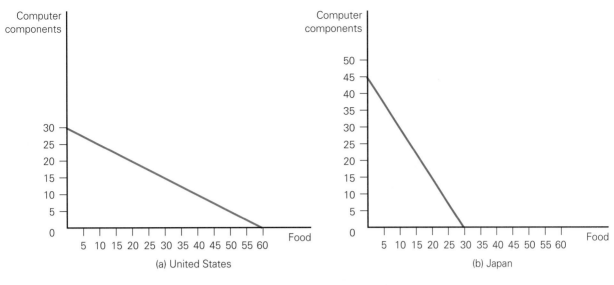

FIGURE 30.1

Prespecialization Production Possibilities Curves

The straight-line production possibilities curves for the United States and Japan indicate that resources can be transferred from computer component production into food production at constant opportunity cost. The different slopes of the two curves indicate that different opportunity costs provide the basis for both countries to benefit from specialization and trade. The United States has a comparative advantage in food production, whereas Japan is relatively more efficient at producing computer components.

Consumption possibilities curve

All the possible combinations of two goods that could be consumed by first specializing according to comparative advantage and then trading at the terms of trade.

both Japan and the United States will fall between $\frac{2}{3}F = 1CC$ (Japan) and $2F = 1CC$ (United States). We might say that the two countries bargain to set the terms of trade, and the bargaining range is determined by each country's internal opportunity cost trade-off. Let us assume that the terms of trade settle at 1 unit of food for 1 unit of computer components, or $1F = 1CC$.

Figure 30.2 illustrates the potential outcomes of this agreement in terms of the production possibilities curves and each country's posttrade **consumption possibilities curve.** If the countries choose to specialize totally according to comparative advantage, the United States produces 60 units of food and Japan produces 45 units of computer components. Each country can now trade for the product it no longer produces; each country is no longer restricted to consuming a combination of goods on its production possibilities curve. Without trade, a country is restricted to consuming whatever it produces. In the absence of trade, its production possibilities curve and its consumption possibilities curve would be one and the same.

With trade, however, each country's consumption opportunities are determined by how much of its specialized output is produced and the terms of trade. A country's consumption possibilities curve shows all the possible combinations of the two goods that could be consumed if production were specialized (according

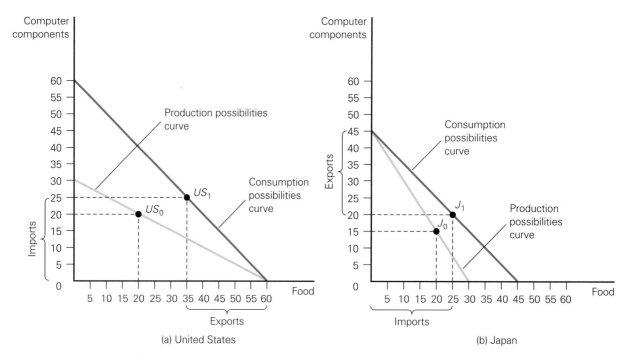

FIGURE 30.2

Production and Consumption Possibilities Curves

The United States specializes in food, producing 60 units; Japan specializes in computer components, producing 45 units. Once trade can take place at the terms of trade of 1F for 1CC, the consumption possibilities curves become relevant. The United States exports 25F and imports 25CC, increasing its consumption (over the pretrade situation) of food by 15 units and computer components by 5 units. Japan exports 25CC and imports 25F, increasing its consumption (over the pretrade situation) of food by 5 units and computer components by 5 units.

to comparative advantage) and trade could take place at the given terms of trade. Of course, only one combination can actually be consumed, so the consumption possibilities curve should be viewed as a menu of alternatives open to the country. The consumption possibilities curve with trade will always lie beyond the production possibilities curve, indicating that specialization and trade will leave the country economically better off. Remember, without trade, the country's consumption and production opportunities are identical.

Given that each country specializes and can now trade (at a price or terms of trade of 1F = 1CC) for the product it no longer produces, the consumption possibilities curves in Figure 30.2 become relevant. In contrast to a domestic opportunity cost of 60F for 30CC, the United States now enjoys a situation in which production of 60F could be traded for 60CC. (Naturally, Japan's resource base will not allow production of 60CC—only a maximum of 45CC.) Japan enjoys a similar expansion of consumption opportunities with specialization and trade. By specializing and trading, both countries are made economically better off. Each has the ability, with trade, to consume a bundle of goods beyond its production possibilities curve. This would be impossible, given each country's resources and technology, without trade. Specialization does not even have to be complete for the two countries to gain from trade. We have used the example of complete specialization here for simplicity.

If we assume that U.S. consumers originally consumed the bundle of food and computer components labeled US_0 in Figure 30.2a, we can note the improvement in their well-being by considering a new, posttrade consumption bundle, US_1, on their consumption possibilities curve. More of both goods are consumed after specialization and trade. A similar conclusion arises for Japan if we compare hypothetical pre- and postspecialization and trade consumption bundles, J_0 and J_1, respectively. Specialization and trade enlarge the consumption possibilities of the trading nations so that both countries can consume more of both goods after trade occurs.

Note that trade between the United States and Japan in this example takes place according to the principle of comparative advantage. Figure 30.3 shows the explicit pattern of trade. The United States exports food (25 units) because it has a comparative advantage over Japan in food production. This is so because 1F costs the United States only ½CC to produce, whereas 1F would cost Japan 1½CC to produce. Japan exports computer components for the same reason. It has a comparative advantage in producing them over the United States. Each country imports the good for which it is at a comparative disadvantage—that is, the good for which its trading partner possesses a comparative advantage. Gains from trade accrue to producers and consumers. In this example, American consumers of computer components benefit from the lower prices made available by imports, while American food producers benefit by obtaining a price for the food they export higher than the price they could obtain by selling it in the United States—which is not to suggest that no one is harmed by free trade. U.S. food consumers must pay higher food prices as a result of the decision to export some U.S. production. Similarly, U.S. producers of

FIGURE 30.3

The Pattern of U.S.–Japan Trade

Japan has a comparative advantage in computer component production; the United States, in food production. This means that Japan will export computer components and import food, whereas the United States will export food and import computer components. The terms of trade, 1F for 1CC in this example, must be between the two countries' opportunity costs of production.

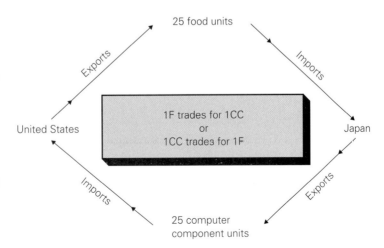

computer components are harmed when Japanese suppliers enter the market and cause prices to fall. On balance, however, gains from free trade exceed losses; free trade leads to improved standards of living in both countries.

Our discussion has been based on a simple example of how the principle of comparative advantage works. In discussing two-good trade between Japan and the United States, we assumed that each country was absolutely more efficient than the other at producing one of the two goods. What if one country is absolutely more efficient in producing both goods? Suppose that productivity in the United States tripled—production of computer components increasing to 90 units and production of food increasing to 180 units. U.S. production capacity in this case would outpace Japan two to one in computer components and six to one in food. Nonetheless, the opportunity cost to the United States of producing each computer component would still be 2 units of food, which is higher than Japan's opportunity cost. It would still be mutually advantageous for the United States to specialize in food and to obtain computer components from Japan through trade. Remember, the argument for free trade is based on the principle of *comparative* advantage. Trade between two countries is mutually beneficial whenever the countries bear different opportunity costs of producing goods. This is true even if one of the countries is absolutely more productive at producing both goods.

Tariffs and Quotas

Tariff

A tax or levy on imported goods.

Quota

A restriction or limit on the quantity of an imported good.

Despite the advantages of specialization and trade, certain barriers to trade exist in the real world. Some are natural costs of exchanges, such as negotiating and transportation costs, and cannot be avoided. Other barriers to trade are artificial contrivances of governments designed to raise revenues or protect domestic producers from foreign competition. The major examples of artificial trade barriers are tariffs and quotas. A **tariff,** or import duty, is simply a tax levied on particular imported goods. For example, the United States imposes a tariff on imported shoes and steel. A **quota** is a partial or absolute limitation on the quantity of a particular good that can be imported. For example, until 1972, the United States imposed a quota on the importation of foreign oil and permitted oil refiners to import only the allowed amount of oil. Both tariffs and quotas reduce the extent of specialization and trade and, therefore, the gains that consumers obtain from free trade. Both raise the prices of imported and domestically produced goods and restrict imports. In these respects, tariffs and quotas are similar.

THE EFFECTS OF ARTIFICIAL TRADE BARRIERS

Free trade

The exchange of goods between countries without the presence of artificial trade barriers such as tariffs and quotas.

With very few exceptions (to be discussed later in the chapter), **free trade**—trade without artificial barriers—leads to maximum economic welfare among nations. Free trade and specialization expand consumption possibilities and deliver goods to consumers at the lowest possible costs. Yet given all the benefits of free trade, the world does not often seem to allow it to work, at least not completely. The reason is that some parties are harmed by free trade. Pressures are brought to bear on governments by producer groups for protection from foreign competition. Sometimes these groups win political favors, such as tariffs or quotas, to reduce the competitive threat. In this section we use economic theory to show how these interferences with free trade reduce the overall economic welfare of a country.

Welfare Loss from Tariffs

Consider the effects of a protective tariff on the society as a whole, using a hypothetical market for television sets. Figure 30.4 represents the domestic market for TV sets, including the domestic supply of the product and the U.S. demand. Prior to the imposition of a tariff, American consumers buy Q_4 units at the world price P_w. Of this quantity purchased, Q_1 are sold by domestic manufacturers and Q_1Q_4 are imported from abroad.

Assume that a tariff is imposed in the amount t, causing the price of TVs to American consumers to rise to P_{w+t}. (For clarity, we have assumed that the foreign TV supply curve is horizontal. A totally elastic supply curve would exist if TV production in the world was a constant-cost industry.) American TV producers gain additional profits or producer surplus in the amount represented by $P_{w+t}E_2E_1P_w$ because of the increased domestic output permitted by the higher price. Imports are reduced to Q_2Q_3, and the total number of sets sold decreases to Q_3. Consumers lose total benefits in the amount of $P_{w+t}E_3E_4P_w$. At the same time, the tariff on imported TV sets creates government revenues. These revenues are composed of the per unit amount of the tariff multiplied by the units of TV sets imported after the tariff is imposed (area E_2E_3AB in Figure 30.4).

FIGURE 30.4

The Effects of a Tariff

Gains in producer profits and government revenue do not equal consumer losses from tariff-imposition. Net consumer losses are shown in the shaded triangles in the figure. Before a tariff on TV sets, consumers purchase Q_4 units at price P_w. The tariff causes the price to rise to P_{w+t}, imports to decrease from Q_1Q_4 to Q_2Q_3, and the total number of TVs sold to decrease to Q_3. Consumers' total loss is represented by $P_{w+t}E_3E_4P_w$ but producers gain $P_{w+t}E_2E_1P_w$, and government tariff revenues are E_2E_3AB. The net loss to society is therefore the sum of the areas E_2BE_1 and E_3E_4A.

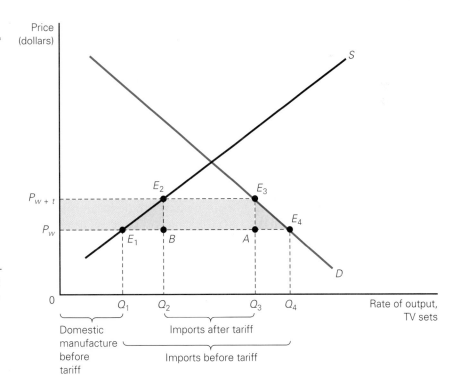

Economists typically assume that the government revenue is used in a manner that produces benefits equivalent to those lost by consumers of TV sets. However, the tariff causes a net loss in benefits to society, of which TV consumers are a part, represented by the sum of the two areas E_2BE_1 and E_3E_4A. The sum of these triangles represents a loss that is not counterbalanced by the sum of producers' gains and government revenue resulting from the tariff. Economists call this loss a **welfare loss to society** due to the imposition of a tariff.

Welfare loss to society
The net loss to an economy resulting from the imposition of an artificial trade barrier.

Why Are Tariffs Imposed?

If tariffs create a welfare loss to society, why are they imposed? Certainly tariff revenue to the federal government is minuscule when compared with other sources of government revenue.

The source of tariff protection is to be found in the urgings of "merchants and manufacturers" as well as from labor in domestic import-competing industries. Consumers of TV sets and of any goods that actually bear a tariff could conceivably convince both producers and the government not to impose tariffs because, as we have shown, consumers lose more than producers and government gain from tariffs. Practically, however, the world does not work this way. Consumers, the gainers from free trade, are widely dispersed and costly to organize in any fight for free trade. Interest in fighting a tariff or quota is also apt to be low among consumers because their *pro rata,* or proportionate, share of losses from artificial barriers to trade is generally small. To an individual consumer, for example, the tariff is a small proportion of the total price of an automobile. The incentive to organize and fight protective tariffs is therefore small.

Not so for producers. The *pro rata* share of the effects of tariff protection is much higher among manufacturers, for they are far fewer in number than consumers. Manufacturers thus have stronger incentives than consumers to form an interest group, and, being fewer in number, their costs of organizing are lower. For such reasons, the consumer interest in free trade is often thwarted.

Nontariff Barriers to Trade

Historically, tariffs and quotas have been the most important types of artificial trade restrictions. In recent years, other types of restrictive practices, which are generally called **nontariff trade barriers** (NTBs), have taken on increased importance. Examples of nontariff trade barriers include domestic content legislation (laws that require a certain portion of goods sold in a country to be produced there) as well as safety or health regulations designed to discriminate against foreign products. NTBs have grown rapidly in recent years because many countries have enacted trade legislation that forbids tariffs or quotas; NTBs represent an alternative form of protectionism. The use of NTBs varies greatly among countries. In the United States, NTBs exist for about 25 percent of imported goods. The corresponding percentage for Japan is about 12 percent. Within the European Community, percentages vary but average about 20 percent.

Nontariff trade barriers
Alternative (to tariffs and quotas) means of restricting trade; examples include domestic content legislation and health and safety regulations.

Although it is difficult to determine the specific effects of nontariff trade barriers, the general effects are quite similar to those of tariffs. Figure 30.4 shows how a tariff artificially raises the price of imported goods and causes the quantity of imports to fall. NTBs have similar effects. If, for example, the United States were to enact legislation requiring that cars sold in this country have a 50 percent domestic content, the Japanese could continue exporting cars to the United States only if at least half of the parts and the assembly were American. The cost of compliance would be higher production costs to the Japanese, but it would be very difficult to determine how much costs would rise. The effect therefore would be identical to the imposition of some specific tariff. Without knowing by how much this legislation would increase production costs, it would be impossible to determine what an equivalent tariff would be.

Nontariff trade barriers have become a major issue in the United States, particularly with regard to the economic unification of Europe. There is some concern that the European Community will implement technical standards that discriminate against foreign firms. Some observers have suggested that U.S. exports to Europe would fall sharply as a result of any such barriers. Although it is impossible to predict what economic policies the European Community will pursue, the complete economic unification of Europe is sure to present certain advantages to U.S. exporters. For one thing, U.S. firms will no longer have to contend with different NTBs in each of the European countries. Also, it will no longer be necessary for U.S. companies to produce a different product for each country in order to meet different standards.

A Quota Is a Quota Is a Tariff

Quota agreements between two countries to voluntarily limit exports from one country to the other have become a popular alternative to tariff controls. One form of quota agreement is called the Voluntary Export Restraint (VER). In 1990, for example, President Bush used the device to restrict imported steel through 1992. The Clinton administration continued to use threats of unilateral import restrictions in trade talks with particular nations. But a precedent for these actions had been established during the Reagan administration with VERs on automobiles.

On April 1, 1981, an international trade agreement between the governments of Japan and the United States was put into effect. Under the VERs, the government of Japan would prevent Japanese automakers from exporting as many cars as they would like to the U.S. market. Japanese car manufacturers were restricted to shipping only 1.68 million cars to the U.S. market per year from 1981 to 1984. What was the economic effect of the VERs on U.S. automobile producers and consumers?

To answer this question, we must first recognize that this "voluntary" restraint was nothing more than a quota of 1.68 million cars. The U.S. government effectively restricted imports from Japan to a level of 1.68 million cars. The next question to answer is: What effect did the imposition of an import quota have on the domestic U.S. market for automobiles?

Figure 30.5 will help answer this question. In Figure 30.5, P_W is the price of a car in the United States before imposition of a quota. Domestic producers sell Q_1 cars, and imports equal Q_4 minus Q_1 autos. Once the quota, equal to Q_3 minus Q_2, is imposed, how does the domestic market move to a new equilibrium? Recall that an equilibrium price is one at which quantity demanded equals quantity supplied. Part of quantity supplied is supplied by foreign producers, the amount of the quota in this case. To find what equilibrium price will be under the quota, we need only find a price at which the horizontal distance between the demand and supply curves equals the quota. At price P_{W+Q}, domestic output, Q_2, plus the quota, Q_3 minus Q_2, equals total quantity demanded, Q_3. Thus, at price P_{W+Q}, quantity demanded equals total quantity supplied. P_{W+Q} will then be the domestic price of a car if a quota of Q_3 minus Q_2 is imposed.

Figures 30.4 and 30.5 are similar in many respects, because tariffs and quotas are similar in many respects. They both raise domestic price and reduce imports, but the tariff works initially by affecting price and letting quantity adjust, whereas the quota directly affects quantity with the result that prices adjust. Whichever method is used to restrict trade, higher domestic prices and fewer imports result.

There are some differences between tariffs and quotas, however. In Figure 30.5, if a tariff had driven domestic price up to P_{W+Q}, the U.S. government would have collected tariff revenue in the amount of area E_2E_3AB. However, under the VERs, no tariff revenue was collected from Japanese automakers. In fact, the United States government merely allowed the Japanese government and Japanese automakers to decide for themselves which companies would fill the quota of 1.68 million units. With the import rights left specifically unassigned (and not charged for) by the U.S. government, the area E_2E_3AB became revenue to Japanese producers (and their U.S. dealers) rather than tariff revenue for the United States. This is one of the

FIGURE 30.5

The Effect of a Quota on the Domestic Market

When the quota is imposed, it is still necessary for quantity demanded to equal quantity supplied for the domestic market to be in equilibrium. Only at price P_{W+Q} will total quantity demanded, Q_3, equal total quantity supplied. Total quantity supplied equals quantity supplied domestically, Q_2, plus imports, Q_3 minus Q_2. The quota raises price, increases domestic producers' profits, and produces welfare losses—just as a tariff does.

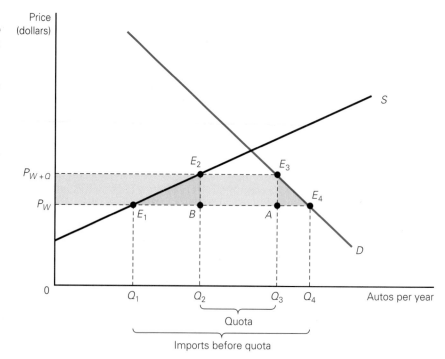

wealth transfers, from American consumers to Japanese producers, of a quota designed in this fashion. (For a further discussion of "voluntary" export restraints, see the Focus "Autos, Peanuts, and Politics: How Quotas Affect You.")

THE CASE FOR PROTECTION

Throughout history, numerous arguments have emerged in defense of protection from free trade. Most of these arguments are but thin veils for producers' interests. All the arguments—both the well-constructed and the questionable ones—deserve scrutiny.

National Interest Arguments for Protection

The two oldest and best-formed arguments in defense of protection and against free trade are the national defense argument and the "infant industries" argument. Both arguments contain a grain of truth, but each should be closely scrutinized before serving as a base for protectionist policies.

FOCUS

Autos, Peanuts, and Politics: How Quotas Affect You

Quotas, like tariffs, raise the prices of the products you buy. While trade has been liberalized through the reduction of tariffs—and through free trade zones such as NAFTA—quotas may be even more insidious at increasing the prices of consumer goods in the United States. Consider some examples. Economist Robert Crandall of the Brookings Institution in Washington, D.C., studied the Reagan administration's VERs in an attempt to gauge the economic effects on consumers and producers of automobiles.[a] He estimated that in 1984 the price of a Japanese car sold in the United States was about $2500 more than it would have been without the VERs. Additionally, the higher prices of Japanese imports allowed U.S. automakers to charge about $1000 more per car than they would have been able to in the absence of quotas. The stock-

holders of U.S. auto companies and the employees of these companies clearly benefited from the VERs. Crandall also estimates that American auto consumers paid approximately $16 billion more for cars in 1984–1985 than they would have in the absence of the quotas.

Quota and tariff concessions to special interests who pressured politicians for favors were a part of the Bush and Clinton administrations' trade policy. For example, the United States Department of Agriculture (USDA) estimates that peanuts cost $491 per metric ton to produce in the state of Georgia, although the world market price is about $300 per ton. The USDA peanut price support program permits U.S. farmers to sell peanuts in the U.S. market for more than $600 per ton. American consumers pay more because there is a virtual ban on the importation of peanuts. Quotas may benefit producers, but they definitely injure consumers and economic welfare.

[a]Robert W. Crandall, "Detroit Rode Quotas to Prosperity," *Wall Street Journal* (January 29, 1986), p. 30.

National Defense   The oldest argument for protection—and the one with superficially the best justification—is that such restrictions are necessary for national defense. As military technology has changed, steel, gunpowder, manganese, uranium, and a host of other inputs have all been commodities essential to making war and they have all been the subject of tariffs and quotas to keep domestic production of these commodities strong.

The logic of protection for defense is clear: Since the ultimate function of government is national defense, any possible threat to national defense, such as the unavailability of some resource during a crisis, must be avoided. A loss in consumers' benefits from protection is thus justified for a greater benefit—the availability of essential materials to be prepared for war. Artificial barriers to trade in these materials are used to protect domestic industries considered essential for national defense.

The national defense argument is plausible for some industries and some products, but consider that cheese, fruit, and watch manufacturers and other, non-defense-related industries have all resorted to the argument. History seems to prove that patriotism is the last and best refuge of a producer seeking protection from foreign competition. The national defense argument has seen double duty as an argument for maintaining unprofitable routes on railroads and protecting truck, air, and railroad companies by setting legalized cartel rates. The telephone industry was long protected on similar grounds.

The imposition of tariffs and quotas is not the only way to handle the national defense issue. A tariff is nothing but a hidden subsidy or cash grant to domestic producers. Thus, if an industry is to be protected for national defense reasons, an explicit subsidy may be more effective than tariff protection. That way, the national defense issue is made clear, and voters know how much defense actually costs them. If, for example, it is deemed vital to national security that the United States have a certain capacity to produce iron and steel, an alternative public policy would be to subsidize domestic iron and steel producers rather than to protect them against foreign competition with a tariff or quota.

Infant industry

A new or developing domestic industry whose unit production costs are higher than those of established firms in the same industry in other countries.

Protection of Infant Industries   Possibly the most frequently heard argument for protection, especially in developing nations, is the so-called **infant industries** argument. The infant industries argument is related to the idea of economies of scale. Economies of scale exist when, as plant size increases up to a point, long-run unit costs decline. This occurs because individual workers become more proficient at narrowly defined tasks, and machines are more closely tailored to individual processes. Scale economies may also occur because both workers and managers "learn by doing" and acquire more experience as output grows. Often, moreover, production of certain manufactured goods results in an enormous initial setup cost. As firm and industry output grow larger, these setup costs are spread over larger and larger numbers of units produced. A number of developing nations use this economies of scale or infant industries argument today in their quest for unilateral tariff protection. One-crop economies, whose foreign earnings are heavily dependent on a single export, seek to use an umbrella of protectionist policies to buy time for diversification.

As much as one might be concerned for the economic plight of poor nations, great care must be exercised in applying the infant industry argument to them. At best, the argument is one for allowing domestic industry to gain a foothold in international competition. Protection for any reason, as we have seen, means lost benefits for consumers. Obviously, any gains from ultimate independence must be balanced against the costs of lost consumer benefits over the period of protection.

A final question that should be applied to the infant industries argument concerns the vagueness of the goal of removing protection when the industry "grows up." It is hardly legitimate to apply the infant industries argument to the present-day steel industry in the United States and Western Europe, but the argument is still being used. Entrenched protectionist interests will always attempt to prolong the "infancy" of any industry. The dangers of giving protectionists a general legal foothold negate any merit the argument might have in limited and specific cases.

Industry Arguments for Protection

A number of other arguments for protection crop up from time to time, usually put forward by domestic firms and industries seeking protection for protection's sake. We characterize these arguments as wrong because they are assaults on the very principle that gains may be realized from trade. They are all variations on the theme that special-interest groups deserve protection from international competition.

The "Cheap Foreign Labor" Argument   A common argument for tariff or quota protection is that labor or some other resource is cheaper abroad, enabling foreign manufacturers to sell goods at lower prices than U.S. manufacturers. This argument is usually heard from producers and workers who fear displacement by imports and foreign competition. Most recently, it has been the argument used by Ross Perot, Pat Buchanan, and others to urge the defeat of the North American Free Trade Agreement. Opponents of NAFTA claim that a massive loss of jobs will result as U.S. firms relocate to take advantage of lower-cost labor in Mexico.

While the argument may be correct—foreign producers may be more efficient combiners of resources—this truth in no way denies the benefits to free trade. The *absolute* level of wages in any other country does not matter. As we have seen, gains from trade derive from *comparative* advantage. Indeed, the request for protection from cheap labor turns the gains from trade position on its head: The reason for trade becomes a reason to limit or restrict trade. Open trade is beneficial precisely because resources may be cheaper or combined more efficiently elsewhere. The opening or extension of trade creates a temporary disruption of markets, including the unemployment of resources. To impose tariffs or quotas on the grounds that some groups of U.S. laborers are temporarily thrown out of work or that some U.S. stockholders are losing wealth is to subsidize special interests at a greater cost to all U.S. consumers of the subsidized product or service. Moreover, the domestic economy may actually gain from the movement of domestic resources into new fields of comparative advantage. For example, resources released from domestic steel production may be reallocated to computer production.

Side issues arise in the cheap foreign labor argument. One common complaint is that foreign governments subsidize the production of exported goods to shore up their domestic industries and prevent unemployment. This complaint is used as a plea for protection from cheaper imports. But to argue for tariffs on these grounds is to look a gift horse in the mouth. The benefits from trade are independent of the reasons that imports are cheaper. If governments choose to subsidize their exports, they in effect tax their own citizens to benefit foreign consumers.

Dumping
The selling of goods in foreign markets at prices lower than those charged in domestic markets.

Dumping, selling goods abroad at a lower price than in the home market, is also related to the cheap foreign labor argument for protection. The practice, an example of price discrimination, means that foreign buyers gain greater benefits from consuming the commodity or service than domestic consumers. In practice, it is often difficult to determine whether goods are being dumped. As defined by U.S. trade policies, dumping occurs when a foreign producer sells in the American market either below costs or at a price below that charged to the foreign producer's domestic customers. In real-world cases, then, a producer could be selling to his or her own customers at monopoly rates and be prohibited from selling to American consumers at lower rates (even though they more than cover costs). Such restrictions, if enforced by trade authorities, work against American consumers.

Special interests in the favored country often complain that dumping constitutes "unfair competition," but the argument for free trade remains intact nonetheless. Consumers in the favored nations are able to purchase goods at lower prices, and overall welfare in the consuming country is enhanced.

It should not matter why foreign prices are low, as long as the foreign supplier who is dumping goods in U.S. markets has no monopoly power. If the producers of Japanese television sets undersell U.S. producers with an eye to putting them out of business and subsequently raising price to a monopoly level, dumping does pose an issue for public concern. More often, "dumping" by foreign producers is a reflection of their lower costs of production and puts competitive pressure on U.S. producers.

The "Buy American" Argument   The "buy American" argument, a call to patriotism, is based on the notion that Americans will be better off by keeping their money at home. More specifically, "buy American" means that imports should be restricted so that high costs or inefficient producers and their employees may be protected from foreign competition.

This well-known argument is fallacious on several counts. First, it asks consumers to pay higher prices for goods and services than are available to them through trade, thereby negating the potential expansion of trade benefits. Second, when money is kept at home, foreign consumers are less able to purchase domestic exports, reducing the welfare of domestic export producers and their workers and other input suppliers.

"Terms of Trade" Advantage   A final argument applies to countries that have monopoly power in international markets. It suggests that a country employ its power to increase its share of the gains from international trade. Thus, if the United States is the world's largest supplier of computers, putting restrictions on computer exports will drive up the price of computers in the international market. Although the United States will then sell fewer computers, it will get a higher price per computer and possibly higher computer sales revenues. In effect, by restricting computer exports, the United States would alter the terms of trade in international transactions in its favor.

Terms of trade argument
Defending the use of artificial trade barriers, combined with monopoly or monopsony power in international markets, in order to produce an improvement in a country's terms of trade.

The **terms of trade argument** suggests that countries exercise monopoly and monopsony power where possible. Doing so is a means for a country to increase its revenues from international trade. The argument founders, however, on a simple point: the possibility of retaliation by other countries. If all countries seek terms of trade advantages, the trading nations of the world *collectively* may be made worse off. The exercise of monopoly or monopsony power to improve the terms of trade for all countries could mean a shrinking of total world production for exports. This negates the gains from comparative advantage and from the division of labor and reduces specialization within nations.

Perhaps the greatest flaw in all arguments for protection lies in the implicit assumption that other nations will lose export markets and will not retaliate. It is improbable that a country could win permanent terms of trade advantages on a unilateral basis while its trading partners sit idly by. U.S. history is peppered with examples of tariff wars. One of the fiercest tariff wars in history took place in the midst of the Great Depression of the 1930s, discussed in the next section. Tariffs or other forms of trade barrier retaliation can only create a reduction in world-wide economic welfare and massive and inefficient allocations of resources. Whatever the initial reasons for protective tariffs, consumers ultimately suffer the costs.

Clearly, the reduction or removal of tariffs or quotas benefits consumers as a whole, producing a *net* benefit to society. But against these gains must be set the losses that occur to laborers (and other input suppliers) in businesses and industries that no longer are protected. Many economists support *temporary* retraining and assistance programs for workers and industries that suffer hardship as a result of freer trade. Further, despite contemporary arguments for "fairness" in trade, economists as a whole continue to emphasize the benefits of free and open trade whenever prices are lower for imports (see the Focus "'Fair Trade' and Protectionism: The Steel Industry").

FOCUS

"Fair Trade" and Protectionism: The Steel Industry

Often one hears of "fair trade" rather than "free trade" in the ongoing debate over protection. Sometimes "fair" trade, advocated by particular interest groups (businesses, labor, etc.) means simply that these groups want only trade policies that will benefit them—consumers be damned. The "fair trade" argument, however, has other variants, variants that appear to provide "fairness." Two of these arguments are the "dumping" issue (discussed in the text) and the "unfair" subsidy issue.

The subsidy issue is often raised because many governments around the world, in common with the United States, subsidize particular areas in their respective economies. These subsidized commodities, such as certain agricultural products within the European Union, then find their way into international markets where, sometimes, they underprice domestically produced products. The point is that consumers benefit from these price reductions, no matter the source. Arguments for free trade are sound, no matter the source of lower prices. Consumers benefit more than producers lose.

Such arguments are, of course, the source of interest-group demands for protection. The dumping ("fair trade") argument was used, for example, in demands for U.S. steel industry protection in the late 1990s. The surge of steel imports led steel laborers and certain domestic manufacturers to demand a limit to steel imports to 25 percent of the U.S. market. President Clinton nevertheless sided with free traders in the U.S. Senate, and the bill was killed in June of 1999 despite a mixed record on free trade of the Clinton administration. The support from both parties was also mixed, with senators from steel-producing states voting for protection. Likewise, the demand for trade restrictions was mixed in that large domestic steel producers who enlarged their inventories from abroad were silent on the issue. Free trade won in this instance, but all kinds of "fairness" pretexts are raised against it. The next time someone argues for restrictions in the name of "fair trade," ask yourself "fair to whom?"

U.S. TARIFF POLICY

U.S. tariff history has been punctuated by cycles of less-restricted and more-restricted trade, with a move toward free trade in the past fifty years that may be more apparent than real. The average tariff rates for the years between 1821 (the year of the first good statistics) and 2000 are shown in Figure 30.6, along with some highlights of our tariff history. In the twentieth century, import duties as a percentage of the value of all imports subject to duty have ranged from almost 60 percent in the early 1930s to about 3 percent in 2000.

Why has the average tariff fluctuated so widely during U.S. history? Before turning to a specific analysis of changing conditions, one broad issue will help us answer the question. With the minor exception of tariffs imposed for revenues to fight wars or to apply foreign policy pressures, the average tariff has varied with business conditions, falling in periods of prosperity and rising during prolonged recessions or depressions. During periods of rising prosperity, manufacturers and workers displaced by free trade find little political support for the imposition of tariffs. When general business conditions turn downward, creating reduced demand for products and increased unemployment, the cry for protection grows louder in the political arena.

Early Tariff Policy

Tariffs were a major source of revenue for our republic in its early years, as they are for some developing countries today. Post-1820 tariffs tended to vary with business conditions, rising during recessions and falling during more prosperous periods of business activity. On the eve of the Civil War, tariff revenues stood at about 19 percent of the value of imports, the lowest level in American history up to that time. In 1861, Congress passed the Morrill tariff under the pretext of generating much-needed revenue for the Union treasury. Whatever the initial intention, the Morrill tariff set off a wave of protectionism in U.S. policy that lasted until the second decade of the twentieth century. Tariffs declined dramatically during the Wilson administration, standing at only 16 percent in 1920.

The dramatic downturn in the economy beginning in the late 1920s had a stark and lingering effect on protectionism in the United States. Manufacturing and commercial interests, coinciding with a willing political climate, produced the Smoot–Hawley Act of 1930, which legislated the highest peace-time tariff in U.S. history. Average tariff levels were raised to almost 60 percent of the value of imports, setting off a frenzy of protectionist retaliations in other nations. The result of what was perceived as American self-interest was falling real incomes, sharply reduced consumer welfare, and a deepened and prolonged depression in the major world-trading countries.

Modern Tariff Policy

Contemporary tariff policy may be viewed as an attempt to overcome the disastrous effects of protectionism embodied in the Smoot–Hawley Act. The first Roo-

FIGURE 30.6

Level of Tariffs

The United States today has lower tariffs, as measured by the ratio of tariff fees collected to the value of imports, than at any other time in its history. Since the establishment of the General Agreement on Tariffs and Trade (GATT) in 1947, tariffs have followed a downward trend.

Source: U.S. Bureau of the Census, *Historical Statistics, Colonial Times to 1970* (Washington, D.C.: U.S. Government Printing Office, 1975), p. 888; U.S. Bureau of the Census, *Statistical Abstract of the United States, 1995* (Washington, D.C.: U.S. Government Printing Office, 1995), p. 824; and author's calculations.

sevelt administration, under the aegis of Secretary of State Cordell Hull, acted swiftly to counteract the protectionism of the Smoot–Hawley tariff. In 1934, the Reciprocal Trade Agreements Act was passed, giving the president power to negotiate bilateral tariff reductions of up to 50 percent with other countries. This act was the important first step in establishing the character of modern U.S. tariff policy. It established a framework within which free trade is envisioned as a policy goal and to a large extent it stripped Congress of its tariff-making power (but not the power to set nontariff barriers). While Congress could legally remove the tariff-setting powers of the president, these powers have been renewed and strengthened a number of times since 1934.

In the post–World War II era, the powers of the president have been expanded to include multilateral negotiations for tariff reductions—that is, negotiations with many nations simultaneously. A manifestation of America's multilateral policy was its support of the General Agreement on Tariffs and Trade (GATT) in 1947. GATT sets rules and conditions for tariff reductions and oversees bargaining with all participating nations simultaneously. Modern U.S. trade policies evolve through GATT, and tremendous gains and an expansion of world trade have occurred since the first GATT talks. Moreover, Congress has expressed some willingness to move toward free trade. In 1962, a Trade Expansion Act was passed, permitting the president to negotiate tariff reductions on all commodities simultaneously rather than commodity by commodity. This act led to the so-called Kennedy Round of tariff reductions (1964–1967), which produced huge concessions on manufactured and industrial products, with special concessions for developing countries. Subsequent GATT rounds have produced additional tariff reductions. A new GATT tariff agreement was reached in 1994 with the so-called Uruguay Round. The World Trade Organization (WTO) was then charged with implementing the provisions of the GATT agreement. Its role is to help negotiate trade agreements and generally reduce tariffs within the member nations. (One sticky point has been the exclusion of China from the WTO—see the Focus "China and the World Trade Organization").

Where Does the United States Stand in the Battle for Free Trade?

Given the rhetoric of recent U.S. administrations and changes in U.S. tariff policy, one can be forgiven for concluding that the United States unabashedly supports free trade. Beyond a doubt, there has been movement toward free trade in recent years. The United States has forcefully worked toward lowering tariffs worldwide in a series of GATT negotiations and, through these same channels, has actively supported measures to free up trade in agricultural products. In addition, the United States and its largest trading partner, Canada, removed all trade barriers between the two countries in 1989, the first step in the creation of a combined North American market (including Mexico) under the North American Free Trade Agreement which went into effect on January 1, 1994. Finally, the disintegration of the Soviet bloc made longstanding trade and finance restrictions against Eastern European countries obsolete—virtually overnight.

The United States is a long way from having completely free trade, however. With three exceptions—Canada, Mexico, and Israel—no country escapes having certain of its imports taxed by the United States. The U.S. tariff policy for the European Community is uncertain, but creation of a free trade zone with the member countries appears unlikely.

In terms of nontariff barriers, the United States has been moving away from a policy of free trade. Since the authority to enforce laws against dumping was transferred to the Department of Commerce in 1980, the number of dumping cases has risen sharply. In the last ten years, the United States initiated about 30 percent of all the antidumping cases worldwide—a percentage exceeded only by Australia. The United States has applied pressure on other countries to enter into "voluntary" agreements to limit exports of various products to the United States. In addi-

FOCUS

China and the World Trade Organization

What is a "world" trade organization when China, the world's most populous nation, is not included? This is the question that advocates of China's inclusion in the World Trade Organization (WTO) have been asking. Opponents suggest that China is guilty of civil rights abuses and unfair trading practices and should not be included.

The stakes are high, with China's foreign trade growing from $20 billion in 1978 to nearly one-third of a trillion dollars in just twenty years. China is the fastest-growing market for American products, totaling $35 billion in 1998. Americans have also benefited greatly from cheap imports such as textiles; however, critics charge that America's trade deficit with China has zoomed to $57 billion in 1998, second only to that with Japan.

The WTO is charged with enforcing the Uruguay Round of the General Agreement on Tariffs and Trade (GATT). The purpose of GATT is to negotiate multilateral agreements between member nations to reduce tariffs and to increase international trade. GATT has been successful in reducing tariff rates, although some critics charge that these reductions have taken too many years to achieve. The WTO will oversee the implementation of the scheduled reduction in tariffs negotiated during the Uruguay Round and help resolve trade disputes between nations.

Nontariff barriers to trade are a big area of dispute. For example, European nations have, in effect, "protected" their local farmers by preventing imports they claim do not meet local regulations that prohibit the use of certain hormones in cattle or pesticides on crops. Such restrictions have been used to keep U.S. beef and Central American bananas out of European markets, but these restrictions could be considered violations of the Uruguay Round by WTO officials.

China has been trying to obtain membership in WTO and GATT for over thirteen years, leading one Chinese official to complain that the negotiation process has "made black hair turn gray." China seeks entry to gain better access to foreign markets, to play a role in future negotiations, and to achieve full status as a major economic power in world trade. China must get permission from the United States and other WTO members to enter the organization.

American interests have several concerns about Chinese membership in WTO, including alleged widespread civil rights abuses in China. Another area of concern is the protection of intellectual property rights, because China has "pirated" rights to products such as music and computer software on a large scale for many years. There are other sources of tension between the two countries such as illegal campaign donations by the Chinese, stealing of nuclear bomb secrets, Chinese military threats against Taiwan, and the United States' accidental bombing of a Chinese embassy. However, one of the largest obstacles is Chinese barriers to imports. The Chinese government still controls large sectors of the economy and can prevent imports without tariff restrictions. China also has import regulations, import quotas, and both indirect and direct subsidies to industries that put foreign competitors at a disadvantage. These nontariff barriers to trade are a big reason for China's delayed entry into the WTO.

tion to the well-known agreement with Japan to limit the number of cars sold in the United States, voluntary export agreements have been negotiated with other countries to limit the amounts of textiles, steel, and various agricultural products that enter the United States. In short, the United States is actively protectionist in its use of nontariff barriers to trade.

The dramatic reduction in tariffs over the last half of this century, as revealed in Figure 30.6, is thus grossly misleading. As long as interest groups (steel, auto, agricultural, etc.) are effective in persuading enough members of Congress to obtain protection, free trade will be subverted. In terms of nontariff barriers, the United States has been moving away from a policy of free trade. At the dawn of the twenty-first century, all sorts of nontariff qualifications are being used as the pretext for "fair" versus "free" trade. It is important to remember that it does not matter *why* prices are lower for goods and services purchased from abroad; the gains to American consumers from free trade are real, nevertheless.

APPLICATION

NAFTA: Free Trade or Free-for-All?

The North American Free Trade Agreement (NAFTA) passed the U.S. House in a close vote (234 to 200) and went into effect January 1, 1994. What is a free trade zone, and what are the benefits of NAFTA for the United States? NAFTA provides for the phased elimination of tariff and most nontariff barriers to regional trade within ten years, although a few "import-sensitive" products will have a fifteen-year transition period. Tariffs are basically taxes on imports, so lowering tariffs will lower the costs of imports. Nontariff barriers include measures such as quotas, the elimination of which will have the effect of increasing trade among the member nations. Along with trade creation, free trade zones, by vastly increasing the size of the market, increase competitive pressures which, in turn, lead to greater efficiency in production and lower prices for consumers.

In reality, NAFTA is not without its shortcomings. On the U.S. side of the issue, complaints have arisen that Mexico has not moved fast enough in particular areas—express-mail delivery, tires, and wine—to open up its markets to U.S. imports as required under the agreement. For example, United Parcel Service (UPS) has cried "foul" with respect to Mexico's restriction that delivery vehicles be no bigger than four tons, a regulation that the firm argues makes it much less efficient and, hence, less competitive in that market. Mexican officials, facing domestic unrest due to a sharp recession in the economy, have acknowledged their fear of political retaliation from domestic delivery services if these restrictions are lifted.

The ability of special interests to influence the political process became apparent in the bitter debate which occurred over the ratification of NAFTA in the U.S. Congress. Industries and their employees who will benefit from increased specialization and growth in the volume of trade had every incentive to support the agreement through the political process. However, some industries and workers will be displaced in the move toward freer trade and could, therefore, be expected to oppose the agreement. A fierce opponent of NAFTA was organized labor in the United States, including the AFL-CIO, arguing that "cheap Mexican labor" would take high-paying union jobs as a result of reductions in tariffs on automobiles, textiles, and other goods. This claim denies the operation of the principle of comparative advantage in directing trade and specialization. Mexico will specialize according to its own comparative advantage in low-tech, low-pay industries due to a relative abundance of low-skill labor. As such industries move south, valuable resources will be freed up in the U.S. economy for investment in high-tech, high-pay industries, where our nation enjoys a comparative advantage arising from a relative abundance of high-skill labor.

It is important to keep the advantages of free trade firmly in mind. The increased value to consumers resulting from higher outputs and lower prices in all three nations will dwarf the costs to certain workers and particular industries with the free trade area. Some studies estimate that the agreement has created about 170,000 new jobs in its first five years of implementation. Job creation resulting from NAFTA has occurred in new, more efficient industries. The challenge for the United States is to help displaced workers make the transition to new jobs. Over the long term, the primary impact of increased trade will be higher incomes made possible by greater efficiency and faster growth. Efficiency in the United States, Canadian, and Mexican economies will be boosted by the tendency of each to export those goods and services in which it enjoys a comparative advantage.

QUESTIONS

If the economic case for free trade is so strong, why did so many politicians fight the ratification of NAFTA? What implications do protectionist demands hold for the future and effectiveness of such free trade agreements?

SUMMARY

1. All individuals possess talents that give them advantages in trade. Nations, like individuals, benefit from specialization and trade. Nations trade not resources, but rather the products and services created with resources. Differing resource endowments are the basis for trade in products because products are ordinarily more mobile than the resources that produce them.

2. Specialization and trade may take place between countries of vastly differing degrees of economic development. The reason for this is the law of comparative advantage, which states that trade is possible when the relative opportunity cost of producing two goods differs between two countries.

3. Specialization according to the law of comparative advantage permits the production possibilities and hence the rate of sustainable consumption of nations to expand. That is, the parties to trade may obtain more of both traded goods after specialization and trade.

4. There are both natural and artificial barriers to trade. Natural barriers are all exchange costs, including transportation costs of moving goods from one country to another. Artificial barriers include taxes on imports of goods, or tariffs, and limitations or prohibitions on imported items, or quotas.

5. Tariffs on imports increase the profits of domestic producers and the revenue of government, but consumers lose more than producers and governments gain. This net welfare loss is the reason most economists oppose protectionist policies.

6. Quotas have similar effects on markets as tariffs, except that the revenue goes not to government but to producer groups.

7. Although tariffs and quotas carry a net loss to society, they are imposed whenever domestic producer-competitors are strong enough to supply gains to politicians. Consumer groups may oppose tariffs but are seldom well enough organized or vocal enough to oppose them successfully.

8. Two substantive arguments are made for protection: the national defense and infant industries arguments. Most economists, however, question the adequacy of these arguments in actual operation. Other arguments—such as "cheap foreign labor" or "buy American"—are regarded by most economists as only thinly veiled protectionist fallacies.

9. U.S. trade policies have historically waxed and waned with prosperity and depression, becoming more protectionist during economic downturns. Although import tariffs have been reduced dramatically in the past fifty years, freer trade has not necessarily resulted. Protectionism lives on in the form of quotas and nontariff trade barriers.

KEY TERMS

specialization
comparative advantage
terms of trade
consumption possibilities curve

tariff
quota
free trade
welfare loss to society

nontariff trade barriers
infant industry
dumping
terms of trade argument

QUESTIONS FOR REVIEW AND DISCUSSION

1. Evaluate and discuss the following statement: Trade across international boundaries is essentially the same as trade across interstate boundaries.

2. How can two countries simultaneously gain from trade? Under what circumstances can two countries not gain from trade?

3. What is the difference between natural barriers and artificial barriers to trade? Was the development of the Panama Canal an artificial encouragement of trade?

4. What does a tariff do to the terms of trade? Are consumers in both countries hurt by a tariff?

5. How are tariffs and quotas similar? How are they different? Would consumers prefer one of these barriers to the other?

6. Who is hurt by a tariff? Who is helped? Who encourages government to impose tariffs?

7. What is the purpose of protective tariffs? Who or what is protected?

8. Evaluate the following statement: Tariffs discourage the movement of goods between countries; therefore, they encourage the movement of resources such as capital and labor between countries.

9. What are the effects of trade on a country's consumption possibilities? After trade, what is the relationship between the consumption and production possibilities curves and what does this imply for the country?

10. What are nontariff trade barriers? Compare the effects of nontariff barriers and the effects of tariffs.

11. What is the difference between "free trade" and "fair trade"?

12. Should China and other countries charged with "human rights" abuses be admitted to organizations whose object is the free trade of goods and services?

PROBLEMS

Nations Alpha and Beta have the following production possibilities for goods X and Y.

Alpha	X	0	3	6	9
	Y	12	8	4	0
Beta	X	0	4	8	12
	Y	15	10	5	0

1. Draw the production possibilities curves for both countries. What does 1 X cost in Alpha before trade? What does 1 Y cost in Beta? If these countries traded, which would export X and which would export Y?

2. If some country Omega can produce 100 units of X with all its resources or 60 units of Y, how much does 1 unit of Y cost? If another country, Gamma, can produce 60 X or 40 Y, what does 1 unit of X cost in Gamma? Which country has a comparative advantage in the production of X?

WORKING WITH THE WEB

1. Go to the following web sites to collect information on U.S.–Canada trade:
   - U.S. State Department's Country Reports: http://www.state.gov/www/issues/economic/trade_reports
   - Statistics Canada: http://www.statcan.ca/english/ Pgdb/Economy/intern.htm

   At the State Department site, access the 1998 Trade report for Canada.
   a. In 1998, what was Canada's percentage of total merchandise exports and imports with the United States?
   b. Why do you think that the United States is such a large trading partner with Canada?

   At the Statistics Canada site, access the (by product) tables for exports and imports.
   c. What were Canada's three largest exports and imports in 1998?
   d. Assume that your response in part (c) predominantly reflects U.S.–Canada trade. Explain whether your findings are consistent with what you would expect from the theory of comparative advantage.

2. One of the best starting points on any data search is the Resources for Economists on the Internet site (http://rfe.wustl.edu/EconFAQ.html). Go to this site, click on the link for "Data," and then click on the subsequent link for "U.S. Macro and Regional Data." Locate the link to the web site for the "Bureau of Economic Analysis" and go there (the web address should be http://www.bea.doc.gov). Once at the BEA site, select the link for "Data" under the heading "International." Go down a few rows, click on "Exports and Imports, Monthly," and look at the tables presented on this page.
   a. The table presents data for the United States. Compare exports and imports of goods and services, and report your findings.
   b. Make a comparative advantage argument supporting your findings in part (a).

3. Go to the Economagic web site (http://www.Economagic.com) and locate data on the government's budget surplus/deficit and the current account for goods and services (trade account). The St. Louis Fed has one of the largest databases there,

so click on this link. Page down until you find "Federal Government Surplus or Deficit (−) (NIPA); annual" and "Balance of Payments: Balance on Current Account; SA" (alternatively, you can use the appropriate Data Headings to find this data).

Create a graph for both data series that covers the time period 1960–1999. To create a graph, you will need to be on the data page you want to graph. Click on the link for "GIF chart," and then set the time period when the next page appears (note that the existing graph only covers the last several years). Make a graph for each series of data (Government Budget and Current Account).

a. Do you observe a relationship between the two series? Explain.

b. Should the Government Budget be related to the Current Account in a typical Keynesian model of the economy?

International Finance

When a car dealer in Alabama buys cars from a Detroit manufacturer to sell in Alabama, both use the same medium of exchange—U.S. dollars. Suppose, however, that the dealer buys cars from Japanese or German manufacturers to sell in Alabama. The Japanese firm will likely want payment in yen; the German firm, in marks. The car dealer thus confronts an international monetary problem. Are the prices stated in yen and marks acceptable? This question brings up others. How are dollars converted into yen and marks? Is there a fixed rate for currency exchange or does it vary? How would changes in exchange rates affect import prices in the United States? American manufacturers sell to citizens in foreign countries and seek payment for their goods and services in U.S. dollars. They must be careful, therefore, to pay attention to exchange rates, because these rates can determine the prices and profits of their foreign sales.

The monetary, or financial, side of international trade concerns the ways in which countries pay for the goods and services they exchange. In this chapter we examine many aspects of the relations among the currencies of the world, relations that reflect a kaleidoscope of changing conditions in each country, from interest rates and inflation rates to exports and imports of goods and capital. When you finish Chapter 31 you should understand

- how international trade takes place when transactions must be made in terms of other countries' currencies.
- how currency transactions are determined when governments fix their respective currencies' value and when the market determines the relative value of currencies.

- how macroeconomic fiscal and monetary policies both affect and are affected by foreign trade and international exchange rates.
- the meaning of the balance of payments, its relation to exchange rates, and its importance for economic growth.

THE FOREIGN EXCHANGE MARKET

Foreign exchange
The monies of countries that are used to facilitate international trade in goods, services, and financial assets.

International sellers and buyers usually prefer to deal in the currency of their own country. American sellers prefer U.S. dollars for their products, and Japanese sellers prefer yen. The currency of another country that is required to make payment in an international transaction is called **foreign exchange.** Foreign exchange is bought and sold in **foreign exchange markets**—typically, large brokers and banks scattered about the globe.

Foreign exchange markets
The interaction of the suppliers and demanders of foreign exchange, through which exchange rates are determined in a flexible exchange rate system.

Sometimes consumers demand foreign exchange; for example, when American travelers arrive at a foreign airport, they often exchange dollars for the local currency. Large firms dealing in international transactions simply keep bank deposits in foreign currencies to cover their foreign transactions. An American importer of French wine will likely pay for its purchases by writing checks on an American bank that holds an account in a French bank. The American bank will use the importer's dollars to purchase the francs needed for payment.

The demand for foreign exchange arises because a country's residents want to buy foreign goods. Conversely, the supply of foreign exchange arises because foreign customers want to buy U.S. goods. For example, we have a demand for francs by the U.S. importer who wishes to purchase French wine and a supply of francs by French customers who wish to purchase U.S. personal computers.

Exchange Rates

Exchange rate
The (relative) price of one national currency in terms of another national currency.

An **exchange rate** is the price of one country's money in terms of some other country's money. It is a relative price, much the same as the relative price concept discussed in Chapter 4, except that it is the relative price of one national currency expressed in terms of another national currency. Like the relative prices of goods, exchange rates can be expressed in one of two equivalent ways. We can talk about one concert ticket "costing" five pizzas, or we can say that one pizza costs one-fifth of a concert ticket. Either way, the relative price of one good in terms of another good (one concert ticket in terms of pizzas or one pizza in terms of concert tickets) is expressed. Which expression we choose is simply a matter of preference or convenience.

So it is with exchange rates. Because they are relative prices of one money in terms of another money, the way we choose to express the exchange rate is a matter of preference and convenience. For example, in April 1999, one U.S. dollar traded on the foreign exchange market for about six French francs (ff), the national currency of France. One U.S. dollar costs about six French francs to buy, or one U.S. dollar sold for about six French francs. This exchange rate is the relative price of the U.S. dollar in terms of French francs. Alternatively, it would be just as accurate to say that one French franc costs, or would buy, about 17 cents. This would

The worldwide volume of trade on foreign exchange markets exceeds $500 billion per day.

be the relative price of the French franc in terms of the U.S. dollar. One is nothing more than the inverse, or reciprocal, of the other. Exchange rates are often expressed both ways. An American in France must use French francs to make purchases. Starting out the vacation, the traveler may have a budget, say $500, that she wishes to spend on meals. By using the U.S. dollar in terms of French francs exchange rate (6 per dollar), she can calculate that she will have 3000 ff (6 ff per dollar × $500) to spend on meals in France. Once in France, if our tourist pays 100 ff for a lunch, she may wish to know how many dollars the lunch cost. A quick calculation using the French franc in terms of the U.S. dollar exchange rate will provide a good estimate ($0.17 per ff × 100 ff = $17).

Of equal importance are changes in exchange rates, for such changes can alter the prices of imports and exports. Suppose that a bottle of French wine sells for 100 ff. Ignoring transportation costs and any tariffs, with a dollar–franc exchange rate of $0.17 per French franc, the wine will cost $17 in the United States. But suppose the exchange rate were to change to $0.25 per French franc. The same bottle of wine would still cost 100 ff in France, but its cost in the United States would rise to $25. Changes in the exchange rate alter the prices of foreign goods in home markets and of domestic goods in foreign markets.

Just as tourists must pay attention to exchange rates in order to make plans and informed decisions, so must businesses and governments. International trade, like interpersonal trade, requires the use of money. The prices of these monies relative to one another are important economic variables. A sudden change in an exchange rate can alter the actual values of any business transaction, making it more or less profitable than at first thought. Such changes

Knowledge of current exchange rates is crucial to tourists traveling in foreign countries.

influence business decisions and can alter the volume of international trade. At issue, then, is what determines exchange rates. Why, in 1999, did a dollar buy (cost) about six French francs and not four or ten French francs? What has caused the U.S. dollar price of French francs, or for that matter German marks, English pounds, Japanese yen, Mexican pesos, or any other country's money, to change from day to day, month to month, and year to year?

Naturally, the existence of multiple currencies has costs. When you take a trip to Europe, for example, exchanging dollars (or some other currency) for national monetary units takes time and resources. The same is, of course, true for businesses exchanging goods and services. Thus, a common currency reduces transaction costs of all kinds. This is the aim of the new common currency for Europe, scheduled to go into effect in 2002 (see the Focus "The Euro, Europe's New Money").

Exchange Rate Systems

Exchange rates, like any other price, are determined in markets by the forces of supply and demand. However, exactly who suppliers and demanders are, and under what constraints the market operates, determines the type of system within which the exchange rate will be determined. One type, the **flexible, or floating, exchange rate system,** is a system whereby the exchange rate is determined solely by the interaction of private demanders and suppliers of foreign exchange. This is the type of system most major trading countries employ today to determine the world market value of their respective currencies. Of course, government fiscal and monetary policies can help determine the exchange rate under such a system by influencing the behavior of private market participants. But government policies usually are not specifically designed to influence the exchange rate directly.

A second system of exchange rate determination is called a **fixed exchange rate system.** A fixed exchange rate system was in existence from the late 1940s until 1971. A few countries today still fix the value of their currencies on world markets in terms of U.S. dollars. Under a fixed exchange rate system, government intervenes directly in the foreign exchange market, either as a buyer or as a seller, in order to fix the exchange rate at some level. Some European countries combine elements of both the fixed- and flexible-rate systems. The values of these

Flexible, or floating, exchange rate system
An international monetary arrangement in which exchange rates are determined by private suppliers and demanders without government intervention.

Fixed exchange rate system
An international monetary arrangement in which exchange rates are set by the government, which then must intervene in the foreign exchange market in order to maintain the pegged exchange rate.

FOCUS

The Euro, Europe's New Money

European nations have been attempting to better integrate their economies since after World War II and the signing of the Treaty of Rome in 1957. The general plan has been to reduce trade barriers and other restrictions that impede the flow of goods across borders in the spirit of the old dictum "if goods don't cross borders, armies will." An important part of economic integration is the establishment of a common currency.

On January 4, 1999, the Euro was launched as a common money of Europe. The Euro replaces the European Currency Unit (ECU), which was used only as a unit of account between European central banks. The idea behind the new currency is that individuals and businesses will be able to use the currency all over Europe, as well as have their accounts denominated in Euros. The situation will be analogous to that of America, where we can spend dollars in all fifty states. The distribution of paper and coin money begins on January 1, 2002, and will consist of eight denominations of bills and eight coins (national currencies will cease to function as legal tender on July 1, 2002).

The value of the Euro is based on a weighted average of the values of the currencies of the eleven participating countries of Europe's Economic and Monetary Union, the EMU. The currencies of large economies like Germany and France carry a larger weight than those of smaller economies like Austria

and Finland. Possessing a Euro will be like having a basket of European currencies all rolled into one.

An important condition of the Maastricht Treaty, which laid the groundwork for the Euro, is that the exchange rate between the eleven national currencies will be irrevocably fixed. This means that the nations will have to keep the value of their currencies in line with all the other members. Fixed exchange rates for paper currencies have been difficult, if not impossible, to achieve in the past; hence as preconditions for membership, nations must meet strict requirements to maintain low inflation, interest rates, budget deficits, and national debt, and they must grant their central banks full independence.

The European Central Bank (ECB) will control the fate of the Euro after the national currencies have ceased to exist. The ECB has been designed with full independence and been given the sole task of maintaining price level stability with inflation at less than 2 percent per year. Detractors feel that the system will collapse politically, while critics fear the loss of national sovereignty and the inflation potential of the ECB if it loses its independence. If successful, this experiment would rid Europe of high inflation, encourage fiscal responsibility among member nations, and speed up economic growth in the stagnant economies of Europe. Could the Euro become Europe's economic hero?

European currencies are fixed relative to one another, but all float against the U.S. dollar.

Since 1973, the exchange rate system determining the relative prices of national currencies has been a blend of these two systems. By and large, the flexible-rate system is in use for the currencies of the United States and other major industrial countries. No country, however, allows its exchange rate to float freely all the time. Wide swings in the exchange rate are controlled by government intervention in the foreign exchange market. For this reason, the present international monetary system is called a **managed flexible-rate system.** In the next two sections we analyze how floating exchange rates and fixed exchange rates work.

Managed flexible-rate system
Primarily a flexible exchange rate system, but with occasional government purchases or sales of foreign exchange intended to influence the exchange rate.

FLEXIBLE EXCHANGE RATES

As we pointed out earlier, U.S. demand for foreign currency arises because U.S. citizens wish to buy foreign products, travel in foreign countries, invest in foreign companies, and carry on other international activities. The supply of foreign currencies to the United States arises because foreigners want to buy U.S. goods, travel in the United States, send their children to school in the United States, invest in this country, and so on. All of these forces of supply and demand affect the exchange rate between the U.S. dollar and other currencies. In effect, they form the basis of the supply and demand schedules in the foreign exchange markets.

Exchange Rates Between Two Countries

We begin our analysis with a simple model of the determination of floating, or flexible, exchange rates. For simplicity, we assume that international trade takes place only between two countries, the United States and Switzerland. The U.S. demand for foreign exchange is thus a demand for Swiss francs; the supply of foreign exchange is a supply of Swiss francs.

Supply, Demand, and the Market for Foreign Exchange   Before beginning our analysis of the factors that determine and change exchange rates, some preliminaries are in order. The exchange rate is determined in the foreign exchange market; it is the relative price of one money in terms of another. As we have indicated, the actions of both the Americans and the Swiss are manifested in this market. But any action on the part of residents of one country is mirrored in the actions of residents of the other. Swiss exports are American imports, and vice versa. This means that technically we would want to look at both the supply and demand of dollars and the supply and demand of Swiss francs to the foreign exchange market in order to examine exchange rate determination. But because the dollar–franc exchange rate is just the inverse of the franc–dollar exchange rate (so that changes in one are mirrored by changes in the other), and because Swiss imports are American exports, we can simplify matters. We need only examine the supply and demand for either francs or dollars on the foreign exchange market in order to discuss exchange rate determination. We will look at the supply and demand for Swiss francs, the foreign exchange in our discussion.

Figure 31.1 depicts the supply and demand for foreign exchange, Swiss francs. What establishes the supply and demand for francs on the foreign exchange mar-

FIGURE 31.1

A Two-Country Foreign Exchange Market

The exchange rate—in this case, the dollar price of one Swiss franc—is measured on the vertical axis. The quantity of francs is measured on the horizontal axis. The equilibrium exchange rate is $0.75 per Swiss franc, because this is the only exchange rate that equates quantity demanded with quantity supplied. At the exchange rate of $0.90 per franc, there exists a surplus of francs, and the exchange rate will fall. At the $0.50 exchange rate, a shortage of francs on the foreign exchange market exists, which will drive the exchange rate back to $0.75.

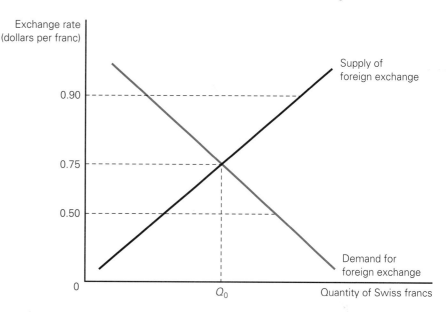

ket? Consider the demand for franc foreign exchange first. American importers of Swiss goods must pay Swiss producers with francs. Thus, American imports from Switzerland are the basis of foreign exchange demand. The demand for foreign exchange slopes downward because, other things constant, a higher exchange rate (more dollars per franc) implies higher import prices, fewer imports, and a smaller quantity demanded (by Americans) of foreign exchange.

The supply of foreign exchange arises from Swiss import activity and, therefore, American export activity. Swiss importers must pay for goods produced in the United States (American exports) with dollars. In order to obtain dollars, they must buy them with francs in the foreign exchange market. The supply of foreign exchange originates with Swiss imports or, what is the same thing, American exports. It is upward-sloping because, other factors considered, a rise in the dollar price of the franc (the exchange rate measured on the vertical axis) means that one franc now buys more dollars, making American goods cheaper to the Swiss. This implies an increase in the desire of the Swiss to import from the United States. They will then offer more francs for sale at the higher exchange rate to obtain additional dollars. The additional dollars are then used to purchase the larger quantity of imports.

The equilibrium exchange rate, like any other price, is one that equates quantity demanded with quantity supplied. In Figure 31.1, this equilibrium exchange rate is $0.75 per Swiss franc. Suppose that the exchange rate were below equilibrium, at $0.50 per franc. The quantity demanded of foreign exchange would then exceed the quantity supplied of foreign exchange. There would be a shortage of francs on the foreign exchange market. As in any other market, a shortage in the foreign exchange market will tend to drive price back toward equilibrium.

Given the fundamental economic factors determining exports and imports in both countries, an exchange rate below the equilibrium exchange rate ($0.50 per franc in Figure 31.1) creates a situation in which Americans wish to import much more from Switzerland than the Swiss wish to sell. At this exchange rate, Swiss goods are "too cheap" to Americans because the dollar price of the franc is "too low." On the other side of the coin, American goods are "too expensive" to the Swiss. Swiss imports are too low, and thus the quantity supplied of foreign exchange is also too low. To stimulate the quantity of Swiss imports and increase the quantity supplied of foreign exchange, as well as to reduce the quantity of U.S. imports and reduce the quantity demanded of foreign exchange, an increase in the exchange rate is necessary. The movement to equilibrium from $0.50 to $0.75 results from the bidding up of the dollar price of francs by American consumers eager to obtain Swiss goods. (Americans demand Swiss francs and *simultaneously* supply U.S. dollars.) The actions of American consumers tend to elevate the price of Swiss francs in terms of dollars, returning the dollar–franc market to equilibrium. Naturally, the rise in the dollar price of francs reduces the quantity demanded of Swiss goods and services by Americans as equilibrium is approached. (The Swiss are willing to supply the additional francs because of the higher price of their currency expressed in dollars.)

Likewise, the exchange rate of $0.90 per franc is too high for equilibrium, creating a surplus of foreign exchange. At $0.90 per franc, Swiss products are very expensive for Americans and American products are relatively inexpensive to the Swiss. As the Swiss demand dollars to get American goods, the price of dollars in terms of francs rises and the price of francs in terms of dollars falls. Simultaneously, with Americans wanting to import less than the Swiss wish to export to the United States, a surplus of franc foreign exchange exists. A fall in the dollar price of the franc will increase American imports and the quantity demanded of foreign exchange. This same fall will also make American goods more expensive in Switzerland, reduce imports, and thus reduce the quantity supplied of francs to the foreign exchange market. Equilibrium is restored, as shown in Figure 31.1, when the dollar price of francs returns to $0.75.

Changes in Flexible Exchange Rates

The foreign exchange market is like any other market studied in economics. Supply and demand determine price, and surpluses and shortages of foreign exchange will move the exchange rate toward its equilibrium value. We now examine why the supply of or demand for foreign exchange might change, producing a change in the equilibrium exchange rate in a flexible exchange rate system.

Appreciation and Depreciation The dollar price of the Swiss franc, or any other currency, fluctuates from day to day and even minute to minute. Trying to explain every small fluctuation in the exchange rate would be a fruitless exercise. However, broad and significant changes in exchange rates have occurred since the collapse of the fixed-rate system and subsequent inception of the managed flexible-rate system in 1973. The late 1970s and the early 1990s were periods of dollar **depreciation.** A depreciation of a country's currency on world markets means that the equilibrium exchange rate has changed such that it requires more of the currency to purchase other money. An increase in the equilibrium dollar price of the Swiss franc from $0.75 to $0.90 constitutes a depreciation of the dol-

Depreciation
A decrease in the equilibrium exchange market value of a country's currency in a flexible-rate system; an increase in the number of units of a country's money required to purchase one unit of a foreign country's money.

lar. It takes more dollars to buy a franc than previously, or equivalently, one dollar buys fewer francs. Another term used frequently by the financial press to describe a depreciation is a "weakening" of the currency on the foreign exchange market. The early 1980s was a period of dollar **appreciation.** An appreciation is the opposite of a depreciation; less of the money is required to buy other monies on the foreign exchange market. A fall in the equilibrium exchange rate from $0.75 to $0.50 per franc signifies a dollar appreciation (and a franc depreciation). A currency that has appreciated is said to have "strengthened" on world currency markets or is a "strong" currency. The basic reasons and fundamental causes of currency appreciations and deprecations are addressed in the following sections.

Appreciation

An increase in the equilibrium exchange market value of a country's currency in a flexible-rate system; a decrease in the number of units of a country's money required to purchase one unit of a foreign country's money.

Price Levels, Money Supplies, and Inflation Rates   One factor that can cause the exchange rate to change is a shift in the price level of either country. Suppose that the price level in the United States were to increase by 20 percent while the general level of prices in Switzerland was stable. Figure 31.2a depicts the effects this would have on the foreign exchange market and the exchange rate. Other things equal, higher U.S. prices would reduce Swiss import demand for American goods.

(a)

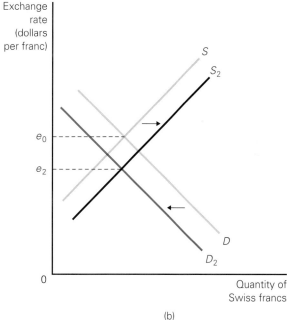

(b)

FIGURE 31.2

Price Level Changes in the Flexible Exchange Rate System

S and *D* are the initial foreign supply and demand curves. In Figure 31.2a, an increase in the U.S. price level, holding the Swiss price level constant, causes the supply of foreign exchange to shift to S_1, while the demand for foreign exchange shifts to D_1. This causes the Swiss franc to appreciate from e_0 to e_1. This can also be described as a depreciation of the dollar. If the Swiss price level increased while the price level in the United States remained unchanged, the supply and demand curves would shift to S_2 and D_2 in Figure 31.2b. This would cause the exchange rate to fall from e_0 to e_2.

This would, in turn, cause a decrease in the supply of foreign exchange, shown as a shift of the supply curve of francs from S to S_1. The rise in the prices of U.S. goods also would make Swiss goods relatively more attractive to Americans. American import demand would increase, and the demand for foreign exchange also would then increase. In Figure 31.2a, the demand for foreign exchange shifts from D to D_1.

The effect is to increase the dollar price of the franc. The equilibrium exchange rate rises from e_0 to e_1, or the dollar depreciates on the foreign exchange market. Of course, one could also say that the franc has appreciated. Had the price level in Switzerland risen by 20 percent with the price level in the United States constant, just the opposite would have occurred. Swiss goods would have become more expensive to Americans, reducing American import demand and the demand for foreign exchange from D to D_2 in Figure 31.2b. Swiss import demand would increase as American goods become cheaper in Switzerland, causing the supply of foreign exchange to increase from S to S_2. The equilibrium exchange rate would fall from e_0 to e_2, and a dollar appreciation (franc depreciation) would have taken place.

Real Income, Exports, and Imports   Other factors also can cause a currency to appreciate or depreciate on world currency markets. Consider the effect of an expansion in the Swiss economy that results in an increase in Swiss real income. As Swiss real income increases, the demand for imports from the United States also increases. More francs are supplied to the foreign exchange market at any given exchange rate, and the supply of foreign exchange increases. In Figure 31.3, the foreign exchange supply curve shifts from S to S_1 and the equilibrium exchange rate falls from e_0 to e_1. The increase in Swiss real income has caused the dollar to appreciate on the foreign exchange market or, equivalently, the franc to depreciate.

FIGURE 31.3

Real Income Changes and the Exchange Rate

An increase in real income in Switzerland has the effect of shifting the supply of foreign exchange from S to S_1. This appreciates the dollar in the foreign exchange market, causing the exchange rate to fall from e_0 to e_1. Should U.S. real income rise, the effect will be to increase the demand for foreign exchange to D_1 and depreciate the dollar, moving the exchange rate from e_0 to e_2.

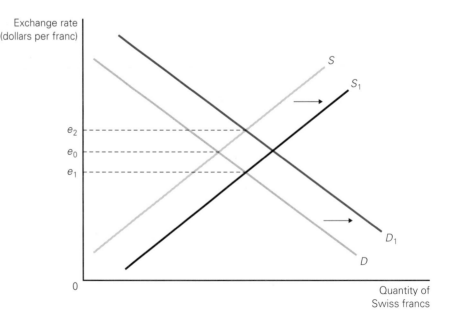

Should real income in the United States rise, the dollar would depreciate on the foreign exchange market. Larger U.S. real income would cause a desire for greater imports from Switzerland. The demand for francs would increase in Figure 31.3 from D to D_1. Given the initial supply of foreign exchange, S, the rise in U.S. real income causes a depreciation of the dollar (appreciation of the franc) on the foreign exchange market. In this case, the exchange rate rises from e_0 to e_2.[1]

Changes in factors that directly affect exports and imports can also cause changes in exchange rates. Should consumer tastes in the United States change in favor of goods produced at home, for example, the demand for foreign exchange would decrease, causing an appreciation of the dollar. Government policies aimed at restricting imports or encouraging exports tend to reduce the demand for foreign exchange and appreciate the country's currency on world markets.

Interest Rates   So far, we have discussed the supply of foreign exchange as arising from the desires of foreigners to buy goods and services produced in the United States. But foreigners purchase real estate and financial assets in the United States as well; for instance, Rockefeller Center in New York was purchased by Japanese investors. Stocks and bonds issued by U.S. businesses and governments (state, local, and federal) are other, less-publicized examples of such purchases by foreign businesspeople. Both such examples are foreign investments in the United States. Just as the purchase of U.S. goods by foreigners creates a supply of foreign exchange, so does the purchase of financial assets or real assets such as automobile or computer assembly plants. Likewise, U.S. citizens purchase the financial assets of other countries, adding to the demand for foreign exchange.

An increased desire on the part of the Swiss to invest in the United States, to buy more U.S. financial or real assets, signals an increased supply of foreign exchange. More francs are supplied to the foreign exchange market to purchase the dollars necessary to buy U.S. assets. In Figure 31.4, the supply of foreign exchange increases from S to S_1 and the exchange rate falls from e_0 to e_1. What would cause this to happen?

Investors everywhere look at many different variables in deciding how to allocate their investment funds among particular firms, industries, or countries. Such factors as risk, liquidity, and the degree of political stability are all important. However, a primary factor that goes into any investment decision is the real rate of interest those funds earn.

The real interest rate, recall, is the rate of interest earned adjusted for inflation. Suppose that the real interest rate in the United States rose. That would make U.S. financial assets more attractive to own and would increase the demand by foreigners to purchase U.S. financial assets. This increase in the U.S. real interest rate would have caused the increase in the supply of francs to the foreign exchange market depicted in Figure 31.4. The effect of a rise in the real interest rate in the United States is dollar appreciation, or, in terms of Figure 31.4, a decline in the dollar price of the Swiss franc on the foreign exchange market from e_0 to e_1.

---

[1] We are assuming that as real income rises, the money supply increases enough to accommodate the extra demand for money.

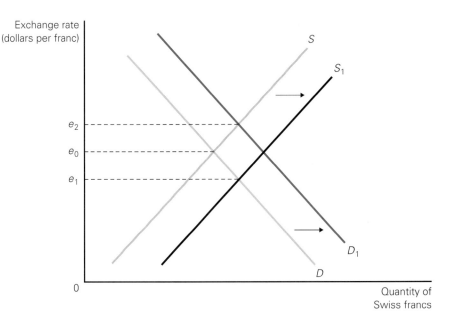

Alternatively, should the real interest rate increase in Switzerland, the demand for francs on the part of Americans would increase, from D to D_1 in Figure 31.4. Given the supply of franc foreign exchange of S, the exchange rate would rise to e_2. An increased Swiss real interest rate causes the dollar to depreciate, or the franc to appreciate, on the foreign exchange market.

FIXED EXCHANGE RATES

As we have seen, a system of flexible exchange rates allows the foreign exchange market to determine the prices at which currency will change hands. By contrast, a fixed exchange rate system does not allow exchange rates to float in a free market. Government intervenes in the foreign exchange market to fix or "manage" the international price of its currency. Once fixed exchange rates are established, governments stand ready to protect the rates through intervention in the foreign exchange market.

The Operation of a Fixed Exchange Rate System

Undervalued

A term describing the foreign exchange market value of a country's money that occurs when the number of units of a country's money that purchases one unit of a foreign currency is greater than the equilibrium exchange rate.

Although the United States and Switzerland no longer trade on the basis of a fixed exchange rate, imagine what would happen if they did. Figure 31.5 illustrates what happens when a fixed exchange rate between francs and dollars does not happen to correspond to ever-shifting market conditions. If the current market equilibrium rate is e_0, but the U.S. government seeks to maintain an exchange rate of e_1, the official or fixed rate is above the equilibrium rate. In this case, the dollar is said to be undervalued relative to the Swiss franc. The dollar is **undervalued** because

FIGURE 31.5

Fixed Exchange Rates Above and Below Equilibrium

If the government sets an exchange rate below equilibrium, such as e_2, a shortage of foreign exchange develops, and the central bank must continuously sell foreign exchange from its exchange reserves to keep the rate at e_2. If the rate is set at e_1, a surplus of foreign exchange is created, and the central bank must continuously buy foreign exchange, adding to its exchange reserves, in order to maintain the fixed rate.

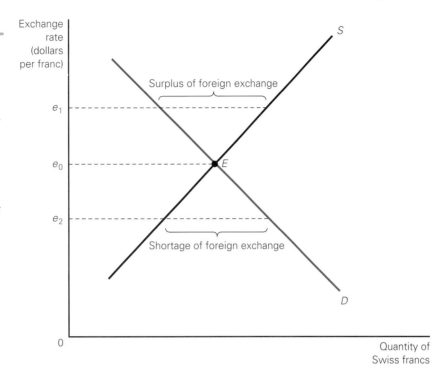

Overvalued

A term describing the foreign exchange market value of a country's money that occurs when the number of units of a country's money that purchases one unit of a foreign currency is less than the equilibrium exchange rate.

Foreign exchange market intervention

Purchases or sales of foreign exchange by government, usually a central bank, with the goal of maintaining a fixed exchange rate or influencing the exchange rate in a flexible-rate system.

Foreign exchange reserves

The stock of a foreign exchange held by a central bank that is available for use in exchange market intervention.

at exchange rate e_1 each dollar will buy fewer francs than it would at the lower equilibrium exchange rate, e_0. Of course, if the dollar is undervalued, then the franc is overvalued. Similarly, if the government were to fix the exchange rate at e_2, each dollar would purchase more francs than it would at the equilibrium exchange rate, e_0. In this case, the dollar (franc) would be **overvalued** (undervalued).

Suppose that the government decides to fix the price of its currency in the foreign exchange market at e_1. To do this, the central bank must continuously engage in **foreign exchange market intervention.**

When the government fixes the exchange rate at e_1, even though fundamental foreign exchange market forces dictate an equilibrium exchange rate of e_0, a surplus of francs on the foreign exchange market is created. At the high dollar price of the franc, quantity supplied of francs will exceed quantity demanded. Without exchange market intervention, as described earlier, the exchange rate would fall back to its equilibrium value, e_0. The central bank can prevent this fall, and maintain exchange rate e_1 only if it intervenes in the exchange market by buying up the franc surplus. The buying of francs, in this case, by the central bank builds up the central bank's **foreign exchange reserves,** its holding of foreign currencies. Such an intervention is not a one-time affair. Each month or year that the exchange rate is fixed above its equilibrium value, the central bank must purchase the surplus of francs in order to maintain the fixed rate. Fixing the rate above equilibrium tends to make a country's exports cheaper and its imports more expensive. Hence, such a policy may be used by governments in an attempt to reduce imports and encourage exports.

Sometimes central banks fix the exchange rate below the market equilibrium exchange rate, such as rate e_2 in Figure 31.5. This creates a shortage of foreign exchange, since quantity demanded at exchange rate e_2 is greater than quantity supplied. Again, without continuous exchange market intervention, the exchange rate would move back toward its equilibrium level, e_0. In this case, foreign exchange market intervention takes the form of sales of foreign currency (Swiss francs) from the central bank's foreign currency reserves. Setting such an exchange rate, one that deliberately overvalues the country's currency in world markets, is not a policy that most countries could pursue indefinitely. Sooner or later the central bank would run out of reserves and be unable to support the fixed exchange rate. Fixing the exchange rate below equilibrium tends to encourage imports and discourage exports.

Fixed Exchange Rates

The fixed exchange rate set by government can stray significantly from the equilibrium exchange rate. A country will therefore experience persistent problems in international trade; namely, it will confront persistent surpluses or deficits in its foreign trade. In the balance of trade between exports and imports, a country whose exports have greater value than its imports is said to have a **balance of trade surplus;** one whose imports' value exceeds its exports' value has a **balance of trade deficit.** What are the options under a fixed-rate system for alleviating such situations?

Balance of trade surplus
Occurs when the value of a nation's exports exceeds the value of a nation's imports; also called a trade surplus.

Balance of trade deficit
Occurs when the value of a nation's exports is less than the value of a nation's imports; also called a trade deficit.

Changes in Domestic Macroeconomic Policy   Consider first the example of Figure 31.5, where the dollar price of the franc is maintained at e_1 while the equilibrium price is e_0. The dollar is undervalued, and the United States experiences a balance of trade surplus, while Switzerland runs a persistent deficit, importing more than it exports. The Swiss will demand that something be done.

One option is to change domestic macroeconomic policies in the two countries. Suppose the United States allows its money supply to rise and Switzerland lets its money supply fall. In the United States the increase in money supply will lead to higher prices and costs. In Switzerland the opposite effects will occur: There will be lower prices and costs. Thus, U.S. exports will fall because they are now relatively more expensive on world markets, and U.S. imports will rise because foreign goods are now cheaper and income is higher. In Switzerland exports will rise because Swiss goods are now relatively cheaper, and imports will decline because U.S. goods are more expensive and Swiss GDP has fallen. The basic tendency in both countries, then, is toward adjustments that erase the surplus of exports over imports in the United States and the corresponding deficit in Switzerland.

An important point emerges from this discussion. In a fixed exchange rate system, where the government chooses to defend the fixed rate at all costs, imbalances in foreign trade must be resolved through macroeconomic adjustment of entire domestic economies. To keep one price—the foreign exchange rate—fixed, the United States and Switzerland manipulate the level of all the other prices in their economies. A flexible-rate system, by contrast, changes one price—the foreign exchange rate—to resolve balance of trade problems.

Devaluation and Revaluation   The second option facing two fixed-rate countries with a trade imbalance is to change the official exchange rate. In this way, the two governments can avoid costly manipulation of their domestic economies to restore foreign trade equilibrium. There are two possible changes in this regard.

Devaluation

An official change in a country's exchange rate in a fixed-rate system; the number of units of a country's money that purchases one unit of another country's currency is increased by the government.

One is **devaluation** of one country's currency. When the dollar is overvalued (e_2 per franc in Figure 31.5), the United States suffers a trade deficit and Switzerland a trade surplus. With Switzerland's agreement, the United States can lower the official exchange value of its currency. In this case, we say that a devaluation has occurred. In terms of Figure 31.5, this means that the dollar price of francs is moved upward, closer to its equilibrium value. This change in the exchange rate changes the relative prices of each country's imports and exports so as to help erase the U.S. deficit and the Swiss surplus without each country's having to resort to costly deflation and inflation of its domestic economy.

Where the official rate is above the equilibrium rate (such as e_1 per franc in Figure 31.5), the opposite process can be applied. In this case, the United States has a trade surplus and Switzerland a deficit. The two countries can support this exchange rate if the United States buys francs or if Switzerland sells dollars or some combination of both. However, to avoid inflation in the United States and deflation in Switzerland to correct the balance of trade situation, the two countries might agree to revalue the dollar. A **revaluation** occurs when the official price of a currency is raised. This means that the dollar price of francs would move downward in Figure 31.5, closer to its equilibrium value. The value of the dollar is thus raised, or revalued, and the corresponding value of the franc is lowered, or devalued.

Revaluation

An official change in a country's exchange rate in a fixed-rate system; the number of units of a country's money that purchases one unit of another country's currency is decreased by the government.

Adjustments in official exchange rates seem less costly than the manipulation of whole economies. However, as we will see later, such adjustments are not always easy to accomplish. The Swiss may reap advantages from a balance of trade surplus and may resist efforts to devalue the dollar or to implement a domestic economic policy that chips away at their surplus. Complex international negotiations are inherent in a fixed-rate system.

Changes in Trade Policy   A third option for resolving balance of trade difficulties under a fixed-rate system is for a deficit country to erect barriers to international trade. Tariffs, quotas, and other barriers to the free movement of people and goods across international borders can be established to try to solve a trade problem. This is not an option that would find much favor among economists, however. As detailed in Chapter 30, such impediments to international trade cost the worldwide economy economic efficiency and gains from specialization.

Instead of erecting trade barriers, another policy is pressuring trading partners to abolish current import restrictions. This strategy has been advocated as a means of reducing the persistent trade deficit between the United States and Japan.

Both floating and fixed exchange rate systems have been used in the past. The most economically powerful countries presently operate essentially on a floating system and have done so since 1973. Before that, starting shortly after World War II, a fixed exchange rate system governed international monetary relations. We will discuss the historical evolution of the international monetary system later in the chapter.

MACROECONOMIC POLICY, EXCHANGE RATES, AND TRADE BALANCE

Foreign trade can have dramatic effects on a government's macroeconomic policy. We consider briefly how monetary policy and fiscal policy are affected by foreign trade.

Monetary Policy

The link between the foreign exchange market and monetary policy depends on whether trade takes place under a system of fixed or floating exchange rates. In the former case, the central bank fixes the exchange rate and allows the money supply to be determined by the economic system; in the latter case, the central bank lets the exchange rate be determined in the market for foreign exchange and manipulates the domestic supply of money.

The Case of Fixed Exchange Rates   To support a fixed exchange rate, the central bank must be prepared to buy and sell whatever foreign exchange is necessary to keep the exchange rate at the fixed level. Suppose that there is a surplus in the balance of trade: At the current exchange rate, the quantity of foreign exchange supplied by exporters exceeds the amount of foreign exchange demanded by importers. In this case, the central bank must purchase foreign exchange by an amount equal to the excess supply to eliminate the tendency for the exchange rate to fall. The central bank purchases foreign exchange by printing more domestic currency, and this increase in the supply of money sets forces in motion that tend to restore equilibrium. Other things being equal, domestic prices rise with a larger money supply, and these higher prices will discourage exports and encourage imports, thus diminishing the trade surplus. In the case of a trade deficit, the central bank will be selling foreign exchange (in effect decreasing domestic currency) to keep the exchange rate from rising. This action will lower the domestic money supply, and the accompanying lower domestic prices will tend to discourage imports and encourage exports. The important point is that to fix one price—the exchange rate—the central bank must give up other money supply controls and allow all other prices to adjust. (The fixed exchange rate system operates like the old gold standard, which is described in the Focus "Should We Return to a Gold Standard?")

The Case of Flexible Exchange Rates   If the government is using a flexible exchange rate system, the central bank can use its domestic monetary policy tools, allowing the exchange rate to be determined by the market. Starting from equilibrium, an increase in the domestic money supply tends to raise prices, and these higher prices tend to encourage imports and discourage exports. Thus, there is a trade deficit (an excess demand for foreign exchange) at the old exchange rate. For individuals to be willing to supply the extra foreign exchange to finance these trade movements, the exchange rate must rise by whatever amount is necessary to eliminate the excess demand. The result of an increase in the domestic money supply is therefore a rise in the exchange rate by exactly the same proportion.

FOCUS

Should We Return to a Gold Standard?

The relatively high inflation rates experienced by the United States during the late 1970s and early 1980s led to a variety of proposals for a return to a gold standard. Proponents of the gold standard argued that linking the nominal money supply to gold would prevent large increases and decreases in the money supply that lead to inflations and deflations. Congress established a U.S. Gold Commission to study the question, and the members not only debated the desirability of again tying the dollar to gold but also considered how to implement a new gold standard.

Proponents of a return to the gold standard argue that the Federal Reserve has neither the willingness nor the ability to follow monetary policies that promote price stability and that some constraint on excessive monetary expansionism is necessary. What are the advantages and disadvantages of gold-backed dollars?

Under a gold standard, currency is freely convertible into gold at some fixed rate, such as $35 per ounce, which was for many years the official U.S. price of gold. Thus, a nation's currency supply is directly related to its supply of gold. The supply of currency can be expanded relative to the supply of gold only by devaluing the dollar in terms of gold—that is, by raising gold's dollar price. A gold standard therefore enforces monetary discipline. In the absence of devaluation, the currency supply can be increased only at a rate equal to the increase in the output of gold, an expansion that has occurred historically at about 1.5 to 2 percent annually. Such a

monetary policy would foster price stability with little or no inflation in the economy.

There are several major drawbacks to a gold standard. Real resources are tied up in money production—gold must be mined, stored, and transported. Also, the supply of gold is relatively inelastic. Expansion in the demand for money as economic growth occurs will generate downward pressure on the general price level. If the supply of gold rises more slowly than the demand, a gold standard will bring about persistent deflation. Discovery of new gold sources or improvements in the technology used to extract gold from existing mines would likely bring about rapid inflation.

Despite the problems, some economists point to the enormous success of a gold standard in promoting sound money and economic growth. It would be difficult to imagine bigger economic success stories than Great Britain between 1717 and 1914 or the United States between 1834 and 1914. Both nations were on the gold standard over these periods (except for brief wartime interludes).

In the United States, the Federal Reserve System has amply demonstrated its willingness to gradually reduce the inflation rate during the 1980s and 1990s. This would appear to take some of the steam out of the argument for a return to the gold standard. But gold standard advocates point out that the Fed's work could easily be undone at any time with a greater degree of political participation in directing the decisions of the U.S. central bank.

Fiscal Policy

The effects of a government's fiscal policy initiatives on exchange rates depend largely on how the changes in government spending are financed. If we assume, for simplicity, that all increases in government expenditures are financed by borrowing, then expansionary fiscal policies stimulate aggregate demand, including the demand for imports on the one hand, and raise government borrowing on the other. The increased demand puts upward pressure on the exchange rate because of the additional foreign currencies required to finance the increased imports. But the increased government borrowing tends to raise interest rates, attracting foreign capital and placing downward pressure on the exchange rate. The net change in the exchange rate resulting from the expansionary policy depends on which of the two effects dominates.

Similarly, contractionary fiscal policies may raise or lower the exchange rate. A lower level of government spending will reduce aggregate demand, reduce the demand for imports, and, at the same time, lower government borrowing. The lower import demand will tend to lower the exchange rate by fostering an excess supply of foreign currencies. But with less government borrowing, interest rates tend to fall. Capital outflows increase, putting upward pressure on exchange rates. Again, the net change of the exchange rate depends on which event—the fall-off in imports or the decline in interest rates—has greater effect.

THE BALANCE OF PAYMENTS

Balance of payments

An official accounting record of all the foreign transactions of a nation's residents, businesses, and governments.

Countries keep track of the flow of international trade and periodically publish a report of their transactions, called the **balance of payments.** The balance of payments is essentially an accounting record of a nation's foreign business. It contains information about the level of exports, imports, foreign investment, and the transactions of government such as purchases and sales of foreign currencies.

The balance of payments, as an accounting statement, is kept according to the principles of double-entry bookkeeping. The concept of double-entry bookkeeping is simple: Each entry on the credit side of the ledger implies an equal entry on the debit side. Thus, each international transaction creates both a debit (–) and a credit (+) item in the balance of payments ledger.

There is a simple rule to follow in classifying debits and credits: Any foreign transaction that leads to a demand for foreign currencies (or a supply of dollars) is treated as a debit, or a minus, item. The act of importing is a debit entry in the balance of payments. Any foreign transaction that leads to a demand for dollars (or a supply of foreign currency) is entered as a credit, or a plus, item. The act of exporting is a credit entry in the balance of payments.

Suppose that a U.S. firm exports computers to France, and the French importer of the computers pays for the purchase with an IOU. The French IOU is entered on the credit side in U.S. balance of payments bookkeeping because the French importer must ultimately demand dollars to pay off its IOU to the U.S. firm. The sale of computers is entered on the debit side as the offsetting part of the transaction. The U.S. firm must give up a computer in return for the French importer's payment. Since each transaction implies an equal debit and credit, the balance of payments must always balance. In this respect, the balance of payment is like any other accounting balance sheet.

Of course, although the total balance of payments of a country must always balance (debits minus credits equal zero), its component parts need not balance. For example, the imports and exports of specific merchandise such as automobiles do not have to balance. But overall, surpluses in one part of the balance of payments must be canceled out by deficits in other parts. This is not to say, of course, that countries do not experience balance of payments problems. Problems arise, as we will see, from persistent surpluses or deficits in the component parts of the balance of payments.

Exports and Imports: The Balance of Trade

Table 31.1 presents the data on the U.S. balance of payments for 1997. Items 1 and 2 represent exports and imports of goods and services. The difference between the sums of these aspects of the balance of payments—exports contrasted with imports—is the balance of trade. Note that trade in merchandise is only one facet of this balance. Merchandise trade figures are the result of a country's international trade in physical goods, such as books, cars, planes, and computers—the visible exports and imports. The data in Table 31.1 show that in 1997 merchandise exports (1a) were less than merchandise imports (2a) by

TABLE 31.1

U.S. Balance of Payments, 1997

U.S. exports enter the balance of payments with plus signs because buyers of these exports must pay U.S. firms with dollars. Dollars thus flow into the United States and are recorded as a plus, or credit, in the balance of payments. U.S. imports receive a minus sign, indicating that to pay for foreign goods U.S. buyers must supply dollars to foreign countries. Dollars thus flow out of the United States, and imports are then treated as a minus, or a debit, in the balance of payments. Similarly, outflows of U.S. capital and inflows of foreign capital are treated as debits and credits, respectively. To classify an item as a debit or a credit, think of whether dollars are leaving or entering the country. If they are leaving, the item is a debit; if they are entering, the item is a credit.

Item		Amount (billions of dollars)
1. Exports of goods and services		1179
a. Merchandise, excluding military	679	
b. Services and other	500	
2. Imports of goods and services		-1295
a. Merchandise, excluding military	-877	
b. Services and other	-418	
3. Unilateral transfers		-37
4. U.S. assets abroad, net (capital outflow)		-479
5. Foreign assets in U.S., net (capital inflow)		733
6. Statistical discrepancy		-100
7. Total		0

Source: U.S. Bureau of the Census, *Statistical Abstract of the United States, 1998* (Washington, D.C.: U.S. Government Printing Office, 1998), pp. 786–787.

$198 billion. This figure is sometimes called the merchandise trade balance and is equal to merchandise exports minus merchandise imports. If the figure is positive, there is a merchandise trade surplus. It was negative in 1997, so there was a merchandise trade deficit.

Many imports and exports are invisible. U.S. citizens and firms supply various services to foreigners, such as transportation, insurance, and telecommunications. Payments are received for these services just as in the case of visible exports. Items 1b and 2b represent invisible exports and imports in the balance of payments. When both visible and invisible exports and imports are considered in Table 31.1, U.S. exports were still substantially less than U.S. imports, yielding a trade deficit of $116 billion.

Net Transfers Abroad

Net unilateral transfers abroad are one-way money payments from the United States to foreigners or United States citizens living abroad. Included in this category are such items as foreign aid and pension checks to retired U.S. citizens living abroad. Nothing tangible comes back to the United States for these transfers, but they do give rise to a demand for foreign exchange. They thus are entered as a debit item in the balance of payments. In 1997, the United States made $37 billion worth of such transfers.

Current Account Balance

The balance on current account is equal to exports of goods and services minus imports of goods and services minus net unilateral transfers abroad. The United States had a deficit on current account in 1997 of $153 billion.

Net Capital Movements

When U.S. residents purchase foreign stocks and bonds, they obtain a claim to foreign capital (buildings, factories, future foreign government payments, and so forth). Funds that would otherwise be invested in the United States are exported, or, to put it another way, capital is exported. When foreign citizens purchase the stocks and bonds of U.S. businesses and governments, foreign capital is imported into the United States. In 1997 capital outflows were $479 billion, whereas capital inflows were $733 billion.

Note what happens in bookkeeping terms when capital flows into and out of a country. Capital outflows are treated as a debit item in the balance of payments because they constitute a payment; they give rise to a demand for foreign exchange with which to make foreign investment. Capital inflows are a credit item because they consist of receipts by U.S. residents from foreigners; they generate a supply of foreign exchange necessary to obtain dollars with which to purchase U.S. financial assets.

Statistical Discrepancy

Item 6 in Table 31.1 is called statistical discrepancy, an accounting fudge factor. When all the data were collected and debits and credits computed, the credits outweighed the debits by $100 billion. The negative statistical discrepancy is added to make the balance of payments balance by compensating for imperfections in data gathering. (Some debits have apparently gone unrecorded in computing the balance of payments. These could include hidden imports or unrecorded capital outflows. Most experts think that the former is the source of most of the discrepancy, which can be quite large.)

The Balance of Payments and the Value of the Dollar

The last entry in Table 31.1 is zero, indicating that the balance of payments must balance. This is the way any double-entry accounting system works. The balance of payments, however, is an aggregate record of a country's international payments for one year. Behind this record are the myriad transactions of U.S. citizens and firms with foreign citizens and firms. These transactions determine how the U.S. dollar fares in the foreign exchange market.

THE EVOLUTION OF INTERNATIONAL MONETARY INSTITUTIONS

Major world trading nations today rely on floating exchange rates. These governments will occasionally intervene in the foreign exchange market when exchange rate changes are significant, but generally currency prices are free to adjust according to the forces of supply and demand. We briefly review the developments over the past hundred years that led the major trading nations to adopt floating exchange rates in 1973.

The Decline of the Gold Standard

Gold standard
An international monetary system in which currencies are redeemable in gold at fixed rates or prices.

In the period before World War I, dating back to the 1870s, most currencies in the world economy were tied to gold. This means that each country was prepared to redeem its currency at a fixed price in gold to both its own citizens and foreigners. The United States, for example, stood ready to exchange an ounce of gold for $20.67 over this period. In addition, countries on the **gold standard** linked their money supplies to their holdings of gold bullion.

The gold standard worked reasonably well in eliminating balance of trade surpluses and deficits over the period 1870–1914. Nonetheless, for a variety of reasons the gold standard broke down after World War I. There were attempts to return to the gold standard in the 1920s, but the shock to the international economy caused by the Great Depression in the 1930s brought the gold system down once and for all.

Bretton Woods and the Postwar System

Bretton Woods System
The fixed exchange rate system established among Western countries after World War II.

Not until after World War II were the problems of the international monetary system addressed in a concerted way. Negotiators for the free-world countries met in Bretton Woods, New Hampshire, in 1944 to develop a new international monetary order. The **Bretton Woods System,** which was in place for almost thirty years, was

International Monetary Fund (IMF)

An international organization, established along with the Bretton Woods system, designed to assist in the efficient functioning of the Bretton Woods fixed exchange rate system.

characterized by fixed exchange rates and an international central bank, called the **International Monetary Fund (IMF),** to oversee the new system.

We have already discussed the economics of fixed exchange rates. The basic idea of the Bretton Woods system was that, over time, countries would obtain or pay for their imports with their exports. There might be temporary periods over which a country might wish to run a trade deficit to obtain more imports than its current level of exports allowed it to obtain. Under the Bretton Woods system, it could do so by borrowing international reserves from the IMF. Over time, the country was expected to return to a trade surplus and pay back the earlier loan of reserves.

The IMF was the bank that held the reserves that allowed the system to operate in this way. When the IMF was formed, each member country was required to contribute reserves of its currency to the bank. The bank thus accumulated substantial holdings of dollars, marks, francs, pesos, and so on, and when member nations ran into balance of trade deficits, the bank would lend them reserves. Each time a loan was made, the debtor nation was encouraged to reform its economic policies to avoid future deficits. Sound economic management might also lead to a trade surplus and a source of funds to repay the IMF loan.

The Bretton Woods system sounds fine in principle, and indeed it functioned tolerably well for a number of years. However, as we saw earlier, fixing the price of a currency is like fixing the price of any other good or service—it is very likely to cause surpluses and shortages in the market. As the conditions affecting imports and exports across countries change, the demand and supply of currencies will shift. Countries can find themselves with overvalued fixed exchange rates, which means that they will face persistent balance of trade deficits. Under the IMF system, the deficit country could draw on its IMF reserves to settle the deficits, but it could not do this forever because it would exhaust its reserves. Chronic deficit countries with overvalued exchange rates were thus said to be in fundamental disequilibrium.

In our discussion of the theory of fixed exchange rates, we reviewed the various courses of action that a country in fundamental disequilibrium could take. First, it could devalue its currency as a step toward restoring equilibrium in its balance of trade. Once its currency was devalued, the exchange rate would again be fixed and defended. Second, the country could attempt to improve its trade balance by imposing tariff and quota barriers to imports and perhaps by subsidizing exports. In other words, the country could move away from free trade to balance its imports and exports. Third, the country could behave as if it were on the gold standard. This would mean adopting restrictive monetary and fiscal policies designed to promote domestic deflation and high interest rates in the hope that such changes would restore the balance of trade to equilibrium. This, of course, is a problematic course of action for any country. For example, if the country's unemployment rate were already high, it is hard to believe that the nation's leaders would be sufficiently disciplined to undertake a deflationary course of action.

Speculation

The buying and selling of currencies on the foreign exchange market with the intent of profiting from possible devaluation or revaluation in a fixed-rate system or from possible future movements in the exchange rate in a flexible-rate system.

Speculation by buyers and sellers of currencies also undermines a fixed exchange rate system. Suppose Great Britain is running chronic trade deficits, and everyone, including speculators, expects that the pound will be devalued (even though British central bankers will deny such rumors vehemently). In effect, speculators are in a no-lose position. Will they continue to hold pounds? Clearly, they will not; pounds are about to become less valuable relative to other currencies. Speculators will sell their pounds for other currencies, increasing the supply of pounds to the foreign exchange market and putting additional downward pressure on the pound. By selling the weak currency and buying a strong currency, speculators make it difficult for authorities to find a new fixed value for the pound. This is why speculation in a fixed exchange rate system is often termed destabilizing.

In the early period of the Bretton Woods system, the United States ran a large trade deficit, and this deficit provided a means of supplying dollar reserves to the rest of the world. It was thought that this deficit was a temporary problem that would soon be replaced by a U.S. trade surplus. This was the premise of the Bretton Woods system. Yet the dollar was overvalued, and the U.S. deficits continued and grew larger into the 1950s and 1960s. The United States was in a difficult position. It was hard for it to devalue the dollar because the dollar was held by virtually every nation as an international reserve asset. A U.S. devaluation would have decreased the wealth of all those countries holding dollars. Several times, the United States tried to impose a restrictive macroeconomic policy to correct its balance of trade. However, when unemployment rose as a consequence, such policies were rapidly abandoned, as political pressures were brought to bear on policy-makers. U.S. deficits continued to grow, and foreign holdings of dollars rose.

Speculators entered again. Many holders of dollars became concerned about what the United States was going to do. There were various runs on the U.S. gold stock, as dollars were traded in by foreigners. In 1950, the United States had 509 million ounces of gold; by 1968, this stock had fallen to 296 million ounces. Confidence in the dollar fell further, and the stage was set for a drastic change in the international monetary system.

The Current International Monetary System

The present international monetary system was born in 1971. In the face of continuing large trade deficits and mounting speculation against the dollar, President Nixon broke the link between the dollar and gold in August 1971. No longer would the United States stand ready to exchange gold for dollars at $35 an ounce. In effect, the dollar was set free to fluctuate and seek its own level in the foreign exchange market. As a result, the overvalued dollar depreciated substantially against other major currencies. There were interim attempts to fix the price of the dollar again, but they failed. By early 1973, all the major currencies were floating.

The international monetary system that has been in effect since 1973 is a managed flexible-rate system. Exchange rates are allowed to seek their free market values, as long as fluctuations are within an acceptable range. If fluctuations fall outside this range, governments may intervene with their reserve holdings to dampen the fluctuations in their currencies. Thus, exchange rates are not completely free; government intervention in the foreign exchange market will be forthcoming if a country's currency falls dramatically in value. In 1978, for example, the dollar fell sharply, and the Carter administration intervened to restrict this decline with international reserves and loans from West Germany and Japan. The central banks of major trading countries also have stepped up intervention activity since September of 1985. It should be remembered, though, that under the managed flexible-rate system, the ranges within which governments consider exchange rate fluctuations acceptable are not well defined as a matter of policy. As a result, it is difficult to tell how far a nation's currency would have to appreciate or depreciate before central bank interventions would occur.

Although the new system abandoned fixed exchange rates, it did not abandon the IMF, which still exists as an international monetary organization. The role of the IMF under the managed flexible-rate system is still evolving, and to this point it has consisted of helping countries that have persistent balance of payments problems by giving them loans and policy advice about how to conduct domestic macroeconomic policy to overcome these problems. The World Bank, which is part of the IMF system set up by the Bretton Woods agreement, has also played an increasing role in the new system. This sister institution of the IMF makes long-run development loans to poor countries. The whole system came under close scrutiny when the Asian financial structure was mortally threatened in 1997. The financial "meltdown" in Asia created worldwide financial problems (see the Application "The Asian Economic Crisis" at the end of this chapter).

Advantages of the Current System   Despite the recent crisis, the consensus view seems to be that the new system has worked very well under difficult circumstances. The following are the major advantages of the flexible-rate system.

1. It allows countries to pursue independent monetary policies. If a country wants to inflate its economy, it can do so by letting its exchange rate depreciate, thereby maintaining its position in international markets without sacrificing its preferred monetary policy.

2. Under the fixed-rate system, a country sometimes had to deflate its economy to solve a balance of trade deficit. With floating rates it only has to let its exchange rate depreciate. Clearly, it is easier to change one price than to change all prices to resolve balance of trade difficulties.

3. The current exchange rate system has proven capable of handling large economic disturbances. When the OPEC countries dramatically raised the price of oil in 1973–1974, the world economy experienced a tremendous shock. The greatest achievement of the flexible-rate system is the way it handled this shock. Oil-importing countries developed large trade deficits; huge trade surpluses built up in OPEC countries. These deficits and surpluses were accommodated by floating rates. Moreover, the huge oil revenues of the OPEC countries were recycled into Western investments. Though exchange rates changed significantly over the period, the new system weathered the storm and got the job done.

Disadvantages of the Current System   The flexible-rate system is not, however, without its critics. Some of the major disadvantages of the current system are discussed in this section.

1. Some observers point out that flexible rates can be very volatile, and this volatility creates considerable uncertainty for international trade. Thus, exchange rate flexibility leads to conditions that can retard the amount of international trade and therefore the degree of specialization in the world economy.

2. A second criticism of floating rates is that they promote increased world inflation rates. Under a fixed-rate system, countries experience a balance of trade deficit if they inflate their respective economies. This link is severed under a flexible-rate system. Hence, domestic political authorities can more easily give in to interests that benefit from inflation.

3. Some countries that have relied primarily on adjustments in exchange rates to resolve trade imbalance problems have found that the solution has been a long time in coming. For example, despite depreciation of the dollar, the U.S. trade deficit with Japan has persisted for years, causing some observers to conclude that dollar depreciation never will solve the problem.

In sum, there are pros and cons with respect to the present international monetary system, but in general the system seems to have worked well over a difficult period in the international economy. Growing problems in the international payments system, however, call for the prospect of further reform of the system.

APPLICATION

The Asian Economic Crisis

In January 1997, a Korean steel conglomerate collapsed, unable to make payments on its heavy debt. In February, a company in Thailand missed its foreign debt payments, and in March another Korean steel conglomerate failed. At the time, the International Monetary Fund (IMF) was confidently proclaiming that there was no reason for the crisis to develop any further. Looking back, we can see clearly now that these were the first signs of the economic crisis in Asia that would devastate local economies, cause violence and political upheaval, and spread economic woes throughout the world.

The summer of 1997 was one of currency meltdown. In Thailand, the Philippines, Malaysia, and Indonesia, the value of currency declined as traders in international monetary markets sold the declining currencies. Local leaders blamed international speculators, such as George Soros, for their problems. Hong Kong, Singapore, and Vietnam all took steps to help stabilize their currencies. Thailand called on the help of the IMF and agreed to financial reforms and budget austerity measures in exchange for a $16 billion bailout package.

As the economic troubles spread throughout Asia and began to have economic ramifications around the globe, violence erupted in Indonesia in May of 1998 in conjunction with the collapse of the long-ruling Suharto regime. Citizens protested and rioted, and the military was called upon to restore order. This social upheaval was the result of the combination of growing unemployment and the skyrocketing prices that resulted from the downfall of the currency. The effect was to further undermine confidence in the currencies and economies of the region.

As the region sank into economic depression and with the regional economic powerhouse, Japan, already stuck in a long recession, Asia began spreading economic problems throughout the world. (Some analysts called it the "Asian contagion.") Asia imports a great deal of food, fuel, and raw materials from around the world to feed its populations and factories. When incomes and production declined, world markets were affected. Agricultural exports from Argentina, Australia, Canada, and New Zealand were all affected by lower prices and less demand for their exports. Oil and mineral exporters such as Chile, Ecuador, Mexico, Peru, Russia, and Venezuela all suffered greatly from lower prices for oil and minerals, their main source of foreign exchange earnings. Stock markets in all these countries fell sharply while unemployment grew. In the United States, certain sectors of the economy such as farming and steel were affected, but falling import prices and expanding technology cushioned the blow to the macroeconomy, and unemployment remained at record low levels. Foreigners were holding dollars and investing in U.S. stock markets, keeping the value of the dollar strong and stock prices firm.

The Asian world had been turned upside down. For the last quarter century, eastern Asia had been the fastest growing region of the world and had gone through an industrial revolution. Led by Japan, the "Pacific Rim" countries such as South Korea, Taiwan, Thailand, Malaysia, Indonesia, Hong Kong, Singapore, the Philippines, and, most recently, Vietnam were considered models of economic development. They were often labeled the "Asian Tigers" because their economic growth and prosperity seemed unstoppable. In fact, income growth was much more rapid in Asia than during previous "industrial revolutions" (see Table 31.2).

What caused this crisis? Most of the traditional causes of financial debacle, such as high inflation, budget deficits, slow growth, and low savings rates were not present. Indeed, the Asian Tigers had a remarkable record of "managing" their

TABLE 31.2

Industrial Revolutions and How Long It Took to Double Income

It took industrial revolutions in the United Kingdom and the United States nearly half a century to double per capita income, but it took South Korea and China only about a decade to achieve the same result.

Country	Beginning of Industrial Revolution	Number of Years to Double Income
United Kingdom	1780	58
United States	1839	47
Japan	1885	35
South Korea	1966	11
China	1977	10

Source: Council of Economic Advisers, *Economic Report of the President* (Washington, D.C.: U.S. Government Printing Office, 1999), p. 227.

macroeconomies. Upon closer examination, this "management" turned out to be "crony capitalism" in which corruption was a major factor in how resources, specifically loans and credits, were allocated. Major companies were granted virtually unlimited credit on favorable terms, were provided with lucrative government contracts, and received special privileges from their governments.

The expansion of credit led to a construction and real estate boom throughout the region. Stock markets rose, but so did debt. Companies were highly leveraged, and as the amount of fixed capital grew, the return on capital shrank and turned negative as the currency crisis and depression hit. The Asian crisis and its "contagion" is a classic case of a rapid and artificial expansion of credit and bad investment that eventually leads to the pain of bankruptcy, liquidation, and even social upheaval.

QUESTIONS

In addition to Thailand, the IMF has provided large bailout packages of loans and guarantees to countries like Mexico, Russia, and Yugoslavia. What effects do these bailouts have? Do you think they encourage countries to act more or less financially responsible?

SUMMARY

1. Foreign exchange is the currency of another country that is needed to make payment in an international transaction.

2. Foreign exchange can be obtained in the worldwide foreign exchange market. The demand for foreign exchange arises from the desire to buy foreign goods. The supply of foreign exchange arises from the desire of citizens of one country to buy the goods of another country.

3. A foreign exchange rate is the price of one currency in terms of another. A currency's value appreciates when its purchasing power in terms of other currencies rises. It depreciates when its purchasing power falls.

4. The demand for foreign currency depends largely on income and relative price levels in the trading countries.

5. Under a floating, or flexible, exchange rate system, a country allows its exchange rate to be set by the forces of supply and demand in the foreign exchange market. Flexible exchange rates change in response to changes in countries' money supplies, price levels, inflation rates, real interest rates, and fundamental factors such as technology, consumer rates, and government export and import policies. Under a flexible-rate system, exchange rate movements act to alleviate balance of trade surpluses and deficits.

6. Under a fixed exchange rate system, governments intervene in the foreign exchange market to set and defend the value of their currency. When a country's currency is overvalued relative to the equilibrium rate, the country will run a balance of trade deficit. It can seek to cure this deficit by deflating the domestic economy, establishing trade barriers, or devaluing its currency to a new, lower, fixed rate of exchange. When the fixed exchange rate is below its equilibrium value, a country will experience a balance of trade surplus and will sometimes revalue its currency upward.

7. An important difference between floating- and fixed-rate systems is that the former changes one price to maintain equilibrium in the balance of

trade, while the latter changes all prices in the economy to maintain a fixed exchange rate.

8. The balance of payments is a record of the international transactions of a country's economy. It follows the principles of double-entry bookkeeping and must therefore always balance in an accounting sense. Transactions that give rise to a demand for foreign exchange are entered as debits; transactions that give rise to a supply of foreign exchange are treated as credits.

9. The modern history of the international monetary system began with the gold standard, followed by a system of fixed exchange rates managed by the International Monetary Fund. The present international monetary system is a managed floating-rate system. Exchange rates are set by supply and demand, but governments can and have intervened if exchange rate movements are too large.

KEY TERMS

foreign exchange
foreign exchange markets
exchange rate
flexible (floating) exchange
   rate system
fixed exchange rate system
managed flexible-rate system
depreciation

appreciation
undervalued
overvalued
foreign exchange market
   intervention
foreign exchange reserves
balance of trade surplus
balance of trade deficit

devaluation
revaluation
balance of payments
gold standard
Bretton Woods System
International Monetary Fund
   (IMF)
speculation

QUESTIONS FOR REVIEW AND DISCUSSION

1. Suppose that the British pound is worth $1.50, and that $1 is worth about 6.5 Swedish krona. How much would a Jaguar automobile cost in U.S. dollars if the British price is 20,000 pounds? How much would a Volvo cost in U.S. dollars if the Swedish price is 84,000 krona?

2. Suppose that the United States and Sweden are on a floating exchange rate system. Explain whether the following events would cause the Swedish krona to appreciate or depreciate.

a. U.S. interest rates rise above Swedish interest rates.

b. American tourism to Sweden increases.

c. Americans fall in love with a newly designed Volvo, and Volvo sales in the United States skyrocket.

d. The U.S. government puts a quota on Volvo imports.

e. The Swedish inflation rate rises relative to the U.S. rate.

f. The United States closes a military installation in Sweden at the urging of the Swedish government.

3. How would you treat the following items in the balance of payments? In other words, would you enter them as debits or credits?

a. An American travels to Canada.

b. A U.S. wine importer buys wine from Italy.

c. A California wine grower sells wine to England.

d. An Austrian corporation pays dividends to American stockholders.

e. General Motors pays dividends to French investors.

f. Several Japanese visit Hawaii on an American cruise ship.

g. A Swedish citizen invests in a U.S. company based in Houston.

4. Explain why capital inflows are a credit entry in the balance of payments and capital outflows are a debit entry.

5. When we say that the fixed exchange rate system requires that all prices but one be changed to overcome a balance of trade deficit, what do we mean?

6. What are the primary advantages and disadvantages of the present international monetary system?

7. Use the following exchange rate tables to answer the questions:

U.S. DOLLAR PER CURRENCY UNIT

	Thursday	Wednesday
Swiss franc	0.7978	0.8003
Italian lira	0.0006480	0.0006474

CURRENCY PER U.S. DOLLAR

	Thursday	Wednesday
Swiss franc	1.2535	1.2495
Italian lira	1543.30	1544.55

a. Did the Swiss franc rise or fall from Wednesday to Thursday?

b. Did the Italian lira rise or fall from Wednesday to Thursday?

c. What happened to the dollar value of the franc?

d. What happened to the dollar value of the lira?

PROBLEM

What happens to the floating exchange rate of a country that has a higher inflation rate than other countries? Show your answer graphically.

WORKING WITH THE WEB

1. Go to the Virtual Economy web site at http://ve.ifs.org.uk. Find the link to "4th Floor, The Model" near the bottom of the page. On the next screen, click on the link "Selected variables form." This site allows you to determine the impact on the U.K. economy from general changes in fiscal policy. Make any changes mentioned below, and then submit those changes by clicking on the "Run Model" button.

   a. What is the effect on the current account ratio and exchange rate from raising the Basic (Income) Tax Rate from £23 per year to £30 per year?

   b. Explain the reason for the changes you described above.

2. Locate the paper entitled "The Crisis in Emerging Financial Markets" by going to the Brookings Institution home page at http://www.brook.edu. After doing a search with the phrase "crisis in emerging financial markets," click on the appropriate link (the web address of this paper should be http://www.brook.edu/pa/conferencereport/cr3/cr3.htm).

   An interesting alternative site houses a video lecture series that addresses this question as well. Go to the Center for Economic Studies home-page at http://www.lrz-muenchen.de/~ces and click on "Video Lectures." Ruediger Dornbusch's lecture is particularly good (to view the lecture you will need to download the program Windows Media Player, which is available at the bottom of the page).

   How did capital mobility play a role in the Asian financial crisis?

3. The IMF was involved in bailing out the economies of Russia, Mexico, and various Asian nations during the 1990s. Go to the Hoover Institution's homepage at http://www-hoover.stanford.edu and do a word search with the phrase "Adios IMF." You should see a link entitled "Uncommon Knowledge, show #320" (alternatively, you can select the link on the initial homepage for "Uncommon Knowledge" and locate show #320).

   When reading the article (note that you can also view it or listen, using the appropriate software), you will find that the discussants take issue with IMF bailouts.

   In terms of how these bailouts affect the risk and return associated with investing in these nations, how might these bailouts affect future capital flows to countries like Mexico?

Peter Tamas Bauer

P. T. Bauer
and Gunnar
Myrdal:
Third World
Development
and Trade

Gunnar Myrdal

P eter Tamas Bauer (b. 1915) is a distinguished critic of development theory. Bauer's studies of the rubber industry and West African trade paved the way for his works on development—*Dissent on Development* (1972) and *Reality and Rhetoric: Studies in the Economics of Development* (1984). Bauer struck his central theme concerning economic development in earlier works: Economic growth, Bauer argued, is the product of voluntary responses and efficient domestic and international markets—not of state intervention or central planning by governments.

Born in Hungary, Bauer was a fellow of Gonville and Caius College at Cambridge (England) between 1946 and 1960 and again from 1968 to 1984. He was also professor of economics in the University of London at the London School of Economics from 1960 until his retirement in 1983. While in these academic posts, Bauer launched attacks on the conventional wisdom regarding economic development, including theories relating to the widening gap of income differences within and between countries, the vicious circle of poverty, the operation of marketing boards and commodity agreements in developing countries, and the operation of foreign aid. Principally, Bauer targeted the economic development theories of Gunnar Myrdal.

Gunnar Myrdal (1898–1987), sociologist and economist, was a joint recipient of the Nobel Memo-rial Prize in economics with Friedrich A. von Hayek in 1974. Myrdal is best known for his work on racial discrimination and social problems. His most famous work, *An American Dilemma: The Negro Problem and Modern Democracy,* began as a study commissioned by the Carnegie Corporation in 1938 and had an enor-mous impact on American attitudes toward integra-tion. His later works explored trade and economic development: *The Political Element in the Develop-ment of Economic Theory* (1935) focused on the philo-sophical foundations of classical free trade doctrine to the problems of economic development.

Myrdal was born in the Gustaf parish of Sweden. He studied law as an undergraduate at the University of Stockholm and received his Ph.D. in law from the university in 1927. In 1924, he married Alva Reimer, with whom he researched and wrote a study of Swe-den's decreasing population, which was published in 1934. After graduation, Myrdal taught economics, trav-eled abroad, and served the government of Sweden both as a representative of the Social Democratic party and as cabinet minister. In 1947, he was appointed executive secretary of the United Nations Economic Commission for Europe, a position he retained for the next ten years. In 1960, he became a professor of international economics at the University of Stockholm.

What Is the Problem?

Both Bauer and Myrdal pursued answers to timeless questions regarding the economic development of Third World nations. Does free trade promote or impede economic development in poor nations? Which is more conducive to economic growth and progress in developing nations—central planning or free markets? What is the nature and what are the effects of economic aid from industrialized nations to poor and developing nations of the world?

Bauer and Myrdal occupy opposite ends of the philosophical spectrum; they could not agree on what the problem of economic development is, much less any solution. Myrdal, for example, would center the investigation around the causes of poverty, while Bauer would have economists investigate the causes of prosperity and development. In other words, the burden of any theory of development is either to explain how certain nations and people got rich (Bauer) or why certain nations remained poor (Myrdal).

Not only are Myrdal and Bauer worlds apart on the definition of the problem of development, they stand apart on the philosophical nature of equality and power. Of great importance here is the concept of "equality," which both economists support, but in vastly different forms. As an important modern commentator on their views has remarked, "Whether Myrdal or Bauer is more in favor of equality depends entirely on whether equality is conceived as equality of economic results or equality of political process. Myrdal clearly believes more in equality of economic results—and Bauer equally clearly prefers equality of social processes."[a] In other words, the goal of economic development, in Myrdal's view, is to promote economic equality—similar levels of development and equitable income distributions—between rich and poor nations. Economic power exemplified by concentrations of monopoly power, Myrdal believed, is the root cause of inequalities. Bauer, on the other hand, believes that economic development requires that social processes and access to economic activity be open to all and be free and unfettered. In Bauer's view, power restricts the choices of others, most often exemplified by government planning and regulation.

The rich, according to Bauer, most often get that way by expanding the choices and opportunities of others.

Trade, Central Planning, and Economic Aid

Not surprisingly, the philosophical differences between Bauer and Myrdal show very different views of key elements in economic development. Here we consider only three of these key elements.

Trade

In Myrdal's view, the principle of comparative advantage and free trade works in favor of rich nations and keeps poor nations locked within a vicious cycle of poverty. The low saving rates of poor countries mean low investment, which means low economic growth, which means low savings, and so on. To Myrdal, trade with other countries does not unlock this vicious cycle. In *Rich Lands and Poor: The Road to World Prosperity* (1957), he writes, "The forces in the market tend to increase, rather than to decrease, the inequalities between regions." Myrdal points to the so-called banana republics, underdeveloped nations that specialize in one product. In Myrdal's view, such overspecialization leaves a country vulnerable to changes in demand and puts its economy in continuous peril. He suggests that tariffs and subsidies would provide the impetus for developing nations to diversify production and to reduce dependence on one or a few exports.

In Bauer's analysis of trade, these views are wrongheaded and counterproductive. In the first place, Bauer denies that there is a vicious cycle of poverty in underdeveloped countries. Saving and investment take place even where people are poor and illiterate. In his classic study of the rubber industry, Bauer showed that very rapid growth was possible as a consequence of voluntary responses by peasants to expanded opportunities and contacts of developed countries in the West.[b] Further, Bauer argued that

---

[a]Thomas Sowell, *A Conflict of Visions* (New York: William Morrow and Company, 1987), p. 159.

[b]A. A. Walters, "Peter Tamas Bauer," *The New Palgrave: A Dictionary of Economics,* edited by John Eatwell, Murray Milgate, and Peter Newman (London: The Macmillan Press Limited, 1987), vol. I, p. 207. For further information on Myrdal, see Paul Streeten, "Gunnar Myrdal," *The New Palgrave,* vol. III, pp. 581–583.

trade restrictions and attempts to substitute domestic production for goods that can be obtained more cheaply abroad were a certain path to welfare reductions and to lower growth and development. Development could be maximized only with free interaction between *all* trading nations.

Central Planning and Aid

Myrdal urged central planning as an extension of his belief that unequal distribution of power and property was the principal obstacle to equitable economic growth. Institutional planning, production goals, and price planning are all parts of the system that Myrdal urged on developing nations as prerequisites to growth and changing attitudes. He had faith that, with enough information and competent managers, planning would be superior to any other method of achieving growth and human development. Further, he believed the role of industrialized countries was to provide aid to poor nations.

Sentiments expressed by Bauer more than two decades ago have a very contemporary feel. Bauer pointed out then that planning, if it works at all, does not maximize an economy's opportunities. All investment undertaken for political motives is wasted. Bauer likewise criticized foreign aid as intergovernmental grants of taxpayers' money. While such aid augments resources in recipient countries, Bauer believes there is no reason to expect that, in the hands of politicians, bureaucrats, and administrators, it will be put to productive uses. With few exceptions, foreign aid promotes centralized and closely controlled economies (factors that choke growth), and it sometimes generates resentment and suspicion toward the donor.[c] Of far greater effect is aid provided on a commercial basis, direct foreign investment in developing nations, and—of ultimate importance in Bauer's view—free and open trade between rich nations and poor.

---

[c]For more on economic aid, see P. T. Bauer, *Dissent on Development: Studies and Debates in Development Economics* (Cambridge, Mass.: Harvard University Press, 1972), pp. 114–135.

GLOSSARY

A

accounting costs Actual money expenditures associated with any activity; payments a firm actually makes to resource suppliers; out-of-pocket costs or explicit costs.

accounting profit The amount by which total revenues exceed total accounting, or explicit, costs; total revenue minus total explicit payments for inputs or out-of-pocket costs.

adjusted income An individual's income after all taxes and all government transfer payments are accounted for.

advertising Any communication or information that firms offer consumers to increase demand for a product.

aggregate supply of land The total amount of land available for use by the entire economy.

allocative efficiency A situation in which the socially optimal amount of a good or service is produced in an industry; the socially optimal amount depends on the tastes and preferences of society and on the opportunity cost of the resources used to produce the good or service.

antitrust policies Regulations established by laws and government agencies that attempt to preserve business competition.

appreciation An increase in the equilibrium exchange market value of a country's currency in a flexible-rate system; a decrease in the number of units of a country's money required to purchase one unit of a foreign country's money.

arc elasticity A measure of the average elasticity between two points on the demand curve.

artificial barriers to trade Restrictions created by the government that inhibit or prevent trade; includes import quotas and tariffs.

asset income Earnings from interest on savings, from capital investments, and from land; all result from forgone consumption in the past.

average cost pricing A regulatory policy that causes a firm to charge a price equal to average cost, inducing the firm to produce an output such that economic profits are zero.

average fixed cost Total fixed costs divided by the level of output.

average product Total output divided by the number of units of the variable input used to produce the total output; output produced per unit of variable input used.

average total cost Total costs divided by the level of output.

average variable cost Total variable costs divided by the level of output.

B

backward induction The incentive each player has to cheat in the last period of the game; exists because there are no future periods left to play in which possible consequences from cheating could occur.

balance of payments An official accounting record of all the foreign transactions of a nation's residents, businesses, and governments.

balance of trade deficit Occurs when the value of a nation's exports is less than the value of a nation's imports; also called a trade deficit.

balance of trade surplus Occurs when the value of a nation's exports exceeds the value of a nation's imports; also called a trade surplus.

barter Direct exchange of one good or service for another without the use of money.

bilateral monopoly A market in which there is only one buyer and only one seller of a resource or product.

binding arbitration An agreement between the buyers and sellers of labor to allow a third party to determine the conditions of a work contract.

Bretton Woods system The fixed exchange rate system established among Western countries after World War II.

bureaus The arms of government that serve to implement and enforce legislation and to administer programs created by legislation.

C

capital consumption A decrease in the capital stock; occurs when the rate of depreciation is greater than the rate of capital formation.

capital formation An increase in the stock of capital due to roundabout production; the process whereby the stock of capital in an economy increases.

capital stock The amount of nonhuman resources available in the economy. These include tools, land, machinery, equipment, and so on; the total amount of capital goods that exists in an economy at any point in time.

capture, or interest group, theory of regulation Argues that regulations are constructed so as to further the interests of the existing firms within a particular industry.

cartel   An alliance of firms that act collusively to reduce output and increase price in an industry in order to increase profits.

cartel enforcement   Attempts by members of the cartel to prevent other members from cheating and thus destroying economic profit potential.

ceteris paribus   The Latin phrase for "all other things held constant."

change in demand   A shift of the entire demand curve to the right or left.

change in quantity demanded   A change in the amount of a good a consumer is willing and able to purchase that is caused by a change in the price of the good or service.

change in quantity supplied   A change in the amount of a good a producer is willing and able to produce and sell that is caused by a change in the price of the good or service.

change in supply   A shift of the entire supply curve to the right or left.

change in the demand for labor   A shift of the entire labor demand curve; caused by a change in the marginal product of labor, by a change in the demand for the product produced by the type of labor in question, or by a change in the price of some other factor of production.

cheating   The act of violating a collusive agreement; may result in an increase in short-run economic profits to the firm that cheats, followed by zero economic profits in the long run.

choices at the margin   Decisions based on the additional benefits and costs of small changes in a particular activity.

Coase theorem   States that the amount of an externality-generating activity will be the same regardless of the assignment of property rights if the bargaining costs are small.

collective bargaining   The process whereby buyers and sellers negotiate, rather than compete individually, in order to determine a wage rate.

common ownership   An arrangement whereby the property rights to a resource are nonexistent or poorly defined; by default, anyone may use or consume the resource.

comparative advantage   An economic entity's (an individual's or a nation's) ability to produce a good at a lower marginal opportunity cost than some other entity.

competition   A market which functions under two conditions—no collusion among sellers or buyers (which occurs with a large number of buyers and sellers) and freedom to enter and exit the market. Competition results in prices equal to the costs of production plus a normal profit for sellers.

competitive labor market   A labor market in which the wage rate is determined by the interactions of a large number of sellers (suppliers) of labor and a large number of demanders (buyers) of labor. Neither group acts in a collusive manner.

complementary inputs   Inputs with a relation such that increased usage of one input due to a fall in its price results in increased employment of the other(s).

complements   Products that are related such that an increase in the price of one will decrease the demand for the other or a decrease in the price of one will increase the demand for the other; two goods whose cross elasticity of demand is negative; $\varepsilon_c < 0$.

concentration ratios   A measure of the degree to which the largest firms in an industry account for total industry assets, sales, or some other factor.

constant returns to scale   As plant size either increases or decreases, long-run average total cost does not change.

constant-cost industry   An industry in which the minimum *LRATC* of production does not change as the number of firms in the industry changes; expansion (contraction) of the number of firms does not bid up (down) input

prices; long-run industry supply is horizontal.

constitutional decision making   The process of choosing which set of rules (voting rules, for example) society will adopt for its use.

consumer equilibrium   A situation in which a consumer chooses quantities of goods that maximize total utility given a budget constraint; equilibrium implies that the per-dollar marginal utility obtained from the last unit of each good consumed is equal for all goods.

consumer-initiated discrimination   Wage discrimination arising from consumers' preferences for goods or services produced by individuals of a certain sex, race, religion, or national origin. Consumers must pay a premium in the form of higher prices or lower quality to exercise such discrimination.

consumers' surplus   The difference between what consumers are willing to pay for a given quantity of a good or service (the total consumer valuation) and what they have to pay (their total expenditure).

consumption possibilities curve   All the possible combinations of two goods that could be consumed by first specializing according to comparative advantage and then trading at the terms of trade.

contestability   Characteristic of a market in which the entry of competitors is possible.

contrived scarcity   A situation in which a monopoly produces an output below what a competitive industry would produce; the contrived scarcity results in price and profits above competitive levels.

costs   An implication of scarcity; the necessary sacrifices associated with making any choice.

Cournot-Nash solution   The likely outcome of a one-shot game or a game with a known end point; in this case, both firms cheat, thus bringing profits below the joint profit-maximizing level.

craft union Workers with a common skill who organize to restrict the supply of labor in their trade and obtain some market power; also called a trade union.

cross elasticity of demand Measures buyers' relative responsiveness to a change in the price of one good in terms of the change in the quantity demanded of another good; the percent change in the quantity demanded of one good divided by the percent change in the price of another good.

D

decreasing-cost industry An industry in which the long-run industry supply is downward-sloping; expansion (contraction) of the number of firms bids down (up) input prices; minimum *LRATC* of production falls as the number of firms in the industry increases.

demand curve A graphic representation of the quantities of a product that people are willing and able to purchase at all possible prices.

demand elasticity coefficient The numerical representation of the price elasticity of demand: $\varepsilon_d = (\Delta Q/Q) \div (\Delta P/P)$.

demand for loanable funds A curve or schedule that shows the various amounts individuals are willing and able to borrow at different interest rates.

depreciation The wearing out of capital goods that occurs with usage over time; a decrease in the equilibrium exchange market value of a country's currency in a flexible-rate system; an increase in the number of units of a country's money required to purchase one unit of a foreign country's money.

deregulation The removal of some or all government regulations from a previously regulated industry in an effort to improve the allocation of resources.

derived demand The demand for factors of production that exists because of the demand for the products that the factors produce.

devaluation An official change in a country's exchange rate in a fixed-rate system; the number of units of a country's money that purchases one unit of another country's currency is increased by the government.

diamond-water paradox Adam Smith's belief that water and diamonds did not follow the same theory of value—a paradox confusing total and marginal utility that is unlocked by the principle of diminishing marginal utility.

differentiated product A product with features that make it distinct, in consumers' eyes, from close substitutes.

diseconomies of scale A situation in which, beyond a point, the long-run average total cost of producing output increases as plant size increases.

disposable personal income Personal income minus taxes; income available to spend.

dominant solution A situation in game theory in which each player has the same best choice no matter what course of action other players may choose.

dumping The selling of goods in foreign markets at prices lower than those charged in domestic markets.

dynamic efficiency A condition summarized in the idea that monopolies may, over time, be more innovative and efficient than competitive firms at developing new products and new production techniques.

E

economic efficiency The allocation of resources that allows maximum benefit to be achieved at minimum cost.

economic goods and services Goods and services that are scarce.

economic mobility The movement of individuals among income ranges.

economic profit The amount by which total revenues exceed total opportunity cost; total revenue minus total opportunity costs of production.

economic system The part of the social system determining what, how, and for whom goods and services are produced.

economic wage discrimination A situation in which individuals in the same occupation who have the same productive abilities are paid different wage rates by a given employer. The wage-rate differences are based on race, sex, religion, or national origin rather than on productive differences.

economic welfare The value society places on goods and services consumed.

economies of scale A situation in which long-run unit costs *(LRATC)* decline as plant output increases.

elastic demand A situation in which buyers are relatively responsive to price changes; the percent change in quantity demanded is greater than the percent change in price: $\varepsilon_d > 1$.

elasticity A measure of the relative responsiveness of one variable to a change in another variable; the percentage change in a dependent variable divided by the percentage change in the independent variable.

elasticity of supply A measure of producers' or workers' relative responsiveness to price or wage changes; the percent change in quantity supplied divided by the percent change in the price or wage rate.

entrepreneur An individual who perceives profit opportunities, organizes resources into productive ventures, and bears the uncertain status of residual claimant of the resulting risky economic outcome.

equilibrium price The price at which quantity demanded is equal to quantity supplied; other things being equal, there is no tendency for this price to change.

ex ante **distribution** The distribution of income before government transfer payments and taxes are accounted for.

ex post **distribution** The distribution of income after government transfer payments and taxes are accounted for.

excess capacity A situation in which industry output is not produced at minimum average total cost. The output actually produced is less than the output that would minimize average total cost.

exchange costs The opportunity costs of the resources used in making trades; includes transaction costs, transportation costs, and artificial barriers to trade.

exchange rate The (relative) price of one national currency in terms of another national currency.

explicit costs Accounting costs.

exploitation of labor A situation in which the wage rate paid to an input is less than the input's marginal revenue product.

externality Benefits or costs of an individual's activity that the individual does not receive or bear.

F

factor market A market in which the prices of productive resources (factors of production, or inputs) are determined by the interaction of firms acting as buyers with households and firms acting as suppliers of resources.

factors affecting demand Anything other than price, such as consumer income and preferences, that determines the amount of a product or service that consumers are willing and able to purchase.

factors affecting supply Anything other than price, such as technology or input costs, that determines the amount of a product or service that sellers are willing and able to offer for sale.

family income The total of all incomes from all sources except

transfers received by members of a household.

firm An economic institution that purchases, organizes, and assembles resources to produce goods and services.

firm coordination The process that directs the flow of resources into the production of a particular good or service through the forces of management organization within the firm.

firm's long-run demand for labor The relationship between all possible wage rates and quantities demanded of labor at those wage rates, given that the firm has enough time to vary the usage of all inputs.

fixed costs The costs of inputs that cannot be varied in the short run.

fixed exchange rate system An international monetary arrangement in which exchange rates are set by the government, which then must intervene in the foreign exchange market in order to maintain the pegged exchange rate.

fixed input A factor of production whose level of usage cannot be changed in the short run.

fixed plant A given amount of equipment and size of production facilities with which the firm can use variable inputs in the short run.

flexible, or floating, exchange rate system An international monetary arrangement in which exchange rates are determined by private suppliers and demanders without government intervention.

foreign exchange The monies of countries that are used to facilitate international trade in goods, services, and financial assets.

foreign exchange market intervention Purchases or sales of foreign exchange by government, usually a central bank, with the goal of maintaining a fixed exchange rate or influencing the exchange rate in a flexible-rate system.

foreign exchange markets The interaction of the suppliers and demanders of foreign exchange, through which exchange rates are determined in a flexible exchange rate system.

foreign exchange reserves The stock of a foreign exchange held by a central bank that is available for use in exchange market intervention.

franchise bidding The privatization of traditionally governmental responsibilities via a bidding process.

free enterprise Economic freedom to produce and sell or purchase and consume goods without government intervention.

free goods and services Things that are available in sufficient amounts and provide all that people want at zero cost.

free rider An individual who receives the benefit of consuming a public good or service without paying for it.

free trade The exchange of goods between countries without the presence of artificial trade barriers such as tariffs and quotas.

full price The total opportunity cost to an individual of obtaining a good; includes money price and all other costs, such as transportation costs or waiting costs.

G

game theory A theory involving decision making in an atmosphere of mutual interdependence and imperfect information.

gold standard An international monetary system in which currencies are redeemable in gold at fixed rates or prices.

goods All tangible things that satisfy people's wants and desires.

government license A legal right granted by state, local, or federal governments to enter an occupation or industry.

H

historical costs   Costs measured by the cost of a resource at the time the resource was purchased.

homogeneous product   A good or service for which the consumer is indifferent as to which firm produces it; each firm's product is a perfect substitute for other firms' products in the eyes of the consumer.

human capital   Any quality, characteristic, or skill an individual has that enhances the individual's productivity, such as education and job experience.

human resources   All forms of labor and skill used to produce goods and services.

I

imperfect competition   Market models, such as oligopoly, cartels, monopoly, and monopolistic competition, in which individual sellers' actions influence price.

implicit costs   Nonpecuniary costs associated with the consumption of a good or service; the opportunity costs of resources used in production for which no explicit payments are made.

in-kind transfer payments   Transfer payments that take the form of goods and services such as public housing, veterans' hospitals, or a mass transit system.

income effect   The change in the quantity demanded of a good that results from a change in real income.

income elasticity of demand   A measure of consumers' relative responsiveness to income changes; the percent change in quantity demanded divided by the percent change in income, holding price constant.

increasing returns to scale   As plant size increases, long-run average total cost decreases.

increasing-cost industry   An industry in which the expansion (contraction) of the number of firms bids up

(down) input prices; minimum LRATC of production changes as the number of firms in the industry changes; long-run industry supply is upward-sloping to the right.

individual income   The earnings individuals receive from their labor, from their assets, and from government transfer payments, minus their tax payments.

industrial union   Workers in a given industry organized independently of their skills in an effort to obtain market power.

inelastic demand   A situation in which buyers are relatively unresponsive to price changes; the percent change in quantity demanded is less than the percent change in price: $\varepsilon_d < 1$.

infant industry   A new or developing domestic industry whose unit production costs are higher than those of established firms in the same industry in other countries.

inferior good   A good that a consumer chooses to purchase in smaller quantities as income rises or in larger amounts as income falls.

inflation   A sustained increase in the general level of prices; inflation reduces the purchasing power of money.

inflation rate   The percent by which the average level of prices in an economy rises; usually expressed as a percent per year.

information   A scarce and important element in the process of economic exchange and growth.

institutions   The sum total of the traditions, mores, laws, and governmental structures of an economy.

interest   The compensation to savers for the act of saving (forgoing present consumption) or the payment made by borrowers; when measured as a percent of the amount borrowed or lent, it is referred to as an interest rate.

interest groups   Collections of individuals with one or more common characteristics, such as occupation,

who seek collectively to affect legislation or government policy so as to benefit members of the group.

International Monetary Fund   An international organization, established along with the Bretton Woods system, designed to assist in the efficient functioning of the Bretton Woods fixed exchange rate system.

L

labor income   The payments an individual receives from supplying work time; equal to the wage rate times the number of hours supplied.

labor union   A group of individual workers organized to act collectively in an attempt to affect labor market conditions.

laissez-faire   A public policy of not regulating to any degree or interfering with market activities (from the French, meaning, roughly, "allow to do").

law of demand   The price of a product or service and the amount purchased are inversely related. If price rises, then quantity demanded falls; if price falls, quantity demanded increases, all other things held constant.

law of diminishing marginal returns   A situation in which adding more and more of a variable input to a fixed plant results in smaller and smaller amounts of additional output produced.

law of increasing costs   As more scarce resources are used to produce additional units of one good, production of another good falls by larger and larger amounts.

law of one price   In perfect markets, the market forces of supply and demand produce a single, equilibrium price for a good or service.

law of supply   The price of a product or service and the amount that producers are willing and able to offer for sale are positively related. If price rises, then quantity supplied rises; if price decreases, then quantity supplied decreases.

legal barriers to entry Government actions that prohibit other firms or individuals from producing particular products or entering particular occupations or industries; such barriers take the form of legal franchises, licenses, and patents.

limit pricing A pricing policy consisting of temporarily setting a price lower than the short-run profit-maximizing price in order to deter entry and maximize profits in the long run.

logrolling The exchange of votes by legislators, usually in order to gain support for particular legislation.

long run An amount of time sufficiently long that all input usage levels can be varied.

long-run average total cost The lowest per-unit cost of producing any level of output when the usage of all inputs can be varied.

long-run competitive equilibrium A market situation in which economic profits are zero for all firms; each firm produces output at minimum average total cost.

long-run industry supply The quantities of a product that all firms in an industry are willing and able to offer for sale at various prices when the number of firms and the scale of operations of each firm are allowed to adjust.

long-run marginal cost The additional cost of producing an additional unit of output when all inputs, including plant size, can be varied.

Lorenz curve A curve plotting the actual cumulative distribution of income in percentages; usually compared to a curve showing a perfectly even distribution of income.

M

macroeconomics Analysis of the behavior of an economy as a whole.

managed flexible-rate system Primarily a flexible exchange rate system, but with occasional government purchases or sales of foreign exchange intended to influence the exchange rate.

manager An individual who organizes and monitors resources within a firm to produce a good or service.

margin The difference between costs or benefits in an existing situation and after a proposed change.

marginal analysis Looking at changes in the costs and benefits of a change from the status quo to a proposed new situation. These marginal changes in the costs and benefits are the basis for rational economic choice.

marginal cost The additional cost of producing one more unit of output; the change in total cost divided by the change in output.

marginal cost pricing A regulatory policy that forces a firm to charge a price equal to marginal cost, resulting in a socially optimal allocation of resources.

marginal factor cost of labor (MFC_L) The change in total costs associated with employing one additional unit of labor.

marginal opportunity production cost The number of units of one good that do not get produced when one additional unit of another good is produced.

marginal private benefit curve A curve, equivalent to a demand curve, which represents the value that consumers place on marginal units of the good or service.

marginal private cost The change in total costs that only the firm bears when output changes by one unit.

marginal private cost curve A curve showing the marginal or additional cost to society—the opportunity cost of scarce resources—of producing additional units of a good or service.

marginal product The additional output produced by employing one additional unit of a variable input.

marginal product of labor (MP_L) The additional output produced that results from hiring an additional unit of labor; change in total output

divided by change in quantity of labor input used.

marginal revenue The change in total revenue resulting from the sale of one additional unit of output; the change in total revenue divided by the change in output.

marginal revenue product of labor (MRP_L) The additional revenue that results from selling the additional output produced by hiring an additional unit of labor; marginal revenue times marginal product of labor.

marginal social cost The change in total cost borne by the economy as a whole (the firm plus all others, or society) that results from a one-unit change in the firm's output.

marginal utility The amount by which total utility changes when consumption of a good or service changes by one unit; calculated by dividing the change in total utility by the change in quantity consumed.

market A collection of buyers and sellers exchanging resources, goods, or services; prices tend toward equality in a market through the continuous exchange between suppliers and demanders.

market coordination The process that directs the flow of resources into the production of goods and services through the price signaling mechanism.

market demand The total amount consumers are willing and able to purchase of a product at all possible prices, obtained by summing the quantities demanded at each price over all buyers.

market demand curve for a public good Obtained by summing vertically, instead of horizontally, all individuals' demands for the public good. Vertical summation is used because consumption is noncompeting.

market demand for labor The total quantity of labor demanded at various wage rates, other things constant. The sum of all individual firms' demands for a type of labor. The firms may or may not all be in the same industry.

market failure   A situation in which the socially optimal (most economically efficient) amount of a good or service does not get produced by the private market; usually stems from unclear property rights assignments.

market for legislation   The interaction between interest groups acting as demanders of legislation beneficial to the group and legislators acting as suppliers of legislation; legislation generally entails some type of wealth transfer.

market power   A situation in which an established firm has influence over price and profit levels due to barriers impeding the entry of rival firms.

market supply   The total amount producers are willing and able to offer for sale of a product at all possible prices, obtained by summing the quantities supplied at each price over all producers.

market supply of labor   The sum of all individuals' supplies of a type of labor. The total quantity of labor people will offer to the market at various wage rates, other things being equal.

mean income   A measure of average income; can be computed as per capita, per family, or per earner of income.

merger   The combining of the ownership of two firms' assets, which results in a single firm.

microeconomics   Analysis of the behavior of individual decision-making units, including individuals, households, and business firms.

model   A simplified abstraction of the real world that approximates reality and makes problems easier to analyze; also called a theory.

money price   The dollar price that sellers receive from buyers; a price expressed in terms of money, not in terms of an amount of another good.

monopolistic competition   A market model with freedom of entry and exit and firms producing similar but differentiated products.

monopsony   A single buyer of a resource or product; sometimes found in labor markets as the single buyer of labor.

mutual interdependence   A relation among firms in which the decisions and actions of one firm have a significant impact on the decisions, actions, and profits of other firms.

N

natural monopoly   A monopoly in which the relation between industry demand and cost structure makes it possible for only one firm to exist in the industry; occurs when decreasing long-run average costs exist up to the level of total industry demand.

natural resources   All those renewable and nonrenewable resources that are given to an economy or society.

negative externality   A situation that arises when an individual or other economic entity imposes costs on others without compensating them.

nominal rate of interest   The market-determined rate of interest; usually expressed as a percentage per year of the dollar or nominal amount of the loan.

nonhuman resources   All resources other than human resources, such as machines and land.

nonmarket activities   Anything an individual does while not working that directly or indirectly yields utility.

nonprice competition   Any means other than pricing decisions that firms use to sell output.

nonproprietary   Relating to nonprivate ownership; entails motivations other than strictly profit motivations; individuals do not always or fully bear the consequences of their decisions.

nonrenewable natural resources   Resources that exist in finite quantities.

normal good   A good that a consumer chooses to purchase in smaller (larger) amounts as income falls (rises).

normative economics   Value judgments based on moral principles or preferences about how economic life should be.

normative public choice   Economic analysis that determines shortcomings and failures of the political process and suggests improvements.

O

oligopoly   Market models characterized by a few firms producing either homogeneous or differentiated products, with entry of new firms very difficult or prevented.

opportunity cost   The highest-valued alternative forgone in making any choice.

opportunity cost of capital   The return that could be received from the next-best alternative investment.

opportunity costs of production   The opportunity costs of resources used to produce goods and services.

overvalued   A term describing the foreign exchange market value of a country's money; occurs when the number of units of a country's money that purchases one unit of a foreign currency is less than the equilibrium exchange rate.

P

patent   A monopoly right granted by government to an inventor for a product or process; valid for 17 years in the United States.

per capita income   Average income per person; the total income of a population divided by the number of people in the population.

perfect information   A situation that arises when information about prices and products is costless to obtain; complete knowledge about the market.

perfect market   A market in which there are enough buyers and sellers that no single buyer or seller can influence price.

positive economics Observations, explanations, or predictions about economic life; scientific economics.

positive externality A situation that arises when an individual or other economic entity creates benefits for others without receiving any compensation in return.

positive public choice Economic analysis of political decision making and other political behavior that aims to understand, explain, and predict such behavior.

poverty A substandard level of income.

predatory pricing The temporary pricing of goods or services below cost in order to reduce or eliminate competition.

present value The value today of a payment to be made or received in the future; a future sum discounted by the current rate of interest.

price ceiling A form of regulation in which a maximum legal price is established by government above which exchange between buyers and sellers is illegal.

price control The setting, by government, of a price in a market different from the equilibrium price.

price discrimination The practice of charging one buyer or group of buyers a different price than that charged to others. The price difference is not due to differences in the cost of supplying the two groups.

price elasticity of demand A measure of buyers' relative responsiveness to a price change; the percentage change in quantity demanded divided by the percentage change in price.

price floor A form of regulation in which a minimum legal price is established by government below which exchange between buyers and sellers is illegal.

price leadership A market where a single firm sets industry price, with the remaining firms charging what the price leader charges. Industry price changes are initiated by the leader.

price searcher A firm that is able to choose a profit-maximizing price from a range of prices rather than have price imposed by market conditions and competition; such a firm faces a downward-sloping demand curve.

price taker An individual seller who faces a single market price and is able to sell as much as desired at that price.

prices The market-established opportunity costs of goods and services obtained through exchange.

principle of diminishing marginal utility The more of a good or service being consumed, the smaller is the marginal utility obtained by consuming one additional unit of the good or service, all other factors equal.

prisoner's dilemma A scenario that illustrates the mutual interdependence of decision making; the basis for game theory.

private choice Choices made through the private (non-governmental) markets.

private costs The opportunity costs of production that are borne, or paid, by producers.

private property Property that an individual (as opposed to a government) holds the right to control.

producers' surplus The difference between the total revenue to producers from selling a given quantity of a good or service and the total cost to them and to society of using the scarce resources in that particular production.

production possibilities frontier The curve that graphs all the possible combinations of two goods that an economic entity can produce given the available technology, the amount of productive resources available, and the fact that these resources are fully utilized.

productive efficiency A condition in which total industry output is produced at the lowest possible opportunity cost of resources.

products market The forces created by buyers and sellers that establish the prices and quantities exchanged of goods and services.

profit-maximizing price The price associated with the quantity sold at which the difference between total revenue and total cost is greatest; the price associated with the quantity sold at which marginal revenue equals marginal cost.

profits The amount by which total revenue exceeds total opportunity cost of production.

property rights Any legal and/or enforceable rights to the use of resources of any kind.

proprietary Relating to private ownership and profit motivation; individuals directly bear the consequences of their decisions.

public choice The economic analysis of political decision making, politics, and the democratic process.

public employees' union Workers employed by federal, state, or local governments who organize in an effort to obtain market power.

public franchise A firm or industry's exclusive, government-granted right to produce and sell a good or service.

public good A good such that, once produced, one individual's consumption of the good does not reduce or exclude the ability of other individuals to consume the good.

public interest theory of regulation Maintains that regulations are contrived so as to promote the public interest by correcting market failures and improving economic efficiency.

pure capitalism An economic system in which most resources are owned, and most relevant decisions are made, by private individuals.

pure communism An economic system in which most productive resources, both human and nonhuman, are publicly owned.

pure economic rent   The total payment to a factor of production whose supply curve is perfectly inelastic.

pure interest   The interest associated with a risk-free loan. The interest rate that produces pure interest is called the risk-free interest rate.

pure monopoly   An industry in which a single firm produces a product that has no close substitutes and in which entry of new firms cannot occur.

purely competitive market   The interaction of a large number of buyers and sellers under the condition that entry and exit are not restricted.

Q

quantity demanded   The amount of any good or service consumers are willing and able to purchase at all various prices.

quantity supplied   The amount of any good or service that producers are willing and able to produce and sell at some specific price.

quota   A restriction or limit on the quantity of an imported good.

R

rate of return on invested capital   Profits earned during a period of time divided by the value of invested capital; usually measured as a percent per year.

rate of return regulation   A cap imposed by a regulatory commission on the allowable percentage that a utility can earn on its capital invested.

rate of time preference   The percent increase in future consumption over present consumption that is necessary to just induce an individual to be indifferent between present and future consumption.

rational self-interest   The view of human behavior espoused by econo-

mists. Given circumstances and preferences, people weigh the costs and benefits of choices in order to do the best they can for themselves.

rationing   The allocation of goods among consumers with the use of prices. The equilibrium price rations the limited amount of a good produced by the most willing and able suppliers, or sellers, to the most willing and able demanders, or buyers.

real rate of interest   The nominal interest rate minus the inflation rate; the interest rate that measures the true incentives and costs that savers and investors face; the interest measured in terms of real buying power.

regulatory policies   Administrative or legal attempts to influence the behavior of firms or industries when competitive goals cannot be realized or when positive goals are to be pursued.

relative price   The price ratio or "trade-off" in consumption between one product (or service) and another product (or service) or between one good and other goods taken as a whole.

renewable natural resources   Those resources that may be reproduced through time if not exhausted by unwise policies.

rent   A payment to a factor of production in excess of the factor's opportunity cost.

resources   Those things used to produce goods and services. These include land, machines, energy, and human labor and ingenuity. Resources are also called factors of production.

resources market   The forces created by buyers and sellers that establish the prices and quantities exchanged of resources such as land, labor services, and capital.

revaluation   An official change in a country's exchange rate in a fixed-rate system; the number of units of a country's money that purchases one unit of another country's currency is decreased by the government.

right-to-work law   A law that prevents unions from requiring that individual workers join the union as a condition of employment by a particular firm.

risk   The chance that a borrower will default or fail to repay a loan.

roundabout production   The current production of capital goods so that greater amounts of consumption goods can be produced in the future.

S

saving   The act of forgoing present consumption in order to increase future consumption.

scarcity   The condition whereby the resources, goods, and services available to individuals and society are limited relative to the wants and desires for them.

services   All forms of intangible but useful activities that are valued by people.

short run   An amount of time insufficient to allow the usage of all inputs to vary.

short-run firm supply curve   That portion of a firm's marginal cost curve above the minimum point on the average variable cost curve.

short-run industry supply curve   The horizontal sum of all existing firms' short-run supply curves.

shortage   The amount by which quantity demanded exceeds quantity supplied at a price below the equilibrium price.

shutdown   A loss-minimizing procedure in which the firm stops production to eliminate all variable costs, although it must still pay fixed costs.

social costs   The opportunity costs of all resources used in the production of goods and services; the sum of private and external costs.

socialism   An economic system in which most nonhuman productive resources are owned by the state.

socialization Government ownership and operation of a firm or industry.

specialization An economic entity's (an individual's or a nation's) producing only one good or service, or the performance of a single task in a production process by an individual.

speculation The buying and selling of currencies on the foreign exchange market with the intent of profiting from possible devaluation or revaluation in a fixed-rate system or from possible future movements in the exchange rate in a flexible-rate system.

static inefficiency A condition associated with the welfare loss due to the presence of a monopoly. The loss can be summarized as the production of too little output sold at too high a price.

strike A collective refusal to work at the current wage or under current working conditions.

substitute inputs Inputs with a relation such that increased employment of one input due to a fall in its price results in decreased usage of the other(s).

substitutes Products that are related such that an increase in the price of one will increase the demand for the other or a decrease in the price of one will decrease the demand for the other; two goods whose cross elasticity of demand is positive; $\varepsilon_c > 0$.

substitution effect The change in the quantity demanded of a good that results only from a change in the relative price of the good.

sunk costs Previously incurred, irretrievable costs of a currently owned resource.

supply curve A graphic representation of the quantities of a product or service that producers are willing and able to sell at all possible prices.

supply of loanable funds A curve or schedule that shows the various amounts individuals are willing and able to lend or save at different rates.

surplus The amount by which quantity supplied exceeds quantity demanded at a price above the equilibrium price.

sustainable monopoly A monopoly that can forestall the entry of competitors in the absence of regulation.

T

tacit collusive solution A possible outcome in game theory when, given an indefinite time horizon and no formal communication, rivals recognize that it is in their best interest to act so that joint profits are maximized.

tangency solution A long-run equilibrium situation in which the firm's downward-sloping demand curve is tangent to its *LRATC* curve; zero economic profits are earned.

tariff A tax or levy on imported goods.

technology Knowledge of production methods associated with producing a particular good.

terms of trade The number of units of one good that exchange in the market for one unit of some other good; a relative price. Although not expressed in terms of money, it is a price nonetheless.

terms of trade argument Defending the use of artificial trade barriers combined with monopoly or monopsony power in international markets in order to produce an improvement in a country's terms of trade.

total consumer valuation The total amount that consumers are willing to pay for a given quantity of a good or service rather than go without it.

total cost of production The total opportunity cost of all resources used in production; the sum of all explicit and implicit production costs.

total costs All the costs of a firm's operations; total variable costs plus total fixed costs.

total expenditures The total amount spent by consumers on a good or service; calculated as equilibrium price times equilibrium quantity.

total product The total amount of output produced.

total revenues Total receipts of businesses; always equal to total expenditures by consumers; calculated as market price multiplied by the amount of output sold; the dollar value of sales.

total utility The total amount of satisfaction derived from consuming any given quantity of a good or service.

total wage bill The total cost of labor to firms; equal to wage rate times total quantity of labor employed.

transaction costs The opportunity costs of the resources directly associated with trade; includes time costs, brokers' fees, and so on.

transfer payment A resource received by an individual from government that is not directly or explicitly paid for by that individual; it may be in the form of money or goods and services such as education or health care.

transportation costs The value of resources used in the transportation of goods that finalize any trade.

U

undervalued A term describing the foreign exchange market value of a country's money; occurs when the number of units of a country's money that purchases one unit of a foreign currency is greater than the equilibrium exchange rate.

unemployment of resources A situation in which some human and/or nonhuman resources that can be used in production are not used.

unit elasticity of demand A condition where the percent change in quantity demanded is equal to the percent change in price: $\varepsilon_d = 1$.

utility A measure of the satisfaction that the consumption of goods or services yields an individual.

V

variable costs The costs of inputs whose usage levels can be changed in the short run. Variable costs change as output changes.

variable input A factor of production whose level of usage may be changed in the short run.

W

welfare loss due to monopoly The consumers' surplus lost by consumers and not gained by the monopolist that results from a monopoly producing a less-than-competitive amount of output and charging a greater-than-competitive price; also called deadweight cost.

welfare loss to society The net loss to an economy resulting from the imposition of an artificial trade barrier; government revenues plus producer gains minus consumer losses.

Z

zero economic profits A condition in which total revenue equals total opportunity cost of production. Firms earn a normal rate of return and $P = MR = LRMC = LRATC$.

CREDITS

INDEX

NOTE: *Page numbers in* **boldface** *type indicate pages on which definitions of key terms appear; those followed by n indicate footnotes.*

A

Account(s)
current, balance of, 818
Accounting costs, **8, 170.** See also Explicit costs
Accounting profits, **172, 358**
Acid rain, 437–439
Adams, A. Frank, III, 103n
Adjusted income, **374**
Advertising, **258**
importance of, 258–259
in monopolistic competition, 257–260
in oligopoly, 280
and price of eyeglasses, 261
pros and cons of, 259–260
AFL-CIO, 322
Africa, AIDS in, and reduced production possibilities, 45–47
African Americans
income of, 379
wage discrimination and, 381
Age, income distribution and, 377
Aggregate supply
of land, **354**
Agriculture, 222–228
antitrust policies and, 402
Freedom to Farm Act and, 227–228
government impact on, 226–227
government programs for, 222–228
move to markets in, 225–228
AIDS, in Africa, and reduced production possibilities, 45–47
Aid to Families with Dependent Children (AFDC), 381–382
Airline Deregulation Act of 1978, 419, 421
Airline industry
deregulation of, 419, 421
price regulation in, 414–415, 419
Allocative efficiency, 93, **213**
"All you can eat" pizza, marginal utility of, 149–150
American Air Lines, 421
American Bar Association (ABA), 322

An American Dilemma: The Negro Problem and Modern Democracy (Myrdal), 829
American Federation of Labor (AFL), 322
American Federation of State, County, and Municipal Employees (AFSCME), 324
American Medical Association (AMA), 322–323
"Anarchy of production," 110–111
Antitrust policy, **97,** 399, **400,** 402–408
agencies of, 403–404
economic view of, 408
enforcement of, 404–407
legislation and, 402–403
multinational firms and, 407–408
Appreciation, of currencies, 806–807, **807**
Arbitration, binding, **333**
Arc elasticity, **120**
Arrow, Kenneth, 459n
Artificial trade barriers, **40,** 40–41, 780–785
Asian economic crisis, 823–825
Asset income, **369**
AT&T, 247, 299, 417
Australia, shipment of prisoners to, 86
Austrian school of economics, 359–360
Automobile industry, 293
economies of scale in, 276
import quotas for, 785
mutual interdependence in, 272
price leadership in, 279–280
Average cost pricing, **413**
Average fixed cost (AFC), **173,** 173–174
Average product, **177,** 177–178
Average total cost (ATC), **174.** See also Long-run average total cost (LRATC)
Average variable cost (AVC), **174**

B

Backward induction, **275**
Balance of payments, **816,** 816–819
current account balance and, 818
net capital movements and, 818
net transfers abroad and, 818
statistical discrepancy and, 818–819
and value of dollar, 819
Balance of trade
deficit in, **812**
exports and imports and, 817–818

surplus in, **812**
Bank(s)
international. See International finance
World, 822
Barbers, as interest group, 102–103
"Barometric" firms, 279–280
Barter, **12**
Baseball players, marginal revenue product of, 309
Bashshur, Rashid L., 47n
Bast, Joseph L., 384n
Bauer, P. T., 829–831
Baumel, C. Phillip, 420n
Beard, T. Randolph, 423n
Becker, Gary, 394–395
Bees, economics of, 469
Benham, Lee, 261
Berlau, John, 328n
Bidding, franchise, **417**
Bilateral monopoly, **331**
Binding arbitration, **333**
Black, Duncan, 459n
Bonds
corporate, 360–362
Botswana, AIDS epidemic and life expectancy in, 46
Bretton Woods system, **819,** 819–821
Briet, William, 138n
Bronze crisis, 433
Browning, Edgar K., 375
Buchanan, James M., 470n
Budget constraint
consumer equilibrium and, 143–145
indifference curve and, 160–161
Bureaucracy, 468–470
Bureaus, **468**
Bush, George, 385
"Buy American" argument, for protection, 788

C

Cable television rates, Telecommunications Act of 1996 and, 423
Canada. See also North American Free Trade Agreement
comparative advantage and, 34–39
health care system of, 385–386
Capacity, excess, **265**
Capital, 6, 343–362
demand and supply of loanable funds and, 346–349

Capital, continued
formation of. *See* Capital formation
human, 312–313, 368–369
net movements of, 818
opportunity costs of, **171**
present value of future income and, 351–352
returns to, 349–351, **357,** 357–358
stock and. *See* Stock
Capital consumption, **345**
Capital formation, **344,** 344–345
benefits of, 352–353
interest rates and, 345–346
roundabout production and, **344,** 344–345
Capitalism, 84
pure, **84**
Capital stock, **32, 345**
Capture theory of regulation, **412**
Carlton, Dennis W., 420n
Carlyle, Thomas, 394
Cartels, 271, **272,** 280–285
antitrust policy and, 404
bid rigging and, 281
characteristics of, 281–282
comparison with other market structures, 286–287
enforcement by, **283,** 283–285
factors conducive to, 285
formation of, 282
government-sponsored and -enforced, 277
illegal, 281
legal, 281–282
operation of, 282–283
Celler-Kefauver Act of 1950, 403, 405
Centrally planned economies, 111
Ceteris paribus, 13n, **56**
Chadwick, Sir Edwin, 86–86n
Chamberlin, E. H., 255, 263, 265
Change in demand, **57**
for labor, 305–306
Change in income, 57–59
Change in quantity demanded, **56,** 56–57
Change in quantity supplied, **63**
Change in supply, **63**
"Cheap foreign labor" argument, 787–788
Cheating, **275**
cartel enforcement and, 283–284
game theory and, 275, 278
Cheung, Steven N. S., 440n, 469–469n
Children, price of, 395
China
property rights in, 7–8
World Trade Organization and, 793
China
property rights in, 7–8
World Trade Organization and, 793
Choices
at margin, 10, **31**

opportunity costs and. See Opportunity costs
private, **31**
public. *See* Interest groups; Politics; Public choice; Voting utility and. *See* Diminishing marginal utility; Marginal utility; Utility
work versus leisure, 386
Chrysler Corporation, 272
Cigarette excise tax, 132–133
Civil Aeronautics Board (CAB), 414–415, 419
Clayton Antitrust Act of 1914, 403, 405
Clinton, Bill, 335, 382, 386–387, 422, 625, 629–630, 641–642, 783
Clinton, Hillary Rodham, 385
Coase, Ronald H., 168–169n, 441n, 448n, 477–479
Coase theorem, **443,** 443n
Collective bargaining, 332, **332**
bilateral monopoly and, 331
need for, bilateral monopoly and, 331
public choice and, 334–335
College athletics, monopsony in, 338–339
Colombian coffee cartel, 282
Common ownership, **434,** 434–439
drilling for oil and, 435–437
fishing in international waters and, 434–435
Communism, pure, **84**
Communist Manifesto (Marx & Engels), 109
Comparable worth, 315
Comparative advantage, 33–45, **35, 774,** 774–780
exchange costs and, 39–45
factors explaining, 38–39
gains from specialization and trade and, 776–780
production possibilities before specialization and, 775–776
specialization and, 33, 36–37
trade and, 37–38
Compensation
interest as. *See* Interest
of professional baseball players, 309
wages as. *See* Wage(s)
Competition, **87.** *See also* Competitive markets
imperfect, 255, **256**
managed, in health care, 385–386
monopolistic. *See* Monopolistic competition
nonprice, **256**
political, 461–462
process of, 194
pure (perfect). *See* Pure (perfect) competition
Competitive equilibrium
economic efficiency and, 92–93

long-run, **207,** 208–210
Competitive labor markets, 297–318, **299**
comparable worth and, 315
demand for labor in. *See* Labor demand; Market demand for labor
marginal productivity theory and. *See* Marginal productivity theory
supply of labor in. *See* Labor supply
Competitive markets, 194–219
campus parking and, 217–219
for labor. *See* Competitive labor markets
private. *See* Purely competitive markets
process of competition and, 194
pure. *See* Purely competitive firms; Purely competitive industries; Purely competitive markets
in real world, 216–217
Complementary inputs, **306**
Complements, **59, 130**
Concentration ratios, **400,** 400–402
Conglomerate mergers, 405–406
Congress of Industrial Organizations (CIO), 322
"Conscript labor," 188
Constant-cost industry, **211**
Constant returns to scale, **185,** 185–186
Constitutional decision making, **470,** 470–472
Constitutional political economy, 470–472
Consumer behavior. *See also* Choices; Consumer equilibrium; Diminishing marginal utility; Marginal utility
basic assumptions about, 140–141
Consumer equilibrium, 139–148, **142**
balancing choices among goods and, 141–143
budget constraint and, 143–145
consumer rationality and, 146–148
indifference curve and, 161–162
utility maximization and, 146
Consumer-initiated wage discrimination, **381**
Consumers' surplus, **90,** 90n
Consumption
capital, **345**
Consumption loans, as source of demand for loanable funds, 346
Consumption possibilities curve, **777**
Contestability, **415**
Contrived scarcity, **244**
Corporations, 185. *See also* Firm(s)
bonds of, 360–362
stock of. *See* Stock
Cosmetologists, as interest group, 103
Cost(s), 5
accounting (explicit), **8, 170**
average, 173–174
economic, nature of, 171–172
exchange, **39,** 39–45

explicit (money), **8**
external, **172**
fixed, **173,** 173–174
  of health care, 383
historical, **171**
implicit, **8, 170,** 170–171
increasing, law of, **30,** 30–31
of making loans, 347
marginal. *See* Marginal cost *(MC)*
opportunity, **9,** 27
private. *See* Private cost(s)
of production. *See* Long-run production
  costs; Production costs; Short-run
  production costs
social. *See* Social cost(s)
sunk, **171**
total. *See* Total cost *(TC)*
transaction, **39,** 39–40
transportation, **40**
variable, **173,** 174
Cost curves. *See also* Long-run average
  total cost *(LRATC);* Long-run production costs; Production costs;
  Short-run production costs
shifts in, 186
Cournot, Augustin, 277
Cournot-Nash solution, 277–279
Crabbing, time and elasticity of supply
  in, 131
Craft unions, **322**
Crandall, Robert W., 785–785n
Credit card calls, Telecommunications Act
  of 1996 and, 423
Crisis, types of, 433, 823–825
Cross elasticity of demand, **129,** 129–130
Currencies
  appreciation of, 806–807, **807**
  depreciation of, **806,** 806–807
  devaluation of, **813**
  Euro, 803
  overvaluation of, **811**
  speculation in, **820,** 820–821
  undervaluation of, **810,** 810–811
  value of, balance of payments and, 819
Current account balance, 818
Curves, **20.** *See also specific curves*

D

Darwin, Charles, 394
Deadweight loss, 246
De Beers diamond cartel, 232, 282,
  287–289
Decreasing-cost industry, **212**
Defense Department, bid rigging and, 281
Deficits
  balance of trade, **812**
Delta Air Lines, 421
Demand
  agricultural, 223

change in, **57**
derived, **298**
elastic, **117**
elasticity of. *See* Elasticity of demand;
  Price elasticity of demand
factors affecting, **56,** 56–60
graphic representation of, 67
inelastic, **117**
for labor. *See* Labor demand; Market
  demand for labor
law of. *See* Law of demand
for loanable funds, **346**
long-run competitive equilibrium and,
  208–210
market, **60,** 60–61
price controls and public choice and,
  72–78
for products, labor demand and, 329
shifts in, 68–72
supply and, 609–610, 615–619, 804
tabular analysis of, 66–67
unit elasticity of, **117**
Demand curve, **55**
  elasticity along, 118–121
  for friendship, 125
  individual, 55–60
  market, 61–62
  market, for public goods, **451**
  of monopoly, 232–234
  of purely competitive firm, 197, 233
  value calculation by demanders and,
    88–90
Demand elasticity coefficient, **116,** 120n
Demand schedule
  individual, 55–56
  market, 60–61
Depreciation, **806**
  of capital goods, **345**
  of currencies, 806–807
Deregulation, **417,** 417–422
  of health care system, 387–388
Derived demand, **298**
Devaluation, **813**
Developing countries. *See* Third World
  countries
Diamond, Jared, 437n
Diamond-water paradox, **146,** 146–148
Differentiated products, **256**
  consumer welfare and, 267–268
  under monopolistic competition,
    256–257
  under oligopoly, 280
Diminishing marginal returns, **176**
  profit-maximizing level of employment
    and, 300–302
  short-run production costs and,
    176–183
Diminishing marginal utility, **138,** 138–151
  consumer equilibrium and, 139–148
  law of demand and, 148–151

misunderstandings about, 151
Direct relations, **20**
Discrimination, wage, 380–381
Diseconomies of scale, **184**
Dissent on Development (Bauer), 829
Division of labor, **28**
Dollar, balance of payments and, 819
Dominant-firm model, 279–280
Dominant solution, **274**
Doomsday predictions, 433
Draft, opportunity costs of, 187–188
Dumping, 788
Du Pont, 247
Dynamic inefficiency, **246**

E

Eastern Air Lines, 421
Eastern Europe, institutions in, 84
Economic and Monetary Union (EMU), 803
Economic crisis, in Asia, 823–825
Economic efficiency, **84,** 92–93, **265**
  allocative, 93, 213
  competitive equilibrium and, 92–93
  of monopolistic competition, 265–266
  politics and. *See* Public choice
  productive, **213**
  in purely competitive markets, 213–217
Economic goods, **5**
Economic growth, 7, 31–33, **32**
  production possibilities frontier and,
    31–33, 742–747
Economic incentives, 453
  property rights and, 85–87
Economic institutions, 84–88
  international. *See* International finance
  private competitive markets and, 87–88
  property rights and economic incen-
    tives and, 86–87
Economic losses, by purely competitive
  firms, 203–205
Economic mobility, **377,** 377–378
Economic profits, **172, 358**
  zero, **107**
Economic rent, **354**
Economics
  definition of, 4
  law and, 443n
  normative, **14**
  positive, **14**
  role of, 13–15
  role of theory in, 13
Economic services, **5**
The Economics of Discrimination
  (Becker), 394
The Economics of Human Behavior
  (Becker), 394
The Economics of Imperfect Competition
  (Robinson), 292
The Economics of Welfare (Pigou), 477

Economic system, **84**
Economic time, 173
Economic wage discrimination, **381**
Economic welfare, **265**
Economies of scale, **184**
   as entry barriers, 276
   natural monopoly and, 232
Economists, roles of, 11–16
Efficiency. *See* Economic efficiency
Ekelund, Robert B., Jr., 103n, 105n, 418,
   423n–424n
Elastic demand, **117**
Elasticity, **116,** 116–133. *See also* Elastic-
   ity of demand; Elasticity of supply;
   Price elasticity of demand
   real-world importance of, 129
Elasticity of demand, 116–127
   cross, **129,** 129–130
   excise taxes and, 132–133
   income, **128,** 128–129
   of monopolist, 236–237
   price. *See* Price elasticity of demand
   for union labor, 327
Elasticity of supply, 130–132
   excise taxes and, 132–133
   time and, 131
Elections, buying of, 463
Elephants, economic incentives to save, 453
Elzinga, Kenneth, 138n
Employment. *See also* Unemployment
   profit-maximizing level of, 300–302
   as union goal, 325
Endangered species, 453–453
Energy crisis, 433
Entrepreneurs, **358,** 358–360, 647
Entrepreneurship, 6
Entry, by monopoly, 240
Entry barriers
   artificial, 277
   lack of, under monopolistic competi-
     tion, 257
   legal, **231,** 231–232
   natural, 276
   under oligopoly, 276–277
Environmental Protection Agency
   (EPA), 95
Equilibrium. *See also* Competitive equilib-
   rium; Consumer equilibrium
   long-run, under monopolistic competi-
     tion, 262–263
   short-run, under monopolistic competi-
     tion, 262
Equilibrium price, 65–72, **67**
   mechanics of price determination and,
     66–67
   price rationing and, 67–72
An Essay on the Principle of Population
   (Malthus), 394
Euro, 803
European Central Bank, 803

European Union (EU), 42
Europe's Economic and Monetary
   Union, 803
Ex ante distribution, **369**
Excess capacity, **265**
Exchange costs, **39,** 39–45
Exchange rates, **800,** 800–816. *See also*
   Fixed exchange rate systems; Flexi-
   ble (floating) exchange rate systems
   fiscal policies and, 815–816
   monetary policy and, 814
   systems of, 802–804
Excise taxes, elasticity of demand and
   supply and, 132–133
Exit, by monopoly, 240
Expenditure(s). *See* Government expendi-
   tures *(G);* Total expenditures
Explicit costs, **8,** 8–9, 170
Exploitation of labor, **331**
Export(s) *(X). See also* International trade
   flexible exchange rates and, 808
Ex post distribution, **369**
External costs, **172**
Externalities, **94,** 94–96, **439,** 439–447
   correlation of, 441–447
   government's role and, 95–96
   need for government intervention and,
     440–441
   negative, **439,** 439–440
   positive, **439,** 439–440
   public choice and politics and, 446–447
   regulation of, 446
   tax-subsidizing approach to, 444–445
Exxon, 257
Eyeglasses, price of, 261

F

Factor markets, **298,** 298–299. *See also*
   Resources markets
   derived demand and, 298
   firms as resource price takers and,
     298–299
Factors affecting demand, **56,** 56–60
Factors affecting supply, **63**
Factors of production. *See* Factor markets;
   Inputs; Resource(s); Resources
   market; *specific factors*
Fagin, Barry, 409n
Fair trade, and protectionism, 789
Family income, **370**
Featherbedding, 328–329
Federal Communications Commission
   (FCC), 412
Federal Trade Commission Act of 1914, 403
Firm(s), 167–172, **168.** *See also*
   Corporation(s)
   "barometric," 279–280
   excess capacity of, 265
   labor demand of, 304–306

   monopolistic. *See* Monopoly
   multinational, 407–408
   partnerships, 178
   production costs of. *See*
     Production costs
   proprietorships, 170
   purely competitive. *See* Purely compet-
     itive firms
   as resource price takers, 298–299
   socialization of, **416,** 416–417
   supply schedule of, 62–63
Firm coordination, **168**
Firm's long-run demand for labor, **305**
Fiscal policy
   on exchange rates, 815–816
Fishing, in international waters, 434–435
Fixed costs, **173,** 173–174
Fixed exchange rate systems, **802,**
   810–814
   devaluation and revaluation and, 813
   domestic macroeconomic policy
     changes and, 812
   monetary policy and, 814
   operation of, 810–812
   trade policy changes and, 813
Fixed input, **173**
Fixed plant, **175**
Flexible (floating) exchange rate systems,
   802, 804–810, 814
   changes in rates and, 806–810
   monetary policy and, 814
   between two countries, 804–806
Food and Drug Administration (FDA), 412
Food crisis, 433
Forbes, Steve, 463
Ford, George S., 418, 423n–424n
Ford Motor Company, 272
Foreign exchange, **800.** *See also* Exchange
   rates; Fixed exchange rate systems;
   Flexible (floating) exchange rate
   systems
Foreign exchange market, **800.** *See also*
   Exchange rates
   supply and demand and, 804–806
Foreign exchange market intervention, **811**
Foreign exchange reserves, **811**
Franchise(s)
   in nineteenth century, 418
   public, **231**
Franchise bidding, **417**
Freedom to Farm Act of 1996, 227–228
Free enterprise, **87.** *See also* Perfect mar-
   kets; Private competitive markets;
   Purely competitive markets
Free entry, in monopolistic competition, 257
Free goods and services, **5**
Free riders, 97, 282, **449**
Free trade, **780**
   barriers to. *See* Trade barriers
   opposition to. *See* Protectionism

trade zones and, 41–44
  United States and, 41–44, 335, 614, 618, 785, 792–795
Friedland, Claire, 419n
Friendship, price elasticity of demand of, 125
FTC Act of 1914, 403
Full price, **53,** 53–54
  and restaurant prices, 54

G

Galatoire's, 54
Game theory, **272,** 272–275
  Cournot-Nash solution in, 277–279
  oligopoly behavior and, 277
  one-shot versus infinite-series games and, 275
  prisoner's dilemma and, **273,** 273–275
Gates, Bill, 409
General Agreement on Tariffs and Trade (GATT), 616–619, 792–793
General Motors, 272, 280, 293, 299
The General Theory of Employment, Interest, and Money (Keynes), 292, 646–647
George, Henry, 356
Germany
  customs union in, 42
Global warming, 433, 437–439
Godwin, William, 394
Gold standard, 815, **819**
Goods, **4.** *See also* Product(s)
  economic, **5**
  free, **5**
  inferior, **58,** 58–59, 150n
  normal, **58,** 58–59, 150n
  private, 447
  public. *See* Public good(s)
Government, 94–97. *See also* Legislation; Politics; *specific branches and agencies*
  agricultural programs of, 222–228
  entry barriers established by, 277
  externalities and. *See* Externalities; Market failure
  ownership of firms by, 416–417
  public goods provided by, 96–97, 452–453
  regulation by. *See* Regulation
  role of, 452
  as source of demand for loanable funds, 346
Government expenditures *(G)*
  bid rigging and, 281
Government license, **231**
Graphs, 19–23
  drawing, 20–22
  purpose of, 19
  slope of curve in, 22–23

of supply and demand, 67
Great Depression, 381, 388, 493
Gross domestic product (GDP), **15**
Gross national product (GNP), **15**

H

Hahn, Robert N., 420n
Hand, Learned, 407
Harris, Patricia, 420n
Hart-Scott-Rodino Antitrust Improvement Act, 403, 405
Hayek, Friedrich A. von, 359–360
Health care, 383–388
  insurance and, 384
  reform of, 385–388
Health insurance purchasing cooperatives (HIPCs), 385–386
Health Insurance Reform Act of 1996, 387–388
Health regulations, 415–416
Hebert, Robert F., 359n
Heilbroner, Robert, 109
Heilbroner, Robert L., 109n
Hispanic Americans, income of, 379
Historical costs, **171**
Homogeneous product, **195**
Hull, Cordell, 791
Human capital, 312–313, 368–369
Human Capital (Becker), 394
Human resources, **6**

I

IBM, 247
Imperfect competition, 255, **256,** 293
Implicit costs, **8,** 8–9, **170,** 170–171
Imports *(M). See also* International trade
  in flexible exchange rate system, 808
Incentive(s). *See* Economic incentives
Income
  adjusted, **374**
  asset, **369**
  change in, 57–59
  family, **370**
  future, present value of, 351–352
  individual, **368,** 368–370
  inequality in, 370–373
  labor. *See* Labor income; Wage *entries*
  maximization of, as union goal, 327
  mean, **379**
  money, 374–377
  national. *See* Gross domestic product (GDP)
  per capita, **379**
  real, **489,** 808
  from savings, 369
  taxes as source of, 369–370
  total, impact of unions on labor's share of, 336–337

Income distribution, 368–383
  adjustments to money income and, 374–377
  age distribution and, 377
  economic mobility and, 377
  interpretation of data on, 370–371
  justice of, 388
  labor income and, 368–369
  Lorenz curves and, 371–373
  marginal productivity theory and, 316
  monopoly and, 246
  poverty and, 379–380
  race discrimination and, 380–381
  savings and other assets and, 369
  single-parent families and, 378
  taxes and transfer payments and, 369–370
  in United States, 373–378
  wage discrimination and, 380–381
Income effect, **150**
  indifference curves and, 163–164
Income elasticity of demand, **128,** 128–129
Increasing-cost industry, **211,** 211–212
Increasing returns to scale, **186**
Indifference curves, **157,** 157–164
  budget constraint and, 160–161
  characteristics of, 158–160
  consumer equilibrium and, 161–162
  law of demand and, 162–163
  substitution and income effects and, 163–164
Indifference map, **159**
Indifference sets, **157,** 157–158
Individual income, **368,** 368–370
Individual labor supply, 309–312
Industrial concentration, 400–402
Industrial unions, **322,** 322–323
Industry(ies). *See also* Monopoly; Purely competitive industries; *specific industries*
  constant-cost, **211**
  decreasing-cost, **212**
  entry into. *See* Entry barriers; Entry
  exit from, by monopoly, 240
  increasing-cost, **211,** 211–212
  infant, **786,** 786–787
Inefficiency
  dynamic, **246**
  in monopolistic competition, 265–266
  static, **246**
Inelastic demand, **117**
Infant industries, protection measures and, **786,** 786–787
Inferior goods, **58,** 58–59, 150n
Inflation, **12**
  flexible exchange rates and, 807–808
Inflation rate, **349**
Information, **7**
  economics of, 196
  perfect, **195**

problems with, lemons and, 215
In-kind transfer payments, **375**
Inputs. *See also* Factor markets; Resources markets; Resource(s); *specific inputs*
  complementary, **306**
  fixed, **173**
  profit-maximizing rules for all, 302–303
  substitute. *See* Substitute inputs
  variable, **173**
An Inquiry into the Nature and Causes of the Wealth of Nations (Smith), 28, 109–110, 146–147, 194
Institutions, **7.** *See also* Economic institutions
Insurance, health, 384
Interest, **345**
  pure, **350**
  as return to capital, 349–350
Interest groups, **101,** 101–104, **466,** 466–468
  comparable worth and, 315
  domination of, 101
  political payoffs from, 105–106
  and price of eyeglasses, 261
  protection from, 348
  unions as, 335
  wealth transfers and, 101–104
Interest group theory of regulation, **412**
Interest rate(s)
  capital formation and, 345–346
  demand and supply of loanable funds and, 346–349
  in flexible exchange rate system, 809–810
  nominal, **349**
  real, **349**
  stock prices and, 360–362
  time and, 347–349
  variations among, 347
International finance, 799–831. *See also* Balance of payments; Exchange rates; Fixed exchange rate systems; Flexible (floating) exchange rate systems
  Asian economic crisis and, 823–824
  Bretton Woods system and, **819,** 819–821
  current monetary system and, 821–825
  gold standard and, 815, 819
International Monetary Fund (IMF), **820**
International pollution, 437–439
  Kyoto treaty and, 438
International trade, 771–795. *See also* Balance of payments; Comparative advantage; Exchange costs; Exchange rates; Fixed exchange rate system; Flexible (floating)

exchange rate systems; Free trade; Specialization; Trade policy
  balance of trade and, 817–818
  importance of, 772–780
  labor union opposition to, 335
  national involvement in, 773–774
  nontariff barriers to, **782,** 782–783
  protectionism and. *See* Protectionism; Quotas; Tariffs
  real-world patterns of, 44–45
  terms of trade and, 776–777, 788–789
  trade zones and, 41–44
International waters, fishing in, 434–435
Interstate Commerce Commission (ICC), 410–411, 419
Inverse relation, **20**
Investment loans, as source of demand for loanable funds, 346
"Invisible hand," 109–110

J

Jackson, John D., 103n
James, Bill, 309
Japanese economy
  international trade and, 776–780
Jevons, Marshall, 138n
Jewkes, John, 247
Johnson & Johnson, 267
Jones-Laughlin, 279–280
Jury duty, opportunity costs of, 188

K

Das Kapital (Marx and Engels), 109
Kassebaum-Kennedy Act of 1996, 387–388
Kennedy Round, 792
Keynes, John Maynard, 292, 646–647
Kirzner, Israel, 359
Kleit, Andrew N., 421n
Koutsky, Thomas, 424n
Kraft Foods, 267
Kyoto treaty, 438

L

Laband, David N., 105n, 260n
Labor
  division of, **28**
  exploitation of, **331**
  foreign, protection and, 787–788
  marginal factor cost of, **302**
  marginal product of, **300**
  marginal revenue product of, **301**
Labor demand, 303–308
  changes in, 305–306
  demand for products and, 329
  long-run, of market, 305
  market. *See* Market demand for labor

  monopoly and, 307–308
  short-run, of market, 304–305
  for union labor, increasing, 328–329
Labor income, **368,** 368–369. *See also* Wage *entries*
  wage differentials and, 368–369
  work versus leisure and, 368
Labor markets. *See* Competitive labor markets; Labor supply; Marginal productivity theory; Market demand for labor
Labor supply, 309–316
  human capital and, 312–313, 368–369
  individual, 309–312
  market, **299**
  wage differentials and, 314–316
Labor unions, 321–339, **322**
  under bilateral monopoly, 331
  collective bargaining and, 331–332, 334–335
  craft, **322**
  decline in membership of, 324–325
  elasticity of demand and, 327
  goals of, 325–327
  impact on labor's share of total income, 336–337
  increasing demand for union labor and, 328–329
  industrial, **322,** 322–323
  under monopsony, 330–335
  as political interest groups, 335
  public employees,' **323,** 323–324
  strikes and, 332–333
  types of, 322–325
Laissez-faire, **417**
Land
  aggregate supply of, **354**
  rent on, 354–356
  supply to alternative uses, 355–356
Landrum-Griffin Act of 1959, 335
Law of demand, 54–61, **55**
  diminishing marginal utility and, 148–151
  indifference curve and, 162–163
  individual demand schedule and curve and, 55–60
  market demand and, 60–61
Law of diminishing marginal returns, **176.** *See also* Diminishing marginal returns
Law of increasing costs, **30,** 30–31
Law of one price, **66**
Law of supply, **61,** 61–65
  changes in quantity supplied and shift in supply curve and, 63–65
Lee, Tenpao, 420n
Legal barriers to entry, **231,** 231–232
Legislation
  antitrust, 402–403

market for, **467**
trade, 616, 790–792
welfare, 381–383
Leisure
choice of work versus, 368
"Lemons," 215
Lewis, John L., 322
Liability
assigning of, 478–479
License, government, **231**
Lighthouses, 448n, 448–449
Limit pricing, **280**
Link, Albert, 359n
Loan(s)
cost of making, 347
as source of demand for loanable funds, 346
Loanable funds, 346–349
demand for, **346**
supply of, **346**
Lobbying. *See* Interest groups
Local phone service, Telecommunications Act of 1996 and, 422–423
Logrolling, **98**, 98–99, **462**, 462–464
Long run, **173**
firm's demand for labor in, 305
monopoly in, 240
purely competitive firms in, 207–212
Long-run average total cost *(LRATC),* **183,** 183–186
economies and diseconomies of scale and, 184
returns to scale and, 185–186
Long-run equilibrium
competitive, **207**
under monopolistic competition, 262–263
Long-run industry supply, **210,** 210–212
of constant-cost industry, 211
of decreasing-cost industry, 212
of increasing-cost industry, 211–212
Long-run marginal costs *(LRMC),* **183,** 183–184
Long-run production costs, 183–186. *See also* Long-run average total cost *(LRATC)*
marginal, **183**
plant size adjustment to minimize, 183–184
Lorenz, M. O., 371
Lorenz curve, **371,** 371–373
Losses
deadweight, 246
economic, by purely competitive firms, 203–205
returns to capital and, 351
welfare. *See* Welfare loss
Luck, wages and, 368

M

Macroeconomic policy
exchange rates and, 814–816
Macroeconomics, **14,** 14–15
Majority voting, public choice analysis of, 459–461
Malthus, Thomas, 394–395
Managed competition, 385–386
Managed flexible-rate system, **804**
Management, 6
Manager, **168**
Margin, **10**
choices at, 10
Marginal analysis, **10**
Marginal cost *(MC),* **175**
long-run *(LRMC),* **183,** 183–184
Marginal cost pricing, **413**
Marginal factor cost of labor *(MFCL),* **302**
Marginal opportunity production cost, **34**
Marginal private benefit curve, **89**
Marginal private cost *(MPC),* **444**
Marginal private cost curve, **91**
Marginal product, **176,** 176–177
Marginal productivity theory, 300–303
income distribution and, 316
profit-maximizing level of employment and, 300–302
profit-maximizing rules for all inputs and, 302–303
Marginal product of labor *(MPL),* **300**
Marginal rate of substitution, **158**
Marginal returns, diminishing. *See* Diminishing marginal returns
Marginal revenue *(MR),* **198, 234**
of monopolist, 234–236
Marginal revenue product of labor *(MRPL),* **301**
of baseball players, 309
Marginal social cost *(MSC),* **444**
Marginal utility, **138,** 138–153. *See also* Diminishing marginal utility
of "all you can eat" pizza, 149–150
misunderstandings about, 151
of voting, 152–153
Market(s), **10, 65, 194**
agricultural, move toward, 225–228
competitive. *See* Competitive markets; Perfect markets; Private competitive markets; Purely competitive firms; Purely competitive markets
factor. *See* Competitive labor markets; Factor markets; Labor demand; Labor supply; Marginal productivity theory
for foreign exchange, 800–804, **804**
information in, 260
for legislation, **467**
for natural resources, 431–434
perfect, **65,** 65–66

political versus economic, 98–99
products, **52,** 53
resources, **52,** 53
Market coordination, **168,** 168–169
Market demand, **60,** 60–61
Market demand curve for public goods, **451**
Market demand for labor, **299**
changes in, 305–306
short-run, 304–305
Market economy
Marx's view of, 110–111
Smith's view of, 109–110
Market failure, **94,** 94–97, 477. *See also* Externalities; Public goods
Market power, **276,** 276–277
Market supply, **65**
of labor, **299**
Marshall, Alfred, 292–293, 477, 646–647
Martin, D. L., 188n
Marx, Karl, 109–110n, 110–111
Maryland crab fishing, 131
Maurice, Charles, 433
Maynes, Steward G., 421n
McDonald's, 293
McKeever, Michelle, 452n
Mean income, **379**
Mercantilism, 230
Mergers, **405,** 405–406
Mexico. *See also* North American Free Trade Agreement
comparative advantage and, 34–39
Microeconomics, **14**
Microsoft, 409
Minority votes, registering of, 472–474
Mixon, Franklin G., Jr., 105n
Model, **13**
Monetary policy
exchange rates and, 814
Money, **12**
banks and. *See* Bank(s)
distribution data, interpretation of, 370–371
exchange rates and. *See* Exchange rates
supply of. *See* Money supply
Money income, 374–377
Money price, **52,** 52–53
Money supply
flexible exchange rates and, 807–808
Monopolistic competition, 255–268, **256**
advertising and, 257–260
characteristics of, 256–257
comparison with other market structures, 286–287
efficiency of, 265–266
long-run equilibrium under, 262–263
product proliferation and, 267–268
pure competition versus, 264–265
resource waste and, 263–266
short-run equilibrium under, 262

Monopolistic competition, continued
  usefulness of, 266
Monopoly, 97, 229–250
  adjustments to scale in, 240
  antitrust policies and, 407
  arguments against, 244–246
  arguments for, 246–247
  bilateral, **331**
  characteristics of, 230–231
  comparison with other market struc-
    tures, 286–287
  demand curve of firms under, 232–234
  distribution of income and, 246
  elasticity of demand and, 236–237
  entry and exit under, 240
  labor demand and, 307–308
  legal barriers to entry in, 231–232
  in long run, 240
  mercantilism and sale of monopoly
    rights, 230
  natural, **232, 408**
  patents as, 248–249
  postal service as, 249–250
  price discrimination and, 240–244
  production costs of, 246
  profits of, 238–239
  pure, **230**
  purely competitive firms compared
    with, 240
  regulation of, 97
  revenues of, 234–237
  short-run price and output of,
    232–240
  sustainable, **415**
  welfare loss due to, 244–246, **246**
Monopsony, **330,** 330–335
  collective bargaining and, 332
  in college athletics, 338–339
  strikes and, 332–333
  unions as political interest groups
    and, 335
Morgenstern, Oskar, 272n
Morill tariff, 790
Motor Carrier Act of 1980, 419
Motorola, 277–279
Multinational firms, 407–408
Mutual interdependence, 271, **272.** See
  also Game theory
Myrdal, Gunnar, 829–831

N

Nash, John, 277
National Anti-Monopoly Cheap Freight
  League, 402
National Collegiate Athletic Association
  (NCAA), 338–339
National defense
  as argument for protection, 786
  as public good, 96

National Grange, 402
National interest, as argument for protec-
  tion, 785–787
National Labor Relations Board
  (NLRB), 334
Natural monopoly, **232, 408**
Natural resources, **430,** 430–434
  nonrenewable, **430,** 431–432
  renewable, **430,** 432–434
"The Nature of the Firm" (Coase),
  168–169
Negative externality, **439,** 439–440
Negative relation, **20**
Net capital movements, 818
Net social value, 93–93n
Net transfers abroad, 818
Neumann, John von, 272n
Niskanen, William A., 468n
Nominal rate of interest, **349**
Nonhuman resources, **6**
Nonlinear relations, 21–22, **22**
Nonmarket activities, **310,** 310–311
Nonprice competition, **256**
Nonproprietary setting, **458**
Nonrenewable natural resources, **430**
  market for, 431–432
Nontariff trade barriers (NTBs), **782,**
  782–783
Normal goods, **58,** 58–59, 150n
Normative economics, **14**
Normative public choice, **458**
Norris-La Guardia Act of 1932, 334
North American Free Trade Agreement
  (NAFTA), 41–43, 335, 614, 618,
  785, 794–795

O

Occupational Safety and Health Administration (OSHA), 416
Oil. See also Organization of Petroleum
  Exporting Countries (OPEC)
  drilling, common ownership and,
    435–437
  market for, 431–432
Oligopoly, 97, 271, **272,** 276–280. See also
  Cartels; Game theory
  advertising under, 280
  comparison with other market struc-
    tures, 286–287
  dominant-firm model of, 279–280
  entry barriers and, 276–277
  pricing under, 277–280
  product differentiation under, 280
Olson, Mancur, 450n, 756n
Opportunity costs, **9,** 27
  of capital, **171**
  and choices, 30–31
  of draft and jury duty, 187–188
  of marginal production, **34**

of production, **169,** 169–172. See also
  Production costs
  of standing in line, 76
Organization of Petroleum Exporting
  Countries (OPEC), 282, 592–593,
  614, 631, 822
Other things being equal, 13n, 56
Overvaluation, **811**
Ownership. See also Property rights
  common. See Common ownership
  establishment of rights of, 441–444
  of firms by government, 416–417

P

Pan Am Air Lines, 421
Parking, on university campuses, 217–218
Partnerships, 178
PATCO. See Professional Air Traffic Con-
  trollers Union
Patents, **231,** 231–232, 248–249
  as entry barriers, 277
Payphones, Telecommunications Act of
  1996 and, 423
Peanut industry, import quotas for, 785
Per capita income, **379**
Perfect competition. See Pure (perfect)
  competition
Perfect information, **195**
Perfect markets, **65,** 65–66. See also
  Purely competitive markets
Perloff, Jeffrey M., 420n
Perot, Ross, 463
Phone service, Telecommunications Act of
  1996 and, 422–423
Pigou, A. C., 444n, 477–479
Pigovian approach, 444n
Plants
  fixed, **175**
  size adjustment to minimize costs,
    183–184
Point voting system, 473–474
Political action committees (PACs), 101.
  See also Interest groups
*The Political Element in the Development
  of Economic Theory* (Myrdal), 829
Political Justice (Godwin), 394
Politicians
  in-kind perquisites of, 105–106
  logrolling by, 98–99
  supply and demand of, 99
Politics. See also Interest groups; Politicians; Public choice; Voting
  buying of elections and, 463
  comparable worth and, 315
  majority voting and, 459–461
  political competition and, 461–462
  political versus economic markets and,
    98–99
  public choice analysis of, 461–470

quotas and, 785
self-interest and, 458–459
Pollution. *See also* Externalities
    international, 437–439
Population
    growth of, 394–395
Positive economics, **14**
Positive externality, **439,** 439–440
Positive relation, **20**
Poverty, **379,** 379–380
    welfare and, 381–383
Predatory pricing, **402**
Preferences
    revealed, **157**
    transivity of, **159,** 159–160
Present value, **351,** 351–352
Price(s), **10,** 10–11, 51–54
    advertising and, 260–261
    agricultural, 223–225
    of children, 395
    circular flow of products and resources
      and, 52
    demand shifts and, 68–69
    equilibrium. *See* Equilibrium price
    full, **53,** 53–54
    law of one price and, **66**
    money, **52,** 52–53
    monopoly, in short run, 237–238
    under oligopoly, 277–280
    profit-maximizing, **238**
    regulation of, 413–415
    of related goods, demand and, 59–60
    relative, **54**
    of resources, cost curves and, 186
    at restaurants, 54
    setting. *See* Pricing
    shifts in both supply and demand and,
      69–72
    supply shifts and, 69
Price ceiling, **72,** 72–73
Price controls, **72,** 72–78
    price ceilings, **72,** 72–73
    price floors, **73,** 73–74
    quality changes and, 74–75
    ticket scalping and, 76–78
Price discrimination, **241**
    antitrust policy and, 406
    conditions for, 241
    model of, 241–244
    by monopoly, 240–244
    by postal service, 249–250
    by universities, 243
Price elasticity of demand, **116,** 116–127
    along demand curve, 118–121
    arc, **120**
    determinants of, 124–127
    elastic, inelastic, and unit elastic
      demand and, 117
    expenditures and receipts related to,
      121–124

formulation of, 116
    of friendships, 125
Price floor, **73,** 73–75
Price leadership, **279**
Price levels. *See also* Inflation
    flexible exchange rates and, 807–808
Price rationing, 67–72
Price searcher, 229, **230**
    demand curve of, 232–233
Price takers, **197,** 298–299
    demand curve of, 232–233
Pricing
    average cost, **413**
    limit, **280**
    marginal cost, **413**
    mechanics of, 66–67
    predatory, **402**
    of public goods, 449–451
Principle of diminishing marginal utility,
    138. *See also* Diminishing
      marginal utility
Principles of Economics (Marshall), 292
Prisoner's dilemma, **273,** 273–275
Private choice, **11**
Private competitive markets. *See also*
    Purely competitive markets
    competitive equilibrium and, 92–93
    efficiency of, 88–93
    supply, costs, and value in, 90–92
    value calculation by demanders in,
      88–90
Private cost(s), **172**
    marginal *(MPC),* **444**
Private goods, 447
Private property, **85**
"The Problem of Social Cost" (Coase), 478
Procter & Gamble, 267
Producers' surplus, **92**
Product(s)
    average, **177,** 177–178
    demand for, labor demand and, 329
    elasticity of demand for, 327
    homogeneous, **195**
    marginal, **176,** 176–177
    proliferation of, monopolistic competi-
      tion and, 267–268
    quality of. *See* Quality
    total, **176,** 178–179
Product differentiation. *See* Differentiated
    product
Production
    factors of. *See* Factor markets; Inputs;
      Resource(s); Resources markets;
      specific factors
    Marx's view of, 110–111
    roundabout, **344,** 344–345
Production costs, 169–187
    economic profits versus accounting
      profits and, 172
    economic time and, 173

explicit and implicit, 170–171
    long-run. *See* Long-run average
      total cost *(LRATC);* Long-run
      production costs
    marginal opportunity, **34**
    of monopoly, 246
    nature of, 171–172
    as opportunity costs, 169–172
    private and social, 172
    shifts in cost curves and, 186
    short-run. *See* Short-run production costs
    supply and, 63–65
    supply decisions and, 187
    total, **171**
Production possibilities frontier, **29,** 29–31
    and AIDS in Africa, 45–47
    economic growth and, 31–33, 742–744
    shifts in, 31–33
    before specialization, 775–776
Productive efficiency, **213**
Productivity
    labor demand and, 329
    marginal, theory of, 300–303, 316
Products market, **52,** 53
Professional Air Traffic Controllers Union
    (PATCO), 324
Profit(s), **197**
    accounting, **172, 358**
    economic. *See* Economic profits
    of monopolist, 238–239
    resource allocation and, 356–358
    returns to capital and, 351
Profit maximization
    for all inputs, 302–303
    employment level of, 300–302
    short-run, by purely competitive firms,
      197–203
Profit-maximizing price, **238**
Progress and Poverty (George), 356
Property
    common, **434,** 434–439
    private, **85**
Property rights, **7,** 7–8, 84–85
    economic incentives and, 85–87
    trading, 360–362
Proprietary setting, **458**
Proprietorships, 170
Protectionism, 785–789. *See also*
    Quotas; Tariffs
    fair trade and, 789
    industry arguments for, 787–789
    national interest arguments for,
      785–787
Public choice, **11,** 98–101, **457,** 457–474.
    See also Interest groups; Politics;
      Voting
    bureaucracy and, 468–470
    collective bargaining and, 334–335
    constitutional political economy and,
      470–472

Public choice, continued
elasticity of demand and supply and, 132–133
excise taxes and, 132–133
logrolling and, 98–99, 462–464
minority voter registration and, 472–474
normative, **458**
political competition and, 461–462
political versus economic markets and, 98–99
positive, **458**
private choice versus, 99–101
Public employee's union, **323,** 323–324
Public franchise, **231**
Public goods, **96,** 96–97, **447,** 447–451
free riders and, 97, 282, **449**
market demand curve for, **451**
pricing of, 449–451
public provision of, 448–449
Public interest theory of regulation, **412**
Public service, compulsory, opportunity costs of, 171–172, 187–188
Pure capitalism, **84**
Pure communism, **84**
Pure (perfect) competition, 194–195, 292–293
monopolistic competition versus, 264–265
other market structures versus, 286–287
Pure economic rent, **354**
Pure interest, **350**
Purely competitive firms, 197–212
demand curve of, 197
economic losses and shutdowns in, 203–205
equilibrium and, 207–210
industry supply and, 206–207
in long run, 207–212
monopoly compared with, 232–233, 240
as price taker, 197
profit maximization by, 197–203
in short run, 197–207
supply curve of, 205
Purely competitive industries
equilibrium in, long-run, 207–210
supply curve of, short-run, **206,** 206–207
supply of, long-run, **210,** 210–212
Purely competitive markets, 87–93, **195,** 195–212. *See also* Perfect markets; Private competitive markets
economic efficiency and, 213–217
industries in. *See* Purely competitive industries
information problems in, 215
real world and, 216–217, 293
resource allocation in, 213–214
Pure monopoly, **230.** *See also* Monopoly
Pyle, Gerald F., 47n

Q
Quality
price controls and, 74–75
price regulation and, 414–415
product differentiation on, 280
Quantity, equilibrium, 65–72
Quantity demanded, **55**
change in, **56,** 56–57
Quantity supplied, **62,** 63
change in, **63**
Quotas, 40–41, **41, 780,** 785
tariffs versus, 783–785

R
Race discrimination, in wages, 380–381
Radio markets, Telecommunications Act of 1996 and, 424
Railroad industry, featherbedding in, 328–329
Rate of interest. *See* Interest rate(s)
Rate of return on invested capital, **357,** 357–358
Rate of return (ROR) regulation, **414**
Rate of time preference, **345**
Rational self-interest, **9.** *See also* Self-interest
Rationing, by price, **67,** 67–72
Reagan, Ronald, 543, 783
Real income
flexible exchange rates and, 808
Reality and Rhetoric: Studies in the Economics of Development, 829
Real rate of interest, **349**
Receipts, business. *See* Total revenue
Reciprocal Trade Agreements Act (1934), 791
Regulation, 408–417
of agriculture, 223–225
capture theory of, **412**
cost curves and, 186
as entry barriers, 277
of externalities, 446
government ownership as alternative to, 416–417
health and safety, 415–416
of health insurance purchasing cooperatives, 385–386
interest group theory of, **412**
laissez-faire as alternative to, 417
of monopoly, 97
of prices, 413–415
public interest theory of, **412**
purpose of, 412–415
rate of return (ROR), **414**
regulatory agencies and, 409–412
Regulatory policies, 399, **400**
Relations, graphical, 20–22
Relative price, **54**

Renewable natural resources, **430**
market for, 432–434
Rent, **354**
Rent control, 72, 74–75
Reserve(s)
foreign exchange, **811**
Resource(s), **4**
human, **6**
natural. *See* Natural resources
nonhuman, **6**
prices of, cost curves and, 186
unemployment of, **31**
waste of, under monopolistic competition, 263–266
Resource allocation
profits and, 356–358
in purely competitive markets, 213–214
Resources markets, **52,** 53, 298. *See also* Factor markets
Restaurant prices, 54
Returns, marginal, diminishing. *See* Diminishing marginal returns
Returns to capital, 349–351, **357,** 357–358
Returns to scale
constant, **185,** 185–186
increasing, **186**
Revaluation, of currency, **813**
Revealed preferences, **157**
Revenues. *See also* Marginal revenue (MR); Total revenue
of monopolist, 234–237
Ricardo, David, 33, 394
Rich Lands and Poor: The Road to World Prosperity (Myrdal), 829
Right-to-work law, **335**
Risk, **347**
interest rate variations and, 347
returns to capital and, 351
Robinson, Joan, 255, 292–293
Robinson-Patman Act of 1936, 403
Roosevelt, Franklin D., 382, 388
ROR regulation, **414**
Roundabout production, **344,** 344–345
Rue, Richard C., 384n

S
Saba, R. S., 423n
Safety regulations, 415–416
Saudi Arabia, OPEC and, 282
Saving(s), **344**
economic incentives to, 453
income from, 369
Sawers, David, 247
Scale
diseconomies of, **184**
economies of. *See* Economies of scale
monopoly adjustments to, 240
returns to, 185–186
Scalping, 76–78

Scarcity, **4,** 4–6
  contrived, **244**
  economizing, and college student's
    time, 5
Schumpeter, Joseph, 247
Scully, Gerald, 309
Securities and Exchange Commission
  (SEC), 412
Self-interest
  and politics, 458–459
  politics and, 98–99
  rational, **9**
Selling rights, 445–446
Services, **4**
  economic, **5**
  free, **5**
Sex discrimination, in wages, 380–381
Shabecoff, Phillip, 452n
Shannon, Gary W., 47n
Sherman Antitrust Act of 1890, 402–403
Shortage, **67**
  price ceilings and, 72–73
Short run, **173**
  market demand for labor in, 304–305
  monopoly price and output in, 232–238
  purely competitive firms in, 197–207
Short-run equilibrium, under monopolistic
  competition, 262
Short-run firm supply curve, **205**
Short-run industry supply curve, **206,**
  206–207
Short-run production costs, 173–183
  diminishing marginal returns and,
    176–183
  fixed and variable, 173–176
Shutdown, **204**
Sidey, Ken, 47n
Single-parent families, income distribution
  and, 378
Slope of curve, 22–23
Smith, Adam, 27–28, 52, 109–110n,
  146–148, 194–194n, 293
Smith, Madeleine, 384n
Smithson, Charles W., 433
Smoke, taxing of, 477–478
Smoot-Hawley Act of 1930, 616, 790–791
Social cost(s), **172**
  marginal *(MSC),* **444**
  solving problem of, 477–479
  total, 93
Socialism, **84**
Socialization, of firms, **416,** 416–417
Social Security, 388–390
Social value, net, 93–93n
Sony, 277–279
Soviet Union, De Beers diamond cartel
  and, 287–289
Specialization, **27,** 27–29, **28, 773.** *See
    also* Comparative advantage
  comparative advantage and, 33, 36–37

gains from, 776–780
  in marriage and roommate selection, 28
  production possibilities before,
    775–776
Speculation, **820,** 820–821
State capitals, politician perquisites in, 105
Static inefficiency, **246**
Statistical discrepancy, 818–819
Steel industry
  "fair trade" and protectionism and, 789
  price leadership in, 279
Stigler, George J., 418–419
Stillerman, Richard, 247
Stock
  capital, **345**
  prices of, 360–362
Strikes, 332–333, **333**
Student governments, as political market,
  100–101
Subsidies, 789
Substitute inputs, **306**
  availability of, 327
  increasing prices of, 329
Substitutes, **59, 130**
  price elasticity of demand and, 126
Substitution, marginal rate of, **158**
Substitution effect, **148,** 148–150
  indifference curves and, 163–164
Sunk costs, **171**
Supply
  aggregate. *See* Aggregate supply
  agricultural, 223
  change in, **63**
  decisions about, production costs and,
    287
  elasticity of. *See* Elasticity of supply
  factors affecting, **63**
  graphic representation of, 67
  of labor. *See* Labor supply
  law of. *See* Law of supply
  of loanable funds, **346**
  market, **65**
  of money. *See* Money supply
  price controls and public choice and,
    72–78
  shifts in, 69–72
  tabular analysis of, 66–67
Supply curve, **62**
  of firm, short-run, 205
  of industry, long-run. *See* Long-run
    industry supply
  of industry, short-run, **206,** 206–207
  market, 64
  shifts in, 63–65
Surplus, **66**
  balance of trade, **812**
  consumers', **90,** 90n
  price floors and, 73–75
  producers', **92**
Sustainable monopoly, **415**

Switzerland, foreign exchange market and,
  804–813

T

Tacit collusive solution, **275**
Taft-Hartley Act of 1947, 335
Tangency solution, 262–263, **263**
Tariffs, 40–41, **41, 780**
  as entry barriers, 277
  free trade and, 780–781
  General Agreement on Tariffs and
    Trade (GATT), 616–619, 792–793
  Morill, 790
  quota versus, 783–785
  reasons for, 782
  Smoot-Hawley, 791
  trade zones and, 41–44
  U.S. policy on, 790–795
  welfare loss to society from,
    781–782, **782**
Taxes
  cost curves and, 186
  "draft," 187–188
  excise, 132–133
  on externalities, 444–445
  health care system and, 386–387
  as income source, 369–370
  on smoke, 477–478
Technology, **7**
  cost curves and, 186
Telecommunications Act of 1996, 422–425
Terms of trade, **37,** 37–38, **776,** 776–777,
  788–789
Terms of trade argument, for protection,
  788, 788–789
The Theory of Unemployment (Pigou), 477
Third World countries
  development and trade in, 829–831
Ticket scalping, 76–78
Timber famine, 433
Time
  economic, 173. *See also* Long run;
    Long-run *entries;* Short run; Short-
    run *entries*
  elasticity of supply and, 131
  interest rates and, 347–349
  price elasticity of demand and,
    126–127
  rate of time preference and, **345**
Torrens, Robert, 33
Total consumer valuation, **90**
Total cost *(TC),* **173.** *See also* Long-run
    average total cost *(LRATC)*
  of production, **171**
Total expenditures, **122**
  demand elasticity and, 122–126
Total fixed cost *(TFC),* 173–174
Total product, **176,** 178–179
Total revenue, **122, 199,** 199–200

Total revenue, continued
demand elasticity and, 122–125
of monopolist, 234
Total social cost, 93
Total utility, **139**
Total variable cost *(TVC)*, 173
Total wage bill, **326**
maximization of, as union goal, 325–326
Trade. *See* Comparative advantage; Free trade; International trade; Protectionism; Quotas; Tariffs
balance of. *See* Balance of trade
terms of. *See* Terms of trade
Trade advantage, **788,** 788–789
Trade barriers
artificial, **40,** 40–41, 780–785
nontariff, **782,** 782–783
Trade Expansion Act of 1962, 792
Trade policy
fixed exchange rates and, 813
Trade zones, 41–44
Transaction costs, **39,** 39–40
Transfer payments, **369,** 369–370
in-kind, **375**
Transivity of preferences, **159,** 159–160
Transportation costs, **40**
Tucker, A. W., 273
Tuition, price discrimination in, 243
Tullock, Gordon, 468n, 470n
TV markets, Telecommunications Act of 1996 and, 424

U

Undervaluation, of currency, **810,** 810–811
Unemployment of resources, **31**
Unions. *See* Labor unions
United Air Lines, 421
United Nations, 47n
United States
economic restructuring of, 328
free trade and, 792–795
health care system of, 383–384, 387–388
income distribution in, 373–378
international trade and, 776–780
leading trading partners, 44–45
macroeconomic policy changes in, 812
North American Free Trade Agreement and, 41–43, 335, 794–795
tariff policy in, 790–795
Unit elasticity of demand, **117**
Universities
parking at, 217–218
price discrimination by, 243
student governments as political market in, 100–101
Uruguay Round, 792–793
U.S. Postal Service, 249–250, 417
Used cars, buying, 215
Usury, protection from, 348
Utility, 137–153, **138.** *See also* Diminishing marginal utility; Marginal utility
total, **139**

V

Value
of currencies, balance of payments and, 819
Van Gogh exhibit, ticket scalping at, 76–78
Variable costs, **173,** 174
Variable input, **173**
Voluntary Export Restraint (VER), 783, 785
von Mises, Ludwig, 468n
Voting. *See also* Politics; Public choice
decision-making in, 99–101
majority, 459–461
marginal utility of, 152–153
minority, registration for, 472–474
point system, 473–474
public choice analysis of, 459–461, 464–466

W

Wage(s)
maximization of, as union goal, 325–326
Wage differentials, 314–316
human capital and, 312–313
income distribution and, 368–369
regional, 316–318
Wage discrimination, 380–381
consumer-initiated, **381**
economic, **381**
Wagner Act of 1935, 334
Water crisis, 433
Wealth
transfers of, interest groups and, 101–104
Wealth and Welfare (Pigou), 477
Wealth of Nations (Smith), 28, 109–110, 146–147, 194, 526, 761
Weidenbaum, Murray, 420n
Welfare, economic, **265**
Welfare loss
due to monopoly, 244–246, **246**
to society, 781–782, **782**
Welfare programs, 381–383
Westbury, Stuart A., Jr., 384n
Wheeler-Lea Act of 1938, 403
Women, wage discrimination and, 381
Work
choice of, versus leisure, 368
Worker(s)
compensation of. *See* Wage(s)
World Bank, 822
World Trade Organization (WTO), 617, 792–793

X

x-axis, 20

Y

Yandle, Bruce, 438n
y-axis, 20
Yellow Pages, 260

Z

Zaire, De Beers diamond cartel and, 288
Zero economic profits, **107**
Zimbabwe, AIDS epidemic and life expectancy in, 46
Zollverein, 42